Penal Philosophy

THE MODERN CRIMINAL SCIENCE SERIES

Published under the Auspices of

THE AMERICAN INSTITUTE OF CRIMINAL LAW AND CRIMINOLOGY

Penal Philosophy

By

GABRIEL TARDE

Late Magistrate, and Professor in the College of France

Translated by

RAPELJE HOWELL

Of the New York Bar

With an Editorial Preface by

EDWARD LINDSEY

Of the Warren, Pa., Bar

AND AN INTRODUCTION BY ROBERT H. GAULT

Assistant Professor of Psychology in Northwestern University and Managing Editor of the Journal of Criminal Law and Criminology

GYAN

Published by

Gyan Publishing House
5, Ansari Road
Daryaganj, New Delhi-110002
Phone: 011-47034999, 9811692060
E-mail: books@gyanbooks.com

Distribution Network
gyanbooks.com
India, USA, Canada, UK, Australia, France

ISBN : 978-81-212-6264-4 (PB)
First Published, 1912

2nd Impression 2022

Printed at: Gyan Press, Delhi.

PENAL PHILOSOPHY
Author: GABRIEL TARDE

THE MODERN CRIMINAL SCIENCE SERIES

Published under the Auspices of

THE AMERICAN INSTITUTE OF CRIMINAL LAW AND CRIMINOLOGY

Penal Philosophy

By GABRIEL TARDE

Late Magistrate, and Professor in the College of France

Translated by

RAPELJE HOWELL

Of the New York Bar

With an Editorial Preface by

EDWARD LINDSEY

Of the Warren, Pa., Bar

AND AN INTRODUCTION BY ROBERT H. GAULT

Assistant Professor of Psychology in Northwestern University and Managing Editor of the Journal of Criminal Law and Criminology

1912

GENERAL INTRODUCTION TO THE MODERN CRIMINAL SCIENCE SERIES.

At the National Conference of Criminal Law and Criminology, held in Chicago, at Northwestern University, in June, 1909, the American Institute of Criminal Law and Criminology was organized; and, as a part of its work, the following resolution was passed:

"*Whereas,* it is exceedingly desirable that important treatises on criminology in foreign languages be made readily accessible in the English language, *Resolved,* that the president appoint a committee of five with power to select such treatises as in their judgment should be translated, and to arrange for their publication."

The Committee appointed under this Resolution has made careful investigation of the literature of the subject, and has consulted by frequent correspondence. It has selected several works from among the mass of material. It has arranged with publisher, with authors, and with translators, for the immediate undertaking and rapid progress of the task. It realizes the necessity of educating the professions and the public by the wide diffusion of information on this subject. It desires here to explain the considerations which have moved it in seeking to select the treatises best adapted to the purpose.

For the community at large, it is important to recognize that criminal science is a larger thing than criminal law. The legal profession in particular has a duty to familiarize itself with the principles of that science, as the sole means for intelligent and systematic improvement of the criminal law.

Two centuries ago, while modern medical science was still young, medical practitioners proceeded upon two general assumptions: one as to the cause of disease, the other as to its treatment. As to the cause of disease, — disease was sent by the inscrutable will of God. No man could fathom that will, nor its arbitrary operation. As to the treatment of disease, there were believed to be a few remedial agents of universal efficacy. Calomel and blood-letting, for example, were two of the principal ones. A larger or smaller dose of calomel, a greater or less quantity of bloodletting, — this blindly indiscriminate mode of treatment was regarded as orthodox for all common varieties of ailment. And so his calomel pill and his bloodletting lancet were carried everywhere with him by the doctor.

Nowadays, all this is past, in medical science. As to the causes of disease, we know that they are facts of nature, — various, but distinguishable by diagnosis and research, and more or less capable of prevention or control or counter-action. As to the treatment, we now know that there are various specific modes of treatment for specific causes or symptoms, and that the treatment must be adapted to the cause. In short, the individualization of disease, in cause and in treatment, is the dominant truth of modern medical science.

The same truth is now known about crime; but the understanding and the application of it are just opening upon us. The old and still dominant thought is, as to cause, that a crime is caused by the inscrutable moral free will of the human being, doing or not doing the crime, just as it pleases; absolutely free in advance, at any moment of time, to choose or not to choose the criminal act, and therefore in itself the sole and ultimate cause of crime. As to treatment, there still are just two traditional measures, used in varying doses for all kinds of crime and all kinds of persons, — jail, or a fine (for death is now employed in rare cases only). But modern science, here as in medicine, recognizes that crime also (like disease) has natural causes. It need not be asserted for one moment that crime is a disease. But it does have natural causes, — that is, circumstances which work to produce it in a given case. And as to treatment, modern science recognizes that penal or remedial treatment cannot possibly be indiscriminate and machine-like, but must be adapted to the causes, and to the man as affected by those causes. Common sense and logic alike require, inevitably, that the moment we predicate a specific cause for an undesirable effect, the remedial treatment must be specifically adapted to that cause.

Thus the great truth of the present and the future, for criminal science, is the individualization of penal treatment, — for that man, and for the cause of that man's crime.

Now this truth opens up a vast field for re-examination. It means that we must study all the possible data that can be causes of crime, — the man's heredity, the man's physical and moral make-up, his emotional temperament, the surroundings of his youth, his present home, and other conditions, — all the influencing circumstances. And it means that the effect of different methods of treatment, old or new, for different kinds of men and of causes, must be studied, experimented, and compared. Only in this way can accurate knowledge be reached, and new efficient measures be adopted.

All this has been going on in Europe for forty years past, and in limited fields in this country. All the branches of science that can help have been working, — anthropology, medicine, psychology, economics, sociology, philanthropy, penology. The law alone has abstained. The science of law is the one to be served by all this. But the public in general and the legal profession in particular have remained either ignorant of the entire subject or indifferent to the entire scientific movement. And this ignorance or indifference has blocked the way to progress in administration.

The Institute therefore takes upon itself, as one of its aims, to inculcate the study of modern criminal science, as a pressing duty for the legal profession and for the thoughtful community at large. One of its principal modes of stimulating and aiding this study is to make available in the English language the most useful treatises now extant in the Continental languages. Our country has started late. There is much to catch up with, in the results reached elsewhere. We shall, to be sure, profit by the long period of argument and theorizing and experimentation which European thinkers and workers have passed through. But to reap that profit, the results of their experience must be made accessible in the English language.

The effort, in selecting this series of translations, has been to choose those works which best represent the various schools of thought in criminal science, the general results reached, the points of contact or of controversy, and the contrasts of method — having always in view that class of works which have a more than local value and could best be serviceable to criminal science in our country. As the science has various aspects and emphases — the anthropological, psychological, sociological, legal, statistical, economic, pathological — due regard was paid, in the selection, to a representation of all these aspects. And as the several Continental countries have contributed in different ways to these various aspects, — France, Germany, Italy, most abundantly, but the others each its share, — the effort was made also to recognize the different contributions as far as feasible.

The selection made by the Committee, then, represents its judgment of the works that are most useful and most instructive for the purpose of translation. It is its conviction that this Series, when completed, will furnish the American student of criminal science a systematic and sufficient acquaintance with the controlling doctrines and methods that now hold the stage of thought in Continental Europe. Which of the various principles and methods will prove best adapted to help our problems can only be told after our students and workers have tested them in our own experience. But it is certain that we must first acquaint ourselves with these results of a generation of European thought.

In closing, the Committee thinks it desirable to refer the members of the Institute, for purposes of further investigation of the literature, to the "Preliminary Bibliography of Modern Criminal Law and Criminology" (Bulletin No. 1 of the Gary Library of Law of Northwestern University), already issued to members of the Conference. The Committee believes that some of the Anglo-American works listed therein will be found useful.

COMMITTEE ON TRANSLATIONS.

Chairman, JOHN H. WIGMORE,
Professor of Law in Northwestern University, Chicago.
ERNST FREUND,
Professor of Law in the University of Chicago.
MAURICE PARMELEE,
Professor of Sociology in the College of the City of New York.
ROSCOE POUND,
Professor of Law in Harvard University.
EDWARD LINDSAY,
Of the Warren, Pa., Bar.
WM. W. SMITHERS,
Secretary of the Comparative Law Bureau of the American Bar Association, Philadelphia, Pa.

INTRODUCTION TO THE ENGLISH VERSION

BY ROBERT H. GAULT

The problem of moral responsibility is as old as philosophy itself. The satisfactory definition of its nature has baffled most painstaking students. Professor Tarde in the chapters that follow describes it as the crux of penal philosophy, and after a review of its historical setting and impracticable solution he presents a new point of view that, in his opinion, may better serve the needs of the criminologist.

The assumption of absolute freedom of choice is involved in many of the discussions of the philosophical aspects of the correction or punishment of misdemeanants. The individual is free to do as he does or to act otherwise. He is the director of his own course. Opposed to this are the doctrines of philosophical and of scientific determinism. According to either of these, conduct is determined by factors that are beyond his reach. He cannot control them. From the philosophical deterministic outlook, he is acting simply in accord with the laws of original nature, and hence of necessity. On the side of scientific determinism, the controlling factors are the patent facts of Physics and Chemistry, of Physiology and Biology, of Psychology and Anthropology, etc. Philosophical determinism is not an absolute denial of the freedom of choice, and, therefore, of moral responsibility — but of this more anon.

Extreme scientific determinism is a denial of the freedom of choice, and where there is no such freedom, there also duty, obligation, moral responsibility are altogether lacking. There is no use that they can serve. Even if they do exist in another sphere than ours, they are of no consequence here. Man is no more morally responsible to his neighbor for having committed a depredation against him than is the oak to a man for having assimilated from the earth nourishment which, had it entered into an apple, might have furnished forth his table. The oak and man belong to radically different classifications. Man and the morally responsible being, if there is any such, are equally distinct. He is played upon by a thousand natural and social forces, and each force is immediately in causal series with a modification in the physiological organism, and at the next step with either the beginning or the performance of an act. Meanwhile consciousness abides, not uniformly distributed upon the series of processes, but like a shimmer of light now here and now there upon the surface of a great water current, and no more effective from the point of view of practical results. This is the extreme deterministic attitude.

Common sense assumes that truth lies not at this extreme. It assumes at the same time, however, that a complete analysis of phenomena would show an invariable causal connection between an act and a physiological disposition, or, more remotely, an element in the physical environment, present, or in the past; or between an act and a social factor present or past. Or for that matter such an analysis would reveal a causal connection among all these factors together. The labor of physicists and of chemists; of physiologists, biologists, and neurologists; of psychologists and anthropologists and sociologists, have contributed each an item toward the general sum of scientific deterministic factors, and lastly the statisticians are casting a gleam upon sources of behavior that are not brought to the light by other agencies.

Herein is the root of a form of positivism; that form which is a protest against speculation; against the speculation of the metaphysician who leaves the phenomenal world aside in his thought and attempts the solution of such problems as that of causation, approaching it the while from so-called fundamental postulates that are regarded as necessary to thought. Let it be observed here, by the way, that the brethren of scientific ideals themselves are not free from speculative tendencies and that on occasion they too may dogmatize a little even while in the main they pursue an ideal of method that has proved to be superior from the viewpoint of knowledge strictly, and of practical control over natural forces as well. This positivism emphasizes here one form of causative factor, there another according to the individual preference or training of the student. Here behavior is said to be determined pre-eminently by anthropological factors, there by social elements. Acts are then benevolent or malevolent, beneficent or maleficent, according as the actor is well or ill endowed from the anthropological viewpoint, or as organized society has provided up-building or down-pulling influences for those who become members of it.

This idea seems to have been suggested by Kant himself when he taught his doctrine of necessity as the key to moral action. As long as man fully responds to the necessity of his nature he is free and hence moral. Any condition, however, that interferes in any degree with his response to that necessity robs him to that extent of his freedom to act, and it can no longer be said of him, therefore, that he is, in a complete sense, morally responsible. In the Principles of the Metaphysic of Ethics, for instance, Kant argues that because moral philosophy rests wholly upon the pure part, it does not borrow from Anthropology, but gives laws to man a priori. But, going on, he says that no doubt these laws require a judgment sharpened by experience, in order to distinguish in what cases they are applicable, and to procure for them access to the will of the man and effectual influence upon his conduct. Acting under the guidance of this idea it is easy to acquit one who is charged with misdemeanor or other crime of any sort; to urge his liberty to come and go according to his good pleasure. Indeed, in all good conscience, we must do so as long as we anchor moral responsibility in absolute freedom of choice, and make the right to punish rest thereupon. While we argue, conversely, that where there is no freedom to choose there is no moral responsibility and consequently no culpability, the idea of punishment must lapse. I say it is easy to acquit. Our expert social workers — and even, be it said, sometimes our profounder students of social phenomena, who should be better guided — do they not pile Ossa upon Pelion to accomplish proof that the accused was determined — fated — by social forces to do exactly as he did? They offer a strong defense of the proposition that environmental conditions have made it impossible for him to do otherwise than he did do. And furthermore, are these conditions not winked at, consented to, or actually invented by society as a whole? Not only could this accused not have done otherwise than he did, but society as a whole is the culprit, and not the individual himself. This is social determinism; determinism run mad; fallacious it is, and consequently dangerous from the viewpoint of those who would develop society after an ideal; who are regretful for past mistakes of omission and of commission; who do not, however, turn flagellant on this account, but confidently face the future and deal resolutely even with the effect of an illy wrought past. As a matter of course, society is blameworthy in some degree for practically every crime committed within it. But for us, *on that account alone,* to swerve one way or another in our treatment either of the crime or the criminal is to confess a weakness for our past, rather than to give effect to an element of strength that has arisen upon the burial of a dead past and the adherence to an ideal for improvement.

The psychologist and the anthropologist, furthermore, dwell upon the inevitable reaction to the "irresistible impulse" and thereupon determinism, and hence moral non-responsibility, follow as a matter of course. The physician thinks of the inevitable consequence of pathological and developmental conditions and once more the idea of determinism and of moral non-responsibility prevails. From this point of view it is a doubtful proposition that, when the act was committed, as alleged, the offender could have done otherwise than he did.

Thus, as long as moral responsibility, the so-called crux of penal philosophy, has its basis in freedom of choice, and as long as we and our experts are inclined toward the scientific deterministic attitude, — and as knowledge grows we are finding ourselves subject to more and more complex systems of natural and inexorable laws — the concept of responsibility will become progressively attenuated.

It appears, therefore, that if the doctrine of responsibility truly is at the crux of penal philosophy, and if responsibility depends upon freedom, we must reconcile determinism with freedom of choice — even identify them — in order to preserve the concept of the moral responsibility of man. This Kant attempted in his doctrine that, normally, life, as the sum of a man's activity, is an expression of the necessity of human nature. To respond to duty and hence to be free and moral, furthermore, is to live according to this necessity — to obey the necessary laws of our nature. Certainly no more could possibly be desired than freedom to live according to fundamental natural law. Philosophical determinism and freedom of choice are so far reconcilable. A single pulley in a system of piston rods and shafts and cogs and cranks is free to do all that its original connections are designed to permit. But the difficulty with this figure is that in the series of connections in human life the pulley is able to stop or wreck the machinery. The individual may at once, or as the effect of a series of choices, throw himself out of social adjustment.

So the partisans of freedom will say that it is only as long as all conditions are normal that the reconciliation is effective. At the point of social or other abnormality, reconciliation fails and we must stake our faith either in the concept of freedom or of determinism. From this difficulty an obvious means of escape is by way of the assumption that anthropological limitations, "irresistible impulses," physiological lesion or arrest, social repression or aggravation, are deterministic factors which interfere with the freedom of choice only when a partial view is taken. Take a wider view, which includes not only the present but the future, not only the immediate but the remote ends of human life, and all these temporary influences of social environment, of physiological disposition, and of mental process are but insignificant segments which themselves play and are played upon according to inflexible omnipresent law.

But this reconciliation is not wholly satisfactory from the point of view of logical and philosophical requirements, and certainly it does not fully satisfy the demands of practical life. The concepts which are involved in its evolution are far removed from everyday problems. Professor Tarde, therefore, in the pages that follow, develops an alternative basis or criterion of responsibility. It is a psychological standard. It has two corner stones: one is in the identity of the self, the other is in the relation of social similarity between the self and the surroundings of self.

When one says that the maintenance of personal identity is a condition of responsibility, one is not necessarily inconsistent with the doctrine of necessity as developed by the philosophers. For wherein consists identity but in the persistence of the self? The self, the psychological self, involves a multitude of elements which enter into the consciousness of the present and others perhaps which extend far backward along ancestral lines of development. Logically, this leads to an identification of the psychological self with all the forces that act or have acted upon it to make it what it is; to an identification of its laws with universal laws. The acts of the self, therefore, assume the character of necessity.

Anyone who analyzes the self *from the psychological viewpoint* finds in its composition the consciousness of his body clad in the clothing he habitually wears; assuming a habitual attitude; moving over a frequented path; the consciousness of a certain complex, of organic sensations which arise from bodily processes and which form a continuous, fairly uniform background of other conscious experiences. These enter into the constitution of the psychological self, but they are not all. Indispensable among these factors is the memory consciousness in which the past is normally maintained in his presence with fidelity, so that last year, last month, and today and tomorrow, he places confidence in a constant group of memories. These include the memories of certain friends whom he has known in the past and with whom the persons he cherishes today are believed to be identical; the consciousness of certain professional, artistic, religious, educational, and occupational ideals toward which he is laboring and which have been, perhaps, during a lifetime, in their general outlines at least, sure guides to his conduct. These, too, go together with other factors to make up the psychological self. But the analysis is not complete with this enumeration. There is also the concrete consciousness of social obligation; of responsibility to one's townsmen, countrymen, and fellowmen in general, in the sense of the recognition of the rights both of one's self and of others, and of the necessity and privilege of co-operation for the accomplishment of practical and even ideal ends. All these and more make up the psychological self and their continuance marks the identity of the self from day to day. And this identity, as I said above, Tarde has made one of the criteria of individual responsibility. We cannot hold one fully responsible who, when he committed a wrong, was not identical with his self as habitually known; who then was one self and now is another.

And indeed, in many individuals, the psychological self is discontinuous. If the above analysis is correct as far as it goes, the self may be broken in various ways. When suddenly the mode of life has been changed, necessitating the casting away of old habits and the assumption of new ones, responsibility must be diminished. When profound physiological disturbances (as in epilepsy) break up the background of organic sensation and blot out the memories of the past and shatter the ideals that have hitherto guided, surely responsibility is decidedly diminished or obliterated.

A second criterion of responsibility, according to Tarde's development, is social similarity. Obviously the South Sea Islander who, unmodified by contact with strangers, has been dropped from the place of his nativity for the first time upon our shore, we do not hold responsible for depredations, to the same extent as our neighbor in the same block with us who has committed a wrong in our community. Against both we provide defense: for both we provide means of adjustment or readjustment to society. But only of the latter do we say that he was under obligation to do otherwise than he did.

These criteria of responsibility have the obvious advantage that they leave out of account entirely all discussion of intention and free will with their frequent theological implications which lead no-whither as far as the practical disposition of a case is concerned. They have the advantage, therefore, of concreteness. An expert can definitely point to alterations in sensibility, organic or otherwise, and losses of memory may be sufficiently patent to the skilled examiner to justify a positive or a negative answer to the question of responsibility or irresponsibility or a modification of either.

No point of view respecting responsibility, however, can lightly brush aside every difficulty, and the one under consideration is not exceptional in this regard. How much modification of the normal organic status, and how much alteration of the normal mental condition must be discovered in order to argue an appreciable change in self-hood and, consequently, of responsibility? The acute insane during the period of their affliction must be adjudged irresponsible. They have suffered sharp alteration both mentally and physically and at the same time they have fallen out of joint with their social surroundings. Of the paranoiac, as far as we understand him today, we must say that he is in a high degree responsible. The congenital idiot and the congenital imbecile are socially dissimilar when compared with their neighbors, but they have not in their lifetime suffered any marked alteration of their physical or their mental condition. While we are thinking only of their social dissimilarity, we shall have to say of them — irresponsible. But let us think of the other criterion as applied to the same individuals. The current of their bodily and mental processes, however narrow and shallow it may be, has always pursued the even course of its way. There have been no interruptions, no sudden changes, to alter the psychological self and consequently the responsibility of the individual must be assumed, according to the criterion. On the whole we would say of such a case — partly responsible.

Another problem arises in consideration of the idiot and the imbecile *by accident.* Because of their social dissimilarity we will have to say of them that they are irresponsible. In view of the sudden accidental transformation that has come about in their body and mind we must pass the same judgment. On the whole we will say unqualifiedly — irresponsible. But after the lapse of time — many years let us say — is the situation not different? Can we not say of them as the day of the blighting accident recedes into what, even for the normal observer, is the dim past; as their current of *unbroken* life processes lengthens; as experiences, such as they may be, accumulate, can we not say of them as we did of the congenitally idiotic and imbecilic — partially responsible? Undoubtedly, yes. But where the line is to be drawn between the presence of responsibility and the lack of it in these individuals, no one is prepared to say. And what of the birth of responsibility in a normal life through childhood and adolescence? No answer is at hand. But at least one can say here, whatever satisfaction it may yield, that no other theory points the way.

Yet once more. Considering the social criterion of responsibility, what is too much social dissimilarity to permit the judgment of responsibility? And what shall we say of him who, albeit he lives in an enlightened community, is nevertheless in advance of it in the sober estimation of a future generation, and is socially dissimilar on that account? Some day, when it is too late for him to profit by the general enlightenment, posterity will remark the unhappiness of the situation that prevented his enjoying in his lifetime, with the full accord of his contemporaries, the judgment that he was absolutely responsible. In other words, the boundaries of our society must be agreed upon and marked before we may know what leeway in the matter of individual social custom and standards is consonant with safety and progress.

Fortunately for the student in his closet, who is already overworked, he is not required to survey the limits. That work is being accomplished incidentally by a thousand shipmasters carrying the commerce of the nations; by the merchant who brings from unknown worlds the products of strange looms; by the school teacher through picture and story; by the man of science or of art who compares and brings back to his own the methods of other peoples; by learned official commissions passing from nation to nation and reporting again to their own, and even by the free-for-all summer tourist, and the perennial traveler with no anchor behind them, who, wherever they go, both become and make acquainted. In short, by means of the extensive social intercourse and the expanding knowledge of our day we are approaching a common understanding without regard to national or even social distinctions; and as we learn to think more and more in accord with one another we more and more approximate social similarity. This suggests that, according to our theory, we are, with the steady increase in the extent of general education and opportunity, slowly elevating the common level of individual responsibility. This is not hypothesis or theory — it is common sense. To whom much has been given, of him much shall be required. Education, wealth, social position, opportunity for good of any kind, enhances individual responsibility for public service. The possessor of such advantages is, for no service or for service beneath his ability to perform, or for positively negative social effect, culpable in common sense.

These and other considerations of individual responsibility are of interest to courts of criminal jurisdiction. Frequently their knottiest problems are to determine the responsibility or the degree of responsibility of the accused. This must be accomplished, if accomplished at all, in the face of ardent and opposing partisans. As a matter of fact, however, the court, as a court, should have absolutely no interest in the question. Its function should be merely to determine the fact that the accused did or did not commit the depredation as charged. If it be found that, as alleged, he did the unlawful act, he is not the man to enjoy the unrestricted freedom of the city. The court should then be empowered in every case in which the question of responsibility has been raised, merely to order the detention of the prisoner pending whatever disposition of him an appropriate commission of experts may determine. This, I believe, is the logical, as well as the common sense, attitude to assume. The problem of responsibility is a minor one to all but those officials who should be charged either with the burden of reinstating the culprit in normal society where he may be a pillar and not a reed, or with the obligation to protect the public against any possible future advances upon their peace and safety which, unguarded, he might be inclined to make. So even in the eyes of the experts outside the court room the determination of individual responsibility is only a means for the accomplishment of a much more important purpose. The educational agencies — the incentives, et cetera

— that we will apply to the fully responsible, or to the partially responsible offender, are not those that will be brought into use in the case of the irresponsible. When responsibility, or the want of it, has once been determined, therefore, we know better than before how to deal with the prisoner. We have no other justification for making the inquiry. We can then more intelligently decide whether the infliction of physical pain, or close confinement or both may be of good service in the particular case — and neither out-and-out positivist nor his diametric opponent can deny that these means, even the anticipation of them, may sometimes be reformative. We can decide how to balance pain and pleasure; the freedom of an occupation in the "honor squad" with the restriction of prison walls.

Throughout the present work, Professor Tarde maintains a sufficient balance between conservatism and progressivism to commend him to those who believe, as the present writer does, that in criminology (including penology) we are in our generation trying many experiments: that in many respects we are wiser than our fathers; that in many other respects we do not yet know how much, if at all, wiser we may be than they. The event of experimentation will prove.

NORTHWESTERN UNIVERSITY, *September* 5, 1912.

AUTHOR'S FOREWORD

This book is an examination of ideas put in circulation and brought into favor, during the last few years, by the school of criminal anthropology. But it is even more a setting forth of personal views. The theories which are herein developed deal with three different matters. In the first place there is an attempt to reconcile moral responsibility with determinism, the human conscience with science, which the conception of free will seemed to have separated with an insurmountable gulf. There is also, and especially, an explanation of the criminal side of societies, in conformity with a general point of view which I felt bound to apply in another work recently published,[1] with the various aspects of social life. Finally, there is a pointing out of a few legislative or penitentiary reforms which are the practical conclusions of these theoretical premises.

In spite of the close tie which unites the three portions of this work, they are distinct and separate. Therefore if some partisan of free will has been displeased with the first part, I will beg him not to anathematize the author before having read the other two. And as it is to be feared that, if the spiritualists reproach me for my determinism, the positivists in their turn will tax me with eclecticism or scepticism, I will also beg the latter to hold in check the impatience which the reading of a few terms borrowed from the vocabularies of their adversaries might cause them. A professional habit of impartiality has often compelled me to be complex, and the desire of accuracy seems to me to demand that a writer should feel it his duty to express not only the precise shade of meaning of his thought, but his degree of confidence in that thought. There are certain subjects upon which it is impossible to be concise, simple, and clear without being dogmatic.

[1] "Les lois de l'Imitation," 1 vol., 8vo., Felix Alcan, publisher, 1890.

EDITORIAL PREFACE

BY EDWARD LINDSEY[1]

To be recognized as an original thinker in three separate fields of knowledge — psychology, sociology and criminology; to pursue successfully the careers of magistrate, statistician and professor of political science — such an achievement is rarely to be recorded. It is a brief summary of the life work of Gabriel Tarde. He was born March 12, 1843, at Sarlat, department of Dordogne, in Périgord, Southern France. His education was received at the College of Sarlat, a Jesuit institution, where he already showed his taste for philosophy and classical studies. He studied law at Toulouse, later at Paris, and began the practice of his profession in his native town. In 1869 he was appointed a judge of the Tribunal of First Instance at Sarlat and in 1875 "juge d'instruction" or magistrate, which position he held until 1894, his judicial career covering a period of twenty-five years. In 1894 he was called to Paris to become the head of the Bureau of Statistics in the Department of Justice.

Meanwhile his writings had established his reputation as a profound philosopher and a scholar of comprehensive learning. He brought to his office of magistrate a high conception of its duties and became intensely interested in the social problems indicated by the cases with which, as a judge of the criminal court, he was obliged to deal. In 1880 he contributed a series of articles to the "Révue philosophique" criticizing the theories of Lombroso, then newly before the public. He analyzed the views of the new "positivist school," criticized their arguments and convincingly attacked Lombroso's theory of an anthropological criminal type. These articles attracted the attention of Professor Lacassagne, of Lyon, who sought Tarde's collaboration in the foundation, in 1886, of the "Archives d'Anthropologie criminelle." Becom-

[1] Member of the Warren (Pa.) Bar and of the American Anthropological Association; Associate Editor of the Journal of the American Institute of Criminal Law and Criminology; and member of the Institute's Committee on Translations.

ing a co-director of this journal in 1893, his connection with it continued to the time of his death and he contributed many brilliant articles to its pages. In his first book, "La Criminalité comparée," published in 1886, fifth edition 1902, Tarde argued that the criminal is a professional type and set forth his theory of crime as essentially a social phenomenon. These views were more fully elaborated in the "Philosophie pénale," the subject of this translation, the first edition of which appeared in 1890 and the fourth in 1903. Tarde's explanation of crime was essentially sociological in nature and was based upon general principles of society and social relations, in some respects strikingly original.

He was as much at home in the general field of sociology as in the province of criminology. In 1890 he published "Les Lois de l'Imitation," in which he set forth his theory of imitation as the fundamental explanation of social phenomena; this was followed by "La Logique sociale" (1895) and "L'Opposition universelle" (1897). These three works were devoted to the development of the principles of repetition, opposition, and adaption and the interconnection of these principles as a system of social science was set forth in a series of lectures at the "Collège libre des sciences sociales" in 1897, published under the title of "Lois sociales," of which an English translation entitled "Social Laws" appeared in 1899. Of his other works the most important are: "Études pénales et sociales," 1891, translated into Spanish, 1893; "Les Transformations du droit," 1894; "Essais et mélanges sociologiques," 1895; "Les Transformations du pouvoir," 1899; "L'Opinion et la foule," 1901; "Psychologie économique," 1902, and "L'Homme souterrain," 19—, English translation, "Underground Man," 1905.

After coming to Paris Tarde was appointed professor in the School of Political Sciences and shortly afterwards (in 1900) professor in the College of France. In the same year he was elected to the Institute as a member of the Academy of Moral and Political Sciences. He died at Paris May 12, 1904. In September, 1909, a marble monument by Injalbert was dedicated to his memory at Sarlat, his birthplace and the scene of his magistrate's career.

Tarde's explanation of crime is simply an application to the phenomena of crime of the general laws governing social relations as he conceived them. All science, in his view, rests on the recognition of certain similarities in the world of phenomena or of repetitions of movement or being, such as, in the physical world, the periodicity of the movements of the heavenly bodies and, in the biological world, the indefinite repetition by each cell of its functions of nutrition, growth, activity and reproduction, which may be denominated habit, together with the repetition or succession of cells themselves, which may be termed heredity. Thus periodic movement is the form of repetition exhibited by the physical world, and heredity that shown by the world of life. Correlative and equivalent to these is imitation in the world of social relations, — the tendency to imitate those with whom we come in contact; this is the essential element in the relation between any two or more persons, as fundamental as is the relation of gravity between two masses in the physical sphere. But, secondly, science rests on the recognition of differences, contrasts or oppositions. In the social realm every imitation, or imitative ray, in the language of Tarde, tends to spread and enlarge itself indefinitely, whence arise interferences between these rays of imitation, thus producing contradictions or oppositions between beliefs or desires, either among the individuals composing a certain social group or in the brain of some individual himself. And finally, in a broad survey of the world of phenomena, we seem to see certain harmonies in the grouping and the totality of these resemblances and these differences. So, in the social realm, distinct rays of imitation — beliefs or inventions — combine or complement each other, and so by adaptation organize themselves into a larger scheme or system. All this applies to crime as to other social phenomena. In proportion to the closeness of their contact is the extent of the imitation by people of each other. Thus in crowds or in cities, where contact is close and life is active and exciting, imitation takes the form of fashion with frequent changes; in more stable groups, as the family and in the country, where contact is less close and the activity is less, it takes the form of custom, with a greater stability and permanence. To this is due the different nature of urban and rural criminality. But to a greater or less degree these two forms of imitation are operative in every society and in a certain irregular rhythm or succession. Fashion spreads a given action, which eventually becomes a custom; but this custom is subsequently uprooted by a new fashion, which finally becomes fixed as custom in its turn.

Under this view crime is primarily a social and not a biological or physical fact, and the criminal must be studied as the social rather than the organic individual. Examined in this light the theories of Lombroso and the positivist school fail of maintaining themselves; the anthropological criminal type dissolves into a professional type; physical and economic causes of crime assume subordinate rôles. The question of responsibility becomes possible of logical solution by treating it as a question of social responsibility, looking to the identity of the social individual and his essential similarity to his fellows as the fundamental elements; by placing the individual not in an abstract realm, but in the actual world where causality rules; and by viewing the question of free will as a question of man's freedom to act according to his own nature.

Tarde does not shrink from the consequences of the application of his principles to every question of crime or criminal law. And these applications are worthy of careful examination. They may not all maintain themselves. Some of us may not believe his distrust of the jury system or his apotheosis of the expert to be well founded, or that his deductions as to the extension of the death penalty are necessary ones. There may be some of the medical profession who, preoccupied with the physical significance of heredity, may quarrel with his view that it matters little whether the causes which produce the social individual "be dispersed in the immensity of the circumambient world or whether they be concentrated, brought into the channel of the nearest of the vital sources" from which he springs. They may doubt his even more striking assertion that "there is no more reason for saying of a man who resembles his ancestors, by virtue of the laws of heredity, 'It is his ancestors acting through him,' than there would be to say 'It is his sons, his grandsons, or, if he is to have none, his social descendants, his future imitators, who are acting through him.'" But his discussions of these topics are all stimulating and suggestive, and if not accepted must be met and answered — they cannot lightly be passed by.

It was Tarde's great merit to have recalled attention to the fact that the problems of crime are social problems, and must be solved by means of sociological principles. However helpful may be the analogies from other fields, they cannot simply be extended and held to explain the more complex relations of social phenomena. The biological world may afford us starting points, but the social world embraces this and more and has its own laws and principles which must be established for themselves. It is still a most opportune time for the emphasizing of these truths in this day when are current so many proposals to remedy social ills by surgery, by "eugenics," in fact by anything rather than by social measures. Tarde's logical and thorough analysis of facts and of principles is most clarifying and salutary. And how keen and logical his analysis is! It is well characterized by Bergson in a letter read at the dedication of the monument at Sarlat: "In the history of philosophy we may distinguish two kinds of thinkers. There is one kind who choose their direction and march methodically toward their objective point, constructing step by step an intentional and premeditated synthesis. The other kind go, without apparent method, where their fancy leads them, but their spirit accords so well with the unity of things that all their ideas are naturally consistent. Their reflections, on whatever subject and by whatever way they set out, arrange themselves in order by always returning to the same point. Their intuitions, which are not systematic, organize themselves into a system. They are philosophers without having sought to be such, without having thought of being. To the latter kind belonged Gabriel Tarde. That which strikes one at first in him is the unexpected fancy which multiplies the new viewpoints, the original and brilliant ideas. But soon the unity and depth of the theory reveal themselves. One grand conception underlies the whole construction and imparts to it its direction."

WARREN, PA., *September*, 1912.

CONTENTS

Chapter III

THE THEORY OF RESPONSIBILITY

Chapter IV

THE THEORY OF IRRESPONSIBILITY

Chapter V

THE CRIMINAL

Chapter VI

CRIME

Chapter VII

THE JUDGMENT

Chapter VIII

THE PENALTY

Chapter IX

THE DEATH PENALTY

PENAL PHILOSOPHY

CHAPTER I

GENERAL CONSIDERATIONS

§ 1. The criminality of savages; prejudices with regard to it. A minority of warlike, criminal tribes must have triumphed over a majority of peaceful tribes. But, moralization of the master by the subject. Also moralization of man by woman: example, cannibalism.

§ 2. The zenith of the criminal law is bound up in the decline of criminality. Another cause of the existing crisis of the penal law; the crisis of morality. Attempts at moral reconstruction in every contemporary school. The modernization of morality. Necessity and difficulty of reforming penal legislation.

§ 3. Prejudice of thinking that free will is the essential foundation of moral responsibility. Kant and his noumenal morality; Fouillée and his ideal liberty. Scholastic origin of this prejudice. Free will and science.

§ 4. Analysis of the conceptions of duty and of right, of responsibility and of justice. Duty derived from finality simply. Consequences of this derivation.

§ 5. The duty of punishing. Criticism of the ideas of Fouillée and Guyau on this subject.

§ 1. The criminality of savages; prejudices with regard to it. A minority of warlike, criminal tribes must have triumphed over a majority of peaceful tribes. But, moralization of the master by the subject. Also moralization of man by woman: example, cannibalism.

The primitive wandering tribes who aspire to establish towns have an ever present danger with which to contend: that of the wild animals which threateningly growl about them. Against this peril labor the Hercules, legendary heroes of every primitive society. Later on, when barbarism is compelled to make way for civilization, there is another tide to be stemmed, that of brigandage or organized crime. Such is the obstacle which has to be overcome in every new country. Catherine II had to overcome this in Russia, and she accomplished it by means of the subjugation of the Cossacks and Tartars, "Christian and Mohametan brigands" as they are termed by Rambaud. Modern Greece, having become the traditional land of brigands, was compelled, and also was able, to exterminate them. Italy renascent is engaged in suppressing them in Calabria and even in Sicily. France has succeeded in doing so in Algeria; would that we might also add in Corsica. And that is not all. There is another plague whose germ is carried and fostered by civilization itself, and of which, nevertheless, it should rid itself if it wants to expand and be at ease: I am alluding to that form of criminality which exists in the great capitals and which is, relatively speaking, polished,—to urban brigandage. And this is not the least arduous of tasks.

Criminality changes from age to age. Is it true that in changing it decreases? Yes, certainly if one goes back no farther than the time of the barbarians. But it does not seem to me to be proved, in spite of the prejudice to that effect which has become current, that the earliest savages were addicted to murder and theft on the largest possible scale. This error, which has served as a foundation for the explanation of the existence of crime by means of atavism, should be avoided at the very threshold of our work. The immorality of existing savages has been exaggerated, as has been shown, among other authors, by Henry Joly in his book on "Crime" (1888), and without the least foundation, the most absolute improbity and inhumanity have eagerly been attributed to the people of the stone age, who nevertheless, as the same author remarks, according to de Nadailhac and the discoveries of the archaeology of prehistoric times, could not have been without all good faith, because they were given to trading outside their own territory, and could not have been wanting in all humanity, because they have left undoubted traces of the care which they bestowed upon their sick. Although among the existing or modern savage races, which alone have come under our observation, pillaging and sanguinary tribes seem to outnumber the others, it does not follow by any means that conditions were always such; that the human race was created wicked, and that goodness, the sentiment of justice and the seed of all the virtues, was the later work of civilization. A hunter implies the existence of game, a warlike tribe the existence of industrious tribes. Let us admit that in the beginning a single warlike tribe, organized along military lines, existed in the midst of many peaceful and laboring peoples. We can rest assured that it would soon have conquered the majority of the other tribes, compelled the remainder to arm themselves, and in this way extended to the entire mass of honest humanity its criminal virus. A little leaven suffices to raise a huge loaf, a Bismarck to enflame the whole of Europe. In this case evil, even in an infinite minority, must inevitably triumph over good. Whence it follows that if, in spite of everything, good exists, even though scattered and as an exception, we are justified in assuming its wide extent in the past. Now it is surprising from this point of view that travelers still point out to us so many peoples who are mild and inoffensive; the Doreyens (New Guinea), for example, among whom theft is almost unknown,[1] and who are at the same time far superior in morality and far inferior in civilization to the Malays, their neighbors; the Negritos, poor little negroes who inhabit Malasia, and who, hunted and persecuted, show us an example of the most exceptional virtue;[2] the Andamans and a thousand other races, of whom Wallace, after having studied them at close range for such a long time, shows us the gentleness, the reciprocal caring for one another, and the spirit of equality and equity. Perhaps it would be only right to add the cave-dwellers of Belgium, who, thus differing from those of Périgord, seem to have possessed no warlike weapon whatsoever.[3] Besides, among those savage peoples of today most given to plunder and to murder, how many would you not find, could you but penetrate the obscurity of their history, who, originally peaceful, began by learning the art of war in order to defend themselves before taking to fighting from any preference for it?[4] The original diffusion of the spirit of good seems to me to be attested, furthermore, by its tendency to reproduce itself and always, to a greater extent, after each great military conquest which has taken place owing to the interposition of the evil principle. It should be remarked, in

[1] See on the subject of these tribes *de Quatrefages*, who cites *Bruyn Kops*. They know no form of theft except child stealing, a monstrous one I admit, but explainable by reason of the institution of slavery, which they apparently acquired from an external source, for it contradicts their customs. Besides, as *Corre* justly points out in "Crime et suicide" (Doin, 1891), as a general rule "the savage has no slaves, or if he has, he ends by absorbing them into the tribe; the barbarian often trafficks in human flesh and blood, treats the slave like a vile beast, kills, or sells him."

[2] This negrito race, according to de Quatrefages, formerly owned all the land where today it retains so little room.

[3] See other developments on this point in my study on "Moral Atavism," which was published in the "Archives de l'Anthropologie criminelle," May, 1889.

[4] The Figians are everywhere cited as the most hardened cannibals. However, they are better than they are reputed to be, and it has required only a few missionaries to transform them morally and socially, according to the English traveler Brenkley (see *de Quatrefages*, "Hommes fossiles et hommes sauvages").

fact, that if evil triumphs, it is in the end to the profit of good. The victory of the most cruel, most crafty, and least moral tribes and nations, although the superior ones owing to their military power, has been a great and unconscious work of moralization, because by its means States come into accord with one another and humanity proceeds in the path of increasing agglomerations, of gigantic levelings of customs, a condition which is indispensable to that higher morality which embraces within its boundaries the entire human race. The Romans were a harsh and cruel people; nevertheless their conquests have had the effect of softening and even of enervating the Mediterranean population to such a point that the barbarians had the opportunity in their turn of invading them. How can this happen? Is it that, perchance, victory will transform the morality of the conqueror? Yes, sometimes; but more often the conquering race in the long run is dissipated and becomes absorbed in the conquered races, always in the majority, which, remaining true or reverting to their original mildness, have gained in defeat union and peace, favorable to the territorial expansion of their influence. This very frequent moral superiority of the vanquished over the conqueror would be a self-evident truth if history were not regulated by or for the conqueror. The conqueror is not satisfied with the destruction of the vanquished, but must calumniate him. Every population which has practised slavery has taken it upon itself to explain it by means of the pretended inferiority of the subjected race or its pretended crimes. It is only with the greatest difficulty that conscientious history or archaeology succeeds in guessing and extracting from under the accumulations of official or officious lies the historical truth with reference to the moral status of the Romans who were replaced by the barbarians, of the Saxons whose property was taken by the Normans, of the Moors who were exterminated by the Spaniards, of the old French nobility which was dethroned by the bourgeoisie.[1] Success is so far from sufficing in the eyes of the

[1] I could also add savages wiped out by white men. But here the dissimilarity between the belligerents is such that the vanquished, after their submission, have been unable to exercise any appreciable moralizing effect on their conquerors; and they have been the less able to do this as their defeat has everywhere, after a short time, been a radical destruction. For example, there remains not one single representative of the Tasmanians. Nevertheless they drew this admission from one of their destroyers, Governor *Arthur:* "We should recognize *today*, that it is a primitive race, but a brave one, and one endowed with noble instincts." Often, it is true, this moral superiority of the vanquished over the conqueror is only due to his defeat, and does not survive that. "The French serf and the colonial slave,"

one who triumphs that he hastens to complete it by justifying it, and to justify it in giving credence to the most impudent fabrications as regards his dead or disarmed enemy.

This great fact, too little known, the moralization in the long run and often the civilization of the master by the subject, should perhaps be brought into closer relation with another fact no less neglected, the moralization of man by woman. A traveler informs us that in the Marquesas islands the women have a deep horror of human flesh, and that this is also true among all peoples who are still cannibals. Is it true, as Letourneau would have us believe,[1] that this disgust, similar to that of the fox in the fable, is founded upon the restriction imposed upon the "weaker sex" against indulging in a dainty too rich for them? This is scarcely likely, if one stops to think of the attraction of the forbidden fruit. Better than any legal defense, the refinement of tastes and sentiments which distinguish woman, even though she be savage, without doubt forbid anthropophagy to her. Whatever else may be the case, the feminine aversion which is here referred to, and on this point we fully agree with Letourneau, must have been transmitted from mother to son, from sister to brothers, from wife to husband, and have contributed in great measure towards uprooting this monstrous custom. Also in this respect, the influence of woman has produced the same effect as the progress of civilization, notwithstanding that, a rebel against every civilizing custom, the "eternal feminine" has kept inviolate that freshness of soul which creates her charm, and in which seems to live again, as in her physical characteristics themselves, primitive humanity. Is this the only point where the power of moralization of the least civilized sex can make itself felt? No; assuredly woman has always had as little taste for homicide as for cannibalism. If then her horror for this latter practice has been contagious, why would her repugnance to murder[2] have been less? As to theft, it

says *Corre* in "Crime et suicide" (1890), "are worth more than the lord and the master, from the point of view of morality [religious and judicial]; emancipated, they equaled them in its attainment, and today the change would tend to show itself on the side of the masses of the people, who are the rulers and the least restrained, while they are the most lacking in education."

[1] In his "Evolution de la morale."

[2] Especially for bloodthirsty murder. *Ferrus* ("Les prisonniers," 1851) says with good reason that, whether in their manner of committing suicide, or in their homicidal proceedings, the most courageous and the most fierce women show "an insurmountable aversion to cutting instruments" and to every sort of death which, in causing blood to flow, disfigures. Is not our increasing horror of the guillotine

cannot have inspired very much repulsion, I fear, to her natural artfulness; also it is to be remarked that theft is on the increase, whereas murder is on the decline in the march of progress. But one can believe, even here, that the gradual replacing of violent and coarse methods of taking away property by processes which are artful and refined is due in a measure to feminine influence. Unerringly the slow, universal transformation of sanguinary criminality into voluptuous and perfidious delictuosity was accomplished under the increasing rule of woman.[1] For this reason criminality became effeminate as it became urban. We could in some respects represent final civilization as the revenge of woman upon man, and also of the herdsman upon the warrior; of primitive tribes, peaceful and oppressed, upon their oppressors. But even then, although there might be some exaggeration in this way of looking at the matter, it would nevertheless be true that the theory of crime as *a recurring phenomenon* is simply a hypothesis, without any justification. If man's ancestors were frugivorous, that is to say, gentle creatures full of tenderness for their own, as are the majority of monkeys, it is not war or assassination which we must seek to explain by atavism, it would rather be family life and the development of the patriarchal virtues.

due to the increasing "effeminization" of our customs, even although on principle we approve of the death penalty? Now among savages and barbarians bloodthirsty murder is by far the most frequent.

[1] Criminal statistics are, in appearance at least, very much in favor of women. There are in France only one-fifth or one-sixth as many women as men accused of crime. In the United States the proportion of women criminals is ten per cent. But in spite of these figures, some writers are not yet well convinced of the moral superiority of the weaker sex. Lombroso wants us to add to the debit side the quota of prostitution, "that feminine vagabondage." Just as though, more often than not, the prostitute were not the victim of man's libertinism, and as though one had the right to confuse the conditions of the offense with the offense itself. Woman, according to *Henry Joly, op. cit.*, is always better than man. Let us accept this formula if you will; that is sufficient for our theory. Let us add that the offenses where, as an exception, the feminine rôle prevails over that played by our sex (immorality, adultery, infanticide, shop-lifting, etc.), are precisely those which are on the increase among a people who are becoming *civilized.* Thus it is permissible to say that delictuosity, while becoming more civilized, is also becoming more effeminate. Thus from the moral point of view, woman seems to have had an extraordinary influence upon the development of the human race, as though to counterbalance, it would seem, the ever increasing insignificance of her share contributed to society from the intellectual point of view. There is not one single invention tending towards civilization, however unimportant, which is due to a woman.

§ 2. The zenith of the criminal law is bound up in the decline of criminality. Another cause of the existing crisis of the penal law; the crisis of morality. Attempts at moral reconstruction in every contemporary school. The modernization of morality. Necessity and difficulty of reforming penal legislation.

We see realized in history every possible transition between organized, triumphant crime and prevailing honesty, or vice versa. We see, on the one hand, brigands, pirates, who, having terrorized a continent, become themselves converted to a relatively honest life and found fine colonies (upon which, by the way, our penitentiary colonies might well be modeled). The permanent settlement of the Normans in the province which bears their name is the most striking example of these conversions "en masse"; there the gradual dying out of the criminal virus was accomplished on a large scale, perhaps not entirely blotted out, but radically changed, violence coming to be regarded as trickery, and cruelty as bad faith. Elsewhere, under the blow of catastrophes which have overthrown an established social order, we have seen honest people give themselves up in despair to brigandage and countries formerly prosperous return to barbarism.

Now when comparative honesty holds sway, the time to recommend penal reforms is not the time when its rule is really threatened by the danger of criminality in insurrection; society which at that time is honest then defends itself as best it can, crushing right and left, without reckoning the force of its blows, as a man surprised by a nocturnal assassin would do. It has its executioners as it has its soldiers. This may account for the atrocity of the penal laws of the Middle Ages. At the time of an epidemic there is no time to care for the sick according to regulation. On the other hand, when the tide of offenses has receded below low-water mark, opinion becomes disinterested. But in the intermediate stage, when the stemmed tide of crime still flows, reaching from bank to bank, the need of preventing possible overflowings and of some guarantee against them by means of ingenious and wise measures is felt; there is time to make a study of the delinquents one at a time, each offense becomes a theme to be discussed by the public and an opportunity for the judge to display his wisdom and his justice. Social utility is not the only aim of the legislator. It is, however, at such a time as this that the conception of a utilitarian body of penal law is elaborated, but in theory only. In fact the penalty becomes less and less severe from day to day, and the penitential reforms initiated by the theorists of utilitarianism themselves demand increasing expenditures of time and money which redound to the benefit of the malefactors.

The zenith of the body of the penal law, the golden age even of penal law, is thus connected to a certain extent with the decline of criminality, and it belongs only to an age of moderated customs, such as ours is in fact, in spite of a momentary recrudescence of offenses, to inaugurate a new era of criminal legislation.[1]

But that is not the principal reason for the infatuation of the public at this time, in the daily and periodical press, in the chairs of the universities and even at the bench and bar, for questions relating to delinquents, to offenses and penalties. One could more readily believe that the slight shudder caused our society by the revelations of statistics and anthropology in relation to that which concerns the steady increase of recidivism and the incorrigible character of the born criminal has caused these problems to become the order of the day. At the same time the true cause lies deeper. The sort of fever which today is pervading the penal law, as well as the economic problems and the political agitation of these times, is but one of the forms in new guise of the great actual crisis which morality is undergoing, a silent and scarcely perceptible revolution except for a few thinkers, but more fraught with incalculable consequences than many a famous upheaval.

This derangement of the internal guiding principle in the very midst of a social upheaval is attributable to many causes, even psychological ones. The crying need for new sensations, be they coarse and strong, or strong and exquisite, which causes the breaking out of the scourge of alcoholism among the lower orders, and among the upper classes of the scientific or artistic disease of hypnotism or of *symbolism*, the frenzy of psychological curiosities or *decadent* novelties and of Russian romances, betrays in this "fin de siècle" a grave nervous crisis, the enervating of superexcited brains. But this morbid condition has its own causes, which are intellectual above everything else. Without a doubt

[1] Since thirteen or fourteen years ago, when all this was written, criminal statistics in France have shown a decided amelioration. The progress of recidivism was checked from 1893, and then forced back. In the "Revue pénitentiare," of 1903, I analyzed and explained the official résumé of the statistics for the twenty years from 1880 to 1900, and while showing the excessive optimism of the conclusions which close this report, I also came to the conclusion that there had been an actual decline of violent crime, if not of crimes of fraud and stealth.

it may seem singular to attach to the ruling positivism, to determinism, becoming more and more a dogma, the abrupt and unexpected reincarnation of mysticism under a thousand different forms in our generation. But it is none the less certain that there is no more any intense realism without its reaction, either idealistic or chimerical, than there is fire without smoke, and often the clearest flame has the densest smoke. I want no better proof than the tendencies manifestly brought out by the most positivist of our contemporary litterateurs, the writers of the naturalistic school. Do not they also, and they especially, dabble in a quasi-mystical pessimism? Do they not allow passion to clear up that which is obscure to explore the monstrous, a sort of repugnant marvel, and for that reason the more feverishly grasped? To this cause may, to a great extent, be attributed the favor which the psychology of the criminal enjoys. Those who, like the neurotic hero of a celebrated criminal trial, would wish to indulge themselves in the sensations of an assassination in order to analyze them, in the style of Dostoïevsky in "Crime et châtiment," are numerous. That material well being, that relative comfort which has cost so many centuries, so many generous efforts, our society has and scorns, and calls for something else. Those proven truths, those stars of foremost grandeur, which so many geniuses have set alight in the heavens of science, it possesses, but it no longer takes the trouble to contemplate them. I am speaking of its intellectual chosen ones. Thus it is dreaming, with open eyes, that realist dream which has nothing in common with the religious visions of the past; and for want of finding what it is dreaming about it says that the earth is insipid and the sky is empty; it is in despair. However, in order to get rid of its despondency or its boredom, it digs right and left, with fury, into that which has never yet been disturbed, that which has always been repulsed with disgust; the shameful miseries, the hideous wounds, the heart of the scoundrel or of the prostitute fallen into the depths of the gulf; pederasty, sapphism, every variety of mental alienism or of moral aberration. It is not that it seriously expects to find therein anything very much; but, little as it may be, this may be capable of appeasing its enormous thirst for the unknown.

Now why all this troubling of the brain? Because certain new ideas have entered it, which have contradicted the former ones. However cold, however much of a stranger to the sublunar world, may be in appearance the quiet working of the thought of the philosophers, it is on this thought that we must fall back as on the high and hidden source of the torrents which ravage us, while hoping that they may perhaps fertilize our own brains. Let us then rise to the level of the doctrines of the masters. Like a superstitious thief who, after having plundered some spot, dares not disturb its landmarks, Kant, in his universal criticism of the ideas of the human mind, stopped short of the ancient notion of Duty and even, as though to have himself pardoned for all the ruin he brought about, made of it the keystone of his new construction or, to put it better, of his artificial restoration. This exceptional timidity of the boldest of thinkers is the striking proof of the prestige which up to the end of the last century religious morality, the only trace of religion yet remaining, had preserved. But at the present time a landmark is only a stone like any other; there is no maxim so venerable as not to be treated as have long since been treated the most sacred dogmas and summoned to produce its authority.

There is no longer any common ground between one school and another, neither on the limitations of rights or of obligations, nor on the fundamental distinction between right and wrong. Perhaps it could be said that there is a better understanding as to what is wrong than as to what is right, and that the same facts are characterized as crimes by persons who attribute to different and some times contrary acts the character of duties. But this agreement is only apparent or fleeting; in reality crime has a concealed meaning of *mortal sin* for some, a meaning of social prejudice purely and simply for others; and as far as each criminal trial is concerned, that which to some is an aggravation of the responsibility is to others an extenuating circumstance. From this there arises among the former as well as among the latter a more or less unfortunate weakening of their moral convictions; for they are only maintained in each case in proportion to the degree of energy necessary successfully to combat egoism upon the condition of having overcome unanimity, at least in the sphere of society immediately surrounding them. Also all the heads of the different schools, appreciating the needs of the present and fulfilling even better those of the near future, are compelled themselves to formulate with strength, and to enforce with authority, the morality which is the result of their theories. While the enlightened depositaries of the spiritual or Kantian tradition — in one word, Christian tradition — Caro, Beaussire, Franck, on the one hand,

and Renouvier on the other, expand the old formulas in order to force into them new desires and new ideas while absorbing them, the materialists, utilitarians, positivists, and transformists coalesce to project, into those minds which are a prey to contemporary instability, the fundamental elements of an infallible school of ethics, as workmen try to build a bridge over a river which has overflowed its banks. On their side eclectic thinkers, Fouillée and Guyau, are working to dissolve the perplexity of consciences into an original synthesis. But, to tell the truth, the ethical Babels of the innovators scarce rise before they are overthrown; the "evolutionary morality" of Herbert Spencer itself, begun on the plan of a pyramid, ended in a leaning tower, resting on a very weak foundation.[1] In truth traditional morality is the only kind which is alive or which survives in our hearts, and the leagues against it have thus far only served to befog it without succeeding in replacing it by anything durable. There lies the danger of the present.

Is the evil as serious, as irremediable as one is led to suppose? I do not believe so. This moral crisis which is causing thinkers so much anxiety is attributable, after all, to that combination of political, industrial, artistic, and other changes which stamp upon modern life its own particular character. Morals themselves are becoming modernized. The old rights and duties are seen to dissolve, but one can also see that new rights and duties are in process of formation, are spreading at a pace unknown to our ancestors, and that, if the sentiment of respect is everywhere undermined, the sentiment of the individual's honor (I do not say that of the family) as an incentive of actions is everywhere spreading from the middle classes to the workingmen, from the workingmen to the peasants, often in the form of a mixture of envy and absurd pretentions, but after all useful and fruitful. The old rights and duties, unchangeable formulae, ponderous precepts,

[1] When I was engaged in writing this passage, the name of Nietsche was still little known in France. His moral philosophy cannot be considered as anything more than an attempt to found a system of morals at one and the same time opposed to Christianity and to democracy. From the aspect of this double negative, it presents a true originality, even should it be deprived of the admirable style in which it is set forth, but that will not suffice to fulfil the requirements of modern society. It should have belonged to contemporary socialism to bring us a new moral philosophy, but the thing which Karl Marx seems least anxious about is the problem of morality, which with him becomes confused with the problem of economics. Georges Sorel is one of the few socialistic writers who have made any attempt to overcome this hiatus.

offering resistance and to a certain extent cumbrous, resembled the furniture of former times, which was so massive as to be immovable; though it lasted in one spot and through centuries, it varied and contrasted from one place to another. Our furniture of today is of a frailness which is compensated for by the ease with which it is renewed and moved about; it is the same with our literary works, our novels, our plays, our pictures, our ideas in general, which pretend less and less to make themselves eternal, but succeed more and more rapidly in universalizing themselves during the little time which is given them to live. In another chapter we will show that this difference can be accounted for by the social laws of imitation. The characteristic which I have just pointed out is, in fact, not peculiar to our age, but belongs to every period wherein the tendency to imitate the contemporary and the stranger prevails for the time being over the necessity, deep rooted and always triumphant in the end, of imitating one's forefathers. From the contemplation of this it is permissible to predict that the deep-seated disturbance of our souls will be brought to an end in our posterity.

In the meanwhile the situation is embarrassing, especially for criminologists. In every country is felt simultaneously the necessity and the difficulty of reforming our criminal laws; the necessity, owing to their flagrant disagreement with the new ideas of morality which are beginning to come to light; the difficulty, owing to the contradiction between these ideas among themselves and their contradiction of old ideas. Under what conditions and to what extent is the individual responsible for his actions which result in injury to his fellow-citizens? This very simple question, which is the fundamental point of the body of penal law, now seems as difficult of solution as the problem of the squaring of the circle. The unfortunate part of it, as we see it, is that it has been too hastily solved, in basing responsibility on free will as upon an indisputable postulate, and that this solution, once accepted without discussion, has given rise to an unending conflict between the determinists and their adversaries. We shall strive to point out in what follows how much the fictitious importance here attached to free will has contributed towards causing a division of minds and leading consciences astray, even towards enervating repression, and consequently how important it is to seek some other support for Duty and responsibility, for morality, and for the penal law.

§ 3. Prejudice of thinking that free will is the essential foundation of moral responsibility. Kant and his noumenal morality; Fouillée and his ideal liberty. Scholastic origin of this prejudice. Free will and science.

In the first place, it is interesting to ascertain at the basis of all rival theories, whether opposed or not to freedom of the will, what is the general belief, express or implied as to the indispensable condition of moral responsibility. A striking example of this indissoluble association of ideas is furnished us by Kant. This great thinker was a determinist; it would have been deeply repugnant to him, the constructor of the most symmetrical and restricted system of ideas which had ever been seen, to admit the existence of a world where a rigorous restraint did not rule. But at the same time the fixed idea of duty blinded him as much as the divine confusion of the starry heavens. Now in order to have the right to maintain this pure firmament at the summit of his system, he found it necessary to imagine for that purpose his "other world," that of "noumena," where he placed freedom, banished from the world of phenomena.[1] Fouillée, like Kant, is a determinist, and, like Kant, he is anxious to preserve duty at any price. But, like Kant, he is convinced that duty without liberty cannot exist. So that disbelieving in noumena, he conceives of the ingenious solution of the problem by means of his "force-ideas." According to him, ideas exist which, upon their appearance in a mind, would make their purpose, till then impossible, possible, and strengthening themselves by means of illusion, in this very illusion would gain strength to become realized by degrees; creative visions, to a certain extent like that God of St. Anselm, the belief in whom implies His existence. He adds that liberty is an idea of this type; and the mistaken consciousness of being free that each one of us has, is the true and gradual means of our liberation.[2]

I admit that I cannot very well understand, if the determination of will is decided upon at each moment by means of the com-

[1] Let us not forget the fascinating influence which Rousseau had over Kant.

[2] "La liberté et le déterminism," 2d edition, 1887. No one has shown as conclusively as *Fouillée,* in his "Evolutionism des idées-forces," that psychic facts are effective realities and not simply "epiphenomena" whose suppression would change nothing in the course of physical facts. He is right in attaching great importance to this demonstration. From my own point of view it has a very great importance. The result of this is that there is between *mental determinism* and physical determinism a profound difference which allows us to found the altered notion of *moral* responsibility upon the former.

bination of external influences and our inclination from within, how this combination will become any the less a determining factor because we have been more strongly influenced for want of any influence to the contrary. All that I clearly perceive in this is that as the consciousness of ourselves, of our personality, I do not say of our liberty, becomes more sharply defined, the preponderance of causes from within, which are ourselves, is surely augmented; and this, in my opinion, is of much more importance. It is the idea of our "myself," of our personal identity, which is really a "force-idea."

But we will come back to this matter. Renouvier rejects these eclectic processes; he refuses to admit either the placing of liberty on a noumenal throne, pre-real or extra-real, or its ultimate realization in an infinite future. As independent a Kantist as he is an ardent one, he denies at one and the same time the existence of noumena and the infinity of phenomena. But as, with that loftiness of soul which alone successfully overcomes the radicalism of his reasoning, he wants above everything to re-establish threatened duty, he undertakes a supreme effort, he replaces liberty, the moral postulate, in the very heart of the world of phenomena from which Kant had expelled it, where Kant had realized its retainment as ridiculous and inconceivable. He advances this theory, that there are, among the things to be seen in this theatre without wings, amid the procession of these spectres without bodies, limited by time and space, which limit he calls the Universe, apparitions which cannot entirely be explained by means of previous or coexisting apparitions, but partly created in all their parts by the unforeseen vibration which nothing could have made it possible to foretell one second beforehand, out of some new source of power, some *first beginning* of a series, introduced into the accumulation of already projected series from that instant of time.

However, if there is one system which logically should have resulted in determinism, it is indeed the "phenomenism" of this author, who before summoning liberty into his world seems to have closed every possible entrance to it, by formulating his dual denial of substance and of the infinite. After all, as there is nothing *under* phenomena, is it not *around* them, in other phenomena, that their cause for existing at all can be found; and if these surrounding phenomena are limited as to number, extent, and duration, is it not incomprehensible that the effect of these exact and definite conditions, which alone exist, can be indeterminable? The indeterminateness of effect cannot be conceived of, it seems to us, except upon condition of the infinity of causes. Never mind, although "the true ambiguity of certain future events," to use the words of the eminent philosopher, may be opposed to the principles of his thought, although it must especially and in vain resist the current of sciences daily becoming more torrential, which have come to besiege this pretended ambiguity even in its final stronghold, the human brain; yet in spite of everything, with the energy of despair, with a redoubled despotism of authority which is in proportion to the disturbance of consciences and can serve as a standard by which to measure it, the head of neo-criticism lays down this dogma: he teaches that Duty exists and that therefore it follows that liberty should exist in the face of all the arguments from the existence of facts. On all sides people have taken to this doctrine, in the schools, as in time of stress they huddle close round a forceful leader.

Thus, because they affirm the existence of Duty, the thinkers whom we have just been discussing believe themselves obliged to affirm the existence of Liberty, even when they declare that they are not able to understand it.[1] Others, the most advanced positivists, because they deny the existence of liberty, think themselves obliged to deny the existence of Duty and moral responsibility.[2] Thus each of them alike is imbued with the same prejudice which indissolubly binds these ideas together.

Unfortunately the legislators share in it. Article 51 of the German Penal Code, which is more explicit and less reasonable on this point than article 64 of ours, demands, in order that there be the commission of a crime, that at the very moment of the act the perpetrator must have been in possession of his "liberty of will." This requirement has as its inevitable result the acquittal

[1] As another example, *Siciliani* in his "Socialismo" (Bologna, 1879) founds responsibility upon *relative* liberty, just as Fouillée founds it upon imaginary liberty.

[2] This conclusion was drawn long since. As early as the twelfth century the example of *Amaury of Rennes* should have shown Christians the danger which lies in founding responsibility upon liberty. "The idea of paradise and of hell," says this author (who is cited by *Franck* in his "Essais de critique philosophique"), "rests upon the belief that we are the authors of our actions; but this belief is a mistake; for it is in God that we have our life, our actions, and our being. *For man there is neither right nor wrong, neither worthiness nor unworthiness,* neither last judgment nor resurrection. Paradise is knowledge; hell is ignorance." During the same period Roger Bacon, who had so many premature intuitions, advanced the utilitarian idea of morality as set forth by Franck.

of many dangerous malefactors. It is becoming more and more difficult for the medical expert, called in an ever increasing number of cases to pass upon the mental condition of the accused, to vouchsafe the opinion that he was free to will otherwise than as he did. If he expresses this opinion he is doing violence to his scientific beliefs. A medico-legal expert, Mendel,[1] has published a work intended to prove that his colleagues, in answer to the question "was the accused in the possession of his free will?" should refrain from giving any answer. Virchow and other medical celebrities adopt this same opinion. And they are perfectly right; to be of any other opinion is, on the part of a determinist expert, to sacrifice logic to utilitarianism, possibly to sacrifice sincerity to routine. On the other hand, during a criminal trial it is becoming more and more easy for a lawyer, with the writings of alienists at his disposal, to demonstrate the irresistible nature of the criminal impulse which carried his client off his feet; and for the jury, as for the legislator, the irresponsibility of the accused follows as a matter of course.[2]

[1] "Archives de l'Anthropologie criminelle," IV, 368.

[2] Thus I cannot agree with *Fonsegrive* that the penal law must practically remain the same, whether we do or do not admit of free will. "Like determinist legislation," says he in his interesting essay on Free Will, "the legislator who is a partisan of free will will take measures of precaution against the violent madman. Both will be more severe in proportion to the perversity shown by actions: only what one will call perversity of will, the other will call perversity of nature." But the legislator who is a partisan of free will ought the more readily to excuse, and to punish and blame the guilty man the less, as this man shall have been driven by a more violent inclination, or by a more perverse nature; the determinist legislator will do exactly the opposite. For example, Fonsegrive is perfectly right in saying elsewhere that the legislator who is a partisan of free will would be more inclined always to hope for the possibility of an improvement in the most perverse, and as a consequence to prohibit irrevocable penalties, the death penalty above all others. Before everything it is important to notice that the substitution of the determinist faith for the dogma of free will should result in the lightening of penalties, and in changing them as well. "As to theft," so aptly says *Carnevale* in his "Critica penale" (Lipari, 1889), "as it was considered to have been due simply to immorality, greed, or contempt for the law, it was natural to suppose that, by means of the condemnation of the guilty to several years imprisonment, society was sufficiently well protected against him and those like him. But when, over and above these causes, one discovers still deeper ones, *of which the former are only the result*, when, for example, one is concerned with the perversity of the thief's predecessors, his education, his shameless mendicancy, the petty larcenies which were his apprenticeship during his childhood, his shameful loves, and his sorry associates . . . then society feels less secure because it feels itself the more threatened. On the whole, free will being denied, society understands that it has not a single force, accumulated and isolated in an individual, to contend with, but that it stands face to face with a complexity of forces converging in an individual; its anger against him becomes less, but its peril is thereby increased."

At the same time, however firmly rooted it may be, the idea of founding responsibility and Duty upon free will is not such a very ancient conception; it is very far from dating back to the time of the origin of Christianity and of spiritualism. It is during the long-drawn-out disputes concerning Grace that the precise opinion of the theologians, and later of the philosophers, came, little by little, to be formed and formulated on this subject. It was said that human liberty was irreconcilable with the dogma of a divine prescience; but it was no less so with that of the creation. Can God create a free being? was the question the doctors should have asked themselves. And they should have replied, "No," for He would not know how to create an uncreated being. In fact, to be an absolute and first cause of one's acts one must be eternal from at least one aspect. However, in default of this happy gift — happy, I mean, politically and socially — of reconciling the irreconcilable, wherein lies the strength of the theological as well as the feminine mind, "grace and liberty, while doing their best to defend themselves, dwelt in peace side by side," as Franck well says, until the fifth century. Pelagius then put forth the first conception of free will and brought about the determinist reaction due to St. Augustine.[1] But Pelagianism, to tell the truth, and Augustinianism as well, had for a common characteristic a new pointing out of that essentially Christian principle, the personal quality of faults, and a sharpening of the idea of personal responsibility as a substitute for the idea of family or *genetic* responsibility.

Every century during which is unloosed, in religion or in politics at first, and later in every kind of social circumstance, one of those great storms of imitative impulse which upset distinctions of caste, of family, of province, and of State, and which cause the taste for strange ideas to succeed for the time being to the cultivation of the example set by our forefathers, — like the propagation of Christianity in the third and fourth centuries, of Protestantism in the sixteenth, of the cult of Voltaire in the eighteenth, and of Darwinism in the latter half of the nineteenth, — is to be recognized by the individualistic (I will not say always *liberal*) character of the prevalent morality. Christianity has made the salvation of the individual soul, and not the preservation of that collectivity known as the town or family, the main object of existence. Prot-

[1] According to Fonsegrive, St. Augustine is a supporter of free will "in spite of all the excuses he makes for it." But these very "excuses" are of such a nature that Bersot has been able to place this father of the church among the determinists.

estantism has individualized the priestly functions and substituted the examination of the Bible by the individual for its interpretation by conclaves. The school of Voltaire appealed to the reasoning power of the individual, and laid stress on the right and interest of the individual, on the feeling of the individual as opposed to traditional and general reason, to the right of the State, to the beliefs of humanity. Evolutionism is founded upon the variations of the individual in order to overcome the idea of species, and in its application to societies, in its attempts at sociology which it multiplies on every side, it justifies individual divergencies and similarities, and the independence of the will in the very face of duty. Besides if belief in free will belongs to Pelagius, the belief in original and hereditary sin, in theological determinism, is firmly anchored in Luther, and the belief in scientific determinism, in the heredity of the good or bad disposition of the soul, characterizes Darwin and Spencer.

The great question, at once theoretical and practical, is not whether the individual is free or not, but whether the individual is a reality or not. The problem was kept stirred up during the entire period of the Middle Ages between the nominalists and realists. Abelard in the twelfth century, — still another century crossed by a great stream of innovation, — was at bottom a nominalist, conceptionalism being only (as has been said) "a reasonable nominalism." As such it especially gave rise to reality in the individual, and burst the bonds of the solidarity which tended more to annihilate than to enslave, which in the eyes of its opponents united the individual being and the surrounding universe. Let us hasten to add that it is true that all individualism is, for the individual set free by its means, simply a transition between his former and future annihilation. There are several ways in which to exterminate the individual. One way, which is traditional (and, if you will, aristocratic), consists in his absorption into the family. Another way, which is natural and scientific, consists in his identification with the race, that is to say, with past generations. Collectivist solidarity in these days has a tendency to become what domestic solidarity was in the past. He who today says in regard to a crime, "It is society that is guilty," or "It is heredity that caused the wrong," would not have failed to have said in the old days, for example in the time of the priesthood of Ephraim, "It is the tribe that is guilty."

It should be observed that the Puritans and the Jansenists,

that is to say the souls who were most under the subjugation of the sentiment of duty, denied freedom of the will. Thus the proposition that freedom of the will is the cornerstone of morality cannot be sustained. With a rare good faith Fonsegrive recognizes this fact after a long and conscientious discussion. "It is well established," says he, in conclusion, "that laws, penalties, prayers, counsels, promises, and contracts are as easily explained by means of the hypothesis of determinism as by means of that of freedom of the will." And as a matter of fact, human consciousness has always refused to accept in practice the effects deducible from current opinion. If Socrates, accused of not believing in the gods of Attica, if Theodore and Protagoras, incriminated in the same way, had sought to defend themselves by showing that in very truth they did not believe in Minerva and in the eponym heroes, but that they were not free to have any such belief; if John Huss and Wycliffe and every heretic both great and small of the Middle Ages and of modern times had thought to escape the stake by proving that they were unable not to deny the dogmas they were striving to overcome, it is more than likely that this means of defense would not have proved of the least avail. Although Anaxagoras might have vowed that his mind, enlightened by astronomical observation, refused absolutely to conceive of the sun as an animated and divine being, he would none the less have been condemned to exile and to a heavy fine for having written that this luminary was an incandescent stone; and Galileo, in spite of similar protestations, would surely have been imprisoned. For example, if Anaxagoras or Galileo could have proved that they had perpetrated the writings with which they were reproached during the course of a dream, they would certainly have been acquitted, not because they would not have been free to dream otherwise, but because their minds asleep and dreaming would have been deemed not to have been identical with their normal and social personality, which alone was responsible to society. To repeat, it is identity and not liberty with which we are here concerned. Has anyone ever thought that he owed no recognition to a benefactor so obliging that it was impossible for him not to have done one a favor?

However, I must give warning of an ambiguity. One might think from what I have said above, that free will is in my opinion the most radical of errors, that in it there is not the slightest vestige of badly expressed truth, and that this is the only or principal reason for which I have felt myself compelled to seek another foundation for morality. But this is not the case; scientific determinism is as far from enlightening us as the dogma of an absolute truth; and concerning this subject we have some explanation to offer. We believe that there is a sense of the notion of liberty which is in no wise contradicted by the general spirit of the sciences, and it may be that understood in this acceptation free will is inherent in the hidden source of personal identity.

The idea of universal necessity, which we should try to conceive of, varies to a certain extent as we reduce beings to forces, a vague term, or to motion, a term which is relatively comprehensive; but in the last analysis it amounts to the same thing, and the important thing is to illumine the unperceived or ill perceived postulate, which belief in determinism implies. If every phenomenal appearance is the effect of an evolution, if every evolution consists in a meeting of elementary forces which have each their own effect separately, *and if it is an essential part of each of these elementary forces never to produce any but the same effect*, one is perfectly right in affirming the existence of a universal predetermination and in denying the actual ambiguity of a certain future. The condition which is here italicized is above all important, for let us suppose that it were otherwise, let us admit the existence of elementary forces whose essence — it is perfectly conceivable — should consist in never repeating themselves, and in constantly emitting what was new, assuredly the world would be no less admirable under such a hypothesis, it would even have a far more obvious reason for existing at all, but it would not be under submission to the law of predetermination. Thus predetermination in the last analysis means the same thing as repetition. In affirming that everything in this world is predetermined you affirm that everything repeats itself. One obtains the same result in explaining phenomena by means of motion. If every phenomenon is the deflection of movements which have met and united, *and if it is essential for every elementary movement to proceed in a straight line, if left to itself*, every phenomenon theoretically at least is a necessity and a certainty beforehand. Here again the italicized condition is of the utmost importance, and in the last analysis is but the preceding one expressed in terms of geometry, with the correct precision clearly to demonstrate the singular, arbitrary, and not in the least "a priori" justifiable character of the determinist Universe. If, in fact, we assume that elementary movements have as the essential characteristic of their fulfilment not only the following of that direction which is ever the same, which repeats itself indefinitely, and which is known as the straight line, but also of following a variable line which is deflected at every moment, and is never the same, we can see clearly that, according to this hypothesis, no phenomenon could be foreseen before its fulfilment.

Now why does every simple and elementary movement proceed incessantly repeating its same direction, until its meeting with another movement, which as incessantly repeating its direction, deflects them both and compels each to carry on an indefinite repetition of another character? Why this peculiarity? Why this exclusion of the countless lines other than the straight line, as though the straight line, which in reality plays so obscure a part in visible and passive nature, were alone capable of realization in invisible and active nature? I realize that habit has made us familiar with this peculiarity; but I am of the opinion that our predecessors were not mistaken in believing that the curved line movement of the elements was apparently a reality in the first instance.

Well, as it is established that universal predetermination indicates an elementary repetition (or an elementary rectilinear form, which is a particular kind of repetition), let us finally ask ourselves if it is permissible to take for granted that universal life consists in repetitions? It is impossible not to be aware that it can be defined either as a varied repetition, or as a variation which is repeated, but that in every case the element of variation is inherent in the very heart of things. Consequently we should consider as insufficient, and as only good for the purpose of a scientific scaffolding, the resolution of the world into forces and into movements. There is something else at the foundation, as there is in the origin of all this; and this something, should it not be the cause of itself, that is to say, free? Liberty is the faculty of primordial initiative or of fundamental initiative. It is to be implied from necessity, as inventiveness is to be implied from imitation, as variation in general is from repetition. It comes under the head of necessity, and by an inevitable downward process, as effort becomes habit, innovation routine, inspiration precedent. Stuart Mill, most determinist of logicians and most logical of determinists, saw concisely that everything could marvelously well be explained by means of laws, excepting the material the laws were made of and the point at which their operation began, that is to say an assemblage of data of facts essentially irrational. There is nothing left to us except to choose between these two conceptions: that of a liberty concentrated into a single being known as God, who shall personify in Himself alone the creative side of things, universally and continually a creator; or that of a liberty which is disseminated among the countless substantial and active elements of the Universe. Universal necessity thus presupposes divine or elementary spontaneity. Let us accept this last hypothesis and we must recognize in the freedom of the will a certain truth perhaps, but which is not the one the moralists say they have need of; a truth not limited to man, but extending to every being; a truth not demonstrated by the illusory testimony of consciousness, but suggested by the observance of the wonders of phenomena, of that which is perpetually new and unexpected in the most regular evolutions of this world.[1] If by means of pantheistic atheism liberty is made a possibility, at the same time it is rendered necessary and universal, which to all intents and purposes brings us back to a denial of free will such as it is understood.

It is nevertheless true that it is important to give its place to that sub-phenomenal autonomy or anarchy which is the foundation of every constraining law and of every despotic regularity of phenomena. It cannot but recall from afar the noumenal liberty

[1] This assumes that we do not deem the perpetual changes in this world sufficiently well explained by Spencer's so-called law of the "instability of the homogeneous" or by the considerations by means of which Darwin is compelled mechanically to explain the appearance of those countless variations in the individual which are the postulate of his system. On the hypothesis with which these thinkers start, that of an absolutely homogeneous substance governed by absolutely inviolable laws and which all consist in the reproduction of counterparts, it seems impossible to me to conceive of even the possibility of a new embroidery on the eternal canvas. One can, it is true, and perhaps one should, look upon variation as consisting in new combinations of former repetitions; but we will be unable to explain to ourselves the change in these combinations without admitting the natural and essential heterogeneousness of the elements of repetition and their eternal originality, otherwise called their liberty. Universal evolution assumes the eternal fixity of an invisible something which does not evolve. It seems as though the knowledge of this truth thrusts itself upon the evolutionists in a confused manner, for they all give as the foundation of their systems the conservation of force and of matter. But why should these two quantities be the only things whose immutability and everlastingness can be conceived of? Why should not these attributes belong just as well, or even better, to the elementary *qualities* of which they are the grand total? Stability, the everlastingness of distinctive characteristics belonging to the final elements of the Universe, and which are all original, seems to me to be far more necessary.

of Kant, that liberty by virtue of which, according to this great thinker, each soul on being born chooses freely its *characteristics*, expecting afterwards to be irrevocably bound by its own decree. Thus he made even identity and the realization of one's own existence rest upon liberty, and it is regrettable that he shrouded the depth of this thought under the fictitious and artificial expressions by which he characterized it. To sum up, the great objection to free will was formerly based upon the divine prescience, and is today based on the conservation of force. But there is this very great difference, that force is inherent in individual beings, while God was external to them. Individual beings, according to existing monism, can thus participate to a certain extent in the liberty of the Whole, whereas they remain strangers to the freedom of God.

But we have sufficiently delayed with these considerations, the net result being that the question of free will, if it should be retained, belongs by right to the field of metaphysics, and not to that of morality; at the same time we must recognize the fact that underlying all morality there are hidden metaphysics, as Fouillée has so well shown.

§ 4. Analysis of the conceptions of duty and of right, of responsibility and of justice. Duty derived from finality simply. Consequences of this derivation.

This much having been premised, we must now, before we enter into any discussion of the Right and Duty to punish, set forth the general ideas concerning Duty and Right, responsibility and justice. We shall give to the idea of duty, over that of right, its logical and chronological priority, and we shall see for what reasons.

According to Littré, the primitive conception of equality, A equals A, is once more to be found in our conception of equity. Justice, says Spencer in support of his view, is equality of treatment. In other words, an action carried out by men who are different, but alike inasmuch as they are agents, should have a similar result from the point of view of punishment or reward, of penalty or of price. It is but just that a similar service should have a similar price, that a similar injury should be repaired by a similar indemnification. In another sense and one conflicting with the former, it is equally just that a similar need should meet with a similar satisfaction. Thus understood, and it cannot be otherwise, justice presents a striking analogy with the determinist postulate, and the axiom of causation according to which under similar circumstances a similar phenomenon is sure to follow. Justice is the relation of the actions of humanity to their price or to their penalty, or the relation of human needs to their gratification, reckoned in terms of the relation of cause to effect as presented by the external world. Justice is so far from denying the universal determinism that she assumes its existence and follows its example. At first sight one might be inclined to think that duty is but the working tool of justice, and that the best means of finding out whether a proposed duty is a real duty is to inquire whether, supposing everybody practised it, the final result of all this obedience to duty would be to place society in a state of perfect justice. But, as a matter of fact, there is no truth in this. In the first place we have just seen that the idea of duty is already implied in the definition of justice, because the latter is conceived of as a relation which *ought* to exist. And now let us go back to the origin of duty. Duty is only a sort, but a very curious sort, of final judgment, the conclusion of what I shall term the practical syllogism, whose major premise is a wish, an object not merely an opinion, and whose minor premise is the perception of a proper means of attaining this end. "I *want* to kill my enemy; now I *know* that a poisoned arrow will kill a man; therefore I *ought* to shoot at him with a poisoned arrow." Thus reasons the savage in the forest. There is not a living creature who at every moment of its life does not unconsciously draw conclusions in reality similar to these. Reflex action is the most elementary expression of this. The purely teleological duty which we have been discussing is transformed into a moral duty, into a duty properly so called, when the major premise of the syllogism, instead of being an object suggested by a need of the individual's organism, is a social suggestion, a collective object, a work in common such as the greatness of Rome or of Athens, the avenging or deliverance of the French fatherland, or "the greater glory of God."

This object began by being the individual wish of a powerful man, of a king-god, a hero or a priest. But it is when, by means of a contagion of imitation, it has been communicated to inferior brains, that it little by little acquires among the latter the authority of the categorical imperative. In fact, reinforced in each one of them by the surrounding reflection of the wishes of all, the wish to accomplish the general object arises with a greater intensity, *practically infinite* as a geometrician would say, and by the very fact of its repetition becomes unconscious; so that being presented apart from its premises, the conclusion seems as though it were hovering in the air without earthly connection, and internally affects the tone of a pronouncement for which no reason is given, and from which there is no appeal, of an order absolute and divine. Those "noiseless ideas which conduct life" are the *final ends* pursued for themselves alone, and which are such because they are strange wishes communicated to one another. Thus under the uncomplimentary name of "heteronomous" morality, it is *social*[1] morality which certain philosophers seek to depreciate. Whatever we may do, whether we replace the commandments of God by utilitarian, evolutionist, or scientific formulae expressing general utility as we may conceive of it, it does not matter; morality will always be heteronomous, or else it will not exist at all. Franklin tells us of a Newfoundland dog and a watchdog who, whilst fighting fiercely at the edge of the sea, together fell into the water; the watchdog would have perished had not his opponent, immediately brought back to a realization of his professional duty (so to speak), by the contact with the water, rescued and brought him to land, only, however, to renew with him the sanguinary struggle. If ever there was a heteronomous morality, it was indeed that which prompted the animal to his sublime devotion. But it is its heteronomy precisely which makes it sublime.

Now is justice the only and greatest object which society thus offers to every right-doing soul, or the only one which can finally triumph? Not at all. The pole, towards which converge all the wishes of a nation and which is responsible for their accord, is some great work to be realized by means of their collaboration, and that same great work more often than not demands the establishment of a military or civil hierarchy of privileges, and not the juxtaposition of equal rights. There are cases where justice cannot be realized without its being to the prejudice of everybody. Let us suppose for, example, that by reason of a bad harvest over the whole of the terrestrial globe, the quantity of rice or of wheat available was not enough to prevent everybody from

[1] *Individual* morality, which makes us realize duties towards ourselves, is certainly nothing more than an echo within us of social morality. Never, without being fostered by civilization, could the refinement of feeling which it assumes have been brought forth.

perishing of hunger. If this amount were equally distributed among all men in equal amounts, or in amounts proportionate to appetites or even to services rendered, all would die of hunger. Thus it would be better to resort to an unequal distribution. And under these circumstances would it be necessary to draw lots in order to ascertain those who should be given the privilege of having something to eat? Yes, if all agreed to accept this way of proceeding, like the castaways on the Medusa raft. But why should they submit to this rather than to resort to violence? It thus follows that in all cases more or less analogous to the one I have just imagined, and which are reproduced on every hand in the history of humanity in a thousand different forms, the will of society would be to have recourse to violence, and the dictates of duty would be to kill one another. Even although there should exist in a society no notion of equity or right whatsoever, the sentiment of duty could not fail to influence all when a common object was in view. Justice is none the less the intense dream of our reasoning faculty which loves equality and symmetry; but to how many of the things we most cherish is it opposed! Beauty, genius, glory, are just so many examples of injustice. What can be more unjust than progress, that superiority of the idle sons over their laboring fathers, which owes its very existence to the work of the fathers!

There is something fanciful about the quest for a proportionateness between an action and its reward or its punishment, if not between a need and its satisfaction; but there is nothing irrational in the pursuit of an adaptation of means to ends. The axiom of finality upon which duty is founded, and which may thus be expressed, "Granted the same object under the same circumstances, the same means will bring it about," is nothing more than the axiom of causality turned round the other way. It is as though one said: "Under the same circumstances, if the same act takes place [the means], the same effect will follow [the object]." But justice is simply the artificial copy of natural causality, duty is its employment by the logic of the will. Granted the will of society, and natural causality being known to science, which furnishes the minor premises of the syllogism of morality, duty, the expression of social finality, follows. Here we have the point it is necessary to set out from, and this is what modern criminologists are doing in asking for a penalty adapted to its object and not exactly proportioned to the offense. As natural causality becomes better known and the will of society becomes more aware of its own existence, duty becomes better defined and is strengthened, while at the same time it loses its character of mystery. As the mind becomes more cultivated, it becomes capable of more accurate self-analysis, in truth, and more rapidly dissipates duties which are instinctive and irrational; and to compensate for all this it gets a better grasp on things, it can take in higher things, vaster planes, more comprehensive benefits and it suggests to the will objects better calculated to force it to appreciate the insignificance of the individual as compared with the achievements of the individual himself, his prospects and his hopes.

The foregoing explanation, which causes moral duty to be derived from teleological duty, that is to say from the will,[1] has no more effect in taking away its essential characteristics so magisterially outlined by the spiritualist philosophers, from the former, than the continued transition from the ellipse to the circle has the effect of taking away the truth of the geometrical formulae based on the sharp distinction of these two curves. But it has the advantage of making us understand why fatalism has from all time been reconcilable with the very deepest morality; it also makes us feel certain that the sentiment of duty can never perish, and enumerates for us its variations of direction and intensity. Just as the sentiment of moral duty is related by its genealogy to the sentiment of the duty of finality, although it is radically different, in the same way, when a moral duty has not been carried out by one who feels it, the remorse which he will then feel, in spite of its distinct origin, will follow the regret felt by him who shall have failed to carry out that which he judged to be for the advancement of his own particular project. Now, although one might conclusively demonstrate to de Lesseps, should he fail in piercing the Isthmus of Panama, that it was an impossibility for him to have overcome the obstacles placed in his way, that he was not free to succeed,[2] his regret would ever remain as keen. And in the same way we must not be astonished that one who is a simple quietist should repent with a sincere

[1] Will, in fact, differs from desire in that the act which one wills is not desired at once and by itself, but is only judged proper for the attainment of that which one desires. Instinctive and immediate desire, which is often unconscious, is the major premise of will, just as will, the fixed, rooted, and almost always unexpressed end, is the major premise of duty. Duty springs from will just as necessarily as will from desire, and almost in the same manner.

[2] Remember the date at which these lines were written.

grief of the sin he may have committed, even though convinced that, for lack of grace at the desired time, he was fated to commit it. Remorse is the more painful in proportion as the sense of duty is more intense, and the intensity of duty is the working of those two sorts of combined quantities, the degree of longing pointed out in the major premise, either conscious or unconscious, from which it flows, and the degree of belief involved in the minor premise.[1] The soldier of France feels his duty of discipline the more keenly as he the more deeply shares on the one hand the national wish to see France triumph over her enemies, and on the other hand, the military conviction that obedience is the necessary condition of victory. Now increase in him the strength of this wish, you will not have accomplished very much if at the same time you diminish the strength of this conviction. It would amount to the same thing if you strengthened this conviction while weakening the wish.

The importance of these waverings is disclosed at the psychological moment of the decision. So always within us there is a battle taking place between two syllogisms, one of which infers an affirmative and the other a negative. Let us suppose that Germany should declare war upon us. Every Frenchman enlisted under the flag would feel in himself the call of duty, "Go and fight," but at the same time he would feel the resistance, more or less weak or strong, of his love of ease, of study, or of pleasure. I do not know what false voice would whisper to him from the very depths of his egoism this advice, disregarded more often than not, "I want to live and to have a good time; now the means by which to attain this end is to desert; so I ought to desert." But at the same moment another and a stronger internal sense of logic would cry out to him, "I want France to triumph; now by my desertion she will be deprived of just one chance of success; therefore I must remain at my post." Or again, if he happens to be a coward, he will say to himself, "I want to live; now if I desert I shall expose myself to the risk of being shot; therefore I must not desert." In this internal struggle of conclusions, which will carry him away? It seems as though there were no solution to the problem, because, generally speaking, the blessings between which one must choose are heterogeneous: safety and honor, money and

[1] Let us add that the intensity of this belief and of this desire is itself a function of the activity of the social life, of the more or less deep and swift contagion of influences.

esteem, the love of a woman and the joys of the family, etc. And this heterogeneousness is, as a matter of fact, one of the great snares for the thought which dwells on these very questions. But everything is simplified if one but observes that, underlying these qualities lacking in a common standard by which to be measured, there are many qualities which to a certain extent have some standard of measurement.

To sum it all up, the conclusion which will win is always the one which bears the most heavily on the desires and beliefs which are the most pronounced. For example, consider what would happen if, when this line of reasoning, "I want to live; the means are to desert, therefore let me desert," was vaguely and unconsciously brought to the mind of the conscript, he were absolutely convinced that the only means of preserving his life was desertion. Wholesale desertion, which is not an unknown thing in the bravest of armies, has no other cause than this, — death suddenly revealed. Let us notice in passing that these cases of single combat of which we are at the same time the battlefield and often the victims, these conflicts by which alone self-sacrifice and devotion are made possible, have themselves as their essential condition the dual nature of the belief and the desire within us, and their independence of each other. For were we free to believe everything it was to our interest to believe, everything which we wished to believe, obviously the protestations of the conscience could never prevail in us over the criminal impulses of our passions. The same internal division, and not any political fiction such as the pretended separation of powers, or the so-called constitutional guarantys, explain why there are limits to the oppression of slaves by their masters, of the people by the government, of minorities by majorities, even in the case where the power of the oppressors is unlimited and where their desire, conforming to their interest, is to exercise it to the limit.

§ 5. The duty of punishing. Criticism of the ideas of Fouillée and Guyau on this subject.

After these general considerations it is time to take up the special problem of the body of the penal law. The result of what has been said is that in our eyes the *duty of punishing* must have been felt by society or by the person injured long before the right to punish, and that the purpose of our subject is concentrated around the question of knowing to what extent and under what conditions this duty should be exercised, and not around the question of knowing what is ideal justice in the meting out of punishment. Unfortunately, the spiritualist school (though it has contributed so powerfully to the perfectioning of the Penal Law), seems too often to have forgotten, in its preoccupation over abstract equity, the importance of finality and of social utility. Its most respected French representatives have, to tell the truth, avoided this forgetfulness more than the Italian masters. But these latter have given way to it to such an extent that penal law in their hands was degenerating into a sort of fictitious casuistry, where the classifying of entities makes us lose sight of realities, and where we are engaged with offenses, with the manner of being of offenses, and their relation to penalties, and never with the offenders and their relation to good people. Here we have neither psychology nor sociology, nothing but *ontology;* the word exists there, and their pupils avail themselves of it.[1] For example, they will go into a long dissertation on the question as to whether recidivism should be treated of in the chapter on the *quantity* of the offense and of the punishment, or in the chapter dealing with their *degree,* or whether the sentence of acquittal or of conviction should be placed among the *natural* or *political* methods of bringing the criminal action to an end. But of recidivists and of the startling increase of recidivism attested by statistics, of observations made on the inmates of prisons and on the efficaciousness of the various courses pursued in the various penitentiary systems, no mention, or very little, is made.

Even the most eminent minds allow themselves to be carried away by the taste for superficial order, of pseudo-rational symmetry. According to Rossi the offense and the penalty which overtakes it should form the two terms of an equation.[2] He does not for one moment doubt the possibility of this equality. One would be surprised, if one were not aware of it from "The Metaphysical

[1] See on this subject the curious and interesting pamphlet by *Innamorati,* professor of Criminal Law at Perugia, "Sur les Nuovi Orizzonti et l'ancienne école italienne" (Perugia, 1887). The author, who belongs to the school of Carrara, that is to say of the last illustrious disciple of Beccaria, seeks to open up the limits of the traditional ideas, of the "national school" says he with patriotic pride, in order to bring within this fold the strayed sheep of the new doctrines. But what his efforts serve best to prove is the urgency of ventilating and animating this old locality.

[2] According to Romagnosi, whom contemporary innovators reckon among their forerunners, we must oppose to the inclination towards crime a *counter-influence equal and similar to it.* Here a regard for the interest of the general public intervenes; but a seeking after symmetry is still perceptible.

Principles of the Law," by Kant, to what excesses the rage for order can carry away a great genius. Kant requires that the penalty should not only be equal, but should also be similar to the offense; and the obvious impossibility of obtaining this similarity together with this equality in a great number of cases does not deter him in the least. On the strength of this principle he pronounces himself in favor of the death penalty. According to his view every homicide should be followed by capital punishment, excepting infanticide and murder committed in a duel. When all is said and done, this philosophy of retaliation is of a surprising weakness; and if one recognizes its author in it, it is to be attributed solely to that passion for symmetry which reveals itself in every part of the architecture and in the smallest part of the structures of his system. One might call it artificial were it not for the fact that nature, in all her physical manifestations, and especially in those which have life, from crystals and worlds to the lower or higher forms of animal life, all stamped with the impress of a radiating or bilateral symmetry, is dominated by the same necessity.

Let us, therefore, not be astonished to see the greatest men adopting the childish conception of the symbolism of the penalty, and its analogy to the offense. It is not the Buddhistic conception of hell alone which rests on this principle, if one is to form any opinion as regards this conception of hell from the subject of their bronzes, where we see depicted liars having their tongues torn out, and sensualists climbing a thorny tree which lacerates them, in their efforts to reach a beautiful and nude woman seated among its branches. Dante's inferno is exactly similar. There gluttons are being gluttonously devoured by Cerebus; the violent and bloodthirsty are immersed in a river of blood; astrologers and sorcerers walk backwards, with their heads thrown back as far as they will go, for having professed to look ahead into the future.[1] And as we are on the subject of Dante's conception of penalties, let us incidentally remark with Ortolan, that the damned are more often punished for their vices than for any specific crime; a very rational point of view, as justice ought to tend to strike at the impulse to do wrong, through the medium of the wrongful act, this impulse being a perpetual danger of the commission of new faults; but a point of view which is irreconcilable with free will given as the very foundation of culpability.

[1] In our old statutes incendiaries were burned alive.

We are not concerned in this book, — which is devoted to an examination of the very latest ideas on the subject of the penal law, — with criticist or neo-criticist theories, nor with spiritualistic theories, whose common characteristic and chief merit is to perpetuate a tradition, to cause a secular tree to blossom again, and not to sow a new seed. It is not that in our estimation the ability more or less usefully expended on this task of strengthening, on this consolidation of Dutch dikes, so to speak, which the older morality offers in opposition to the flood of modern desires, cannot equal that of the modern engineers, who are sometimes nothing more than destroyers. But we are not engaged in a comparison of authors and of writings; we are engaged in the study of ideas which are now making their way into the world for the first time with a certain lasting publicity. So we should bring all our energies to bear upon the positivist innovations, which will be laid bare in the next chapter and whose value will be estimated in all the remainder of this work. At the same time, however, it is advantageous, before doing so, to put in their right place the eclectic ideas of the two very distinguished thinkers whose names have been mentioned, — Fouillée, and his disciple Guyau, prematurely taken from us in the full bloom of a train of thought so poetic in its very severity, so religious in its irreligion.

Fouillée fully appreciated the fact that the question of penal law comes down to asking oneself what the nature of human association really is. He asked the solution of this problem with all the fulness of which it admitted. Is the tie which binds associates together anything more than a manifestation of organic solidarity? or is it an agreement either implied or expressed, an accord of their wills which is not forced? He attempts to lay the foundation of his two conceptions of the *social organism* and the *social contract*, and by this means he hopes to reconcile naturalistic positivism with spiritualistic idealism and to have the right to perfect the utilitarian reason of the material trouble which it introduces into organized society, by means of the ethical reason of the motives underlying an act which is offensive. An illusion, we think. He does not tell us what he understands by the *organic* relations of the members of society, as distinguished from their *contractual* relations.

What is it which allows us to attribute to the social body a real and not alone a metaphorical similarity with the body of an animal if it is not the unanimity of disposition? And what is this unanimity except the slow and toilsome result of imitation, regarded as a credulous or submissive passivity, in other words of that internal work of social logic, of intellectual agreement, which is called religion or science, and of that internal work of social teleology, of voluntary agreement, which is called morals or legislation? Now what are contracts except one of the principal means of social teleology? Therefore society is not so much to be distinguished in so far as its organism is concerned, from society in so far as its contractual relations are concerned. The first point of view takes in the second just as the genus embraces species; which, moreover, is enough to serve as a motive for the objections which the partisans of the first conception, for example one of the most learned of its promoters, Espinas, have directed against the second. Now, according to Fouillée, the result of the social contract is that the condemned has consented to submit to his punishment beforehand, and that consequently according to the way in which this philosopher looks upon justice, his punishment is just. Is this strictly true? No; but it is true that, more often than not, impressed unconsciously and in spite of himself by the convictions of his environment, the convicted man who has been *sentenced*, *believes* that the penalty imposed upon him is just, though he may be far from *willing to have it imposed.* Though ordinarily he does not go so far as to feel "the duty of being punished," to use the happy expression of Beaussire, he recognizes the duty of society to punish. Now, is not his punishment as much justified by reason of this unison of the wrongdoer's thought with that of all, as it would be by reason of the supposed harmony of his will with the general will? If the social contract has seemed to be wholly imaginary, it is because it has not been completed by means of the social union of minds, which is far more manifest and no less important from a legal point of view than the union of feelings. It is seldom that a man, unless he be a monster or a fool, does not come within at least one of these unions; sometimes a dissenter intellectually, he stays a conformist as to feelings and to action; sometimes, which is the case of the ordinary malefactor, a heretic as far as will is concerned, he remains orthodox in his beliefs.

After all, if it were true that the convicted man consented to his own punishment, the question would always be whether this punishment, even though consented to by him, should be allowed by his judges, and if this "contractual penalty" is necessarily reasonable. A contract is only a reciprocal subjection of wills in place of their unilateral subjection; it does not suffice to prove the utility of that to which we may agree to consent, nor does it prove the agreement of wills united with uniform beliefs. Philosophical criticism strives to attain this agreement, ever incomplete, by pointing out unperceived contradictions and inconsistencies. This criticism goes back to the premises of the syllogism which has as conclusion judgments and moral sentiments (consolidated judgments), and it shows, or believes that it shows this conclusion to be a *survival* of vanished premises which have been replaced by new premises which contradict them; that for example, our Christian morality, our ideas as regards chastity, humility, and the despising of riches, are contradicted on many points by the main objects of our life which have reverted to paganism, and by the discoveries of our sciences. It thus teaches us to reform our ideas of morality, not in making them conform to an ideal justice which should exist outside of our social logic and teleology, but in carrying out the irregular task of this double co-ordination. Only the surest means of hastening the achievement of this harmony is to suggest more and more to the association of wills, as their main object of attainment, the worship of right, because the most contradictory tendencies of mankind are ingeniously reconciled from the moment when they contract the habit of taking on the aspect of rights, that is to say, by taking as their objective point their very limit.[1]

Thus expressed as general views, the rival interests seem no

[1] The idea of right which *Fouillée* imposes upon himself, and which he looks upon as marking the limits of liberties and their mutual recognition, is unfortunately based on a postulate which he himself knows to be a delusion, that is free will, or rather the shadow of this phantom, the ideal of this illusion. "We place," says he, "this basis [that of the moral responsibility for punishment] in the category of a liberty which is entirely ideal, and not in that of an already existing liberty, like the free will of the spiritualists. In our eyes this liberty is an end, and not properly speaking a cause. In a word, the moral justification for punishment is deduced *from ideal liberty conceived of as the underlying principle of right*, according to us, and its justification socially is deduced from the general acceptation of this ideal by means of the contract." ("Science sociale contemporaine," p. 282.) Why has not Fouillée given as the underlying principle of right, instead of this ideal liberty whereby he leaves it up in the air, and with so much eloquence and profundity too, the identity of the individual which is at the same time real and ideal? When I feel myself bound to keep my appointments, is it necessarily because I feel that I was free not to make them? Is it not, before everything, because at the very time that their fulfilment is expected of me, I feel myself to be the *same* person, or very nearly the same person, as at the time I made them? An identity which as a matter of fact is always imperfect, but which appreciates its own existence better and better in thinking itself to be itself, a "force-idea" if such exist, as I have already pointed out.

longer to antagonize one another so keenly, and the logical solution of their teleological conflict becomes a more simple matter. Then, instead of being disputatious, one becomes litigious, and pleadings in court supplant blows dealt upon the field. When the advantages of this legal guise, or disguise, are well understood, it becomes so much generalized as to be applied not only within the limit of two particular interests, but also to a particular interest and a general interest at one and the same time. One seeks to put in terms of law even the need of reaction which will be aroused among the entire mass of honest people by the criminal violation of some right. This need, this spontaneous force, whether called a thirst for vengeance, or indignation, hate, or repugnance,[1] is in direct opposition to the needs and the personal interests of the offender; he is anxious to live and to be happy, society wants him to die or to suffer; and the object becomes, from the legal standpoint, to dissimulate this opposition which cannot be destroyed in oneself, and to change it into an apparent accord, just as when my neighbor covets my vine which I am desirous of keeping, the absolute contradiction of our desires is compensated for by our common respect for the same hedge or the same ditch. So the legislator, there as here, will have to set a limit; he should specify to what extent the social appetite for punishment shall be satisfied and do nothing beyond this. Shall we say with the utilitarians that it is only to the same extent as death or suffering, demanded with loud cries by an outraged mob, can serve to prevent by means of intimidation, the recurrence of wrongful acts attributable to that imitation of oneself which we call habit, recidivism, or the imitating of someone else? I am perfectly willing to admit this; but you must admit that general utility is susceptible of a broader interpretation. Why could you not just as well say that the desire for death and pain clamored for (or not), in the case of a particular criminal by the multitude, should be carried out to the same extent as its carrying out would benefit this aggregation of common ends, designs, or caprices which, taken together, are called general utility? Indeed, if in order to realize some caprice of a political

[1] "Malefactors," says *Garofalo*, "are the object of universal hatred. For the conditions which explain the anomaly whence crime is derived cannot be known by the people, they are only made a study of by the learned and by specialists. Besides, even among these latter, if the recognition of causes makes hatred disappear, another feeling which is almost equal to it cannot help but assert itself, I mean repugnance towards beings who are so unlike us and so malevolent." ("Criminologie.")

nature which might occur to them, or to pass from one form of government to another, all that a people would need would be the head of some man, or his exile, the thing would soon be done; and there would not be lacking historians to prove that progress purchased at such a price was not too dearly paid for.

In fact, one can scarcely see what authority the utilitarian philosophers would have for admitting that there can be crimes committed by a nation against a man, even by a majority against a minority, although this occurrence, exactly the reverse of ordinary crimes, is frequently found in history. This takes place every time that the mob violates an individual right which annoys it, but which it must recognize (belief and desire being, as we know, independent of each other). The situation is the same whether the question be one of a primitive people in revolt against their king, whose divine right is not doubted for an instant by any of the rebels, or whether it be of a popular form of government incited against a small class of citizens whose essential liberties violated by it are a component part of the Rights of Man recognized and proclaimed by itself. Here I maintain, and my principles uphold me, that there is the commission of a crime, and that the perpetrators of these outrages realize that they are criminals; but once again the historians, with their habitual utilitarianism (as inconsistent as it is profound), forgive all these transgressions. If one looks at it from this all too common point of view, I fail to see why one should be more greedy for the shedding of the blood of the criminal than for that of the innocent. Why should not the need of vengeance or of indignation, of expiation or of infamy, be included among the number of those desires, of those projects, or of those passions which are haphazardly understood by the collective name of social interest?

It follows that there is no more reason to limit this need than any other; it ought to receive full gratification. Thus I cannot see why the penal law of expiation should be so unanimously combated by the utilitarian philosophers, who, to be sure, are more idealistic than they give themselves credit for being. I could more readily understand why it should be so combated by their opponents, who are, in fact, its decided champions (always excepting Franck, who is in this, and not in this alone, one of the most enlightened of spiritualists).

Possibly you may say: These outraged feelings, these "virtuous hatreds" which an offense gives rise to and which drive us to torment the offender for the very pleasure of tormenting him, even without the slightest interest from the point of view of intimidation for the sake of example, and which cause us to dream the evil dream of a terrestrial hell, as a successor to the vanished dream of the terrestrial paradise, are passions created by virtue of a mistaken conception. This mistaken conception, free will, being out of the way, we can no longer, without contradicting ourselves, despise the murderer who was forced to kill, nor be outraged by that fatalism of which he was the instrumentality, and the logic of society demands that this inconsistency should be dissipated. My answer is: Should this be demanded, then how many other inconsistencies does any society carry in its train, which the legislator upholds and which he should uphold, and upon which he is compelled to rely! But this demand is not made if it be true that free will has nothing to do with the case and that what we despise in an act is the perversity of a nature and not the freedom of a will. However, I will add that outraged feelings can be carried to excess and that hatred is an evil to be contended with, and to be stemmed by means of the co-operation of every kind-hearted person; and this no doubt is partly responsible for the gradual lightening of penalties which is one of the historical laws of criminal law. Nevertheless, hatred is one of the great and irresistible stumbling blocks of the heart, and it will take centuries to overcome it. Let me as far as this is concerned, share in the hopes of Guyau! "Already," says he, "in our time, there are none who are capable of feeling hatred except the ambitious, the ignorant, or fools." Three exceptions he thus names which constitute a numerous category. Now as long as man has absolute need of hating something, would it not be a good thing for him to turn his hatred against crime and the criminal? What better can hatred accomplish than to take itself for its own object and its own sustenance? Is not the execration of an assassin in a way but to feel a hatred of hatred?

The sympathy which society feels towards the victim of a crime must necessarily be given expression, even among the most educated people, by means of a profound antipathy against the criminal by reason of his crime and apart from any thought of the crimes which he is still capable of committing or that his example is capable of suggesting. If one thinks this ardor of antipathy irrational, one must judge the ardor of sympathy to which it is united, and from which it is inseparable, with the same severity.

It is said that our indignation, in so far as it is excessive, makes us want a penalty for the wrongdoer which is of no benefit to us. Possibly; but it can also be said as well that our sympathy felt for its victim causes us to feel a grief which is often useless, which will not bring back to life the person who has been assassinated and will not restore the stolen property to the person who has been robbed. Will anyone go so far as to bar this feeling which does nothing, this powerless wish? The unfortunate part of it is that the very day these fine and useless sentiments and others similar to them shall have disappeared, all the useful ones which are left will lose their value and the charm of life will be broken. But when the honest masses, sympathizing with some unfortunate, slain or mutilated by this criminal, desire but are not able to repair his injury, they betake themselves to the author of this powerlessness and despise him all the more and obtain for themselves a momentary satisfaction in punishing him.

So remarkable is the tenaciousness of this sentiment in spite of every calculation and of every line of reasoning, that it almost seems as if a higher law here intervened, — as if a social echo of the mysterious physical law of a reaction, which is equal to and contrary to action, makes itself vaguely felt in the inclination which irresistibly drives us on to avenge ourselves because of a wrong, as though to contradict an error, to oppose will to will (*i.e.* in a criminal trial ending in a punishment), or to oppose judgment to judgment (*i.e.* in a civil trial). In civil trials one may believe, and one is supposed to believe, that the violation of the legal right by one of the parties took place owing to inadvertence, and this mistake is disproved by the enacting part of the decision. In criminal trials the violation of the legal right has been intentional, and herein lies their essential characteristic (just as the simple, elementary nature of the legal right which has been violated), and this bad will on the part of the wrongdoer is redressed by that of society which causes the sentence to be carried out. We take vengeance, after all, for the same reason as we spontaneously deny, often without any need, as is proved by the many cases of ruinous litigation over a trifle.

This deep-rooted and strange need of symmetry, which I have already combated in Kant, and which I shall often keep coming across and must continually reckon with at the same time as I combat it under certain forms, has not failed to cause instructive astonishment to the thorough moralists. Some of them are seeking to find a place for it. "The good should be happy"; Fouillée concedes this, but according to him it by no means follows that "the wicked should be unhappy." On the other hand, Janet seems disposed to give up the idea of the compulsory relation between merit and reward, but he persists in upholding the relation between demerit and punishment. The truth is that one of these positions is no more easy to defend than the other. In vain does Fouillée think to justify his position by calling attention to the fact that suffering is never an end and can be nothing more than a means of attaining happiness. But is happiness itself, and especially its element pleasure, its proper end? Physiologically, pleasure, that physical happiness, is nothing but a stimulant and a warning for action; socially, happiness, that social pleasure, is in the same way nothing but an encouragement to activity. Is that as much as to say, in parenthesis, that action itself is the final end? Not at all, for the goal is the work and not the doing of it, the victory and not the combat, the universal empire of Rome and not the gradual romanization of the universe, the absolute triumph of hellenism, of Christianity, of modern civilization, and not their propagation by degrees.

But what is the work other than the conception of the work, its scheme, which never can be realized in full? That is the end. It still remains to be seen why one plan is decided upon rather than another. It is not always because one anticipates more happiness from its execution than from any other, or, if one does anticipate more happiness from it, it is just for that very reason that one has chosen it. There are men and peoples who are just like children. A capricious child will refuse to eat the dish he is fond of, to drink the syrup he has a preference for if you do not serve it to him in such and such a plate or glass, or at such a place or in such a position, simply because this *idea* has flashed across his brain and he has seized it on the wing while imitating someone just as he would have grasped no matter what idea. These caprices of children are not as far removed as one would be inclined to think from the perverseness which causes a nation not to want to be wealthy, prosperous, or happy, excepting under such and such a form of government acclaimed this evening, brought on by a current of imitation, and overthrown tomorrow morning for no better reason. Now children, it seems, are the more capricious as they are more intelligent. Their caprice is already idealism, the sacrifice of pleasure for the sake of the idea, alone and disinterested. There is a great moral lesson to be drawn from these observations of the psychology of children and of peoples.

But let us come back. Guyau very concisely states this problem: "Is it true," he asks, "that there exists a natural or rational bond between the morality or immorality of the *will* and a recompense or a punishment applied to the *feelings?* Does any kind of reason exist, outside of social conditions, why the greatest of criminals should receive, because of his crime, simply a pin-prick, and the virtuous man a price for his virtue?" He cannot understand "that in the profound order of things there can exist a proportionality between the good or bad condition of the will and the good or bad condition of the feelings." But, let us ask, do there not perhaps exist, "in the profound order of things," reasons which compel the will and the feelings, in order that they may expand, to improve upon the social surroundings? And from the time when society becomes a necessity, does not the bond which seems unjustifiable to Guyau thrust itself upon us, and will it not impose itself upon us for all eternity? As society assumes the reward of intentional services, logically it must also rest upon the punishment of voluntary acts which are to its prejudice. Let us demonstrate that logically this is a necessity.

Whether we found the economic world upon *to each according to his works* or upon *to each one according to his capacity,* it is a certainty that the price of a service should decrease in proportion as its usefulness or that of its producer is judged to decrease. If its usefulness goes down to zero, its price is zero. But following this, if its utility becomes negative, that is to say if the service becomes changed into a detriment, what should happen then? The principle of continuity, at the very foundation of evolution, demands that the motion should not then cease; utilitarian evolutionists could not very well contest this. Now it must be one of two things, and it is just here that the difficulty begins to appear. Either logic demands that, instead of *receiving* a price the man responsible for the detriment should *give* a price, called an indemnity, to his victim, or else it exacts that, instead of receiving a *price,* the author of the misdeed should receive the *opposite of a price,* a punishment proportionately heavier as his act shall have been more injurious or his will more depraved. But of these two different deductions, which is the better reasoned out? And, in the first place, must we necessarily choose between the two, or can we not adopt both of them together, as has been done by all legislation? The first one, the one which gives the indemnity as the counterpart of the price, has this advantage over the second, that it impliedly includes a portion of the latter, whereas the latter in no way includes the former. When the thief pays the man he has robbed the money damages for his wrongdoing, this payment is at the same time a punishment for him, a sorrow often the most keen. On the contrary when the thief is imprisoned, the man he has robbed does not become any more wealthy. Thus it seems as though we should give pecuniary or other compensation for offenses the preference over every other penalty.

And I hasten to add that in fact it is far from being practised as it ought to be; Garofalo is absolutely right with respect to this.[1] But the unfortunate part of it is that all too often in a case where this sort of punishment would be applicable (*i.e.* where rich or solvent wrongdoers are concerned), it would be insufficient, and that in a case where it would be sufficient to check poor wrongdoers whom the payment of an indemnity would compel to a long and difficult expenditure of labor, it would not be applicable, because of the laziness and lack of energy of this class of delinquents. That is why *the inverse of the price* and not the *inverse of the receiving of the price* was chosen principally as being the logical and analogous consequence of the remuneration of the services, for the suppression of offenses. Thus it was necessary to inflict sufferings which should not be simply the grief of having to deprive oneself of one's money in order to indemnify one's victim or to do work for him. Kant, too, was able to define the right to punish: "The right which the sovereign has *painfully* to afflict the subject by reason of a transgression of the law." It is a good thing to insist upon this, should it be alone to justify from the historical point of view, I do not say from the humanitarian point of view, the cruelties perpetrated by our forefathers in the enforcement of the penal law and to explain the persistence of corporal punishments, such as flogging[2] and the bastinado, among European peoples and not the least civilized of them. If originating from the instinct of punishment, from the first paternal correction,[3] the spirit of punishment in order to combat

[1] His ideas have found an echo upon this point everywhere. See especially the "Bulletin de l'Union internationale de Droit pénal," no. 3 (1891).

[2] The penalty of flogging has been re-established in England for some years past, and it is suggested that Parliament make a study of its application.

[3] Read on this subject the forceful pages of *Eugène Mouton*, former magistrate, in his book on the "Devoir de punir" (1887).

the spirit of crime rivals the latter in its atrocities and its horror, and also in lack of inventive powers, from an irregular rotation in a narrow circle of ideas which are ever the same, let us say in justification of our forefathers, that an energetic feeling of justice and of logic led them astray on this point. Among them vengeance was judged to be a duty as imperative and on the same order as gratitude, and in the same way as they believed it to be their duty to reward a past service, independently of any reckoning as regarded future services, so they thought it their duty to punish "quia peccatum est" and not only "ne peccetur." By good fortune, the need of seeing services more and more remunerated, by means of the raising of prices, is ever on the increase in the progress of civilization, but the desire to see injuries paid for in suffering does not make any headway; on the contrary, pity increases with the disposition to associate with others, and that, I repeat, is why penalties are becoming less harsh.

Let us conclude that Caro was not wrong, in his "Problèmes de morale sociale," in seeking at the bottom of the principle of expiation, although in another sense, a soul of truth. Further on we shall have to come back to these considerations. We shall see how, from the historical point of view, expiation could be conceived of as the strongest expression of penal utilitarianism, *i.e.* conceived, as a means to purify an entire people from the stain with which (as they believed) the crime of an individual stamped them or to obtain for the guilty individual himself, imbued with the ideas of his surroundings as to the purifying effects of suffering, the happiness of re-establishing himself in his own eyes.[1] To be one's own executioner, to be the avenger and the offender at one and the same time, nothing can better prove than this ancient and mystical notion the unconquerable force of the need of vengeance, as well as the depths to which the contagion of surrounding beliefs descends in the inner conscience of the individual. Notwithstanding, can one deny that penal law thus understood, outside of any idea of defending it, or of any social utility, responded to a desire, which was very noble and (from a social point of view)

[1] Guyau sees, and not without penetration, the need of an artistic and aesthetic restoration underlying the feeling which, in the presence of moral ugliness, makes us wish for its effacement by means of an expiation, just as in the presence of some beautiful marble which has been mutilated or of a beautiful verse of Virgil's which remains unfinished, we dream of supplying what they lack. This feeling may be fanciful, but it is so universal and so persistent in an infinite variety of forms that it becomes necessary to take it into account.

very useful, for moral perfection? A man flogged himself, fasted, suffered in all sorts of ways, sometimes even gave himself up to the judge in order in the end to give himself the inner joy of feeling his conscience to be pure. Looked upon from this point of view, the most peculiar and extravagant penances, — of which be it understood there can be no question except as a memory, — barefooted processions, in a shirt and with a candle in one's hand, pilgrimages to Jerusalem with the pilgrim's staff, etc., had an incomparable utilitarian efficacy, which the costly therapeutics of our houses of correction has not equaled up to this time.

CHAPTER II

THE POSITIVIST SCHOOL

§ 6. Origin of the positivist school; its existing representatives; its success and the progress it has made.
§§ 7–12. Statement of its doctrines. Preliminary remarks. (I) What is responsibility? (II) What is a criminal? Classification of criminals. (III) What is crime? Its characteristics and its causes. The three *factors*. (IV) What is the remedy for wrongdoing? Criminal sociology.

§ 6. Origin of the positivist school; its existing representatives; its success and the progress it has made.

Before taking up the doctrines of the positivist school by means of an analysis of the best writings on the subject, it is desirable briefly to trace the history of its formation. It would be an easy task if this school, following the example set by the idealistic school, had shown itself anxious to clear up its own origin, and to supply within itself the precise consciousness of its previous condition. But nothing of this kind exists,[1] and in the first place we shall have to observe this peculiarity, that it is the philosophy of the absolute, of the categorical imperative, of the distinctions drawn between principles and beings, which is to be distinguished by its amenability to historical research, by the importance which is attached to the genealogy of ideas; and it is transformism which excites a distaste for its former manifestations. This contrast, however, is easily explained. Positivism, which pretends to apply itself exclusively to the observance of facts, can only see in the case of its own history a more or less useless preface to its demonstrations; but dogmatism, which finds in tradition its firmest support and its chief argument, at the same time that its discussion seems rational in manner or in aspect, makes of this preface its principal chapter. So, if evolutionists sometimes show themselves to be revolutionists in social science, it is not an inconsistency on their part, whatever may have been said of it. Also positivism is progressing, and dogmatism is

[1] We have an exception to make in favor of *Marro*, who preceded his book on the "Caratteri dei delinquenti" (1887) with a historical notice, rather dry but complete enough in itself.

losing ground, and it is never at the moment of its prosperity that a family is most preoccupied with its genealogy.

However much of a revolutionist one may be, one is always something of a traditionalist. It is not because of any chance coincidence that the initiative of the serious reforms in penal legislation, ever since the Middle Ages, has had its origin in Italy. Lombroso, the founder of the new school of criminal anthropology, in giving this steadfast direction to his mental activity, has, more than he is aware of, obeyed an ancestral suggestion. He wrote "L'Uomo delinquente" partly because his compatriot Beccaria had written the "Traité des délits et des peines," and because in the sixteenth century, Farinacius, Hippolytus of Marsiliis, and other great criminologists who, says Esmein,[1] "shine with incomparable brilliancy," had, so to speak, made of the soil of Italy "the fatherland of the criminal law." Let us not forget the school of Bologna in the twelfth century, which compels us to go back to the "Corpus Juris" of the ancient Romans, the first and final source of all these diverse and opposed currents. However, it is permissible for a Frenchman, not exactly because of patriotism, but because of a habit of clear and precise analysis which is a national characteristic, to reclaim for France a good part of the germs of the ideas which, having been exported, flourished on the other side of the Alps. Beccaria, whose book appeared in 1754, that is, two years after the punishment of Calas and the eloquent protestations of Voltaire, is a child of our eighteenth century; in him is reflected and concentrated all its sentimental philanthropy, unaffected optimism, and excessive individualism, and he owes to this faithful echoing of our philosophers his reception at their hands, and the universal enthusiasm which this reception earned for him.

Lombroso, it is true, seems to have been more directly inspired by English ideas, at least in the *form* of his doctrine. As to the scientific facts which go to make up its *content*, they obviously have no nationality, and only the method by means of which they are disclosed can have one. But from this point of view French influence is far from being insignificant. To dress up in the Darwinian and Spencerian manner the results furnished by the observation of lunatics in asylums, by the measurements of skulls or other parts of the body in the laboratories devoted to anthropology, and finally by the registrations of statisticians; in other

[1] "Histoire de la Procédure criminelle en France," p. 288.

words, to interpret physiologically, and not socially, crime and the criminal; to present one as the phenomenon of recurrence in which is reproduced in miniature and as an exception that which was formerly the rule, and the other as a savage driven to crime by his very nature, wherein we should see the enfeebled image of our ancestors of long ago; such was the first conception of the celebrated professor of Turin. Later on it became more involved. Even he, to his sorrow, found himself compelled to recognize in the criminal less of a primitive man than of a madman, less of an ancestor than of a patient, and he thought to combine these two interpretations by means of a third. Then came Enrico Ferri, and with his rare qualities of assimilation and deduction, of lucidity and strength which go to make him a classifier and popularizer of ideas to an equally prominent degree, he has completed the work of the master. He had for auxiliaries a whole phalanx of m nds who were fond of innovation, such as those of which the new Italian renaissance can muster so goodly an array, and especially a magistrate, Garofalo, the most fine-spun logician of the group, who made himself carry the doctrine even to the point of use by the judicial majority, which is more apparent than real, where tentative legislative reforms are formulated of their own accord. And if the hope of having their innovations adopted at this day by the Italian Chambers, where the spirit of Beccaria has just had its triumph, has since had to be abandoned, one may be sure that some day or other it will reappear, when we take into account the supple tenacity and the steel-like flexibility which characterizes the intellectual temper of our neighbors. Whatever may have been the result of this collaboration, Lombroso's point of view has broadened, considerable importance has been attached to the social causes of the offense as well as its psychic and physiological causes, statistics have been plunged into as greedily as anthropology, there has been as much ardor to strive to decipher the hieroglyphic figures of the former as the confused and contradictory descriptions of the latter. New problems have sprung up, the question of the death penalty, previously settled by Lombroso in a Draconian way, has split the school, and other divisions have been brought to light within it.

Now, to come back to our search for origins, at the starting point of all the ways which have converged in the "nuova scuola" as though into their cross roads, we will find Frenchmen. Its *formal* conception was furnished it by means of an ingenious combination of the Darwinian or Spencerian evolutionism with the utilitarianism of Stuart Mill and Bentham; but behind Darwin do we not perceive Lamarck; behind Spencer, Auguste Comte; and behind Stuart Mill and Bentham all our encyclopaedists and even all our idealists?

Its *material* substance has been supplied by means of the happy concurrence of two new and rapidly growing sciences, those of statistics and anthropology, not forgetting legal medicine and mental pathology, which, having preceded anthropology, contributed to bring about its creation and are always engaged in fostering it. But emanating from the quasi-Frenchman, the Belgian Quetelet, — for I do not suppose that we will go back to the rough outlines of this nature by the Florentines of the thirteenth century, — the science of statistics has undergone in France itself its finest developments from the point of view with which we are concerned. Guerry has been since 1829 the true precursor of the statisticians of the new school, with naturalistic tendencies; our criminal statistics, which have been in regular use for more than half a century, are the most fertile and pure source from which Ferri, who does not cease to express his admiration and recognition, has drawn.

Anthropology, on the other hand, has Broca as its father, even though it may have Gall for its more or less legitimate grandfather; psychiatry had its origin at the end of the last century in Pinel, and was carried on during ours by Esquirol and by a whole line of great contemporary alienists, our compatriots, among whom we must mention Lucas, Morel, and Despine, who expressly and long before Maudsley,[1] stated and supported the theory of native criminality looked upon as a variety of insanity; and lastly legal medicine, which is partly confused with the preceding science, numbers among us its most illustrious representatives, from Orfila to Tardieu, and Brouardel.[2]

Such was, in brief summary, the part contributed by our nation to the deposit or the first working over of the materials afterwards

[1] "Jacques le Fataliste," of *Diderot*, "did not know the name of vice nor of virtue; he pretended that one was either happily or unhappily born. When he heard the words 'recompense' or 'punishment' pronounced, he shrugged his shoulders." Still another French predecessor of the "nuova scuola."

[2] *Despine's* "Psychologie naturelle," dated 1868; *Morel's* work on "Dégénérescences" is dated 1857, and *Prosper Lucas'* is dated 1850. Before this had appeared *Lauvergne's* book, on "Forçats considérés sous le rapport psychologique, moral et intellectuel observés au bagne de Toulon" (1841). *Maudsley's* first work, "Mental Responsibility," is dated 1876.

made use of by the Italian criminologists. The share of Germany is practically nothing; it can be reduced to the ancient conjectures of Gall and Lavater, the conscientious works of Benedikt being later than the "Uomo delinquente," the first edition of which appeared in the reports of the Institute of Lombardy from 1871 to 1876. On the other hand, England, as we already know, made a powerful contribution to the common work, and not only by means of the famous names already mentioned, but by means of that blossoming forth of original psychologists which has been peculiar to it in all times, and among whom it will be sufficient for us to mention Thompson ("The Psychology of Criminals," 1870) and Maudsley (1873).

Furthermore Lombroso's worth is scarcely lessened by the researches of his predecessors; in our opinion it is still more lessened by that absence of method, by that insufficiency of criticism, by that disordered confusion of heterogeneous facts, by that inclination to take an accumulation of exceptions as proving a rule, and lastly by that nervous hastiness of judgment and that obsession of fixed ideas, I mean fleeting ideas, which is noticeable in all his writings, and which his absorbing ardor, his prolific observation, and his original ingenuity cannot make one forget. This enthusiastic seeker is none the less the true promoter of what he calls criminal anthropology, a name unsuitable enough too; and the impetus which, even outside of Italy, keeps so many distinguished minds occupied in the many different lines of this branch of study, emanated from him. In France, Lacassagne, professor of Legal Medicine at Lyons, was one of the first to follow him, less as a disciple than as a competitor. Essays on the tattooing of criminals, on the criminality of animals, on the criminal calendar, have aroused interest by means of their stimulating originality and have held it by means of their scope filled with possibilities.[1] To the first edition of "L'Uomo delinquente" he replied with "L'Homme criminel" (1881), just as later on to "L'Archivio di Psichiatria," a periodical organ of the new Italian school, he replied with the "Archives de l'Anthropologie criminelle."[2] He accounts for innate criminality not by means of atavism, but by means of arrested development and degeneration, an explanation which tends to prevail, and no less successfully does he throw into relief the social aspect of the question, which

[1] "Les Tatouages" (Paris, 1881); "L'Homme criminel" (Lyons, 1882), etc.

[2] The first number appeared January 15, 1886.

his rivals on the other side of the mountains have a manifest tendency to keep in the shadow. He in his turn has founded a school whose pupils are enriching the library of the criminologist,[1] with instructive works, and if the French public has already become so keenly interested in theories and ideas which amount to a passion on the other side of the Alps, it is to him especially that they owe it.

In Italy, Lombroso has perhaps aroused a legion of writers rather than of workers,[2] among whom we must mention besides Ferri and Garofalo, Messrs. Virgilio, Morselli, Sergi, Puglia, etc. Also with each new edition of "L'Uomo delinquente," in 1878, 1884 and 1887, this work, thanks to successive tributaries and the continual ferment of its author's brain, always rather ready to generalize, but to suppress as well, became considerably augmented. I will say as much for the "Nuovi Orizzonti di diritto penale," by Ferri, which, a slim pamphlet to begin with, has not ceased to grow like the ranks of his adepts.[3] It must be admitted that neither he nor his collaborators have neglected any of the known means to stir up opinion: special reviews, public conferences in the principal towns, controversies with schools opposed to them, and at last, a Congress. The Congress held at Rome, in 1885, under the name of "First International Congress of Criminal Anthropology," brought together about a hundred learned men more or less imbued with the new doctrines and who came from quite far away, even from Russia, to profess and to attest the propagation of their positivist belief.[4] Nevertheless it enabled

[1] "Du suicide dans l'Armée," by *Mesnier* (1881); "De la criminalité en France et en Italie," by *Bournet* (1881); "De la criminalité chez les Arabes," by *Kocher* (1884); "Criminalité en Cochinchine," by *Lorion* (1887), and a number of more recent works.

[2] Also of passionate and sagacious adversaries. One adversary, as much by reason of his moderation as by reason of the solidity of his learning, is *Alimena*, author of a fine work on "Premeditazione."

[3] Since these lines were written, the ranks of which I am speaking have become strangely thinned.

[4] It is none the less true that the classical school still preponderates, as well in Italy as elsewhere. A table of *Bournet's* (see "Archives de l'Anthropologie criminelle") shows that there are published in the Peninsula thirty papers or reviews dealing with criminality, and that only five serve as organs of the positivist school. The Italian Penal Code has recently been revised in the manner of the old school and not of the new. I must add (May, 1903) that at this very time the enthusiasm of the Lombrosians has cooled off a great deal; some of them have delved into Marxism, which causes them to forget about criminal anthropology; the others limit themselves to questions relating to the system of punishments. No one believes in the criminal type any more, excepting Lombroso.

one to observe the delineation of the dissensions which have begun to affect the school and will not be long in splitting it up, and which would have been much more pronounced had the programme of the second section, that of *criminal sociology*, been as complete as the programme of the first, that of criminal biology. If the influence of religions, of governments, of education, of wealth, of social conditions, and of the period of history upon criminality had been discussed as were the influence of physiological heredity, of mental alienation, of epilepsy, of alcoholism, of age, of the temperature, and of the seasons, the socialists would have had a fine opportunity for showing that poverty and not cold or alcohol, is the cause of crimes, and for laying the responsibility for the offenders at the door of so-called honest society. But the school, to tell the truth, is still destitute of a sociology which properly belongs to it; it reserves an undetermined place for the "social factors" of the offense, without explaining itself concisely on this subject, whereas it is, or it seems to be, well settled as to the "anthropological factors" and the "physical factors" and flatters itself with having sketched the criminal type or types with a precision unknown until its own time and which unfortunately is deceptive.

The same hiatus was to be observed in it at the second international Congress which it held in Paris in August, 1889, and which was, moreover, a brilliant affair. Much too large a place in it was usurped by the criticism of Lombroso's hypotheses; but we must not regret it after all, if, as the majority of the learned men who have followed these sciences have thought, the pretended criminal type emerged from it greatly crippled, or rather reduced to the condition of a phantom in process of vanishing. A science which is being created should consider as a gain the loss of its chimeras, which might have led it astray in the beginning. It is time, however, to replace shadows by substance, and conjectures by certainties. Also the most obvious result of this interesting Congress seems to me to have been the bringing to light of the preponderance of the social causes of offenses and the social remedies for offenses and, as a consequence, the urgency of treating criminal anthropology as a form of psychology before everything, and as a form of criminal sociology.

We must recognize the fact that these first founders, alienists or medical experts for the most part, were to be excused, by reason of the nature of their habitual occupation, for having felt themselves compelled to exaggerate the influences of vital importance; and if the adherents which it later recruited among the Faculties of Law, at the bar, among journalists, and even among the magistracy, reacted against this tendency of exclusion, the only ones among the latter who have brought a clear and systematic point of view in social science, a radical and practical remedy (none call it impracticable) for the evil of wrongdoing, belong to the socialist Church. To number these men, Filippo Turati, of Milan and Napoleone Colajanni, of Sicily, among others, with the supporters of the "nuova scuola" is perhaps an illusion due to the relations of political intrigue which it has maintained with them. But when we compare the courteous chivalry of which it has given proof while fighting them, at least in formerly combating the first of them, with the tone of its controversies with the champions of the classical school, with the successors of such men as Rossi, Romagnosi, and Carrara, we are unable to think it as hostile to the former as to the latter,[1] and the notion strikes us that these adversaries who are so much in sympathy are allies in disguise, who are rather compromising. At the same time, if this is so, and if socialism is, in fact, the only hope of development which is offered to the sociological aspect of the doctrine, we can say that it is destined to contradict itself or to become ruptured, for the socialistic idea is just the reverse of the naturalistic idea. This is already apparent from the hostile reception given by Lombroso and his supporters to Colajanni's last book on "Sociologia criminale" (1889), which is very remarkable as a criticism if not as the advancement of a theory. The school contains still many other contradictions as we shall soon see, without counting the minor divergencies, notably on the policy, one must not say on the legitimacy, of the death penalty; and finally, accord seems to hold sway only on its fundamental points, the belief in evolution, the denial of free will and of moral responsibility. Again, on this last point, I personally am able to hope that, since the last Congress of Paris, a belief to the contrary is far from being unshaken.

In spite of everything this school has made its way in France

[1] In response to an impassioned pamphlet of *Turati*, on "Il Delitto e la questione sociale," which created a great stir in Italy (1883), *Ferri* published "Socialismo e criminalita," a very substantial and powerful pamphlet, but showing sympathy for his adversary. This is entirely different from the volume entitled "Polemica," where personalities abound. I must add (May, 1903) that since these lines were written, Enrico Ferri has become a convert of Marxism.

and in Europe. In France the Congress of which we have spoken enabled the rapidity of its progress to be measured. Opened by the Minister of Justice, it numbered among its presidents or its most active members, Doctors Roussel, Senator, Brouardel, Magnan, Motet, Manouvrier, Lacassagne, Magitot, Féré, Bournet, Coutagne, Madame Clémence Royer, Messrs. Bertillon, Prince Roland Bonaparte, and many others. Mr. Herbette, Councillor of State and Director General of the Penitentiary Service, had frequent applause during his eloquent speech. More than two hundred persons became members. Belgium was represented especially by Dr. Semal; Holland by Mr. Van Hamel, professor in the Faculty of Law at Amsterdam, as official delegate of the Dutch government; Switzerland by Dr. Ladame; Austria by Mr. Benedikt; Spain by Mr. Alvarez Taladriz, who founded two years ago in Madrid a review of "Anthropologia criminale" on the model of "Archivio di Psichiatria" and of the "Archives" of Lyons. Though Spanish America, where, however, the writings of the new criminologists have met with great success, and even serve as authority for judicial sentences,[1] was not able to send any representatives, Russia had several, such as Mr. Bajenoff, director of a lunatic asylum at Moscow, and Mr. Drill, a distinguished publicist. The United States had sent Mr. Thomas Wilson, curator of the section of Prehistoric Anthropology in the Smithsonian Institution at Washington, and Mr. Clark Bell, president of the Medico-Legal Society at New York. It would take too long to enumerate the representatives of Italy, but we already know the names of the most celebrated of them. However, a place apart belongs to Senator Moleschott, whose youthful old age and courteous authority contributed no little to moderate and wisely conduct the debates.

It seems that since this Congress, the need of reuniting on a common ground which is truly positive and practical all the supporters of the new ideas, all the minds convinced of the need of reform, has made itself more keenly felt than ever. It is from this time on that the International Union of Criminal Law, whose members are recruited from the whole of Europe, entered upon a course of prosperity destined some day to bear fruit in legislative results. This society has as its fundamental principle the pre-

[1] Last year a sentence of conviction rendered against a poisoner, by the Criminal Chief Justice of Buenos Ayres, is based upon two passages of Garofalo . . . and of mine.

ponderance, thenceforth established, of the social causes of the offense, and it is from this point of view that it is making a study of questions relating to punishment.

The time is ripe, also, to encourage the progress of reformers. The sudden revival of the marvelous during these last few years, under the learned form of hypnotism, and the remarkable impression caused in the whole of Europe by the experiments at the Salpêtrière and at Nancy with suggestion, by means of the wonderful seances of various "fascinators," have seemed to cast a terrible light on the innate error of free will and to have brought to bear crushing arguments upon the theory of irresponsibility. Liégeois, in his pamphlet on "Hypnotic Suggestion in its Relation to Civil and Criminal Law," was the first to point out the vital problems which this new line of psychological discoveries raises or revives, resuscitates or exhumes. But without having read it, the first comer who assists at the exhibitions of a Donato takes fright and says to himself: Can it be that man is an automaton who believes himself to be self-governing, an unconscious marionette of the strings which operate his will and determine his very consciousness itself? What becomes of culpability after this? What becomes of the penalty? From now on in the bottom of our hearts, a moral anxiety which, fostered also by other causes, by the uncertainty of so many of the things around us, and by the rising tide of our delictuosity which is preoccupying even our Parliaments, lends to the lessons taught by the new criminologists the powerful interest of its actual existence. The crisis in which penal law finds itself is also increasing, as is that of morality, of which it is only a symptom and an effect, and reveals the imminence of a revolution affecting laws and customs.[1]

§ 7. Statement of its doctrines

After this historical preamble we shall review and make a careful analysis of the doctrine with which we are here concerned; and then we shall attempt to form an opinion as regards it from our particular point of view. The shortest and best way in which to state it, it seems to us, is not successively to review the principal

[1] (May, 1903) I have nothing to retract in the historical review which is given above, neither have I anything much to add to it. In fact the divers Congresses which have since taken place (at Brussels in 1892, at Geneva in 1896, at Amsterdam in 1902) did nothing more than reveal more and more clearly the overthrow of the masters of the "nuova scuola" and the disillusionment of its latest disciples.

works which it has brought forth, but to bring out the answer which it has furnished to some problems of vital importance; which are: 1st. What is responsibility, free will being left out of consideration? 2d. What is the criminal, according to the most recent results of the science of man, anthropology and psychology? What is the most natural classification of offenders? 3d. What is crime? What are the causes which act upon it, according to the information obtainable by means of statistics? 4th. What should the punishment be? What are the judicial and penitentiary reforms which are needed? After some preliminary observations which we shall borrow from the introduction of the "Nuovi Orizzonti" by Ferri, we shall proceed with our statement in the order indicated. In conforming to it we shall follow almost step by step the volume which we have just cited and which, in spite of the youthful sound of its title, is at least the most substantial, if not the ripest, fruit of the school of innovations.

§ 8. Preliminary remarks.

The old school, says Ferri, started with those abstract things, offenses, which it considered apart from the criminals; its system of penalties was an "a priori" construction, founded upon these two postulates: in the first place, free will; and in the second, the error, borrowed by Beccaria from the optimistic and sensitive eighteenth century, that man is born good and that if he does wrong it is, without any doubt, a passing deviation, easy of redress by means of a slight correction, unless it should be the fault of society. This illusion is preserved even to our day by the socialists. But pessimism, no less than determinism, both so widely spread in our day, compels us to reject these two axioms, and in this way exhaust the sources of a liberal spiritualism in criminal law. Beccaria is a counterpart of Adam Smith; the economic point of view of the one in his explanation of productive activity, just as the penal point of view of the other in his explanation of destructive activity, is dominated by this conviction that man is everywhere engaged in the pursuit of his happiness, and warped by his exclusive concern with the aims and rights of the individual, without any regard for the aims and rights of the State. Now just as political economy saw the rise, caused by reason of a reaction against the individualism of its founder, of the school which has been given the name of the Socialism of the Chair, so the "nuova scuola" arose in opposition to the classical school of penal law. It is inspired with the same spirit and conforms to the needs of our times, being at the same time more comprehensive and more penetrating, taking in with a broader view the complexity of social facts and grasping individual facts the more closely. It is concerned with the classification of offenders rather than of offenses, and with observation rather than with deduction. Before everything else, "it proposes to bring into the science of offenses the life-giving breath of the latest discoveries made by the science of man, revived by the doctrines of evolutionism. Who would have said that the observations of Laplace on nebulae, that the voyages of discovery in savage countries, that the early studies of Camper, of White, of Blumenbach, on the measurements of the human skull and skeleton, that the researches of Darwin on the variations obtained in the raising of domestic animals, that the observations made by Haeckel in embryology and those of so many other naturalists, would one day become of interest to the penal law?" In substance the divergencies between the old and the new doctrine bear upon three distinct points: 1st. free will, affirmed by one, denied by the other; 2d. the delinquent, looked upon by one as a man of some description, and represented by the other as a physiological and not simply a psychological anomaly of human nature; 3d. the offense, regarded by one as a future contingency which will or will not arise according to the free caprice of the individual, which must be curbed by means of the prospect of punishment, and regarded by the other as a natural and necessary phenomenon which has its physical, anthropological and social causes, which cannot be neutralized, unless to a very slight extent, by means of the fear of punishment, however severe it may be, and, in a very much stronger measure, by means of the reform of civil institutions. Having said this much, let us see how the school replies to our first question.

§ 9. (I) What is responsibility?

The criminal, had he so wished, external or internal circumstances remaining the same, could have not committed his crime; he himself was aware of this possibility; therefore he is guilty of having committed it. Such is the postulate of the old school. This is completely overthrown by the general spirit of modern science, which has for guiding principle the belief in the necessary repetition of similar phenomena under similar circumstances, and especially by the discoveries of experimental psychology (not to mention hypnotism). There are thus so many contradictions of the illusion of the inner sense on this point that, in a number of cases which are daily increasing, the demonstration of its falseness becomes palpable. From this there arises a real social danger: the lawyer finds in the alienist a more and more extensive and firm support, and, as the latter conclusively shows that the accused was unable to will not to commit the crime, he insures immunity to this criminal. This is logical because the foundation of responsibility is freedom of will. But this result points out the necessity of changing the principle. As to the provisional solution which is suggested by eclecticism, that of a limited freedom and of a partial responsibility, it is useless to insist on the frailty of this compromise. However, if we leave out free will, on what are we to base responsibility? Like good transformists let us seek for the sources of the "penal function," as well as of criminality, in the prehistoric, even in the animal world. Theft and assassination are not monopolized by the human race, and neither is punishment. "Every being fights for its own existence," such is the Darwinian principle upon which we must found all penal law. The necessity of fighting implies that of defending oneself against every aggressor.[1] This defense is a double one; an immediate hitting back, as in a duel, or a hitting back postponed, called vengeance. Vengeance is already a step in advance, for it presupposes memory and foresight, a resentment and a calculation. Under this double form the defense is made use of by individual organisms, from the proteids to mammals and to man; and by social organisms as well, which, from the lowest to the highest degrees of the animal scale, compose a series not only similar, but parallel to that of the former.[2] In

[1] One could, to go still deeper, connect the *penal function* of societies with the *irritability* of the live tissues; a comparison, let me remark in passing, which would have the advantage of showing the insufficiency of the definitions of life which are founded on irritability as the only vital quality. This quality, entirely defensive, entirely negative, assumes a positive aspect, which is possibly unknown but nevertheless affirmative. Irritability is no more the fundamental characteristic of a living being than is punishment the fundamental characteristic of a society.

[2] This remark, which bears on observations to a certain extent accurate, deserves to be developed and to be corrected. It holds within it at least this truth, that the social world is not a consequence of the living world, but accompanies and enlarges the latter, not, however, without considerable dissimilarities which the already hackneyed metaphor of the *social organism* does not recognize. Furthermore, the parallel between vital development and social development is not without very marked exceptions. *Letourneau*, in his "Evolution de la morale," points out how much inferior the monkey is, as regards social instincts, to the ant. Again,

every society, whether it be animal or human, the personal revenge of the individual injured exists side by side with the collective revenge of the group to which he belongs, but more and more is the latter coming to be substituted for the former. Is it desirable still better to define the nature of this sort of vengeance? Spencer is correct in saying that the "defensive reaction" of a society is always the same thing at bottom, whether it be against an aggressor from within or one from without. The malefactor is nothing more than an enemy on the inside. Thus the same causes which have little by little changed the defense by individuals against outside aggressions into a collective defense, in the form of armies and battles will inevitably operate to change the defense by the individual against aggressions from within into a defense by society. Thus the development of the military spirit and of the criminal law keep pace with each other.

Let us point out, parenthetically, how much happier a comparison this one of Spencer's is than is, in many ways, his perpetual antithesis between the military spirit and the spirit of industry. Contrary to his views we find all through history, in Egypt, at Athens, at Florence, in France, in Germany, alas! industrial prosperity and military supremacy as allies and not as opponents. It would be a surprising thing, however, if, parallel on the one hand to the progress made by the bench, the spirit of militarism, so scorned by the illustrious philosopher, were opposed to industrial progress; just as though industry could exist without the security which criminal justice assures it! If there is no army then there will be no police force. Undoubtedly, though in its character of defender the army is responsible for those judicial institutions worthy the name, it has its aggressive side, which is historically the most important, by means of which it is responsible for the institutions of oppression which allow of the subjugating and ransom of the innocent as the conquerors reduce to a state of servitude or burden with tribute the most peaceful of the neighboring peoples. Oppression is nothing but an aggression from within and which starts at the top.

But even under this aspect the matters we have been comparing are not without their possible justification in the eyes of the

the remark is not true, unless we proportion social elevation to the degree of social cohesion and discipline, of the apportionment of labor pushed to the rule of castes. . . . If one looks at it from the point of view, which I think is a broader one, which I developed in my "Lois de l'Imitation" (pp. 67 *et seq.*) the exception disappears.

historian. What great nation could have been formed had it lacked the spirit of conquest? What powerful national unity could have been established without a centralizing and organizing despotism?[1] Aggressive militarism has thus this very great use; it leads us towards the immense accumulations, without which no lasting peace is possible; and oppressive government is responsible for the foundations of the powerful centralizations without which no great State is capable of existing, and upon which may later on be built flourishing democracies. It will be a good thing if, in the course of our work, we often recall this analogy, this radical identity between war and criminal prosecution, and especially will it be so when we come to deal with the death penalty. It is the *putting out of the fight*, and not the death of the enemy, which is the object of the combatants; it is also the putting out of the fight, and not the death of the guilty which is the aim of the courts. If one objects to these fearful slaughters of the battlefield which ought by comparison strangely to lessen the horror of a few instances of capital punishment here and there, it becomes a case for the application of the distinction made above by Ferri, and for noting this difference that the "defensive reaction" of society against the enemy in the shape of blows with lance or cannon is an immediate hitting back, while its defensive reaction against the criminal is always a deferred hitting back, a revenge. There are many other differences, however, and they are no less instructive than the resemblances.

Let us come back to our review. Is one concerned, while repelling an attack, with knowing to what extent the aggressor is guilty? Not in the least. The conception of culpability is of mystic origin; the usurping superiority of the power of the priest, when societies were still young, alone can explain the character of *trespass* which attached to an offense. The priest placed the divine vengeance above the public vengeance and here brought in ritual formalism, which is dear to him. But his influence is on the wane. Considered in its entirety, the evolution of feeling and ideas relative to punishment embraces three phases: the religious phase, the ethical phase, and the social or judicial phase. Among us, classical science has remained at the second period, and legislation still more behindhand, is only at the first. But positivism leads us to the last, by which we are brought back to the starting

[1] Also give us an example of a brave people which has not been warlike, or a great people which is not courageous?

point, or to the principle of social utility, that is to say, of law. Law is "the specific force of social organisms"; a society without law is as inconceivable as an animal without the spark of life, as a chemical substance without affinity. But there are two ways, one metaphysical, the other positive and utilitarian, in which law should be understood. Starting from this point one perceives that society does not have to ask itself, in order to punish injurious acts, whether they are intentional and voluntary, because it does not demand that useful acts should be intentional and voluntary in order to reward them; and the unconscious influence "of the residue of religious traditions" alone can account for the importance which we attach to intention in the criminal law.[1] Intentionally or unintentionally, the act has resulted fatally, and an inborn perversity is no more reason for giving rise to indignation than is a corruption of the blood. Today we pity the insane who used to be burned. A day will come when delinquents too will inspire pity; which will not prevent us from protecting ourselves against their attacks.

The remedies against offenses are of four kinds: 1st. preventives; 2d. measures of redress; 3d. repressive measures; 4th. measures of elimination.[2] In order to apply these different remedies to the different cases, what shall be the rule? Garofalo has answered, the degree of "temibilita" (of "redoubtability," if my creation of a new word may be overlooked) of the offender. This answer is true, but it is insufficient. We must at the same time take into account the more or less anti-social character of the agent. With this last distinction is intimately connected the distinction between delinquents of various categories. One can see the importance of this classification which leads us to propound our second problem.

[1] Carmignani is still more logical than Ferri. He rejects the terms "offense" and "punishment" as themselves contaminated with the spirit of mysticism, and only wishes to hear "offense" and "defense" spoken of.

[2] Garofalo's classification is simpler; he only distinguishes reparation of the detriment and the elimination (temporary or final) of the malefactor, measures of prevention being set apart. It is hard to understand just what *repressive* measures consist of, considered as distinct from preventive, restorative, and elimination measures: imprisonment prevents and eliminates temporarily, the fine prevents and repairs *socially*. The place given to *repression* is thus an unconscious and illogical concession to the theory of expiation, and illustrates the force of the repugnance in us which is opposed to the suppression of one punishment for the sake of another, symmetrically counterbalancing the offense.

§ 10. (II) What is a criminal?

It is by means of a close physical study of delinquents, both living and dead, that we have arrived at the ability of discerning among them differences in their natures more or less sharply defined, and of classifying them according to a principle which has in it nothing artificial. In the first place it is remarkable that all competent men, after a prolonged contact with prisoners, especially the directors of penitential establishments and medico-legal men, are agreed in recognizing a class of incorrigible malefactors, a fact diametrically opposed to the optimistic illusions of classical spiritualism; and, on the whole, the great distinction which is recognized at the base of every proposed classification — and there are a great number of them — is that of delinquents *from habit* and *from opportunity*. It is, moreover, a distinction which could be applied even to honest people. How many there are whose honesty is entirely due to opportunity and depends on the happy circumstances of their lives! It may be that these are the very ones who, bearers of the *criminal* type without having any criminal court record, constitute an apparent objection to the theory of Lombroso and those like him. The kinds and varieties of offense provided for by the various systems of legislation are numerous, about one hundred and fifty in our Code, and two hundred in the German Code; but habitual wrongdoing is localized only in some of these forms. In every country it bears principally on theft; in Italy it also applies to assaults, carrying of weapons, perjury, and counterfeiting[1] much more than in France; much less than in France does it apply to offenses or crimes against morality. As to murder and assassination they have also a very strong tendency to become habitual, especially when they have stealing as their motive; but murderers are not always given the opportunity to become recidivists.

At the same time the proportion of recidivism is greater in the case of crimes properly so-called, including bloodthirsty crimes, than in the case of offenses. This is so in all countries. The difference is eighty-four to thirty-two per cent in Italy, ninety to thirty-four per cent in France, eighty-six to thirty per cent in Belgium. The coincidence of these figures is striking.

[1] This is or was owing to the compulsory circulation of paper money in the form of a small fractional currency. The best remedy for this species of crime is thus, according to Ferri, the return to a metal currency.

Let us leave out insane delinquents, and when we see individuals such as Sergeant Bertrand, Verzene, or Menesclou, exhuming dead bodies in order to defile them, defiling women after having strangled them, or defiling a child of seven, and then cutting it into pieces, can we have any doubt as to the morbid principle of these aberrations? Let us now draw a distinction, as was said above, between delinquents from habit and delinquents from opportunity, but let us subdivide them. Among the former we must set apart delinquents who are incorrigible because of inborn perversity, from delinquents who are incorrigible because of an acquired habit. Among the latter we must make a special division to include delinquents by reason of passion, who in one sense are related to insane criminals, irresistible passion being nothing but temporary madness.

Two psychological characteristics, whether they be united or separated, characterize criminals, no matter to what category they may belong; lack of moral sensibility and lack of foresight. Let us add an immeasurable vanity. Lack of moral sensibility accounts rather for wrongdoing from habit, and lack of foresight for wrongdoing from opportunity. The criminal by reason of passion has a very acute perception, but is extraordinarily lacking in foresight. Precocity is one of the most striking indications of the delinquent who is destined surely to become a recidivist. Numerically compared, these various classes differ no less among themselves. Out of the total number of malefactors, delinquents because of passion or madness represent but five per cent; delinquents from birth or habit amount to the number of forty or fifty per cent. Here are the individuals who bear the physical description traced, not without many erasures and contradictions, by the anthropologists of the new school. It is worth noticing that the proportion pointed out, forty or fifty, is far from being equal to the proportion of recidivists (offenses and crimes taken together) which is fifty or sixty.

This classification of Ferri's, I should observe, has not been unanimously accepted. At the Congress of Rome it gave rise to lengthy discussions. But it is the most complete thing which the school has produced up to the present time, and its underlying principle has not met with too great an amount of opposition. One is, as a general thing among the innovators, prone to accept its clear enough distinction between criminality from birth and madness, and it is not one of the least of the originalities of the "nuova scuola" to have resisted on this point, by the choice of an ingenious support, discovered on the very field of the natural sciences in their most recent state of development, the allurements of the alienist group. This support is the theory of Darwinian atavism and transformism.[1] Anatomical, physiological, psychological, and even social similarities have been imagined to exist or have been stated to exist, between the primitive savage, such as he may be imagined to have been according to what is known of existing savages, and the criminal by birth. From his handle-like ears, very far apart and very large, from the heaviness of his lower jaw, from his low and receding forehead, from his ferocious physiognomy, from the length of his arms compared with his legs, a characteristic in which one feels the near parentage of the four-handed animals, from his insensibility to suffering and to pity, from his tendency to tattoo himself, from his slang, an ignoble and rudimentary language, from his associations for purposes of brigandage, the criminal from birth might be in a way a very old family portrait reappearing from time to time. If this be so, and this was Lombroso's first theory, the born criminal is not necessarily or habitually either a madman or a monstrosity, for diseases of the brain or other diseases are not ordinarily recurrent phenomena, any more than monstrosities properly so-called. This position seemed a strong one; but from the time of the second edition of his book, Lombroso began to lose his foothold in admitting that the born criminal presented undeniable analogies to the madman, as well as to the savage or the pre-human animal. With good reason the objection was made to him that he ought to choose between these two theories; they are in fact contradictory, madness being the outgrowth of civilization, whose progress it follows, being even now an exception in our rural districts,[2] and a rarity not to be found among savages. In attempting to solve the difficulty Lombroso made it more confused; he brought in epilepsy, which, whether manifest or "larvated" (that is to say concealed), would be more intimately related than any form of madness to congenital criminality and would effect the fusion of the opposed points of view. But in order for this to be so it would be necessary for epilepsy to have been the normal state of primitive

[1] According to *Topinard* ("Revue d'Anthropologie," November, 1887), this idea was put forth for the first time by Bordier.

[2] I allude to madness, and not to idiocy, which abounds in rural communities. It is true that idiocy strangely resembles the last stages of madness, dementia. Dementia is an acquired idiocy, and idiocy an innate dementia.

populations, a gratuitous assertion if ever there was one. Furthermore, nothing was better established in a certain sense than the relation existing between epilepsy and a tendency towards crime. To be sure epilepsy has often the character of crime; but it does not follow that every criminal has a predisposition to epilepsy. I read in the curious "Etudes sur la sélection" by Dr. Jacoby (1881) that in Italy "the medical investigation made in 1874 ascertained that among all the inmates of the penitentiaries of the kingdom there were but ninety epileptics and insane persons, including feeble-minded and idiots." The proportion of epileptics and madmen, according to this author, would be three, four, or five in every hundred inmates.[1] However this may be, in the most recent expression given to his thought we maintain that Lombroso, without absolutely giving up the anatomical characteristics of the delinquent, insists much more on the anomalies of a pathological order which would distinguish him; little by little he departs from his first idea and approaches the theory advanced by Despine, Morel, and Maudsley.

Then came Marro, whose book on "Caractères des délinquants," a review of work done according to the anthropometric method of the professor of Turin, but more orderly, more well defined, and clearer, marks another step in advance in this line of reasoning.[2] The conclusions drawn by the master were, as he tells us, based on observations made on nearly 4000 malefactors,[3] a pretty large figure; but they had been examined either to a limited extent by himself, or by other scholars, often superficially and always only partially and from different viewpoints, and compared with an undetermined number of honest people of some kind or other, not always of the same race, nor belonging to the same class in society. The disciple limits himself to the study of 507 male and 35 female criminals; but the examination of each one of them thoroughly by himself, from top to toe, after an exhaustive research of their parentage and their antecedents, is the subject of a separate study, and they are compared with one hundred honest individuals, whose honesty was verified and guaranteed, all of the same Piedmontese origin as were the former, and belonging to approximately the same social surroundings. Every

[1] This hypothesis of criminal epilepsy is the subject of a strenuous attack by *Colajanni* in his "Sociologia criminale" (1888).

[2] See our accurate account of this work in the "Revue philosophique," for December, 1887.

[3] Without counting three hundred and eighty-three skulls of criminals.

instrument for measuring or which was known to contemporary medical science and to psychophysics, the sphygmograph, dynamometer, aesthesеometer, etc., had already been employed by Lombroso for the purpose of characterizing in the language of figures or of graphic curves, singular arabesques, the manner in which thieves or assassins breathe, in which their blood flows, their heart beats, their senses operate, their muscles contract, and their feeling is given expression, and by this means to discover through all the corporal manifestations of their being, considered as so many living hieroglyphics to be translated, even through their handwriting and their signatures submitted to a graphological analysis, the secret of their being and of their life. In this manner he had discovered, especially by means of three sphygmographic tracings, that malefactors are very responsive to the sight of a gold coin or of a good glass of wine, and much less so to the sight of a "donna nuda," in a photograph to be sure. He had above all furnished the proof of that remarkable insensibility to variations of temperature and to physical pain which accounts for[1] two other no less striking characteristics among malefactors; first, their profound indifference to the sufferings of another, and second, that which has been called their "disvulnerability," the marvelous rapidity with which, by a strange favor of Providence, they recover from their injuries and their wounds are healed, and in the case of the girl-mothers who are the perpetrators of infanticides, their confinement comes to an end without any medical assistance and without any unfortunate complication.

Now Marro has taken all these measurements and ascertained all these data over again and he has found gaps in them, which he has filled in by measuring, for example, the hands of murderers, which are strong and large, and the hands of swindlers and thieves, which are long and narrow. — Thus, if the criminal type exists, there is reason to believe that it will most decidedly become detached, and will now be drawn with all the preciseness which is dreamed of by the essentially precise mind, precise even to the point of minuteness, as we can see, of the new and patient searcher. However, there is not the shadow of a doubt as to its existence in

[1] This insensibility considerably reduces the worth of that stoicism which almost strikes one with admiration when one reads, for example, the "Maison des morts," by *Dostoievsky*, a book of intense interest in which the author, condemned for a political offense, has reviewed the memories of ten years of compulsory labor. On every page convicts are referred to who submitted without flinching to five hundred or one thousand lashes with the whip.

the eyes of the latter, and he carries far back into the past, with an erudition not very familiar to those like him, the imaginary genealogy of the predecessors who presented it. He tells that Porta in the twelfth century drew a portrait of the professional rogue which very much resembled the Lombrosian characterization: large ears, long cheeks, etc. He does not even seem to smile in reminding us that Socrates held a poor opinion of Thetitus, because the latter had a flat nose. The day he said this, moreover, Socrates had apparently forgotten his own physiognomy, which was so repulsively ugly. Thus Marro carries on his researches with a prejudice which is very favorable to the ideas of his celebrated fellow-countryman. Let us see, however, to what results they will lead.

He is compelled to admit that previous research has suggested conclusions which are sometimes divergent "and even opposite," that the cranial capacity, the stature and the weight of delinquents seemed to some to be greater than the average, to others less; he tells of the disagreement among anthropologists when it was shown (in 1882) by Giacomini that the quadripartal division of the frontal lobe where one learned man had thought to discover the cerebral characteristic of the malefactor was in no way peculiar to the latter, and implied no approach whatever to the carnivorous type. As far as he himself was concerned, he found only an insignificant variation between the height of criminals and that of "normal" people (it is thus that he calls honest people, at the risk of contradicting the German professor, Paul Albrecht of Hamburg, according to whom the truly normal man would be the criminal and honesty would be an anomaly).[1] As to weight, according to him that of delinquents is perceptibly less, which perhaps shows that prison diet is not fattening. To be sure he confirms the observation of Lombroso as regards the great arm-spread of delinquents, but the atavistic theory does not gain much thereby, for he establishes at the same time that the "stupratori," the "violators," that is to say precisely the most bestial category of criminals, have short arms.[2] If he finds the proportion of beardless adults thirteen times greater among delinquents than among "normals"

[1] This is the *result* of anthropological deliberations very seriously developed by him at the Congress of Rome, with examples to bear them out. There were smiles: an assemblage is always indulgent to the person who affords it amusement.

[2] At the Préfecture of the Seine, following the anthropological system of Bertillon, we were assured that notorious criminals as a general thing have shorter arms.

and is fully sustained on this point, the same as it is with regard to the bushy hair of the former, according to the observations made by Lombroso and Lacassagne, we must admit that after all here are details which are of comparatively secondary importance. Ambidexterity and "mancinism" are however of greater importance, and he reckons, still agreeing with his master, twice as much ambidexterity and left-handedness among delinquents as among "normals"; but can this be an effect of atavism, of a reverting to bestiality? Animals are not left-handed. It is much more important to observe the exaggerated development of the jaws, the narrowness of the forehead, the decrease in the size of the frontal and truly noble part of the brain, among malefactors, "conclusions which we can draw," says Marro, "from all the cranial measurements."

Again there is nothing to prove that this preponderance of a low type of life over a higher, which has been pointed out, denotes the reappearance of the former type rather than the holding back from the development of the existing type. One of the most ingenious and prettiest arguments invoked by the atavistic theory was founded upon the frequent tattooing met with in the case of malefactors. This had already been answered [1] by explaining the fact as a simple course of examples which, traditional among certain barbarous tribes coming into contact with our civilized people, sailors or soldiers, was communicated as a fashion to the latter, and then to prisoners, as a result of the habitual isolation and the long periods of idleness favorable to its propagation among the former as well as among the latter. Thus prisons sometimes become, they are almost bound to, true studios of tattooing. Marro interprets things in the same way. "A spirit of imitation, vanity, and idleness, these are the motives which, generally speaking, have prompted delinquents to tattoo themselves," not all over the body and in order to scare the enemy, as savages do, but most frequently on the forearm only and in order to amuse themselves.

Marro, however, gives its place to atavism; but let us see what place. He classifies all anomalies, all individual variations judged to be defects, into three kinds, according as their probable cause goes more or less far back into the past. He qualifies them as atavistic if their cause is an apparent defect manifested among the ancestors of the individual; as irregular or teratologic if

[1] See in the "Revue philosophique," June, 1885, our very extensive criticism of "l'Uomo delinquente" under the title of: "Type criminel."

their cause is an accident which has taken place during the embryonic life of the individual himself; and lastly, as pathologic if the cause is a circumstance happening after their birth. By accurate statistics he discovers the following facts: the anomalies of the first category, exaggerated frontal cavity, receding forehead, oblique eyes, etc., are almost as frequent in the world of honest people as they are in the world of criminals and cannot in any way serve to characterize the latter. Anomalies of the second kind, deformations of the skull, squinting, lack of facial proportion, nose crooked, prominent ears, goitres, hernia, rickets, etc., serve still less to distinguish criminals from "normals," although it might seem natural to attribute to moral monstrosities the better fate of physical monstrosities. But anomalies of a morbid nature, scars, facial paralysis, disturbances of the circulatory system, deformity of the genital organs, etc., are found in much greater proportion among criminals; the difference is even "enormous" and "clearly shows that in anomalies of this type resides the most important physical characteristic of the delinquent." For example, lesions of the head are met with one hundred and twenty-five times in the group of five hundred and six vagabonds of our author, and only nine times among his one hundred honest people.

Now these lesions are of very great importance if, as we are led to believe, they account for many cerebral changes which follow upon blows received.[1] The lack of physical feeling of delinquents, that is to say the principal key to their psychology, comes partly from these changes, and partly from illnesses such as typhoid fever or from the abuse of alcoholic liquors. After all, the delinquent is before everything a sick man, often a madman; his intellectual inferiority, besides, is attested by all observers, who are unanimous in this respect, and this is no occasion for surprise, when we learn that the only characteristic of his cerebral organization which is truly evident, the sum total of all his being, his final formula, is "the insufficient nourishment of his nerve centres." Badly nourished brain, misfortune, poverty; here is all then that remains of the *criminal type*.

One might as well say that, in the naturalist acceptation of the

[1] "It follows from statistics compiled in certain institutions for the insane, and especially by Lunier, and from other considerations, that artificial deformations of the skull do not produce insanity, but that they create a strong predisposition towards it. So artificial deformations of the skull, according to the same means, therefore should create a predisposition towards criminality." *Topinard*, "Revue d'Anthropologie," November, 1887.

word, nothing is left; but in a sense which is entirely social, it is susceptible of being revived. We have ventured the idea [1] that each profession in the long run will create its social physical type, and that the distinction between the classes of society corresponds "grosso modo" to that of the more prominent professions, such as agriculture, industry, arms, religion, each class having both its anatomical and physiological characteristic more or less easily recognized among the majority of its members. This does not simply mean that the exercise of a calling develops and adapts to its own ends the organs which it makes use of; the arm of the locksmith, the legs of the postman, the lungs of the lawyer, and even in an indirect way the organs which it does not make use of, as is pointed out by Darwin with respect to cobblers who would have the frontal region of the skull very much developed because they are in the habit of stooping their heads.[2] It shows besides that a calling, if it be open to everybody and freely recruited, draws to itself preferably the individuals best constituted to make a success of it, and if it be a limited class, accumulates and fixes by means of heredity its direct or indirect consequences upon the organs of the successive generations who transmit it from one to another.

Either in one way or the other, by the choice of vocation or by the force of heredity, it must come about that the majority of people who are engaged in the practice of a profession are born for it, that they have "the physique of the occupation." So we are perfectly right in calling the professional type the collection of special characteristics, often incongruous and without any apparent justification, which are ordinarily to be noticed among fellow-members and colleagues of all sorts and who make of the "confraternity" a sort of true fraternity, with or without kindred. Why, then, should not crime and wrongdoing, which if not callings are at least characteristic occupations, very ancient customs inherent in our societies as is the mushroom in the tree, have their professional type also? It is exceedingly probable, and the criminal type thus conceived would have this advantage over the atavistic conception that it would be applicable not only to

[1] See the article already referred to in the "Revue philosophique," for June, 1885.

[2] Darwin says, in the way of a general theory, that the attitude compelled by a trade is enough considerably to modify the cerebral and cranial conformation. If this is so, a revolution in all branches of economics, which are absolutely controlled by the brain, ought necessarily to follow.

the born criminal, but to the criminal of every class. Now it is noticeable that this viewpoint has made its way among professional anthropologists. Manouvrier in a very clear article[1] has welcomed it, and Topinard,[2] in turn, accepts it after having energetically combated Lombroso's point of view. Corre gives it a place in the classification of delinquents.[3]

Finally, and to return to Ferri's classification, his second class, that of the born criminal, is either nothing more than a dream, or is covered by the first, that of the insane criminal, or else by the third, that of the criminal from force of habit. On the other hand the fifth, that of the criminal from passion, also manifestly constitutes a part of the first, passion driven to paroxysm being nothing more than temporary madness. Thus there are left only the delinquent from force of habit and the delinquent from opportunity, to face each other; but to tell the truth how are we to distinguish them with absolute accuracy? Is it not always the opportunity which creates the robber and the murderer as well? What habit is there which has not an accidental happening for its underlying principle, and what accidental act is there which has not a tendency to reproduce itself, and to become crystallized into a habit? In the very heart of the school itself some of these objections have come to be formulated. One can see that it is far from having firmly established, of having even definitely laid the first course of its conception and explanation of the criminal. As a consequence it would be astonishing if its conception and explanation of crime were perfectly clear. However, now let us ask what it is.

§ 11. (III) What is crime?

Crime differs from the criminal as the *act* differs from the *power*. One must be examined separately from the other. It is in the light of the natural sciences that the delinquent is revealed and explained; wrongdoing is especially made clear by means of statistics which allow of observing it collectively, "in abstracto," and of discerning the influences which give rise to it. One is justified in supposing that nature alone is responsible for true delinquents, sometimes without a record of conviction, for the

[1] Published in the "Archives de l'Anthropologie criminelle," March, 1887.

[2] See the "Revue d'Anthropologie," November, 1887.

[3] See "Crime et suicide," pp. 84 *et seq.*, 492 *et seq.* *Corre* admits of many criminal types.

force does not always result in the act, but one can have no misconception as to the part which society plays in the production of the offense, either in giving rise to its opportunities, or in more or less arbitrarily attributing to certain acts the character of an offense. Thus it is that the man of genius is a purely biological phenomenon, but that the conception of genius, which is always necessarily aroused by means of previous inventions or discoveries which it combines and whose success paves the way for its own, is before everything else a social phenomenon. So we will not reproach the positivist school with a contradiction which consists in making social causes play a more important part in the production of misdeeds than in the production of malefactors. It could, without having contradicted itself to any greater extent, have enhanced their importance still more.

The question which we have asked is divisible into two parts: what are the characteristics belonging to the offense, and what are its causes? Let us begin with the first. If the arbitrary will of the legislator sufficed to render wrongful an act in itself the most innocent, if the variations in criminal legislation were not inclosed in an impassable circle, and were not connected with an unalterable scheme, it would not be worth while to discuss the anomaly of the criminal by birth. The most honest man in the world of our time, might, according to this hypothesis, from the point of view of *absolute relativism* so to speak, have been a born criminal in another country and at another period of history. How avoid this pitfall without falling into another, into moral dogmatism? The difficulty was felt by Garofalo, but he thought to overcome it by his way of defining what he called "the natural offense." It would perhaps be more accurate to say "the essential offense."

What inoffensive act is there which has not somewhere been made a crime? and what monstrous act is there which has not somewhere been called innocent or applauded? It is useless while on this subject to repeat the horrors and the exaggerations which travelers and analysts have been pleased to relate to us, in order, as they think, to broaden our ideas on the subject of morality, and not without sometimes putting our credulity to a severe test. But if we scrutinize them closely, leaving aside "some savage tribes which are degenerate or not capable of development and which represent, in the human race, an anomaly similar to that of malefactors in the very core of a society," and limiting ourselves to a consideration, even beginning with their known origin, "of the superior human races" [1] we see that through the infinite shades and transformations of superficial morality under the sway of superstitions, customs, institutions and the most diverse legislation, a deep layer, always the same, of moral feelings elaborated during the long night of the previous ages, never ceases to be apparent, and to serve as a mold for the varied blossoming forth of the most delicate and sublime virtue. In order to recognize the fact that this elementary moral sense has existed from all time and has been common to every people within the broad limits indicated above, one must observe that the individual equipped with the feelings of which it is made up has always given them vent in favor of those persons alone looked upon by him as his fellow-creatures, and that the circle of these, at first limited to the restricted group of the family or of the tribe, expanded by degrees to the point of taking in the whole of humanity. What are these feelings, as persistent as they are universal, and which are the fundamental inheritance of every normal man born into this world, the exceptional absence of which characterizes the born malefactor, and whose exceptional violation characterizes the true crime or offense? [2]

One is only able to mention two, a certain minimum of pity and a certain minimum of probity. Others are often added to these, as modesty and patriotism; but they may entirely disappear, and never is their disarrangement, though necessarily characterized as a crime or an offense by the positive law, felt to be directly criminal or wrongful by everybody. Between the political crime [3] and the crime without a name; between adultery, "this political offense of the family," and theft there is the same difference as exists between the artificial and the real. I leave out of consideration the precedents, the distinctions and the

[1] See the "Criminologie" and the article published in French, by *Garofalo*, under this title: "Délit naturel," in the "Revue philosophique," for January, 1887.

[2] Unless, the author tells us, the feelings in question should be violated in view of their more exalted gratification. This is the case with the surgeon who is unaffected, even through pity, by the cries of his patient; it is also the case with savages who, by reason of filial compassion, sacrifice their aged parents, or with such men as Agamemnon and Jephthah, who sacrifice their daughters for the salvation of their country.

[3] Political purely and simply; if there be an attack on persons the question becomes more complicated. On *political offenses* see our study published under this title in the "Revue philosophique," (1890), and relating to *Lombroso's* last work, "Il delitto politico."

niceties of the Italians, which lend to this vague generalization an appearance of strictness, and ably conceal the omission of that which it excludes of the conclusion come to, the conception of right and of duty. Just as though the conception of crime did not imply as an essential and natural thing that of a right or of a duty violated, and not merely an outraged feeling; just as though this very feeling were anything but an accumulated and consolidated belief in right and in duty! The most striking thing to be here observed is the sight of an evolutionist making this desperate effort to attach himself to some fixed point in this unfathomable flood of phenomena and cast anchor exactly in what is the most fluid and evasive thing in the world, that is to say, feeling.[1]

The characteristics of crime having thus been specified as being within the range of possibility, let us seek its causes. Ferri draws a distinction between the physical, anthropological, and social "factors" of the offense. Does this distinction correspond in his mind to that of the three concentric spheres of reality, the physico-chemical sphere, the vital sphere, and the social sphere? No, physics here signifies cosmology and takes in the whole of the external world, animals and plants, to the exclusion of our species. Very well; but why place among anthropological factors profession, civil status, social class, instruction, and education, which are all primarily social matters? One can see that Ferri, like all the minds of this century, intoxicated by the new wine of the natural sciences still in course of fermentation, is carried to the point where he confuses the social with the vital to the detriment of the former. However this may be, criminal statistics, to which our authors are quite right in attaching great importance, allow the particular contingency to be isolated and figured on, up to a certain point, in its bearing towards criminality in general, during a given period and in a given State, by the influence of temperature in the form either of heat or of cold, of climate whether northern or tropical, of the harvest whether abundant or insufficient in wheat or in wine, of country or town residence, of profession whether agricultural, industrial, or liberal; by means of ignorance or learning either primary, secondary, or above the average; of religion or the lack of the same; of celibacy or marriage, of youth, middle age, or old age; of alcoholism or of sobriety, of poverty

[1] The "Nueva ciencia," by *de Aramburu*, Vice-Rector of the Academy of Ovideo, contains a very profound criticism of this theory of the natural offense and a general one of all the ideas put forth by Garofalo.

or of riches, of barbarianism or of civilization; of political events, etc.

When I say, however, that statistics allow us to proceed with so high and delicate an analysis, I am expressing myself badly; they would allow of it if they covered the operations of fifteen centuries past, and not merely of some ten years, and if, with the same penal code and the same legal institutions operating, let us suppose, throughout an entire continent such as Europe, they supplied information which would be useful for purposes of comparison among nations, and not as now only among provinces, or among departments. Under these conditions they would allow of the observance of the varied behavior of different European races, religions and latitudes as plainly as of the varied effect of different callings in each State. But criminal statistics fall far short of this high state of perfection, which partly explains why the positivist school has refrained from a direct attack on the problems we have just been enunciating. However, in default or rather as a complement of statistics, archaeology even better than history properly so called, can be of assistance in their solution by throwing light upon moral conditions during the times gone by. Among other documents of the past, memoirs, books of reasoning, and official acts preserved among the archives are precious traces which should be the subject of research.

Unfortunately our new criminologists either scorn these ancient sources or they are unaware of them; it is seldom that a utilitarian is an archaeologist and that a naturalist is a scholar. Also, the positivist school has up to now but gleaned a few sparse glimpses from the field where a sheaf of fertile ideas awaits a reaper. It is either silent or else disparaging on the effect of religious beliefs; it would, however, be very unlikely that this effect, even though ascertained by means of statistics as to the number of divorces, legal separations, or suicides,[1] should be absent or without any statistical manifestation in the matter of offenses. It has not added very much to what the professional statisticians since Quetelet had taught us as to the proportionate effect, which is almost invariable, of different ages, and also of different civil status. In all of this its researches have been lacking in consecutiveness and in definite scheme, being, most frequently, inspired by the needs of discussion. They were concerned with combating the idea of free will; so they insisted, with an extraordinary

[1] See the fine monograph on "Divorce" by *Bertillon*.

partiality, upon the criminal efficacy of heat or cold, of a good or bad harvest, of alcoholism, of the "physical factors" in general.

On the other hand, in order to reply to the socialist group, who sought to establish by figures the relation of poverty to crime and thus to lay the blame on the social condition,[1] they were compelled to show that on the contrary the increase of well-being is parallel to that of delictuosity, that years when prices are high or harvests are good are especially signalized by a recrudescence of offenses against morality, of assaults, woundings, and murders.[2] Or again, in order to demonstrate that the existing system of statutes and of penalties was in need of reform, they invoked what had resulted therefrom, they triumphantly computed the increase, truly alarming, if not of crimes of blood, at least of cunning offenses, of cheating, and of corruption during the last half century which had passed under the sway of these institutions; an argument, to be candid, which was a contradiction of the principle of the school that penalties, whatever they may be, are the least efficacious of the causes which serve to counterbalance delictual tendencies. A few essays which were partially generalizations have appeared, but they have had but a short-lived success. Poletti thought he had discovered a fixed, a quasi-mathematical relationship between the rapid increase of wealth, of productive activity, and the slower increase of criminality, of destructive activity; whence he deduced the optimistic paradox that the *absolute* increase of our criminality is the equivalent of its *relative* repression.

This singular theorem was not very well received in France and Italy. The ingenious calendar of criminality, gotten up by Lacassagne, has not removed many of the objections; but the inverse relationship established by some authors between criminality against persons and criminality against property has met with contradictions, as has the geographical location of the former in the South and of the latter in the North.[3] Another inverse relation, which made quite a stir, was that which Morselli perceived, in his fine work entitled "Suicidio," between suicide and homicide. But this latter theory itself, in spite of the lavishness

[1] See the pamphlet by *Turati* with which we were concerned above. See "Alcoolismo" and also "Socialismo," by *Colajanni*, and the "Dinamica del delitto," by *Batagglia*, and especially "Sociologia criminale."

[2] See *Ferri's* "Socialismo e criminalita," especially the chapter entitled "Benessere e criminalita."

[3] See the "Revue philosophique," January, 1886, as well as a pamphlet of *Colajanni's* on "Criminalité sicilienne."

of the statistical tables invoked in its behalf, has not been able to withstand the blows of criticism.

Thus, on the question with which we are concerned, the new school is a pretty tumultuous workshop, where plans abound, where constructions struggle with one another and where demolitions are piling up.

§ 12. (IV) What is the remedy for wrongdoing? Criminal sociology.

The answer is a whole vast programme of reforms, moral, political, or even industrial, or finally, legislative, both judicial and penitential, which are set forth in the "Nuovi Orizzonti" and the "Criminologie." Before going over them it is worth while noticing that the extreme ardor with which our authors labor to make prevalent the methods of examination, of sentencing, and of administering punishment, which are dear to them,[1] is hard to reconcile, in them, with their theory of the almost utter uselessness of punishment. But first it behooves us to listen to them for a moment on this subject. In a given physical and social state, they say, the climate, the seasons, the harvests, commerce, and social relations of all kinds being such as they are, a fixed amount and a fixed nature of criminality exactly corresponds to this state, as an effect corresponds to its cause. This is what Ferri terms the law of criminal saturation, by a metaphor borrowed from chemistry; but *what* is for each State that degree of criminality which suffices and is necessary in order to saturate a society, this is what the law omits to tell us. So the law is only a picturesque and *particular* expression of the parent idea of determinism in general.

We did not even think it necessary to refer to it above. It does not any the less follow that, among all the favorable or contrary influences the meeting of which determines the number of offenses of each period, the leniency or the severity of the punishments represents an almost insignificant value. "Just as oidium and phylloxera," says Ferri, "are of more value than severity of punishment in the lessening of the number of blows and wounds, so want is more efficacious than the best locks and dogs let loose in the prison yard in preventing the escape of prisoners," the latter under these circumstances appreciating the advantage of being fed at the expense of the State. For this same reason, while in

[1] Ferri, legislator, in his speeches in the Chamber of Deputies in May, 1898, on the proposed reforms of the Penal Code, may be opposed on this point to Ferri, professor and lecturer.

1847 all sorts of thefts considerably increased in number, one saw a decrease in the number of thefts committed by servants, who had no wish to have themselves driven from the house where they found the means of support. The efficacy of punishments, adds this same writer, has been exaggerated. In Rome the excessive penalties inflicted on the celibate did not check the progress of depopulation. The tigers and the lions of the amphitheatre did not hold back the propagation of the Christian faith; the atrocity of the tortures of the Middle Ages did not prevent a superabundance of crimes to such a point that truces had to be established limiting the ability to commit crime to certain days of the week. It is not to a weakening of repressive measures that the increase in criminality in France, for at least fifty years, is to be imputed, because, on the contrary, if one is to judge by the proportion of acquittals, repressive measures have become more severe. In fact, this proportion has decreased by degrees, from thirty-two per cent in 1826–1830 to six per cent in 1877–1881. In Italy and even in England it has been the same.[1] "The discerning husband relies on anything but the Code provisions against adultery in order to preserve the fidelity of his wife." Smuggling has been terribly punished for centuries, by death or cutting off the hand, but it has continued to flourish. Now, the customs tariffs having been lowered, it is rapidly declining, because the gain which it aspired to has lost much of its attraction. In reality "a little uncertainty takes away far more from the fear of suffering than an uncertainty even though great does from the attraction of pleasure. Furthermore, the guilty have so many chances of escaping justice and of being acquitted!"

It is, however, only fair to add that all Ferri's co-religionists do not go as far as he does in this same direction. Garofalo, who is a magistrate, makes some reservations; Lombroso[2] cites historical examples of vigorous repressive measures crowned with success. Under Sixtus V, more than a thousand executions in five years stamped out brigandage for the time being in the Romagna;

[1] Ferri forgets to notice that the desire, experienced by magistrates and better and better realized by them, to avoid acquittals, and to adapt themselves more and more to the ever increasing weakness of the judges and even of the criminal judges, which is ever becoming better known, is amply sufficient to account for this gradual lowering of the proportion of acquittals. There is in all this a phenomenon of judicial adaptability as inevitable as it is unconscious. Repression is, in reality, weakening from day to day.

[2] See his "Incremento del delitto in Italia."

the Austrians in 1849, by means of an equal severity, drove it out of Calabria; more recently the law of Pica has checked it at Naples. There is one penalty, at all events, whose efficacy the majority of our authors recognize and even proclaim, and that is the death penalty. However, they are not unanimous in upholding the expediency of its being kept at the present time. Ferri thinks it inopportune today. But they all bear witness to its great usefulness, in the past at least, and to its legitimacy at all times. It is curious to observe, after this, that the paradox of inefficacious punishment was originally put into circulation by the opponents of the death penalty, whose favorite argument it is.

It is undeniable that the true and sovereign remedy against the offense would be the elimination of its causes, if care had been taken to study them in their entirety. Again, the most active causes must necessarily be those depending on man; for, if "physical and anthropological factors" such as climate, season, race, individual idiosyncracies, over which the will has practically no control, preponderate, as our new school criminologists pretend, there is practically nothing left to do but to cross one's arms in the face of the advancing flood. We cannot really accomplish anything except by acting upon social causes, and again only upon a portion of these. Now, as we have seen, the school has very much neglected going into these and nowhere does it lay before us a methodical table of them which is detailed and complete. From such premises none but a vague and insufficient conclusion could arise. This is just what has happened. When he wants to unroll the list of his great preventive measures which he calls "substitutes for punishment," Ferri gives us nothing save a bare sketch,[1] the first conception of which is the only thing worth retain-

[1] Against infanticide he suggests the re-establishment of turning boxes and of the right to investigate the child's paternity; against duelling, the jury of honor; against adultery, divorce. On this subject he relies on the statistics of Massachusetts, the result of which shows that from 1865 to 1878 the number of divorces increased from three hundred and thirty-seven to five hundred and sixty-two, while the number of adulteries (in which there was a prosecution) decreased from one hundred and ninety-five to one hundred and thirty-six. But I would like very much to know whether the divorces in question were not in a great measure decreed or sought for on the ground of adultery. Ferri could have chosen examples less liable to be contested, such as the forbidding of the carrying of weapons which, in Corsica, had decreased by four-fifths the number of assassinations under the Second Empire. See as regards this "En Corse," by *Paul Bourde*, "Reforme pénitentiare et pénale," by *Labroquère*, Advocate-General at Bordeaux, and "Criminalité en Corse," by *Bournet*.

ing; that is to ask for reform in laws and civil institutions, especially the stemming of the tide of criminality. But as a matter of fact laws and institutions are but the outer skin of society, and their kernel, whence comes the surface, is composed of a sheaf of ingenious ideas, of discoveries, and of inventions to which we always have to revert, just as to the feelings and the primitive needs of the organism, when we want to explain beliefs and customs, religions and State institutions. Unfortunately genius is not made to order, and like the rain and the sunshine it escapes man's power. It is quite possible, as Ferri somewhere insinuates, that the gradual disappearance of drunkenness among the upper classes among European nations, during the last two centuries, was brought about among them by the spread of the custom of coffee drinking since the time of Louis XIV. Thus the discovery of this precious tonic has been a splendid antidote for wine, that other very ancient discovery, and has restrained in a great measure the abundant source of offenses which the latter had given rise to. This remark may even become the subject of generalization. The invention of steam applied to navigation has caused piracy to disappear; railways cause brigandage to disappear wherever they may penetrate. In Anatolia, according to a traveler,[1] excepting in the parts traversed by the railways, the entire territory "lives almost without interruption in terror of assassins and of plunderers. Recently they even came into the streets of Smyrna, pillaging shops and holding the merchants for ransom." These examples, which it would be easy to multiply, are of a kind to make us think that if such and such a discovery or invention still in the limbo of future generations had just blossomed forth, such and such a branch of the tree of wrongdoing, actually in bloom, as forgery, arson or theft, would begin to wither, having been affected in its very sap. But this sovereign specific is a secret which the future holds, and it escapes our will.

That is why as a matter of fact we have to fall back on the small means at our disposal, for want of a grasp of the great ones. Let us therefore quickly run over the legislative reforms which are in contemplation, and which are of two kinds. One kind has to do with criminal procedure and justice, the other bears on the system of punishment and the course to be pursued in penitentiary institutions. The first arise from this idea, which is a perfectly

[1] *Emile Bournouf*, article on "La France dans le Levant" ("Revue des Deux Mondes," October 15, 1887).

justifiable one, that it is important to substitute in matters relating to crime the point of view of sociology, which is a far broader and higher one, for the strictly juridical point of view. Consequently an assemblage of aptitudes and of special enlightenments, quite distinct from the qualities which go to make up a good judge in civil matters, should be demanded of the magistrate called upon to pass judgment on crimes and on offenses; the scholarly or law-student's training which would be expedient for the former would not be expedient for the latter; the habits of mind peculiar to the former, the taste for syllogism and quibble would lead astray the judgment of the latter, who should especially shine by reason of the talent of observation, of a love of facts, a keenness of vision; and it is a very great error to make use of the same personnel of judges turn and turn about and without any distinction, to fill the requirements of two such diverse occupations. It also follows from this that the jury, "which is to the magistracy what the national guard is to the army," is not fit for the task imposed upon it. It is lacking in the requisite amount of education and experience. But we are here pointing out the impassioned attacks of the new school directed against the jury merely that they may be borne in mind; they are deserving of having a separate examination given to them further on.

If, notwithstanding, we are determined to preserve this detestable institution, born of the Anglo-mania of the last century, at least we must try to ameliorate it. To the two verdicts of acquittal and of conviction with or without extenuating circumstances, it would be a good thing to add this third one, the verdict of *insufficient proof*, analogous to the "non liquet" of the Romans. In a great number of cases it would permit the jury better to express the real truth of what they think and to avoid the scandal of an exoneration pure and simple. Furthermore, the decree of no ground for prosecution *until further charges are brought* is perfectly permissible; why then should not something of a similar nature be permissible in the case of judgments? The Austrian and the German Codes have already recognized that society has, on principle, a right to a revision of criminal trials when new proofs are brought to light. We must also find a remedy for the abuse of recourse to appeals by reason of formal defects and the equal abuse of special and general pardons, "those jubilees of crime."

Garofalo has spent a great deal of time on a reform which presents the characteristics of a high form of justice.[1] The victim of an offense should no longer be obliged to go to the expense of making himself a party to a civil action in order to obtain a sentencing of the offender to pay damages; this reparation of the wrong should be required by the Public Prosecutor before any other penalty is imposed. A theft is committed; the thief is not entirely insolvent, and the person who has been robbed could be compensated, if the State did not first of all demand the fine which is payable to itself. Is this not strange? The State benefits by offenses which it was wrong in not preventing, and it gets the benefit at the expense of those who are entitled to reproach it by reason of its negligence.

Whether it be before magistrates or before juries, the nature of the argument between the prosecution and the defense ought to be changed. There should no longer be any question of moral responsibility. If it is a case of homicide, it is not premeditation which ought to be the circumstance of aggravation,[2] it is the anti-social character of the motive which has driven to murder or to assassination. When it has been proved that the motives of some delictual act are anti-social, acquittal should no longer be pleaded for. Between the Public Prosecutor and his adversary, the only difficulty which remains to be solved is whether the guilty man ought to be placed in the category of *insane, born, habitual,* or *accidental* criminals. It would be of very great advantage if for a tilt on common grounds of oratory, there were substituted a similar discussion wherein scientific arguments alone were admissible, and where the part played by the expert would come to preponderate. The expert should furthermore be chosen from an official list, and in difficult cases recourse could be had to the luminaries of a great college of experts, such as already exist in Germany, Austria, and Russia. A medico-legal examination would determine the class to which the condemned should belong, and we would no longer see a jury, which, moreover, realizes its unfitness to pass upon the conclusions drawn by a doctor-lawyer, believing itself bound to solve the most arduous problems of morbid psychology entirely alone. Ferri attributes this assumed competence of the first comer in cases of diseases of the brain to the influence of spiritualist ideas.

[1] See especially his pamphlet entitled "Riparazione alle vittime del delitto" (fratelli Bocca, 1887).

[2] On this point the classic school agrees with the new school. See on this subject "La Peine de mort," by *Holtzendorff* (chap. 22 *et seq.*). See also the "Premeditazione," by *Bernardino Alimena* (fratelli Bocca, 1887).

Let us now take up penitential reforms. The foremost among them consists in the creation of criminal refuges, a kind of prison-asylums[1] where madmen would be incarcerated who should benefit by a decree of no ground for prosecution by reason of their madness; madmen acquitted as such; convicts showing in prison sure signs of mental alienation, and lastly, ordinary insane people who have committed acts characterized as criminal in their sanitariums. As to born criminals, incorrigibles, the question arises as to whether it is right to apply the death penalty in their case. Its legitimacy is no more doubted by anyone in the positivist camp than is its illegitimacy in the opposed camp. But a number of our writers believe that under normal conditions the exercise of the right of society to *eliminate* the obstacle in the path of social ends is useless and may advantageously be replaced by deportation. We will come back to this subject in a special chapter. In what concerns individuals judged to be dangerous, Garofalo has always championed the penalty of *indefinite* terms of imprisonment, of a duration which is not determined upon in advance and which varies according to the conduct of the condemned while in prison. For that matter this idea has been advocated by other authors, especially by Kraepelin in Germany. Ferri would seem almost to approve of corporal punishment to a certain extent, that which Roncati calls the "maternal system," by way of a delicate allusion to the spankings which good mothers give their undisciplined children.[2] Electric shocks, cold douches would be useful processes according to absolutely modern and scientific ideas. Wrong-doers from force of habit, though often not very dangerous, need severe repressive measures. The penalty should increase in geometrical progression according to the number of the recurrences of the offense. Everybody is agreed in condemning the futility of short sentences applied to recidivists. Delinquents because of opportunity should be compelled, in prison, to pay by means of their work the expenses of their maintenance and the damages sustained by their victim. For them, as for the preceding class of prisoners, the system of placing them in cells is effective; but

[1] In England, Bedlam; in France, Gaillon, can give us an idea, but an imperfect one, of this species of establishments.

[2] In France a former magistrate, *Eugène Mouton*, in the "Devoir de punir," (1887), had the temerity to point out that the bastinado and flogging are in use today even among people who are our contemporaries in civilization. *Beaussire*, in his "Principes du Droit," does not categorically pronounce himself as opposed to this method of punishment.

the Irish system of repression by means of establishments divided into large classes of prisoners is still better. As no punishment has any effect on offenders by reason of passion, there is no occasion to inflict any punishment on them other than the strict reparation of the injury occasioned by their offense.

In the final chapter of his book, Ferri places *Criminal Sociology*, which he has just sketched, and which we have been reviewing according to his method and that of his school, among the other social sciences. He shows the penal law henceforth being reconstructed with the data furnished by psychology, anthropology, and statistics; he predicts that before very long the need of a thorough revision based upon the same inspiring studies will be felt even in the civil law.

CHAPTER III

THE THEORY OF RESPONSIBILITY

§ 13. Preliminary remarks.

§§ 14–16. (I) Moral responsibility founded on personal identity and social similarity. (II) The ideal of perfect responsibility. Conditions of the affections, sociable and unsociable; opposition to this point of view as between the desire to produce and the desire to consume, objective and subjective beliefs. The psychological conditions of personal identity are generally also those of social similarity. (III) Comparison with the collective responsibility of a nation. Its numerous analogies to individual responsibility.

§§ 17–20. What must be understood by social similarity. (I) It has nothing to do with physical similarities nor even with every kind of physiological similarity. The moral sense. The teleological syllogism. Good and evil, their sociological significance. Social subjectivism. The duty of believing or of not believing. (II) Unanimous judgments of blame or of approbation; necessity of this conformism. (III) Importance of defining the bounds of a society. This limit is always extended, and in several ways. Extradition treaties.

§§ 21–26. What must be understood by personal identity. (I) Identity, permanence of the individual. What is the individual? The individuality of the individual made clearer by the individuality of the organism and especially by that of the State. Logical and teleological co-ordination. The immortal soul and eternal cities; similar conceptions. (II) A difference in spite of analogies, the identity of the "myself" much deeper than the identity of the State. The hypothesis of monads. (III) The State is to the nation what the "myself" is to the brain. The "force-ideas" of Fouillée. Identity *makes* and unmakes itself, it has its degrees. (IV) Foundations of the limitation of criminal prosecutions; reforms which should be introduced therein. (V) Civil responsibility.

§§ 27–31. Our theory agrees with the historical one of responsibility. (I) Family solidarity of primitive times; vendetta. Survivals of these past times, reprisals. (II) Royal justice took for its model, not the domestic tribunals of a former era, but warlike proceedings; malefactors everywhere treated as enemies. (III) Expiatory character of punishment: individual transition. (IV) Review and completion.

§ 13. Preliminary remarks.

What is the result of the preceding chapters? A conclusion which does not appear to be very encouraging. As we have seen, responsibility made to depend on free will adjudged to be in actual existence is ruined at its very base by the progress of scientific determinism; responsibility made to depend on free will looked upon as an ideal to be realized is nothing more than an illusion, and responsibility based on social utility to the exclusion of everything else has nothing in common with responsibility as understood in the preceding senses except its name; while its name is refused it, and justly so, by the more rigorous of the utilitarians.

Does it follow from all this that it is impossible to find a rational foundation for an idea which is plainly visible to all of humanity, which enlightens every man coming into the social world, and which is no superstition in process of receding before the advance of civilization, but an exact conception, spreading as civilization increases and expands? We do not believe so. The best means, as we look at it, by which to combat or to acquire control over the various theories hereinbefore set forth, is to oppose to them some theory which has in it nothing scholastic, but which evolves itself and ought to formulate itself, if one closely scrutinizes what men in fact have always meant when they say that in their opinion one of themselves is responsible, either civilly or criminally. Have they thought that he was responsible for some action because in carrying it out he, through his voluntary decision, through his freedom of choice, made necessary a mere possibility which, previous to this decision born "ex nihilo," would have had not one of the characteristics of a necessity? Never has human common sense entered into such subtilties. From all time a being has been adjudged to be responsible for an act when it was thought that he and no one else was the author, the willing and conscious author, be it understood, of this very act. The problem solved by means of this judgment is one dealing with causality and identity and not with freedom. Just as soon as free will shall be a truth and not a hypothesis, the fact alone that its existence is denied almost universally by the learned men of our time and an ever increasing proportion of educated people should make us feel the urgency of seeking elsewhere for the support of responsibility. In fact, when consulted by justice on the point of whether an accused is responsible in the classical interpretation of the word, the medico-legal expert ought always to reply, and as a matter of fact does more and more reply in the negative; and from this arise acquittals as scandalous as they are logical. Our utilitarians have indeed felt this danger and they have endeavored to avert it. But they have not been successful in doing so. By reason of the obligation which they believe to be imposed upon them after having denied the existence of free will, of defining responsibility as being a thing apart from any idea of morality, that is to say of decapitating and destroying it, they appear to justify this pretension, so often advanced by the partisans of free will, that, their principle having been destroyed, morality falls to the ground.[1] There is in this a prejudice so dear to the spiritual conscience, and so eloquently propagated and supported by the noblest minds, that we cannot hope to see broken up this association of ideas entirely opposed to morality, as long as we limit ourselves to the undermining of the pretended foundation of the latter without having carved out or unearthed some new foundation on which to rest it. The importance of and the opportunity for this attempt should be an excuse for its very boldness. So we are going to take the liberty of outlining in the following pages, in a theoretical way, our way of looking at the matter; after which we shall endeavor to show that it is in accord with the historical evolution of responsibility and enables us for the first time to establish a connection, and for the first time to avoid any hiatus between the older conception, which is fading out, and the new positivist conception, which has a tendency to triumph.

§ 14. (I) Moral responsibility founded on personal identity and social similarity.

The problem of responsibility is connected with the philosophical search for causes and is but an application of the latter, but a very arduous one, to the study of the facts relative to man living in society.

It is just because of this slim connection between the two problems that the conception of free will came into existence. In fact it came into existence, and it must logically have come into existence, at a time when the idea of the unlimited and absolute guilt of the sinner was the rule. If being guilty of an act means primarily being the cause of the same, it follows that being guilty of it absolutely and without limit, in the opinion of everybody and without any restriction, as is necessary in order to justify the notion of eternal damnation, must indeed mean being its absolute and first cause, in other words, the free cause, beyond which it is impossible for us to go back along the chain of the series of causes. Liberty used in this sense is an "ex nihilo" creative power, a

[1] "Man," says Dally, "could no more be morally responsible for his acts than he is for the illnesses he brings with him at birth or which he has contracted during the course of his life." Declarations as radical as the above were made during the Congress of Rome amid general applause.

divine attribute conferred upon man. The free agent resists and is able to check God; he is in reality a little god opposed to a great one. To refuse to man this creative power, this privilege of suspending the divine laws by means of a sort of incomprehensible *veto*, and at the same time to judge him to be deserving of punishments without end for having placed an obstacle in the path of the will of God, would unquestionably be to contradict oneself. But if, instead of an absolute and unlimited liability, henceforth left out of the discussion, the only question is one of a relative and limited liability similar to every real and positive thing, a causality itself relative and limited, a *secondary* causality, so to speak, will suffice. Consequently liberty becomes a useless postulate. We have arrived at that point. The question is to know finally whether, in order to be simply a stitch of the tissue bound about by phenomena and woven by necessity, the "myself" has lost all right to be called a cause, and whether there is no true cause excepting the first cause which is hypothetical and imperceptible. The question is to find out whether, instead of being founded upon the supposed indeterminateness of the act, responsibility will not be conditioned upon the special nature of its very determination, its internal determinism.

Let us suppose that we are looking at it from the point of view of the determinist. Do I any the less exist because I must of necessity exist? Am I any the less myself because from all time it has been ordained that I should exist, because billions and billions of chains of causes, rivers, and streams of force have converged in my direction, unknown to themselves, but inevitably, since the world has been in existence? This is not all; it will not even suffice to say that I have been from all time the inevitable flowing together of so many evolutions in the past; we must go so far as to say that an immense fan of causal evolutions, extending into the infinite future, emanates from me. I am the point of intersection of this double infinity, I am the focal point of this double convergence. For in truth why could you not say, *if necessity is the universal rule*, that my true cause is in the future, which is not yet, as well as in the past, which is no more? Is it not because of an entirely subjective illusion, and because of a remnant of unconscious, but deeply imbedded belief in *the contingency of the future*, that we refuse to account to ourselves for the actual fact, the existing phase of an evolution, by means of its later phases, and that we insist upon explaining it, always insufficiently, by means of its previous phases? There is no more reason for saying of a man who resembles his ancestors, by virtue of the laws of heredity, "it is his ancestors acting through him," than there would be to say, "it is his sons, his grandsons, or, if he is to have none, his social descendants, his future imitators, who are acting through him." If one only thinks of speaking of one's ancestors, it is because one knows only them, it is because man's imperfect intelligence is in general deprived of the faculty of seeing into the future, — unless it be with reference to astronomical phenomena of a certain kind, — and is reduced to the faculty of remembering. Thus, *I must always have existed, I must exist forever*, and I will not truly be — I am. Now, if I am and as long as I am, it is but a farce to seek any cause for my acts other than myself.

However, we must recognize the fact that there is nothing more obscure than the idea of a cause and the relation of causality, nothing has given rise to more discussion among the philosophers. Hume and Kant, the positivists, and the critical philosophers, scarcely agree on this subject; and if the question had to remain unsolved until they had reached some agreement thereon, one might look upon it as impossible of solution. But human consciousness is not engaged in this debate; it has never here asked itself, what is the cause? Taking this word in its most obvious and practical meaning, it has merely asked itself, *where* is the cause? It has replied, in various ways according to the period of time, by circumscribing the more or less narrow circle of reality judged to be indivisible, within which the cause should be found inclosed. We say when we see an assassin who has just committed a crime, it is in this brain, in this soul that the cause of this homicide lies. A few centuries ago we would have said in a more vague way, it is within this individual, and at a time still more remote, when the individual was bound to his family as the member is to the body, we would rather have said, it is within this family. The essential thing is not to mistake one family for another, one individual for another, one soul, one brain for another; let us now add, for this progress continues, one "myself" for another. A family changes during the course of time and is renewed, an organism is transformed, a "soul" is modified, a "myself" is altered; but as long as the family, the body, or the person endures, the transformations taking place in them are variations upon a theme which remains more or less identical and whose identity, attenuated but not destroyed, gives us the right to look upon these circles of reality as always inclosing the cause of an act previously committed, the same cause or very nearly the same. Psychologists have attached far too great an importance to the feeling which we have of our liberty and not enough to the feeling, firm in every other respect, which we have of our identity. Moralists have expended treasures of analysis as a loss simply, in setting up the scale of the degrees of liberty; and the degrees of identity have escaped their vigilance. It is, however, easy enough to say at a certain moment of time, when one scrutinizes a person very closely, to what extent that person has remained the same as at a previous date; but no one can say just to what extent that person was a free agent. Let us admit free will, be it so; but at least we ought to recognize the fact that there is a most incontestable practical advantage in making responsibility rest upon identity which is a patent fact, rather than upon liberty which is a latent force.

Is that as much as to say that the idea of *individual identity* alone is sufficient?

No, we must add to it that of *social similarity*, as we shall see, and it is only in combining these two notions that we can find the plausible solution of the problem. In order for me to judge an individual to be responsible for a criminal action committed a year, ten years ago, is it enough for me to believe that he is the identical author of this action? No, for though I might have brought the same judgment of identity to bear in the case of a murder committed on a European by a savage of a newly discovered isle, yet I would not have the same feeling of moral indignation and of virtuous hatred as a similar act carried out by one European on another, or by one islander on another, would inspire within me. Therefore one indispensable condition for the arousing of the feeling of moral and penal responsibility is that the perpetrator and the victim of a deed should be and should feel themselves to be more or less fellow-countrymen from a social standpoint, that they should present a sufficient number of resemblances, of social, that is to say, of imitative origin. This condition is not fulfilled when the incriminating act emanates from someone who is insane, or from an epileptic at the moment he is seized with a paroxysm, or even from one addicted to alcoholism in certain cases. This sort of people, at the very moment when they have acted, have not belonged to the society of which they are reputed to be members. But when the two conditions pointed out above are met with and are together developed to a high degree, the feeling of responsibility bursts forth with remarkable strength. Among every people, such as the ancient Egyptians, the Romans, the Chinese, the English, wherever, on the one hand, the assimilation of individuals to one another, or the homogeneity of society, is well developed, and where, on the other hand, faith in the identity of the person is pushed even to the dogma of the immortal soul, one can see that fellow-citizens in their mutual relations feel that they have a grave responsibility as far as their faults and their obligations are concerned. In China, for example, in spite of what has been said as to the want of integrity of this nation, "the guilty man," Simon tells us,[1] "is *convinced* before being sentenced. I have seen," he adds, "Chinese convicts themselves hold out their legs for the irons which were to be placed upon them." More than this, the law of the Central Empire in certain cases authorizes the substitution by one for another to undergo the penalty of death. So that we find old scoundrels who, being the shame of their family, are willing to serve as substitutes on the scaffold in order that they may rehabilitate themselves in the eyes of their relations.[2] Nothing can better picture for us the family spirit in the Far East than this characteristic; but at the same time, "all this assumes a conception of justice [in the dealings with one another of the Chinese] carried to an extreme of power."

§ 15. (II) The ideal of perfect responsibility. Conditions of the affections, sociable and unsociable; opposition to this point of view as between the desire to produce and the desire to consume, objective and subjective beliefs. The psychological conditions of personal identity are generally also those of social similarity.

Let us endeavor to ascertain what constitutes the fulness of moral responsibility. First of all it is essential that the agent while acting should have been possessed of all his habitual and characteristic faculties, that he should in nowise have departed from his normal state of being. But is not a man, born irascible and debauched, in his normal state of being when he cries out and vociferates, and when he is a prey to voluptuous transports? Undoubtedly. So it becomes necessary to fill out our definition. If the normal state of a man is in no way similar to the normal state of the majority of his associates, there exists in him irresponsibility; he is not absolutely responsible except when his normal state,

[1] "Cité chinoise."

[2] Here the penalty is essentially of an expiatory nature and nevertheless presents, precisely because of this character, a great and profound social utility.

because of which he has acted, is as similar as possible to the average state in question.

Now from this point of view we can distinguish the psychological states of various individuals under two great headings: states which are susceptible and states which are not susceptible of lasting association; a division which admits of this subdivision, states which are, or, are not, compatible with the time some sort of an association lasts, and states which are only compatible or incompatible with the time a kind of association peculiar to some period or to some country will last. Most assuredly there are very few states whose compatibility or incompatibility absolutely corresponds with the stability of any imaginable society. However, we are quite right in advancing the proposition that violent states, as a general thing, are essentially incapable of association, and not capable of generalization without prejudice to the common interest, and that if a great society supports them, it is to absorb and to merge them, thin-sown, into itself. When the proportion of the irascible, the excessive drinkers, the gamblers, the envious, the politicians, and the vindictive gets beyond a certain limit, the social tie is relaxed or is broken. Moderate states alone are habitually capable of association. I refer to moderate states as relating to desires or needs to be fulfilled, or as relating to subjective beliefs called self-respect. For as regards desires and needs of production, and similarly as regards objective beliefs called dogmas or knowledge, the most excessive states, if they succeed in becoming general, realize on the contrary the most absolute unanimity.

We see warlike or peaceful activities, on a battlefield or in an industrial market, let loose together and alike, and with great violence, in Europe or in America, and the strength of the military or national tie feels not the slightest effect, but just the opposite. We see burning convictions, having the same religious dogmas or the same scientific truths as their object, assert themselves with energy and at one and the same time to the extent of several millions, and, if they are affirmative or negative in the same sense, this group of fanaticisms is always the most tenacious of unions. But we do not see, unless a society is in jeopardy, appetites unbridled therein more rapidly than activities are extended, and pride and absurd self-confidence dilate more rapidly than convictions and knowledge are strengthened therein. The more appetites resemble one another, that is to say pursue the same prey to devour, and the more they conflict, the more similar to one another are activities, that is to say they pursue the attainment of the same goal, and the more they agree or are capable of agreement. The more alike different sorts of self-esteem are in their nature, each one believing itself superior to others in the same relation, the more they contradict one another; the more similar in nature are beliefs, and the more they mean the same thing, the more do they confirm one another. It follows that a social state which is excellent and truly stable is at all times and in all places made up of strong convictions which are alike and of feeble prides which are unlike, of great needs of concerted action and of little needs of private pleasures. History proclaims this truth, and the illusions which our century may choose to create for itself on this point will not prevail against it.

Therefore, just as soon as a man is one day seized with a conviction, called a hallucination, which is not shared with other men and which he can never make them share, because it is contradictory to their beliefs, which they call certitudes; or, again, just as soon as a man is suddenly filled with a swelling of unusual conceit, with a confidence in himself out of proportion to that which conforms to the social life of his surroundings, and as a consequence gives himself up to the delusion of persecutions, the delusion of greatness, or to any other aberration of a similar kind; or as soon as a disordered and irresistible passion drives this same man either to some strange occupation or one contrary to every trade, or to a satisfaction which is intense and out of proportion, and contrary to the social and legitimate pleasures of others; from that very moment this same man ceases to belong to his society, he *disassimilates* himself at the same time as he *alienates* himself. If he was born with a temperament which led him into these extravagances, these eccentricities which set him apart, it is true that one cannot say that he alienated himself or disassimilated himself by giving way to them, as they are natural to him; but because of them he is born outside of the association of his fellow human beings. In the one case as in the other he is morally irresponsible.

At the point at which our races, civilized for so many centuries, have arrived, a man who is not born sociable is an abnormal being, and in the case of a man who is sociable, a condition not marked with the stamp of society is an abnormal state. The conditions of personal identity are generally also those of social similarity, although the latter assumes the effect of surroundings upon the person, and the former a relative independence of the person as far as the surroundings are concerned. In fact, persons associated together have more influence over one another, are better able to exchange with one another their best ways of doing things or of thinking, the more each one of them is influenced by the recollection of himself through their own previous experiences which they have preserved and accumulated; personal identity is nothing but this preservation and this accumulation, this consequence and this development resulting from experience, that is to say from recollections properly so called and from habits. The aptitude for the imitation of others thus bears a relation to the aptitude for the imitation of oneself, in other words with the accuracy of memory.[1]

But among all the ideas and all the actions, among all the nervous exciting causes and all the muscular contractions of our past, which are the ones which bear the imprint of the identical person to the highest degree? They are the ideas upon which our attention has successively been brought to bear; they are the actions which each in turn have been the object of our will. The mind, or to put it better the soul — a vague and vast name which well suits a thing so obscure and so large — is like a sky in which there is but a single star, yet a star ever wandering as its caprice may dictate and changing its color, that which is called the "myself." Again one can say that the soul is an inextricable and vast labyrinth in which is unrolled the thread, tenuous and continuous, of our many colored attentions and volitions whose inexhaustible ball is the "myself." — On the other hand a society is a collection not of organisms exactly, nor even of souls, but of "myselfs." It is the "myselfs" alone which are bound together by social and legal ties; it is the "myselfs" alone which mutually serve one another as examples to be imitated or not to be imitated; it is the "myselfs" alone which are able

[1] Social assimilation is so far from being contrary to individual identity that it constitutes the latter. We have two Christians; one of them a Christian at heart and in his faith, the other, only so far as external habits and practices are concerned. Both of them are this because of imitation of others, because of tradition and the influence of their surroundings; but with the former, this contagion has been far more profound than with the latter. Now which one of the two is it who, in acting in a Christian manner, puts more of his own personality into his acts, who more completely realizes the "conscium" and the "compos sui"? Assuredly the former. The solidity, the personality of his character are to be measured by the extent to which surrounding actions have influenced him.

to contract, to give, to make their wills and commit crimes or do virtuous acts as well.

From this and for these two reasons, it follows that the responsibility for an act shall be so much the more absolute as it shall have been the more voluntarily and attentively deliberated upon.[1] So in proportion as the increasing complexity of civilized life develops and facilitates the action of that "mechanism of attention," so well described by Ribot, and the exercise of the will; in proportion as this double centralization of the soul spreads itself and is strengthened, does the individual become more fully responsible for his actions. Unless, however, because of the effect of a civilization which is too oppressive or too severe for him, he becomes mad; in the latter case his act may in vain be voluntary, it is not *his;* it emanates not from his "myself," but from a corner of his brain which has revolted, and which has nothing in common with society; and the murder he may have committed under these circumstances is no more a crime than is the killing of a Frenchman who has disembarked upon his shores in the eyes of some savage who is an absolute stranger to our form of society.

§ 16. (III) Comparison with the collective responsibility of a nation. Its numerous analogies to individual responsibility.

A comparison which is not a comparison merely will make the preceding statements more readily understood.

Let us ask ourselves under what conditions the collective responsibility of a nation as a nation is fully and undeniably brought into play. Here the equivalent of memory and habit, foundation of individual identity, is tradition and custom, foundation of national identity.

When a people are the faithful guardians of their beliefs and of their customs, China for example, they feel themselves, even after the lapse of centuries — though perhaps they are unwilling to admit as much — responsible for the decisions and the acts of their ancestors, and though they may exclaim, in reality they

[1] That is why, — I recall it to the experience of every magistrate, — the sitting of a civil court is often more disgusting than the sitting of a court dealing with misdemeanors, and there is more true immorality brought into play in certain proceedings wherein the cynical bad faith of a litigant in full possession of his faculties is displayed than in the majority of the cases of petty larceny or of small cases of blows and woundings wherein is seen the effect of a passing misconduct. That which jurists call "fraud" is a sort of "civil criminality," as has been very well said.

never find it surprising that a neighboring people should call upon them to make good the injury caused to the latter by their ancestors at a remote date. But in order that the justice of this claim may be felt in this way, the State making the claim must present a civilization analogous to that of the State which is called upon. China is far from believing itself to have as much responsibility towards a European people as it would have towards Japan or Korea. The Christian Principalities of the Middle Ages believed themselves to be bound by their treaties among themselves, even though very remote, in a way quite different to that in which they were bound by promises, even though of recent date, with the Saracens. The small Greek republics scattered throughout the entire Archipelago, along the entire Mediterranean shore, showed a noteworthy constancy as regards their reciprocal treaties if it be compared with their relations with even their nearest barbarian neighbors.

Responsibility, I repeat, implies a social tie, a collection of similarities in nature which are not organic merely, between the great and the small, the States or the individuals judged to be responsible; and responsibility implies, furthermore, a psychological tie between the former state during which the being adjudged to be responsible acted or contracted and the later state during which he is called upon to answer for his act or to carry out his contract. Is it also necessary that there should be a psychological connection between the former and the later state of the one who makes the claim himself? Yes I believe so. When, following a conquest or a revolution, a people has been thrown into disorder from top to bottom, it is hardly the time to invoke against another people rights based upon an insult to the flag of its former government which has been overthrown, or even upon an agreement made with the leaders of this former State, whose name is all that is left of it. In Europe the French Revolution itself did not result in any such confusion as the cancellation of every diplomatic treaty previous to 1789 could have brought about; but assuredly the social transformation which resulted therefrom brought to bear on these treaties an effect at least equally far reaching. Similarly, I do not feel that I am obliged to carry out a promise made to someone who has become insane since my obligation was incurred, unless it be when it relates to the discharge of a debt the amount of which the guardian of this lunatic, or his heir after his death can collect. As a matter of fact, in such a case the law establishes the fiction of a legal person who never dies and who continues to exist without change. I will add that neither do I feel myself bound to discharge a debt which I contracted when I was five or six years old, before the absolute determining of my person, no matter with whom.

Several cases may arise. 1st. A nation which is very persistent as concerns its national identity is surrounded by nations also very steadfast, but which differ greatly from it, ancient Egypt, for example, a neighbor of the Israelites, of the black-skinned Africans, of the Phoenicians; the Byzantine empire, a neighbor of the Arabs and of the Turks; Christian Spain, a neighbor of the Moors, etc. In such a case there might occur a series of wars and of massacres between these heterogeneous societies, but there never would be any important treaties, never any *law of nations*. It is the same with two individualities who are exceedingly original or eccentric meeting each other; they always clash, and, if they attempt to form a partnership, neither one of them has any scruple about soon violating the rules.[1]

2d. A very changeable nation and one which readily forgets its traditions and usages is surrounded by nations which are also very variable, and, furthermore, very different to it at each moment of their incessant changes. I doubt if this case has ever been presented in history; for, as a rule, if not invariably, *internal variation* has for its cause the too hospitable reception given to the imitation of neighbors, and, as a consequence, it is accompanied by *external assimilation*. If, however, this supposition should be realized, we should have to see in it the ideal of international irresponsibility. This supposition is indeed realized, but only in the individual sense, in lunatic asylums, and we know that no legal tie can exist between madmen, separately carried away and denatured by their morbid evolutions.

[1] I do not say that they are right in violating these rules. In all of this, of course, I am explaining *what is*, and not *what ought to be*. Some writers have misunderstood my thought, which has seemed *odious* to them. They have thought, for example, that I justified the bad faith or the barbarity of civilized people which are so frequent in their relations with the races thought to be inferior. I protest with all my heart against such an interpretation. In my opinion the individual *ought* to feel himself the more responsible towards every animate being, often even towards animals, in proportion as he is more distinguished and educated. Every being which *feels*, which is liable to suffer, has rights; and every being which *has understanding* has duties towards those even who would be incapable, through lack of intelligence, as yet to have duties towards himself. But, here again we are concerned with responsibility as it is experienced and put into practice, and not as it ought to be.

3d. A changeable nation is surrounded by peoples who are also changeable, but who constantly resemble it, by reason of a continuous flow or of an exchange of imitative actions and reactions. The responsibility of one of these States towards the others is then very keenly felt, but only for a very limited time. This is just the case with the existing European peoples. They can be compared to young fellows, to students who make progress together, live the same life, change as far as appearances are concerned, but all of them at the same time, and who recognize the fact that they are firmly bound to explain to one another their common offenses, to pay one another their mutual debts, provided always, that the offenses shall be of recent date, and the debts as well.

4th. A contented nation, grown up and fixed as to its final structure, movable or immovable, furthermore, but at bottom unchangeable, contained within its customs either like a lake, or like a flowing river is between its banks, is surrounded by peoples just as ripe, just as solid, just as peaceable as itself, and, at the same time very similar to it in language, religion, legislation, government, culture, and customs. This was to be seen in Europe during the splendid feudal period, in the twelfth century, and, later still, during the fine monarchic period, in the seventeenth century. The various European States, during these two periods, formed a veritable federation, and in spite of the frequency of internal wars and conflicts, explainable by the excessive parceling out of territories and the violence of passions, there occurred then this remarkable thing, very justly pointed out by historians, that international differences it seemed to everyone should be settled by the decisions of the higher courts, to the same extent as litigation between individuals.[1]

Such are the relations which are to be observed as existing between men of a ripe age having the same fatherland, belonging to the same class, and having the same political opinion. These relations reveal the feeling of mutual responsibility elevated to its greatest power. From this it follows, among other consequences, that if ever the modern nations of our continent, as we should hope, bring to maturity their brilliant civilization which is still young, and settle themselves anew, despite the exalted complexity of their elements, into an equilibrium which is at the same

[1] This essentially legal character of the relations between States during the Middle Ages has forcibly struck *Cournot*. See his "Considérations."

time stable and flexible, without ceasing to assimilate more and more, the United States of Europe may become a reality. Each new step towards national stability, each new step in the direction of an international resemblance carries them along towards a final phase in which — if some gigantic conquest has not already united them by violent methods — their federation will become established, and will of its own accord become consolidated, because each one of them will feel itself strongly bound by its treaties, and obligated on account of its wrongful actions or its mistakes as regards the others, in the same way as honest fellow-citizens would feel themselves bound towards one another.

It is worth while observing, in following our analogy, that whether it be in the relations of one people with another, or in the relations of one person with another, the slightest degree of identity or of similarity is sufficient to give birth to the feeling of civil responsibility only in order that it may arouse that of criminal or quasi-criminal responsibility. Such a State, after passing through a revolutionary crisis, believes itself to be exempted by reason of its metamorphosis from any reparation to another State arising from some offense to the latter before the revolution on the part of the displaced government, but it nevertheless believes it ought to honor the signature of this former government by conforming itself to the clauses of a former diplomatic agreement. Such a civilized people recalls without the slightest remorse having carried on the slave-trade with Guinea, having poisoned Chinamen or massacred Indians,[1] but would feel some scruples about not conforming to the terms of a bargain struck with these inferior races, who, after all, are a part of the human race.

In the same way a private individual would laugh if reparation were asked of him by a duel-challenge for an insult dating back ten years, or two years even, especially when, during the interim

[1] And even in our day what do we not see? "In Zanzibar," says *Corre*, in "Crime et suicide" (1890), "Germans are civilizing negroes by compelling, through the lash and the rifle, the granting of that which is not given to them willingly. In Senegal I was able to admire the proceedings owing to which our big merchants attain, in the mother-country, fortune and honors: they have no hesitation, among Europeans, about relating with a laugh, the sleight of hand tricks with the scales. . . ." We know to what sort of treatment Stanley and his companions submitted the negroes of Africa whom they were going to *civilize:* Commander X indulged himself in the re-creation of scenes of anthropophagy in order to have the pleasure of photographing them. With this object in view he bought negro children with the express purpose of giving them to the cannibals to devour. Has English justice pursued the perpetrator of such deeds? I think not.

a great illness or a disaster of some sort had greatly changed its character; but he would take seriously the demanding of a sum borrowed by himself without any right and at a period even more remote. He gaily recalls the annoyances which he caused Asiatics or Africans, providing they do not amount to real crimes (in this he is better than a nation would be in his place), but he would deem himself to be disgraced were he to fail to pay these foreigners what he owed them. It is perhaps because of a vague realization of this truth that the periods of limitation in criminal cases are much shorter under all legislation than are those of limitation in civil cases. It is worthy of notice that criminal jurisprudence in England, during the last century, seemed to take precisely the opposite point of view to the truth set forth above, when it demanded a greater degree of madness, that is to say a lesser degree of identity, for the acquittal of a man accused of crime than it did for the cancellation of a will or a contract. This peculiarity is rightly criticised by Maudsley. He refuses to admit that a man judged to be sufficiently mad to be incapable of contracting can be condemned to be hung for having killed someone.

If the similarities between national responsibility and individual responsibility are instructive, the differences are no less so. Everybody knows, and it may have been noticed incidentally in the preceding statements, to what an extent the former, despite the progress it has made, always stays behind the latter. Foreign policy, that morality of the nations, tolerates duplicity and cruelties, a cynicism and an egoism, a lack of scruple and of pity, which the morality of individuals would severely reprove, and, in the midst of the most humane civilization, it remains barbarous.[1] Proceedings which, as between individuals, have disappeared centuries ago, such as the duel at law, principles which, morally speaking, have had their day, such as the right of vengeance, retaliation, and pecuniary composition, survive in political dealings as between States, under the name of war, reprisals, and indemnities. This should be so, from our point of view, since national identity is always very far from being the equivalent, in truth and depth, of personal identity, and international similarity never as a general rule approaches the average similarity existing between the citizens of the same State.

[1] One can say as much of internal politics, this morality of parties and of classes, in so far as these parties and classes act as different societies and not as the united fragments of the same society.

§ 17. What must be understood by social similarity.

But we have insisted enough on the preceding comparison. Let us now devote ourselves to a closer grasping of individual responsibility, and let us ask ourselves just what must be understood, first by social similarity, and in the second place by personal identity, which constitute its two elements. Let us begin by explaining the former and moreover the least important of the two.[1]

§ 18. (I) It has nothing to do with physical similarities nor even with every kind of physiological similarity. The moral sense. The teleological syllogism. Good and evil, their sociological significance. Social subjectivism. The duty of believing or of not believing.

In what should the resemblance of individuals consist in order that they should feel responsibility towards one another? Is it necessary that they should resemble one another in the features of their faces, the conformation or the capacity of the skull, the coloring, or the physical abilities? Not at all; if they resemble one another in this respect so much the better, because the similarities from another source, of imitative and not of hereditary origin, will by this means be the more readily acquired; but it is the latter which are the important ones. Is it necessary that they should have the same tastes, and should one look upon them as strangers to one another socially if they are born with certain eccentricities of taste, such as aberrations of the sexual sense, so well studied by our alienists? Not any more, and for the same reason. But their natural inclinations, whatever they may be, must, to a great extent, have received from surrounding example, from common education, from the prevailing custom, a particular direction which has designated them, which has specified the kind of hunger in the need of eating French or Asiatic dishes, the kind of thirst in the need of drinking wine or tea, the kind of sexual desires in a taste for wordly affection or rustic idyl, in a love of

[1] *The least important one.* I should have insisted upon this much more than I have done. The condition of *social similarity* is, in fact, secondary and accessory, if it be compared with that of *personal identity*. This latter is the foundation which is permanent, and ought to become the more and more conscious foundation, of moral responsibility, whereas social similarity should be demanded less and less and should end by not being demanded at all, at least among the superior civilized beings. My theory of responsibility, because of the lack of this necessary explanation, has been misunderstood and has seemed far more complicated than it really is.

dancing in France and of "flower boats" in China, innate curiosity in the form of a passion for travel or for reading, for such and such forms of travel or of reading, etc. When society has thus recast in its own image all the functions and all the organic tendencies of the individual, the individual does not make a single movement or gesture which is not directed towards an object designated by society.

Furthermore, the brute feelings furnished by the body and by external nature in the face of one another must, to a great extent also, have been deeply elaborated by means of conversations, by instruction, and by tradition, and by this means converted into a collection of definite ideas, of opinions, and of prejudices in the majority conforming to the beliefs of others, to the propensity of the language, to the spirit of the religion or of the philosophy which predominates, to the authority of forefathers or famous contemporaries. Whatever the individual may think, after this, he will think by means of the social brain, he will believe on the strength of what is said, in his boldest flights of the mind, and will but repeat a lesson learnt from society, or but combine, if he be unfettered and resourceful, such repetitions into an original composition.

Now let us observe that all our conscious and thought out actions, a thin but continuous current, stretching from the cradle to the grave, are the practical conclusions, formulated or implied, of what we may call a teleological syllogism, whose major premise is a desire, an object which one suggests to oneself, and whose minor premise is a belief, an opinion bearing on the best means to be taken in order to attain this end. I want to eat some bread; now, I believe that the best means by which I can satisfy this desire is to labor; therefore I *ought* to labor. Here we discern the germ of duty; it is not the social duty as yet, it is but the purely individual duty, but we shall soon perceive the analogy between the two, and that the latter is but the underlying principle of the former. However that may be, it follows from the preceding statement that, while the major and minor premises of the syllogism of finality formulated by the individual, that is to say his objects and his ideas, are the products of social manufacture, it is the same with the duties, be they individual or social, of the individual, conclusions of this usual and universal formula of reasoning.

Is it necessary, at least in order that the required similarity should be obtained, that individuals be born with a store of sympathetic instincts which are together called the moral sense? One may hesitate before replying in the negative; for this collection of tendencies favorable to life in a society and which have passed into the blood is a social alluvium, a deposit of long centuries of history. But strictly speaking it is sufficient, in default of these native tendencies, for one to have learned to bring to bear upon the same acts the same opinions of approval or of blame as one's contemporaries, to share in their conception of good and evil, to agree, as a general proposition, with them upon the lawful and illicit ways of teleologically pursuing one's ends. Let us explain clearly what we mean in this respect.

We are told to cast aside, as appertaining to mysticism, those old notions of culpability, of responsibility, of right, of duty, and, to go to the bottom of things, of good and evil. But is it true that positivism, that transformism even, demand this sacrifice? No, and if they do not demand it, there is no occasion to convert the idea of an offense into that of an injury, the idea of unworthiness into that of social menace. There are two teleologies, two finalities, bound up in the conduct of each one of us: individual teleology and social teleology. Their distinction is radical and justifies the preceding notions which belong to one of them; opposition to them accounts for crime, their concurrence accounts for the prosperity and nobility of humanity. Certainly a being who should be devoid of needs and without wishes would have no idea of right or of duty; a being who would not know pleasure and pain would not conceive of good and evil, a rightful action and a wrongful one, merit and demerit. But it is not enough for a being to have needs and wishes in order to have a conception of right and of duty, nor to have pleasures and sufferings in order to conceive of good and evil, let us add of beauty and ugliness. It is furthermore necessary for this being to live in a society. Living in contact with other beings, he learns by means of repeated clashes to distinguish concisely and thoroughly the needs, the wishes, and the individual pleasures which are opposed to one another, from those which do not collide with one another or which even assist one another.

Now pleasures which do not conflict, that is to say which are not bought by means of one another, and sufferings which do not conflict as well, that is to say which are aroused among all, or nearly all, associates by the same causes, create in each one of them a pleasure and a pain of a new kind entirely characteristic — the pleasure of seeing one's pleasures multiplied and the pain of seeing one's sufferings multiplied. Here we have the double feeling of good and of evil. The individual calls that which makes everybody suffer, evil, and also that which gives pleasure to some while causing pain to the majority of others; he calls good that which pleases all and also that which is injurious to the minority or to the "inferiority," but is useful to the majority or to the "superiority" (for, in time of aristocracy or of absolutism, the egotistical interest of the leader by itself counterbalances the interests of all his subjects, even in the eyes of the latter).

But this is no more than the unformed embryo of that vast idea of good and of evil. We have merely been applying this to the relation of feelings; it remains to extend it to the relation of wishes and of understandings; it is, in fact, a *categorical form* so to speak, a category of social logic, which imprints its stamp upon every faculty of men assembled in towns and imposes upon them a proper manner of feeling, of wishing, and of understanding. When a man has experienced the joys of sympathy and the pain of antipathy, at the same time that he continues to hold dear the things, be they acts of man or natural phenomena, which are agreeable to him, and to hate those which are painful to him, he begins to direct an affection of a nature which is peculiar to itself towards the things which please the majority of his associates or the more important of them, and to direct a hate also of a kind peculiar to itself towards the things which are painful to them. This love and this hatred are the *perceptible* feeling of good and evil.

In a similar way, the needs and the wishes which accord with one another — and I have said that it was especially the productive needs and the wishes called work — suggest to him, by the happiness of their coincidence, a need and a wish of a new kind — the desire, the wish to develop the desires and the wishes of that privileged kind, which have become duties properly so called, social duties. As for the appetites and the wishes which conflict, they no less surely suggest to him the desire, the wish to put an end to their struggle in ascertaining their limit and in striving to concentrate all their intensity upon their very limit. When this limitation, when this concentration is put into operation, this is called the feeling of right, an original and entirely social change in direction of the individual need and wish. Before it is even realized, the accord obtained or sought by the collection of the limits with which we are concerned is admitted as being something of an objective nature.

In the mind of each one of the associates of no matter what society, either savage or civilized, there exists thenceforth the representation, not only of a system of duties, but of a body of rights in the midst of this society, — in its midst only and not outside its confines, — whose essential characteristic is that they are unable to contradict themselves. When right is opposed to right, when duty is opposed to duty, as it is on a battlefield for instance, it is as between different societies, between two armies, each one of which is an example of admirable agreement and whose coming together is a terrible discord. But as between fellow-citizens, as between companions in arms, conflicts of rights or of duties, when they may appear, are always supposed to be merely apparent and are judged to be so by the magistrate who settles these differences which are called legal proceedings. A right which has been overthrown in a trial is considered as never having existed, unless it be in the misplaced imagination of the party who invoked it by mistake.

Right and not-right, the duty of doing and the duty of not doing, that is the category of good and evil applied to tendencies and acts, to qualities and activities, that is *functional* good and evil. Let us add that there is always, even at the time of the greatest freedom of thought, an *intellectual* good and evil, which are known as truth and error and which consist in the duty of upholding the ideas in which one believes one sees the virtue of producing (at the present time *or later*) the greatest accord of minds and in the duty of denying ideas which are opposed thereto. We will come back to this.

Indeed, in the midst of a nature where the essence of every force seems to be to struggle, where every being kills its fellows in order to live, where fratricide is the law, this conception of essentially harmonious faculties, in absolute contrast with this spectacle, is a singularity which does credit to the soul of man. And I do not see how the doctrine of evolution can continue and can, without sustaining any shocks, account for this phenomenon. But as a matter of fact the miracle is not so great as it appears to be, for it is not as true as it has been said to be that the fight for life, the radical hostility of beings and of their elements, is the first and fundamental principle of the Universe.

The first one is, as we have pointed out, the associating together in order to sustain life, the solidarity within of the very beings whose battling is their external manifestation. Man living in society has thus had no need of creating a harmony of every part in order to conceive of it; he has found the pattern for it within himself; I do not mean to say in his *organism*, as the theory of the social organism so dear to our sociologists assumes, but more especially and primarily in his mind, in that famous organ known as his brain, whose every function operates with a consonance equal to their complexity. The question is not precisely to create a single organism out of thousands of organisms, but a single soul out of thousands of souls. However, this does not matter very much for the time being.

So when we contrast the "altruistic" tendencies which the social atmosphere develops in the higher brain, with the egotistical impulses of the organism, we are contemplating truths which differ less than they may appear to. I do not mean to say by this, following an opinion which is common, that altruism is a refined egoism. I would say, rather, that the egoism in question is, to look at it closely, the result of a conspiring together of the various organs, of the various tissues, of the countless elements of the body, principally of the brain cells, and that it expresses a sort of organic patriotism by virtue of which each fragment of the whole devotes itself, sacrifices itself if necessary, to the common end. It follows that egoism is no more than a sort of devotion, sacrifice is the universal rule, and the vital "consensus" is merely being carried on, under new forms and on a larger scale, by means of the mutual assistance of the workers, by the disciplined worth of the soldier, by the generous self-denial of the citizen. Whether it be called vital principle or nutritive and functional irritability, or no matter what, it is certain that there exists in each living cell an acquired discernment of specific good and evil, of duty, of the rights of the cells, a vital form rather than force, without which the continual assimilations and disassimilations of this life would not take place, and which organically fills a part which may be compared to the social part played by our ideas of morality and justice.

As to the reproach of mysticism which is directed against these latter, we are now able to understand what that means. It means simply, from our point of view, that they are to society, or, if you prefer it, to man considered as a social being, what subjective ideas are to the individual, to man considered as such. What is there more eminently subjective than pleasure and pain, the emotional element of sensations and of any of the manners of being of the "myself"? At the same time, is there anything more real and more important from the individual's point of view? And those other universal qualities of our perceptions, expansion and duration, space and time, and even those no less universal characteristics of all our perceptions, substantiality and energy, matter and force, are they not also subjective things according to Kant and his disciples, who have triumphed over so many adversaries on this point? That, however, is the most solid basis of our thoughts. So that when I shall have conceded to the utilitarians that these ancient ideas of fault and of virtue, of worthiness and of unworthiness, of evil and of good, are infected with social subjectivism so to speak, it will not by any means follow in my opinion that the reality of things interpreted or symbolized by means of these ideas should have any the less weight and value. The day they shall have taught us to study geometry without the subjective and altogether mystical idea of space, and mechanics without the ideas of space, time, and force, I will be ready to admit that one can study sociology after having eliminated the ideas of good and evil. In the meanwhile I ask in what is the idea of force more clear than is the idea of duty?

An incidental assertion thrown out above demands an explanation. I have spoken of a duty of believing and of a duty of not believing. The fact is that the conformism to which a society subjects all its members is not limited by the desires, major premises of the syllogism of finality; it extends to the beliefs which are its minor premises. From this there arise at all times, two sorts of offenses: offenses in the form of acts and offenses in the form of opinions, because there are two sorts of non-conformism, that of the will and that of the understanding. Let us be sure that we understand each other. If the dissimilarity of one citizen, as compared with the mass of the nation, goes beyond a certain limit, he ceases, in a moral sense, to belong to that nation, and his moral responsibility (I do not say his political or his penal responsibility, which are and must often be different) becomes less or is blotted out altogether, because, as we have said, a certain similarity is a condition of responsibility in the moral sense of the word. Thus it is necessary that the divergence be partial and very limited.

However, how can it be, if wrongdoing be essentially a non-conformism, that the responsibility of the delinquent should be full and absolute? The answer to the problem is very simple. The wrongdoer will feel himself to be fully responsible, in the sense in question, every time that he shall be compelled in the bottom of his heart, by virtue of the conception of good and evil which he has received as a consequence of his honest surroundings, himself to condemn the act he has committed. It will be the same, up to a certain point, of the dissenter, of the heretic, every time that, by virtue of the dogmas taught by society and held by himself as articles of his belief, as *duties of belief*, he shall be compelled to recognize the mistake he has fallen into in giving expression to a theory contrary to these predominant principles.

There is, however, a difference which strikes one forcibly, from the point of view of social importance, between a conflict of words and a conflict of actions, and society should not strike at discordant speeches excepting in such measure as they appear fraught with prejudicial actions. But this measure is and will always remain a very large one. Although it is a common practice today to declare that there are no more offenses of opinion, there are always offenses by the press; no government has yet been able to allow journalism to overflow without any restraining dike, and, though the fires of the stake may be extinguished, the tacit and frightful excommunications of the mob have not ceased to fall upon persons bold enough to think differently to it on certain points of vital interest. A certain spirit of tolerance, it is true, has spread through a part of Europe during the last two centuries, perhaps as a consequence of lassitude; but a new wind is arising, and, in order to be hypocritical no longer, the exigencies of the democracy of tomorrow, in the matter of political or anti-religious orthodoxy, will probably be no less than those of the former theocracy. Now the incontestable fact, let it be said in passing, that there have existed, that there still exist everywhere men who are punished, be it only by discredit, destitution, injustice, and ruin, due to the misfortune of having had convictions contrary to the current ideas, information contrary to popular legends, this fact evidently proves that free will never has been considered, excepting in words alone, as the true and necessary foundation of responsibility. In fact everyone is agreed in recognizing that one is not free to think as one may wish to. All the "auto-da-fés" are thus a striking protestation against the accredited theory.[1]

§ 19. (II) Unanimous judgments of blame or of approbation; necessity of this conformism.

There is a class of opinions which, be they implied or verbal, are of the greatest importance in their bearing on our subject and whose similarity is especially requisite. They are the opinions of blame or of approbation brought to bear on the acts of another. In a society which is in a critical condition, in process of gestating a new world, the same acts are often applauded by some and stigmatized by others; anarchists praise up to the skies assassins whom our juries condemn; and, in the most serene regions, the spiritualistic and utilitarian, metaphysical and positivist principles, as bearing upon punishment, often clash, as we know. But in proportion as this critical unrest settles itself, which is sure to happen, unanimity comes into operation, at least as far as the rules of thought which regulate blame or praise are concerned, and it almost always embraces the victims of these decrees of opinion. In effect, the malefactor who, after all, has breathed the social air since his birth, and who is certainly too little inventive by nature to realize within himself the strength to resist the suggestions brought to bear upon him by his surroundings, is bound logically, after having blamed such and such a criminal, to blame himself in the commission of a crime of a similar nature.

It is worthy of note that even though he may have experienced an irresistible desire to commit this action, even though he may have had a consciousness of the inherent *irresistibility* of this desire, — for is one more at liberty to desire or not to desire than to believe or not to believe? — yet he will not cease to judge his act as blameworthy and bad and to judge himself to be responsible for the same, unless he has become impregnated in some school of philosophy with the prejudice which subordinates responsibility to free will. If, on the contrary, we suppose that the society in the

[1] There is still another very important difference between theoretical dissent and practical prejudice. The suggestive force is far greater in the matter of beliefs than in the matter of acts, one receives, one absorbs the prejudices of the small surroundings within which one lives and which may be contrary to the great social surroundings in a far more irresistible manner than one reproduces the examples set by it. Social causality in the matter of opinions is thus a more difficult investigation than it is in the matter of actions, which renders the persecution of thought particularly delicate.

midst of which he was molded is imbued, and consequently like himself, with determinist and utilitarian principles, he should, as we look at it, believe himself to be responsible for an act which in his opinion he could not have avoided committing. In fact, these principles, if they came to be generally accepted, would have as a consequence not the banishment of the ideas of responsibility, blame, and praise, but the taking of them unto himself. Surely neither determinism nor positivism, nor even utilitarianism, forbid us these strong and noble sentiments, indignation, admiration, the worship of duty, a passion for justice, and a hatred of injustice.

These sentiments are the hereditary molds into which all doctrines, whatever they may be, should be poured, as purely intellectual material, in order that they may play a moral and a social part. Did the determinism of St. Augustine and of the Jansenists prevent them from believing in sin and in the guilt of the sinner? No. In the Middle Ages the wrongdoer was vowed to infamy because he had offended God, as they believed and as he believed himself; at the present time he is sent to prison because he has violated some right of mankind; neither here nor there is there any question of free will or of future contingencies. It is not the constraint exerted or not exerted over the will which is of interest to us; it is the fact of knowing whence this constraint proceeds, if it be from within the person or from without. It is also the fact of knowing whether by means of our act, we have wounded someone who is dear to us. The feeling of culpability is in fact derived, among other sources, from that peculiar and very acute pain which the child feels within himself when he has just had a passing quarrel with a person who is close to him, who serves him as an example and has authority over him, as his father, his mother, or his elder sister. He is humiliated and disconcerted at the same time as he is grieved. *A humiliating sadness*, an isolation consequent upon exile or ruin; is not this all there is to remorse? And the child only succeeds in escaping from this anguish by means of a reconciliation. An offense in so far as it is a trespass is a *quarrel* just the same, and the suffering which is a proper consequence of it *from this point of view* ought to be a *reconciliation* of the sinner with society.

Conformity as far as judgments of blame and of praise are concerned is demanded, we maintain, and it is because these judgments, which are the conclusions of teleological syllogisms, assume that there exists a unanimity as far as the premises are concerned. But it may happen that, while agreeing with his fellow-citizens on the ends to be sought for, that is, on the major premises, a man may differ from them in his own personal opinion as far as the minor premises are concerned, as to the best means of attaining these same ends. In such a case as this he is logical in praising that which everyone condemns, and in condemning that which everyone praises. We must notice that under these circumstances, the stronger his conviction may be, the more absolute is his contradiction to the general public, and the more is his moral guilt extenuated in the eyes of an interested onlooker, if he has, for the greater glory of his fatherland and for the greater happiness of the human race, thrown a bomb under a royal train or set fire to a palace. In the first place because his divergence upon a point of as vital importance as moral opinion separates him from the society of other men, though not entirely, by reason of the conformity of his ends with theirs; and, in the second place, because the praiseworthy character of the latter pleads in his favor. If instead of loving his fatherland, he despised it and hoped for the triumph of its enemies, the separation between himself and his fellow-countrymen would be still more absolute. But assuming this, it will happen more often than not, that he himself in committing an act of treason in order to satisfy this passion contrary to nature, will succumb under the lash of his own moral opinions, which are in conformity with those of the general public, and, in every case, he will be treated as a monster more to be hated than held responsible, to be eliminated rather than punished. One pities a fanatic even while protecting oneself against him; he frightens but does not horrify; one hates a wicked nature, even though it be justified in its own eyes by reason of its strange convictions, slaves to perverseness. But neither such a wickedness, nor such a fanaticism, and still less the former than the latter, is fully analogous to moral responsibility in the proper meaning of the word, with its so-called similarities.

§ 20. (III) Importance of defining the bounds of a society. This limit is always extended, and in several ways. Extradition treaties.

We have been able to appreciate by means of the developments set forth above how important it is to specify the extent of a society, as it is only on the near side of this line that the power of conciliation, the teleological and even logical function of the notions of good and of evil, of right which is respected and right which is violated, of duty which is put into practice and duty which is disregarded, of worthiness and of unworthiness, is exercised or is displayed. In order that there may be an offense, culpability, evil, right which is violated, duty disregarded, it is necessary that the perpetrator of the act which is blamed be judged to belong to the same society as his judges and that he recognize willingly or unwillingly this profound community. There are cases in which it is hard to solve this problem, which, however, is a fundamental one of criminal law. Such and such a riot is with good reason looked upon as a crime; such and such a great insurrection as an event of war. A raising of shields which suddenly cuts an abyss between two classes or two parties which are too unlike to remain united in one and the same nation changes the fellow-citizens of yesterday into belligerents whose struggle has nothing in common with that of honest people against the robbers and the assassins who are their fellow-countrymen.

Again, after the combat it is time to make prisoners of war and not to hold criminal trials. I hasten to add that in my opinion this case was not presented in 1871 when the partisans of the Commune and the "Versaillais," in spite of the hatred which they bore one another, joined together in the indissoluble union of the same fatherland. Their character of fellow-citizenship was attacked far more than was that of the leaguers and the French Huguenots in the sixteenth century. It is none the less true that, in similar cases, the dissimilarity of the adversaries who are face to face and the relaxing, if not the dissolution, of the patriotic bond between them, should count, in the eyes of the moralist at least, as a great lessening of responsibility.

Even at a time when conditions are normal a peasant believes and feels himself to be more guilty if he has robbed a peasant like himself than if he has robbed a townsman, or a great landowner who is his neighbor, and similarly a man of affairs who would have scruples about deceiving one of his colleagues in a deal will sometimes have no hesitation in causing a stranger to fall into a snare of a similar nature. It is certain that under the old régime a cleric had more remorse after having killed a cleric, a gentleman a gentleman, and a villein a villein, than if the victim of the homicide had been a stranger to their caste. Let us note that the extension or the drawing in of the moral domain, the displacing of the frontier which separates the two standards of morality coexisting in each one of us, the one relative to those like us, and the other to those who are unlike us, or rather to the individuals judged to be such, depends upon a thousand accidents, and oftentimes on the most fortuitous circumstance. As soon as Alexander had conquered Asia and the Greek was able to say *my, mine, ours,* as far as everything which was Asiatic was concerned, the Orientals became Hellenized in his eyes; before having really assimilated to themselves the Hellenic civilization, they ceased to be barbarians, and from that time on, as Denis has so well pointed out in his fine history of moral ideas in ancient times, the practical field of Duty and Right received an unlooked-for, an enormous enlargement which caused the philosophical conception of Humanity, conceived of according to the enormously enlarged model of the ancient City, to take a giant stride in advance. From this the universal City of the Stoics was born, and the City of God of St. Augustine, when the Roman Empire, true successor of Alexander, came to complete his work.

The unfortunate part of it is that the limit of societies is far from being distinct and visible to everybody, as is that of organisms, which, moreover, is equally important. Within the confines of the living body there may be maladies which force the "vis medicatrix" (either with or without the assistance of doctors) to curb or to expel the diseased cells; there are no battles for life except outside it. The error of our Darwinians in relation to criminality is the consequence of their error in relation to biology. They only want to see in the finest internal harmony of an organism the effect of a vital concurrence, at bottom entirely similar to the other, and, for a similar reason, they only want to see in malefactors *enemies* with respect to an honest society, forgetting that these pretended enemies are true associates, that crime is in no way a hostile act, and that, consequently, the penalty could scarcely be a simple act of defense or of retribution. Among the learned men of whom I am speaking it is true that the Darwinian point of view alternates with the alienist point of view, which has a tendency to prevail and which shows us the criminal as a patient to be cured rather than as a foreign body to be destroyed or eliminated.

Let us picture to ourselves, during the period of the Norman invasions or during the Hundred Years War, a monastery in the midst of the woods. Inside, peace, security, union, an intelligent apportionment of work in common under a community rule, the converging of every heart towards the same hope of heaven; outside, murder, pillage, incendiarism, anarchy. Such is the difference which exists between the interior of a living body and the outside world. Also, in the same way as during the most evil days of the Middle Ages, the monasteries, sole refuges from the surrounding chaos, never ceased to fill their ranks and to expand, and, having arrived at a limit beyond which it was impossible to go from a practical standpoint, were prolonged in some other manner, by serving as a model for the still more vast aggregations, for the brotherhoods and the lay corporations which were formed outside of them, so in a similar manner, from that far-distant age when the first living beings, at first microscopic and monocellular, made their appearance, their bulk and their weight have not ceased to increase and their structure to grow more complicated and to allow of a greater aggregation of elements within their breast. At the same time, or else following thereon, in the likeness of those organic societies which could go no further for physical reasons in the advancement of their frontiers, animal and human societies have been constituted, free and original aggrandizements of these latter, pursuing the same unconscious end under some new form.

But this is not all; human societies, in primitive times limited to a single family or to a narrow group of families, have carried on this great movement, and the thing which is most manifest in history is the salutary necessity which drives them, through the vicissitudes of defeat or victory, to extend themselves, to increase themselves, to constitute together but a single gigantic State or a single federation of lesser States. By means of the continual and universal spreading of examples of all kinds outside of the tribe or the town where they were born, this majestic end is being pursued, the unknown pole of the small ambitions which find their way towards it without seeing it.

At the threshold of history, — and when I say at *the threshold* I do not necessarily go back to the unknown origin of the first human association, but rather to the *re-beginnings* of history which have taken place much later at divers points of the globe, to periods which are even historical, among the early Greeks, among the early Romans, and among the early Chinese, — at the threshold of every history, to state it more accurately, not only are States of very small dimensions, for they do not go beyond the circle of relationship, at first natural, and later adoptive, but even societies whose scope is always of greater extent than is that of States, are exceedingly restricted, for the reason that the scope of similarities between different individuals is very contracted. From this it follows that each man feels himself to be responsible towards a very small number of people and irresponsible as regards the majority of mankind; bound by pity, by justice, by love, as far as a very small minority is concerned, and relieved of every obligation as far as a vast majority is concerned.

What Letourneau says about the Mandingues (African negroes), according to Clapperton, may be applied to all savages and to the majority of barbarians. "In their eyes theft is only criminal if it wrongs a member of their tribe or little State; as against a stranger it is in no way to be regarded as worthy of blame." But in proportion as the progress of assimilation accomplishes its work, the territorial proportion of responsibility and of irresponsibility changes and is in the end overturned, until one of the terms disappears. When an *extradition* treaty has just been concluded between two peoples, it proves that each one of them begins to feel itself affected by the crimes committed among the other; that the citizen of the neighboring people has in its eyes ceased to be a being apart against whom everything is permissible. Now, such a feeling can only come into existence, as a matter of fact, when the dissimilarity between the two peoples has greatly decreased, as a consequence of a prolonged exchange of examples from every point of view. So, extradition treaties may serve us as a means of estimating, of approximately setting a date to the progress of international assimilation, and of the territorial scope of responsibility as well.

The first treaty of this nature in Europe was made in 1376, between the Count of Savoy and Charles V. It proves the great strides made along the way of European leveling following the vast conflict of the crusades and even during the Hundred Years War. But here we have an isolated treaty. We must next go to the eighteenth century in order to see fresh diplomatic conventions of this nature — 1736, 1759, 1765, etc. (See du Bois.) Our century, *thanks to the railways*, has seen extradition treaties multiplied. England, *by reason of its character of insular originality*, has been the country to remain the most deaf to the demands for extradition. This exception proves the rule. Let us add that the principle of *extraterritoriality*, by virtue of which each State judges itself to have the right and to be under the duty of following up against every individual residing within its territory the suppression of every sort of crime of at all serious a nature committed even outside of its territory, tends to spread itself in our modern legislation. It is to the credit of the new Italian Penal Code, so much opposed, moreover, by Messrs. Lombroso, Ferri, and Garofalo, that it has allowed this principle to play a more important part than hitherto it had dared to allow it.

This continued extension of the realm of responsibility and duty, even more than the perfecting of their nature, is the chief benefit conferred by civilization as far as morality is concerned; but moral cosmopolitanism, which it in this way substitutes for the exclusiveness of former times, is infinitely precious. It is not really by means of its extension alone, it is still further by means of its profound investigation, that the scope of morality has increased; for, at the same time as it was taking in new peoples, it was annexing to itself new classes among each one of them. If for example woman, — who was man's first domestic animal, — has by degrees acquired rights which are recognized by her lord and master, in other words, if man has, little by little, felt himself to be responsible towards her, it is to the same extent as, because of the circumstances, she has been able to imitate our sex, and resemble it in manner of living, in ideas, and in customs. One would deceive oneself if one thought that it was according as man has been softened by means of civilization.

During the Middle Ages, despite the barbarity of customs maintained by reason of perpetual wars, the rights of woman were everywhere undisputed, as a consequence of the Christian beliefs without a doubt, but also because feudal isolation, as Guizot has so well pointed out, threw the husband and the wife together, and compelled them, during the interval between combats, to lead a life in common. In ancient Greece on the contrary, in spite of the incomparable soaring of souls in the purest heights of art and even of science, woman was treated as a slave, because the habits of the gymnasium and of the public square on the one hand, and of the women's apartments on the other, absolutely separated the life of the two sexes. What a contrast with our French eighteenth century! Among every savage tribe given to war and to the chase, the women who are unable to make war or to hunt are treated as beasts of burden. Among pastoral and agricultural tribes they are looked upon by man as companions. Let us add that, if the dissimilarity between men and women prevents men from feeling themselves to be responsible in a moral sense towards women, to the same extent also does it prevent women from being conscious of their moral responsibility towards the men. They may bend under the fear of blows, but they are lacking in a feeling of duty. They acquire it in the attainment of rights.

When one wishes to measure in a fair manner the morality of a person, at a given date and in a given country, it is by means of that person's relations with his fellow-countrymen in a social way and recognized as such that they must be judged. We must not judge the English according to their relations with the Chinese, nor the Chinese according to their relations with Europeans. Still less must we judge of the moral value of the savage hordes, as so many travelers have thoughtlessly done, according to their dealings with these latter. We would create for ourselves far too dark an impression, as we would certainly debase the travelers themselves beyond measure if we were to judge them according to their manner of behaving with the inhabitants of these islands. It is well known that the Polynesians are savage and not to be trusted as far as foreigners are concerned, but among themselves, within the confines of their own people, they are full of kindness and gentleness, according to Porter, Cook, and many other observers.

§ 21. What must be understood by personal identity.

It does not suffice, as we are well aware, in order that there may be moral responsibility, that the author of an act shall be compelled, by means of his habits of judging inspired by someone else, and by means of his social intercourse with his victim, to judge of this act as being blameworthy; it is furthermore and above everything necessary that he be compelled to recognize himself as the very cause of this act. Let us therefore examine in what consists and what is the value of the belief of each one of us in his own identity, the basis of our final judgment as to our powers. If it be demonstrated that this belief is an illusion, that the person is an entity similar to a river, whose identical persistence under the changing of its waters is but a name, responsibility is a chimera, and we will have profited little by having changed its base. Unfortunately it is a fact that the schools which are incited to combat free will are also carried away so far as to deny personal identity. But their temperament and not logic carries them away to this extent; they cannot undermine this principle except by exposing themselves to absolute scepticism, to intellectual nihilism; they cannot shake this last column of the temple of science without running the risk of an overthrowing. Let them deny absolute and everlasting identity, so be it; but a relative and temporary identity suffices for us.

§ 22. (I) Identity, permanence of the individual. What is the individual? The individuality of the individual made clearer by the individuality of the organism and especially by that of the State. Logical and teleological co-ordination. The immortal soul and eternal cities; similar conceptions.

Identity is the permanence of the person, is the personality looked at from the point of view of its duration. What is the person and in what does its permanence consist? In order to make the nature of personal individuality more clear, Ribot has compared it to organic individuality,[1] into which it thrusts itself by means of every one of its nerve roots and rootlets. It will remain to compare it to national individuality which is nourished and lives in it. These three individualities have this in common; they imply a solidarity of elements and of numerous functions converging in a sheaf of ends [2] and they maintain themselves by means of a continual renewal of their elements and of their functions, in the same way as their ends, under more or less similar forms. The living individual is an assemblage and a connection of infinitely ingenious secrets which, from cell to cell, invisible to us, but visibly directed towards the pursuit of certain general or special objects, are transmitted until death with the direction proper to the initial ovule, with that style or that manner which makes them resemble one another while they are being transformed, repeat themselves while they are being varied, and which raises the slightest living variations to the rank of true creations.

The psychological individual, the "myself," is an assemblage and a connection of states of consciousness or of *subconsciousness*, that is of information and impulses, of external information called sensations, or internal called "cenesthesia" by the new psychologists, *feelings of the body*, of external impulses called

[1] "Revue philosophique," August, 1884, "Les bases affectives de la personnalité."

[2] In the "Revue philosophique," for January, 1890, *Paulhan* has very well shown, as regards "associationism," that the laws or so-called laws of the association of ideas by reason of contiguity and resemblance explain nothing, unless they be subordinated to a more general law of finality (we ourselves would say, of logic and of finality, of theoretical and practical co-ordination) which dominates the whole of psychology.

tastes, or internal ones called appetites. And if these states are simultaneous they have as a characteristic a concurrence towards a same theoretical or practical action, and their logical agreement in entering into, for example, the general system of opinions as regards location, called space, or of opinions as regards the naming of things, called language, and to agree in a teleological manner in serving for the play of those complicated mechanisms called instincts or habits. If they are successive, they have as a characteristic the indefinite, and, for the most part, almost identical, repetition of themselves, either in the form of images and memories, or in the form of that sort of a soundless murmuring in the very depths which is the continuous base of consciousness, upon which the diversity of outside sights soon becoming monotonous casts light modulations, phrases themselves reverberated in a thousand echoes of memories, and developed in a sort of long discourse; the whole marked with the stamp of a special physiognomy which the greatest changes in feature scarcely alter. However, I do not say that the "myself" consists in nothing more than this; but it is certain that it does consist in this. Finally the social individual, the town or the State, is an assemblage and a connecting together of social states, that is to say of states of consciousness again, but of states of consciousness, beliefs, or needs, belonging to different persons and persons who are influenced by one another.

Furthermore, these states, like the preceding ones, are information and impulses, but information more often received from another or perceived through another, called knowledge, and impulses communicated by another, called ambitions; and these states, like the preceding, are in more or less close and durable harmony. If they are simultaneous they agree in the majority of instances, not only by virtue of those general systems of opinion or of those general employments of acts of which mention has already been made, as space or language, locomotion or war, etc., but again by means of the sanction of those co-ordinations of thought which are more especially social,[1] which are called religion, philosophy, the sciences, and those still more vast co-ordinations, which are called callings or institutions. If they are successive, they reproduce themselves in the form of inexhaustible and almost

[1] We must, however, observe that language is a social thing in the same way as religion is, but I have been forced to speak of it already, in defining the "myself," because the "myself," in my opinion at least, has awaited, before being truly hatched out, the heat of social surroundings.

unvarying counterparts, known by the vague name of tradition and custom, which are to society what memory and habit are to the individual; and they also repeat themselves with a continuity, even with an almost equal unvaryingness, unless it be in time of crisis, in that confused buzzing of conversations, of writings, of demands, of complaints, or else give expression to ideas and needs which are unceasingly reborn, which are commonly called in politics popular sentiment and will, and which could just as well be called social cenesthesia; while upon this dark background the genius of inventors and of innovators of every kind stands out in vivid relief, in revelations and in creations depending upon one another, themselves immediately repeated by means of imitation, and which have fallen one after another into the domain of the commonplace, the traditional, and the customary; all this is imprinted with the national stamp, which gives the most varied products of a society a resemblance as indubitable as it is incapable of definition.

This is not the place to develop all the relations which exist between the three individualities which have been the subject of comparison, and I am only permitted to point them out in passing. Not only do they resemble one another, but to a certain extent, they are of mutual assistance to one another. Espinas has well said that "psychic individuality and physiological individuality are parallel"; he could have added social individuality; for, if consciousness disperses itself or becomes united with the organism, it lowers or raises itself, contracts or enlarges, lets go of itself or fortifies itself in conformity with its social surroundings. I hold especially to this last comparison, because it is particularly instructive. We are in fact marvelously well informed as to what is going on in the intimacy of the social life, whose primary element is our own life; but we are entirely ignorant of the secrets of organic life, whose effects as a whole are the only ones revealed to our vision.

Thus if, in order to clear up a psychological fact, we point out its similarity to a vital fact, this statement, interesting in other respects, will not satisfy our curiosity; one cannot clear up semi-obscurity by means of complete obscurity; whereas if we establish the similarity of this same fact to some social fact, it will be easy for us, in elucidating the latter to its very depths, to elucidate by analogy the familiar phenomenon. Sociology is the solar microscope of psychology. This remark finds its immediate application in that which concerns our subject. It is important for us to know in what this scale of the degrees of our personal identity consists, that scale of which we have a vague and constant feeling, and which, in going deeply into mental alienation, has as its supreme pinnacle the ideal of energy and of stoical wisdom. What is this maximum and what is this minimum of identity, between which our existence oscillates? Upon this subject observing our body teaches us nothing, unless it be that the maximum of its own identity is realized in its perfect health, the minimum in the invasion of an illness, true vital alienation, or in the congenital evil of an infirmity which renders it abnormal. But observation of our societies teaches us more than this.

Illness is a discord, health is a harmony of the organs, physicians vaguely tell us; as to the nature of this discord and of this harmony they remain silent. But politicians, when they boast of the vigor or the prosperity, or deplore the weakening and the decadence of a State, know very well what they understand by this. A vigorous and prosperous people is the one among whom unanimity to acknowledge a belief in common, a science in common, overrules the petty discussions of a secondary nature and the contradictions due to selfishness, among whom unanimity in the pursuit of the same goal of patriotic action, in the realization of the same plan of work which is binding upon everybody, overrules all egotistical rivalries, all contests of the appetites. An ill and enfeebled people, in process of going insane and disappearing, is the one among whom the proportion of inconsistencies and of reciprocal obstacles decidedly outweighs that of corroboration and of mutual assistance, among whom, in other words, individual pride and opinion contradict each other more than prevailing principles corroborate one another, and among whom the greed of gain is in opposition among individuals more than their activities aid one another and associate together. Undoubtedly there is no nation so united and powerful as not to harbor some hidden germs of discord, as there is no reason so sane as not to enclose some speck of madness. Inconsistencies and opposition in weak doses, under the pseudonym of freedom of mind and of concurrence, are the necessary leaven of progress. But there is a degree of incoherence beyond which a society, just as a mind, may not go without incurring the danger of a radical change for the worse.

During the periods of the relative immutability of societies and of persons, it is not the reality alone, but it is the immortality of the three individualities in question as well, which has been an article of belief. Each ancient nation, once established and ruling, believed itself to be immortal, for the same reason that, later on, each human body or each human "myself" judged itself to be immortal. The Egyptian idea of embalming, in view of the resurrection of the body, is founded upon the belief in its imperishableness; then the belief in the imperishableness of the consciousness was added; but already the imperishableness of the great nations and of the great dynasties had been established for a long time in the minds of the peoples, and Rome is not the first, it is rather the last, of the cities reputed to be eternal. These three great beliefs, which have played so important a part in history, and especially from the point of view with which we are concerned, still survive in China, where the stability of everything has preserved them. In our modern Europe the frequency of social or of mental revolutions has swept them away.

We are absolutely ignorant as to how mental alienation, the crisis by means of which a new "myself," generally formless and incapable of living, is substituted for the former and normal "myself," comes into existence and grows; we only know that this internal working of the brain proceeds sometimes from an unwonted invasion of external feelings and exciting causes which trouble the mind by reason of their strangeness, or the strangeness of which denotes the trouble of the mind, sometimes from a no less strange modification supervening in the general tone of the internal sense. We know far better how social alienation originates and increases. When a young and powerful State, having attained an internal harmony of its constituent elements, primitive Rome for example, enters into relations with its neighbors, acquires something of their arts, of their customs, and even of their gods, and in this way becomes modified by means of its successive expansions, its identity does not suffer by reason of this importation so long as it assimilates that which it absorbs. Rome assimilated for itself that which Etruria and even Greater Greece had which was best or rather which was compatible with its own ideal of religious citizenship, which was heroic and avaricious. But, after the taking of Corinth by Mummius, after the conquests in Asia, the Roman constitution received a severe blow, because a new ideal of philosophical aestheticism which was artistic and voluptuous entered into the soul of the old aristocracy, and then of the old Roman populace, with the sophisms of Carneadus and the marbles of Lysippus. Between this ideal and the former one, between the old catechism and the new doctrines, agreement was impossible, just as it is between yes and no, between pro and con; the two could therefore do nothing but combat each other and mutually seek to expel each other, or, if they did not succeed in this, give rise to a schism, whether it were a schism manifested by the division of society into two camps divided from each other, that of the votaries of the former cult and that of the votaries of the latter, or a schism masked by the trouble inoculated into each individual consciousness which, in accepting the contradiction within itself and becoming accustomed to it, as so often happens, becomes false to and annihilates itself.

The identity of the person in the same way is but a greed which gratifies itself by means of an incessant appropriation from without. The "myself" is but a word, or else is but the *mine own unceasingly enlarged.* Now, one only appropriates to oneself that which one adopts to oneself, only that by means of which one assists or strengthens oneself; when one meets with a denial of one's habitual system of regulating ideas, an obstacle to one's system of chief aims, every effort which one makes to assimilate all this tends to disorganize. Thus the "myself," in its incessant changes from one perception to another, from one act to another, proceeds in the same way as does society in its transition from one discovery to another, from one invention to another. So long as a society absorbs more innovations favorable to its principles than innovations opposed to them, it strengthens its identity; under the opposite circumstances it alienates itself.

One may ask, it is true, what there is which is contradictory or contrary to the previous ideas or tendencies of the person, in the unaccustomed states which lead a man to madness. Here, where is the internal system contradicted or opposed, and which is analogous to that of the national beliefs or institutions? I answer that it is the sum of memories and of habits, of previous perceptions and of acquired talents. When I suddenly attribute to myself the office of pope or of emperor, I am contradicting the system of my memories in placing alongside of it a past other than my own. When, alone in my room, I believe that I hear voices of invisible and nearby persecutors speaking, I am placing alongside the system of my actual perceptions (for, let it be noted, that sensations experienced at one and the same time have a tendency to create a true synthesis by means of the collection of immediate judgments which they call into being and of which they are the incorporation) perceptions which are contradictory to the former. In the case of bilateral hallucinations, when "one ear is obsessed by threats, by insults, and by evil counsel, and the other comforted by kind words" or when "one eye sees only sad and unpleasant objects, and the other sees only gardens full of flowers," the contradiction is patent.[1] When, temperate and peaceful under ordinary circumstances, I suddenly feel depraved tastes within myself, or homicidal impulses, are not these tendencies contrary to my habitual state? And would not imputing them to me be but to confuse me with my enemies? And would not holding me responsible for their consequences in the same way as for the consequences of my normal "myself" be but to confuse all under the pretext of method and of science?

§ 23. (II) A difference in spite of analogies. The identity of the "myself" much deeper than the identity of the State. The hypothesis of monads.

I would not, however, wish to push my comparison to its very extreme. There are preceptible differences between mental alienation and social alienation. There is, first of all, this one, that the latter, because of the less concise character of the corresponding identity, is able to lead from an old régime to a new régime which is just as capable of living, and consequently just as much responsible as the former one; whereas the former is always a disastrous or an annoying perturbation whose only possible issue is death or a return to the old state.[2] If, by chance, a new "myself" is definitely substituted for the previous "myself,"[3]

[1] It seems perfectly simple to us to have two hands and two legs agreeing in all their motions, helping each other, proceeding together towards the goal. But among the demented this very agreement is often broken. One sees some of them whose left hand stops the right hand when the latter wants to do something, and, among all of them, the division of the person into two "myselfs" who fight against each other is a common occurrence, as we shall see.

[2] When there is an alternation of two personalities, which reminds us of revolutions followed by restorations, one of the two "myselfs" ends by expelling the former one little by little; for example in the case of Félida.

[3] Again we must notice, with Ribot, that there always remain important traces of the preceding "myself," "bodies of habits" so to speak, "gait, speech, manual labor, purely automatic activities, which are almost unconscious, and which are slaves ready to serve every master," in this resembling those "trade bodies," those administrations which the revolutions failed to reach and which serve for every régime.

this change is always a fall, whereas social revolutions sometimes constitute progress.

If this is so, I have said, then it is because social identity is a very inferior thing, as far as its reality and depth are concerned, to psychological identity. "We lend our personality," says Beaussire,[1] "to a fortuitous and passing collectivity, to a mob for example, which in a public square or at a theatre, assembled more often than not by reason of curiosity alone, manifests to such a degree common passions and a unity of will, that it seems difficult to see in this only the result of the passions and of the wishes of each individual. What dramatic critic has not noticed the unanimity of the demands of propriety among the public at a theatre where one meets, as everywhere among humanity, together with a small number of noble spirits, every degree of moral indifference and of vice?"

But here, as the author points out, there is but a pseudo-person which we can explain to ourselves by means of the laws of imitation. Undoubtedly a nation, which is an assemblage which is not fortuitous, a living aggregation of souls, mingled together in an irregular scheme of thoughts and of designs, and not in the preoccupation of a moment, attains to a far higher degree of personality. At the same time is this comparable to the personality of a man? If we were to hold ourselves bound by the definition which we have given above, the latter like the former would not be *identical* with itself except in so far as it is made up of *similar* thoughts and actions although emanating from distinct consciousnesses.

Now, that identity thus resolves itself into similarities alone is not strictly true, even in the case of society, at least in the case in which it is despotically ruled over by the "king-god" of primitive monarchies so well understood by Spencer. In him the State is incarnated; he is the central monad in which every nature is reflected and which lends to the faithful reproduction, to the harmonious combination of their reflections, the substantial support of his own lastingness as long as his life endures, fictitiously prolonged after his death by his apotheosis and the conformity of his successor to the example set by him. The human person is perhaps to be compared to this ancient theocracy, the "myself" is perhaps the king-god of the brain, the centre and the field of a group of vassal and suggestive consciousnesses. To build up the personal consciousness, as is so often attempted, by means of the

[1] See "Revue philosophique," February, 1885.

simple juxtaposition of states of consciousness, is the same as though one attempted to explain the formation of society by means of a combination of social states. To cause the "myself" to spring up from a simple placing in relation of varied consciousnesses no one of which would be the "myself" and the grouping together of which would alone constitute it, is to create a hypothesis infinitely more mystical than all the monadologies. Whether we say nerve cell rather than monad makes little difference; the essential thing is to recognize in the brain the supremacy of a central element, always the same throughout its continual modifications, and whose familiar states, an echo but not a result of the states belonging to the innumerable elements which surround and are subjected to it constitute the normal person.

It is very important in fact, from our point of view, to know whether one looks upon the "myself" as disseminated, in some incomprehensible manner, in almost the entire brain, — moreover one could scarcely say within precisely what limits, nor by virtue of what marvelous property, — or whether one looks upon it as localized in an extremely small, infinitesimal point of the brain substance. Let us for a moment admit this last hypothesis, however strongly it may go against our prejudices. The inner sense, in truth, that fallacious organ of knowledge, seems to assure us that the "myself" is everywhere present in the head; but it assured the Greeks of the time of Homer that the "myself" also resided in the breast, it still tells us that the "myself" is at the tips of the fingers during the processes of active touch, and if we were reduced to the sense of vision, it would lead us irresistibly to believe that the "myself" fills the entire field of our vision.

The unfortunate part of it is that, if its mistakes as to its proper extra-cerebral localization can easily be rectified by means of the reciprocal control of the different senses, its intra-cerebral localization is beyond the reach of this rectification. In spite of everything, let us once more suppose that the "myself," localized within very narrow limits, is simply an interweaving, but a true and actual interweaving, of information and of influences, a *place* and at the same time a *bond* of instructions and of impulses, emanating from all the neighboring cells. Thenceforth the problem of free will, translated and transposed into our language, becomes singularly simplified, and rids itself of the obscurities with which the confused conception, which is contradictory and mystical, of the "myself" endowed with *cerebral ubiquity* had surcharged it. The freedom of the "myself" becomes its authority over the other "myselfs" of the brain. The extent of its freedom is the measure according to which it is well informed and well seconded by these latter. It ceases to be free at the precise moment when it is more opposed than served, more contradicted than confirmed by them, that is to say when the information and the impulses which it has already received from some of them and which it has appropriated and assimilated to itself by its adhesion, not free but necessary by virtue of its nature, are contrary to the suggestions which it receives from others, which cannot be appropriated, and as a consequence cannot be assimilated.

In a case in which these latter should overpower it, it would no longer be the "myself" which was *itself the cause* of the act carried out, and its responsibility would be released. But there is no occasion to make this distinction if one admits that the "myself" is the whole brain; in fact, assuming this to be the case, if an act has had as its point of departure a cerebral nervous centre whatever it may be, the "myself" is responsible for that same action. In vain one may say, this individual is morally a madman, his volition is the consequence of a morbid evolution which is produced in his cerebral substance, which is manifested by periodical attacks and whose phases may be foretold with certainty. It makes no difference, the evolution of the brain, be it owing to illness or not, being itself the development of the person, or at the most its deviation, but never its substitution, it is the person who wished the act to be committed and who should answer for it.

On the contrary if the "myself," a spiritual atom as indispensable to psychology as the nameless atom is to chemistry,[1] is but a point, an heir in the direct line of the initial ovule, a substantial point, whose substance consists in the innate aptitudes which it manifests in habits acquired in the course of its life, by means of a series of perceptions or movements, of affirmations or wishes; an infinitesimal point, but one which is the seat of an unlimited ambition aspiring each day to extend and consolidate more and more, as it has done since its embryonic life, its omnipotence on a number of similar points which have been subordinated and disciplined; in this case the "myself," against whom a portion of its subjects

[1] *Taine*, one of the first, understood this truth very well in "l'Intelligence" long before the learned speculations of Haeckel on the "myself" of the atom. There has been nothing since then to weaken his ideas on this subject, far from it.

is in revolt, is no more responsible for the consequences of this riot than was a king of Persia for the revolt of a satrap, and every part of the brain which escapes its domination becomes an absolute stranger to it.

I certainly have no wish to change the nature of my thought and to weaken its bearing by establishing an indissoluble bond between the hypothesis of monads, revived in a manner unhoped for by contemporary science, and my way of understanding responsibility. One may cast away all monadology and yet retain this last point of view. However, we must admit that the latter has a right to hope for special favor at the hands of the monadologists. So I must be pardoned for still insisting upon this digression and upon this useful illustration of our subject, and for pointing out in two words how this "spiritual atomic philosophy," by which all the truth of materialism is resolved and transfigured, is justified. The point is to know after all, whether the individual be a reality in very truth, if the countenance be anything but a silhouette. Am I or am I not? That is the question.[1] If one wishes the in-

[1] Both here and further on I make use of the words "person" and "myself" almost synonymously. However, I will concede to Richet (see "Revue philosophique," March, 1883) that the personality within us can change, — by hypnotic suggestion in certain forms of madness or in dreams, — without the subject ceasing to say "I." In vain may he attribute to himself a past other than his own, take himself for something which he is not, something of his previous being persists in him. This something would be, according to Richet, the "myself" properly so called, which would be quite distinct from the *personality*. This author only sees in the personality a phenomenon of the memory, a "collection of particular recollections," and in the "myself" but a phenomenon of sensibility and innervation, a collection of actual perceptions and impulses.

Very well; but if, in order to *collect* the recollections of the states of our past, a collection of present states be necessary, would nothing be necessary in order to collect the latter? I believe that in this case, as everywhere else, phenomena do not stand unsupported except for themselves. Every true reality is something other than a collection of phenomena; it is — as Stuart Mill well saw in his definition of matter — a possibility, that is to say a conditional necessity of phenomena almost all of which have not occurred, are not occurring, will not occur, but would occur or would have occurred if such and such a circumstance had been presented. Furthermore, let us beware of confounding these conditional pasts and futures with the contingent pasts and futures of the partisans of free will. The conditional necessity of the first contradicts the supposed ambiguity of the second.

I fully realize that my past, this more or less wretched succession of incidents which constitutes my life and which has created my social person, is *mine* rather than *myself*, for it could have been other than it was. The profound essential "myself" of each one of us is — not a bundle of actual sensations, as Richet, who, moreover, here forgets the inseverability of sensations and images, would have us believe — but an infinite virtuality indeed, whose existence has at the same time been its very limited realization and its tremendous mutilation, its development along a certain line and its abortion following an immense sphere. Particular

dividual to be purely and simply the effect of what one considers as his cause or as his causes, that is, the sort of parents he comes from and the physical or social acts of his surroundings, one must first of all explain oneself on the question of this bond between cause and effect, and, from the phenomenist point of view, clear up the mystery of an entirely phenomenal reality which, already out of existence, for the cause is always assumed to be previous to its effect (although after all, that which has been may be a pure nothingness in the same way as that which is not yet) has given rise to the appearance of another, truly another reality! One must inevitably recognize something that persists, under these transformations of phenomena, one of which disappears when the other makes its appearance. But what? This something of which we catch a confused glimpse through the multitude of facts is called by a vague word, "force," just as one calls a mass of men seen from afar and very indistinctly the "crowd" or the "army."

Let us draw near, we will distinguish these men by means of their gestures, their faces, the sound of their voices. If we were able in this same way to resolve that other nebula, force, energy, matter, is it not likely that it would astonish us by the exuberant richness of its elements? Before everything we should be convinced that these elements are distinct, discernible, characterized. That is the only possible justification for the variations which continually play upon the surface of things which appertain to the greatest progress of the world, and which would not be able to spring from the bosom of universal repetitions under the assumption of perfectly homogeneous elements made use of by laws obeyed without exception. I defy anybody to discover the least foundation which is not a delusion for this great scientific prejudice which puts the fundamental homogeneity of the elements in the form of a dogma, and also the infiniteness and the eternity of this despairing monotony. It is a delusion to create the variation out of the theme too late, the varied out of the invariable, by

circumstances of my organism, accidents of my life have developed me in such and such a way and have at the same time closed the entrance of an infinite number of other paths to me. It is because I know this, because I have an inner certainty of it, that I judge myself to be a real being. But, this having been said and expressly recognized, I ought to add that, once having entered into or fallen within the bonds of a determined personality, *I* have identified myself with it. And that is why I will continue to say, the "*myself*" or the *person* without, as a general thing, distinguishing between the two.

means of the so-called "instability of the homogeneous," differentiated one knows not how. Every law is the instrumentality of regulation and of leveling; consequently, if they were to be exercised over materials already regular and absolutely similar, one asks oneself from whence could the least note of approval result in the midst of the universal sing-song.

So let us have no doubt but that matter, energy, force, this pretended indifference which is all-powerful, only owes its all-powerfulness to the tempestuous variations, each separately acting and working towards its own end, of which it is composed. From thence originality, from thence freedom, from thence individual realities. Of what use, without this, is the individual, who is a new and superfluous copy of an edition which is already more than sufficiently large? Each individual, without a doubt, has as his reason for existing at all his personal distinction; and his distinguishing feature, his original identity, from birth until death has as its cause the persistence of some first element which, affected, it is true, and influenced by others and even owing to their co-operation almost the whole of its stored-up power, of its virtuality which it can dispose of at each moment, has no less appropriated to itself, in stamping them with its seal, all those outside actions. Certainly one cannot say that at the very moment when this element, which reveals itself in the "myself," thus revealing itself more clearly to itself, arrives at a decision, it has the privilege of deciding otherwise; but one can say that in wishing this act it makes the act *its own*, and that it is precisely because this act could have been none other that it is its own. It follows that at the foundation of every individual existence, if the individual really and truly exists, there is something very special which seeks to be extended and to become universal, and something which seeks to live, that is to say, to endure.

The individual is more than a sum total, he is a living unit. It is really strange to see, in a century as individualistic as ours, learned men go to such pains gradually to lessen, to annihilate the individual, the "myself," as though this lessening and this annihilation were the necessary conclusion of their research in relation to the illnesses of the person, to madness, to dreams, and to hypnotism. For the responsibility of criminals is unceasingly denied altogether or lessened for the same reason that the worthiness of men of genius is depreciated as much as possible. The discoveries up to now attributed to Newton and to Christopher Columbus would be in reality collective works signed with their name, just as the crimes of a celebrated assassin or robber would be the consequence of a social suggestion combined with a vital impulse, of a carrying away by example combined with a hereditary tendency. But if this be so then what is individual existence? A pure nonentity. This assumption that the individual exists for the species or for society is too easily adopted; in a deep sense the converse is true. My species, my race belongs to me, in the same way as my language, my religion, and my government; I make use of these things and they are *mine*, and, in so far as I utilize them they are for my benefit. The individual was born yesterday; but in being born he has appropriated to himself his family and his race, an ancient thing; and life, an antique thing; the physical forces, the chemical atoms, which are everlasting, we are told, which he subjugates and directs. He has thus become eternal himself by means of this conquest, "causa sui," and, as a consequence, truly free, in the only true and plain sense of this word.

§ 24. (III) The State is to the nation what the "myself" is to the brain. The "force-ideas" of Fouillée. Identity makes and unmakes itself; it has its degrees.

This is metaphysics; well, I admit it; now, the evil, as we know, is not so much in being metaphysical as in being so without being aware of that fact. However, abandoning a dangerous shore, let us limit ourselves to extracting out of what has just been said, as a review of the whole of it, the following conclusion: the "myself" is to the brain what the State is to the nation; the State, that is to say the guiding personality which advises and commands, which, depositary of the traditional legacy of institutions and of principles, of the powers and of the enlightenment accumulated by its predecessors which it carries on, utilizes and augments this legacy by means of its decrees and instructions, by means of its conscious and voluntary acts of each day, in the long run converted into administrative habits added to those already existing. It is a certainty that the State has no existence except through the nation. However absolute may be the monarch in whom it has its incarnation, there is not a single one of its acts which is not necessarily brought about by the revelations of the learned bodies, which are analogous to the perceptions of the senses, or by the new productions of industry and art, which are sources of new needs, new powers, and new ambitions; and, from another standpoint, there is not a single one of these innovations which does not in its own manner interpret this national chorus of confused warnings and summonses which are to be more or less heeded, and which I have compared above to the bodily feelings, vague and constant, afflux of millions of nervous activities brought from every point in the body by the centripetal nerves, in which Ribot sees the absolute basis of the personality. From each point of the social body, in fact from each corporation and from each brotherhood, emanate small thoughts and small wishes which are continually being given expression in talk, in complaints, in letters, in telegrams, in newspaper articles, in comments, finding a higher and a broader expression in the discoveries of science and the inventions of industry, in the works of literature and art, until they finally become realized in protestations of belief and acts of government. When we say that literature is the reflection of society, that men of genius are the representatives of their times, that the true government is opinion, we are interpreting under different forms this truth, that the social personality is the result of the social life.

Moreover, this truth must be completed by this other one, that, to a great extent also, the social life depends upon the State, as the organic life depends upon the "myself." Some decisions, suggested by particular theories, may have the effect of transforming the education of the young; some wishes, arising from accidental meetings and perceptions, may have the effect of profoundly modifying cenesthesia; as, for example, when the organism, obeying an arbitrary desire for travel, for venturesome undertaking, changes its physical and social surroundings. Does this modifying action of the State and of the "myself" upon their own foundation have a tendency to lessen or to increase? To increase without any doubt. Each new step along the way of political or of organic centralization places greater powers in the hands of the directing force. So we are not permitted, with the criminologists of the positivist school, to look upon the question of knowing whether an action which is prejudicial to another emanates from the will or merely from the organism of its author, as being of secondary importance; we might as well say that it is of little importance to inquire whether the State of France has participated or not in the injury caused by some of our nationalists to a foreign nation. However, I do not mean to say by this that an act which is deliberate, absolutely conscious and willing, is the only one which creates responsibility. For, if I have made myself clearly understood, perceptions and movements, reasonings followed by conclusions, and deliberations followed by decisions are but the "myself" in process of being formed, in the same way as the doubts and discussions of Chambers or of Cabinets followed by laws or by decrees are but the State in process of formation. The State acts, it is the deep stratum of institutions, in conformity with the national spirit; the "myself" acts, it is the collection of habits and of knowledge, of talents and beliefs in conformity with the slowly changing character. Thus, if a crime is committed by reason of habit with the ease of a reflex action, which is almost unconscious, our point of view demands that the responsibility of the agent be involved even more strongly than if it had willingly been done after deliberation. The classical doctrine of responsibility founded upon free will demands the opposite; but one can see here to what a disastrous consequence it will lead.

Besides, one may deny the reality of our person which is original and identical with itself; but one cannot cast any doubt upon the idea which we have of it, that is to say our consciousness. Now if the theory of Fouillée on the "force-ideas" is an illusion, as we have seen it to be in so far as it applies to freedom, it seems to me that it could to better advantage be applied to identity. It is not true that by reason of believing ourselves to be free we become independent in the slightest degree in the world of the ties of causation, external or internal, of which our voluntary decision is the complex effect; it is not true, it is a contradiction in terms, that belief in this ideal indeterminateness of our will determines the gradual realization of it. But it is certain that our personality becomes accentuated in the same degree as it is strengthened and that the perfect identity of our "myself," an ideal conceived of by so many souls who are religious and sure of their posthumous immortality, is realized better and better at each step taken along the way of logic and finality. More and more does the studious man become absorbed in his parent-idea, the man of action in his chief aim, the artist in his own shade of beauty. Thus is the person strengthened, the features become hollow or are brightened, and the foundation of responsibility gains strength.

§ 25. (IV) Foundations of the limitation of criminal prosecutions; reforms which should be introduced therein.

Let us point out in closing one of the legislative corollaries from our point of view. The normal alterations of the personality not being accomplished with an equal slowness either among different individuals or at the various ages of life, it will be advisable to give some attention to these differences in fixing the period of limitations in criminal procedure. The period of these limitations should be lengthened in proportion as there shall be occasion to believe these alterations to take place more slowly. I am more or less what I was yesterday, the day before yesterday, a year ago, ten years ago. During certain outbursts of passion I am very far from being myself. Personal identity comes and goes, subject to alternate rise and fall, to periodical fluctuations. But in the midst of this undulation which no formula is able to fix, it is an easy matter to establish this general fact; that after having been transformed with relative rapidity during childhood and adolescence, the person stops, becomes ossified, and, from this time on, is but slightly modified, assuming that he is undergoing modification. It is therefore not true that one is at all ages as much more different from oneself as more time shall have elapsed since a given date. This presumption, upon which legislation which establishes the same period of limitation in criminal cases for young people and for full grown men is partly founded, is contradicted by the observation of facts. There comes an age when, far from proceeding to differentiate itself more and more, the "myself" proceeds to become more and more identified with itself so to speak. Without taking into account every one of these shades it seems as though the law might at least prescribe two periods of limitation for the prosecution of crimes: the one, much shorter, in cases in which minors and persons not arrived at puberty are concerned, and the other in cases in which those who have attained their majority and adults are concerned, much longer. However this may be, one will have no difficulty in recognizing the importance attaching to the point of knowing to what extent a person, just as a State, has remained identical with itself between two given dates. The credit of a State no less than its responsibility depends upon the greater or lesser degree of stability and of permanence of which it gives proof to the eyes of its neighbors; a State stirred up by continual revolution cannot hope for any lasting alliances.

§ 26. (V) Civil responsibility.

Our theory of responsibility, let us observe, has the advantage of being applicable to civil cases as well as to criminal cases. Now civil responsibility has remained outside of the discussions stirred up by the question of free will; this means that it is understood by everybody as resting on a foundation other than this mysterious faculty. I know very well that, according to moralists and jurists, a contract does not bind the man who has signed it unless it was *freely* consented to. But the liberty which is here involved, as everywhere in the subject of obligations, is not free will, that inherent quality of the will of having been able not to decide as it has done; it is the absence of *external* restraint, that inherent quality of the act of being in conformity with the will of its author. The maker of a promissory note might say in vain that in signing it he yielded to an irresistible passion for a woman or for gambling, he would not any the less be held bound to pay it; he is gallant, he is a gambler, it is his character. Perhaps it might be otherwise (here the suspicion of madness would come into existence) if, in signing this paper, he had yielded to an incentive which was entirely an exception in his life; if, for example, having up to that time had a horror of gambling, he had contracted this debt in order to play baccarat. Why this difference? Because the question is *whether he was himself when he signed.*

In the case of the civil responsibility for an obligation one has to take into account the presence of *two personal identities*, that of the creditor and that of the debtor, just as, in the case of criminal responsibility, we had in contemplation, and face to face with each other, that of the guilty man and his victim, *or of the representatives of the latter.* Just as in fact the person of the debtor is carried on by that of his heirs or of his assigns, so is the person of the victim carried on, at first in old times, by that of his near relations, and later by that of his fellow-citizens, of his compatriots in the ever broadening meaning of this word. This fictitious carrying on of the person of the victim implies a high social state which has increased the bonds of solidarity between the members of the same nation. Thus is the guilty man held liable to liquidate a sort of debt towards society as a whole personifying his victim. But let us notice the important distinction which has arisen between the two evolutions of civil responsibility and penal responsibility.

The effect of this progress has been to enlarge the group of those interested in defending the victim to the point that in the end they forgot the fiction with which they started out, which was, that the man who denounced or the man who accused someone of a crime was the person who was the representative of the victim and had a right to denounce and to accuse only because of this representation. So in criminal trials the responsibility has little by little ceased to be considered as a bond between one person and another, and it has come to be regarded as the bond between a person and a purely impersonal being. On the other hand, progress has left the person of the debtor limited to the debtor himself or localized in a narrow circle of assigns; so that the civil obligation has never ceased to be and to seem a bond between two persons, and I will add between two persons more or less alike socially.

§ 27. Our theory agrees with the historical one of responsibility.

It is easy to review in two words the theory which has just been set forth. The responsibility of one person towards another assumes the following concurrent conditions: 1st. That there exists a certain degree of social similarity between the two persons. 2d. That the first, the cause of the incriminating act was *himself* and has remained or seems to have remained identical with himself. Moreover, as we shall see, penal responsibility, no less than civil, is always in the nature of a debt, that is to say, its nature is to produce a satisfaction judged to be useful to the person or to the group of persons who have the right to invoke it. Penal utilitarianism, in this sense, is as old as the world. Now let us show that this is no metaphysician's system, but that responsibility has always been thus understood in every period by popular instinct. If founded upon free will, this idea is very hard to reconcile with the history of the penal law, and, if it seems to agree with existing legislation, it has a tendency to create a gap between the latter and reforms in the near future, such as are demanded by determinist science. If founded upon identity and similarity, it accounts for the past and allows the present to bear some relation to the future, and the old prejudices to the new principles.

§ 28. (I) Family solidarity of primitive times; vendetta. Survivals of these past times, reprisals.

In primitive times the social tie is as energetic and as persistent as it is restricted, and strongly binds together the members of the same clan and segregates them from the rest of the world. This clan appears to the other clans as a living unit, as a single person who never changes or dies. It is true that sometimes the various clans resemble one another very much in language, superstitions, the rudiments of industry, and in customs; but again they are often very unlike, although placed alongside one another. When they differ very much, they look upon one another as absolute strangers and no true tie of responsibility whatsoever could exist between them. They can but alternately serve one another as quarry. But when they resemble one another in a varying degree, they feel themselves in a certain measure to be socially fellow-countrymen. Under these conditions, if the theory outlined above is the true one, responsibility for crimes committed by one clan upon another should be collective and not individual; but it ought to make itself felt very deeply in all directions and to last indefinitely. Now this is precisely what takes place, the phase in question is characterized by the prevalence of fierce and irregular *vendettas*,[1] a reciprocal form of punishing from whence proceeds our justice. It is not that during these same periods individual responsibility was unknown; the crimes committed by a relation against his own kin, within the clan, aroused its intense feelings.

But these crimes which at that time appeared more monstrous than they do at the present time revealed a character of madness, or rather of family suicide, which often tended to disguise their nature; moreover, they remained hidden in the bosom of the family, guarded and walled in, where the observation of the legislator would not penetrate. From this, for example, arises the

[1] If originally families who were a part of the same tribe resembled one another very much, the tribes scattered over the land must have been very unlike. Also the vendetta between one family and another is more persistent than the hostility between one tribe and another, and we must not confuse the feeling of savage, but deep, justice, which inspired vendettas, with the need for extermination which drove certain heterogeneous tribes to massacre one another. Let us add that, as we shall have occasion to say later on, for wrongs committed within the *family* to the prejudice of its own members, the penalty, which had in it nothing revengeful, was inspired by a feeling of what was right very much more profound and far more pure.

omission not only by Draco, but by every barbarian legislation, of parricide from among the crimes susceptible of punishment. It is not at all, as has been innocently imagined, because the severe Athenian legislator did not allow for the possibility of such a transgression; it is because parricide, an *intra-family* crime, falling under the special law of the family, was only cognizable by the *domestic tribunal*, a sort of paternal court of appeals too often forgotten by our criminologists,[1] when, for example, they derive penal justice from revenge and retaliation as its only primitive source.

Their error, which is very excusable, arises from what they have not seen, and have not sought to see, and that which was never shown them: the action of that occult and private justice where remorse, repentance, pardoning, and the feeling of morality such as we understand it played a great part, if we are to judge by the remains which are left in China, in Kabyle, and especially in a gorge of the Caucasus, among the tribe of the Ossetes. As serious an error, indeed, as would be that of a political writer who should take the Federal Constitution of the United States to be the sole law of that great federation, without taking into account the particular laws of each State. But in spite of everything the theoretical consequence of this forgetfulness has not been as annoying as one might have feared, and the conception which has been taken of the evolution of the punishment of crime has not thereby been radically perverted, at least from the *formal* point of view. In fact the domestic tribunals have unfortunately contributed in a small measure only, as we shall see, to the origin of our judicial courts, to which they have only lent, what is still important, the spirit animating them, the character of moral stigma which belonged to them and which they have added to the vengeful and atrocious character of the penalties of the latter. The odious nature of punishments in the Middle Ages, for example, is thus explained by this enforced spiritualization of brutal ferocities.

This much having been noted, let us continue.

When a barbarian who had been wronged thought it legitimate

[1] See, on the subject of these tribunals, the learned work of *Dareste*, "Etudes sur l'histoire du droit" (1889), especially pp. 148 *et seq.* See also "Evolution juridique" (1891), by *Letourneau*. The first of these two authors saw the contradiction which the existence of this domestic justice offers to the accepted theory of the entirely material and brutal conception of crime and its punishment among our far distant ancestors.

to *punish* another barbarian, because the latter was the brother or the cousin of the offender, obviously the *culpability* of persons depended in his eyes upon a totally different principle to that of the pretended freedom of their will. Here the *man punished* had been neither free nor otherwise to commit an act of which he was not the perpetrator. Nevertheless we find written everywhere, at the head of ancient customs, this law of family solidarity, of hereditary reversibility of penalties as well as recompenses, which shocks our narrow rationalism. Proofs of this universal singularity abound. In the world of savages it is the rule without exception.

"For the Australians," says Letourneau,[1] "no death is natural, every decease is the work of witchcraft planned by an enemy, and the strict duty of relations is to avenge their dead by killing, not exactly the presumed author of the murder, but some member of his tribe." It is needless to cite other examples. Among the barbarians the universal custom of vendettas, of vengeances from family to family, from tribe to tribe, shows the persistence of the ancient prejudice in this respect. The Gallic law permitted the family of the offender to buy back, for a money consideration, the right of revenge which belonged to the family of the offended against the guilty: but, "a peculiar thing," remarks Beaune,[2] "the latter did not alone have to bear the expense of the indemnity. He only paid a part of it; the rest was defrayed by his relatives, both paternal and maternal, the former paying twice as much as the latter. Responsibility only ceased with the ninth degree."[3] Similarly in the Frankish law, every family has a right to take vengeance for an outrage committed upon one of its members, unless pecuniary composition has been made. The half civilized States of the ancient Orient, Persia, Syria, Assyria, and India, all inflicted upon the wife and the children of the criminal the punishment, generally of an atrocious nature, to which he himself was condemned.[4] China also, previous to the third or fourth century of our era, attributed to crimes and penalties in general (excepting of course that which has just been said as to offenses within the family itself) this collective character. A great step

[1] "Evolution de la morale" (Paris, 1887).

[2] "Introduction a l'étude du droit coutumier," p. 59.

[3] In this old Gallic law, relationship which we would term *near*, extended to the eighteenth degree. From this one sees what a powerful collectivity the ancient family formed.

[4] *Thonissen*, "Droit criminel des anciens peuples de l'Orient," Vol. I, pp. 70 and 158.

in advance accomplished by the law of Moses consists in not compelling "the father to die for the sake of the children, nor the children for the sake of the parents," [1] which goes to prove that until the date of this prohibition the family guilt, because of the fault of a single individual, was recognized in Israel.

In England, it is only from the ninth or tenth century on that the woman ceased to be beaten for the crimes of her husband; but under Edward the Confessor again, each guild was responsible as a whole for the offense committed by one of its members. Moreover, even among the more or less civilized peoples who have for a long time admitted the individual character of offenses and of punishments on principle, the old principle survives or is resuscitated in certain particular cases, for example, on the occasion of crimes of a religious or of a political nature. In Egypt "the mother, the children, the whole family of the conspirator was given over to the executioner." [2] In Mexico under the Aztecs, not only was the vestal guilty of having broken her vow condemned — just as in Rome, singular coincidence — to be buried alive, but even her relatives were banished and her native town destroyed.[3] In the same way, in Peru, if one of the wives of the Inca were convicted of adultery, the relatives of the two guilty persons were put to death together with them. In Greece, during the war against Persia, a senator having been of the opinion that the proposals of the enemy should be heeded, he was stoned, and the women ran to his house to stone also his wife and his children. When the accused, in Athens, died in the course of a criminal procedure directed against him, it did not abate, as with us; it was carried out against his children. "In striking down the children of criminals," says Thonissen, "the judges thought to imitate the gods." We often even see the *neighbors* in the same village criminally liable for one another.[4] This was so in Germania, where the inhabitants of the same "march" not only "ab intestat" succeeded one another and were able to exercise against the purchaser of the share of one of themselves a sort of "repurchase by neighbors," a survival no doubt of the former indivisible nature of their community property, but again "were responsible for the crimes committed upon the territory of the 'march' or of which the

[1] Deuteronomy.

[2] *Thonissen, op. cit.*

[3] *Lucien Biart,* "Le Mexique."

[4] See on this subject, *Dareste, op. cit.*, and *Glasson,* "Histoire du droit et des institutions de la France."

perpetrator had therein taken refuge. . . ." Certainly this solidarity of neighbors is nothing more than an imitation of family solidarity, or even in the last analysis rests upon a presumption of relationship.

Is there any necessity of recalling that in France, in the case of crimes of high treason, this fearful archaism of family responsibility survived until the eighteenth century? The relatives of Damien were banished as had been those of Ravaillac. But even in our own day does there not remain something of this old historical prejudice in the fiction which makes us consider the members of a ministerial cabinet as mutually responsible for the misdeed committed by one of them? The immunity of parliament, by virtue of which a deputy or a senator may not be prosecuted without the authorization of the assembly of which he is a member, as though the latter judged itself to be in a measure responsible for his honor, is derived from the same source. Moreover, among the illiterate classes the old prejudice is still alive. A few years ago, for example, according to Ferri, an Italian stabbed a soldier whom he did not know, because another soldier had offended him some time before this.

What does this ancient custom signify? It means simply that in the eyes of primitive communities all the members of the same natural group, be it tribe or patriarchal family, went to make up an indivisible, an indissoluble whole, a truly identical and immortal person. In vain might they be aware that the perpetrator of a crime was such and such an individual and not his brothers, they struck at all his brothers along with him,[1] just as nowadays, though we may believe that the cause of a crime resides only in one portion of the brain of its perpetrator, we sometimes make his entire head fall under the blade of the guillotine. Then we take as our basis the limited solidarity which binds together the organs of the same individual; at other times, that which is fictitiously reputed to unite the ministers of the same cabinet and to make of them but a single being. Our forefathers took as their basis the solidarity, in their eyes no less exacting, which in their times bound together the members of the same race.[2] When

[1] In the beginning, in fact, collective responsibility was always understood in this sense that *all* the relatives ought to be punished at the same time. But later on, owing to the modification of customs, it was understood in this sense, which was more human, that *some* member of the family ought to be punished.

[2] Artificial families having everywhere come into existence after the model of natural families, the same fiction was applied to them. Even in the very midst

the relaxing of the patriarchal sheaf allowed them to distinguish between the guilty man and his family, they began to admit the principle of the individuality of penalties. In the same measure as the progress of medicine and psychology allows us sometimes to distinguish between the diseased and the healthy portions of the same brain, between the madness and the person, we are led to spare the latter while defending ourselves against the former only. So the nature of the conception of responsibility has not really changed, and, without breaking the thread of historical evolution, we are able to advance along the new paths opened up by the alienists.

Possibly the objection may be made that collective responsibility sometimes rested on the assumed complicity of the relatives, or else on the fear of their vengeance reputed to be likely. Be it so; but even this presumption of complicity and of vengeance bears witness to the strength of the family solidarity which universally suggested the former. We must not confuse, moreover, with the examples given above, certain facts which seem to resemble them. Under Augustus, when a master was assassinated by one of his slaves who remained unknown, all his slaves were put to death. Here, obviously, the penalty only fell upon the entire group because the disadvantage of hurting the innocent seemed preferable to that of leaving the guilty unpunished.

But everywhere in the legends of the far-distant past fratricides, parricides, to say nothing of infanticides, abound; how reconcile with this fact the character of close union, of absolute indivisibility, which so many other facts justify us in attributing to the primitive family? The difficulty resolves itself if one recollects that the ancient family was an entrenched camp, assailed upon all sides and constrained to enforce an iron discipline under penalty of destruction. What happens in all barbarian armies must have happened therein: there was no medium between criminal rebellion and passive obedience, between treason even to the extent of murder and devotion even unto death. Furthermore, that domestic ties have gradually lost their force and their extent, in the same proportion as political ties have gained strength and

of the seventeenth century, the Criminal Ordinance of 1670 admits that the communities of towns, boroughs and villages, corporations and other legal persons are *capable of committing crimes*. In such a case their syndic represents them; he has to undergo the interrogatory and all the different phases of the examination (including the rack?). See *du Boys*, "Histoire du droit criminel chez les peuples modernes."

extent, cannot admit of the shadow of a doubt. Is it necessary to give one of the thousands of existing proofs? I shall seek it in the midst of full-fledged democracy, at Florence, where in the thirteenth and fourteenth centuries, by virtue of the formidable "Ordinances of Justice" of 1293, a crime committed by a "magnat" against a "popolano" rebounded upon his relations to the seventh degree inclusive. Compare 1293 with 1793; assuredly our "Law of Suspects" can rival the sanguinary product of Florentine legislation as far as arbitrariness and despotism are concerned. But the idea of incriminating the brothers, cousins, and cousins' children of the aristocrats he was pursuing did not even occur to the revolutionary legislator. As a matter of fact the *suspicion* was well understood to apply to the relatives of the *guilty;* but they would not have dared to write that this should be so in law.[1]

At the same time, the object was, under the Terror, to slay especially the families of the nobles. Now, in every country and at all times, the nobility has been distinguished by the high degree of its family solidarity; and it is noticeable also that it has always been especially reached by the principle of collective responsibility, which confirms my explanation of the latter. It seems, "a priori," that plebeian families should everywhere be the more united, the greater weakness of the individuals calling upon them to bind themselves together the more in order to protect themselves; but let us not forget the military origin and life of the noble families, especially let us not forget their relative splendor which arouses the self-esteem their members have in belonging to them. Still more than to a need of mutual protection is social cohesion due to a need of reciprocal pride; from this the former family spirit,

[1] Even since the beginning of this century, the family has continued to be very rapidly dismantled. The causes for the challenging of witnesses, as they are formulated by the legislator of 1805, are proof of this. The relation to the fourth degree is exceptionable, as well as the servant: this shows that as late as 1805 the servant was a servitor, an integral part of the household. If the law were to be amended, I do not believe that it would be upon a presumption of deference towards their masters held by servants, or of the mutual devotion of cousins, that they would contemplate founding the challenges. The fact of belonging to the same political or religious corporation would have an entirely different import in the eyes of the legislator. Despite the individualism which reigned in the theories of the eighteenth century, the French family was still so much of a unit in 1789 that quite a number of the Memorials of the Three-Orders proposed to give a legal sanction, in serious cases, to the orders of an assemblage of relatives, organized in the form of a domestic tribunal. (See *Desjardins*, "Les Cahièrs des Etats généraux," 1883), and several Memorials do not even absolutely reject the idea of causing to weigh upon a family of a condemned person the consequences of his crime (*op. cit.*).

the present patriotism, arises. The nations which are most exposed to invasion are not always those among which patriotism is deepest; those defeats which imperil the fatherland do not always thereby make it the more precious to the citizens whom they have humiliated.

As the "gens" at Rome and in Greece, so the noble family at Florence formed the clan and served as an example for the families of the "popolani" who strove to imitate it. The same thing happened in France. Again, every time the political current has turned against the aristocracy, whether it has been in ancient times, in the Middle Ages, or in modern times it is in compact masses that its members have been banished or sacrificed, and, in all times, these families have been more prone than others to be looked down upon or dishonored because of the fault of a single member. Let us cite in the case of France a passage from the Memorials of 1789. A large number of them ask for the maintaining of arbitrary orders of arrest in the interest of families. "We must indeed take into account," says one of them, "the prejudice which, especially in the case of the nobility, causes the family to be responsible for each one of those of whom it is composed."[1] Again it was necessary that this solidarity should be very acutely felt in order to check the excessive individualism with which the Memorials, even those of the nobility, are generally imbued.

The right of reprisal has always been exercised in time of war: everywhere, when *one* soldier of an army has perpetrated some cruelty upon a soldier of the enemy's army, the latter believes that it has the right to be revenged not only upon the guilty man, but upon every one of his companions in arms and even against every one of his fellow-countrymen. This is an old military tradition, very hard to justify at our period of individualism, but which did not astonish anybody in the ages steeped in the sentiment of national and family solidarity.

During the Middle Ages, even in time of peace, the right of reprisals was recognized, and, in the Italian republics, it had become raised to the height of an institution. If a merchant of Pisa by reason of his insolvency or bad faith caused a Florentine merchant to lose a certain sum of money, the town of Florence demanded reparation of this loss from the town of Pisa, and upon the refusal of the latter to comply, the merchandise or property

[1] *Desjardins, op. cit.*

belonging to no matter what inhabitant of Pisa was seized in Florence until payment was made of the sum due. "In the year 1329 alone," says Perrens,[1] "Florence had six hundred livres worth of reprisals against Perugia, two thousand worth against Fano, two hundred and fifty worth against Spoleto, fifty-five worth against Pisa, and twenty-four hundred against Forli, because of loans not paid back, or of stolen merchandise. Neither did Viterbo, Venice, nor Padua, though farther off, escape the reprisals of Florence; sometimes they took the initiative." The Italians of that time thought this was natural. "They saw therein a right, and it did not enter into the mind of any of them to blame those who made use of it. Never, as has been justly said, did the chroniclers give the name of depredation to reprisals." Why in time of war, why during warlike times, does collective responsibility tend thus to be substituted for individual solidarity if it be not because the social tie is very binding between fellow-citizens? Between these latter there is no longer any similarity, there is identity; there can no longer be any question of similarity or of dissimilarity excepting in the relations of belligerent States.

§ 29. (II) Royal justice took for its model, not the domestic tribunals of a former era, but warlike proceedings; malefactors everywhere treated as enemies.

We have said that, from the very earliest times, two sorts of criminality, two different sorts of responsibilities existed side by side: one sort of criminality and responsibility, which is collective and which applies to the injuries caused by one member of a small State to a member of another, and an individual criminality and responsibility which applies to the wrongs of a member of a society towards his associates. It is clear that this distinction must have existed from all time, and that consequently a corresponding distinction must have been applied to the primitive punishment of crime. The chief of the clan, the head of the family in old times had two principal attributes: he was doubly a judge, both as protector of his children, and as the depositary of the ancestral vengeances and hatreds, of the honor of the ancestors. Through him, for want of a higher authority, his family took justice into its own hands as against strange families, at the same time

[1] "Histoire de Florence." See also *Cibrario*, "Economie domestique au moyen age," Vol. I, p. 143. This right of retribution, under the name of "stamp duty," remained in full force until the fifteenth century.

as he rendered justice to his children who had disagreed. When, after this era of patriarchal parceling out, monarchies began to make their appearance, in other words simple federations of families gathered together under the shelter of a sceptre, the need of a new form of justice began to be felt. Crimes committed by a member of one family to the injury of another, within the limits of the empire, urgently called for a special jurisdiction, distinct from that of the domestic tribunals and from that military jurisdiction as well, which punished by means of war the crimes of one nation as regarded another. Now this royal justice could be organized by taking as an example either the merciful procedure of the domestic tribunals, or warlike usages and customs. But while both derivations seemed to be equally admissible, it is a fact that only the second was realized, except that — and in truth it is very important — something of the moral spirit and feeling peculiar to domestic justice has passed into official justice. The penalty has remained vindictive as at the time of the vendetta, but has become dishonorable, humiliating, like the family excommunication which fell upon the children who were guilty: a characteristic which punishment by means of the vendetta did not have, for a capital execution of this nature in nowise made the relatives of the person executed blush. In Corsica and in Sicily it is still the same.

Moreover, for him who has no concern excepting with external forms and proceedings, *public vengeance* has been modeled upon warfare. Spencer, in a passage upon which we have commented, has very justly remarked that militarism and penal justice have advanced with the same stride. The atrocity of the proceedings employed by the latter even until modern times could suffice to demonstrate that it was modeled after the image of the carnage of war and not after that of paternal repression. "One need not be very well versed in ancient history," says Thonissen, "to know that primitive peoples [read the great primitive States] were in the habit of compelling malefactors to undergo the treatment to which they far too often submitted their prisoners of war." Thus it is that in Egypt captives were employed in the mines, and mingled with the great criminals, and that in Persia they mutilated the latter as well as the former. The origin of torture which goes so far back into the past, especially into the past of the time of the Pharaohs, cannot readily be understood unless one looks at it from this point of view. One sees in the Ramesseum a picture "where Egyptian soldiers are giving the bastinado to two enemies who are prisoners, in order, says the hieroglyphic inscription, that they may be compelled to reveal what the Khetas do." This brutality vented upon one's enemy in order to compel him to say *that which one is sure he knows* is odious, but in no way absurd; it should attain its object. Also, it is as old as combats. Later on, this usage having once become established, it is quite conceivable that, after its advantages were recognized, its employment for the discovery of crimes by means of the submission of the accused or of witnesses to tortures of a similar nature was thought of. But then one could not be certain that they knew the thing that was being asked them, and this semi-obscurity of the proceeding here added to its ever present barbarity forbids us to believe that the idea of its use by the judiciary was arrived at independently from its use by the military. Perhaps ordeals originated in the same manner through the imitation of the diviners or by virtue of the same principle. It was natural to consult the gods on what decision to take in a criminal proceeding after having interrogated them on the probable outcome of a battle.

Let us observe, in passing, that neither torture nor the ordeal were in use before the domestic tribunals. In every case the custom, which was so universal during the barbarian ages, of pecuniary composition is manifestly connected with this military origin of the punishment of crime. There has been a desire to see therein the proof of an absence of the moral sense among our forefathers. It is as though the indemnities which we exact from a foreign nation for an injury of a criminal nature occasioned to one of our own nation served as an argument for the outcries directed against our immorality. Besides this, we have reasons for the belief that the "Wergeld," introduced during the period of barbarism as a slow progress and with the object of pacification, in the beginning offended the moral feelings of many a warrior; witness the Danish chieftain who, having been unable to accustom himself to this innovation, cries out in popular song: "Who would formerly have dared to receive money as the price for a father assassinated?"

§ 30. (III) Expiatory character of punishment; individual transition.

We can see that it is an historical error to contrast the principle of *expiation*, in the case of criminal punishment, with the principle of social utility. As long as the belief in national defilement because of individual wrongdoing persisted, the punishment could not have any greater utility than this very function of expiation, that is to say, of purification. And it has always been utilitarian in its nature as well as under other aspects, in so far as it is exemplary and intimidating. It is true that even after the advent of purely individual responsibility, or rather after its extension to take in crimes in general (for domestic crimes had always had an individual character), the penalty did not at once cease to be looked upon partly as an expiation. But we must fully realize the sentiment to which this conception answered. First of all, when, while recognizing in speech the personal character of faults, one believes that the nation is concerned that the penalty should be in the nature of an expiation, this really indicates that, contrary to the principle which is being upheld, one feels the need of effacing a public stain and not only one which is of a private nature. In the second place, when it is in the interests of the guilty man himself that this purging by means of the punishment is demanded, this proves that the new relation established between the sinning soul and the outraged god has been conceived of, while partially reckoning it from the old relation between two families divided by an ancestral vendetta. These families were, or seemed to be in their essence, similar and immortal; from which it follows that their responsibility should have been very great or unlimited. In their image, the souls of individuals were also reputed to be immortal, immortal like the god whom they had offended and after whom they were supposed to have been modeled, — for, in the last analysis what greater mystery can there be than the possibility even of death?

From this there followed, according to our principles, an idea of culpability which had nothing of the mystical in it, whatever may be said as to this. On the contrary, it was perfectly logical in starting with the belief in the absolute similarity of God and the sinner, and with the belief in the identity of the guilty soul pushed to the extent of believing in its immortality. The everlastingness of the person, the depth of its reality, seemed as though they had every reason to be connected with everything which emanated from it, with its demerits as with its merits, with its hatreds as with its loves, with its sufferings as with its joys, and to give it a right to punishment without end just as to eternal reward. Now the lesser conception of the "myself," frail flower of the organism, which we create for ourselves, has no less logically changed the notion of the fault and of the penalty; life has become infinitely lowered in value in our estimation, and, as one can expect but short-lived joys therefrom, it seems reasonable not to have to fear any but evils of a temporary character.

But, as long as this austere and disparaging conception has not come to light, the "myself," proud and sure of itself, of its importance and of its future, should be concerned, even at the price of the most cruel torments, with sparing itself from a dishonor of an indefinite duration and extent. When a man has sustained an affront, he seeks to re-establish himself by means of some brilliant action. In the eyes of a nation which a crime sullies, whether it be admitted, or whether it unconsciously feel this stain, the penalty which is striking and atrocious is analogous to this exploit of a warlike nature. It is the revenge of public and private honor at the same time against the injury caused by the offense; it is an indignant protest which is the equivalent of a rehabilitation. Even among our ultra-civilized societies, this feeling is still alive or is revived at certain times.

Thus *expiation* has been the primary form which the utilitarian side of the punishment of crime has assumed. The secondary form, which later on became the principal one, was *exemplariness*. The last one will be *amendment* in so far as that is possible. Putting it in another way, the first advantage which was expected to result from punishment was to give the mass of honest people the satisfaction of feeling themselves relieved of all complicity, from all solidarity with the criminal, to see between themselves and him a gulf opening up. The second has been to inspire within those who shall be anxious to follow in the footsteps of the malefactor a salutary terror. The third shall be, whenever possible, to make the guilty a better man.

§ 31. (IV) Review and completion.

In conclusion let us review what we have said. Originally the family of the one who is offended took up the feud as a unit, but only against the family of the offender, of the criminal. There are two forms of solidarity here which are about equal: that which binds together the relatives of the latter and that which binds together the relatives of the victim. But later on, one of these forms of solidarity lessens and disappears, whereas the other extends outside of its own field: in proportion as the individual character of faults is the more felt, the interest of society as a whole in repression is also better understood, and responsibility which is purely private is formulated when *public action* appears. Perhaps there is occasion to remark that this contrast cannot be explained in an entirely rational manner. If the multiplying of the relations, even between our relatives, as a consequence of social progress, has tended to lead us to realize that everybody is interested in restraining murder and theft in the case of a single person, the same reason might have caused the admission of the vague and indirect complicity of all when a single individual has struck or has stolen. And, in fact, this last truth also has a tendency to compel its own implied acceptance: does not the increasing indulgence by means of which, and even beyond all measure, so many malefactors benefit, have its source in the confused feeling of the fact that the criminal is in many respects the fruit of the social tree?

Our exaggerated individualism is at the same time contrary to our naturalism, which does not cease to remind us of the solidarity of fathers and children, of the living and the dead, closely united by heredity, and to our socialism, which shows the no less rigorous solidarity of fellow associates, of the living among themselves, as a consequence of their imitation of one another. Society in punishing its delinquents too often resembles those libertine fathers who cruelly punish the libertinage of their sons. But, on the other hand, the following consideration justifies the more and more individual character of responsibility. The criminal act, like every other act committed in the midst of a society, is the result of two combinations which are themselves combined together: one combination of physiological and psychological attributes accidentally met with and transmitted by heredity, the *character*, and one combination of examples crossing one another, the *social surroundings*. Now the more the elements of these combinations are multiplied, as happens in the case of the first by means of the progressive mingling of races, and in the case of the second by means of the progress of civilization, — two effects which are generally parallel, — the more is the act emanating from the individual under these conditions peculiar, original, and unique in itself. Thus, in proportion as a society becomes civilized, should responsibility become individualized.

Let us now add that, after having led us gradually to affirm the individuality of every fault, social progress ought to go still further and be carried on under new forms. How can this be? By means of the development of mental pathology, or, if you will, of criminal anthropology, which will allow us to pick out from this very complex being called the individual the distinct elements, though they may not be severable, of which he is composed, to take them to one side and to apply to the special treatment of each one of them the appropriate remedies. So, in occupying ourselves in the chapter which follows, with the limitations or with the suppression of penal responsibility under the sway of certain abnormal states, such as madness and drunkenness, we will only be applying to these exceptional cases the general ideas which are set forth above, and engaged along the lines to which the historical evolution of the punishment of crime has forced existing societies.

CHAPTER IV

THE THEORY OF IRRESPONSIBILITY

§ 32. Preliminary remarks. Reply to Binet. Different causes of irresponsibility.

In the eyes of the philosophers who are inclined to resolve notions of morality into moral feelings instead of recognizing the fund of implied opinions and accumulated ideas of which every feeling is but a condensation, and of which it is but the sheaf, the preceding theory must err because of an evident insufficiency. Binet it is true adopts it,[1] but he explains it in his own way. According to him, we judge a man to be morally responsible for a bad action which he has committed when we believe that we have

[1] See his short and remarkable article on "Responsabilité morale" in the "Revue philosophique," September, 1888. It should be observed that the germ of our theory of responsibility had been indicated by us in a previous writing, but in a succinct and incomplete manner.

the right to carry back to this man the feeling of indignation which his action has caused us to feel, that is to say, when this action conforms to the nature of its perpetrator, when the agent has remained the same since he acted; let us add when the indignation thus brought back to the guilty man is stronger in us than the pity which is inspired by the thought of the punishment incurred by him. If, on the other hand, pity is stronger, we judge him not to be punishable. Thus the conflict of two feelings would give rise to all the difficulty in the problem and the result of this duel within the enclosed field of our sensibility and our imagination, and in no way of our reason, would bring about the result of the decision sought for. According as the jury is the more impressed by the punishment of the crime or the prospect of the guillotine, it convicts or acquits. Whence Binet concludes that moral responsibility, being a purely sentimental thing, our penal legislation should cease to be dependent upon it.

I reply, first of all, that this conclusion does not follow from the premises. Were it true that the idea of moral responsibility had in it nothing but emotions, it would not follow that the law should take no account of it. Who has better shown than Binet and his friend Féré the importance of the ways of feeling in psychological and social life? Their fault lies in often exaggerating it, as when, for example, convictions seem to them to be passions in disguise. I would say rather that passions are convictions which are accumulated and deep rooted. Do they not know that our hatreds, our repugnances, are the unconscious expression of former experiences of an *injurious* nature, and our likes of former experiences of a useful nature? At the bottom of that horror which a crime inspires is there not, so to speak, the condensed utilitarianism of all mankind, a mass of acquired certainties? With the moralist who reasons out his feelings, the latent convictions of the past seek to become conscious once more, that is all. He justifies his indignation in his own eyes, or rather he displays or reveals it to itself, in maintaining that this murderer who has just killed someone without being molested for it, and not during an attack of insanity, will kill still more people unless he be put out of the way. And why does he maintain this, if it is not because he believes that this murderer has remained identical with himself since his crime? It is not true that this opinion of identity alone serves to cause the feeling of indignation provoked by the contemplation of the act, to be carried back to the agent; this opinion gives rise to this feeling; without this opinion, this feeling would not be produced by the contemplation of any crime. We will never feel indignation against the entity of the crime, hypothetically detached in an abstract manner from the criminal being; we would not begin by being indignant against an assassination "in abstracto," excepting that we would afterwards become indignant against the assassin. No, it is against the assassin, directly and primarily, that our indignation is directed, at the sight or the recital of the assassination; and, I repeat, the first condition of our becoming indignant, is that we should judge the guilty man to be identical with himself when acting.

The second condition is that we should judge him to be similar to ourselves; without this neither indignation nor compassion are possible. It is to the extent that the malefactor reflects our own image for us that we do him the honor to be indignant against him or to feel pity towards him. Moreover, from the point of view which concerns us, let us beware of placing these two opposite feelings in the same rank. The natural effect of the crime and the criminal is to arouse our indignation; it is accidentally, it is secondarily that they arouse our pity, when the law imposes a punishment upon them which we *consider* excessive. If the law were to impose a lesser penalty upon them, our pity would diminish and would be surpassed by the opposite feeling. This shows that the level of pity rises or falls with the changes in legislation, that it is a *function* of legislative variations. The level of indignation, on the contrary, remains unchanged by these external modifications; it is only influenced by the variations within the criminal, whence, in certain cases, may result his *insanity*, and by the variations within society, whence may result the inoffensive character of an act formerly characterized as a crime, or the malevolent character of an act formerly lawful. Thus it is this latter feeling by which responsibility should be measured, to the exclusion of the former. And the jury knows this perfectly well, when, while acquitting because it finds the law to be too severe, it judges the guilty man to be worthy of a lesser punishment, or at least of a severe censure.

As a matter of fact, censure, or the verdict of reason, is the essential punishment, the hidden spirit of every chastisement worthy the name. There is nothing so very sentimental in this. But is it only when we are aroused, are filled with indignation, that we censure, that we flay, and that we judge a man to be punishable from a moral point of view? If the jury is the slave of its impressions, the true judge is not. Being accustomed often to pass judgment as to responsibility at once deadens the feeling of indignation, while, on the other hand, the strength of this judgment increases. There is an inverse ratio between this way of judging and this way of feeling; thus the former does not spring from the latter. The latter rather proceeds from the former; for the ideas which our reason elaborates within us upon the nature of duty and the scale of faults act as a powerful modifier of the emotions, which appear to be spontaneous and which the contemplation of acts which are wrongful, or which are judged to be so, suggests to us. An exhibition of nudity such as an Athenian would have applauded scandalizes the modern public, because it is Christian. It is thus that our admiration for the aesthetic, our most enthusiastic plaudits at the theatre or concert, are for the most part the result of our aesthetic opinions and not vice versa.

Our object, in this work, is precisely to investigate and to test the principles upon which our feeling of indignation at the sight of the misdeed and the malefactor is founded, has been founded, or ought to be founded. Now this emotion is the complex result of two different sorts of ideas, and is proportioned, either according to the degree of responsibility which our reason, by virtue of certain principles which are conscious or unconscious, attributes to the delinquent, or according to the degree of gravity which, by virtue of other principles, it attributes to the crime for which we judge him to be responsible. In the present and the preceding chapter, we limit ourselves to the study of principles of the first kind; we shall deal with the others, but more briefly, in the course of a later chapter. Let us not confuse these two sorts of considerations as Binet seems to do.

This objection having been set aside, let us go on with our investigation.

To what extent, and for what reasons, do certain states, such as madness, epilepsy, intoxication, old age, and hypnotism cause one to be irresponsible? We shall attempt to answer this difficult question. Our theory of irresponsibility should serve as an annexation and a counter-proof to our theory of responsibility; and, just as the latter pretends to agree with the historical evolution of the penal law during the past, so does the former pretend to be in accord, I do not say with the radical revolution which our new criminologists dream of, but with the necessary reforms which their complex effort is preparing for the future. Indeed it cannot be denied that the field of irresponsibility has grown out of all proportion in our day and that its unceasing extension is the characteristic of contemporary penal science.[1] Still very restricted in the eighteenth century, limited to cases of *absolute* madness, it has increased by means of a series of encroachments, owing to the thorough observation of Pinel, to Esquirol's doctrine of monomania, to that of Morel in regard to hereditary degenerates, and lastly, to the recent researches of our hypnotists and anthropologists. A violent, irresistible current drives science to its usurpations and to its conquests. But the question is whether they should be without limit and whether logic condemns us, as one of the first of these men, Dally, has dared to say in the course of a discussion which has remained famous in the annals of the medico-psychological society, to the absolute assimilation of the criminal and the lunatic. Is it indeed true that of this old and venerable idea of moral responsibility there is nothing worth retaining and that it is urgent that it be razed to its very foundations in order to erect in its stead, as so many of the young savants suggest, Féré for example, the new Bastille of social responsibility, which, moreover, is no less formidable than the old one? Many distinguished alienists, Paul Dubuisson among others,[2] are not of this opinion, and I believe that they are quite right in resisting the general enthusiasm.

We have above made a study of responsibility, but we have scarcely mentioned that responsibility which is perfect, ideal, and unlimited. To tell the truth this latter implies a contradiction. As a matter of fact, it assumes, according to our principles, these two conditions: the greatest possible similarity between the members of the same society and the most lasting, the most absolute possible identity of the author of a wrongful act. Now personal identity is the more perfect as the internal harmony, the persistence of which it is, is the more complete, that is to say, as the individual is the more moral; and the progress of social

[1] In his "Nueva ciencia pénal," a book of incisive and heated criticism directed against the new Italian school, *de Aramburu*, in spite of the classicism of his ideas, makes this sad admission. He is compelled to recognize the fact that "the number of patients is greater than it was thought to be up to this time, and the number of criminals is less," and that thus "the field of teratology is extended while that of the old penal law is becoming more limited."

[2] See his remarkable study entitled "Essai de théorie positive de la responsabilité" published in the "Archives d'Anthropologie criminelle." We will speak of this again further on.

similarity is not possible beyond a certain degree except by means of the progress of morality. It is only given to very honest people to imitate one another more and more without society becoming disorganized. Thus the maximum of individual responsibility implies not only the maximum of individual, but of general honesty as well. So that my hypothesis of a man absolutely and fully responsible in the criminal sense of the word is that of an absolutely moral man who in the midst of surroundings which are also absolutely moral should be constrained to commit a crime. This is contradictory.

Again one can say that, in immoral surroundings, a man conforming perfectly to these surroundings would only commit crimes which were excused or approved by opinion, that is to say, would, properly speaking, never have anything criminal about him. Besides this, the accentuation of individual identity, of individual originality, would be unable to progress beyond a certain point without coming into conflict with the progress of social assimilation. The ideal of socialism and the ideal of individualism cannot be realized at one and the same time and without damaging each other. From this it follows, and this consequence has its bearing, that the necessity of joining the two conditions of moral responsibility impose upon this man, in a given social state, a *maximum* which cannot be exceeded, but which civilization tends to extend unceasingly.

Unlimited speed, unlimited force, unlimited duration, are not less contradictory than unlimited guilt. There is also in each given physical state, an impassable maximum of speed, of force, of life, etc. That which is realized at each instant is the hypothesis to which the idea of finite, limited, precise responsibility is applicable, that is, the hypothesis of a man more or less honest who, in surroundings which are pretty nearly honest and which he resembles only to a certain degree, has a moment of failure.

The idea of absolute irresponsibility is no less contradictory than that of absolute responsibility, for it assumes, if not a radical heterogeneousness of the social surroundings, which would make all society impossible, at least a radical alteration, a total and incessant transformation of the person which would be incompatible with the simplest phenomenon of the consciousness, still more with the carrying out of an act which was criminal.[1] Again,

[1] Let us observe a difference between these two contrary ideals. That superlative degree of logic and finality which makes personal identity perfect, imperiously

even in the case of the lunatic who has come to the last stages of incoherence, in the case of the demented, absolute irresponsibility, properly speaking, does not exist. It is never anything but "practically" absolute, to borrow one of their phrases from the geometricians. This is so true that the directors of asylums often inflict upon the most incurable madmen certain punishments in order to avert the recurrence of serious infractions of discipline. If madmen were entirely irresponsible, chastisement would be absolutely ineffectual in their case, which is not the fact.

Between the positive ideal and the negative ideal of which I have just given a definition, or, better still, in reality between the slowly changing "maxima" and "minima," the immense scale of the degrees of real responsibility and irresponsibility is interposed. Let us now run over these latter and let us first of all give our attention to madness.

§ 33. (I) Madness destroys assimilation and alienates at the same time. The moral sense.

Madness makes us irresponsible for two reasons: because it *destroys our assimilation*, and because it *alienates* us, because it makes us strangers to our surroundings and because it makes us strangers to ourselves. It recasts the "myself," although more often than not it may cause the latter to take the direction towards which it already inclined, and the new "myself" which it substitutes for the old is in its essence unsociable, and takes away from the action and reaction of imitation which radiates from all sides. The normal "myself" says, thinks, and feels nothing, even when alone, which is not said, thought, and felt under the unconscious and all-powerful domination of example. The abnormal "myself" only listens to and believes itself; from this there results, among other consequences, that swelling up with pride which is one of the first symptoms of insanity; for as soon as it ceases to be impressed by the salutary contradiction of the self-esteem of others, the self-esteem of the "myself" swells up beyond all limits, and nothing less than their pressure upon one another

demands first of all a full organic harmony, and then, and before everything else, a noticeable social harmony. "Mens sana in corpore sano" is only to be found "in societate sana." But the very greatest cerebral derangement does not demand, or at least does not to the same extent demand, the overthrow of society, and the maddest madman can exist in the midst of a society which is in admirable equilibrium. This proves that the normal person is a social thing, and that the insane person is simply a pathological thing.

is necessary in order to keep the pride of men, like the cells of a honeycomb, within the desired limits. This is why our principles forbid the punishment of the madman, even after the series of his mental transformations has been arrested, as so often happens, in the form of a delirium henceforth unalterable. If, in such a case in fact, the condition of individual identity is, or rather seems to be sufficiently well fulfilled, that of social similarity is not in any way fulfilled.[1] All madness is an irregularity which isolates us, and it isolates us the more in proportion as it is the more fixed, consolidated, and chronic.

Let us be more specific and let us go into the details of the different forms of madness. They can be classified without difficulty as far as our subject is concerned. The moral sense, a collective name by which we designate an assemblage of repugnances towards certain acts and towards certain weaknesses, is the brake upon the train of life; it is given us by nature or else by social culture, but may be supplied by the fear of punishment. The will is the engineer of this train; by itself it has no power whatever, and all of its power is in the greater or lesser energy of the moral sense, just as all the power of the percussion cap is in the powder within the gun. There is a normal degree of morality which will permit a man, if his will intervenes in time, to resist temptations of every kind, either from within or from without, provided that they do not go beyond a certain limit, which is very seldom passed in reality.

Now it may happen that the temptation from without, as a consequence of exceptional circumstances, may become excessive and that in such a case the brake may be insufficient. Such a failure to act as this taking place during the Terror or the Commune can be accounted for in this way. Or else it is the impulse from within or which at least comes from the brain which has gone beyond the limit of the brake, under the sway of morbid exciting causes. Attacks of intermittent mania, of epilepsy, of hysteria, and of alcoholism are a realization of this hypothesis. When the murders or the thefts committed under the influence of such disorders are studied by the courts, it is more difficult than in the preceding cases to decide whether the tempting force did or did

[1] When a character which is savage in the beginning is advantageously transformed, having become more social, the new "myself" which results from this beneficial mental alienation is still more responsible than the former one, for being due as a general rule to social action, it is in every case more fitted than the other for the life of society.

not exceed the normal force of an ordinarily efficient moral brake. In fact, this force is here hidden within the individual. However, the estimation of its intensity up to a certain point is attained by means of a comparison of the symptoms which show this force, with the entirely similar manifestations of madness which have already been observed.

It may also happen that the external or internal, enveloping or nervous impulse, remaining within normal bounds, the train may leave the rails, because the brake has become rusted or has been broken. This is the case of that moral perversion without impulsive attacks, which, for example, precedes the outburst of general paralysis. It is given the name of moral madness.

Finally, it may happen that the impulse not exceeding the desired degree, and the brake retaining its habitual force, the accident takes place as a consequence of an error committed by the signals of the line. Here we have the likeness of delirium of the intellect [1] which is the most striking, but perhaps not the most frequent form of madness.

This is not all. Generally the very cause which rouses exceptional impulses smashes or weakens the moral brake and disturbs the understanding. Thus all the causes of misfortune are here encountered at the same time.

In all these hypotheses, which from our point of view exhaust every category of mental alienation, the individual is irresponsible, not because his action was *inevitably* determined or caused, but because it was determined by a cause external to the "myself," to the social being. The whole problem will be to know whether, in certain cases, the morbid impulse not being very pronounced, having been such that a good brake could have resisted it, the absolutely abnormal weakness of the individual's brake is to be attributed to a pathological evolution or is not rather the result of a whole life of vices and the lesser infractions of the social laws; of a whole series of acts which did not have madness as their cause, but which are to be explained in the same way as are the customary acts for which the individual is responsible; so that, as St. Augustine says, by means of his "bad will" the individual has in the end lost his "power for good."

Such are the problems which madness gives rise to. Having

[1] For example, someone suffering from hallucinations believes that he hears someone insult him, call him "bugger," "pederast," like a man judged by the Criminal Court of Pas-de-Calais, in 1855 (cited by Tardieu), and kills this man.

said this much, we must admit, in accordance with common sense, that in the great majority of cases the impulses, be they from without or from within, are inferior to the force of the moral resistance which the individual harbors within himself, but which he is far from making use of all the time. What shall we indeed say of this most frequent of cases, where the individual, in the same way as the fireman at the Opéra-Comique who had a faucet close at hand which he could have made use of to extinguish the fire at its inception and to which he did not give a thought, does not think of bringing into play the moral energies virtually enclosed within his nature or within his memory and yields to a temptation against which he would have struggled successfully had he wished to do so? There is here this difference between the will and the fireman at the Opéra-Comique that the latter really did not think of turning on the faucet, because he never had to do this simple thing under similar circumstances, whereas the will is always brought into play from the beginning,—because that is the essential part it plays, as all the psychologists show, especially Ribot,—to resist our desires. Thus, if the will has not had as its object, at the opportune moment, the employment of moral forces to which it held the key, it is because the "myself," of which it is the purest expression, was in sympathy with the tempting cause and *appropriated* it to itself, *making it its own*. Undoubtedly the "myself," *this being so, was not able to wish that which it has not wished*. But this proves precisely that the "myself" *is bad*.

It is one thing, therefore, *not to have been able to wish* to resist temptations and another *to have wished to but to have been unable to resist them*. There are here two kinds of necessity which are very distinct. The former shows the perversity of the "myself," the latter bears witness to its misfortune. A ruinous inactivity is called a fault when it is due to laziness; it is called misfortune when it is due to an infirmity. An injurious act is called a fault when it is voluntarily committed; it is called a misfortune when it is carried out during an attack of madness. Can it be said that the difference arises from the fact that one is not free not to be inactive by reason of laziness, or not to wish to do an evil act? But however little of a determinist one may be, one is forced to admit that in many cases laziness is incurable and bad will is irresistible.

Now do laziness and crime seem less worthy of blame to us when they appertain to the very character of the individual? Far from it. Why then do an incurable laziness and an inborn criminality arouse our indignation, whereas a permanent infirmity and an incurable homicidal madness arouse our compassion? I say that it is because infirmity and madness are always strangers to the "myself," even when they have taken root forever within us. A chronic madness is no more a new personality than is a chronic state of anarchy, like the one which held sway in France during the Hundred Years War, a new government. Though an illness may be prolonged, it does not follow that the physiological nature of an individual is to be ill. Although a madman and an epileptic may remain mad and epileptic all their lives, their essential physiological nature does not cease to protest against the morbid oppression which annihilates it and to repel the acts accomplished under the constraint of this yoke. Even when the individual brings with him at birth a latent predisposition to madness which must some day burst forth and drag him down to crime, and then to death, one cannot say that this organic vice constitutes a part of him himself. This germ, hostile and with murderous intentions, is contrary to him and consequently a stranger to him, like the traitor which a secret society numbers among the members who were its founders and who is soon to lead it to its destruction.

Maudsley, in "Crime and Madness," cites cases in which wrongdoing occurring in a hitherto honest life is but the symptom of a general paralysis which is beginning,[1] which is, moreover, recognizable to an experienced eye, by a slight impediment in speech together with an unequal dilation of the pupils; the experienced physician is able by means of these indications to foretell exactly the fatal progress of the fearful malady thus revealed. What is the misdeed committed in a case of this sort by an unfortunate who does not himself realize the mischance of which he is the victim? It is one of the proofs of the fact that this individual is each day losing a fragment of himself, today the moral sense, tomorrow his understanding, soon all the senses one after another, and that, having become insane in the true meaning of the word, he will therein find death. Moral perversion, aberra-

[1] General paralysis is the illness of our time. Its progress is parallel to that of our civilization. According to the statistical researches of *Régis* ("Manuel des maladies mentales"), there are three men suffering from general paralysis and two women in every hundred insane persons in the country; twenty-three paralytic men in every hundred insane workmen in towns; thirty-three paralytic men and two and one-half women in every hundred insane persons of the upper classes of society. Among the latter the proportion of men is *thirteen times* greater than that of women.

tion of the judgment and the senses, imbecility, as well as difficulty of pronunciation and the condition of the pupils are but the phases of a morbid dissolution. Can one perchance say that an illness which results in the death of an individual is an essential part of him? No. Nothing can be an essential part of us except that by means of which we live, that which causes us to be and to endure. A man born immoral does not die because of his immorality, he lives by means of it; the longevity of born criminals has been demonstrated.

These are distinctions which have in them nothing subtle and about which a society at the same time has no occasion to be anxious so long as they are not perceived. But the day it becomes sufficiently enlightened to see them, or that alienists and psychologists have placed them before its eyes, it ought to take them into account. As the light of analysis is beginning to penetrate within this complex whole called the individual, it ought to do as it did formerly, when the family, another complexity, allowed itself to be analyzed little by little and to be resolved into individuals who could be separately punished.

§ 34. (II) Internal duality of the insane: Félida and Rousseau. Responsibility or irresponsibility of great men.

One no longer dares to pronounce the name of Félida, so ordinary has her peculiarity become after so many instances of it. I must therefore apologize for here recalling, in passing, the case of this celebrated unknown, who had two alternating spirits, not in an artificial manner, as certain people who have been hypnotized have, but naturally; two spirits separated by a short interval of vertigo and lethargy, the one sane and good, the other morbid and evil. But although in the end the evil one carried her away in point of duration, I look upon the good one as alone being the normal spirit, and I hold the responsibility of Félida as incited by the acts of the latter quite otherwise than as by the acts of the former.

A psychological phenomenon which can be likened to the preceding one, and which was of vital importance in the history of the last century, is offered us by Jean-Jacques Rousseau. He, too, always had two spirits which dominated him alternately. The first is quiet, frank, and confiding, naïvely affectionate, innocently egotistical, indolent, and careless; this is the spirit of the musician, the poet, and the botanist within him. It is found again identically, it is seen to be reborn at every period of his life. It is awakened at the age of five by the old romances told him by his Aunt Suzon, blooms at the first glance from Madame de Warens; at Turin, at the house of the young tradeswoman; at Lyons, under the starry sky. It rests and is master of itself at Charmettes, inspires the "Devin du Village," is finally concentrated in study and the love of nature at Motiers, in the island of St. Peter, and until the time of Ermenonville. It is like a line of rest through which he passes and repasses, or like an inland lake which he does nothing but cross, driven by an unconquerable wind. The second is gloomy, false, and mistrustful; it must have invaded the other by degrees, have led it to the delusion characterized by persecution and to the final suicide. It can be thus followed all through his life.

This belief in the nature of a hallucination, which was his undoing, in the form of a sort of European league formed against him and in which great ministers and even his most devoted friends would have participated, is not a passing straying of his being limited to his last years; and the thing which proves absolutely that the germ of terror and hallucination existed in him is that, admitting a thousand times that he had been mistaken in his suspicions—with regard, for example, to the Jesuits, whom he had accused of misrepresenting the "Émile" and of conspiring against this book at court at a time when their expulsion was imminent,—he never cures himself of his fatal inclination. One sees this aberration recurring under different and periodical forms, even at Charmettes, where the reading of the works of the Jansenists gives him a mortal dread of Hell, or the reading of the works of physiologists gives him so great a fear of all the illnesses whose description he has read, that he undertakes a long and expensive journey to Montpellier in order to have an absolutely imaginary "tumor of the heart" cured. Would one not say from reading his account of the happy period when his whole life was wrapped up in his books, his garden, his flowers, his turtle doves and the love of Madame de Warens, that his heart at that time never for one instant ceased to be of the same color as the Italian sky? A piece of verse,[1] composed by him in this much regretted period, shows us that this happiness was not without a cloud. One there sees the same contrast which astonishes us in his other works: the words "plot," "crime," "fury," "hatred," "remorse,"

[1] It is entitled "Le Verger des Charmettes."

"punishments," "horror," the thought of hidden enemies who threatened his home and his friend, were noticeable therein alongside of the oft-repeated words "innocence" and "virtue." A strange contrast of which the Revolution, its image and its child, was soon to be the violent and terrible development.

This idea of a plot thus already hovered over Rousseau as a youth, before settling upon him; it twisted within his heart, like those black specks of enfeebled sight, which are a slight inconvenience, until they become fixed and foreshadow blindness. Conversely, at the height of the storm which troubled his old age, the indolent sense of security which had been with him in all the tribulations of his unstable life did not desert him. Driven from France, a fugitive and in disguise, running the risk at each moment of being discovered, he wrote the "Lévite d'Ephraïm" in post-houses, a work of pure imagination, wherein, a thing to be remarked, there is not to be found a single word of any return to himself. And, later still, after that hail of stones which came near to being his finish at Motiers, having taken refuge for a few days in a small island where religious animosity does not allow him to sleep long in peace, he forgets his troubles, lies down for entire afternoons at the bottom of a boat, and there goes to sleep, happy, as he used to go to sleep formerly when he was twenty, without money to pay for a bed, on the threshold of a garden, on the banks of the Rhône or the Saône, in that delicious night which he has described for us in his most bewitching style.

Only, Rousseau would not have been the man of genius who made his mark in revolutionary France and left a lasting stamp upon French literature, if his two natures had only been able to clash and to come together in a sterile manner, like those of so many ordinary lunatics. They often penetrated each other or harmonized with each other, the one lending its strength to the other, which tempered it with its mildness or reflected in it its own light; and their accord, which meant for us masterpieces at the age of virile maturity, caused the glory of Jean-Jacques, as their final discord and their schism, during the age which followed, caused his misfortune. Now, although the evil nature here again finally smothered the good one, the good one is the true one, and if the shame which hangs over the life of the great writer spring from the other, it should but feebly stain his memory. It is, however, to a certain extent to be imputed to him, precisely because of the partial accord and of the reciprocal penetration of his two personalities.

This would be the occasion, if the subject would not carry us too far, to deal with a difficult question; the responsibility or the irresponsibility of great men. We will only say a word with regard to it. There is assuredly no one less free than the great man; and, however guilty he may be, however disastrous his act may have been, we should, as a consequence, absolve him from the point of view of the old school. Poet, soldier, magistrate, artist, heresiarch, publicist, engineer, no matter the way into which he flings himself and along which he carries us, this spurrer on of societies is never anything but an *impulsive man*. Sometimes his greatness is nothing but the opportuneness of what is really his madness. He then becomes the most dangerous of the insane and at the same time the least responsible, as his madness feeds on the very applause with which it is received. How many madmen and madwomen have there been whose names have been inscribed in letters of gold in the list of martyrs of parties or of cults, from Marat and Cola of Rienzi to so many famous visionaries! More often one sees fictitious great men whose sole merit is that they so much resemble the mob that it cannot help gazing at itself and admiring itself in a *generic portrait* which has been a success up to this point. Their artificial superiority is thus nothing but condensed mediocrity, raised to a great power. Here the condition of similarity demanded by our theory is admirably fulfilled; but to make up for it the condition of identity is so little fulfilled, and the overestimated person is so much a slave of his flatterers, so constantly overthrown and changing, that the benefit of extenuating circumstances should generally be granted, and even with a liberal hand, to the popular idols with which we are dealing.

This is not the case with the true great man, of the one which the crowd does not create and does not guide, but who rather in a sense creates it and most certainly directs it. For Sainte-Beuve has given an illuminating definition: "Genius is a king who creates his people." In order to appreciate the accuracy of this formula, it must be applied not only to those kings of literature of whom the great critic meant to speak, but to the kings of thought, of politics, of the military art, of industry, etc. Everywhere the genius is presented to us as a fruitful originality, as an unusual thing which, while thrusting itself upon us, becomes a superior being recognized by all. He is not great because he is born in conformity with the multitude, but because he reforms it and little by little makes it conform to himself. Hugo, in this sense, created his public, slowly, by an irresistible overflowing of his style of mind, of his manner of verses, even of his bad habits, strange coins in 1830, currency today. Darwin, as well, engendered the immense number of his readers, and also Spencer, and before them Plato, Aristotle, and so many others. In the same way Napoleon — reread Taine on this point — created his administrative and military France; Mahomet gave birth to Islam. Imagine a manufacturer who, in order to make of it a new outlet for his product, peoples a new world; or else imagine a great culprit who, in order thereby to secure his acquittal, himself constitutes his own tribunal.

Such is the great man. After his triumph his victims have disappeared, he is no longer judged except by his children. Racine was judged and consecrated by the classics born of him; Plato by the Platonics; Luther by the Protestants or the free-thinkers who were more or less affected by Protestantism; Hugo by his disciples; Napoleon by his soldiers and his legists; Darwin by the Darwinians. Is this right? It is a necessity. If the great man is responsible, he cannot be so in so far as he is a great man except to those who resemble him in the direction which has made his greatness. He is a stranger as far as others are concerned. With reason is it said that he is above the law, I understand by this the law of literature, of art, of industry, of politics, the usages and customs which it is his mission to reform; but he should be judged by his own laws, by virtue of the very reforms which he has introduced, of the rules which he has laid down and which he sometimes transgresses. With him the condition of identity is realized in its highest degree in the originality which characterizes him, by his constant pursuit of a fixed goal, a fixed idea; but the condition of similarity is only realized to a certain extent. His resemblance to other men, under the special relation which fame manifests through him, is of a kind which stands by itself and creates in him a responsibility which also stands alone. It is a one-sided and not a reciprocal resemblance. He does not imitate, he makes others imitate him. Thus he is only halfway in relation with the other men who have *become* like him. In reality he is born, on the side which distinguishes him, *extra-social;* or, rather, he is born on the borders of society of which he seems to constitute a part and of nature and the different societies which he looks upon with curiosity. A learned man who discovers truths contrary to dogma, a traveler who brings with him new usages, an inventor who renders old processes useless, he has lived alone, a wanderer, independent of his sphere; socially he plays the part which the peripheral cells of living bodies play in an organic way, anxious sentinels always ready to gather warnings from without in order to transmit them to the interior. He is not entirely extraneous to the social world, as is the madman; he does not live steeped in it, as does the ordinary man, as does the criminal himself who is rather an anti-social being than an extra-social being; he keeps close to this world and enlightens it without penetrating into it. Whence, when he is called upon to give an account of himself before the jury of history, arises the peculiarity of his attitude. This creator-king would surely scarce be able to participate in the royal privilege, which is always fictitious, of irresponsibility; but those who alone have the right to impute to him as a crime the abuse of his power proceed from him! They strike at themselves in condemning him. The more numerous they are, the more responsible he is; thus his responsibility, in the same way as the recognition which is due him, increases with his success. This is what historic common sense had already decided, and it is a good thing to note that the logic of our system leads us to the same result. But let us leave genius at this point and return to madness.

§ 35. (III) Duel within the insane. Psychology of the mystics. The various forms of madness.

Every kind of madness is preceded by a cerebral disturbance, by a mental anxiety which denotes the intrusion of a strange element, the contradiction from within to which the subject is a prey. "A great change of character," such is, as Maudsley reiterates, the first and necessary symptom of madness, and especially of moral madness. It is necessary that the individual "be no longer the same." If one had any doubt, moreover, as to the internal duality which constitutes insanity, one has but to read in the writings of the alienists the picture of these terrible states of consciousness wherein the madman struggles against the temptation which obsesses him. The best proof that one has two individualities is that one fights a duel against oneself.[1]

[1] This duel, this inner struggle, is the most constant characteristic of madness under every form. In what, for example, does drunkenness pure and simple differ from dipsomania, which is only a variety of madness? In that the drunkard takes pleasure in it and enjoys feeling himself carried away by the desire to drink, his will and his passion being in accord, whereas the dipsomaniac is compelled, in

Maudsley has been present at these psychological combats and this is how he speaks of them: "Like the demoniac of old, into whom the impure spirit had entered, he [the madman] is possessed by a power which constrains him to do an act of which he has the greatest fear and the greatest horror; and sometimes, when crushed by this incessant struggle, and in a fearful agony, he consults the physician, his appeal to science passes anything one could imagine which is most sad and moving." Honest hypnotic subjects offer the same spectacle [1] when an immoral act which is absolutely repugnant to their nature is suggested to them. "One could scarce imagine," continues Maudsley, "unless one had seen it with one's own eyes, in the case of impulse to suicide for example, with what industry is prepared, with what determination is consummated the fatal act, by the very one who, during the entire time never ceases to have a horror of it." Calmeil gives an instance of a son who, in order to resist the unhealthy impulse to kill his mother whom he dearly loved, had enlisted, and, having returned home, had begged to be shut up in an asylum. Analogous cases are not very rare. If, in spite of all the precautions ordered by themselves, sufferers of this kind commit the crime which they dread, must we then, in conformity with the wishes of the new Italian school, send these unfortunates to the "manicomio criminale," to the house of the criminal insane, pellmell with the most repulsive scoundrels? Obviously this would be an enormity.

So madness is the redoubling of the person, something like the moral equivalent of a double monstrosity. Now let us suppose that one of the Siamese twins should be a member of an association to which the other remained a stranger and that the second one, and not the first, had incurred the penalties embodied within the statutes of the society against the members convicted of an infraction of the rules. If this infraction had been committed by the brother who was not a member while the one who was a

spite of himself, to get drunk, becomes saddened thereby and is caused to suffer. In what does the incendiary differ from the pyromaniac? The debauchee from the erotomaniac? The thief from the kleptomaniac, etc.? In an analogous characteristic. It is to be observed that, by means of researches entirely independent of those of the alienists, Binet and other authors have to their own astonishment arrived at the discovery that, within the normal man himself, there exists a subconscious person distinct from the conscious person. It is especially to be seen in the movements of persons who are absorbed. See on this subject the remarkable works of *Binet* ("Revue philosophique," February, March, August, 1890; "Revue des Deux Mondes," February, 1891).

[1] See, for example, the works of *Beaunis*, *passim*.

member was asleep, the latter should purely and simply be acquitted; this is the case of absolute madness.[1] If, the second one having wished to commit the wrongful act, the first one, awakened, had sought to prevent him, but in a weak way, and without making use of all the forces which were known to be at his command, there would be occasion for a condemnation, but not to the same degree as if, instead of allowing the thing to be done where little would have been necessary to prevent it, the culprit had taken the initiative in the misdeed. Finally, if the one not a member, while acting, merely placed his superior strength at the disposal of the evil desires of the one who was a member, we would have to condemn the latter with less of extenuating circumstances. Times when there are disturbances are full of these cases of dangerous madness which, auxiliaries of a native wickedness and hatred, add strength and audacity to the wish to injure. They carry out what the "myself" has wished.

At the same time is it right, even in such cases, to punish the will which is the accomplice of the illness, as in the Middle Ages in Germany and Italy they used to punish the instigators of assassinations by means of procuration, so numerous at that period and in those countries, or as we ought to punish the man addicted to the abuse of alcohol who, having had experience of the murderous character of his drunkenness, purposely gets drunk in order to kill someone, or the hypnotic subjects of the Salpêtrière, who, according to Charcot, have some one of their companions hypnotically suggest to them the petty larcenies which they want to commit without having the courage to do so in the normal state. No, for one does not become mad at will, and if the "myself" has too well received its guest who has become its bravo, it has not been the seeker; but Charcot's patients must have begged a person who was agreeable to do so to produce for them the suggestion in question; the drunkard in question wished for his drunkenness, and the Sicilian lords who revenged themselves by means of the gun of a brigand deliberately resorted to him.

The psychology of the mystics, interesting in an entirely different way in many respects to that of the insane, might here

[1] The common sense of peoples has always seen clearly that the acts of the madman did not emanate from him; and it is this belief, which is at bottom a very just one, which has, at all times and in all countries, given rise to the explanation of madness by means of a demoniacal possession. When they saw a man acting in a manner contrary to his character, they supposed that *another spirit* had entered into him, and they were not very far wrong.

furnish us with more than one figure of comparison. It abounds in strange things and in infinite delicacies, which are not all morbid. The impossible love which it describes for us, in the same terms, of Plotinus for St. Theresa, and which it shows us to have been recompensed at long intervals by unhoped-for delights, by the incomprehensible possession of its divine object, is itself but a redoubling of the single "myself." It is not necessary, in order to be convinced of this, to be raised to the summit of a full ecstasy, it is enough to stop at the less troubled states, of persuasive gentleness, to which Marcus Aurelius attained, or in which Fénelon delights, and, after him, Maine de Biran. But what a difference there is between this internal duality which the visitation of the ineffable god creates for them, that is to say the sudden novelty of their joy without motive, and the separation of the person due to madness! Auto-suggestion, if you will, imaginary vision, or the *hearing* of one's own voice, the timbre of which has become altered, it does not matter. The mystic "myself," just as the "myself" which loves and is transformed by the agitation of a fixed image, is only redoubled in order that it may be reunited to itself in a pleasant way; the insane "myself" struggles, tears itself ordinarily, and, even when it enters into a compact with its internal enemy, is unhappy and anxious.

A man afflicted with the monomania of suicide has been seen to avoid getting into a railway carriage for fear of yielding to the irresistible temptation of throwing himself out of the doorway. Has one ever seen a lover fleeing from the opportunity of meeting the woman he loves and thus reanimate the ardent dream wherein his thought is being ruined? And always, however intimate may be the *union*, however dear to the heart may be the alteration caused by it to the mystic spirit, this spirit is altered, this is enough for it not to be entirely responsible for the eccentricities which it may commit, even willingly and gladly. I will say the same of the carrying away by passion. A miser who, having fallen in love, spends foolishly, is more to be pitied than blamed. The "myself," if it sins in such a case, should be judged to be but an accomplice; the chief author, passion, whose source is essentially organic and not social, escapes from the effects of society.

In cases of melancholia, of lypemania, of hypochondria, organic disturbances give rise to new states of consciousness which, not being in any way connected with the system of habitual states, are first of all attributed by the patient to someone other than himself. "At first," says Ribot,[1] "this new manner of being seems to the individual to be strange, to be something outside of his "myself." Little by little, by force of his becoming accustomed to it, it makes a place for itself within the "myself," becomes an integral part of it, changes its constitution and, if it be of an intrusive nature, transforms it in its entirety." But for a systematized, coherent "myself," molded and fashioned by the social surroundings, there has been substituted in this way a contradictory, incoherent, savage "myself" which is unlike those which surround it, and consequently is irresponsible.

It is not the same thing as regards puberty; here sensations and feelings hitherto unknown break out in the person and take possession thereof in an imperious manner. Their incorporation is normal and the "myself" which is transformed by them, far from being less logical and less sociable than the previous "myself," is to be distinguished by a far superior degree of finality and sociability. Also its responsibility has increased. Conversely, castration, which prolongs a childish "myself" within an adult body, or one which has remained so in many ways, and which makes a masculine "myself" effeminate, has a tendency to lessen responsibility. The guilty eunuch has a right to the same indulgence as the woman or the youth. Let us remark, with respect to this, how deep is the mental transformation effected by this barbarous mutilation. For madness changes the person within us, but more often than not without changing sex or age. The renewed spirit which it inaugurates stays feminine in the case of a woman, or masculine in the case of a man, youthful in the case of a young man, or senile in the case of an old man, excepting in the very exceptional case of those sexual aberrations of which Glay has made such a thorough study.[2]

Madness, like magnetism, may be said to have two opposite poles, between which are shared or are met with in a superficial way the forms of mental alienation which, by reason of their cause or of their evolution, are the most heterogeneous. I have called "mania" and "melancholia" the proud exaltation of the imaginary all-powerfulness and the oppression of despair; two contradictory states which alternate in the madness which is called successive. From the point of view of responsibility, it is difficult, if not im-

[1] "Revue philosophique," August, 1884, "Les bases affectives de la personalité."

[2] "Revue philosophique," January, 1884.

possible, to decide which one of these two deviations of the "myself," by reason of *excess* or of *deficiency*, by reason of equally sickly optimism or pessimism, is greater than the other. Between fury and stupor, between the perturbed individual who struggles feverishly all day long in his cell or his yard, and the excited individual who never tires of absurd purposes and senseless whims, and the despairing individual who, huddled in one corner of his cell or his yard, not eating, not moving, stupefied, terrified, follows in his conscience the unending spectacle of frightful hallucinations and dramas, there seems to be a great difference. But in the one case as in the other, the personality is broken; broken also is the relation of the person with surrounding society.

There is, in lunatic asylums, a third category of individuals who, as to their general aspect, differ in nothing from ordinary people. These are the *partial madmen.* The characteristic of partial madness is not to be tied down to a constant ground of excitation or depression. Furthermore, delirium is as well defined and as limited as in cases of general madness. But, outside of his special form of delirium, the partial madman reasons and acts like everybody else, and for the most part regains his responsibility; the general madman always thinks and acts as a sick man. Now we shall prove that in having become localized in this way madness has become strengthened. General madness is curable, partial madness is not. Partial madness is qualified as "essential" by Dr. Régis. We also see, by means of the observation of its phases, that the result of this morbid work is really to implant a new "myself" within the old one. Its progress, according to this author, is always as follows: 1st. Period of analysis, the patient feels symptoms which frighten him, strange feelings (hypochondriacal madness). 2d. Delirious explanation, the patient accounts to himself for this thing either humanly (delirium of persecution), or divinely, by the action of supernatural beings (mystic madness). 3d. Finally *his personality seems to him to be transformed,* he imagines himself to be now a great personage, now a god or a demigod, the Virgin or Antichrist (ambitious madness).

Still looking at it from the point of view with which we are concerned, it is useful here to establish a distinction of an entirely different nature and to investigate whether madness has been a veritable upsetting or has been but a pathological reinforcement of the primitive character. There are cases in which it substitutes violence, mistrust, and hatred for mildness, confidence, and kindness; at other times it is nothing, more often like drunkenness, but exaggeration of the hypertrophy of a natural tendency. Such a man has always been hard, unfeeling, he has become cruel; such another, born irascible, has become frenzied, impulsive; a third, a libertine in temperament, has become a veritable satyr. Generally speaking madmen have begun by having a remarkable egoism, which their madness accentuates beyond all measure. It is evident that madness, when it makes us fall in the direction in which we were leaning, is not so profound an alienation as when it upsets us in a contrary direction, and that it does not make us irresponsible to the same degree.[1]

§ 36. (IV) Epilepsy, intermittent madness. Analogous illnesses of the social body.

After the above developments we could dispense with a discussion of epilepsy, if this nervous affection were not very well fitted to make us understand what mental alienation is. Epilepsy is an intermittent form of madness, which is often seen to come into existence, to grow, and to die. The days which precede the attack are marked by a change of humor in the patient; in him is accumulated the darkening of a storm, a sort of *nimbus* which insists upon bursting. It bursts in three ways, as Maudsley and the majority of alienists observe. The crisis, in fact, only termi-

[1] With respect to this, *Lévy-Bruhl*, in the very kindly article which he has devoted to the present work ("Revue philosophique," December, 1890), makes an objection which demands a reply. "Such an individual," he says, "has not become frenzied because he was irascible, or 'strupator' because he was a libertine; on the contrary it is very probable that he was irascible because he already had in him the germ of impulsive madness, or a libertine because he already felt the influence of his sexual aberration. Hence, should not these cases be interpreted in the following manner: an insanity of a slow and progressive kind [this is the most frequent sort] which only makes the individual incapable of living in society from a certain moment of time when it manifests itself through some criminal act, but which persisted under the form of a power which became ever more ready to pass into the act?" There is here a question of fact which it belongs to the alienists to solve and which often makes us feel the necessity of their intervention in the domain of penal justice. Should we, however, decide that, in the event of this progressive alteration of the character by its very reinforcement in a certain sense taking place to the extent of a complete rupture of the person's equilibrium and its downfall into out and out madness, the irresponsibility belonging to this latter state ought to retroact in going back to the previous states? No, for, though it may be the cause of the alteration which has taken place, the only question of importance from our point of view is to know from what moment it sufficed to destroy the person's equilibrium. It is difficult but not impossible to tell. Besides, every gradual and continued change gives rise to difficulties on the same order as these.

nates in one of the following discharges, only to form again later on: 1st. *Convulsion*, the succumbing of the patient who struggles against himself; this is the most usual result. 2d. A *fixed idea*, a strong hallucination which manifests itself and which takes possession of the subject. [1] 3d. A *fixed desire*, an irresistible need of committing some act of violence, such as a murder or a rape. Shall I be reproached for an abuse of analogy, if I take the liberty of comparing epilepsy in all this, in order to explain it better, to its social equivalent, to that great intermittent disturbance which, almost periodically, agitates certain European societies? We all know that this agitation — which is sometimes salutary, in which respect it differs from the other — is always produced by the appearance and the imitative propagation of some belief or of some desire opposed to the convictions and the needs upon which rests the order of things established.

Now, the disturbance having thus been amassed, when literature and the press, science and the arts have long set forth the germ of contradiction with which we are concerned — the germ of Christianity under the Roman Empire, for example, the germ of free investigation in the sixteenth century, the germ of free-thinking in the eighteenth, the germ of socialism in the nineteenth, — either settles itself of its own accord if it is not deep seated and intense, which reminds us of the case of masked epilepsy, or else is bound to result in one of these three issues: 1st. A civil war, social convulsion. 2d. An enthusiasm, an extravagant cult, a fixed and unjustifiable faith in a man or an idea, in a family or in a dogma, true delirium of a nation; it is thus that every apotheosis, every dynasty and powerful religion is to be

[1] "In the same way as the function of the motor centres," says *Maudsley* (page 131, "Crime et Folie," Paris, 1874; a French translation of "Responsibility in Mental Disease," London, 1873), "is motion, the most noble function of the nervous centres is thought; and just as a morbid state of the motor centres produces convulsive movements, a morbid state of the psychic centres produces that which, for lack of a more appropriate term, we may well call 'the convulsion of the idea.'" This mental convulsion is *delirium*, which in this respect corresponds to *chorea*. — Furthermore, while spreading itself, the morbid state of the idea centres is inevitably communicated to the centres of motion. Is thus to reduce everything to the idea of motion to materialize the spirit? I do not think so. In fact motion is but the innate symbol of the change *directed towards an object*. That is the reason why every motion is necessarily divided for us into rectilinear motions. The straight line which vain attempts have been made to define has as its essential property the idea of the object. It essentially implies an *objective point*. To say that all motion elementarily takes place in a straight line is to say that every phenomenon is composed of finalities which are elementary or complex, hidden or visible, "sub-real" or real.

explained,[1] that is, like one of the inevitable solutions of a problem set by social logic. 3d. Finally, an outside war, which, without any other usefulness moreover, offers itself as a necessary consequence of the internal difficulties of a people. How many unjustifiable aggressions have there been whose true cause is a contradiction within a society! In all this it is apparent that nothing is explainable except by means of the division of the social group into two parts which struggle together and one of which ends in prevailing, owing to civil war, to the invasion of dynastic or dogmatic belief, or the warlike attack of neighbors. Thus epilepsy, and in the same way madness,[2] can be, in no matter what form the manifestation takes place, but the result of the schism within, of a combat which is, so to speak, fratricidal.

Furthermore, whatever may be the outlet, the channel through which the epileptic attack escapes, the patient cannot be responsible for the acts committed during the time it lasts. The second outlet is no less formidable than are the first and third. It is thus that the fanaticism of a visionary people can make them commit as great excesses as can the fury of civil wars and of battlefields. During the night of the second to the third of February, 1886, a man named B . . . committed in Belgium a five-fold assassination on the persons of divers members of his family, and it was demonstrated by medico-legal experts that he had acted during a nocturnal attack of epilepsy, under the domination of a hallucination. He had thought that he saw two murderers against whom he had sought to defend his life by throwing at their heads the weight of his clock. He was shut up in an asylum. Surely there is no one more dangerous than an insane man of this type, but no one more irresponsible morally. Let us observe in passing, this fact, that attacks of epilepsy occur

[1] How many times, among convulsionary peoples, and when least expected, do attacks of delirium burst forth, and are reproduced those prostrations and bowing of the knee before an idol, which is either abstract or alive, which are enigmas to the historians! These latter, when these infatuations persist, never have any doubt but that the object of the general adoration has a value proportional to its success. It is as though one were to judge of the beauty of a woman according to the passion which she inspires. The *heroism* of a man (in the sense in which Carlyle understands this word) is more often than not but a subjective quality, I say *socially subjective.*

[2] It is a remarkable and instructive fact, says Maudsley, that the convulsive energy of the homicidal impulse (in the case of the insane) is often preceded by a morbid feeling originating in some part of the body and rising from thence even to the brain, absolutely similar to the one which precedes the epileptic attack and which is known in medicine by the name of "aura epileptica."

especially during the night, and after midnight. "During twenty consecutive months," says Echeverria,[1] "seventy-eight epileptics had two thousand eight hundred and ninety-six attacks between two and five o'clock in the morning, and only ninety-two attacks between two o'clock in the afternoon and two o'clock in the morning." May it not be that the great frequency of nocturnal crimes is, to a certain extent — to a very small extent at any rate — attributable to this cause? What is certain, and what must be conceded to Lombroso, is that there is within every epileptic virtually a murderer. But this murderer is an unfortunate and not a guilty man. And the danger which he presents does not thus give us the right to infer that the epileptic and the criminal are identical.

§ 37. (V) Consolidated madness. Moral madness, state opposed to true madness. Heredity, in no way contrary to individual responsibility.

We have not finished with the difficulties which the responsibility of neuropaths gives rise to. The problem is liable to become complicated, as we shall see. The transformation which is so frequent, of over-excited and general madness, of mania, into a special form of madness, into monomania,[2] is at the same time its limitation and its consolidation, as we already know. By this means the "myself" appropriates its ills to itself, and identifies them for itself; but this does not mean that the individual thus becomes more responsible; for though he may have come to an agreement with himself up to a certain point, he has more and more detached himself from his fellow-men, whom he resembles less and less.

Now the phases of madness, instead of unfolding themselves in the course of a single life, are able, like very much enlarged waves of the sea whose breadth exceeds the length of a vessel, to take in several successive generations. To a maniac father, insane on all points, succeeds a son who is only eccentric and exaggerated in certain respects. The latter is a monomaniac born such and who has not become such, an attenuated monomaniac moreover. Here the appropriation of the eccentricity or of the exaggeration in question by the "myself" of the individual is far more profound than in the preceding case, and it follows from the statistics of

[1] "Archives de l'Anthropologie criminelle," No. 9.

[2] In the same way, general melancholia is often resolved into "lypemania," to make use of the expression of Esquirol, into "chronic melancholia," as the modern alienists say. These two transformations recall the termination of epileptic trouble in a fixed idea or a fixed need.

Morel that whereas simple hereditary madmen are cured fifty-eight times out of a hundred, the degenerate madmen in question are absolutely incurable. This anomaly, this "originality" of the individual, to make use of the usual euphemism, is essential to him;[1] but it creates a partial dissimilarity in this respect, between other men and himself.

If, therefore, it consists, for example, in the quest of decorations or superficial honors of some sort with an unreasonable greediness, or in experiencing strange appetites in love, the wrongful acts which he may commit in order to satisfy these depraved passions can be imputed to him, for, on the one hand, he actually is a member of society, and on the other hand, he has wished for these wrongful forms of satisfaction, he was not even able not to want them and has thus shown the inherent vice in his constitution. But they can only partially be imputed to him, by reason of his partial heterogeneousness. It is not because of his not being free. Let us suppose that another accused has given way to a constraint which is just as overpowering, but caused by a motive which is very well known in its surroundings, by the passion for gold in mercantile surroundings, by the passion for the circus or the theatre in the surroundings of gladiators or of strolling players, by the passion for statues and pictures in artistic surroundings. The delinquent, in this case, which seems strange, will seem far less to be excused in the eyes of everybody than our absolute monomaniac.[2]

[1] It is to be observed, with Maudsley, that those eccentricities which, were they to occur during the course of his life, would be "a sign of evil omen and would presage a serious end," can, if they be innate, last in the case of the individual till the end of his days "without disturbing the lucidity of his reason in every other respect." Precisely because monomania, even when acquired and not innaté, is an *assimilation of its insanity by the "myself,"* it is very rarely curable. In order to uproot it it would be necessary, as is well said by this same author, whom I cannot too often cite, "to tear out the foundations of the character." Nevertheless it is sometimes cured, which proves, in spite of everything, that the assimilation with which we are concerned is not absolute. And, let us observe, it is more readily cured when it is sad than when it is joyous, for in the former case the very suffering of the spirit proves that "its derangement has an extrinsic origin." At the beginning of general paralysis the patient experiences a depression, arising from a painful feeling of trouble; if after this an excitation, a feeling of pride and joyfulness bursts forth in him, this change indicates that the malady has become firmly rooted. The inevitable end in which every form of incurable madness terminates is *dementia*, "acquired imbecility." Dementia is not simply a dividing up of the "myself," like madness; it is the parceling out, the crumbling of the "myself" into as many fragments as there are absurd ideas and tendencies placed alongside of one another in the same brain; an absolute incoherence which may be compared to the complete anarchy to which perpetual civil wars will lead a people.

[2] It is the incoherent and *unsocial* character rather than the irresistible

It is true that in the one case as in the other the irresistible character of the inclination to which the individual has yielded is due to the insufficiency or to the absence of the moral *brake* of which I have spoken above. We must therefore say a word as regards this *moral madness,* so much contested, which would consist in a cerebral gap or lesion confined to the seat of the emotional feelings, without any alteration of the intellectual abilities.[1] Let us clearly distinguish the case where there may be a gap, that is to say innate absence, from that in which there may be a lesion, that is to say a destruction, as a consequence of blows received by the head, for example, as in several cases cited by Marro. Garofalo and several of the criminologists of his school refuse to recognize as a special kind of madness native perverseness. One must admit that it is difficult not to connect the latter more or less closely with acquired perverseness, which only differs from it in the accidental character of its appearance, and not to see in this latter an illness of the brain.

Féré contrasts with this opinion of the learned Italian magistrate the almost unanimous conviction of observers, and in fact their accord is imposing. "The study of criminals," says Maudsley,[2] "has convinced all those who have had experience of them that the partial or total lack of moral sense is very often, in this special class, the result of a defect of the organism," and on the other hand, the observation of the insane by the most distinguished physicians "establishes the fact that the absence of a moral sense is one of the occasional effects of the existence of madness in a family." Thus two very distinct branches of research come together in the same conclusion. The moral sense has an organic base (which does not necessarily mean to say a cerebral *place*), and consequently its disappearance or its deadening can only be explained by means of a gap or a lesion, by an atrophy or an injury to the brain, or by an imperfect nutrition of its cells; by some misfortune in other words.[3]

character of his impulses which causes the irresponsibility of the insane man. With the *degenerate* who is not mad, the impulse is more irresistible than with the madman. (See *Saury,* "Etude clinique sur la folie héréditaire," 1886, p. 50). Notwithstanding, the degenerate is, in the opinion of everybody, less irresponsible than the madman, for he is less illogical and less strange.

[1] In the first volume of the "Sociologia criminale" (1880), *Colajanni* gives some excellent reasons against the hypothesis of this cerebral *localization* of the moral sense.

[2] "Crime et Folie."

[3] It would be surprising, moreover, if it were otherwise, for the moral feeling

It is certain that it is a misfortune to be born perverse, as it is to be born stupid, on the condition, however, that we continue to punish the manifestations of perverseness, to become indignant at them, to condemn them and to hate them, as we laugh at foolishness. If, on the contrary, one were to feel sorry for rascals, under the pretence that they are such by birth, it could not fail to happen that the moment this compassion, accompanied with absolution, became general there would no longer be any occasion to be sorry for them in any way. Foolishness, in many respects, would be a benefit conferred by nature if nobody made fun of it.

Furthermore the enormous part played by heredity in all of this cannot be contested. The researches of Marro with respect to this (they covered 456 malefactors and 1765 honest persons) have given him the following results. Among assassins, the proportion who were born from parents more than forty years of age at the time of the conception is fifty-three per cent, a very much larger proportion than that of the other criminal classes, and especially than that of honest people, which latter is one half less. Forty-six times out of one hundred, the delinquents had fathers or mothers who were addicted to the excessive use of

is after all nothing but one of our emotional faculties, and intellectual forms of madness themselves furnish us with the manifest proof that the emotional states are connected with the modes of being of the brain. Let us take, for example, two forms of delirium which have been very thoroughly studied, the *delirium of persecutions* and the *delirium of magnitudes* (see as to the first the masterful work of *Legrand du Saulle*). Both of them are connected with the same overflowing of the personality, which moreover could have flowed out in other channels. At the same time pride or vanity is but a predisposition to madness. The true effective cause is another one: it consists in a cerebral lesion. Though a man may be proud and distrustful, he can never be persuaded, if he remains sane of brain, that the police are at his heels, that the magicians have vowed his destruction. What is requisite in order that his distrust, reinforced by his pride, should lead him to a hallucination of the mind or of the senses of this kind? It is necessary that an organic disturbance of a certain nature should take place within him. The patient then, says Legrand du Saulle, feels "a sort of undefinable anxiety . . ., and, astonished by so novel a situation, he asks himself the reason of it. . . . This uneasiness which is so great, these impressions which are so painful and so absolutely justifiable must have a secret cause." Thence arises the idea of a persecution by hidden enemies. This is exactly the opposite of what takes place under normal conditions. A man who is sane learns of a great danger, and he feels a great anxiety because of it; here the patient feels a great anxiety, whence he infers the existence of a great danger.

It is the same thing with many other kinds of delirium: one feels a great and sudden expansion of one's self-esteem, and one concludes that one has had literary or dramatic successes; one feels an acute satisfaction of the heart, and one concludes therefrom that one has a fashionable wife, etc. All this amply proves that each mode of feeling has a cerebral base which is peculiar to it.

alcohol, — a brief but eloquent reply to Colajanni and to Fournier de Flaix, — and fourteen times in every hundred, they had parents or direct ancestors who were insane. If one adds those who had epileptic parents who were themselves hysterical or delinquents, one arrives at a total proportion of ninety per cent of morbid heredity. There have been twice as many deaths from cerebral illness among the parents of malefactors as among the parents of honest people. This gives quite other food for reflection than do anthropological measurements. But on the whole do not the conditions under which a man is born form a part of himself, and are they not the only ones under which he could and should have been born?

And as the opportunity of touching upon this question of heredity is presented, let us remark how strange it is to see the determinists themselves preoccupied, from the point of view of responsibility, with the solution which should be given to it. From the time one becomes a determinist, from the time when one ceases to believe in creation "ex nihilo," one admits that all the characteristics, all the inclinations brought by the newly-born have external and pre-existing causes. Whether these causes be dispersed in the immensity of the circumambient world or whether they be concentrated, brought into the channel of the nearest of the vital sources whence springs the individual, it matters little. In this last case, it is true, all the effects taken together, that is to say the individual, will be presented as similar to all of its causes taken together, that is to say to his progenitors; whereas, in the other case, this similarity of the aggregate will not exist and one will only have the resemblance of each particular effect to its special cause. But again what does it matter? The question is whether the individual has or has not, appropriated to himself and identified with himself that of which he consists. Is this appropriation in any way prevented by the fact that what he consists of is similar to that of which other individuals, his parents, consist? I do not see any reason why this similarity should render this identity more difficult. I will suppose that a man is born by spontaneous generation, by a divine miracle like Adam. Here heredity plays no part at all; is he any the more free because of this in the eyes of the determinists? No, he is neither more nor less than a *hereditary degenerate*. If hereditary madness engenders irresponsibility, it is not so much that it is hereditary as that it is madness.

Let us apply our principles here, and we shall see that innate moral madness, or, to put it better, moral imbecility, is precisely the opposite to true madness. This latter is an *alienation* of the person; whence it follows that such and such acts, reputed to be ours, in reality do not emanate from us; the fundamental condition of our responsibility, that is *our causality*, is lacking. Moreover, this perturbation which makes us differ from *ourselves*, does not prevent this normal "*ourself*," which is virtually latent under our madness, from remaining similar to our fellow-citizens in the essential relations, and does not break our ties with their society.[1] Here *identity* does not exist, but *similarity* subsists. On the contrary, here we have a Brinvilliers, a Tropmann, a man born pitiless, unfair, shameless; he poisons, he stabs, he rapes a woman or a child; can one say that he is *another* in carrying out this heinous crime? No he is always only too much *the same*. But the more he thus conforms to his essential nature, the more does he demonstrate and accentuate his profound dissimilarity in one respect to his social surroundings. Not only did he not have at his birth those hereditary instincts of humanity, of justice, and of honor which are as necessary to the civilized child as the seed-lobe is to the embryo plant, but even education has not been able to replace them in him by good habits. Not only did he lack the germ, but even the proper soil for the development of the germ brought in from outside. Thus he came into the world deprived of one sense[2] with which every honest man is provided.

[1] If I have said above that madness *disassimilates* at the same time as it alienates us, this means that the abnormal "myself," the new "myself" created by means of the madness, is as dissimilar to our surroundings as it is different from the normal "myself;" but the latter, the only one which bears any legal and moral relation to society, remains none the less, during its slumber, cast in the image of our fellow-men.

[2] I say "sense" in order that I may conform to the usual metaphor, which, moreover, too many learned men seem to abuse. Not any more than Paul Dubuisson do I believe in this metaphysical entity, the *moral sense*, which we should have at our birth and which would be "charged with discerning good from evil, in absolutely the same way as sight causes us to distinguish day from night." The moral feeling, at least in its delicate part, is a cerebral depository of the social life which is relatively recent; and it is perhaps for this reason that it is the first faculty to be affected by the morbid disturbance from which madness springs. It is a remarkable thing that the alienists agree upon this point: the loss of the moral sense among the insane precedes the loss of understanding. Esquirol gave as the base of mental alienation *moral alienation*. Now, as a general thing, that which the declining brain loses at the first is that which it acquired as the last thing. It is the most recent memories which are the first to be destroyed in the case of old men. See the fine monograph of *Ribot* on the memory.

Now although a man may lack sight or hearing, though he may be color-blind, near-sighted, or deaf, while this may make it difficult for him to accomplish certain social duties, certain forms of employment, as to be a station-master, a judge, or a sailor; yet this will not prevent him from fulfilling a rôle of some kind in society, or at least from remaining fundamentally similar to his fellow-countrymen, conforming to them in a number of the more important ideas and feelings. But if the sense of which I am speaking, if the ability to suffer by reason of sympathy for the sufferings of another, to love the beauty of certain duties and the bitterness of certain sacrifices, is lacking in a man, although this man may share all our physical sensations and even acquire all our scientific knowledge or all our artificial needs, live according to the fashion and speak with the purest accent, yet he has nothing in common with us excepting his features and his external appearance.

But this is a great deal, and it would be a ridiculous declamation to refuse him all resemblance to ourselves, especially when an artistic civilization like that of the Renaissance, or an industrial one like our own, in developing exclusively the intellectual side of man, has given it the preponderance over the moral side and has spread the habit of appreciating talent and mind more than character and heart. Neither Benvenuto Cellini nor the Borgias were monsters in their times; their anomaly was certainly not sufficiently exceptional to be the cause of their moral irresponsibility, as it could have been up to a certain point if it had made itself manifest in a universally and rigidly moral country where the most brilliant gifts are counted but for little if honesty be not joined thereto. In surroundings of this sort a well brought up rogue resembles his fellow-countrymen as a hollow nut does full ones. Among us he resembles them as a worm-eaten apple does a healthy one. Yet the difference is important. Thus we may conclude that here the condition of *identity* is completely fulfilled, but that that of *similarity* is but imperfectly fulfilled. From the moment it judges the criminal to be a being apart, radically dissimilar to other men, the positivist school is founded, according to our principles, upon judging him to be morally irresponsible. But it is his radical dissimilarity which I contest.

Native criminality, moral monstrosity, is, therefore, from our point of view, almost the opposite of madness. It is true that, in the first case no more than in the second, are the two conditions of responsibility both fully met with at the same time; but in the second case one of them, the principal one, is absolutely lacking, and, in the first case, the accessory alone is lacking, and that only in part. In the second case it is proved that the person, the individual, as far as he is a social being, is not at all the author, or is but in a slight degree the author, of the offense which is imputed to him; in the first case it is proved that the person is the author, but that social in many respects, he is non-social or rather anti-social in a way which is important. The decrease of responsibility can thus go to the extent of its elimination in the second case, but never in the first.

Furthermore, this decrease, which is due to two very distinct causes, could not have the same nature here as there, nor could it produce the same effects. The half insane man, an accomplice for the time being of his own insanity, demands a treatment which is especially medical which, in curing him, corrects him; he remains a member of the society which owes him vigilant care and a maternal severity. But the innate malefactor is incurable and incorrigible, — a rare case moreover, — and there can be no question of either curing him or of reforming him. On the other hand, it cannot suffice to strike him down like a wild beast straying in our streets, for he resembles us sufficiently to cause us shame and not merely fear, and to justify our indignation against him. He still belongs to our association, and that is why we must drive him out of it, by means of the judicial ceremonies of a social excommunication which is unfolded every three months before our courts of criminal jurisdiction.

§ 38. (VI) Theory of responsibility by Dubuisson. Mistake of contrasting moral responsibility with social responsibility.

I will add that it is not sufficient thus to excommunicate him; we have still to guard ourselves against his offensive return and against the contagion of his example. It is here that we can give its place to a theory of responsibility set forth by Paul Dubuisson.[1] We cannot accept it, as the author in spite of the positivism of his methods borrows from spiritualism the old idea of responsibility founded upon free will. But he rejuvenates it by the manner in which he understands it. According to him, this comes to the same thing as saying that responsibility, in that which concerns criminals by reason of temperament, is founded

[1] "Archives de l'Anthropologie criminelle," 1887, 1888.

upon the penalty. In appearance it is the upsetting of the logic of things, as it is clear that the penalty, on the other hand, assumes a pre-existing responsibility. In reality, the formula set forth simply means that it is right to apply a penalty to the man who is born perverse precisely because the threat of the penalty, before his crime, had been made to him,[1] and owing to it, he had found a counter-weight within himself which the moral man finds in his conscience alone. He was thus able to lean on this counter-weight in order to resist his vices; therefore he was free, therefore he was responsible. It is the idea of the "contra-spinta" of Romagnosi. Obviously this doctrine is inadmissible according to our principles; it leads us to maintain that, in the case where the apprehension of the penalty has been weaker than the depraved impulse, there has been irresponsibility. Well, precisely this case is realized every time a crime is committed. The prospect of the penalty is the same for all; but some will think themselves sure to escape it, rightly or wrongly, and this involuntary confidence, which is fatal like every belief, will bring it about that the penalty in their opinion will be as though it did not exist.

Thus these latter will be irresponsible, according to Dubuisson, because, all penal counter-weight having been taken away from them, they will no longer have the disposal of their free will, such as he understands it to be. Others will believe more or less strongly in the possibility, in the probability of incurring the legal punishment, and, according to the degree, which is always involuntary and inevitable, of this belief, they will or will not resist the temptation. So much the better for those who shall have sufficient belief to hold themselves back upon the declivity of evil, so much the worse for those who shall not believe to the required degree. As to those who, while being convinced that they will be punished, shall sin, it will be proved either that they are mad because of the anomaly of their reckoning in certain cases, or that society, as far as they are concerned, has not fulfilled its duty of sufficiently protecting them against themselves. To exceptionally audacious and perverse natures it would be necessary to oppose the risk of punishments so horrible that one would never feel one had the courage to apply them, which would make this spectre ridiculous.

[1] "It is," he says, "because there exists a penal law, that the man who is lacking in intelligence ought to be considered as being responsible for his actions, this penal law being in reality only the compensatory influence thrown by society into the scale of human inclinations."

Or else, if one did not recoil before this application, the social logic of analogy would compel one to strike with an excessive severity the great majority of less evil natures which lesser punishments would have sufficed to have guaranteed against being carried away by themselves.

In any event, between the absolute conviction of escaping the penalty and the absolute conviction of being reached by it, there is an immense scale, and, as one descends or ascends it, the fear of a penalty varies from *zero* to m or from m to *zero*. It also results from the preceding considerations that the bugbear of the penalty being given, equally threatening to all, the one most perverse, most strongly driven to wrongdoing should be judged to be the least responsible, that is to say, the one to be the least punished. In order that he may avoid this last result, Dubuisson, like so many other criminologists, is obliged to distinguish between two sorts of responsibility, the one called moral, the other called social; the latter as much stronger as the former shall be the weaker.

Happily our point of view allows us to avoid these hopeless complications, which are analogous to the cycles and the epicycles of Ptolemy. Is that which is opposed to the *social* in all matters, the *moral?* No; because the moral is a part of the social. But it is the *individual.* I could therefore understand it if they opposed to social responsibility individual responsibility, giving this latter a special and a very narrow acceptation. The first, to tell the truth, is the only one with which criminality and even morality need be concerned; it is the corollary and the converse of our external causality, the legitimate rebounding upon ourselves of our own acts in so far as they affect others; by others being understood a family or a nation, a man or a group of men, it matters little. As to responsibility which is purely individual, such as we understand it to be here, it is, for example, that of the Christian or of the stoic who examines his own conscience and punishes himself for his past faults, even though inoffensive, in the opinion of those like him. But in order that responsibility, be it social or individual, may exist and may be felt as such, certain subjective *moral* conditions must necessarily have been fulfilled. For to understand responsibility in an entirely objective and materialistic sense would be to retrograde to the primitive times when the unconscious incest of Oedipus was judged to be criminal as though it had been conscious and willing. The Christian does not repent of having eaten meat on Friday without knowing it and without wishing it; and, for the same reason, society, which has a duty not to be a collective monster of egoism and harshness, when the individual has already for centuries been imbued with feelings of sympathy and delicacy, could not condemn a man for an injury, for a homicide even, involuntarily committed. Here we have very simple distinctions, but distinctions which the positivists have often neglected to take into account.

§ 39. (VII) Partial responsibility of the insane, Falret. The criminally mad and mad geniuses.

In all that has been said above we have virtually solved a question which has greatly divided and still divides alienists; that of knowing whether the responsibility of the insane can or cannot be partial.• In a very well known work,[1] Falret has upheld the theory which is contrary to ours, basing his arguments on the insurmountable difficulties which were presented, according to him, by the medico-legal estimate of the phases of the transition between complete responsibility and absolute irresponsibility. Thus here there is no mean between everything and nothing, between infinity and zero. It is much more concise, I agree, and of an extreme simplicity; but if it be true that "natura non facit saltus," how artificial it is! It seems to us, moreover, that with the assistance of the rules and the distinctions given above the problem judged to be incapable of solution by Falret loses a great deal of its arduous aspect. We must add that he himself, when he passes in review the different forms of neurosis, often forgets his idea so *squarely* formulated;[2] and it so happens that, concerning cases of incomplete degeneracy, of native perversity, or of alcoholism, he admits an *attenuated* responsibility, if not a partial one.

Partial or attenuated, I do not see a very great difference. Others do not see it any more than I dó. Henri Coutagne[3]

[1] "Dictionnaire encyclopédique des sciences médicales." Article on "Responsabilité légale des aliénés."

[2] Maudsley is not less inconsistent and wavering. Is a madman who, imputing an imaginary injury to someone, kills him in order to be revenged, which would have been an inexcusable thing to do even had the injury been real, punishable? No, he says, for the disturbance of his brain upon one point allows us to infer that it is weakened and contaminated all over. However he adds: "In order to be absolutely just, one must admit a certain measure of responsibility in some cases, but never the full responsibility of the reasoning man." *Saury* ("Folie héréditaire") expresses himself in the same way as Falret.

[3] "Manuel des expertises médicales en matière criminelle." (Lyons, Storck, 1887).

establishes, while congratulating himself upon doing so, that the theory of attenuated, or partial responsibility, for he makes no distinction, "looked at in a bad light by alienists who are confined to the study of clinics, every day gives evidence of its practical value in the domain of judicial examinations, where one may say that it has acquired an absolute right to be invoked." Legrand du Saulle estimates that the insane affected with the delirium of persecutions are partially responsible. Ball, professor in the Faculty of Medicine of Paris, upon the occasion of the mysterious crime of Villemomble, gave out his opinion to the same effect in a masterly way. Called upon to make a study of Euphrasie Mercier, her antecedents and her family, he succeeded in unraveling the radical dual personality of this complex nature, of this visionary combined with a very practical tradeswoman, endowed with a great deal of good sense, "of a very remarkable intelligence, and a very energetic will." What do we see also? [1] "Upon the one hand a crime committed not only with premeditation, but with an extraordinary lavishness of precautions and clever combinations, a remarkable ability in the scaffolding of financial operations destined to cause the fortune of the victim to pass into the hands of the assassin . . . ; and upon the other hand, a state of hereditary madness, extending to all the members of the same family almost without exception and presenting the most obvious characteristics of religious delirium. On the one hand, the finished type of intelligence in the service of crime; on the other hand, the most manifest indications of mental alienation." How are we to escape recognition of the fact that the greedy Euphrasie is responsible if the mystic Euphrasie is not so? And is it so hard here to separate the two? Ball does not hesitate to make his opinion a general one. "The insane," says he, "and they are numerous, who have preserved a considerable portion of their intellectual endowments, are undoubtedly governed to a certain extent by the *same* feelings, the *same* instincts, and the *same* motives *as are other men, and that is why*, in some particular cases, one is right in applying to them the principles of the common law."

One could not with more force impliedly adopt the part of our theory relative to the required condition of social similarity than is done in this passage, as well as the connected condition of personal identity, in the case of penal responsibility. Ball ends with

[1] "De la responsabilité partielle des aliénés," by *Ball* (J.-B. Baillière and Sons, Paris, 1886).

a consideration more brilliant than firm at first sight, but which after reflection is still more firm than brilliant; for it bears upon that social need of symmetry between the penalty and the recompense of which we will have occasion to show all the importance later on. "Men of the greatest genius," says he, "historical figures of the highest fame have presented undoubted indications of mental alienation.[1] Has any one ever taken exception to them in order to diminish their merit or to renounce the debt of recognition which we have contracted in their behalf? Because he passed through a period of madness, none the less did Newton found the system of the world; because of having been sequestrated in a sanitarium, none the less was Auguste Comte one of the greatest philosophers who ever lived. Because of having been very deeply affected by hallucinations, none the less did Luther carry out one of the most gigantic revolutions of modern times. Did the visions of Joan of Arc prevent unbiassed history from rendering justice to the nobility of her feelings, to the loftiness of her patriotism, and the grandeur of her faith? If the insane can thus deserve reward, how can one maintain that they are incapable of deserving punishment, and that neither blame nor chastisement should ever reach them? The first of these two propositions logically carries with it the denial of the second."

There is one thing more to be said. Let us grant to the alienists everything they attempt to prove. Very well! so be it; genius, madness, criminality are different anomalies, but anomalies just the same. There is nothing normal excepting the flat, the ordinary, and the mediocre; nature is like the ancient tyrants, it has a horror of all superiority in good or in evil and chastises it by impotence or sterility to the third and seventh generation. But, I ask, from the point of view of our theory of responsibility, does this prove the least bit in the world that the man of genius and the criminal from birth, I do not say the madman, are irresponsible or even less responsible in fact than the man called normal? Is there anything which can be more particularly our own than an anomaly which characterizes us and which, moreover, allows us to resemble our fellow-countrymen in the majority of our other characteristics? Does the *normality* of the ordinary man, shaped after the common pattern, belong to him any more than his peculiarity belongs to the man of genius? As to the

[1] With respect to this consult "l'Uomo di genio," by *Lombroso*, 5th edition (Turin, 1888), where examples of mad or half insane geniuses abound.

madman, it is not the same thing if, by madness one understands, not an individual exception to the typical rule, but a disturbance brought to bear upon the development of the individual himself, a "disindividualization," so to speak. If, on the contrary, we are concerned with an innate extravagance, which is persistent and logical, one should apply to this pretended insanity what I have said concerning genius and crime. It is the normal man, perfectly ordinary and mediocre, who would rather deserve to be absolved as being irresponsible when he has submitted in a docile and unresisting manner to the external rule of example.

§ 40. Drunkenness. Homicide by reason of imprudence and homicide in a state of intoxication, madness due to alcohol. Should drunkenness be more of an extenuating circumstance as it is more inveterate? Contradiction between the determinists and their adversaries upon this point. Amnesia.

Although easily solved with the help of the foregoing conclusions, the problem of responsibility as raised by drunkenness, to a certain extent must be dealt with separately in this section. In Morel's classification, after those forms of madness which have heredity as their cause, come those which must be attributed to the habitual use of alcohol, opium,[1] hashish, and morphine. It is certain that if the individual is in no wise responsible for the breaking out of the first, he is so to a certain extent for that of the others, which he could have prevented. I say that he could have had he so wished, which does not prevent us from recognizing the fact that he was not able to so wish; his character together with the circumstances of his life being given. The habitual opium smoker and alcohol drinker have thus been constrained, in this sense, to enter upon their fatal course. But this constraint arises from a necessity which is principally from within, inherent at the bottom of their being, in which respect it differs from the essentially external necessity, that is to say, the pathological necessity, which constrains them when madness, induced by their destructive habits, has at last burst forth.

But it is not with madness induced by alcohol, it is with the attack due to alcohol that we are concerned. Let us draw a

[1] The question was discussed at the Congress of Legal Medicine of 1889. Consult also *Pichon's* book: "Morphinism," etc. (Paris, Doin, 1889). See also *Corre*, "Crime et suicide," chapter III. According to Magnan, forty out of one hundred mental diseases would be attributable to alcoholism, which in these last few years has been progressing among us.

distinction, with Vétault,[1] between involuntary and voluntary intoxication, and let us subdivide the first into either accidental intoxication, or else that which is occasioned by the artifices of a third person; and the second into either exceptional intoxication, or else that which is habitual, or that which is intentional (with the object, for example, of giving oneself *courage* to commit a crime), or finally that which is *complicated*, as a consequence of a defective organization which makes it disastrous. In this last case, its consequences, the first time that the subject gives himself over to it, could not have been foreseen by him because of their exceptional character. The excuse which is the result of this is thus much stronger than in every other case; but from the very moment when experience has warned the drinker of the fearful danger which his excesses of drinking cause others or himself to run, he becomes blamable in a very high degree for again having become intoxicated. Is this as much as to say that thenceforth he can be as responsible for a homicide committed while in this state as he would be if, while in the normal state, he had carried out the same murder? Not at all.

A man has a pistol in his hand; someone, behind him, grasps his arm and compels him to fire a shot with his weapon in the direction of a group of persons. Obviously, if one of these persons be wounded this man will neither deserve to be prosecuted nor to be censured. Such is the case of homicide by reason of madness. But this same man, to amuse himself, to practise shooting, and without taking the trouble to find out whether anybody is passing or not, discharges his revolver in the street. If he hits a passer-by, his responsibility will be involved. It will, however, be less so than if he had intentionally aimed at and hit this passer-by. His fault can be reduced to not having sacrificed his pleasure at the risk of injury to his fellows. He did not wish for the death of one of his fellows, he did not even wish for the possibility of this death; he was only in the wrong in not having repulsed the prospect of this possibility and in having permitted it to happen rather than in having accepted it.

This kind of responsibility, in order to be well understood, must be compared with that special form of responsibility, which is so hard to account for under the theory of free will, which

[1] "Etude médico-légale sur l'alcoolisme des conditions de la responsabilité au point de vue pénal chez les alcoolisés," by *Vétault*, of the Faculty of Paris (Paris, J.-B. Baillières, 1887).

affects, in every Code, the authors of wounds and homicides by reason of carelessness or awkwardness, and with that other form of responsibility, called civil at the Palais de Justice, which punishes the father or the master for the faults of his children and his servants. One is "civilly" responsible for the intentional torts committed by one's sons, as one is both civilly and penally responsible at the same time, for the injuries which one has unintentionally oneself caused to others, and fundamentally for the same reason. In the one case as in the other, one has been the indirect cause, in not watching with sufficient vigilance the active elements over which one has charge, whether they be the nervous and muscular elements of one's own body, or whether they be the personnel of one's household. Organic solidarity in the one case, domestic solidarity in the other, is the foundation of this responsibility by reflection. Well, the responsibility of the drunkard, once it has arisen, is of the same kind with respect to the acts which he has committed during his intoxication. There is no occasion to acquit him; nor is there any occasion, if he has killed or stolen during his short delirium, to treat him as one would treat an ordinary assassin or thief. The latter is a continual menace; the former is but a conditional menace, depending upon whether he becomes intoxicated again. One can say the same thing of the smoker of hashish or the hypnotic subject.

Habitual drunkenness, whether it be caused by opium or alcohol,[1] here puts a delicate question to us. On the one hand the habitual drunkard, as he becomes rooted in his chronic evil, takes a more and more exact account of the peril which he causes society; but on the other hand he is driven to become intoxicated by an ever increasing attraction, and one which is always more irresistible. Conversely the accidental drunkard, who is habitually sober, is less well informed as to what danger there may be to others in his intoxication, but the desire which drives him to it is less in his case and it is more easy for him to resist the temptation. From the point of view of the theory of free will what is the consequence of this? It follows that the individual who is the most strongly tempted, and as a consequence less free, is less responsible.

[1] Let us, however, draw a distinction. Possibly alcohol and opium stupefy to an equal extent, says *Lorion*, who has seen the effects of both in Cochin-China ("Criminalité et Médecine judicaire en Cochinchine," Lyons, Storck, 1887); but there is this difference that the man who has become an idiot through opium is not wicked, and that the man suffering from alcoholism is dangerous. China, from this aspect, thus runs far less danger than does Europe.

It is true that, had he been by nature good, the more exact realization of the misfortunes made possible or probable by his intoxication would have aroused in him a repulsion greater than was the appetite for this impure pleasure. But what does it matter, from the point of view of the theory of free will, that he may have been shown to have been naturally bad? His innate badness is a thing which he could not help bringing with him when he was born.

After all, an unconquerable attraction, fought against by means of an insufficient repulsion, and which must have been such because of his native perversity, has carried away this unfortunate; therefore he is irresponsible. Therefore all the indulgence of the judge must be reserved for this inveterate victim of alcohol and severity must only be shown in the case of the occasional drinker.[1] Fortunately, the different legislatures have not been of this opinion; the majority punish the habitual drunkard with an exceptional severity. There is nothing more fitted to strengthen our point of view. In the first place the native badness of the agent is inherent in his person; and in proportion as his inevitable habit becomes deep rooted, being more and more voluntary, the more does it become an integral part of his being.

When on coming out of an attack of drunkenness, one has lost all recollection of a wrongful act which one has committed while in this state, one should, according to Vétault, be judged irresponsible for this deed. Why is this? Why is amnesia, in a similar case, according to him, bound up with irresponsibility?[2] Does it prove that the intoxication was complete, that the alienation of

[1] "What is the degree of the responsibility of a smoker or of a hashish eater?" asks *Lorion, op. cit.*, following *Kocher* ("Criminalité chez les Arabes"). He solves the question by means of the same distinction as the latter: 1st. If the use of hashish is accidental, *acute*, the individual, according to the conclusive experiments of Moreau, still preserves enough consciousness, even in the most terrifying hallucinations, to feel that he is delirious. *From which these authors conclude* that he is responsible. 2d. If the use of hashish is *chronic*, the responsibility is done away with, and the impulse towards homicide may become irresistible.

According to these authors, the same distinction should be applied to alcoholism. If acute, it leaves the responsibility intact (as though the man who accidentally becomes intoxicated were in possession of his consciousness and his will!) but, if chronic, he is irresponsible. Ought we not rather to think the contrary? The proposed distinction is, however, logical enough if one wishes at any price to make responsibility depend upon *apparent* free will. It is more apparent (although neither more nor less real) in the case of the acute than in that of the chronic hashish eater and alcohol drinker.

[2] It is a good thing to note that Vétault, whose conscientious work is worthy of praise, is constrained, in doubtful cases, to pronounce himself for and not against responsibility.

the moment was profound? No; but, says this author, "willing acts leave a more or less lasting impression upon the mind," and consequently, "when one establishes that certain acts were done in a state of amnesia, it means that they were carried out without deliberation, without resolution, and without consciousness."

This reasoning is far from being conclusive; it is contradicted by all that one knows as a consequence of the observations and the experiments of Alfred Maury, of Delbœuf, and others, upon the altogether insignificant importance which must be attached to the remembering or the forgetting of that which one has done during a dream or during hypnotic delirium. There is not the slightest relation between the deepness of sleep and the deepness of forgetfulness after dreaming. The same dream is sometimes forgotten and sometimes remembered upon awakening; this depends upon entirely accidental circumstances. If it be forgotten, it has not been any the less conscious, and the imaginary acts which go to make it up have not thereby been any the less willing, deliberated even, *or felt to be so* by the sleeper or the hypnotized subject. They may not have left any trace in the memory of the normal "myself"; but later on in a new dream, during another state of hypnosis, and during another attack of epilepsy as well, they will be or may be recollected by the abnormal "myself" which belongs to these states. Thus it is not the so-called unconscious or even voluntary character of an act which is attested by its being forgotten when one awakes, it is rather its character which is foreign to the social person,[1] and, moreover, the recollection of it would in no way prove the contrary. This fact has thus not any very great significance and cannot acquire any except by the favor of our interpretation.

§ 41. Hypnotism and identity. Hypnosis and dreaming, two forms of the association of images, which imply the reality of the identical person. Voluntary decision is thus something other than a complicated suggestion.

Hypnotism is so hackneyed a subject that we almost scruple to deal with it. The responsibility of the hypnotized and of the hypnotizer has been treated of by Liégeois,[2] Messrs. Binet and

[1] Of course, a great importance should be attached to the question of whether the drunkenness has been a *denaturing* of the person or merely an *exaggerating* of his nature. We strongly approve of the remarks of *Garofalo* upon this point: "We must observe whether the sort of crime committed during intoxication corresponds to the character of the individual, if the inhumanity or the improbity of the act corresponds with the inclinations of the delinquent."

[2] "De la suggestion hypnotique dans ses rapports avec le droit civil et le

Féré, Campili,[1] Ladame[2] and many other learned men. It is easy to apply our general point of view to this question. But a double interest, at the same time practical and theoretical, obliges us to pause here. A practical interest: Thefts, murders, and arson hypnotically suggested are perhaps (I am far from saying *probably*) to be called upon in the near future from the laboratories, to unfold themselves before the criminal courts,[3] which have perhaps already had to take them into account without being aware of it, — for example, the court at Var in 1865 in the Castellan case. This does not at all mean that they will be called upon in the near future to play in the midst of our civilization the bloody part which was filled in the feudal past, in Florence and in Germany, by *assassinations by appointment*, which are still made use of, it seems, in Corsica. An interest which is especially theoretical: hypnotism, that madness at will, throws light on all the forms of mental alienation which we have just been studying. Finally, hypnotism is the experimental junction point of psychology and sociology; it shows us the most simplified sort of psychic life which can be conceived of under the form of the most elementary social relation. And especially, in that which concerns the responsibility which attaches to the various sorts of neurosis or of disorders even, which are due to social causes, there is nothing more instructive than hypnotism.

droit criminel," (Picard, 1884). In spite of the criticisms of which this memorandum has been the object on the part of Binet and Féré, it still retains the incontestable merit, and this is not the only one, of having drawn the attention of the public to these questions. The article of *Binet and Féré*, entitled: "Hypnotism et responsabilité," appeared in the "Revue philosophique" in March, 1885.

[1] "Il grande hypnotismo nel rapporto col diritto penale e civile" by *Giulio Campili* (Turin, Bocca, 1886).

[2] "Archives de l'Anthropologie criminelle," Nos. 10 and 12. See also *Gilles de la Tourette*, "L'Hypnotisme au point de vue Médico-légal," and the works of *Pitres*, of *Bernheim*, of *Beaunis*, etc.

[3] This prediction was soon fulfilled. We know the part played by hypnotism in the Eyraud-Bompard case (December, 1890). Did Gabrielle Bompard obey a hypnotic suggestion? The question was asked and was, I think with reason, answered in the negative. But the general problem exists none the less, whether and to what extent criminal suggestion is a possibility. It can be answered in a pretty broad general sense, while refusing to hypnotism, with us, the power of transforming the character in its very depths, to change an honest man into an assassin. In fact it may be sufficient to suggest to an honest man the illusion of lawful defence in order to suggest to him a murder. At the same time we must admit that, from a practical standpoint, the hypnotic suggestion will always be the most perilous and the most inconvenient of criminal proceedings. It could rather serve to falsify the testimony of children, who are already without it, so eminently the subject of warnings.

Also there is nothing better fitted to cure us of the illusion of free will. The hypnotic subject awakened, or at least awakened as far as appearances are concerned, who, under the persisting domination of a command received during his sleep, steals a watch or hits one of his friends, believes himself to be free to act in this way and bases his conviction upon the false pretexts which are furnished him by his imagination in order to justify in his own eyes his absurd act, to appropriate for himself in an illusory manner an initiative from a foreign source. It is true that in reply to this it may be said that here the illusion of personal identity seems to be as completely contradicted as does that of liberty. However this is not so in the least. Our somnambulist is mistaken in believing that he was able not to have wished to do his act; but he is not mistaken in believing that *he* wished it and that consequently it really is *his*. Only this *he* is not his normal "myself," it is a quite special "somnambulistic myself," which nevertheless retains the moral character of the other "myself." For it has never been demonstrated by a single authentic example that hypnotism has transformed a good and straight nature into one which is cruel and false; and the thefts of watches and the blows which have been suggested to various honest and mild subjects have either only been carried out because the person hypnotized was conscious of playing a part in a comedy, or else could not be carried out because the moral base of the being has obstinately resisted this suggestion.

The hypnotized person, in fact, is not purely an automaton, especially when in this state of apparent awakening, which is in reality very incomplete, and which Delbœuf well calls somnambulistic wakefulness. They are at this time, and even during deep hypnosis, "persons who have their character, their aversions and their preferences," say Binet and Féré. Character, aversions, and preferences, moreover, which distinguish them from their habitual personality. Is it however sufficient that it be a person such as the latter for the responsibility of the person hypnotized awakened, that is to say of the other person, to be involved up to a certain point, as the authors who have been cited are led to think, as do Pitres and Ladame? I think not and for two reasons. First of all, the person whom one supposes to be responsible is not the guilty person; in the second place, the latter is not more responsible, for this person is essentially withdrawn from social action and unlike the social surroundings. It is true that this person has a relation to the hypnotizer; but this person has no more a social relation to him than has the dog to his master, although it is permissible, as we look at it, to regard this unilateral action of a "myself" upon another as the first element and the analytical explanation of this reciprocal action which constitutes the true relation of society. From onesidedness to reciprocity, in fact, is here very far, it is also very far from dreaming to awakening, or from the animal soul to the human soul.

One wakes up every morning, every morning one passes by degrees from the dreaming "myself" to the "myself" awakened. In the same way, and though one generally passes suddenly, without transition, from hypnosis to the normal state, it is allowable to imagine a series of stages by means of which, owing to an intricacy of simultaneous suggestions, in an ever increasing number and whose termination is ever farther off and more indefinite, one would connect the suggested action of the most thoroughly asleep somnambulist with the deliberated action of the most balanced and sane will. It is in the same way as voluntary action has been connected with reflex action. Without a doubt this can be conceived of in the abstract; but does that prove that the final state does not radically differ from the initial state? Without any discontinuity one can change a straight line into a circle, a circle into an ellipse and a parabola, all of which does not prevent these lines or these figures from being precisely defined by means of their proper formulae and their particular theorems.

I have said that hypnosis, and I could just as well have said ordinary sleep, is an extreme simplification of mental life. This mutilation is its radical transformation. The marvel of hypnotism as far as this is concerned is scarcely more astonishing than is the phenomenon of dreaming,[1] and, in the last analysis, is to be explained as is the latter, simply by the play of the association of images, wherein the English have mistakenly wished to see the supreme law of psychology. If they had spoken the truth, one would have to say that the normal "myself" is the "myself" of

[1] To compare hypnosis to natural sleep has ceased to be a hypothesis; one can say that the proof of their fundamental identity was furnished by Delbœuf. He was the first to show that one could easily recall to hypnotic subjects who had been awakened the memory of the singular state from which they had just emerged. Now how do the subjects of Delbœuf describe that which they have experienced? "I have scarcely closed my eyelids," says one of them, "when I feel an overwhelming calmness; I feel no other sensation save that of a great well-being. I do not feel that I am asleep, I hear everything and remember everything. It is only when I am awakened that I perceive that I was asleep."

the dreamer, for it is only during the course of a dream that images and ideas are linked together by virtue of the single fact of their previous connection. One ought to say the same thing of the hypnotic "myself." The mind of the dreamer is a dark firmament, with about one star, I mean to say with about one image in it, which evokes therein another, and so on and so forth; the mind of the hypnotic subject is in the same way emptied of its entire contents, excepting the sight and sound of the magnetizer, and, when the latter speaks a word, a sentence, or makes a gesture, the idea or the action *associated* with this sign is at once reproduced. Suggestion is therefore nothing but a species of association, and, conversely, association is nothing but a species of suggestion. Images which are really associated are those which suggest one another; the first one to appear evokes the second and thus plays the part of the sentence spoken or the gesture outlined by the hypnotizer. When we dream we thus at each moment hypnotize ourselves, and the succession of images which constitute the dreams are nothing but a continuous auto-suggestion. Or to put it better, it is no more *I myself* who suggest to myself while dreaming all the absurdities at which I laugh upon awakening, than it is the hypnotized subject who suggests to *himself* the misdeeds which the one hypnotizing orders him to commit.

If one is here forced to recognize that the instrumentality and the cause of the act are two distinct things, logic compels one to draw this same conclusion in the case of dreaming and in the case of madness as well. What essential difference is there between hypnotism and the somnambulism which is called natural? The spontaneous somnambulist who gets up during the night, without suggestion from anyone else, in order to kill somebody, is no more the true author of his crime than would a hypnotized subject be under the same circumstances. Now, between him and the insane man who commits homicide there is not the slightest difference in this respect either. This duality which I have often pointed out in the core of the diseased or weakened brain is merely the reproduction within of the duality of the magnetizer and the magnetized.

This means, that every time the law of the association of images alone predominates, there takes place within us the action of some one other than ourselves. If this is more evident in the case of hypnotism, it is primarily because here the *other than ourselves,* who is visible to everybody, is the hypnotizer, a person like ourselves, and in the second place, because the bond of association, in this case, is extraordinarily rigorous. There is no more close and fixed association than that of the verbal sign or of the gesture with the idea which it expresses, and consequently, with the act which is a realization of this idea when it is an idea of an act. It is therefore not astonishing that the hypnotized subject mechanically obeys the one who magnetizes him and manifests a blind faith in his word, for ordinarily but one possible hallucination, but one possible act, corresponds to one sentence or to one gesture of the latter, whereas several other images are as a general rule bound up in a given image. From this arises the irresistibly settled character of the illusions of the hypnotized subject and the capricious appearance of the illusions of the dreamer, in spite of the no less absolute bindingness of the latter.

Furthermore the efficacy from the point of view of hallucination of the image which has been suggested, by the word of the magnetizer or by the antecedent image which the dreamer has seen, is easily accounted for if one picture to oneself the brain as continually disposing of a certain amount of credulity and docility which, normally, is distributed among all the simultaneous feelings and reminiscences, always in considerable numbers. When as a consequence of a momentary and almost absolute paralysis of the senses and of the memory, the mind finds itself reduced to but a single feeling, as in the case of hypnosis, or to a single image, as in the case of a dream, the whole force of its belief and desire which calls for one direction, which needs to strive for or to realize a given thing, throws itself on this side, and that which was but a light shadow during wakefulness then becomes a vision.[1] However it is certain that there never has been a dream which has had the intensity of effect proper to hypnotic suggestion, upon the depths of organic life, or even upon the muscular system, which has even healed wounds and which, without any difficulty, brings

[1] The singular strength of the beliefs and impulses of the insane can be partly accounted for in the same manner, that is to say because of the extreme poverty of mind of the madman who, by reason of the paralysis of the governing centres of his brain, never thinks of more than one thing at a time, but is so much the more strongly impressed thereby. Then, says Morel, "dread becomes terror, courage a carrying away which nothing can stem; the doubt, the suspicion which have the very slightest foundation can become a certainty. *The mind is on the declivity of exaggeration in all things;* the slightest impulse seldom fails to carry it away." From thence also, still as in dreams, arises the rapid succession of the most opposed passions, of convictions which are the most contradictory within the mind of the insane.

into play all the muscles of the patient. But does not this difference depend upon that which exists between the circumstances under which the two kinds of sleep compared by us occur? Ordinary sleep is produced by exhaustion of strength, at the moment when the need of believing and of acting has fallen below low-water mark; hypnosis, on the other hand, takes place through the damming and ebbing of the strength, at the time when the double current of credulity and docility of which we are speaking still flows from bank to bank. Thus one can understand that the dream induced by hypnosis, the only channel for this stream, should be active and powerful in a different manner to the dream induced by sleep, which is the humble bed of a little brook.

Now, between the state of dreaming and the state of awakening, once more, is there nothing more than a difference in degree due simply to an increasing complication of the elementary fact of association or of suggestion? But the first condition which is requisite in order that this complication may be possible, is that there exist a central rallying point wherein are stored and mingled the memories and perceptions which are increasing. And, in fact, during wakefulness, we establish with Paulhan that the law of the association of images is always subordinate to a superior law, to the law of logic and finality. This latter really constitutes the person, and, among the many ideas, which are concurrently offered by means of their ties of similarity or of contiguity with others, designates, and chooses the idea which conforms to the end pursued, to the chief pre-occupation of the moment. Already, moreover, we shall have been able to perceive both as a germ and in operation this essential need even in the deepest dream. The dreamer, in fact, and especially the hypnotic subject, is far from presenting this absolute passiveness which we assumed a little while ago for the convenience of our discussion. We know that he has "his aversions and his preferences," which means his dominant feelings or prejudices which have an influence over the progress and the unfolding of his phantasms; but we also know that this influence is too insignificant to involve his responsibility.

It is important to notice this clear distinction between the inconsequent, unstable, and ever changing "myself," of the hypnotic subject, and the incoherent, tenacious, and long identical "myself," of the man who is awake. Otherwise, one might say that the concurrence and accumulation of the innumerable examples and influences of surrounding society determine the crime of the most thoroughly awake and healthy man, in the same manner as the example and the influence of the magnetizer alone determine the acts of the most thoroughly asleep hysterical woman. Society taken as a whole would thus always be the true author of the misdeeds carried out by some one of its members, and the sociability of the individual, far from being proportional to his responsibility, would be in inverse ratio. Now it is certain that "hypnotic suggestion," as Ladame says so well, "is of the same nature as persuasion during the state of wakefulness"; it is also certain, according to us, that the social relation being imitation, the most thoroughly social being is the most thoroughly imitative being. But we must notice this very important point: absolute imitativeness, the faculty of submitting to influences of all kinds and from every side, and not merely from one single direction, as is the case with the hypnotic subject, must essentially imply the faculty of resisting an isolated example, a particular influence. A universal impressionability assumes an extraordinary originality which consists in a profound finality and logic, a regular combination of scattered impressions under the domination of one of them which the "myself" has made its own and by means of which it incorporates all the others. It is not only here that the combination is opposed to its elements, the resultant to its components. Also it is not alone by their anonymous character that the many influences, call them the suggestions of the social surroundings if you will, which are combined in each one of us are to be distinguished from hypnotic suggestion; it is especially by their character within and not foreign to the person, by their personal incorporation and their integration which has in it after all nothing more mysterious than all the other integrations and incorporations of the universe. If there were here a simple delusion, like that of free will, the monosyllable "*I*" would be the most insignificant of all words.

And at the same time we must admit that very often, much more often than one would suppose, the controlling influence of an enchanting man, a fascinator of mobs, a sort of Donato on a large scale, exercises over his contemporaries an absolute rule which ought in a great measure to cause the responsibility for the vices or the crimes bearing his effigy to be brought home to him. Again it is only over natures predisposed towards this contagion that it acquires this absolute power. And this remark applies to the very much simpler cases where madness is propagated from father to son, from wife to husband, from sister to sister, from a lover to his mistress. One sees many examples of this, of which one can become convinced by reading Legrand du Saulle's "Délire des persécutions." While studying these phenomena of the "delirium of two," "and when the two patients are undergoing treatment, the physician will notice that one of them dominates the other, that the latter is but the echo of the former, that the first one is intelligent and the second is far less endowed." Often the imitative force goes so far as to cause the same hallucinations of hearing to pass from one to the other. Euphrasie Mercier, according to Ball, was possessed of a power similar to this over her brothers and sisters.

But it frequently happens that, when one suffers example to carry one away, one was perfectly willing to have it do so. Those who resemble one another assemble together; the malefactor who has drawn from the surrounding suggestion of his companions the daring to murder or to steal began by choosing his friends and by creating for himself the society which suited him. This case in which companions having become accomplices reinforce their depraved tendencies by means of mutual suggestion, cannot but recall the case of the hysterical women of the Salpêtrière who have suggested to them, as we saw, the larcenies which they would not dare to commit were it not for this.

Before we draw to a close, let us also notice that the indirect responsibility of the drunkard, who is always guilty of having willingly exposed his fellow-men to the danger of his intoxication, is not applicable to the hypnotic subject without a distinction being made. Hypnosis is a form of madness at will, but sometimes at the will of the hypnotizer only, and not of the hypnotized. Certain subjects without knowing it present hypnotic zones, contact with which alone, without any consent on their part, plunges them into a deep sleep and gives them over without any defence to the one who has touched them. Such is the case, pointed out by Pitres,[1] of a young girl who, when her elbow was pressed, and who immediately went to sleep, was the unconscious victim of a rape and was astonished to find herself pregnant. Ladame believes himself to be able to establish the frequency of rape committed upon people who have been hypnotized. He cites a crime of this sort the discovery of which hypnotism alone

[1] See in the "Archives de l'Anthropologie criminelle," No. 10, p. 325, the account of this fact.

made possible, the patient having been put to sleep by the expert and having then revealed and given the circumstances of the fact which was forgotten by her in her normal state. It is especially, in so far as false testimony in criminal cases is concerned, that hypnotism is to be dreaded in the future. Bernheim has demonstrated the possibility of suggesting to a witness a retroactive hallucination.

§ 42. Old age. Age and sex.

If madness, epilepsy and hypnotism are accidental alterations or alienations of the person, extreme old age is their inevitable decomposition. The question of knowing up to what point the old man is still responsible for his acts is therefore of far more practical importance than the problems treated of above. We will, however, only say a word as regards it, for everything that has already been said helps in its solution. To what extent is senile degeneration a *denaturing* of the person? Is it not rather, as is often the case with drunkenness, a strengthening and a development? Such and such a man, born economical, becomes sordidly avaricious as he advances in age; such and such another, born distrustful, becomes ridiculously suspicious; very rarely is the character inverted as a consequence of old age. Old age is the shriveled fruit of life, an evil old age is a certificate of an evil life; thus the passions to which the old man gives way make him resemble the driver who is crushed by the wagon which he has set in motion. However, this is only true in part, and we could not agree with Chauveau and Faustin Hélie that, far from being able to aspire for an extenuation of his culpability, the old man who is not insane should be judged to be more guilty than other men, by reason of his characteristic experience, foresight, and reflection. Can one say that the old satyr, driven to indecent assaults upon children by a sickly passion, is deserving of more severity than a mature man who rapes a woman? We ought to say with Tardieu, that "the more advanced the age of criminals becomes, the more does that of their victims recede," and this contrast bears witness to a softening of the brain which brings us back to mental alienation.

A question which is also rather a delicate one is that of the responsibility of the deaf-mute. The latter, according to Tardieu,[1] would come very near to being irresponsible, if at least he

[1] "Etude médico-légale sur la folie," — Especially consult *Lannois:* "La surdimutité et les sourds-muets devant la loi." In "Archives de l'anthropologie criminelle," No. 22, 1889. (Lyons, Storck.)

were not brought up according to the perfected methods which are in use in these days. If he did not have this special education, in fact, he would be a stranger all his life to the society of other men, one could not say of his fellow-men.

Should I not, finally, say a word as to an influence which, without having in it anything morbid, deserves attention from our point of view: that of sex? According to all statistics, men are far more forcibly impelled towards crime than are women; one cannot harbor the slightest doubt with respect to this. Thus it is an annoying fate for an individual to be born a boy, at least as far as morality is concerned. Is this as much as to say that the fact of belonging to the male sex ought to be considered as an extenuating circumstance in the case of various offenses, especially that of crimes of a violent nature? Nobody has put forth this ridiculous opinion; at the same time what reason is there for not admitting it if one believes one ought to invoke in favor of an assassin or a thief the assassinations or the thefts committed by his parents, or every other deplorable condition of his origin? I limit myself to asking this question. Most assuredly my sex is no more an essential part of me than is the nature of my parentage.

§ 43. Moral conversion, salutary insanity. Slowness of great conversions. Necessity of surrounding suggestion. Great extent of moral transformations obtained by the founders of sects or religions. Effects of penal transportation. Remorse and repentance.

We have just gone over all the morbid causes which have the effect of more or less deeply transforming the person, and we have seen that, to the same extent as they affected his identity they decreased his responsibility. But are there not transformations within, moral regenerations of oneself by oneself, which are as salutary as the preceding are destructive, and which, without having anything pathological about them, sometimes rival these latter in their depth? If any such exist, must one extend to these beneficial alienations of the "myself" the same privilege of irresponsibility? This twofold question is worth while looking into.[1]

[1] This is the occasion to draw a general distinction which I had neglected to bring out in the first edition of this work, and which was responsible for my seeing very clever minds among the anthropologists reject my theory of responsibility at the outset and without examination. "Let us not confuse," I have since said ("Revue philosophique," May, 1890), "the identity of the person in the biological and individual sense of the word with its identity in the social sense. Identity

The naturalists of the penal law, imbued with the idea, unfortunately only too well justified in the majority of cases, that the mysterious powers of life alone can modify within us their own work, our character, which is the expression of the organism and the race, have very little belief in "the conversion of sinners" and only speak of it with a smile. Their scepticism, concurring on this point with our pessimism which is derived from other sources, has been contagious; our century, which has so often been the dupe of words, says that it is undeceived by appearances, and, even in fiction, it has begun no longer to tolerate the hackneyed type of the repentant sinner, and still less that of the regenerated brigand. We have here a fashion, the reverse of the artificial optimism which ruled during the last century. Let us endeavor, if that be possible, to free ourselves from both of these influences. If the moral character of a man were something as

always signifies change, as rest always signifies motion, but a *minimum* of change and of motion, or else a *sort* of change and motion, with which one need not be concerned *relatively to the object which one has in view.*

"Now such a degree or such a kind of modification as would perfectly suffice to operate a complete transformation of the person in the eyes of the moralist can perfectly well allow the wholeness of the individual character to continue in existence in the eyes of the natural psychologist. For the latter the person is characterized by the singularity of a certain group, of a certain equilibrium, Paulhan would say of a certain system, of innate tendencies, diverse and unequal, which are moreover susceptible of being made use of for the most contrary social or anti-social ends; but for the former, for the sociologist, it is essentially characterized by a certain system of customary ends, which are at first voluntary, of *acquired* feelings, wherein the natural person finds its special occupation, which could have been otherwise. An individual has not become physiologically or even psychologically another, because his native audacity, after having been for a long time exercised in maritime adventures, in the savageries of brigandage, has been turned into military bravery, in scientific voyages of exploration; but he has become socially another; and, as a consequence, to judge him to be guilty or worthy of blame because of the crimes committed by him before his conversion would be from a social and a moral point of view, as unjust as to impute to the madman who had been cured the extravagant acts committed during an attack of his madness which is past. That which is true of individuals is also true of peoples. When a people, such as the Scotch people, which, scarce two centuries ago, exceeded in bloodthirsty and vindictive cruelty, in the number of homicides, Sicily and Corsica, is now shown to us as the most gentle and inoffensive people of Europe, classed *as the most white of all* on the map of murder and assassination; when the Bulgarians, the Servians, the Cossacks, the Piedmontese, the inhabitants of the Romagna, the Swiss, and many others, without forgetting the Islanders of the Marquesas, those former cannibals changed into peaceful laborers, show us a similar phenomenon; and when, on the contrary, modern Greece as compared with ancient Greece, Calabria compared with Greater Greece, show us the passage of the most humanitarian civilization into the most cruel barbarity, are we not justified in saying that the ethnical character of peoples from the social point of view, the only one which interests us, has changed to the very greatest possible extent?"

limited as his physical shape, one could judge it to be as unalterable; the efforts of the will would succeed no better in changing it than do movements and attitudes in changing the form of the body, or even than does the play of the physiognomy in perceptibly altering the features of the countenance. This is what happens whenever the nature of an individual is ruled over by some exact and strong vocation, which is as tyrannical, as special as the instinct of bees; a hereditary impulse towards the calling of arms, to agriculture, to the life of a seaman, sometimes even to murder or to theft.

But this case is far more rare than people seem to think. Under the influence of a few missionaries, the Fijians, those ferocious cannibals, have been marvelously softened, in the same way as have the descendants of the bloodthirsty Aztecs. Darwin at the time of his extensive voyage had declared the Fuegians (the inhabitants of Terra del Fuego) to be absolutely incapable of becoming civilized. Some few years later, as we are informed by his Correspondence (Vol. II, pp. 449 *et seq.*), he became convinced, by means of evidences worthy of credence, "that their progress was marvelous," that these bandits who had been baptized had become remarkable for their honesty, and at once sent a check for five pounds Sterling to the Society of English Missions. These phenomena taking place in our own times, account to us for others which have taken place in the past. The rapidity with which the Normans, those sea-wolves, became transformed into shepherd dogs in the tenth century, the Bretons into Christians in the seventh, and the Gauls into Romans under Caesar, shows the degree of the plasticity of those human instincts reputed to be the most untamable by reason of their antiquity. In less than a century, Ozanam was able to say, "Great Britain, that island of pirates, had become the island of saints" and "the horror of blood was remarkable among the grandsons of Hengist and Horsa." Formerly, if one is to believe Onésime Réclus, the inhabitants of English Cornwall "led vessels upon the reefs by means of moving lights" in order to capture them, whereas now, without their race having changed, they have "become salvors always ready to lay down their lives."

Undoubtedly during the period of transition between these two extremes, there were to be found many individuals who, after having had the traditional passion for crime, had that for salvage. There are very few men in fact, whose *nature*, a vague virtuality, an undetermined problem, does not admit of several realizations, of several different solutions which are so many distinct or even contrary personalities between which as a general thing the chance of their life alone makes the choice. This ought to be so if the personality, the identity, as we understand them, consist in the domination of some unheard conviction, such as a certain pride or a certain religious belief, or of some deep sentiment, such as ambition, avarice, or love, which has dictated according to its convenience, and more often than not unknown to us, our thought and our conduct. When a Roman patrician, a refined Athenian, after having listened to the inflamed speech of a Demetrius (first century) or of a Demonax (second century), took it upon himself to lead as they did, the life of a cynic in all its roughness, to sell his goods, to sleep on straw, to drive from his heart all desire and from his mind all curiosity, it was a turning upside down of his life from top to bottom. The day when, combated by a new inspiration, our master-idea, our mother-passion, is laid bare before us and loses its force; the day when, being our own surgeon, we succeed in driving it out and, for example, in sowing on the ruins of vanity a resignation to absolute nothingness, on the ruins of dear illusion the hard truth, on the ruins of egoism, of hatred and of envy, pity, kindness, and self-denial, that very day there arises within us an entirely new person, and we are able to sing like Dante our "vita nuova." Only more than one day is required in order that this day may dawn, and no more here than elsewhere does life admit of a sudden turning point. I know quite well that a bitter crisis in the midst of their lives, and this coincidence is remarkable, is credited to the majority of the great founders of religions or of religious orders, from which they will have come out in a few days miraculously altered. Buddha and Christ, as well as Mahomet, had their Hegira, their retreat into the desert or the woods; Pythagoras, in Crete, passes a month in meditation in the sacred cave of Mount Ida. St. Paul falls upon the road to Damascus, Augustine has his decisive ecstasy under his fig tree, Luther in his cloister. Ignatius Loyola, wounded in the leg, recreates a new soul for himself in a few weeks of meditation in his castle.

But these are either legendary or exceptional facts; and these great men were themselves so well convinced of the slowness of true conversions that they generally imposed upon the chosen among their disciples a long period of preliminary tests which were judged to be necessary for their regeneration. Pythagoras, in his marvelous philosophical monastery at Crotona, demanded of his ascetics a novitiate of five years before authorizing them to don the white tunic bound by a cord of flax, which signalized the Dominicans of a later age. Not only the monastic orders of every religion, Buddhistic or Christian, but even the civilized armies of all times, have gone through such experiences. Everywhere, even though cut down by the application of the wisest methods of training, the military novitiate, which, out of a cowardly laborer must make a soldier "in spirit," of a Circassian slave a Mameluke, of a mountain bandit a hero, lasts several years. As to the education of children, which, under favorable conditions, also works miracles, one knows that it is scarcely ever complete in less than ten years. But one can easily conceive that, when the transformation takes place without the preliminary consent of the one who undergoes it, as in the case of the Mameluke and the schoolboy, it must be slower in its accomplishment than when it is wished for by the novice.

That which is important to notice, however, is that, reduced to its forces alone, the will of the individual is always powerless, with the very rare exception of a few great men, to change the trend of his heart. The help of grace is necessary for this, say the Christians; that is to say the assistance of a sudden, a deep emotion, enthusiasm or suffering, affection or anguish; especially is the suggestive co-operation of examples necessary, the reciprocal carrying away of the neophytes gathered together under a common faith and a common rule, and each one of whom is fortified with the strength of all. That transformation of the personality which, in the case of the hypnotic subject, is momentary and more apparent than real, becomes a continued and durable reality in the case of the neophyte, thanks to that continuity of simultaneous suggestions which he assimilates to himself.

Religions, up to the present time, have had almost the monopoly of these great recastings of souls, and this is the explanation of their vitality. If one wishes to see in them only a museum of ancient superstitions and of children's tales, it is impossible to understand their secular and universal domination. But they are something else, that is, the support which is necessary for the moral renovations which the individual has dreamed of and which he cannot realize all by himself, and for the lasting intellectual settlements as well, for the stable convictions of which the individual feels the need and which few minds can themselves found without the imitative pressure of the prevailing unanimity around them. Religious, pseudo-religious, or quasi-religious, every institution which has been truly regenerative has been one of these; the convents of Thibet or of the Aztecs, the Porch or the Port-Royal, the schools of the Cynics, "those mendicant friars of antiquity" or the Catholic Seminaries, the Geneva of Calvin or the Florence of Savonarola, the noisy meetings of the Quakers or the silent walks of the Pythagoreans, the great secret societies. Artificially if you will, but not superficially, a second nature is thus formed within each associate, which is the collective work of all the others as well as himself, the fruit of an ardent collaboration. But is it any the less his because his co-religionists have worked for its accomplishment? No, it is indeed his own, just as much, if not more so than his first nature, which he had not even concurred in forming.

However this may be, the depth of the moral metamorphoses which often take place during the course of a human life cannot be denied, and scepticism upon this point would be but ignorance. Undoubtedly it is a good thing not to accept without reservation what the sacred writers tell us as to the conversions, instantaneous and "en masse," of an entire people, as to the Franks for example, who were regenerated between one evening and the next day because of the baptism of Clovis. But is it permissible to dispute the efficacy of the Christian missions in Germania,[1] in Ireland, in Saxony, and even, despite the remoteness of time, the power of the preachings of Pythagoras? "This was somewhat of an analogy to the preaching of Buddha in India," says Lenormand.[2] The inhabitants of Crotona were laid low by a recent disaster: he raised them up again, gave them new life, victory and prosperity. The proof that their conversion was thorough is that their propaganda spread far in time and space; all the towns of Greater Greece borrowed its institutions from Crotona, so much so that, having become alike through imitation of this common model, they were able to have a national currency. Monetary unity is generally the clearest indication of social unity. When one sees Greeks, and Greek inhabitants of Italy, neighbors

[1] We must not only consult Ozanam and Montalembert on this subject, but also Littré. — The republic of Paraguay is another more doubtful, but no less convincing example. One can read with respect to this the *Marquis of Argenson* in his "Considérations" (1764). His enthusiasm is exaggerated, but curious.

[2] "La Grande Grèce," Vol. II.

of Sybaris, become chaste and silent under the influence of this extraordinary man, and practising fraternal communism; when one sees the high culture and the exquisite charm of the Pythagorean women, as reserved in their customs as they are lofty in their minds, grandmothers of Hypatia, blossom forth in the midst of the gynecium or the markets for courtesans, one cannot doubt but that the apostleship of the master had the virtue attested by the whole of antiquity. The least one can admit in this case and in all the other analogous cases is that some few souls were stirred to their depths and that, through the action of this leaven, a town, a nation was raised up little by little, gained over to the new feelings, to the new customs, to a varying and ever increasing extent. A legend tells that Pythagoras would have tamed an ordinary bear which followed him in the streets of Crotona and a white eagle which was flying above him; this recalls, says Lenormand, the taming of the wolf of Gubbio by St. Francis of Assisi. These symbols are transparent. The fact is that the moral conversion — I do not say recantation because of interest — of a man can be compared to the domesticating of a wild animal, and it is natural to attribute this second power to him who has given proof of the first one.

The ideal prison would be one which was a moral novitiate: this is the object striven for by the cell system, but one plainly sees what it essentially lacks in its attainment. Isolation may be harmless, but, as we know, it cannot but be powerless. Though very far from the perfection dreamed of, penitentiary colonies have sometimes given better results. The being sent abroad, the complete change in climate and way of living impresses upon many a person who has been deported the moral stirring up which disposes them towards a change of heart, and the power of example is such that, if the new surroundings into which they are thrown are honest or practically honest, they are there regenerated in all seriousness.

Such has been the spectacle offered by the convicts in Australia, at least in the various centres where the colonists who have come of their own volition mingled with those who had been transported and where, as Michaux [1] says, these latter "separated from the others by a little integrity, were led away by their mutual con-

[1] "Etude sur la question des peines," by *Michaux*, sub-director of Colonies, (Paris, 1875). An excellent pamphlet, especially interesting by reason of the details which it furnishes on the history of English deportations.

tagion"; for in the island of Norfolk, where an attempt was made to colonize with the convict element free from any alloy, and to create order out of nothing but disorder, the emulation of vice and crime was seen to result in a paroxysm of depravity and savageness. On the contrary, at Sydney, even eight years after the colony was founded, there had not been committed one single assassination. Also "one who had been freed, distinguished for his good conduct, was provided with the office of a magistracy." In a quarter of a century, "a population of 40,000 souls, among which there were more than 2000 convicts, had been agglomerated, formed, organized, policed, already giving evidence of its vitality and its virility by means of noteworthy actions." Australian civilization grew out of this foundation. I do not know the part played in this very fruitful rebirth by the Protestant propaganda, but one must believe that it was a powerful auxiliary. If I am to believe the "Chronique de Nouméa"[1] upon this point, there too "the material and moral raising up of the condemned is no longer a philanthropic abstraction, it is a reality. In Nouméa, your tailor as well as your bootmaker, before having become those who supply you, were members of the '4th. Marines' [that is to say are transported criminals, who jokingly pretend they followed the three regiments of Marines]; they are now very honest fellows." Often "confiding colonists close neither doors nor windows and have no reason to be sorry for it. They point out such and such an unfortunate, who, condemned upon his own admissions, for qualified theft, is today numbered among those to whom one makes a payment without taking any receipt for it."

Why should we be astonished at these facts? Cannot one consider as a sort of penal colony those great capitals of ancient times, Athens, Thebes, Rome, which were originally simply places of refuge hospitably open to the malefactors who came from all the surrounding country? Was not the *refugee* in such a case a sort of a *willingly transported man?* Now, the most brilliant civilizations of the old world began thus. Finally, as prostitution, according to Lombroso, is one of the principal forms of female criminality, I am very much inclined to look upon the conversion of the beautiful sinners as coming within our subject. Now to be sure Magdalenes are exceptional enough; but after all, are they never to be found?

[1] Under this title there appeared a very curious article by *Kernwoor*, in the "Archives de l'anthropologie criminelle," No. 11.

Very well! these facts not being capable of being contested in certain cases, I maintain that, when they are proved and manifest, one could not legitimately, nor legally, impute to the new man the crimes committed by the old man. An excellent Superior Officer of the French Navy, according to Maxime du Camp,—had begun by being a thief; to remind him of his offense would have been not only cruel, but a mistake. To reproach a convict, who is now an upright business man of irreproachable probity, with a theft or a murder of his former life, would be an indignity. It may be that this theft or this murder was not one of which he had been convicted, that it was an act only recently brought to light and prosecution of which was not yet barred according to law; no matter, if the public prosecutor judged it to be proper to carry out a prosecution against this man, the public conscience would be revolted.

Why is this so, however? And how can the partisans of responsibility founded upon free will justify this revolt of the moral sense? Is it that the change which has taken place in the nature of a criminal since his crime causes his crime to have been any the less free? No. He should thus have remained just as punishable as ever. If one refuses to come to this conclusion, it means that without knowing it one makes moral responsibility rest upon personal identity and not upon personal liberty. We all feel in the bottom of our hearts that, however great may have been the fault, pardon is due to sincere and deep repentance when it clearly denotes a radical conversion.[1] This feeling stays active in penal practice, in spite of that style of Draconian severity which has a tendency to prevail in theory. Religions believe they have the right to pardon, because they believe, and not without reason,

[1] Repentance, remorse is the state of transition between the old and the new man. On the one hand it attests identical persistence since the act which we attribute to ourselves when we repent; on the other, it reveals the work of transformation from which we will come out free from all shame, from all remorse, from all repentance which is obligatory. At all events, repentance does not in any way prove our liberty. In a dream, when we have just committed an imaginary evil deed, we feel a true remorse because of it, for, as Bouillier ingeniously remarks: "that which we approve of or which we condemn in the daytime, be it in ourselves, or be it in others, we equally approve of and condemn in our dreams. Perhaps even, it is with respect to the notions of morality of each one of us that there is the least alteration in the transition from real life to the life of dreams." Moreover, once awake, we no more blush, we no more repent of our real or imaginary actions committed during a dream, than does the madman who has been cured blush and repent of the acts which are prejudicial to another which he may have committed during his attacks of madness.

that they have the power to convert; it is not because they would attribute to themselves the virtue of being able to render inevitable an act of the past which would have been freely brought about. Their Penal Code which is so indulgent, that which they call penance, implies, in the last analysis, the truth which I am developing. In the same proportion as a religion shows itself to be powerful in transforming men does it show itself to be indulgent in absolving them. What I am saying about cults is just as true of civilizations. If our own were inclined towards a greater power of honest assimilation, of deeply bettering its prisoners, one would see it exercising upon a larger scale the right of pardon and general pardon. When a society shows itself to be without pity, one can conclude from this that it has little hold over hearts.

Thus like madness, like epilepsy, like hypnotism, moral conversion gives rise to irresponsibility; but there is none the less, in this very respect, an important difference between the pathological alterations and the voluntary transformations of the personality. In the first case, the new "myself" is not only not responsible for the acts committed by the old one, but again is not or is scarcely responsible for its own acts, as it is a stranger to the social world and scarcely identical with itself; on the contrary, in the second case, the new "myself" of the convert, superior to the old one in sociability and in identical persistence, is still more responsible for its acts than was the latter. The more advanced one is in honesty, the more does one feel oneself to be, and in reality the more one is guilty of an act committed in a moment of backsliding.

We have seen above that the crisis which causes transformation of the person is sometimes undergone involuntarily, and sometimes willingly brought about or welcomed by the subject of it. The Christian slave of whom a Mameluke has been made only resigned himself to his fate with tears, and it is the same thing with the child caught in the cruel machinery of our schools; but the Jesuit has entered upon his novitiate of his own free will. In the eyes of a partisan of free will, the distinction must seem to be important, and when the person has been transformed in spite of himself, he could not impute to him even the acts which conformed the most to his new nature, which he commits as a consequence of habits originally due to constraint and to violence. At the same time the transformation can be as absolute in the first case as in the second, and I do not see why the Mameluke or the graduate forcibly recast by means of an education "ad hoc" should be less guilty because of their faults than a monk or a Pythagorean are because of theirs. Common sense forbids us to draw a distinction here, and we see that it once more upholds in this our point of view.

§ 44. Sovereignty.

It remains for me to say a word as to a kind of irresponsibility which does not come under the preceding heads, that of the primitive despots with relation to their subjects; whence, by reason of survival, has issued the fictitious irresponsibility of our constitutional monarchs. Like the idiot, by reason of his inferior nature, so the absolute monarch is rendered irresponsible by reason of his presumed superiority; for both the one and the other are or seem to be outside of society, the one above, the other below.

According to Stuart Mill, this irresponsibility of the autocrat would bear out his way of explaining the feeling of responsibility which would consist simply in foreseeing the possibility of being punished, that is to say, of feeling pain at the hands of someone else as a consequence of an act. Thus the king-god of primitive times would only be reputed to be irresponsible because he was known to be guaranteed by his armed forces against the possibility of punishment. Just as though the most holy character of this sovereign, supreme legislator, and consequently a person above the laws which he enacts and the social sphere which he rules, were not sufficient to justify his privilege in the eyes of his subjects, who would obviously not dare to compare themselves to him in asking him to render an account of his acts! He is judged to be irresponsible, firstly, because he is judged to be incomparable, and then because he is judged to be impeccable and infallible, but not because he is known to be unpunishable. It is known that the neighboring kings dispose of a power equal to his own and can punish him; but the conclusion that he is responsible as regards them is not drawn because of this. I will add that, when a savage tribe has killed a member of a neighboring tribe not related and not allied to it, without affinity of race or of custom with the former, it does not judge itself to be in any way responsible towards the latter, although it expects reprisals will soon be taken. Thus, at the base of the idea of responsibility, there is something else besides the expectation of a penalty, of pain; there is, I repeat, the feeling of a social tie and of individual identity.

The despot is, moreover, less a stranger to surrounding society than is the slave or the idiot. He is in a relationship with it which, though not reciprocal, is yet unilateral, just as the man of genius in so far as he is a man of genius. If he does not deign to imitate anybody, it often happens that his people rise up to take him for their model. Consequently, and because of his assumed infallibility, he can be worthy of merit, although he cannot be unworthy of merit; and although he cannot be held liable for a debt owed his subjects — for to be a debtor is to be responsible — he has over them many of the rights of a creditor. Praise is due him and not blame. Thus the reverse of responsibility appertains to him.

Let us show, in closing, that exemption from punishment founded upon the causes of irresponsibility enumerated in this chapter could never have any results which would be prejudicial to society. A crime is excused or not prosecuted because the author of it was either overtaken by madness, or a prey to an attack of epilepsy, or hypnotized in spite of himself; or because he has since his crime been sincerely converted; or, finally, because he is an absolute monarch. Could the knowledge of this fact ever encourage anyone who was well informed[1] to commit a crime under the same conditions? No, for there is no such thing as a madman or an epileptic at will, and, if one could be so at will, one would take care not to wish to become so; no more is one willingly hypnotized *in spite of oneself;* there is no such thing as an absolute monarch at will; as to wishing to commit a crime and wishing at the same time to be sincerely repentant afterwards, this would be a manifest contradiction.

Supposing that one were to condemn a madman, an epileptic, a hypnotized person, a convert, or a despot for a crime committed under the above conditions. The penalty, in all these cases, excepting the last one, might prevent the public from repeating this crime, it would thus serve as a *warning* for them: but it would in nowise prevent the author from eventually repeating it himself, it would thus not serve as a *warning* as far as he was concerned, or it would only do so *in a useless manner*, I mean to say for the convert, who has no longer any need of this penal menace. In the last case, that of the despot, it would be just the opposite. The penalty (supposing it to be applied, an inadmissible hypothesis

[1] I say "*well informed*"; an acquittal based upon our principles could in fact only have disadvantages if the public were informed of it without having any knowledge of its motives. This is frequently the case; but ignorance of the motives of a judgment which is made public can no more be assumed than can ignorance of the law itself.

moreover, as it is a contradiction to be an autocrat and to be punished) might prevent the author from doing the same thing again, but it would have in it nothing which would intimidate the public, who would not believe itself in any way threatened by the punishment of a superhuman being. Thus it will never combine the two advantages whose combination, in our opinion, is required for the absolute justification of punishment. Our theory requires penalties to be useful, but it requires this utility to be absolute.

CHAPTER V

THE CRIMINAL

§ 45. Preliminary remarks.

§§ 46–53. (I) The criminal type. (II) The "natural offense" and native criminality are two different things. Impossibility of localizing this complex tendency, criminality, in the brain, before having localized its elements. (III) The criminal is not a madman. (IV) The criminal is not a savage who has reappeared among us. Illusory foundations of the hypothesis of atavism: physical anomalies, tattooing, slang. (V) The criminal is not a degenerate. (VI) Is the criminal an epileptic? Refutation of this theory taken literally. The example of Misdèa analyzed. What may possibly be true at the basis of this idea. Essential periodicity of psychological phenomena. (VII) The criminal type is a professional type. Physiognomy and handwriting. (VIII) Psychology and the criminal. The criminal is partly the result of his own crime and of criminal justice.

§§ 54–57. (I) The classification of criminals should be psychological above everything else. The rural criminal and the urban criminal. (II) Rural brigandage in Corsica and in Sicily. Its characteristics. The rural police and the urban police. (III) Continuation, the Sicilian Maffia. (IV) Urban brigandage. Criminality in Barcelona.

§ 45. Preliminary Remarks.

An estimate of the contemporary doctrines relative to the penalty absolutely demanded the development of the subject which has been given above. In order that there may be a penalty there must be a crime, and not only an injury; and that there may be a crime it is necessary that the act to be punished should be really imputable to its apparent perpetrator. Thus, the keystone of every penal system ought to be a theory of moral responsibility. But up to this time all the schools of philosophy have admitted on principle that moral responsibility was based upon the postulate of free will; all of them, including those which, denying free will, believe that they have established, as a consequence, the complete moral irresponsibility of human agents. Now, we have seen that the early schools established imputability upon a foundation which was in ruins, and, without having to commit ourselves upon the absolute value of determinism, we have come to agree with the later schools upon the necessity of finding some other support than freedom. The positivists thought they had discovered it by inventing a responsibility which was purely social, and which, despite the absolute irresponsibility of the man, would be connected with every one of his actions injurious to another, even though committed involuntarily or during an attack of madness.

This position has seemed untenable to us; it is as outrageous for society as it is dangerous for the individual, for it likens society to a brute which strikes back blindly after a blow without seeking to discover whether it is or is not intentional or excusable. Moreover, it injures logic as much as it does humanity; it only leaves to responsibility its name, and, so to speak, its fossil form. If it makes any pretense of preserving the ideas of crime and punishment, and of satisfying the human conscience upon this point, it pays the latter with illusory words. In the last analysis it only serves as a disguise and in no way serves to bring about the disappearance of the fatal consequence which follows from determinism if it is true that free will be postulated by the responsibility of the individual. This consequence is that there is occasion to treat the criminal, if he be a savage who has reappeared among us, as we treat the islanders of Oceania who attack us, or, in other words, to exterminate him; or else, if he be a species of madman, an epileptic, or a degenerate, to send him into some sanitarium where he will be more or less confined; and that it is right, moreover, to modify the physical, physiological, or social factors of the crime by applying as soon as possible the rules of hygiene and radically reforming the social condition. To speak frankly, this would mean that it is important not to correct, but absolutely to do away with the Penal Code. To reason about the penalty after this is the same thing as giving a dissertation upon theodicy while professing atheism, — a thing, however, which is sometimes seen.

This is why we have been constrained in the three preceding chapters to set forth our own theory of responsibility. If this exposition had been lacking, in fact, admitting neither the spiritualistic theory upon this point nor the positivist compromise which we have absolutely overthrown, we ought necessarily to confess that the ideas of crime and penalty are chimerical, and give up all thought of concerning ourselves with criminal law. If our point of view is the true one, if it is at least acceptable, if it agrees with psychology and with mental pathology, with sociology, — in other words, with science, and, what is more, with history, — then we are entitled to pursue our labors.

But it still remains to build up something upon this foundation. The conditions of responsibility or of irresponsibility in general having been laid down, it is now well worth while to seek the conditions of penal responsibility, that is to say, to ask ourselves first of all what is a crime and what is a criminal, under what physical or social circumstances they are produced, how they are formed and transformed in the course of the progress of civilization, and what are the natural categories of crime and criminals. And, in the second place, it is worth while to find out what punishment is; what is, what has been, and what should be its object; what transformations it has undergone and has to undergo, in the same way as criminal procedure. I say that at present it is worth while raising these questions, for, if moral responsibility had not been securely established, their discussion would be far from affording the same interest.

For example, the problem of knowing if influences of a natural order or influences of a social order have predominated in the production of an offense is of very great importance, practically as well as theoretically, from our point of view; but, from the point of view of the various factions of the positivist school, is it as important? For us, to say that a crime is due principally to social causes, or even to physical causes, is to say that it is due to causes of a social *origin*, or else of a physical *origin*, but which have been individualized by the adhesion of the person to their action, by their consonance with the nature of the agent, who has rather appropriated them for himself than obeyed them, and who has rather made use of them than been their instrument, — unless we refuse to this "*he*" every reality worthy of the name. Thenceforth he should always be punished, but his punishment should differ according to whether natural causes shall have carried him away or not. In one of these cases it will be proved that one has to deal with an incorrigible, and there might be a question of eliminating him; according to the other hypothesis, there would be some hope of repairing by means of social influences of a new kind the moral evil which bad surroundings had produced.

On the contrary, if one looks upon the physical *factors* or the social factors of the offense as its true causes, and if the delinquent has only supplied a name for them, what is the use of alienists and socialists disputing as to the more or less preponderating part which these two great anonymous criminals have played in the carrying out of some particular crime? It is these guilty fellows that must be reached; but, as it is no easier perceptibly to modify society than nature, if one attacks these apparently guilty ones, at the same time knowing perfectly well that they are only guilty in appearance, one should treat them, in one case as in the other, as incurables, and, consequently, — assuredly, with no hatred nor anger, and even pitying them greatly, — decapitate them.

However, let us approach an examination of the various subjects which we have pointed out; and, in order to keep as nearly as possible to the order already followed in our setting forth of the positivist doctrines, let us deal with: 1st, the criminal; 2d, the crime; 3d, the judgment; 4th, the penalty. First, in this chapter, we will deal with the criminal.

§ 46. (I) The criminal type.

What is a criminal? — At the death of the great Lama, the priests of Thibet agree to seek for the newborn into whom his immortal soul has transmigrated. They recognize him by certain characteristics, by true anthropological description, which they firmly believe never deceives. The Egyptian priests proceeded in exactly the same way, in order to pick out the bull Apis among all the bulls in the Valley of the Nile. Thus, there was for them, as there still is for the clergy and the people of Thibet, a divine type; and it is thus that in the eyes of Lombroso a criminal type exists which will allow of recognizing the malefactor from birth. Such, at least, was his first conception; but we know that in being developed it could not help becoming complicated in order to accommodate itself to the facts that contradicted it. At the present time, what is there left of it? Apparently, there is little, but, at the same time, something essential, as we shall see. If it had only served to give us more precise knowledge as to what the criminal is not, without giving a single indication, moreover, as to what he is, it would not have been in vain. But it has done more. It has accumulated curious observations, which will doubtless be useful later on; it has outlined in characteristics which will not perish the psychology of the delinquent, and has paved the way for a sociological explanation of him.

First of all, owing to the partial failure of its attempt, the school of Lombroso seems to us to have absolutely demonstrated that the criminal is not a product of nature; that is to say, that he does not correspond to any natural idea in the Platonic sense, nor in the scientific sense either. The Chinaman, the Negro, and the Mongol correspond to realistic schemes of this nature. Combine by Galton's process ten or a dozen photographs of Chinamen, and you will obtain a generic portrait wherein, with their differences blotted out, their similarities alone will appear in a curious relief, a living abstraction and individual incarnation of the ideal rule, of which the individuals are the oscillating deviations. This picture-type has this particular thing about it, that it embellishes that which it combines and it explains that which it sums up. Carry out the same operation with twenty or thirty other Chinamen; the new synthetic picture will resemble the preceding one still more than the photographs which compose it resemble one another.[1]

But now endeavor photographically to integrate in this manner the several hundred photographs of malefactors which fill the album annexed to the French translation of "L'Homme criminel." Assuredly, the thing is possible. Galton's process must always give a result, for the same reason that the repeated looking at external things and the stirring up of recollections in one's memory must always result in the human mind in general ideas. Only, between the violent and artificial fusion of heterogeneous pictures which we can produce in the latter case, and the mutual commingling of congeneric pictures which we have called forth above, there is the same dissimilarity as between a generalization which is purely verbal and a generalization founded upon the nature of things.

One would perceive this by operating separately upon various groups in this album. The number of groups would determine the number of results, which would differ very greatly from one another and would have scarcely any more relation with the elementary portraits which had been violently disintegrated and artificially combined in them. Can one at least hope that in separately photographing groups of malefactors belonging to the same category, — "caroubleurs" (thieves who use false keys), "cambrioleurs" (robbers of apartments), "escarpes" (assassins), swindlers and "stupratori," — one might be more fortunate? Not at all. Each nation and each race has its swindlers, its thieves,

[1] In "La Photographie appliquée a la production du type d'une famille, d'une Tribu ou d'une Race" (Paris, 1887), *Arthur Batut* gives us several examples of type-pictures obtained by means of this process, and one can see that they are to be distinguished from the pictures which go to make up their elements by a greater degree of harmony and regularity. But these pictures were always of members of the same race.

and its assassins, who are bearers of the anthropological characteristics that distinguish it. With any physical type, under certain social conditions, and being given certain cerebral peculiarities that are too profound to reveal themselves in the external anatomy, one can create delinquents of every kind. Thus there are no more *several* criminal types than *one* criminal type in the *Lombrosian* sense of the word; and Marro, when he attempts to substitute the plural here for the singular, is no less conjectural and has no better foundation than his master.[1] One of two things must be so. Either the delinquent is physically, if not physiologically, normal, and in this case he bears the very type of his country, or else he is abnormal, and then he does not belong to any type; and it is his very lack of type that characterizes him. But, to say at the same time that he is an anomaly and that he conforms to a natural model is to contradict oneself. There is another hidden contradiction in looking upon the social life as so essential to man that a human being who is "dishumanized," so to speak, can alone be anti-social, and to assume that nature has taken the pains to make a special creation in order to bring forth this individual who is contrary to nature.

For Topinard, the criminal, when he was not a sick man, would be an individual who was perfectly *normal*, at least as far as he was concerned physically. He finds that the collection of pictures brought together by Lombroso reminds him of the photographic albums of his friends. "With the exception of the filth, the naked breast, and the weariness," he says, "and often the poverty stamped upon his face, the head of a rogue, as a general thing, resembles the head of an honest man." I would not go so far as that; Vidocq was not of this opinion, nor were the majority of the clever detectives. Maxime du Camp, it is true,[2] somewhere expresses the same impression. "When one sees these people close to," he says, speaking of malefactors, "when one speaks with them and knows their antecedents, one is surprised to see countenances similar to those of other men." But a few pages further on,

[1] Sometimes the school allows discouraging admissions with regard to this to escape it. "It is neither correct nor accurate," says *Benedikt* at the Congress of Rome, "to pretend that one must always find something abnormal in the criminal individual. It is neither correct nor accurate because the psychological fact is partly the product of molecular phenomena, and because science is still very far from having discovered an anatomy of molecules and a molecular physiology." At the Congress of Paris (1889), the same learned man accentuated the same opinion supported by Senator Moleschott and a number of his associates.

[2] "Paris, ses organes et ses fonctions."

dealing with a highway robber of the worst type, he writes: "I had the opportunity of seeing him; he is very large, and his strength must have been colossal; *his powerful lower jaw*, his large mouth, almost without any lips, *his receding forehead and very shifting eyes*, give him the appearance of an *enormous chimpanzee*, — an appearance which *the excessive length of his arms* does not belie." Lombroso could not have put this better. This is one of those meetings, — which are not very rare, moreover, — which lend to the atavistic explanation of the criminal a certain apparent support. However, they are far from being sufficient to establish it. This simian type, appearing here in such an evil form, has served elsewhere as an envelope for remarkable personages of a high degree of morality. Robert Bruce, the liberator of Scotland [1] had, as we know, a skull formed like that of the man of Neanderthal, who was the most monkey-like of prehistoric men.[2]

From the social point of view crime may be a monstrosity, but not from the individual or organic point of view, because it is the absolute triumph of egoism and of the organism over the brakes of society. The man who is a true born criminal could thus be nothing more than a very fine animal, a sample which was a credit to his race. Were the tyrants, were the artists of the Italian Renaissance, who were as lavish with their assassinations as with their achievements and masterpieces, monsters? They were not monstrosities physically, that is certain; and, socially, it is open to discussion. If the social characteristic of this historical phase was, as Burckhardt demonstrates, the fading away of individuality, it was inevitable that it should be fertile in criminal manifestations, The Borgias [3] are not at all an exception in their time. The same lack of scruples and of moral feeling characterizes all the Italian princes of the fourteenth and fifteenth centuries, — born in crime, living in crime, and dying as soon as they cease to be criminals.

[1] *De Quatrefages*, in "Hommes fossiles et Hommes sauvages," cites several other facts of this nature.

[2] In a profound and substantial book ("Les Criminels," Doin, 1889) *Corre* seems to me to have wisely avoided the two opposite extremes that I have just pointed out. On the one hand, with the French School, he makes the social causes of the offense preponderate; and in doing this he combats the exaggerations of the Italian School; but on the other hand, he knows enough to give its proper place to the criminal type understood in the professional sense of the word. As a general thing, he takes the same point of view as Lacassagne.

[3] See an interesting article by *Gebhard* in the "Revue des Deux Mondes," December 15, 1888.

Crime among them takes on the disguise of punishment. They massacre in order to intimidate, at the same time as they take vengeance. For them crime is a necessary part of government, just as the government is for the people a necessity for order and for existence. Crime has its place, and its place of honor, in this magnificent blooming forth of all the arts in festal array; they are bound up in it "as the pearls are in the dagger."

This is the very thing which was bound to kill this beautiful aesthetic civilization when it was in full bloom. For a civilization which glorifies the criminal is no more capable of living than that which casts the most honest people among the criminals, a spectacle so often met with in times of revolution. The criminal is the man that society, when it is capable of living and is regular, is compelled to eliminate. The criminal is thus, to tell the truth, no more a social product than he is a natural product; he is — forgive me the word — a social excrement. And that is why it is interesting to the very highest degree to examine closely into which are the types of people to be found in the convict prisons and in ordinary prisons, rowing in the galleys or mounting the scaffold, in all times and in all countries. When the nature of these people happens to change it is always a serious symptom. If a society *excretes* excellent elements which it does not know how to utilize, — the Protestants under Louis XIV, the "aristocrats" under the Terror, — it is dangerously ill, rather like a man suffering from diabetes, and for a reason which is at bottom analogous.

Now, what society, in varying degrees, does not present this cause of weakening? The ideal would be for a society only to reject from its midst the *downright scoundrels*, individuals who are absolutely incapable of being assimilated and disciplined. We must do this justice to our modern Europe, by saying that it is making great strides towards this end; the people in its jails are really the refuse, more and more vile, of its rural districts and its towns. But perfection is still very far from having been attained. Thus, if there existed a criminal type, this type would be subject to fluctuation and changes which, from century to century and from latitude to latitude, could not fail to render him exceedingly unlike himself. A few skulls, a few brains of assassins, weighed and measured in our time, — this is all very well. But have there been submitted to the same anthropological examination the thousands of thieves hanged yearly upon the gallows of England within the last half century, the people sacrificed at Montfaucon, the corpses swinging in the breeze before the gateways of the feudal castles, upon all the hills, before the entrance of every town of the Middle Ages? The twenty thousand heretics and sorcerers burned in eight years by Torquemada, the Romans condemned to be given to the beasts or to be handed over to the games of the circus, and the Egyptians condemned to labor in the mines or upon the pyramids? All those pirates of Barbary who infested the Mediterranean until the end of the last century, all those highwaymen who devastated France during and after the Hundred Years War, — who will tell us the form of their skulls and their cerebral or corporeal anomalies, if anomalies there were? Who will verify, by referring to them, the exactness of the pretended proper types, we are asked, of the malefactors of every race and of all times?

§ 47. (II) The "natural offense" and native criminality are two different things. Impossibility of localizing this complex tendency, criminality, in the brain, before having localized its elements.

However, the very remark which I have just made implies the recognition of the fact that there actually exist a certain number of true criminals, whose criminality has about it nothing conventional. By true criminals are we to understand those who would have been criminals in any society which one can conceive of? No; most assuredly, there are none of this sort. Then must we understand those who would have been such in any stable society? Perhaps. However, let us clearly explain what we mean. That there may exist forms of offenses which are incompatible with the stability of any people I admit; such are murder and robbery committed without any provocation which can be thought to justify them, and to the injury of the fellow member of society or the man thought to be such. But that there exist people, who, under all social conditions, of no matter what nation and at no matter what time, would have been murderers and thieves of this type, I deny. Let us only consider, if you wish, as absolute crimes, or, to use Garofalo's expression, natural crimes, murder and theft, leaving aside not only every offense against morality — even adultery and rape — which hardy people have fostered, but even abortion and infanticide, which certain nations have elevated to the rank of praiseworthy actions.

Does it follow from this that all our incorrigible murderers and thieves are stamped with the seal of absolute criminality, and that they are the only ones who are so stamped? Not in the least. Neither one nor the other of these two propositions seem to us to be correct. On the one hand, a number of our assassins and our pickpockets, if they had been born rich, and if they had not had the bad luck to be born and to be brought up in an evil suburb, and to be subjected to the example of perverse comrades, would never have killed or stolen. And we must not here allow the atrocity of the crime which has been committed to lead us astray. When we think of a Pranzini strangling the woman with whom he has slept, and then her servant and the child of the latter, it seems as though we had to deal with a being who was essentially a destroyer, born for homicide as Mozart was born for music. But those Cossacks and Prussians, who were so numerous, and who in 1814 [1] raped women and then slaughtered them before their husbands who were bound, were honest citizens in their own villages, where they had never committed the slightest misdeed; and more than one of them must have won the military medal of honor.[2] It is possible that under certain social conditions even a Pranzini might have made himself useful, or, at least, would not have committed either theft or murder, although his depraved nature would undoubtedly have driven him to other kinds of offenses, but to offenses which were *relative*, such as adultery or rape. On the other hand, as a result of this last conjecture, we may presume that among the individuals punished by our tribunals because of even the most relative of offenses, — whether it be for poaching or for smuggling, — there are to be found some who are thoroughly dangerous, sometimes even more dangerous than many of the Sicilian or Corsican murderers.

From this it follows that the "natural offense" and essential criminality are two things, and that the former cannot serve to account for the latter. If there exist, as we believe without being prepared to prove it, natures which are essentially anti-social, there is reason to believe that their inborn criminality was susceptible of revealing itself in other times, in other surroundings, and under other circumstances in very different forms from those with which it has clothed itself under our eyes. A man who is a slanderer in our times would have been a blasphemer in the Middle Ages; a man who would have been shot for rebellion and the execu-

[1] See on this subject an article by *Henry Houssaye* in the "Revue des Deux Mondes" of October 15, 1887.

[2] I do not wish, however, to liken them to Pranzini. The great difference is that Pranzini acted alone and they excited one another by their mutual example. The following chapter will show how great is this difference.

tion of hostages after the Commune would have been burned as a heretic under the Inquisition. At the same time, can there be any more relative, more conventional crime than blasphemy or heresy? It is the same thing with regard to delinquency as it is with regard to predisposition and neurosis, — those pathological turncoats, whose transformations are infinite.

There are, moreover, a very small number of people, without doubt, who everywhere and always would have committed offenses, whether natural or not, just as there are a small number of people who would under no circumstances yield to the temptation of sin. The great majority is composed of persons who are kept within the bounds of honesty by their fortunate fate, or who are driven to crime owing to the misfortune of circumstances. It is none the less true that the criminality of one class belongs to them just as the honesty of the other class belongs to them, for each of these qualities has its source in the nature of the men, which, under the conditions in which it has been developed, or has been realized in revealing itself to itself and to others, admits or does not admit of crime.

Now, the ground having been cleared, let us once again ask ourselves if there are any external signs which allow one to recognize and to point out absolute criminality. I answer that so far none have been discovered that are very clear, any more than it has been possible to discover the external marks of unshakable honesty. If the former can be recognized by the heavy jaw, the receding forehead, the scanty beard, ambidexterity, great length of arm, and insensibility to touch, then the latter should be signalized by the small size of the maxillaries, a straight forehead, a tufted beard, a constant and well-marked superiority of the right side over the left, short arms, and an exquisite sense of touch. Is this correct? Has there been any attempt to verify it?

By this I do not mean to deny the connection which very probably exists between the tendencies of character and certain anatomical, or, rather, histological, peculiarities of the brain and the whole of the nervous system; nor even the more doubtful connection between these hidden peculiarities and the bony and muscular conformations which it would be possible to define. But I maintain "a priori" that the characteristic tendencies which result in crime, which must even inevitably result in crime, are related to one and the same anatomical description. For crime is a crossroad of hidden ways coming from diametrically opposite points, and the absolute insociability which goes to make up the born criminal arises sometimes from an immeasurable pride, which makes him ferociously vindictive, — as in Corsica, Sicily, Spain, and the majority of the primitive ancient races, — and sometimes from an incurable laziness, which, combined with the most varied vices, — with libertinage, ambition, gambling, and drunkenness, — drives to murderous theft the unclassed or the degenerates of the fallen race. Thus, there must be not a small number, but a very large number of physical indications, often contradictory, which would disclose propensities to crime to an eye capable of unlimited penetration.

Experience confirms this line of reasoning. There are as many different criminal types as there are anthropologists. Marro does not agree with Lombroso, nor does Lombroso agree with himself. For example, "the cranial volume, which is found to be above the normal in the skulls of assassins by Bordier, Heger, and Dallemagne would, on the contrary, be inferior according to Ferri and Benedikt;"[1] it would be equal, according to Manouvrier; and, according to Topinard, who happens to agree with Lombroso on this point, it would be at one and the same time inferior and greater. "Among criminals," he says, "there are no other differences with respect to normal skulls [after having corrected many defective measurements and comparisons] excepting a certain number of excessive volume [which can be accounted for by means of cerebral hypertrophy, which is a cause of madness, or criminality, or genius] and also a certain number of very inferior volume. . . ." "Consequently," he adds, "there are *at least* two criminal types in this respect, and not merely one."

To sum the whole thing up, the cerebral localization of criminal propensities is today at the point where the cerebral localization of the faculties in general was a little before the time of Broca. Anatomists had indeed pointed out such and such a lesion of the skull as being sometimes related to such and such an illness; and observations of this nature accumulated, but without throwing any very decisive light upon the subject until the day when Broca discovered a very clear and well established relation between the changes in the third left frontal circumvolution and disturbances of articulated speech. From that time on all observers have confirmed this relation; from that moment the cornerstone of the science of the brain had been laid, and this partial but brilliant

[1] *Marro, op. cit.*

success was an encouragement for the hopes of all. If the discovery that a learned man believed himself to have made one day relating to a certain quadripartite division of the frontal lobe which was the cerebral indication of an assassin had been upheld, criminal anthropology would then have had its Broca. But the unfortunate part of it is that this was merely an illusion. It is none the less true that, even before the time of Broca, being familiar with this science was deemed sufficient for the maintaining of the cerebral localization of the faculties, although one might not yet be prepared to prove it.

Let us add that the success or failure of research is dependent upon the idea that gives it its direction. If our eminent anthropologist, instead of seeking the seat of language, — that is to say, of a simple, daily phenomenon, constant in the mental life of man, and, consequently, worthy of having a very obvious place in the brain, — had sought the seat of insults, blasphemy, or any other act, accidental as well as complex, occasioned by excess or lack of certain simple qualities joined together, it is very likely that he would have died without having discovered anything. This means that it is undoubtedly an illusion to suppose that one can localize crime in the brain, an act or a quality which is so complex, when pride, egoism, sympathy, justice, the thirst for vengeance, etc., tendencies which are relatively simple, and whose exaggeration or atrophy accounts for the tendency towards wrongdoing, are not yet localized in the brain. Let us not interfere with the alienists;[1] when they shall have begun to open up the pigeonholes of the brain, the work of the criminologists will be well on its way. Meanwhile, the only clear thing one can say is that the skulls and brains of criminals, taken as a whole, present a proportion of anomalies, a lack of symmetry, far above the average, and, as Corre says, "a predominance of occipital activity, which is probably related to the impulsive sensitiveness, over the frontal activity, which today is recognized as being entirely intellectual and devoted to thought." *Less reflection and more action,* — thus is their nature to be summed up, according to Bordier.

With respect to stature and weight there is no more agreement among anthropologists than with respect to the skull. "Lombroso

[1] Let us also not interfere with the unclassified anthropologists. "A comparative observation of races," says *Corre* ("Les Criminels," 1889), "according to Mme. Clémence Royer, already allows one to see a connection between certain instincts and certain physical characteristics of the skull and brain."

found delinquents to be larger and heavier, on the average, than honest people; Thompson, Virgilio, and Lacassagne established absolutely the opposite."[1] Lombroso found that the "spread," that is to say, the length of both arms extended in a cross and measured from one hand to the other, more often exceeds their height among criminals than among ordinary men. Topinard disputes this fact. When these authors accept the same data they are divided as to their interpretation. Where one sees a symptom of madness the other sees a phenomenon of atavism; others, among whom I can mention Manouvrier, Topinard, and Féré, reject both explanations; and I admit that I am of the opinion of the latter.

§ 48. (III) The criminal is not a madman.

Before going any further let us first of all, and as quickly as possible, deal with the two hypotheses with which we are here concerned. There are madmen who commit crimes, but is every man who commits a crime a madman? No; in our preceding chapter we believe we have already impliedly proved this. If there are analogies, even anatomical ones, between them, they are far from being sufficient to allow of these two types being confused. For example, from measurements of the skulls of one hundred and thirty-two assassins made by Heger and Dallemagne the result would seem to be that in the case of these malefactors the posterior of the brain is noticeably more developed than among honest people; and I was struck by seeing that Rodriguez de la Torre[2] in taking similar measurements of five hundred and thirty-two insane persons in his asylum has established the excessive predominance of their latero-posterior lobes. But this relation between crime and madness has nothing in it to surprise us, because both are a lowering of the human type; nor has it anything in it which ought to hinder us.

Go into a lunatic asylum, and what do you see? The excited or the depressed, each one pursuing his dream, — idle, incapable of any work, and strangers to one another. Visit a prison; you will there see convicts working, walking about in groups, whisper-

[1] *Marro, op. cit.*

[2] "El craneo i locura" (The Skull and Madness), Buenos Ayres, 1888. — Another characteristic which it seems is much more marked among madmen than among criminals, to judge from this author's atlas, is lack of symmetry. Every one of the one hundred and fifty-six skulls a section of which he has drawn is asymmetrical.

ing with one another, acknowledging the superiority of one of their comrades, and showing indications of a mass of humanity where the social leaven has begun to ferment. Among the convicts, Dostoievsky tells us, recalling his memories of imprisonment in Siberia, there were some who were more intelligent and more energetic who had *moral influence* over their comrades. Conspiracies are hatched, revolts break out, in prisons, and never in asylums. The lunatic is incoherent, the criminal is logical. Gazine, one of Dostoievsky's companions in misfortune, was, it seems, a sort of Tropmann. "He liked to kill little children whom he had succeeded in enticing into a lonely spot; there he would terrify the little one, would torment him, and, after having fully enjoyed the fright and shudderings of the unfortunate child, he killed it slowly, steadily, and with delight."

Here, indeed, one would say, was a case of clearly defined insanity. However, our author, who is an observer and a psychologist of great sagacity, says that he never noticed in Gazine anything abnormal excepting when he was in a state of drunkenness. "So long as he was not drunk he behaved himself very properly; he was always quiet, he never quarreled, and he talked very little. His appearance was not lacking in intelligence, but his expression was hard and sneering." Orloff was another great criminal: "He was a malefactor capable of assassinating old men and children in cold blood; he was gifted with an indomitable will power and filled with a proud consciousness of his strength. *This man had perfect control of himself;* he had only contempt for punishment and was afraid of nothing. The thing which predominated in him was an unlimited energy, a thirst for vengeance, an inflexible will and activity when he wished to attain some object." In other words, Orloff personified the very opposite of insanity and degeneracy, — that is to say, the highest degree of persisting and original identity.

"After eighteen years' residence in prisons and experience with criminals," says Bruce Thomson, "I believe that nine-tenths of them have an intelligence which is above the average, but that they are all exceedingly cunning." Here is a remark which a familiarity with madmen has never called forth. Here is another statement of this same author's: he declares that he never knew a single convict (which is an exaggeration, moreover) endowed with the slightest aesthetic talent or capable of making a sketch, a verse, or any piece of ingenious machinery. Is this the same with regard to madmen? No. "We know," says Maudsley, "that they often show a remarkable appreciation of beauty, and that they possess quite exceptional artistic talents and aptitudes."

§ 49. (IV) The criminal is not a savage who has reappeared among us. Illusory foundations of the hypothesis of atavism: physical anomalies, tattooing, slang.

If he is not a madman and is not always a degenerate, is the criminal a savage? No more so.[1] It is true that the skulls of assassins often, but not always, bear a stamp of pronounced brutality in which it is sometimes excusable to see a retrogression towards the hypothetical bestiality of our distant ancestors. Their characteristics, according to Manouvrier, "can be summed up as follows: A relatively small frontal development, a small development of the cranial arch as compared with that of the base of the skull, and an excessive development of the jaws as compared with that of the skull." Only upon this point have observations coincided. As early as 1841, Lauvergne, who was an ardent disciple of Gall, gave the following description of *cold-blooded assassins*, "a rare species," he says, "and which ordinarily comes from the mountains or out-of-the-way countries. They have telltale protuberances, and have a special 'facies' that indicates in the most striking way a brutal and impassive instinct. . . . Their heads are large and *flattened at the top*. . . . They are remarkable for their lateral protuberances;[2] these heads seem to be accompanied by *large and thick jaws*, and enormous masseter muscles, which project under the skin and *are always in action*."

But is there any need for the intervention of atavism and the

[1] *Lombroso* still persists in upholding this theory. In a letter written to Moleschott (see the "Revue scientifique," June 9, 1888), he invokes in support of his favorite idea the result obtained by the *composite photographs* of the skulls of six assassins and six highway robbers. These two photographs he says resemble each other to a remarkable degree "and show us the characteristics of the criminal man with an evident exaggeration and *in certain respects* the characteristics of the savage man: very strongly marked frontal sinus, zygomatic apophyses, and very massive jaws, very large and very wide apart orbits, asymmetry of the face, petriform type of the nasal orifice, lemurian appendix." Very well; but these skulls have been likened to one another, we are then told, because they formed a homogeneous group. It is to be noticed that the skulls of six swindlers and thieves resulted in "a less accentuated type," and that the one photograph obtained from all of these eighteen skulls at one time presented anomalies which were still more obscure. What would it have been if one had photographed one or two hundred skulls together?

[2] Lombroso has often pointed out the exaggeratedly long arms of assassins; but this characteristic is much contradicted and varies greatly according to race.

imagining of the miraculous resurrection of a prehistoric ancestor, separated from us by we know not how many superimposed and intercepting races, which in their turn invade the others, in order to account for so simple a result? Little frontal development and a heavy jaw, this simply means, says Bordier, "less reflection and more action;" this cross type is frequently met with among the most peaceful populations, but such as are backward and devoted to the rude work of the fields; and it is natural that assassination should choose its adepts from among individuals marked with this stamp. The evidence of Bordier is all the more precious because he seems to have been the first, if one is to believe his friend Topinard, to have conceived of accounting for crime by means of atavism. "He compared," the latter tells us, "the assassins of Caen to Broca's series of the 'Dead Man's Cave,' and found them to have characteristics in common. Now, both series are familiar to me, and I must say that it is hard to find, either by examining them or by analyzing them, two sets of skulls that are more unlike." [1]

I know perfectly well that the partisans of atavism support the preceding data, with a few other considerations drawn from cranial asymmetry, which is more frequent among criminals than among the masses of honest people, from their badly formed or *prominent* ears, from certain forms of their nose, and from some peculiarities found in convicts, such as tattooing and slang. But asymmetry, Topinard replies, is the rule and not the exception, even for ordinary skulls. Lannois, in an instructive monograph on "L'Oreille humaine," maintains that he has not established more anomalies of this organ among forty-three young prisoners under his observation "than it would have been possible to find among an equal number of subjects with a clear conscience." [2] And Marro himself admits that the prominent ear is found more frequently among the Turks, the Greeks, and the Maltese than among the barbarians and the negroes of the Soudan.

We must add that in his conscientious comparison of five hundred and thirty-nine criminals and one hundred honest people

[1] I will allow myself one last consideration. The size of the jaws is dependent upon the nature of one's habitual food: among carnivores they should be stronger than among frugivores or granivores. As a consequence, among a race of men who pass from a life of hunting to a pastoral and farming life the maxillary development should decrease. Now, I ask, when among hunters, who have a big jaw, an individual as an exception shows us a small jaw, is it right to see therein a phenomenon of prophecy? If you reply in the negative you cannot logically see in the appearance of a heavy jaw in the midst of small jaws a characteristic of atavism.

[2] "Archives de l'Anthropologie criminelle," No. 10.

Marro was not a little surprised to find among these latter the frequency, which was at least as great among them as among the former, of anomalies of an atavistic origin, or one supposed to be such. In the case of "the receding forehead, a characteristic to which Lombroso attaches so much importance," the proportion was found to be four per cent among the honest people and three and one tenth per cent among malefactors; in the case of an ear having Darwin's tubercle (a projection which would seem to be a vestige of the tip of the former animal ear) the proportion among the malefactors is seven per cent and among honest people *less than* one *per cent.*[1] In the case of the *frontal sinus* delinquents are in the majority but by very little; the proportion is only eighteen to twenty-three; but with regard to the "torus occipitalis" normal persons regain their strange advantage, which can be expressed by the excess of nine over four and seven tenths, which is pretty nearly a double proportion. It is true that ambidexterity and left-handedness, — characteristics, moreover, which are irregular rather than atavistic, — according to this same author, are twice as frequent among malefactors as among "normals." But this difference may be due, at least to a great extent, to the difference in their education; the malefactors have much oftener than "normals" been abandoned, been left to themselves and their bad habits, during childhood; and we know how many times the vigilance of attentive parents corrects a natural tendency among children to use the left hand.[2]

The nose among criminals, compared with that of madmen and honest people, has, it is true, been the subject of special and far-reaching studies in the laboratory of Lombroso. Out of it all there has come a curious monograph from one of his pupils,[3] from which it would seem to result that several anatomical anom-

[1] There appears in the "Rivista di antropologia criminale" of October, 1888, a study by *Frigerio,* very profound and very well developed, on the *external ear* among madmen, criminals, and the rest of humanity. The author merely comes to the conclusion that his work "has not been absolutely barren"; and, to tell the truth, nothing very concise results from all these measurements and all these figures.

[2] In his monograph on "Gauchers," *Jobert,* a pupil of Lacassagne (Lyons, 1885), comes to this conclusion: that the cause of left-handedness is not precisely known, but that "it seems to be especially due to habit and to education." In the more recent thesis of *Etienne Rollet* (Lyons, 1889), Lacassagne gives another theory and attributes this marked predominance to the localization of language in the left brain.

[3] "La squelletto e la forma del naso nei criminali," etc., by *Salvator Ottolenghi,* (Turin, fratelli Bocca).

alies (only visible on the skeleton) of the nasal orifice are very much more frequent among criminals than among honest people in the same country and of the same race. Now, these anomalies would seem to have an animal character, according to the author, who, upon this point, moreover, seems to me to disagree with Topinard. But, if this explanation is to be admitted because of atavism, one ought — and this is no easy thing to do — to make the origin of the anomalies with which we are concerned go back very much farther than the inferior human races, and even much farther than monkeys, and, as our learned man expressly does, agree with Albrecht, who, in his amusing report to the Congress of Rome, places man below the monkeys in the rank of the insectivora. Let us add that, if the dead and mutilated nose of malefactors places them so low in the animal scale, their living and complete nose places them at the head of the human races in some respects. According to Ottolenghi, their nose is straight and long much oftener than that of honest people which is a good characteristic. These results are too hard to reconcile to be worthy of having any confidence placed in them.

What can we say with regard to slang, excepting that it does not in any way remind one of the little that is known about the languages of savages? The latter, according to Taylor, are superficially characterized by an abundance of onomatopoeia, and by frequent reduplication of the same syllables in the body of the word, — a habit which is quite childish. Such words as "papa," "bébé," "nounou," which are habitually found in the mouths of our children, and which are so rare in the mouths of civilized men, abound in the speech of the native Oceanians and Americans. Now, a few slang terms — "ty-ty," typography; "bibi," Bicêtre; "coco," friend, etc.; "fric-frac," release from prison expressed by the noise of the lock, etc., are apparently related to this double type; but it is in a spirit of mockery, owing to a need of belittling and disparaging, that the familiars of crime speak in this way in imitation of our children, and not in the least in imitation of the Neo-Caledonians or the Red-skins. Moreover, the so-called puns, the evil jokes, the degrading pictures which make an animal of man ("cuir," skin; "ailerons," arms; "bec," mouth) go to make up the foundation of their vocabularies, together with many words borrowed from foreign languages, — from the "calo" language of the gypsies, from Arabic, and from Italian, — an obvious indication of the cosmopolitanism acknowledging no fatherland. But the language of primitive peoples is serious in its very puerility, poetic in its picturesqueness; it has its own particular vocabulary, which is patriotic and original, and, furthermore, its own grammar. It is as different from slang, an excrescence of our languages, as a wild appletree is from a poisonous mushroom.[1]

As to the tattooing of malefactors, it will be well to compare the plates in Lombroso's atlas, where a few examples are given of these obscene and stupid designs, which are recreations of captivity, with the fine engravings in "Hommes fossiles et Hommes sauvages," by de Quatrefages (especially, pp. 488, 489 and 433), showing tattooed Maoris. Here we have strange but expressive arabesques, which do not conceal, but which rather accentuate the countenance, and which have as their object the completing of its terrifying effect upon the women or the enemy; a decoration and an armor at one and the same time, a mark of the religion or the tribe upon the forehead of the individual who belongs to it body and soul, and who glories in so belonging to it.

On the other hand, in the former case there is nothing like this; but, upon the forearm oftenest, never upon the face, we have devices and cynical symbols, profiles of women, and everything which is intended to remain hidden, and which recalls the caricatures made by a scholar in his exercise book. If this shameful tattooing were a vestige of or a reversion to the habits of primitive savages it would be more often met with among women who were criminals than among male malefactors, for it was in the feminine sex, as we know, that the prejudices, the rites, and the ornaments of former ages, — for example, earrings, — took refuge a long while after they had been given up by men. But, on the contrary, it is male criminals almost exclusively who have a taste for tattooing. The old sacrificers used to cut up the corpses of captives or animals offered to the gods in order to divide them up according to the rites; in the same way assassins of our own time, owing to one of those criminal contagions which are not the least of the arguments that may be invoked in favor of the social origin of the offense and the delinquent, conceived of the idea of cutting up their victims into pieces in order more easily to escape the investigations of the police. Can one say that this criminal cutting up[2] proceeds from the religious cutting up of former ages to which it presents

[1] I have dealt with this point and the following point more fully in my "Criminalité comparée."

[2] See on this subject a pamphlet entitled, "Dépeçage criminel," by *Louis Ravoux* (Lyons, Storck, 1888).

an apparent similarity? There is no more and no less reason for admitting this origin than for connecting the tattooing of criminals with the warlike tattooing of savages. Taine has brought to light several traits of cannibalism which were seen in the events of the most tragic days of the French Revolution.

Can one also explain those temporary aberrations, such as anthropophagy, which held sway for a few days upon the raft of the Medusa, by atavism? It is quite possible that some advanced disciple of Darwin might go as far as this. Frigerio, one of the most distinguished alienists of the new Italian school, told at the Congress of Rome of having observed a "moral madman" who, during a periodical attack of exaltation, suddenly changed in character and became "quarrelsome, arrogant, and pugnacious," and at the same time "was then driven in an irresistible manner to model in clay a great number of figures of a quite special originality and form, the grotesqueness and improbability of which recalled the symbolic bas-reliefs or other crude sculptures of the centuries of the decadence." According to Bournet, we have here "forms which, unless we are mistaken, recall the attempts of the early Christians." Now, Frigerio seems almost to think that many generations of heredity might here play a certain part. If one accept such conjectures as these, I can conceive of one's being disposed to receive those of Lombroso upon the subject with which we are occupied. But it seems infinitely more simple and more probable to see in the inscriptions and scrawls with which malefactors cover their skins only the effect of an accidental contact with primitive populations; for it is especially among sailors who are criminals that this custom is to be noticed. At the same time it is quite possible that the opposite should also be true, and that many backward people owe to their relations with our civilized sailors the advantage which they derive from practising these incisions of the skin. "Tattooing is rare among the natives of Cochin China," says Lorion;[1] "those who bear these designs made by means of various colors injected into the skin have lived among the Europeans; they have most often been sailors, firemen, or servants on board the war or merchant ships." The Arab, who is much more civilized than the inhabitant of Cochin China, but who is much more closely in touch with Europeans, tattoos himself still more[2] and often the nature of the

[1] "Criminalité en Cochinchine," (Lyons, Storck).

[2] *Cocher*, "Criminalité chez les Arabes."

design produced by him clearly shows that he has copied our fellow-countrymen.

But we are delaying too long upon a point which is of such secondary importance. Let us conclude with this final remark. Admitting that the likening of a criminal to a savage could never have had the least foundation, it each day loses its probability in proportion as crime is recruited less and less among the backward populations of rural districts and more and more from the corrupt and subtle surroundings of great cities.[1]

§ 50. (V) The criminal is not a degenerate.

If madness and atavism (I do not say heredity) have nothing to do with the inclination towards crime, then what is a criminal? Shall we say with Féré that he is a degenerate, or with Lombroso in his last work that he is an epileptic? A few words will be sufficient with regard to the former of these two theories, which, however, is the more firmly established of the two. The second one will detain us a little longer.[2]

It is certain that there is an agreement between the anomalies known under the name of the "stigmas" of degeneracy, of prominent jaws, of squinting, of asymmetry of the face, malformations of the ears, etc., and the characteristics out of which the pretended

[1] *Colajanni* in the first volume of his "Sociologia criminale," after having devoted the first part of this volume to overthrowing the physical atavism of the criminal and the other theories of Lombroso, — and with a great deal of vigor, moreover, — devotes the second part to an endeavor to demonstrate the *moral* atavism of the criminal. In this there is at least an apparent contradiction. I opposed this theory in my study on "Atavism morale" ("Archives de l'Anthropologie criminelle," May, 1889), to which I take the liberty of referring the reader.

[2] Dr. *Emile Laurent* was for two years resident physician in the central hospital of the prisons of Paris. While there he saw and observed more than two thousand prisoners with whom he was in perpetual contact. Now, in his book on the "Habitués des prisons" (Storck, 1890) he maintains that the anthropological measurements more often than not have only led him "into contradictory results." He did not perceive anything that resembled a criminal type. Just like the hospitals, "the prisons abound in pointed and flattened skulls, in flattened noses and elongated jaws," in cases of stuttering, squinting and lameness. "It is not possible to say that one meets with such and such a malformation invariably, as one encounters reddened sputum in pneumonia and albumen in Bright's disease. All the malformations of all the organs can be met with among all criminals; that is the truth." Among them an anomaly which is very rare elsewhere is relatively frequent: "the exaggerated and pronounced development of the breasts in men at the time of puberty." This coincides with the opinion of Lombroso and other observers in the greater resemblances between the two sexes in the world of crime, whether it be that the men become effeminate or the women have a masculine appearance.

criminal type has been built up. But do these stigmas, which are merely frequent, and not constant, among the degenerate, seem more especially to predispose those who bear them to evil actions? Not at all.[1] Many *stigmatized* as imbeciles deserve the name of *innocents*, which their habitual harmlessness has earned for them. Conversely, as Féré himself recognizes, many of the born malefactors "are remarkable for the regularity of their physical conformation," and Magnan, at the last congress of criminal anthropology, showed several of them who might serve as excellent artists' models. Thus, if degeneracy — that is to say, loss of equilibrium, a sort of physical loss of class — is often allied to criminality, or, at least, to criminality that is due to congenital weakness, one cannot say that degeneracy is the cause of this criminality; and as to criminality which is due to an excess of energy and audacity, it is so far from being related to degeneracy that it is, so to speak, the opposite of degeneracy. True and perfect criminals, such men as Pranzini, Prado, and Lebiez, are as little degenerates as it is possible to be. Can one even say that, assuming degeneracy to be added to a certain given moral characteristic which does not tend to crime, this characteristic would thereby give these men a criminal tendency? So long as it is permissible to base one's reasoning upon a hypothesis which cannot be verified, but which can be conceived of, it seems as though one ought to reply in the negative.

Without attaching too much importance to general statistics in a matter of this kind, I am rather impressed by a table drawn up by Colajanni[2] from which it results that the Italian provinces in which the greatest number of bodily illnesses and deformities that characterize degenerates, especially alcoholic degenerates, are to be met with (according to which tables, however, the thesis of Féré seems to be all the more confirmed) are precisely the most moral ones, — those of the North; whereas, the most criminal provinces, those of the South, are to be distinguished by the fine health of their inhabitants. At the same time, does this comparison give us the right to conclude that "degeneracy constitutes the best condition for the increase of morality"? Assuredly not; nor do I think that this is Colajanni's idea. The truth is that the violent and bold criminality of the uncultivated provinces of Italy,

[1] These marks, furthermore, as Lacassagne has demonstrated, do not denote "the actual or eventual disturbance of the cerebral faculties."

[2] "Sociologia criminale," Vol. I, table annexed at the end of the volume. See also pp. 315, 317.

by reason of its very character, excludes enervated and degenerate natures from participation in it; whereas, the voluptuous and astute criminality of the cultivated provinces allows of weak natures among its agents. Féré makes a remark which is worth while remembering with regard to degenerates. "They are easily subjected," he says, "to the influence of their surroundings; they allow the emotions and the passions of the moment, of which they often become the passive instruments, to be communicated to them; we see them subject to the contagion of suicide, as well as the contagion of murder." This is undoubtedly true; and it follows from this that degeneracy, when it is connected with crime, results in the latter, not by virtue of some affinity and attraction, but owing to the lack of resistance to a criminal impulse that comes from outside.[1]

§ 51. (VI) Is the criminal an epileptic? Refutation of this theory taken literally. The example of Misdéa analyzed. What may possibly be true at the basis of this idea. Essential periodicity of psychological phenomena.

At present the question is whether this impulse might not possibly come from an epileptic constitution. Let us pause for a few moments at this hypothesis of Lombroso's, however singular it may seem to be. Lombroso does not say that every epileptic is a criminal,[2] but he claims to prove that every true criminal is an epileptic, more or less in disguise. Epilepsy would be a species, of which criminality would be the most widespread variant. He passes in review every kind of criminal, the born

[1] *Schopenhauer* reproaches Gall with having sought for the bumps of crime or moral qualities in the brain. He rightly sees therein a denial of his doctrine which (see "Le Monde comme volonté et représentation," translated by *Burdeau*) incarnates the moral nature of man, the will and the *character* in the *entire organism*, and only localizes in the brain intelligence, an accessory and secondary phenomenon, according to the celebrated German thinker. Thus it would be contradictory to this point of view — so deep in many respects, so full of scientific foresight, especially on the subject of hypnotism — to admit of a criminal type which was principally characterized by cerebral anomalies. On the other hand, it seems to me to be quite in conformity with this system to consider instinctive criminality as being connected with the bodily anomalies of degeneration. Now, this is what seems to be most conclusively proved.

[2] According to the researches of Totini, cited by himself, the numerical proportion of liars, of thieves, and of the perverse of every category, among epileptics, would not be more than four or five per cent. (It is true that it would be equal to sixty-three per cent according to Cividali.) *Laurent*, in his work cited above, tells of having met with hysteria far more often than epilepsy, and the latter only rarely in the antecedents of criminals.

criminal or the criminal through moral madness, the criminal from passion, the criminal from madness, from hysteria, from alcoholism, and even the occasional criminal and the "criminaloid"; and underneath all of them he discovers traces of an epileptic constitution or an "epileptoid." A generalization which is at first sight as illogical as this one, and which conflicts with the restrictions which the author here and there brings to bear upon it, but which an instant later he forgets, does not seem worthy of examination. At the very outset it clashes with the boldness of his figures. Dr. Marro of Turin is one of the pupils of our author, his fellow-countryman; and at the time when he wrote his excellent book upon "I carrateri dei delinquenti" he could not, therefore, be ignorant of the importance which his master attributed to epilepsy. Thus his attention was directed toward not allowing the slightest signs of this disease to escape him in the study of his subjects. At the same time, out of the five hundred and seven delinquent men whom he had under observation, he only found twenty cases of epilepsy; and, again, he adds that *only one* of these twenty had committed an offense under the direct influence of an epileptic attack, — a thing which is truly surprising if we are to maintain that epilepsy is the special organic exciting cause of criminality. Better still, the proportion of epileptics in Italian prisons, according to the statistical studies of the same writer, is at the most .66 per cent; and Lombroso himself admits that it is only five per cent.

The refutation of the idea with which we are concerned, if one takes it literally, is thus easy, — too easy, even; and it is hard to believe that so learned a man could deceive himself to such an extent through hastiness of judgment. On the contrary, one is convinced, I know not why, after having read his work attentively, that under a mass of observations and conjectures a very deep thought is stirring, just as a spring stirs under the crumbling earth. He has sought, and in this we see the only new aspect of his book, a connecting link, a single virtual or real focal point for the various forms of criminality; he has endeavored intimately to connect these various forms with one another by the bond of the flesh, — the cold ferocity of the thorough-going assassin, without fear and without remorse; the homicidal delirium of the insane man, who weeps after having committed his crime; the murderous outburst of the man who is guilty because of passion or drunkenness; the disastrous aberration of the fanatic or the "mattoid"; the professional routine of the thief by opportunity, who has fallen into the meshes of recidivism; the unpunished wickedness of the latent criminal, of the robber statesman, — that privileged person of times of equality, or that favorite of the courts according to the prevailing system.

Now, I really believe that he is mistaken in specifying so close a connection as this, but I think that this connection has some existence, and that there is some truth in that *physiological* and not merely juridical *importance* attributed to crime. I can, as far as I am concerned, accept this physiological importance without having any difficulty, as we shall see, in reconciling it with my explanation of crime, which is above all sociological. Now, whether this sad social phenomenon has its deep roots in the brain is what we must first of all conjecture, owing to a fact upon which Lombroso incidentally insists, but from another point of view. This well known fact, that certain classical forms of mental alienation, such as homicidal monomania, kleptomania, pyromania, and erotomania, correspond with the different and permanent forms of crime — with murder, theft, arson, and rape — does not in the least prove, in fact, the common origin of crime and madness. But, on the other hand, it does show that the criminal act is not an ordinary act as far as the brain is concerned, and that there would still be reason to admit the possibility, if not the probability, of special localization, even though at the same time one should reject the localization of all other methods of activity.

One may be struck by seeing that there are categories of madness characterized by an irresistible impulse to kill, to rob, to rape, and to destroy; whereas, there is not a single one which is characterized essentially by an irresistible impulse to row, to labor, to dig, and weave cloth, etc. The latter, however, are very old forms of action, repeated and multiplied for centuries by innumerable generations. It seems that this repetition, which has been so long drawn out, has not been sufficient to fix a desire to carry out these actions in the physiological instincts which have a distinct seat in the cells of the brain. Thus it is inevitable, as it seems to be otherwise with crime, that crime, in spite of its lesser repetition, if not its lesser antiquity, should have played a stronger part in humanity in the deepness of the impression which it has produced than have the acts of ordinary life. Just because it has always been the exception, it has been the monster, the acute feeling which places its stamp upon the moral being, and even upon the physical being. Crime divides this privilege with those other acts which, although coarse and very common, are of exceeding interest to the organism, — the drinking of stimulants (dipsomania), gluttonous eating (certain forms of hysteria), abuse of sexual pleasures, etc.

But let us return to epilepsy. I shall not follow Lombroso through the various "boges" of the Dantesque inferno to which he leads us. In order to give some conception of his method, let us limit ourselves to a review of his line of argument relative to the *moral madman*, or, in other words, to the born criminal, with whom, according to our author, the moral madman is almost confounded. Moral madmen, according to him, resemble epileptics in the following characteristics. The same backwardness in the *personal equation* with respect to people who are normally constituted. The same vanity. The same inclination to contradict themselves and to exaggerate everything. The same morbid irritability and bad character, whimsical and suspicious. The same obscenity. (Incidentally, "coitus" is likened to the epileptic convulsion in the same manner as the *attack of genius* and the criminal frenzy. The *attack of genius*, especially because of its instantaneousness, its violence, and the amnesia following it [?] is epileptiform. . . . One asks oneself what is the precise meaning of epilepsy thus understood.) The same invulnerability. (Let us observe that the invulnerability of *rural* malefactors, who are illiterate, is common to them and to all persons of their class; the invulnerability of urban malefactors, who are more crafty is imaginary.[1]) The same cannibalism: Cividali has seen an epileptic "eat the noses of three of his companions." (So be it; but in fights taking place after drinking bouts among peasants we often see one of the combatants, who is not in the least epileptic, tear away with his teeth a piece of the nose or the ear of another. In this case the persistence of the habits of savages dating back to distant ancestors may be invoked as an explanation. But in the case of the epileptic the excesses with which we are concerned have a different origin, as we shall see.) The same tendency to commit suicide. The same inclination to be sociable: in sanitariums epileptics are to be distinguished from the other insane by a taste for associating together, which is common to them and to the inmates of prisons. (Let us add, and to honest people. If the epileptic is sociable, it is merely because he is not a mad-

[1] See "Le Crime," by *Henry Joly*, on this subject.

man[1] whatever Lombroso may say. For madness is in its very essence an isolator of the soul.)

Do not offer to all these similarities, more or less artificial,[2] the objection that in two ways at least, the intermittence of the attack and the following amnesia, the epileptic contrasts with the born criminal. They will answer that, according to the keepers of prisons, prisoners have a "bad time" during the day, and that, according to Dostoievsky ("Maison des morts") the return of spring stirs up the instinct of vagabondage among the imprisoned. (We shall see later on that everything, from a psychological point of view, and not only criminal tendencies, is periodical.) Lombroso and his colleague, Frigerio, tell of having observed that on stormy days, when the attacks of epilepsy become very frequent, the inmates of prisons become more dangerous, tear their clothes, smash their furniture, and strike their keepers. In certain cases, we are told that there is a sort of criminal "aura" which precedes the offense and causes it to be foreseen; and we are cited the case of a young man "whose family could perceive that he meditated a theft when he continually held his hand up to his nose, a habit which ended by deforming his nose." As to the blotting out of memory after such an attack, it has been observed by Bianchi in the case of four moral madmen; and we also know that children, those temporary criminals, have the faculty of easily forgetting their misdeeds. But what is there that children do not very quickly forget, whether misdeeds or good deeds?[3]

[1] What I mean to say is that he is not mad during the interval between his attacks, in spite of the permanent imprint which the epileptic temperament stamps upon the character. As to the epileptic attack, one should see in that an intermittent madness, a passing *mania*.

[2] Another very unexpected analogy between born criminals and epileptics. Their way of walking, when studied according to the method of Giles de la Tourette, is the same and differs as compared with other peoples. Conversely to the latter, the abnormal individuals with whom we are concerned walk with a slightly longer stride with the left foot than with the right; furthermore, still contrary to the normal gait, they diverge from the line of axis a little more to the right than to the left, and their left foot when placed on the ground forms with this line an angle of deviation greater than the angle formed by the right foot. Such are the three characteristics by means of which, according to the measurements of Perrachia and Lombroso himself, the gait of rogues no less than their conduct would differ from that of honest people and would resemble that of the unfortunates affected by epilepsy. Unfortunately, we are not told on how great a number of observations his conclusions are based; and it is quite possible that a new anthropologist, taking up the researches of Perrachia, might arrive at entirely different results, as has happened only too often in criminal anthropology.

[3] It is, moreover, the same with epileptic amnesia as it is with hypnotic

We must not forget that there is a sort of epilepsy that is not accompanied by any convulsion, which consists of vertigo. This sort, which causes a most profound disturbance according to Esquirol, is accompanied more often than the other form by tendencies which are venereal, homicidal, fraudulent, and incendiary, among people who were previously reputed to be of good character. Every time that we observe among young delinquents a certain intermittent periodicity of impulse to commit crime, there is thus reason to suspect that they are of an epileptic nature. According to Trousseau, when an individual, *without any motive*, commits a homicide, it can be said that he has acted under the influence of epilepsy. Of epilepsy, or of some other nervous affection? At any rate, whether he be an epileptic or not, the man who commits a murder *without any motive* cannot be, as a general thing, except in the case which we shall take up later on, characterized as a criminal. There are cases, they say, where epilepsy, having lain dormant for a long time, is only revealed after the committing of some offense, which is committed, no doubt, under an unperceived influence. This is true, and it is unfortunate; but it does not prove that it is always thus, nor that we must always liken a thief who steals owing to his habitual and fundamental character, to a thief who steals owing to his morbid and temporary character, grafted upon his normal character because of some cerebral disturbance. In the former case the subject is responsible; he is irresponsible in the latter case. Again, they tell us that when they have complete information with regard to the parentage of criminals and epileptics, they find that among their relatives and their ancestors epilepsy alternates with criminality. But alternations and identity are two different things. Madness also often alternates with genius in a family, and night with day in the sky.

In order to bring out the nature of the dissent which, to my great regret, divides me from Lombroso, I will cite an example which is dear to him, — that of the famous Misdéa. Here our author seems to triumph, because, in fact, native criminality and epilepsy are confused to the point of making an analysis seem hopeless. It is not, however, impossible to separate them, if one takes into account our principles of penal responsibility. Briefly, Misdéa was a bad Italian soldier, crafty, full of hate,

amnesia, which is not without numerous exceptions, as has been proved by Delbœuf's subjects.

violent, vain, lazy, devoid of feeling, and with all this an epileptic; and during a final attack brought on by the most trivial wounding of his self-esteem, he shut himself up in one of the rooms in the barracks and from there set to work to shoot down his comrades against whom he thought he had a grievance. A regular siege was necessary before he could be disarmed.

Now, we are told that in him "lack of feeling, laziness, vanity, violence, and hatred driven to the point of ferocity, — all those characteristics which we find again in the born criminal and the moral madman, are exaggerated by reason of epilepsy." They may be exaggerated, but they are not created. Was there not in the case of Misdéa, independent of epilepsy, the stuff out of which criminals are made? And if, assuming that this stuff was lacking in him, — that is to say, if he had been neither lazy, nor boastful, nor vindictive, nor cruel, nor a liar, — would he during an attack of epilepsy have committed the murders which brought him to the scaffold? The last epileptic vertigo which seized him seems only to have furnished his criminal powers with the occasion to reveal themselves. And this occasion could just as well, if not better, have been afforded him by certain circumstances of his social life, in which malefactors other than he have found themselves, as, for example, if a really serious outrage had been inflicted upon his pride, or if excessive poverty had driven him one fine day to the inevitable choice between work, which was rejected because of his laziness, and assassination, which was accepted because of his lack of feeling. In the latter case, how many homicides which he would have committed, which would perhaps have been less atrocious in their form, would, however, have been more worthy the name of crimes! His character, manifesting itself in this way, under a new aspect, would in reality have remained the same; whereas, its manifestation through epilepsy, besides the exaggeration, was also the partial *denaturing* of it. The noticeable thing is that out of a coward it made a brave man, a sinister hero, who alone resisted an entire regiment. In this way the habitual Misdéa became partially morally irresponsible for the crimes which have been imputed to him, and by reason of which I hardly regret, moreover, that he was executed. But let us assume that Misdéa in ordinary times had been industrious, modest, good, frank, and generous; if by chance during an attack of epilepsy he had killed one of his comrades, do you suppose that he would have been found guilty?

He would assuredly have been acquitted and confined in some asylum.

And yet a murder committed by him, assuming this to be so, might have been brought about in the same way by a wounding of his self-esteem. It is sufficient to assume that the alteration in his personality would have affected his modesty, which had been suddenly changed into sickly vanity, just as it had affected his cowardice, which had been changed into intrepidity. Lombroso seems to think that when we see an act of violence or fraud committed by an epileptic or a madman preceded by a motive, — however great may be the disparity between the futility of the motive and the seriousness of the act, or, better still, between the temporary and accidental character expressed by this motive and the permanent character that is an essential part of the person, — we cannot reasonably distinguish an act so committed from an analogous act committed by a criminal indisputably judged to be such. But this is an error. Perhaps there is no murder committed by a madman in a moment of insane impulse which is not caused by a passion that belongs peculiarly to this insane man at that very moment. If we take into account the intensity of this passion, conjugal jealousy or the madness of exasperated vengeance, we shall see that more often than not a proportion exists between the (imaginary) motive and the act. But this proportion is not sufficient to prove the criminality of the agent.

Conversely, there may be the greatest disproportion, at least in appearance, between a homicide and the circumstances which determined it, without the murderer ceasing to be fully responsible for it. Such and such a Negus of Abyssinia and such and such a King of Dahomey, who sees that one of his subjects does not prostrate himself quickly enough when he passes by, falls into a rage and cuts off the man's head with a blow of his sword. But, differing in this from Misdéa, this crowned bandit has not even partially changed his character in carrying out so ferocious a vengeance in order to punish so slight an offense. Again, his moral responsibility, according to us, is complete, excepting that, intoxicated by his absolute power, he might possibly be the victim of a sort of chronic *delirium tremens*. But many urban or rural brigands, whether civilized men or barbarians, who have not the same excuse to advance, in the same way, after a long career of assassination inspired by cupidity or revenge, come to a point where they kill a man in order to gain a few centimes or because of a mere insult, or even, in very rare cases, for the mere pleasure of killing. Although here the crime may be reputed to be without motive, the guilt of the perpetrator is not in the smallest degree lessened. For in the long run the thirst of blood for blood in the case of the murderer, just like the thirst of gold for more gold in the case of the covetous man, is not an anomaly and not in itself a symptom of insanity, but, on the contrary, the expression and the result of their innermost nature, of that nature which they have created themselves, little by little, by the consolidation of their will into a habit.

Lombroso goes to a great deal of useless trouble in trying to discover traces of epilepsy as the underlying cause of the actions of the delinquent by opportunity. What I am very willing to concede to him, moreover, is that it was a mistake to create a gap between the accidental delinquent and the habitual delinquent. The unfortunate part of it is that opportunity is always the beginning of a habit. Only opportunity merely acts by means of its meeting with an internal condition of the subject, a condition which is produced either by heredity or by education, or, rather, by a combination of the two, but, at any rate, by the direct or indirect action of the social surroundings in which the ancestors of the individual have been constantly immersed, just as he himself has been. Let us draw a distinction, if you will, between delinquents because of *heredity* and delinquents because of *education.* Now, in this last case, that is to say, when the internal condition of the offense is the result, not of heredity especially, but of imitation under all its forms,[1] what has epilepsy to do with it? Lombroso himself tells us of a band of assassins composed of ten brothers and sisters; the youngest sister alone, who was

[1] In this connection I cannot refrain from observing once more the fruitfulness of this social force of imitation, which has expressed itself in the most contradictory results. When he takes his first step in crime the man who has gone astray has momentarily broken with his usual distrust of novelty, he has made an innovation like the inventor; but a moment after he inevitably falls back under the weight of habit and custom, or nearly so, when it is a matter of a new habit or a different custom which is limited to the little world of the high class or low class thieves. Thus the same cause which holds us back on the declivity of our first misdeed, which is obedience to habit and to custom, the imitation of ourselves and of those who are about us, causes us to lapse back into crime once the first wrong has been committed. The reason why honest people remain honest is the same as that which makes delinquents become recidivists. This progression of recidivism, so often pointed out in our day and so striking, is therefore one of the best counterproofs of my sociological principle. I admire the simplicity with which that law of segregation, which extends to the whole of nature, thus operates in our societies.

quite a child (what becomes of the criminality of children here?) refused to steal and to spill blood; but, forcibly compelled to follow her relatives, in time she came to be the most ferocious of them all. Was she an epileptic? He does not tell us.

Thus we believe that we are able to assert that he has not proved his theory. But in reading it we have the feeling that it hinges upon a truth. I do not pretend to be able completely to bring out this truth. At the same time, there is one aspect of this unknown thing which it seems to me is visible here and there, and the idea of which is suggested to me by the explanation which the author finally makes with regard to the nature of epilepsy. It was indeed time, to tell the truth, that he should explain himself on this subject. He acquiesces in the definition of it given by Venturi, which is not lacking in depth, and especially in broadness. The epileptic temperament, according to Venturi, is merely an exaggerated temperament, which is excessive in everything, in good as well as evil: "to the movements, to feeling, to emotion, to blushing, to tears, to the judgment of the normal person, correspond the convulsions, the hallucinations, the terror, the rage, the congestion and foaming mouth, and the delirium of the epileptic;" in both of these cases it is the same nervous life that is more or less strongly expressed. We can accept this point of view if, with this author, we observe that among the sanest subjects a sudden and strong excitement can give rise to manifestations of anger, of fear, of jealousy, and of erotomania, which are rather like attacks of epilepsy, *and, like the latter, tend to reproduce themselves spontaneously later on* under favorable circumstances.

How true this is! Which one of us during the course of his life has not felt someone of those violent shocks of the heart, those enormous disturbances, originally having some motive, but later on coming into existence of their own accord and upon the slightest pretext, as though their imprint had remained in us during the interval? A horse which has been quiet up to that time, and which has been terrified at dusk by a shadow or a white stone, thenceforth rears from time to time at the same hour before some phantom from within. Can we not say that from this day on he has to a certain extent become epileptic? An attack of some kind of passion which has become fixed in a distinct cerebral negative would thus be the beginning of epilepsy. Epilepsy in this sense would only be passion which had to a certain extent become firmly fixed.

Now, there is no need for me to remark that, even understood in this way, epilepsy does not sufficiently account for crime, because it accounts equally well for the opposite of crime; and it is obvious, at any rate, that it could be the social explanation of crime as well as its natural explanation. We can also say that, in broadening out to this extent, the circle of epilepsy has become entirely changed. However, an essential characteristic, and one which it is instructive to consider, remains, — that is, its intermittence and its periodicity. Had it not been for epilepsy properly so called, the importance of this characteristic, which is common to all psychic phenomena, it is true, but which is more marked in epilepsy than in any other phenomenon, might not have been so striking. But by means of epilepsy we may learn that there are within us many invisible wheels that are turning unknown to us in order to release periodically the tension on some terrible spring and to cause the explosion of one of those internal explosive substances which we carry within us without knowing it.

These innumerable and incessant rotations, which are the unconscious life of our memories, of our plans, of our latent feelings, — the continual repetition of everything that has once entered into us by means of accidental impressions — are carried out within the interior of the cells of our brains. It is owing to these endless turnings, which are multiplied and confused, that meetings sometime take place within us whence spring unexpected acts of audaciousness, of perversity, characteristics of madness, of genius, which astonish us ourselves; just as it is owing to the complicated centripetal forces of the heavenly bodies that their conjunctions take place, whence result eclipses or moments of sublime brilliancy. Everything is periodic in the "myself," whether it be the normal one or not; and sickly ideas or inclinations are not the only ones which have a tendency to repeat themselves without being called upon, but they are the ones which succeed best and most irresistibly in repeating themselves.

Moreover, however reasonable, however free from all neurosis we may be, we cannot prevent ourselves from gravitating in an ellipse of thoughts, actions, and emotions which are repeated from day to day, from season to season, and from circumstances to analogous circumstances. The sort of enchanted and poignant sadness, always the same, which the return of spring invariably brings to many souls and which forces them to suspend all work then, has its sources in the sorrows of love of their first youth, forgotten and resuscitated confusedly with the accompaniment of other deceiving reminiscences, harmonics of that note, and "timbre" of that sound. This forms a sort of spontaneous concert of the heart, a sort of internal hand-organ, plaintive and heart-rending, which it is impossible to stop. Certain predispositions to joy without any apparent cause which last for weeks at a time are to be accounted for by the vague resurrection of former happiness. But there are also among the unfortunate, who have suffered great privations, great humiliations, or bad treatment during their childhood or their youth, days when a silent, inexplicable rage mutters within them, a confused need of hatred and vengeance and envious greed. And if during such moments someone offends them, or if some prey tempts them, a homicide, arson, a theft may be the result of this fatal coincidence. And, once the crime has been committed, there will be days, months, during which a sort of criminal appetite, vague and insatiable, will come back to them, one knows not why; for crime sets its stamp upon the character, and, as there is no stronger feeling than this, there is none which is stamped more indelibly.

But, for the very reason that this periodicity with which we are concerned extends to the whole world of our consciousness and of our unconsciousness, it will not suffice for us to establish it and to discover it where it is less marked as compared with the phenomena where it is more marked, to justify us in judging the individual to be irresponsible for that which appears or breaks forth in him spontaneously. There are here some distinctions to be drawn. More often than not, the ellipse of memories and habits of which I have just been speaking is really ours because it is with our support or according to our initial wish that it has been traced; or else, because it is the internal perpetuation and assimilation of accidents which have become essential to us, of scars which form a part of our description; like a curve described by the planets, as a general thing it only compels us to traverse states that are not very unlike one another, — at least, not obviously contradictory.

On the contrary, the enormous ellipse along which madness projects us, like the comets precipitated from extreme heat to extreme cold, and vice versa, leads us astray and changes our nature at each instant. One will say that between these opposite characters there are many intermediate ones. Yes, no doubt, but there are fewer than one might think; the planets are, after all, rather clearly separated from the comets; and, if in the past there have existed hybrid celestial bodies, they have been destroyed; the borders of madness, whatever one may say, form a rather narrow zone; and semi-madness is a state of unstable equilibrium wherein one never sojourns very long. Within the soul, just as within society, there is scarcely any middle ground between order and disorder. That which is called order in the life of the individual or in the life of society is only a chain of periodic ideas and actions with the smallest possible periods of conflict. Then we have social identity. But, when these periods of eruption occur, when the substance of the periods that are linked together, — and which we call work, industry, justice, health, or mental equilibrium, — comes to be torn by these eruptions, the result is disorder or madness, anarchy or epilepsy. And from one of these states to the other the transition is, after all, always brief.

A certain order, to tell the truth, can even, in the long run, creep into disorder; but it still remains subordinate to the latter and only serves the more to accentuate it. For example, it is noticeable that repetitions of morbid attacks, that are irregular to start with, have a tendency to become regular. Among people addicted to the abuse of alcohol who become firmly rooted in their vice the recurrence of their trouble brings about, says Vetault,[1] "a regular period." It is the same thing in the case of dipsomaniacs. A drunkard mentioned by the same learned man, every time he had drunk too much, mechanically repeated an offense which was identical; he took possession of a carriage and horse which had for the moment been left by their owner.

There are other conclusions to be drawn from the foregoing remarks. The hereditary repetition of the intellectual and moral qualities presented by one's ancestors enters as a curious instance into the general periodicity of psychological facts. This case is the one in which the period exceeds the lifetime of the individual, and sometimes even takes in several generations. All of a sudden, just like an attack of epilepsy, in a calm spirit, a vicious or perverse organization breaks out in an honest family. Work, the repetition of the same acts and of the same ideas at very short intervals; habit, properly so called, memory and instinct, the repetition of acts and ideas at intervals which are already a little farther apart; finally, heredity and atavism, a repetition of tendencies towards certain acts and certain ideas after the expiration of a considerable time; all these are just so many concentric undulations, which go

[1] See his work on "Alcoolisme."

along their way, extend themselves and become more complicated, and graft themselves upon one another. Let us add that upon these various forms of imitation *of oneself*, of the imitation which is a slave and prisoner of organic life, there are grafted in their turn all the superior forms of imitation of others, of imitation which is free and emancipated in the immense world of society. But at the centre of all these rotations, as the prime mover, there is always a will to which society has suggested its object. Whatever road we take, we come back to this source of the offense.

§ 52. (VII) The criminal type is a professional type. Physiognomy and handwriting.

If the group of malefactors, which is as variegated as it is numerous, as changing as it is persistent, is not united by a single bond that is truly vital; if there exist between them neither that pathological relationship which a similar form of degeneracy or mental alienation would establish, a same group of maladies with which they would be affected, nor that physiological relationship which their common resemblance to supposed ancestors would bear witness to, of what nature, then, is the bond which brings them together and often gives them a special physiognomy more easily perceived than formulated? In our opinion it is a bond which is entirely social, the intimate relation which is to be observed between people carrying on the same trade or trades of a similar character; and this hypothesis is sufficient to account for even the anatomical peculiarities, especially the physiological and psychological peculiarities by which delinquents are distinguished. Let us first deal with the former.

We have told in a previous chapter why every profession, whether it be open to everybody or enclosed in a caste, must in the long run recruit its members from among those individuals best endowed and best fitted to succeed in it, or develop among its members, through heredity, the talents and, consequently, the forms which it prefers. This is so not only with regard to every profession, but with regard to every class and every social category that is more or less clearly defined. For example, a series of the skulls of *distinguished men* — by this is understood the chosen of the liberal professions collectively — is typified, according to Manouvrier, by a face which is relatively small, a fine frontal development, and especially a cubic capacity that is far above the average.[1] When we go into detail in the separate study of artists, learned men, philosophers, or engineers, we shall certainly be led to draw a typical portrait which will have rather strong characteristics drawn from each one of these groups. It is even probable that it might easily be clearer and less doubtful than the famous criminal type.

As a matter of fact, of all careers, the career of a criminal is indeed the one that is least often entered into by a person having freedom to choose, and is the one where, as a consequence of the rapid extinction of vicious families, the hereditary transmission of aptitudes has less time to be carried out. One has been thrust into it from birth; this is the ordinary case. The majority of murderers and notorious thieves began as children who had been abandoned, and the true seminary of crime must be sought for upon each public square or each crossroad of our towns, whether they be small or large, in those flocks of pillaging street urchins who, like bands of sparrows, associate together, at first for marauding, and then for theft, because of a lack of education and food in their homes.[2] Without any natural predisposition on their part, their fate is often decided by the influence of their comrades. However, there are others whom the fatal logic of their vices has driven to the dilemma of crime or death. And, even with regard to the former, one can say, as a general thing, that the preference which they will give to the example set by a small minority of rascals over the example of the immense majority who are laborious denotes in them some anomaly of nature; although one can reply that it is the same thing with imitation as with attraction which is exercised inversely to the square of the distances. Thus it would be permissible for the child who was the most normally constituted to be more influenced by half a score of perverse

[1] People have been astonished to observe in England that the class of clergymen was distinguished from the rest of the nation by a proportion of births of male infants far greater than the general mean. Bertillon, moreover, has established that each profession gives us a different proportion and establishes in relation to each one of them the proportion of births of male children compared with that of female children. If one stops to reflect that the act of generation is a confluent and a condensation of all the organic activities, one will be led to see in the preceding remark a reason for believing that every class and every trade has its physiological characteristic and its anatomical characteristic as well.

[2] The majority of thieves, says Lauvergne, "have been children of the streets, sons abandoned by a father who had no resources" or of a prostitute. See in the "Criminalidad en Barcelona," by *Gil Maestre,* one of the most competent of Spanish magistrates (1886), interesting details as to these bands of precocious malefactors. We give an outline of it further on.

friends by whom he is surrounded than by millions of unknown fellow-citizens. In spite of everything, there is no doubt that advancement in the trade of murder or theft ordinarily assumes a true vocation, more or less vaguely recognized by an experienced eye. Also, Topinard and Manouvrier are each separately drawn to this conclusion, that criminals form one of those "professional categories" that we have just been discussing.

Thus, despite the failure of previous attempts to attain the unattainable and to prove scientifically the correctness of that which the sight of malefactors often makes us feel, we can explain why the existence of a special "scent" which reveals the criminal tendencies of a man of "evil mien" to the skilled detective and the wise observer cannot be contested. Of phrenology nothing remains, but there have been phrenologists who have often given proof of a striking divination. Lauvergne cites several diagnoses of this sort in his book on "Les Forçats." Of the science of physiognomy there is very little left; but there have been and there still are physiognomists since the time of Lavater. Of graphology, which is rather in vogue at this time, what will be left in ten years? I do not know; but it is certain that for a long time to come there will be handwriting experts who, seven or eight times out of ten, upon inspecting a sample of handwriting will be able to tell the character of the writer. Well, without at all wishing to humiliate criminal anthropology by this comparison, I will take the liberty of adding that, should it one day perish, the criminal anthropologists would not fail to survive it, and to show that their wisdom was equal to the occasion. Moreover, the enumeration of so many consecutive failures has in it nothing to discourage this science. How many times have we not seen in science and elsewhere a persistence of successive defeats merely attesting the strength and power of certain causes and presaging their future triumph?

Only, let us remark that the special "scent" which sometimes makes one discern among honest people the man who is dangerous and "capable of anything" is much less guided by a vague feeling of a certain anatomical description that applies especially to vagabonds than by that of a physiological description.[1] It is not the eye, it is the look; it is not the mouth, it is the smile, it

[1] But, above everything, the most essential quality of a good detective is an excellent memory, which enables him to recognize after months and years every one of the malefactors that has ever passed before his eyes.

is not the features, it is the physiognomy; it is not the figure, it is the carriage, that enlightens the diviner without his knowing it. The clear-sighted handwriting expert bases his inductions not upon the finished writing, but upon the running writing; not upon each one of the written characters by itself, statically considered, but upon their relation of dynamic solidarity, to a certain extent, whereby the impulse of the spirit portrays itself in the movement of the hand. To a certain extent, in fact, the pen is to the action of the mind what the sphygmograph is to the action of the heart; both of them make a drawing of the action. In spite of his absolute faith in the system of Gall, Lauvergne writes this admission: "A pickpocket, a swindler, a thief reveal themselves as much by the play of their physiognomy as by significant protuberances; *the latter are not even recognized until one has read upon the faces of the condemned that they ought to exist.*"

Now, there is nothing that is so quickly modified in us by the influence of education and the circumstances of life as the mobile expression of the visage and the body, that which is called "the air and the manner"; a further reason for believing in the preponderance of social causes in the formation of the malefactor. Moreover, anatomical characteristics themselves are not subject to the influence of these causes. If a good hygiene has the virtue, while strengthening a child, of modifying even his structure, a bad hygiene has this power as well; and that which is true of the whole of the body is especially true, as Dubuisson remarks,[1] of the most plastic of our organs namely, the brain. "Our power of modification is dependent in everything on the complication of the object which is to be modified. The very multiplicity of the functions of the brain opens the door to more modifying agents than any other organism of the economy."

There is not one of even the most precocious of the young monsters of seventeen or eighteen years whose exploits appall the press who has not behind him years of criminal apprenticeship during his entire vagabond and soiled childhood. For the trade of crime, like every other, has its special schools. Also, like every other trade, it has its special idiom, namely, slang. What old and deep-rooted profession has not its own slang, from sailors, masons, and coppersmiths to painters and lawyers, — to the very police agents themselves, who say that they "camoufler" them-

[1] "Théorie de la responsabilité" ("Archives de l'Anthropologie criminelle," 1886, 1887).

selves when they mean to "disguise" themselves, and "coton" for a "resemblance," etc.? We can read Maxime du Camp on this subject. Finally, there are special associations, temporary or permanent, epidemic or endemic. As an example of the former, the rising of the peasants in 1358, and in certain respects Jacobinism, which temporarily ravaged France; as an example of the latter, the Camorra and the Maffia, which are traditionally prevalent in Italy. These are great professional syndicates of crime, which have played a far more important historic part than one might suppose. How many times has a warlike band, organized in the very midst of pastoral tribes, been a society of brigands? How many times has this brigandage been the necessary leaven that has served to raise an empire and establish peace through the triumph of the strong?

So, do not reproach me with doing too much honor to crime by placing it among the professions. If the petty criminal industry which languishes in the depths of our towns, like so many little shops where a backward manufacture survives, does nothing but harm, the great criminal industry has had its days of great and fearful utility in the past, under its military and despotic form; and, under its financial form, people pretend that it renders appreciable services. Where would we be if there had never been any fortunate criminals, eager to overcome scruples, rights, prejudices, and customs in order to drive the human race from the pastoral poem to the drama of civilization? And must we not, unfortunately, recognize the fact that from the out and out criminal to the most honest merchant we pass through a series of transitions, that every tradesman who cheats his clients is a thief, that every grocer who adulterates his wine is a poisoner, and that, as a general thing, every man who misrepresents his merchandise is a forger? And I do not mention the great number of industries that exist more or less indirectly through the profits of crime, — low taverns, houses of prostitution, gambling houses, old-clothes shops, — which are just so many places of refuge for the receipt of stolen goods for delinquents. They have many other accomplices. Among the upper classes, how much extortion, how many doubtful bargains, how much traffic in decorations, demand the complicity of people who are rich and reputed to be honest, who profit by them, not always without their knowledge! If the tree of crime, with all its roots and its rootlets, could ever be uprooted from our society, it would leave a giant abyss. It is a good thing to overcome the repugnance which prevents us from examining the criminal heart, were it only to help us in overcoming the very keen attraction which leads us to delve into the vicious soul. A tree should be judged by its fruit, vice by crime. The psychology of the prostitute and the debauchee, almost the only subject upon which the realism of our writers of fiction and our poets is exercised, would undoubtedly not be quite so interesting if one knew the psychology of the thief and the murderer a little better.

§ 53. (VIII) Psychology and the criminal. The criminal is partly the result of his own crime and of criminal justice.

Perhaps one is born vicious, but it is quite certain that one becomes a criminal. The psychology of the murderer is, in the last analysis, the psychology of everybody; and in order to go down into his heart it will be sufficient if we analyze our own. One could without any very great difficulty write a treatise upon the art of becoming an assassin. Keep bad company; allow pride, vanity, envy, and hatred to grow in you out of all proportion; close your heart to tender feelings, and only open it to keen sensations; suffer also, — harden yourself from childhood to blows, to intemperateness, to physical torments; grow hardened to evil, and insensible, and you will not be long in becoming devoid of pity; become irascible and vengeful, and you will be very lucky if you do not kill anybody during the course of your life. And, in fact, the psychological characteristics that I have just enumerated are indeed the most striking ones among the inmates of prisons.

Let us, for example, enter with Dostoievsky his "Maison des morts." There is no more fitting document than this book, wherein ten years of imprisonment, unjustly undergone, in Siberia are reviewed, to make us intimately acquainted with the damned of this world. "All the prisoners," he tells us, "with the exception of a few who were gifted with an inexhaustible gaiety, and who for this very reason drew down upon themselves a general contempt, were morose, *envious, horribly vain*, presumptuous, susceptible, and *excessively formalistic*. Vanity was always in the foreground. . . . The newcomer who sought to get his bearings unconsciously submitted himself to this feeling, and acquired the general tone, — a sort of personal pride, — with which each prisoner was affected. The satisfaction of feeling themselves all right was developed in them to the point of childishness. They looked down upon peasants from the heights of their greatness, although they themselves, for the most part, were peasants." Let us observe this titanic conceit of criminals; just as of all mistakes there is none which is more easily reconciled with the apparent errors of others than this exaggerated esteem of oneself, so there is no greater cause of insociability; also, it is remarkable that in all times and in all countries, among the bandits of Corsica and Greece, or among the Sicilian "maffiosi," just as among the degraded of our large towns, pride is the dominant note of their character. It is true that they worked in this prison, but because of compulsion, or because there was nothing better to do to while away the time. This was fortunate. Had it not been for work, these people "would have destroyed one another like spiders enclosed within a glass jar." One did indeed see "a few good and mild faces in this sombre and hateful crowd," but they were the innocent ones, or the ones who had gone astray.

In this prison the great pleasure to be attained from the profits of one's work is to satiate oneself all alone, without inviting any comrade to participate. The convicts, an inconceivable thing, could while at exercise, in spite of their chains and their guards, carry on at rare intervals some coarse idyl with the women "ad hoc"; but, as they could also with less difficulty procure brandy for themselves, they ordinarily preferred to use their money in the latter way. This agrees with the sphygmographic experiments of Lombroso upon the impression which the sight of a glass of wine and that of a "donna nuda" cause criminals to experience. The stoicism of prisoners is wonderful; it is partly because of their conceit and partly because of the physical lack of feeling, which is a characteristic of the lower classes. A frequent punishment was that of a hundred or five hundred strokes of rods or canes falling like a shower of blood upon the sufferer who ran between two lines of soldiers.

Now, "all the prisoners, without exception even the most faint-hearted of them, courageously bore this penalty." This lesser capacity to feel pain may allow of one's understanding another privilege which malefactors enjoy, that of the extraordinary facility with which their wounds heal. This is common to them and certain barbarian peoples, who show the same rapidity of healing coupled with the same lack of feeling. I observe that Lorion among the Annamites and Kocher among the Arabs have, independently of each other, pointed out this twofold gift of nature. Certain experiments carried out by Delbœuf, who in suggesting to hypnotic subjects that they could not feel the pain of their injuries singularly hastened their healing, throw light on all these facts which have been gathered together from various directions.

Because of his concern as to the effect he produces on others, because of the very envy and hatred which he bears for others, one can indeed feel that the criminal bears some social relation to the rest of mankind. Their example carries him away, their opinion matters to him; and it would be to misunderstand him if we were to believe that he is a stranger to their society. "That which continues to justify the criminal in his own eyes is that he has no doubt but that the verdict of the neighborhood in which he was born and where he lived acquits him; he is sure that a minority of the people will not look upon him as absolutely lost, excepting, however, if the crime has been committed against people of his neighborhood, against his brothers." One ought to read the account of the Easter celebration in the Siberian prison. The convicts celebrated this solemn occasion with all the pomp that they were allowed to; they got up a theatrical performance, many of them fulfilled their religious duties. "Outside of the high respect which they have for this great day, they felt within themselves that in observing this festival *they were in touch with the rest of the world.*" Also, on that day "neither the quarrels nor the habitual insults were heard; it seemed as though a sort of friendly feeling existed among them," although ordinarily they were "hard and sharp" in their mutual relations.[1]

Far from presenting that absolute lack of foresight which Lombroso makes a characteristic of the criminal, the companions of Dostoievsky showed a calculation and a rare perseverance in the carrying out of all their plans for their purchases of brandy or their escapes in the spring; and the idea of their eventual punishment never ceased to be of concern to them. The impulsive type was absolutely an exception. Petrof is the perfect incarnation of this type. This man had few ideas, but at long intervals a violent and sudden desire aroused by some insignificant object. "An individual such as Petrof would assassinate a man for twenty-five kopecs, in order to have enough money to drink a half litre; on

[1] Note this: they are led to group themselves under the rule of some influential comrade. They are not yet capable of really caring for one another. The earliest societies are thus always formed by the unilateral tie of prestige before recognizing the reciprocal tie of sympathy.

every other occasion he would disdain hundreds of thousands of roubles." He was "the most determined man in the jail"[1] because he put his whole strength of will and convictions at the disposal of his temporary desire, of his one idea, in the same way as the hypnotic and the madman. His responsibility was not complete.

To sum up, the character of the criminal is already very much easier to trace with precision than is his physical type. His type changes according to race; his character scarcely varies. Besides this, we must not exaggerate the psychological differences, especially the intellectual differences, which distinguish the delinquent from ourselves. When we compare the various sorts of books, — fiction, literature, history, science, etc., — that are read with more or less enjoyment in the Parisian prisons for both sexes with the reading that is more or less preferred in the municipal schools of Paris, we observe that the relative proportion of readers for each kind of writings is about the same in the former as in the latter.[2] More than one-half of the books read by prisoners consist of fiction; the books of Alexandre Dumas chiefly. They also greedily devour the "Magasin pittoresque," the "Tour du Monde," and even the "Musée des familles."

As to the moral characteristics which we have endeavored to point out with some precision, the two most often betrayed, vanity and lack of feeling, are far from belonging exclusively to the criminal and can be the effect of crime as well as its cause. I can say the same thing of laziness and lack of remorse. In the first place, is the criminal as devoid of feeling, — at least, physically, — as Dostoievsky, Lombroso, and the majority of the Italian authors maintain? Their observations seem contradicted by other testimony. "I inquired," says Joly, "at the central infirmary of the Santé, where all the men from the prisons of the Department of the Seine who are seriously ill are taken care of, if they had ever noticed *invulnerability* among them. They

[1] "But in the convict prison as everywhere else," says the author, "men of determination are rare." And he adds that we must not confuse the determined man with the man who is desperate, who plunged into his evil course in the intoxication of his criminal "vita nuova," of his infernal emancipation, because of the disorder created within him by a first murder which could be accounted for, and which caused him to commit five or six other murders without any reason. The convict prison sobers him, and "one would never say to see him that this wet hen had killed five or six men."

[2] "Archives de l'Anthropologie criminelle," July 15, 1888, an article by *Henry Joly* on "Les Lectures dans les prisons de la Seine."

replied that, far from it, they always found them very sensitive to pain. They distinctly told me that to one who had worked in this special infirmary and in some of the ordinary hospitals of Paris (as almost all the internes have done) the difference was striking. The brave fellows, the honest workmen, the fathers of families, who go to be cared for at the Charité or the Hôtel-Dieu, undergo operations with very much more courage than the patients at the Santé."

Here is something which scarcely accords with the facts of the stoicism in penitentiaries that were related above, and to which the memory of some examining magistrate in the provinces could very easily add still others. Nine times out of ten the girl mothers who kill their new-born children go through their confinement clandestinely and under conditions such that a lady, if she allowed herself to take such risks, would surely die. I know of one prisoner — among a thousand — who, being overcome by the pains of childbirth upon a washday, at the very time when she was preparing a meal for five or six laundresses, went up to her room, went through her confinement, smothered her child, and three quarters of an hour afterwards came downstairs again and went back to her household duties, standing up, coming and going, and, moreover, without any injury to her health. But the apparent contradiction which faces us here is easily removed, I believe, by the very simple consideration that Dostoievsky and Lombroso, like the majority of the Italians and the provincial magistrates, have had to deal with rural criminals, who have little physical feeling, like all the illiterate; whereas, the malefactors cared for in the Parisian hospitals participate in the general and characteristic hyperaesthesia of the inhabitants of cities.

The idea of attributing the lack of pity in the criminal to his relative exemption from pain is thus merely a conjecture without any proof. Another hypothesis seems to me to be more probable. It is, I repeat, that the monstrous egoism, and the prodigious conceit as well, which are noticeable among criminals are perhaps rather the consequence than the source of their crimes. A study has been made of the effects of crime upon the surrounding society which becomes terrified at it, upon the followers of the malefactor who are going to imitate him; but have its effects upon the perpetrator himself been sufficiently explained [1] outside of a few

[1] *Joly* (*op. cit.*) has touched upon this question, the importance of which he seems to have seen, in passing.

theoretical or sensational novels? The most that has been done has been to attempt to portray the impression, the sudden and ineffaceable stamp, produced by the criminal act upon the imagination of the criminal agent. But no less than his imagination are his judgment and his will, his reason and his feelings and his self-esteem, changed or deformed by this terrible blow.

The idea of, the determination upon, the preparation and the execution of a crime can be regarded as the progress of a special kind of fever which has no name, like the cerebral fermentation of an image, to be placed psychologically, — not socially, be it understood, — in the same rank as those other internal fermentations which are known as the impulse to suicide, love, or poetical inspiration. Now, there are crises in constitutional illnesses from which the organism comes forth remade; and this is one of them. There are fermentations which are no sooner completed than they begin again under new forms, which are more dangerous than the former. After alcoholic fermentation comes acetic fermentation; and of such a nature is the criminal fever. Before acting the future criminal is agitated, disturbed to the very depths, by the fascinating thrill of the persecuting idea, which it is impossible to drive out and horrible to contemplate. Shall he plunge into it or shall he not? Up to the last minute he is still in doubt. However longed for it may be, his own downfall astonishes and stuns him as much as it alarms and appalls the public. He is astonished when he finally does escape from his delirious obsession. He is astonished at having so easily overcome everything which but lately seemed to him almost insurmountable, — honor, right, pity, morality. He feels himself at one and the same time strangely freed and lost, plunged into a new world which has opened up before him, and driven forever from the house of his father.

In his surprise there is something of that which the youth feels when for the first time he has tasted illicit pleasures, or the scholar who has just composed his first good verses. He is proud of his isolation. He tells himself that he has become a new man. An abyss has been dug out, a sudden chasm, between his compatriots and himself; he compels himself thenceforth to prove to himself that they are strangers to him, and, although he never entirely succeeds, and although the all-powerful force of their example compels him to listen to and to repeat within himself the blighting echo of the judgment which they will pronounce upon him, his strenuous effort to free himself from them has merely the effect of increasing his conceit and his egoism. He swells with pride, like the lover after the conquest, the general after the victory, and the artist after his masterpiece. The lover, the inventor, the artist, and the conqueror are in this way similar to the mountaineer or the inhabitant of sparsely populated countries, whose self-esteem expands in his real isolation as theirs does in their imagined isolation. The withering of the heart, the lack of feeling with regard to that multitude from whom they isolate themselves, follow as a consequence of this. There also follows, little by little, in proportion as they progress in this feeling of absolute division from the multitude, a lack of remorse. For, by virtue of our principles, in believing himself to be heterogeneous, the criminal ought to believe himself to be irresponsible.

Also, it has been possible to say with a certain depth of meaning that he experiences "remorse *before* the crime, and not *afterwards*." Before the crime he still looked upon other men as being like himself; afterwards this is not so. Moreover, he becomes indifferent to his friends and to his acquaintances and is no longer in sympathy with anybody excepting his nearest relatives and his brethren in wrongdoing. He dreams. Thus is his laziness accounted for. It is the characteristic of the dreamer of every kind, — the lover, the poet, even the inventor. The criminal is a great dreamer, and Dostoievsky has not failed to reveal this trait.

Whoever has in his memory some very prominent recollection which he knows does not exist in the memory of his fellow-citizens nurtures within himself a growing faith in his strangeness, and very soon in his superiority. This is the case with the murderer, even before he has been found out. A murder is for the man who has committed it a fixed idea similar to the idea of genius in the case of the inventor, and similar to the image of a woman in the case of the lover. This idea, no doubt, is not always present in the very centre of the consciousness, but it is ever roving and turning about the horizon of his mind, like the low sun of the polar regions. There is nothing of the nature of an illness in this tyranny; it is perfectly normal; the fact of its not taking place would be abnormal. The harder the tongue of the bell is struck, the more prolonged will be the vibrations of the bell; the more striking a sensation has been, the more does it vibrate and repeat itself within the conscience. This incessant preoccupation betrays itself by a thousand indications; by drawings, such as the one which Tropmann drew of one of his crimes, often by means of tattooing, or by compromising words wherein is revealed the necessity of saying the thing which is still known only to oneself; by silence also, and even by sleep and dreams. I knew of an assassin who was going to be set free for lack of proof when a word which he had spoken while dreaming, and which was overheard by the keeper of his prison, made it possible to question him to some purpose, to disconcert him, and to obtain his confession.

Thus, of all the actions of our past life, crime is the one which must be repeated the most in imagination, because it is the most energetic; and, as a consequence, it is also the action which must have the greatest tendency to reproduce itself in reality. The propensity which drives a man to the repetition of crime is thus a fatal one, still more fatal than the tendency to an amorous, artistic, or poetic repetition, to erotomania, melomania, and metromania. One error is sufficient to make of an honest woman a Messalina, one poem is sufficient to make of a notary's clerk a perpetual versifier. And in the same way a first theft committed at the age of thirty-four is sufficient to change a brave officer into a Lacenaire. But why? It is not merely because of that disturbance of the imagination which I have just been dealing with.[1]

Ordinarily, we account for the sudden downfall produced by the first step along the path of vice or crime by saying that a taste for the forbidden fruit or the taste for blood has awakened vicious or precocious instincts. Again, we say that the fault lies with society, which is all too ready to repel the one who falls and to force him to seek shelter in the company of the depraved. But in speaking thus we forget the essential thing, which is the verdict by means of which the internal jury, an echo of outside opinion, cuts off the guilty man from the honest multitude, even before the latter shall have cursed or even blamed him. This imaginary division, with the morbid swelling of self-esteem and the hardening of the heart which follow it, complete his ruin. The more a man feels or thinks himself to be separated from his fellow men because of a fall, or even an assumption of it, because of an infrequent depravity, or even because of an exalted passion, the more dangerous he is. If the prostitutes of our sex are, even more than courtesans, capable of every heinous crime, it is because the feeling of their degradation is especially intense and deep within them.

Again, as long as the fault remains hidden, this ditch which the conscience of the sinner digs between honest people and himself

[1] See *Carlier's* "Deux prostitutions."

is capable of being filled in. But, when prosecution against him has taken place, and when he has been condemned, the gulf within him becomes singularly widened and deepened by being revealed to the outside world, in the same way that his evil nature, in being revealed to itself because of the crime, had become accentuated and fixed. A woman whose one fault is made public is lost forever. Inevitably, the criminal is the result of his own crime just as much as his crime is his own work; also, inevitably, the criminal is partially the result of criminal justice.[1] Excommunicated in everybody's eyes by this justice, he cuts himself off still more in his own eyes, almost, but in an opposite way, as an artist or poet who, after having been the only one to be aware of his talents, is touched by a ray of fame and at once sees the pedestal which he is erecting for himself grow a thousand cubits.

It is none the less true that, because of the opinion that they hold as to their separation from surrounding society and as to their dissimilarity to it and their independence with regard to it, both the artist and the criminal furnish the proof of their close similarity in spite of everything, and of their forced communication with that common herd which they disdain or curse. In the case of fame, just as in the case of condemnation, the "myself" reflects the opinions of others within its obscure chamber; it cannot help admiring itself even more when it is praised, and disparaging itself even more when it is disparaged; only, this latter attitude of self-esteem being unnatural, the "myself" often compels itself to give back to the honest multitude contempt for contempt, which is only another means of reflecting it while repelling it. Thus the "myself" still remains sufficiently similar to society to retain its responsibility towards it; and, on the other hand, its alienation within itself, which is rather a revelation of a disturbing nature, is far from being sufficiently great to place any obstacle in the way of its responsibility.

The new Italian school repeats to satiety that it is important to study and to punish the reality known as the criminal, and not the entity known as the crime. We see at present with what

[1] Perhaps it is this which causes *Emile Gautier* ("Archives de l'Anthropologie criminelle," 1888) to say that there exists a *penitentiary type* rather than a criminal type. In their physiognomy especially, according to him, as we have seen above, do prisoners resemble one another. It is because the prison life, with its twofold irresistible influence of disciplinary routine and reciprocal corruption, accomplishes that which a life of crime had outlined, the psychological recasting of the malefactor and the feeling of his being transplanted into another environment.

restrictions we ought to accept this opinion, and that the old school was not without some reason in taking the opposite point of view; or, rather, we perceive the easy and complete reconciliation of the opposite points of view. We also understand why the perpetrator of a great crime, even though it be committed by accident, has from this time on become more dangerous, and should be more severely punished than a petty habitual malefactor. In fact, the more serious the crime that has been carried out, the more honest has the consciousness in which it has burst forth remained up to that time, the deeper and the more terrible is the revolutionary crisis within the "myself" which is the consequence of it. But when from childhood a man has accustomed himself to committing larcenies which are at first insignificant and then become progressively more important, this violent shaking up of his personality has been avoided, and he has never ceased to feel those close ties that he has with surrounding society. To confuse these two categories of guilty men by dealing out to assassins and to recidivists who are misdemeanants the same fate in the colonies is an injustice which is based upon a mistake.

§ 54. (I) The classification of criminals should be psychological above everything else. The rural criminal and the urban criminal.

If the foregoing considerations and views are correct, they will permit of our applying very simple elements of solution to one of the most discussed but least settled problems of the new school of penal law, the classification of delinquents. The thing to do is to divide the latter into natural categories which will group side by side individuals who are truly similar to one another. Up to this time, no doubt by virtue of that implied principle that similarities in vital order are the only ones that are important, and that they relegate to the background those of a social order, the bases for a rational division have been sought for in physiology, in mental pathology, or, at the most, in psychology. From this, as we have seen, there have resulted many attempts at a distinction between insane criminals, criminals because of their temperament, criminals by reason of passion, etc.

I am astonished that no one has suggested a division based upon dolichocephalous or brachycephalous malefactors, or, in conformity with Marro's analysis, upon the atavistic, atyptic, or pathological character of the anomalies of their skulls or bodies. But can one imagine a penitentiary establishment which would divide up the prisoners into dolichocephalics and brachycephalics! To tell the truth, however, the mixing in each compartment would not be less if all the delinquents through passion and all the delinquents through temperament were lodged together pell-mell, even though they should be subdivided according to the nature of their passion or their temperament without at the same time taking into account distinctions of class, profession, and rural or urban surroundings. The best received of the distinctions put forth consisted in dividing malefactors into criminals because of opportunity and criminals because of habit. In this the social point of view already in a vague way begins to come to light. But what criminal is not a criminal because of opportunity, and what crime that takes place accidentally has not ordinarily a tendency to become repeated because of habit, if there be no opposition offered to it? If by criminals because of opportunity we are to understand the less dangerous criminals, the truth will scarcely correspond to this hypothesis; for the perpetrators of the most monstrous crimes, who are arrested and condemned for the duration of their whole lives for their first offense, have scarcely leisure to recur to crime. The most incorrigible and the most perverse recidivists — understand, most *perverted*, for, being as a general thing pickpockets, swindlers, and petty thieves, they are not in the least *born malefactors* — are not the great criminals. The latter present at the same time a greater danger and a lesser perversity.[1]

We ought to start from a different point of view. The plastic clay of our natural innate qualities being only a material whose form is modeled by the social world, it is to the resemblances of the social life, that is to say, of class, profession, and surroundings, that we must adhere in order to rank together the delinquents who are really similar to one another. But we must not forget that at the same time it is necessary not to place together offenses which are too dissimilar. Leaving to one side delinquents who are more or less insane, with whom we are not concerned, let us then begin by accepting that rather clear cut separation which in every period and in every country divides in half the multitude

[1] "Felons condemned to a corporal and disgraceful punishment, of which the duration is at least five years and at the most ten years, are as a general thing, *as all those who have experience of prisons know*, far less perverse than the majority of persons who are condemned for misdemeanors, for which the penalty is, however, according to the code, *neither corporal nor disgraceful*, and who are only condemned to an imprisonment whose term varies from a year and a day to five years." ("Les délits et les peines," by *Acollas*.)

of criminals according to the nature of the rights which they have violated; on the one hand, we have murderers or violent aggressors, and on the other hand, thieves in the broad sense of the word. Our statisticians, in drawing a distinction between crimes against persons and crimes against property, merely translate this real and ever living duality into an abstract symmetry. Furthermore, let us beware of exaggerating the importance of this distinction which our statistics have abused.

This much having been said, let us classify murderers and thieves separately according to the nature of their occupation and of their habitual life before they are condemned. What I mean to say is, let us classify them according to the social category to which they belong. It seems difficult here to establish precise limits; for, be it understood, there can be no question of a subdivision of prisoners into as many classes as there are various trades. At the same time, an important contrast strikes us, and because of the greater part which it has always and everywhere played in our societies, it is one which deserves to be taken into consideration. It is the contrast between two groups of professions and populations, — on the one hand, agricultural professions and rural populations, and on the other hand, industrial and mercantile professions and urban populations. These two groups are surely jointly and severally responsible for each other, and the distinction between them is rather vague; but they are opposed in so many characteristics, — one is so faithful to customs and traditions, the other is so open to infatuation and novelties; one is so submissive to the example of its domestic or patriotic ancestors, the other to the influence of strangers; one is so violent in its coarseness, the other so depraved in its refinements, — that we cannot possibly confuse them. The difference is such that the word "profession" is amphibological when applied at one and the same time, as we have just applied it, to trades which are recruited very often by means of heredity, a thing which takes place in the country, and to trades ordinarily recruited by means of a free choice, which is what happens in towns.

At the present time one of two things must have happened. First, the condemned lived by means of an honest trade apart from his offense, from which he expected, — like the majority of thieves who are sentenced in police courts, or even at the assizes, — only a supplementing of his resources which was entirely secondary, and, if it was a question of blows and physical injuries or murder for vengeance, expected absolutely nothing. In this case we will classify him according to his origin among the rural convicts or urban convicts. Thus he will live with his equals; not with his physiological equals, which is of secondary importance, but with his sociological equals, which is of more importance. Common interest in their former work will establish between fellow prisoners a relation which may be salutary; but when among convicts of various social classes the only characteristic they have in common is their offense, what must we expect from their coming in contact with one another?

The other alternative is that the prisoner had as his only or principal trade some specialty in the nature of an offense, — picking pockets, passing counterfeit coin, stealing by means of false keys, the assassination of wealthy prostitutes, stealing flocks ("abigeato") in Sicily, horse stealing in the Spanish mountains, etc. Now, in this case, also, the best thing is to class him with his equals, because he and they cannot make each other worse; but, if one wishes this to be so, if one wishes to avoid every heterogeneous mingling together, and that terrible pell-mell of Corsican brigands, for example, mingled with assassins from the large towns which angered Lauvergne in the convict prison of Toulon, it seems to me essential to establish between the rural criminal and the urban criminal a distinction which is analogous to the preceding one.

§ 55. (II) Rural brigandage in Corsica and in Sicily. Its characteristics. The rural police and the urban police.

To really feel the necessity of this distinction it is a good thing to look upon its two terms in their most perfect and highly organized form. The criminal of the *town,* just as the criminal of the *fields*, is not complete until he has succeeded in associating himself with men similar to himself under conditions which are, moreover, favorable to his liberty. He always has a tendency towards this sort of completeness, as the pieces of a snake which has been cut seek to unite again. That professional partnership which consists in killing in order to rob, or in robbing by means of terrorizing by threats of death — often followed by the deed itself — or in stealing with the determination to kill if it be necessary, is called brigandage. Starting with this, it is not difficult to see that there are two sorts of brigandage: brigandage such as has been practiced or is still practiced in the majority of the uncultivated or mountainous countries [1] in Italy, Spain, Greece, Hungary, and Corsica; and that brigandage, less romantic, but no less dangerous, which is rife in our big towns. The former is on the decline, the latter is increasing.

I know quite well that these are two manifestations of the same social malady, and that the desire to live and to become rich by means other than work, talent, or chance, that is to say, at the expense of someone else, is the common source of these two malignant eruptions. But the cupidity of the rural brigand has as its object only the satisfying of simple needs; it is linked rather more with conceit than with vanity, with the taste for the power exercised by terrorism over the stricken minds of the populace. The urban brigand, who is more often vain than proud, more vicious than ambitious, only aspires to gratify his desire for luxuries and orgies, with which he has been inoculated by civilization. The rural brigand has most often been led to his existence apart from his fellow-men, to his final downfall as a professional criminal, by a homicide carried out in a "vendetta," as happens in Corsica, or because of a feeling of revolt against actual social oppressions, as happens in Sicily or Calabria; the urban brigand, by the loss of his fortune, which has been dissipated in debauchery, through some indiscretion of his youth, or because of his immoderate appetite for pleasures. The intensity and the tenacity of resentment, hatred or ambition in the case of the former; the intensity, the great number of vices and the covetousness of the latter have been the force behind the criminal impulse.

Less important in reality, although more striking in appearance, than the distinction between urban and rural brigandage, is that between brigandage on land and on sea. This latter distinction, which is founded upon the wholly physical difference between continents and seas, which compels the criminal to modify hi; of proceedings as a consequence, does not in the least establish great social inequality between the bandit of Calabria and e, in pirate of the Mediterranean. In fact, the sea rover is only a hinks, remarkable and peculiar variety of the rural brigand. orsican stocracy

[1] In many countries, in Sicily, for example, the brigand of the mou... "maffia." be contrasted with the brigand of the plains or of the sea coast; but th... is, after all, identical with that of the rural brigand and the urban ... plains and the sea coast being in those countries the centres of civilizati... *urnet*, "Crimi- tively speaking, in our time. There was a time when towns, on ... e la criminalité sought the inaccessible heights and not the shores of the sea.

regard to this it must be remarked that brigandage on land existed before brigandage on the sea and survived it, or is said to have survived it. At the present time piracy has ceased in our European waters, and yet there are still bands of malefactors in our country and in our towns. However, we have seen the prosperity of piracy continue after the criminal associations on the continent were driven back; and, whether in olden times, when Pompey was compelled to lead a regular expedition against the Corsairs, — or in the Middle Ages, when in the eleventh century, for example, the pilgrims preferred to take the route by land to go to Jerusalem rather than the route by sea, on account of the pirates, — or in modern times, when up to the eighteenth century the maritime plunderers of Tunis and Algiers captured women and children upon our coasts, — always and everywhere, long after the mountains have been in a great measure purged of their pirates, the seas still remain infested with theirs.

Why is this so? No doubt because the need of security in the case of land routes, which are constantly in use and an absolute necessity, made itself felt long before the need of securing communication by sea; yet, when finally they did decide to take the costly measures necessary to make war upon piracy, it was possible completely to exterminate it, to do away with its fleets, its ports, and its arsenals; whereas, mountain brigandage, because of its equipment, which is much more simple and easy to hide, can never be radically destroyed, even with the best police force in the world. There is also a deeper reason than this. The seas are a neutral territory, an international one; no king and no State is personally and exclusively interested in establishing security for voyagers, and the attacks of the Corsairs are looked upon as a professional risk, and one which the navigators have no right to complain of to anyone. The Corsairs do a great deal of harm; as much, if not more harm, than the brigands of the mountains; but they arouse less indignation because, as a general thing, they are of another nationality and of a different religion and a different social species from their victims. On the contrary, the mountain brigands and their victims are generally speaking fellow-countrymen and of the same religion. Also, the fight between a merchantman and a pirate ship has the character of ordinary warfare, and from this arises the warlike aspect which maritime commerce retained after it was lost by land commerce. — But having said this, let us return to our previous distinction and continue to justify it.

Let us see, for example, how one becomes a brigand in Corsica.[1] One begins by becoming a bandit. The life of a bandit is there a type of life recognized by everybody, even the authorities, and which does not disgrace anybody. A Corsican, after having revenged himself, in order to escape the rural police, plunges into the woods, his gun slung over his shoulder, alone or accompanied by his relatives; and his life thenceforth is passed wandering in this desert, suffering from hunger and thirst, sleeping with one eye open under the stars or in a cave.

Now, "so long as he does not become a brigand, the bandit keeps people's sympathy," says Paul Bourde. But often he does become a brigand. One must eat and drink in these waste places, so one begins by holding the traveler for ransom in order to have something to live on; in the end one holds him for ransom in order to make one's fortune. In all times the same causes have produced the same effects. In England, for example, statutes of Edward I and Edward III show us that there existed in the thirteenth and fourteenth centuries true organized bands of brigands, who are called "Wastours" or "Robertsmen," and against whom it seemed necessary to decree a true law of suspects. Now, how were these terrible corporations recruited? It was, no doubt, among the vagabonds and the beggars of that period, among those sham pilgrims and sham preaching friars, those sellers of false relics, and those suspicious minstrels who infested the roads at that time, as do at the present time pickpockets, pretended laborers out of work, and peddlers; but above all else it was among the outlaws. The peasant sentenced for the very slightest of misdeeds took to flight; by this very fact he became an outlaw, in the eye of the law he was nothing more than a wolf's head, which could be hunted, as one text says, forcibly. Such were the men who had become but were not born perverse, who nourished English brigandage, and from whom the great revolt of 1381 recruited its soldiers.

At other times it is to escape the humiliation of his fate, in order to make for himself a better social position, as he thinks, than that of the class in which he was born, that the Corsican or the Sicilian becomes a brigand. There exists an aristocracy of crime in those countries of traditional "vendetta" or "maffia."

[1] Consult the "Archives de l'Anthropologie criminelle," 1888; *Bournet*, "Criminalité en Corse"; *Kocher and Paoli*, "Notes sur Rocchini et causes de la criminalité en Corse," (Lyons, Storck).

"The way to inspire respect in a great part of Sicily is to be reputed to have committed some homicide," says Franchetti.[1] Also, many a peasant treated in a lofty manner by the steward of a great landowner, his neighbor, cannot resist the temptation to carry out his little exploit in order to obtain the consideration that his conceit requires, — that immeasurable conceit which is the characteristic of the inhabitants of this island. His ambition is soon to become a "capo-banda," head of the band, and the terror of those who used to scorn him. It is not so easy to become an urban brigand. As a general thing, an earlier preparation is needed, an apprenticeship begun at an early period under the eyes of experienced masters; this is what takes place among children who have been deserted or not very well watched over by their parents. However, a despair caused by the consequences of debauchery or gambling, by some financial catastrophy, is sometimes sufficient to plunge a civilized Frenchman into a loss of class, that jungle of civilization. Thus, desertion of children and loss of class, — in other words, vagabondage under various forms, — are the urban equivalent of bandit life. They are, to the low cafés of assassins and robbers, speaking their slang, which is endlessly renewed in our capitals, what the bandit's life is to the caves of assassins and robbers, speaking their maternal and unchanging dialect in the Corsican mountains. When one has seen the number of bandits increased for the last twenty years in the District of Sartène[2] by those individuals who, — either after having revenged themselves, or in order to revenge themselves, or to escape the vengeance of an enemy, — live like vagabonds, with neither fire nor lodging, in the woods and beyond the pale of the law, it is not astonishing to see the holding-up of carriages on the highroads increase. In the same way, when we find our statistics revealing the uninterrupted increase of the offense of vagabondage and mendicancy and of child desertion, we should not be surprised to find the increase of nocturnal attacks, of burglary and robberies by armed men, that are committed in Paris, Marseilles, and Lyons and the majority of the large cities.

It is not less true that one must be careful not to confuse murder inspired by vengeance, where it is accounted a duty owed

[1] Cited by *Alongi*, in his interesting monograph upon the "Maffia," from which we shall have to borrow much more information. Alongi is a Sicilian, and his judicial duties have enabled him to obtain an intimate knowledge of the special customs of the great criminal class which he describes with a great deal of insight.

[2] "En Corse," by *Paul Bourde*.

to a man's honor, with murder inspired by cupidity; and there is as great a distance between them in primitive countries as there is between adultery or libertinage and robbery in the more advanced countries. "With regard to a contested ballot at the elections of January 13, 1888, at San Gavino of Garbini, one Nicoli killed one Pietri who was presiding over the bureau. A 'vendetta' followed between the two families. Three of the Nicoli and one of the Pietri were successively killed. About twenty of the members of both families had taken to the country, and other assassinations were imminent."[1] The Prefect and a Deputy intervened, and the two families were made to sign a veritable treaty of peace, similar to a diplomatic document of the same kind. But, as only two of the Pietri had been killed, the Nicoli thought it was only just to break the treaty in order to carry out their revenge. A third Pietri was killed, as was fitting, and other executions took place from time to time.

Can one liken this type of criminality, in truth, to that of our assassins in Paris, and mix them up together as our statisticians do? Where the family solidarity has preserved its primitive force, to avenge a dead relative is to defend the family which is still alive. This is like defending oneself against a mortal attack, and the excuse drawn from the "vendetta" is really not without some relation to that of lawful defense. Between *customary* homicide, whether one call it "vendetta" or duel (the "vendetta" being in the last analysis, as has been very well said, "only an American duel prolonged for many years") and criminal homicide there is no similarity excepting their name. Thus it is that Chinese or Japanese suicide, which is due to vengeance or animosity, and the Roman suicide, which is due to stoicism or sometimes to Epicureanism, and the Hindu suicide, which is due to devotion, without mentioning the heroic and legendary suicides of a Codrus and a Decius, have nothing in common with our suicide, which is due to despair or madness.

Is it necessary to say that the moral type, and the physical type as well, of the Troglodyte brigand should differ strangely from that of the miscreant of Paris or London? "A priori,"

[1] This is the southern portion of Corsica, and also the most backward, the most firmly rooted in the old usages, — not because it is the most southern portion, but because it is the furthest removed from the Continent. The same thing applies to the south of Sicily, and for the same reason. This seems to me to be obvious, although the Italian criminologists have not been able to resist a desire even here to make the influence of climate and latitude play the most important part.

one can affirm this with entire certainty. Their manner of living is no less dissimilar. The former is picturesque in an entirely different way from the latter. Far from seeking to disguise himself, he has his particular kind of costume, — at least for his show days. The Sicilian "maffiosi" had formerly a traditional uniform, of which they were as proud as our officers are of their epaulets; a "béret" (flat cap) with a great silken tuft, and a velvet jacket. It is with regret that they have had to give up this compromising insignia. They have no slang, but only a special laconism and a characteristic accent. A strange thing, parenthetically, if slang should be a phenomenon of atavism, for, according to this hypothesis, is it not among the most primitive and least civilized criminals that one should expect to see it flourish, which is just the opposite of what we actually find? By these characteristics and many others a member of the body of suburban criminals contrasts with his colleagues of the mountains and the deserts. He uses a distinct idiom composed of scrapings of languages, and he conceals himself under a great variety of disguises or under the most commonplace clothing. It is in low cafés and restaurants, as we have said, and not in rocky chasms, that he holds his secret meetings. A progressive man, he recognizes the division of labor. He has his specialties, as we shall see; whereas the rural brigand, like the village workman, is compelled to do a little of everything at one and the same time, but with a simplicity of action which is in strong contrast with the elaborate tricks of his town rival.

Moreover, in the annals of all peoples, and especially in Italy, the rough brigand has a much more conspicuous position than the subtle brigand; he has played a historic part; kings and emperors have not been afraid to have dealings with him[1] and to depend upon him; for example, King Ferdinand of Naples during the French Revolution. The other, on his part, up to this time has only been associated with a few conspirators; but he is destined to see his importance grow, perhaps to such a point that he will one day eclipse his contemporary of the Sierras and the Apennines; I cannot tell. The ambitious novices have as yet only dared to

[1] A statement has been found of the sums paid by the Council of Ten to a great number of bravos as fees for assassinations ordered by the Council. The number of homicides by order is incalculable in the Middle Ages, in olden times, and even more in the sixteenth century during our frightful religious wars. But in these cases the rulers and the republics employed a criminal as a useful instrument. On other occasions, and it is of these I mean to speak, they negotiated with him, treating with him as one power treats with another.

depend upon modern vices; we cannot, however, be sure that they will never call upon modern crime to assist them.

Moreover, crime is ever ready to take back its old power, and at the slightest disturbance of the dikes that keep it within bounds it threatens to overflow. It has been necessary to combat it by instituting bodies of men which are at the same time contrary to and like these mysterious associations; and, as "naturam morborum ostendunt remedia," the distinction between the rural police under various names and the urban police has for a long time come about naturally, in order that it may exactly correspond to the two forms of rural and urban brigandage. Imagine the finest brigade of the Corsican rural police transported to Paris and charged with carrying on the duties of a brigade of the agents of public safety, and vice versa. Taken from its own sphere, each of these bodies of men would be ridiculous in its impotence. Half of the strength of the rural policeman is in the traditional fear which is connected with his three-cornered hat and his shoulder belt, just as half of the power of the mountain brigand has sometimes consisted in the fear which the mere sight of his costume inspired, the mere sound of his commands and his threats according to the established formulae. The rural policeman, like the brigand of the mountains and the woods, is the legendary and traditional man; his prestige is wrapped up in this. "The promptness and the invariable obedience with which six or seven persons, even when they are armed, will throw themselves face down upon the ground at the first traditional command ('Giorgio, à terra!') of a mere vagabond is a remarkable thing," says Alongi. In the same way one has noticed a hundred times the magical effect produced upon a rebellious crowd by the appearance of two mounted rural police.

As to the police spy, — who must not be confused with the mere guardian of the peace, who is to be recognized by his uniform, — his only care is not to show himself wearing any distinctive badge; he goes everywhere dressed like everybody else, sometimes in disguise, as astute and versatile as his quarry. It has been claimed that every hunter finally comes to resemble his game to a certain extent. If this is so, one must believe that the urban criminal is singularly superior to the rural criminal in shrewdness, in skill, in flexibility, and especially in individual initiative and personal power of imagination. It is permissible for the rural policeman, like the fisherman, to use means of investigation which are always the same; they are always successful because they are opposed to manoeuvres which never vary; the more he conforms in this to his regular habits, which are excellent, the better does he fulfil his mission. But the good detective is only worth while because of the inexhaustible fertility of his imagination.

The part played by the town policeman has not ceased to grow during our time, whereas that played by the rural policeman, at least in so far as he is an auxiliary of criminal justice, — for it joins to his other duties a quantity of administrative work which tends to supersede the former more and more, — is every day relatively upon the decline.[1] This is quite natural, because we know that criminality, like population, emigrates from the country into the cities at the present time. As a general thing, this movement of urban emigration, which is an intermittent phenomenon of societies, denotes an unusual rush of inventions and new ideas, whether they be spontaneously brought forth or imported from outside, which have just caused to break forth in the heart of cities a hundred springs of new example, of new imitations, which have quickly become streams and rivers of wealth. The "*imitation-fashion*," then, — if I may be permitted thus to name that imitation which is connected with new examples, — each day makes greater gaps in the "*imitation-custom*," until finally — a time which has not yet come for us — the latter absorbs and assimilates those currents of example which in their turn have become traditional, somewhat as the sea swallows up the rivers. While awaiting this inevitable abatement of the fever of progress, or, if you will, this consolidation of progress by a return to broader tradition, there are still many prosperous days left for crime, upon condition that it shall be altered in the same way as the general alterations that are taking place.

Just as in all industries and in every path of art and thought, the prestige of novelty has been substituted for that of age; just as at the same time as they are renewing their equipment of tools, all trades are being recruited in a more liberal and less hereditary manner, and often in choosing their personnel give the preference

[1] The differentiation of the rural police and the urban police is only developed in the long run, but it always takes place; and, just as rural development precedes urban development, the organization of the rural police, or of a body which fulfils its function (as, for instance, the horse police under the old French system), precedes the organization of the urban police. The urban police was only really formed in France by de Sartine, about the middle of the eighteenth century; the horse police, under Louis XI, exercised the functions of a provost, principally against the peasants.

to a stranger rather than to a fellow-countryman, in the same way the criminal profession is now adopting new methods, such as the cutting up of the bodies of its victims or disfiguring them by vitriol, and shows itself more hospitable to every recruit. In other words, it is becoming less and less rural and more and more urban. A band of Corsican brigands was only opened with great difficulty to any other men but Corsicans; a band of Sicilian brigands has from time immemorial made use of the same ways of intimidation or plunder, "lettera di scrocco" (swindling letters), "abigeato" (stealing of cattle in the fields), sequestration of persons (in order to get a ransom from the captive), etc. But a band of the Parisian vagabonds welcomes the scamps of every country; it is essentially cosmopolitan as well as progressive, and its instruments are as varied as its members.

§ 56. (III) Continuation, the Sicilian Maffia.

A few examples are necessary if one wishes to verify the accuracy of these remarks. As we have been speaking of Sicily, let us make known its "maffia" rather than the Neapolitan "camorra" which has already become far too citified to serve as a good example of rural crime.[1] With regard to that criminality which belongs to the fatherland of Theocritus, we will set forth in a few words some specimens of urban crime. We shall here and there rely upon information furnished by writers who, being magistrates or functionaries raised up from the rank and file of the police, have learned to know while they hunted them out the malefactors of their country. The criminal in prison has been studied too much; a sufficient amount of observation of him when free and at work has not been made. One who has only seen the lion and the fox in a menagerie knows little about them. The anatomy and the cranial measurements of the lion may interest a naturalist, but the least tale of an African hunter will better teach the common mortal as to the nature of this splendid beast. Leroy teaches us more about animals which he has hunted than many indoor naturalists.

Similarly, it is the memoirs of prefects of police or magistrates

[1] *Bournet* ("La Criminalité en France et en Italie," 1884) very rightly compares the camorra of Naples to the high class thieves of Paris. He adds: "During our stay at Naples, in the Borgo Loreto, where the members of the camorra are numerous, we witnessed the assassination of a detective by a 'piccioto' (an aspirant to the camorra). Acclaimed by the whole crowd, the assassin became a member of the camorra that very night, and a great banquet was tendered him."

charged with the repression of offenses that one must read in order really to know the delinquent. Then it is that we perceive by means of the similarity of the processes employed by malefactors of the same region and of the same period, by means of the local color and the historical color which distinguish the criminal fauna adapted to each locality and to each time, the preponderance of the "social factors" in the production of the offense and the delinquent. The criminal always imitates somebody, even when he originates; that is to say, when he uses in combination imitations obtained from various sources. He always needs to be encouraged by the example and approval of a group of men, whether it be a group of ancestors or a group of comrades, whence arises the duality of the crime because of custom and the crime because of fashion. It is precisely in this respect that the criminal is a social being, and that he is a member of society, and that as such he is responsible.

The madman, on the other hand, does not imitate another madman, or anybody else. There may exist vague resemblances between acts of madness committed by different madmen; but this similarity, which, moreover, is always less than in crimes of the same kind, is never the result of imitation. Also, attempt to classify the insane into two categories corresponding to our preceding distinction of criminals and you will not succeed. The manifestation of mental alienation is the thing most varied in individuals, although in the same individual it may be identically repeated. One may, indeed, if one wishes to, call this identical repetition *habit*, but it has nothing in common with the habit of picking pockets for example, or robbing the intoxicated. The pickpocket, more or less consciously, imitates himself as each new theft takes place, at the same time as he, more or less consciously, imitates others; and each time he profits by the experience acquired by his comrades and by himself. The lunatic who reproduces from hour to hour, from day to day and from month to month the same extravagances obeys an organic impulse, a habit which is simply physiological and not in the least psychological, — more often than not without the slightest recollection of his previous strange and similar doings.

At any rate, if one can say, strictly speaking, that there is such a thing as *habitual* madness, it is quite certain that there is no such thing as *customary* and *traditional* madness; for to give this name to religious hallucinations and cases of persons possessed by demons, for example, would be the same as to take the changing and entirely superficial reflection of a piece of material for its actual and permanent color. It would not be any more correct to liken the intermittent epidemics of madness to the criminal contagions which are spread at certain dates as a fashion of the day. The latter, which consist of imitations, often take place among individuals at great distances from one another; the term *contagion,* which brings to mind *contact,* is not, metaphorically speaking, applicable. The former, which are pathological phenomena before everything, require the physical coming together of the subjects who are affected by the passing of the scourge.[1] It is generally within the narrow and shut-in confines of a convent that one has seen the latter flourish.

Having closed this parenthesis, let us return. The maffia is in Sicily what the clan spirit is in Corsica, but on a larger scale. The members of the same clan conspire together with a view to obtaining possession, by every lawful or fraudulent, peaceful or bloodthirsty means, no matter which, of all the electoral functions, to place their hands upon the "sugillo" (mayor's seal) and to carry out for their own advantage every possible annoyance against the adverse clan. The "maffiosi" pursue the same object against all those who do not form a part of their association. Analogous political circumstances, the prolonged absence of the central power, reassuring, firm, and just, have developed in both islands that need of solidarity "per fas et nefas," that keen freemasonry, wherein the member obtains the security which he cannot find anywhere else. Let us not be astonished at this; this fact, which is today an exceptional one, was universal at one time, and Corsica as well as Sicily, remains of the Middle Ages carefully preserved by the Mediterranean for our instruction, may teach us as to our past. It seems to me that I am right also in seeing in this a confirmation of certain particular views with regard to imitation. Did not the clan spirit rule formerly upon the Continent, shutting up each small town and each feudal jurisdiction within itself? If it has been gradually replaced by a wider *consciousness,* is it not in the same proportion as that in which the various peoples became like one another through the continual exchange of examples of every sort? And cannot one thus account

[1] The alienist criminologists thought they could liken the distinction between madness consisting of attacks and madness that is chronic to the distinction between criminality because of opportunity and criminality because of habit. But the analogy is here nothing more than apparent and is not supported.

for the fact that, having remained strangers to this incessant reciprocity of influences, just as lakes are free from the movement of the tides, Corsica and Sicily have kept the original exclusiveness and the inhospitable narrowness of their moral sense, which to our eyes is so strange?

Moreover, brigandage is only one of the manifestations, or, to put it better, one of the excrescences of the maffia; but the maffia makes use of it and fosters it, and it is the strength of the maffia just as it is its sustenance. The same relations are established in Corsica between the clan and the brigands or the bandits who belong to it. We have seen and we still see municipal councils voting annuities to bandits who are members of the dominant clan. And, in fact, popular sentiment lends a mission to these nomads who are transfigured into knights-errant; the assassin seems like a sort of administrator of justice. Through him, in fact, one obtains justice; for one cannot obtain it in any other way. We have seen in these last few years a band compel a mayor of the District of Sartène to set right his relations with his former mistress whom he refused to marry. In 1886 another band, playing the part of rural policemen, prevented a duel from taking place at the gates of Ajaccio. It is the same thing in Sicily.

Must we see in the Sicilian brigand a *born criminal?* The Prefect of Messina will answer us.[1] "All these people," says he, speaking of farmers who have become malefactors, "are sober, of a gentle nature, very respectful to the middle classes, and would always have shown themselves incapable of committing offenses had they not been compelled to take a part in the dark intrigues, the private vengeances, and the rivalries of a few privileged persons," whose hired assassins they are. It is worthy of note that the famous chiefs of brigands, "from Don Peppino to Reggio and from Don Pasquale to Raia," have sprung from the peasant class. Here we are concerned with the typical rural brigand. Sicily,

[1] Although he is a partisan of Lombroso and of the theory of the criminal by birth, Alongi allows such admissions as this to escape him: How are we to account for the fact, he says, that at Palermo, where leisure and education flourished, the maffia came to be developed? This cannot be, he replies, an effect of *atavistic heredity*, "for, if we think that born delinquents are in a minority, this minority must have long since disappeared under the repeated blows of justice," whereas, on the contrary, the blood of assassins is the seed from which new scoundrels spring. — He concluded very correctly that "the principal cause of the maffia does not lie in the economic condition, but in the mind and the heart of the peasant, in the *historical and moral conditions of his environment.*"

moreover, just as Corsica (in spite of the contempt of Corsicans for agricultural labor) is an essentially agricultural country, dotted here and there with small villages. The "maffiosi" have as their rendezvous the fairs.

Shall we say with the social writers that poverty is the social cause which has driven the Sicilian peasant to turn brigand? Alongi begins by admitting it, but afterwards he finds himself greatly embarrassed to account for the rapid progress made by the maffia under a refined and urban form, it is true, in Palermo and its surroundings, in that golden "conch-shell," a marvelously rich and fertile region, where property is very much split up and the farmer is very comfortably off. It is because, rich or poor, the Sicilian peasant is vain to the highest degree; if he be rich he hastens to ruin himself in luxurious extravagances, in festivities and in fine clothing,[1] in order that he may rival the upper classes; and when he has been ruined he is compelled to become a "maffioso"; if he is poor he spontaneously becomes a "maffioso," in order to raise himself above his station.[2] One fine day, without any reason, "disgusted with his tiresome existence," he puts on the costume of the brigands; and, after a solemn initiation, surrounded by a great assembly of relatives and friends, he goes armed and with his baggage into the camp of the vagabonds. Moreover, he has learned at an early hour to arm himself. "At Palermo and at Bagheria and in the Southern districts the peasant invariably leaves the fields with his mattock under his arm and his gun slung over his shoulder; and his knife has no difficulty in finding victims." "A man lends neither his gun nor his wife," says a Sicilian proverb. Still another analogy with Corsica. Under the brigand the peasant always survives. A Sicilian brigand

[1] And in sweets also. "Each festival, each saint, has its special sweetmeat, and one might make a calendar from the various kinds of sweetmeats."

[2] This pride, or this vanity, whichever one chooses to call it, may be a source of heroism as well as of crime; but it is certain that such a *faith in oneself* is one of the primitive mistakes that is most contrary to the ideas of civilization. "The Sicilian loves his island, the Palermitian adores his Palermo. Every inhabitant of the smallest village professes the same great love for the four walls within which he was born and grew up. . . . The Sicilian does not say *my father, my mother*, but *the father, the mother*, as though his were the father and mother 'par excellence.' He affects not to admire anything." — This exaggeration is "*greater in the interior and the little places, less among the cultivated classes of Palermo and in the great centres.*" It is rather, in fact, largely, by reason of ostentation that the Sicilian, like the Corsican, is generous and hospitable to excess. — The victim of a theft in Sicily feels the humiliation of having been duped far more than the actual injury that has been done him.

never dies outside of his own canton; homesickness, in spite of the greatest dangers, will bring him back to his birthplace.

We have said above that the methods of procedure employed by the rural brigands of Sicily are the "lettera di scrocco," the "abigeato," and sequestration; let us add to them the "grassazione," — that is to say, armed highway robbery, or the holding-up of carriages. These methods are not only traditional, but sometimes hereditary. We have seen the office of the "capo-banda," like the crown of a monarch, transmitted by heredity. A great landed proprietor residing upon his estates one day receives a letter which is as respectful as it could possibly be, wherein his excellency, his most illustrious lordship, is begged to be kind enough to provide some honest people who are overtaken by misfortune with a little assistance in the shape of two, three, or four thousand "lire," if his lordship does not wish to have something unpleasant happen to him. This is called a "lettera di scrocco." If this letter remains unanswered a second, more urgent, letter is sent. Finally, a third letter comes, which states laconically, "Pay or you die." A few days later the threat is carried out; the recalcitrant is either killed or "sequestrated." In the latter case, taken by surprise and carried off in the night to some cave, he is taken care of with deferential respect until the time when his family decides to buy him back at the price of an enormous ransom.

The "abigeato" or driving off of vast wandering herds in the immense pastures is a kind of robbery which goes back at least to the time of Cacus, the Troglodyte giant, the mythological brigand, who stole the heifers of Hercules. The domestication of animals, having been one of the first and most fruitful forms of inventive genius, domestic animals have for a long time been the best kind of capital and, consequently, the object of the most bitter envy.[1] The possessor of cattle has been looked upon for centuries in the same way as a great modern capitalist, — that is to say, more liable than anyone else to be robbed. When a faithless cashier takes to flight carrying one or two millions with him he is not considered a common thief. In primitive times the stealer of domestic animals inspired an analogous "consideration." When one of Attila's sons

[1] In his profound research in juridical archaeology *Sir Henry Sumner Maine* has indeed shown this, especially in his "Primitive Institutions." He there shows us that at the very beginnings of the known races we always find a state characterized by an abundance of land and a scarcity of animals; then it is that nobility consists in a wealth of herds. From this there result many of the peculiarities of the old law of Ireland, Rome, and the Hindus.

wished to make a little kingdom for himself "he gathered together," says Jornandès, "cattle thieves, Scamares, and brigands from all countries, and took possession of a tower called Herta." There, "pillaging his neighbors in the same manner as the rural thief, he proclaimed himself king of the malefactors who obeyed him."

This audacious type of robbery has very old roots in Italy. In the thirteenth century in the neighborhood of Florence rich "contadini" (peasants) allied themselves with gentlemen in order to steal their neighbors' pigs.[1] There are tribes, even peoples, who have specially devoted themselves to this kind of pillage. In Spain the gypsies [2] have given themselves up from time immemorial to the stealing of horses; encamped in the Sierras in the midst of the ruins of a feudal castle, sometimes between the four uprights of an old gibbet on which several of their ancestors must have been hanged without doubt for similar misdeeds, they spy out horses or mules to be stolen and are very skilful in the art of disguising them after having captured them, to such a point as to make them unrecognizable by their rightful owners. If they cannot find these beasts of burden, however, they are sometimes content with taking a pig in passing; but this is enough proof of the respectable antiquity of this rural offense.

As an example of an old and traditional form of offense one might cite the counterfeiting of money. Bands of counterfeiters inhabit, it would seem, at least on the Spanish slope, the caverns of the Pyrenees. Gil Maestre tells us of having roamed "for long hours in the night" around their haunts, and of having often heard the conversation and the laughter of women, "the whole thing accompanied by little sharp and regular taps of hammers." But this crime savors of civilization and the town.

There are, in fact, transitions between rural brigandage and urban brigandage,[3] and the maffia itself is the proof of this.

[1] "Histoire du brigandage en Italie," by *Dubarry*.

[2] "La Criminalidad en Barcelona," by *Gil Maestre*.

[3] Our century knows them well, for through the intervention of railways it has given a most decided impulse to the urban transformation of criminality. One can no longer stop the trains as one could stop the stage-coaches. Until 1840 or 1850 the last bands of malefactors who drew any attention to themselves were of an obviously rural character; the band of "chauffeurs" at the end of the last century, the brigands of Vienna in 1834, etc. In 1857 the "Graft" band had already industrial elements mingled with it. From then on the famous bands have had their headquarters in the great towns; for example, in Paris, the "Vrignault" band, in 1876 (one hundred and fifty members); the "Abadie" band, in 1878; the band of the Bois de Boulogne, in 1888, etc. I do not mention the little bands of Parisian counterfeiters that are always cropping up.

Under the form that we have just described it has been on the wane since 1877, owing to the energetic repression exercised by the Italian Government; but, on the other hand, it is growing under its urban forms. In descending from the mountains to the seacoast it changes its character; from its wild mountain character it has changed to mere brutality. Influenced by the life of the sea and the city it has become perhaps still more sanguinary, but especially more crafty and subtle; its organization is being perfected, its implements are being replaced. The working class begins to affiliate with it. Already associations of workmen are constantly pledging themselves, either impliedly or expressly in their by-laws, to provide a lawyer for every member "who may be accused of an offense" and to support his family during his detention. Associations of criminals have been formed, the last "avatar" of the maffia, which, spreading their nets at one and the same time over agriculture and industry, including both the fields and the town, ransoming on the one hand landowners, but in a more ingenious manner than in the past,[1] and, on the other hand, disposing of credit, causing at their will the rise and fall of the market upon the public square of Palermo, awarding public works or ecclesiastical property which has become secularized, may be considered as a synthesis of the two forms of brigandage which we are comparing, or as a transition from one to the other. They bear alluring names, — the "fratellanza," the "fratuzzi," the "amoroso," etc.

§ 57. (IV) Urban brigandage. Criminality in Barcelona.

This hybrid form leads me to the pure and absolute form of high grade urban brigandage, which is centralized, powerful, and raised to the dignity of an institution, and which finally is a worthy match for the high grade rural brigandage, so to speak, that we portrayed a short time ago. Circumstances analogous to those which, as we have seen, have given birth to the maffia in the rural districts of Sicily cause to arise from time to time in the very midst of civilizations in capitals some frightful sect which

[1] The chief seeks out a landowner and tells him *respectfully* that he has a bad gamekeeper, and that he must change him and take another, — that is to say, a member for whom a lucrative employment is sought. The landowner yields, or, if he resists, he finds in his orchard which has been devastated a cross, a symbolic threat which he does not need to have repeated. It is to be noticed that the same threatening symbol was frequently made use of by the Holy Vehme and is still made use of by the Corsican bandits.

terrifies the world, and of which even the historian is afraid, — so much so, frequently, that, unless a man has the courage of Taine or Maxime du Camp, he dares not say what he thinks. When the regular power in a great city suddenly becomes weak or gives way, or else, conversely, when an excessive despotism arouses rebellion therein, each citizen, no longer being able to count on any authority to protect him, seeks out the support of a coterie. From thence spring up clubs and secret societies which are seen to multiply; the most violent of these clubs, the most dangerous of these societies, soon absorbs or annihilates all the rest because of its relative strength, and soon, whatever may have been the honesty or the original loftiness of its object, draws to itself criminal natures that get possession of it; detestable malefactors, who are also tigers and hyenas, but of a new and complicated kind. Thus broke forth the sect of the "Maillotins," the "Ecorcheurs" and the "Cabochiens," during the anarchy of the Hundred Years War; the faction of the Jacobins at the beginning of the French Revolution, the Commune of Paris in 1871, or, still more recently, the nihilist conspiracy.[1]

The evil here has the characteristics of an epidemic, and not of an endemic; for the time being it ravages the whole of some vast territory instead of taking root during centuries within a narrow compass. It is a fashion, and not a custom. The malefactors who become the chiefs of these historic bands are not farmers, but artisans, shopkeepers, rhetoricians, actors, and artists. They are not tied to the place of their birth, it is not to their birthplace that they return to die; the majority of them are foreigners or cosmopolites. They practice, not the "grassazione," but the robbing of the public coffers; not the "lettera di scrocco," but the abusive demand, lists of proscription, laws of suspects; not the "abigeato," but the confiscation of property "en masse," the despoiling of the adversary in innumerable ways; not the sequestration in a grotto or the murder of a single man, but the filling of prisons, the shooting and drowning on a large scale, the decimation of a class by the guillotine and explosions of dynamite; not the burning of a barn or the destruction of a harvest, but the burning and pillaging of palaces. And they unceasingly vary these methods of procedure, adapting them to the taste of the day with a fertility of imagination which puts to shame the time-honored routine of rural brigands.

[1] In ancient history the conspiracy of Catiline showed the same characteristics.

But one should recognize the fact that they very much resemble the latter in one remarkable characteristic; in the popular legend which is attached to their names. The most ferocious, the most crafty and the most rapacious of the highway robbers, an Antonino Leone or a Di Paschati,[1] has his picture hung up and venerated in the cottages of Sicily; Marat, Hébert, Robespierre, and others have their busts in the place of honor in many a man's study.[2] Still another resemblance deserves to be pointed out. The rural brigand would not be possible without numerous direct and indirect accomplices, either active or silent, who smooth his way for him. In Sicily they call "manutengolismo" (literally, the fact of *holding the hand*) that complicity of every degree, from that of the false witness, who out of fear keeps silent as to the crime which he has seen to that of the receiver of stolen goods, who acts from cupidity. What a part does this double "manutengolism" play in our towns terrorized by a handful of agitators!

But in normal times the police prevent urban brigandage from organizing in the face of history under the triumphant exterior of the type just mentioned. It is opposed to its organization, its conquering centralization, and it disperses if it does not destroy it. For the criminal industry on a large scale civilization thus substitutes criminal industry on a small scale, which is exactly the opposite of the transformation that it causes honest industry to undergo. Being no longer able to act in considerable numbers for the carrying out of glorious exploits, the detestable and wicked outcasts are reduced to plot obscurely some ordinary crime in the company of two or three comrades or apprentices, or else with more skill to work up some bad scheme of extortion, some gambling house, some kind of a machine for the public to speculate in. In one case as in the other they often frustrate prosecution by the variety of their inventions. It is not because they are individually imaginative, but because, being placed in a good position to keep themselves posted on innovations of a rascally or fraudulent nature, they hasten to adopt them. And up to this time only high grade rural brigandage has been in

[1] It is rather interesting to note that these two great chiefs of bands were enemies, and that the former ended by killing the latter.

[2] This popular veneration for brigands dates back a long way. The minstrels of the thirteenth century in England sang the praises of Robin Hood, the immortal outlaw, "how this pious man . . . boldly despoiled the great lords and high prelates, but was merciful to the poor, which was an indirect way of advising the brigands of that time to discern on their rounds between the tares and the wheat." (*Jusserand*, "La Vie nomade et les routes d'Angleterre au moyen age").

question, — brigandage which does not hesitate at murder, arson, and rapine on a large scale.

But there is still a low form of rural brigandage, with habits no less traditional, of marauding, of petty thefts of chickens, wheat, wine, and wood. The customary frauds practiced by the farmers and the boatmen, who water their wine according to custom, with a perfectly clear conscience, etc. To this relatively slight form of criminal tendency, to this ground floor of rural offense, corresponds an urban outcropping which is truly luxuriant of pilfering, of swindling, of abuses of confidence, infinitely more numerous and changing. It is to this delictual expansion much more than to great crimes that our great centres owe their remarkable number of cases before the courts. Often enough this lesser criminality in cities conceals itself behind the mask of mendicancy. This was so in old Paris, where sham beggars and sham cripples, veritable bands of swindlers, had as their quarters the Cour des Miracles. In Pekin this formidable organization is still extant. Maurice Jametel ("Pékin," 1888) tells us that the beggars there constitute a formidable corporation, that they have a chief who is elected, and a general meeting place, and tax the shops just as the camorra of Naples does. It is useless to go into the details of criminality in the Paris of today; the writings of Maxime du Camp and d'Haussonville have given us information on this subject, as have the works of Macé. Let us talk of Barcelona, for example, which, not being a capital, will better serve to give us an idea of the average large city.

In Spain, as everywhere else, civilization seems to substitute fraud for violence, but is in reality merely showing itself more ingenious in renewing fraud than in bringing violence into the paths of progress. In the sparsely populated and wild provinces the "vendetta" still reigns and crimes against persons predominate; but in places where the population is dense and where the railroads have penetrated, assassinations, according to Gil Maestre, become rare and attacks upon property (under less brutal forms, moreover) are on the increase. In Barcelona forgery, pilfering, and swindling flourish especially. It is not that murderers are unknown there; the people greatly fear the "atracador" (the "thug"), the panther of assassination who pounces upon his victim and strangles him. He is the hero of his own world; he it is whose praises will be sung by the blind should he be so unfortunate as to be captured. The "minadores" (miners) are scarcely less terrifying. The latter make a specialty of entering houses by means of subterranean galleries. They proceed in a methodical and strategic manner, hiring first of all a cellar or a store alongside of the house which they wish to enter and hiding behind barrels, either empty or filled with earth, the entrance to their mine. Well dressed in the daytime, at night dressed as excavators, they must associate together to the number of four or less for the carrying out of their difficult excavations under the direction of one of them who acts as an engineer. Moreover, the malefactors of Barcelona have their rendezvous and their secret meetings. Their motto is, "Bread and bulls." They are very versatile; such and such a fellow who yesterday was dressed as a villager today is dressed as a young leader, and tomorrow he will wear the blouse and the cap of the workingman. To discover them under these disguises is the task of the able policeman. The "topista" (in Paris the sneak thief) has the specialty of robbing unoccupied apartments. He is essentially vicious, has a profound contempt for the tradesman, they tell us, and only holds his own kind in esteem. Peril attracts him as much as pleasure. The "espadista" (robber and housebreaker) knows neither lock nor bolt that can resist him. He often begins by laying siege to the heart of the servant of the household, who becomes his accomplice without knowing it. Let us add that the "santeros" (thieving servants) are very numerous in Barcelona; and one is never better served than by them. Shall we enumerate the infinite varieties of swindlers, — the banker swindler, the promoter swindler, the administrator who is the delegate of companies which he has founded, etc.? The species are innumerable. One useful specialist is the "guitarist," who by means of an ingenious instrument in the shape of a guitar passes his time in swindling the other swindlers.

There, as in all towns, the making of counterfeit banknotes flourishes, a civilized rejuvenation of counterfeit coin. Gil Maestre points out the frequent emigration and the continual renewing of the population of petty thieves. Once their tricks are played out they go somewhere else, where they recognize their brothers by secret signs; and, thanks to these meetings, "they communicate to one another the information they have and perfect their processes." This magistrate maintains that there exist schools for the training of pickpockets.

There is a kind of stealing, which is very Spanish, which one might call stealing "with an embrace." Two women, — one of them young and pretty, the other elderly and appearing to be the duenna, — seem to be looking into the window of a shop alongside of a man who appears to be rich and ingenuous. The pretty one turns round and throws her arms about the neck of her neighbor. "What! is it you! What a pleasure it is to see you again!" and she prolongs for a moment this affectionate effusion, to which she suddenly puts an end. "Ah, I beg your pardon; I have made a mistake." And both women disappear with a rapidity which seems to be accounted for by the desire they have of hiding their confusion. But after their departure the recipient of this all too tender embrace discovers the loss of his pocketbook.

For the use of children there is the robbery of lawns, of a local color which is still quite marked. These young thieves steal during the night the linen and clothing left upon the lawns of houses. They form a body of skirmishers of crime under the direction of chiefs. They scatter to carry out the plan of campaign and then meet one another again to divide the booty. Pillagers like sparrows, they have an extraordinary ability for robbing people; having carried out their exploit, they laugh, play cards, and huddle together in some corner, the "seat of an abominable corruption," in order to sleep soundly. They begin by robbing lawns and pigeon-houses; it will not be long before they are robbing the upper stories of houses. They fight among themselves with knives, just like the *grown up persons* whom they imitate. Their only occupation is robbery, and this was bound to be so. The child is born a parasite; if he does not live at the expense of his parents, who abandon him, he must live at the expense of society. And, if his father and mother neglect to teach him some occupation, he will learn the first one that presents itself to him, and one which is so captivating and so amusing, — a trade which has nothing mechanical about it, a profession which is essentially a liberal one in his eyes, — the criminal profession. But the proof that this novice is not born bad is that as a general thing he is loyal and kind to his comrades.

A few figures may help to make these considerations more precise. In the individual tables, so full of varied information, which Marro has added to his work, "I caratteri dei delinquenti," I have counted a number of malefactors who from the age of eighteen years on, or under eighteen (often from early childhood), are noted as having *abandoned their family*, which assumes, according to my point of view, that their family had previously greatly neglected them. I have counted one hundred and sixty of them out of four hundred and seventy-two male malefactors, without mentioning forty-seven who at the age of eighteen or before had become orphans by losing either their father or their mother. Now, out of ninety-seven honest individuals of the same sex I have not counted a *single one* who, without being an orphan, had abandoned his family at such an early age. Out of these ninety-seven "normals" there were fourteen orphans of the age pointed out, which is a slightly larger proportion — quite by chance, without doubt — than that of orphans who are malefactors.

Furthermore, from a table drawn up by Marro it is shown that with regard to the premature death of their parents malefactors are not found to be placed in a situation which is less favorable *in appearance* than is that of "normals." But we must not be too hasty, as is the author, in concluding from this that the bad conduct of the malefactors is a result of their nature much more than of their education. In fact, what does it matter that these unfortunates have had their parents as long as the others, if, as the author shows us elsewhere, their parents present a proportion of madmen, drunkards, epileptics, and unbalanced people far greater than that of the parents of sons who have remained honest? They have not been brought up any better than if they had remained orphans.

It is to be observed, — and this remark also comes from Marro, — that out of seventy-six delinquents whose parents were neither drunkards nor insane nor delinquents themselves, fifty had become orphans at a very early period, — a proportion which is truly enormous. Here we see the premature death of the parents playing the same part as that of the vices of the parents who are alive; and these two causes cannot be equivalent to each other excepting as to the bad education which is a common result of them. Is it not possible, even probable, that the lesser criminality of women is partly to be accounted for by the fact that society has been much more concerned up to this time in founding orphan asylums for girls than for boys, as has been proved by the report of Théophile Roussel (1882) upon these charitable establishments in France?

To return to Gil Maestre, it is quite certain that the future "espadistas" and "minadores," whom he depicts for us in the condition of thieves in the grass, are less guilty than the auxiliaries of crime, dealers in old clothes, or keepers of low lodging houses, receivers of stolen goods and receivers of thieves themselves. Gil Maestre says that he knows of a "casa di dormir" where in one airless room, tapestried with cobwebs, all the guests, — men, women, little boys, and little girls, — sleep pellmell and, on account of the suffocating heat, in a condition of absolute nudity, but, knowing one another only too well, take good care not to go to sleep unless they hold their clothing clutched in their arms for fear of being robbed.

This brief sketch of the criminality peculiar to large centres [1] would be too incomplete were I not to add a word or two as to that crime at once essentially urban and essentially masculine which is called an indecent assault. Overexcited by the very ease with which they can be satisfied, the desires of the feelings acquire among agglomerated populations an acuteness which amounts to a disease. I do not wish to deny the action of physical causes upon the crime in question, because its annual statistical curve rises regularly in summer, but its geographical redivision clearly reveals the dominating action of social causes. In France, for example, upon the charts drawn up by Lacassagne,[2] the criminal infection of which I am speaking is graphically depicted by four blotches, by four radiations of contagion, having as their centres the great cities of Paris, Nantes, Bordeaux, and Marseilles. The central plateau and a few mountains alone emerge entirely above this deluge. Thus we have every reason to believe that the majority of men who are found to be guilty of this crime have been so because they have had the misfortune of being born or of going to live in the midst or in the vicinity of our Babylons, instead of being born or living in Auvergne. But this consideration, as we know, does not place any obstacle in the way of their responsibility; a virtuality which was truly *theirs* was in them; it was realized owing to their sojourn in the cities, but belongs to them none the less because of this.

To sum up, in its external and internal characteristics, in its more numerous and better concealed manifestations, as well as in

[1] The bad name of towns from the criminal point of view dates from far back, and, without going so far back as Sodom and Gomorrah, I notice that when in the twelfth century the Countess Mathilde, who had become old, was wandering about from castle to castle, her chaplain Donizo recommended her, *Perrens* tells us, "to flee the populous towns, where crimes are multiplying with the frauds of the merchants." ("Histoire de Florence.")

[2] "Archives de l'Anthropologie criminelle," No. 5, p. 433.

its more astute and more voluptuous nature; in its more ingenious and less routine methods, just as in the more varied and more exotic social origin of its agents, urban criminality contrasts strongly with rural criminality. One ascends as the other descends. It is well to notice that a contrast of the same nature takes place in the long run, from the point of view of time and not of place, between *primitive* criminality and *advanced* criminality. One can see the advantage of not misunderstanding this fundamental duality, all the more as in certain respects it coincides with that of delictuosity because of opportunity and delictuosity because of habit, which has absorbed and usurped the attention of learned men far too much. As a general thing, delictuosity because of habit, — that which the individual is more prone to implant in himself by the repetition of a first misdeed, — in any country takes on the same forms as a delictuosity due to *custom*. We know that in Italy it consists more than in France in blows and wounds, in "coltellate," an old national custom, and that in France it consists more often than in Italy in indecent assaults, an old Gallic weakness.

But we must apologize for having rather encroached upon the subject matter of the following chapter. It is true that it would have been difficult to talk about the criminal without concerning ourselves to a certain extent with crime.

CHAPTER VI

CRIME

§ 58. PRELIMINARY REMARKS: The biological and sociological interpretation of statistics. Existing statistics; the rudimentary eye.

§§ 59–62. 1. PART PLAYED BY PHYSICAL AND PHYSIOLOGICAL INFLUENCES.

(I) The repetition and even the regular variation of statistical figures imply the non-existence and lack of the exercise of free will. From the social point of view, they show that man living in a society imitates far more than he innovates. (II) The three factors of an offense, according to Ferri. (III) *Physical Influences.* Lacassagne's Criminal Calendar. Criminality and climate. Climate and mortality. Climate and the birth rate, according to statistics. Decreasing importance of the part played by physical influences corresponding to the progress made by a society. Their effect upon industry and art. (IV) *Physiological Influences.* Race and sex.

§§ 63–78. 2. PREPONDERANCE OF SOCIAL CAUSES.

(I) The tendency towards imitation, its force and its forms, its study by means of the phenomenon of crowds. How a suspicion soon becomes a conviction among a crowd. Genesis of popularity and unpopularity. The spirit of sect and the spirit of the group. The group, as well as the family, a primitive social factor; double origin of societies. (II) The laws of imitation. Men imitate one another in proportion as they are in close contact. The superior is imitated by the inferior to a greater extent than the inferior by the superior. Propagation from the higher to the lower in every sort of fact: language, dogma, furniture, ideas, needs. The great fields of imitation; formerly aristocracies, today capitals. Similarity of the former and the latter. (III) Application to criminality. Vices and crimes were formerly propagated from the nobles to the people. Examples: drunkenness, poisoning, murder by command. Deliberations of the Council of Ten. Counterfeit money. Pillage and theft. (IV) At the present time they are propagated from the great cities to the country. Women cut to pieces. The lovers' vitriol. (V) The crime chart of France, drawn up by Joly. Its division by watersheds, fields of criminality; Hérault, Normandy, Eudes Rigaud. (VI) Criminality of great cities. Progress of homicide. Murder because of greed alone. Rape and indecent assaults upon adults and upon children. Abortion and infanticide. Alleged law of inversion between crimes against property and crimes against persons. Both increase in the same proportion in great cities. At the same time civilization improves mankind. How can this be made reconcilable? (VII) By means of another of the laws of imitation: the law of insertion, the alternate passing from fashion to custom, an irregular rhythm. Examples drawn from the history of languages, of religions, of industries. The same law applies to feelings of morality or immorality. (VIII) The meeting of different currents of imitation; their struggle or their concurrence governed by the laws of social logic and expressed by means of statistics. (IX) Application of these ideas first of all to the influence of teaching upon criminality. (X)

In the second place, to the influence exercised by work and industry. (XI) In the third place, to the influence of poverty or wealth. (XII) And fourthly, to the influence of civilization in general. (XIII) Analogies offered by the historical transformation of offenses with that of industries, of languages, of religions, of law, etc. At first *internal* changes in each sort of crime, which has nominally remained the same, general meaning of this transformation. Importance of this consideration in criticising impartially the judges of the past. Irreversibility of the transformation pointed out above. (XIV) In the second place, change in the accusation, crimes which have become torts, and have then been legalized, or vice versa. Comparison with the variation in values. General meaning and irreversibility of these slow revolutions. Garofalo's theory of the "natural offense." (XV) In the third place, changes in criminal procedure. Same order as that of the succession of tools. Irreversible order. (XVI) A summing up of the chapter. Characteristics which differentiate crime from the other social phenomena. Crime and war. Historical passing from the unilateral to the reciprocal.

§ 58. Preliminary remarks. The biological and sociological interpretation of statistics. Existing statistics; the rudimentary eye.

WITHOUT wishing to detract from the worth of those anthropologists who seek to reform the body of the penal law, we should admit, after the foregoing developments, that judicial practice cannot yet be inspired by their efforts, unless it be to draw therefrom, when the most incontestable anomalies presented by them are to be found in the person of an accused, an indication which is more or less unfavorable. The bad and more especially the good information furnished by a mayor is, moreover, not always most worthy of credence. On the other hand, it is to be regretted that the alienists of this school should so seldom be consulted by magistrates and lawyers.[1] The countless observations of insane persons or of moral monstrosities, accumulated by Morel, Tardieu, Maudsley, Legrand du Saulle, etc., have actually achieved positive results, which the numerous measurements of the skulls and bodies of delinquents are still far from having attained.

Thus, in this respect, the positivist school, — for mental pathology, I assume, is a positive thing, at least to the same extent as anthropology, — is already worthy of being given a hearing at the Palais de Justice and the Assize Courts, where ignorance of these matters is so profound. The field of irresponsibility, I repeat, has greatly increased as a result of the work of which I am speaking;

[1] Or, to put it better, it is unfortunate, as a distinguished magistrate, Sarraute, very justly remarked at the last Congress, that magistrates refrained from indulging in criminal anthropology in this sense because the lawyers of the criminal courts are already indulging in it — unwittingly. We therefore join in the wish expressed by this criminologist upon this subject.

and this is precisely the reason why it is important exactly to define its limits for fear of leaving to responsibility no part in the matter. Let us not forget that the born pervert, the "moral madman," is not in the slightest degree an insane person, although the alienists may have furnished us the best information which we possess with regard to him as yet.

Even admitting as certain the anthropological ideas of the new school, it has been possible to observe that they allowed of a sociological interpretation far preferable to the too exclusively biological interpretation which its founders have formulated. In the same way we shall see that, to a lesser degree, it repeats the same mistake in interpreting the statistical statements which are the most serious and perhaps the most lasting foundation of its work. After having, by means of anthropology and mental pathology, sought the typical characteristics of the criminal, it seeks, by means of statistics, to find the natural laws of crime. It accords, as we have said in our statement, a greater part to social causes in the production of crime than in the production of criminal tendencies. In fact, it speaks of the "sociological factors" at the same time as the physical or anthropological factors. Its mistake, in our opinion, is in having placed in the same rank causes so heterogeneous and in having misunderstood the peculiar nature as well as the greater intensity of the first of them. This reproach is not addressed to the socialists of the school, but, among the social causes of crime, the latter refuse to recognize any but economic causes, and their point of view upon this subject is no less imperfect than that of their brother naturalists.

This much having been said, we cannot too highly praise the efforts and the attempts, even though they be sometimes without result, of these distinguished statisticians. Had they done no more than bring to light the regular progress of recidivism in all countries and to bring about the necessary measures to deal with recidivists, they would have a right to our gratitude. Theoretically, they have accomplished more than this. If however they have so far given us nothing more than an outline, if they have not worked for a common object, though they have limited themselves to working out a few isolated problems of social arithmetic, such as the relation of the seasons to the curve of crime, or the relation of the curve of homicides to that of suicides, of the curve of crimes against the person to that of crimes against property, etc.; the relations between certain facts which they have established are valuable acquisitions to science. In this they resemble the psycho-physicians whose contributions to psychology bear upon points which are as yet secondary, but have the advantage of introducing for the first time precision and certainty, "aliquid inconcussum," and are stepping-stones to the future. Only, the psychologist who, upon the limited basis of his own experiments, should hasten to reconstruct at the present time the whole of psychology, would run a very serious risk of being mistaken.

The same thing applies to the criminal statistician who, upon the faith of his figures, which are still so few in number, should wish to recast the criminal law. However, let us be careful, even under these circumstances, not to blame him. When, in the depths of the sea, the first rudimentary eye was long since opened, scarce admitting of a distinction between light and shadow, or the vague contours of an enemy or prey, the animal which allowed itself to be guided by these imperfect indications must often have made very great mistakes and reproached itself for not having continued to grope as its forefathers had been wont to do. None the less was this animal progressing along the fruitful way upon which its very falls were the preliminaries to bounds in advance. Very well, statistics are to some extent a social sense which is awakening; they are to societies what sight is to animals, and, by reason of the conciseness, the rapidity, the increasing number of their tables, of their graphic curves and their colored charts, each day they make this analogy more striking. Is the eye, in fact, anything more than an admirable apparatus for the rapid, instantaneous, and original counting of the optic vibrations which it shows us in the form of ceaseless visual pictures, a sort of atlas which is continually being renewed?

But assuredly statistics are far from having reached the point where they will be capable of realizing such an ideal as this, if they should go so far as ever to realize it. Now when a man, recently operated upon for cataract, begins barely to see, what should he do? Can he depend entirely, for directing his steps, upon the weak information furnished him by his sight? No, he ought merely to use it to assist him, and supplement its imperfection with the assistance of his memory and his reason. Thus it is that criminologists and legislators as well, in the stage in which criminal statistics are to be found today, are under a duty to take these statistics into account, but at the same time combining their statements with the light furnished by history and archaeology, this memoir of the people, and with social science, that rational consciousness which advanced societies end by themselves acquiring. We shall take this point of view.

I. Part Played by Physical and Physiological Influences

§ 59. (I) The repetition and even the regular variation of statistical figures imply the non-existence and lack of the exercise of free will. From the social point of view, they show that man living in a society imitates far more than he innovates.

When statistics first came into operation, the facts primarily revealed by them seemed completely to overthrow accepted ideas. Then great was the surprise at the fact of the establishment of that annual reproduction of figures which were approximately the same with respect to the same offenses.[1] At first this unvarying contingent was looked upon as being irreconcilable with free will, and, as it was customary to base responsibility upon free will, the conclusion was soon arrived at that the criminal is not responsible for the crime committed by him. No doubt in the beginning the invariableness of the part contributed by the criminal, with which we are concerned, was greatly exaggerated; but the variations which were noticed in it later on also showed themselves to be regular, and subject to periods of very high or very low continuance.

Now in what way is the regularity or merely the continuance of these variations here less capable of being opposed to the assumption of individual liberty than is the exactness of these repetitions? Thus, the objection which was made at the outset continues in full force, and only habit has in the end weakened it. As to the replies which have been made to this objection, they can be classified into two parts, the one of a despairing weakness, the other of a despairing obscurity. The most specious of them consists in saying with Quételet, that free decisions, in so far as they are peculiar and accidental, play the part of the disturbances of an astronomic curve and neutralize one another.

This is an illusory explanation. Let us assume an astronomical curve resulting from the combined effects of disturbances exclu-

[1] And with respect to the same voluntary acts of life of whatever kind, marriages, purchases and sales: births and deaths do not occur with any more regularity than do these consequences of the will.

sively. This is indeed our very case, as all crimes, all marriages, and all the purchases carried out in a certain situation during one year are considered as emanating from the independent initiative of individuals. It remains to show in what manner these initiatives can neutralize one another, and how, a deduction having been made for their so-called neutralizations, we arrive at a numerical remainder equal to or in conformity with a certain empirical law of increase or decrease. Now, this absolute or relative uniformity would be incomprehensible if we did not admit that wills, looked upon as independent *in law,* make, so to speak, absolutely no use *in fact* of their independence, and that they constantly correspond to a sum which is equal, or regularly increasing and decreasing, of influences of a social, or vital or physical order, in comparison with which the part which can be attributed to their freedom is a negligible quantity. Thus it is that the ellipse described by the earth around the sun is regular, because its cause, the mutual attraction of these two bodies, is immeasurably greater in energy than the reciprocal attraction of the earth and the other planets, which is the cause of the periodic and complicated disturbances which indent this curve. Certainly if the earth were free to drift in space, or if its motion, although necessary and inevitable, were dependent upon a complication of accidental influences coming from every point in space, it would not describe a path capable of being geometrically formulated. During each moment of time the attraction of the sun upon the earth *is repeated,* equal to itself and similar; or, if you prefer, at each moment of time the undulations of the ether, the hypothetical cause of this attraction according to many physicists, are repeated equally and similarly. That is the true explanation of the regularity presented by the curve of the heavenly bodies.

Why do the measurements of anthropologists bearing upon the height, the weight, the pulsations of the heart and other physiological and anatomical characteristics of a sufficient number of men, provided they belong to the same race, or the same nation consisting of various races, but always in the same proportion, constantly give the same results? For a similar reason. All these men are hereditary copies of one another. Each one of their features is the reproduction of another, by means of procreation. And the constancy of the figures furnished by anthropometrical measurements simply proves that the sum of the repetitions through heredity is far greater than the sum of the variations which are individual and irregular because of an inexplicable innateness. As to the regular variations, which anthropometry would have no difficulty in disclosing, were it to be applied to hybrid races in process of formation or disappearance, their regularity would also demonstrate the preponderating effect exercised by the hereditary propagation of certain organic modifications. If, to assume what is impossible, all these were but original variations in the living being, if each individual were a species apart, though one were to count a thousand, ten thousand, ten million statures or heart pulsations, one would never arrive at figures which would be approximately reproduced when one began to take these same measurements on other subjects. The law of great numbers would serve no purpose, and again, the more the number of observations was increased, far from becoming less, the greater would become the inconsistency of the figures.

Everything I have just said is applicable, "mutatis mutandis," to moral statistics. If, in the determining by each citizen of each one of the acts of his life, marriage for example, the part played by free initiative, released from all physical, vital, or social suggestion, preponderated or were even appreciable, we would not see the number of marriages, in a given locality and during a stated period of time, recurring every year with a striking monotony, or following a progress no less remarkable. But the concurrence of the three sorts of influences pointed out exercises upon the total number of wills an all-powerful effect, because here more marked, there less marked, — as we see the printing of a same negative result in proofs which are either too pale or too dark, but generally resembling one another, — it is only combated to a very small extent by individual spontaneity.

The three sorts of influences are very clearly to be distinguished in the example which has been chosen by reason of the sensitive test of statistics; for it is quite certain that it is an impulse which is physiological, hereditary, and which varies according to age, as well as an impulse which is physical and varies according to the season, which drives men to marriage. But it is also a social impulse, a carrying away by custom or surrounding example. Were it not for this there would be nothing but free unions, and not any official marriages, civil any more than religious. Thus the regularity of the statistics of marriage only proves one thing, which is, that the force of *imitation-custom* is constant in this respect, or else regularly increasing or decreasing because of its coming into contact with *imitation-fashions* whose propagation is favorable or unfavorable to it, and that it is far more intense than the force of individual initiative, independent of tradition or opinion. *The quantative superiority of voluntary energies subjected to Imitation over voluntary energies employed along the lines of Innovation;* here indeed, we have the sum total of what is expressed by the regular figures of social statistics.

It does not follow, it is true, that the part resulting from the innovating activity should be considered as nil. Fortunately this part is very real, and its value is a thousand times greater than its apparent volume. But is there any occasion to credit the human free will with those unfortunate disturbances which true initiative brings into the world? Not the least, although it is permissible, as we have said, perhaps to see in them an indication of elementary liberties which would be carried out underground, a thousand leagues below the luminous surface upon which the psychological life is displayed. Moreover, let someone show me an invention, a discovery, which cannot be resolved into combined copies, into various currents of imitation which have one day met by chance in a well endowed brain; let some one show me an individual originality which is anything other than a peculiar intersection of things commonplace, or pretty nearly so. Thus, the explanation offered by Quételet falls to the ground, and the disturbing element even of statistical curves escapes the partisans of free will. The terror of consciences was thus not without some excuse when, imbued with the old conception of responsibility, they saw an enemy in nascent statistics. But, our conception of responsibility being different, we ourselves have no reason whatever to be afraid. Far from it, the results pointed out by statistics are the most fitting to make us of the opinion that criminals are really responsible for their acts. Responsibility, as we have said, is based upon similarity to others and the persistence of the personal identity.

Now, the peculiar series furnished by statistics show us that the first condition is fulfilled to a very high degree, as they prove the physical, vital, and social resemblance of the individuals who go to make up the same nation or the same class. And they prove that the second condition as well is fulfilled, if at least, after examining the matter, we have occasion to believe that they imply the preponderance of social influences over physiological or physical influences. In fact, the individual only remains identical with himself in being subjected to an influence in so far as he appropriates that influence to himself. Physiologically, organically, he can appropriate to himself a natural influence, such as the sight of prey or the feeling of heat, and act in accordance with his temperament in giving way to it. But psychologically, he can only appropriate to himself motives or moving causes suggested by the psychological surroundings, that is to say the social surroundings, into which he is plunged in his capacity of a *person*, and it is his personal and not his organic identity which is in question here.[1] The malefactor, in submitting to the persuasions of his comrades, acts in conformity with his own character. It is as a social being, not as a living being, that he is responsible. Thus in proportion as he is affected by the suggestions of surrounding society, so does his responsibility increase. We know already that the progress of man in his own personal identification is generally proportional to his progress in social assimilation with others, and conversely, that in becoming gradually dissimilar, he estranges himself.

In fact, the enormous social organism advances assimilating the little individual organisms just as the latter advance assimilating the molecules and forces from without; and it is as a consequence of the former assimilation that individuals are responsible for their acts to one another, just as it is as a consequence of the latter that the molecules of their bodies are bound together among themselves and subject to be eliminated if health should so demand.

Consequently, it is especially important to find out what is the true part played by suggestions of an economic or religious, political or domestic order, of social order in a word, in the production of the offense, and to decide whether the suggestions of a natural order have been subordinated to them or not. This is the question which is being discussed by the naturalists and the socialists of the new school. With the latter I agree in admitting

[1] I insist, and I cannot insist too much, upon pointing out that the identity of the person, upon which I base my theory of guilt, should be understood in the social and not in the vital sense. From a biological point of view, a criminal who has been converted, become an honest man, has remained identical with himself; but from the sociological point of view it is entirely different. The very transformations which madness brings about in the personality are never of such a nature that they can make the individual *organically otherwise* than he was before. But they make him different from the civic, civil, and social point of view. Many of my adversaries, naturalists by profession, have criticised this theory because they have failed to grasp this point.

the superiority of social causes over external causes; but instead of concluding from this, as they do, that society alone is guilty of every crime, I conclude from it that the individual is really and justly punishable.[1]

§ 60. (II) The three factors of an offense, according to Ferri.

As you see, I maintain that, first of all, the division of the causes of an offense into *three factors*, as Ferri has magisterially set forth, is correct. To the same degree as his classification of delinquents into five categories is disputable, is this threefold analysis striking by reason of its correctness and its clearness. With great wisdom he has often drawn from the confusion of figures the action of each cause taken by itself. But he has a marked tendency to exaggerate the importance of natural impulses, and not sufficiently to recognize the fact that, though every force used in our social actions flows from that impulse, at the same time every guiding of this force comes from elsewhere. He has not, as it seems to us, had sufficient regard for the hierarchy of the realities which he distinguishes and which are superimposed upon one another. From this there arise inevitable errors in interpretation. The superior, frequently, while appearing to adapt himself to the inferior, is merely molding the latter to his own ends.

Thus does life sometimes pretend to adapt itself to chemical forces, thus does society sometimes pretend to adapt itself to races and climates. The temperature of each day seems to hold in its dependence the growth of the stock of plants; the hotter it is, the more the plant grows; and the nature of each soil seems to impose upon the growth of the stock of plants special manners of growth and properties. It is none the less true that, under this apparent subjection of the vegetable germ to external exciting

[1] I must point out one thing, once and for all. Imitation in the social life, I mean normal and not sickly imitation, is to a great extent voluntary, even with respect to language and customs, but it is none the less a determining factor. One voluntarily, deliberately sometimes, imitates such and such a person in order better to realize such and such an end, to satisfy such and such a need, an end and a need it is true, copied from others more passively but not unconsciously. If, in our opinion, a person is still responsible for acts committed in imitation of others, although without this example they would certainly not have been committed, it is because the entire person, persisting and original, has participated in this act of imitation. When, on the other hand, in an excited crowd for example, imitation is absolutely unconscious and blind and contrary to the habitual character of the person who is subjected to it, it is a phenomenon of momentary insanity which lessens responsibility or eliminates it.

causes, the naturalist perceives the aptitude of this germ to utilize outside forces, to command them and even ingeniously to derive something from all the obstacles offered by them. In the same way the physical vigor of the workmen of a factory is the first condition of its operation; the better fed they are, and the more vigorous they are the better it operates; and the particular temperament of the workmen of a factory stamps the progress of that factory with a special character.

The railway service is not carried out in Spain and Italy in the same manner as it is in France; in France itself the Southern Railway Company is clearly to be distinguished from the Northern Railway Company. But, in the last analysis, this means that the invention of railways employs the various degrees of force of the agents which it brings into play and causes these peculiarities to work for its own profit. No doubt it is correct to say that the ripening of a bunch of grapes is caused by the concurrence of two factors, the temperature and the soil on the one hand, and the direction given by the germ on the other. No doubt it is correct to say, also, that a manufactured product results from three factors acting together: 1st. climate and the season; 2d. race and health; 3d. supervision of the employer (a momentary incarnation of the invention which he is developing). But one can equally well say that this page which I am writing results from three conditions: 1st. the existence of paper, ink, and pens; 2d. the good condition of my hand, it is not paralyzed, not impeded; 3d. my knowledge of the art of writing and my wish to write. Let us not confuse *cause* with *reason;* upon this point it is well to read Cournot again. The true and only reason for the bunch of grapes is the seed; the true and only reason for the manufactured product is the employer; the true and only reason for this page is the education which I have received and the contagion of manifold examples which have made me decide to want to write this.

§ 61. (III) Physical influences. Lacassagne's Criminal Calendar. Criminality and climate. Climate and mortality. Climate and the birth rate, according to statistics. Decreasing importance of the part played by physical influences corresponding to the progress made by a society. Their effect upon industry and art.

These preliminaries are long, but they have seemed indispensable to me. By means of the light shed by them, we shall from now on be able to appreciate the ingenious "Criminal Calendar" drawn up by Lacassagne.[1] This author has shown that the enumeration, month by month, of crimes against property, and that of crimes against persons, is expressed by means of two annual curves which are almost the opposite of each other. The greatest number of "person-crimes" are to be found in June,[2] the smallest number of "property-crimes" in June and July. Let us deal with the former.

Must we see in the rising of the temperature the only explanation of the recrudescence in summer? Ferri answers "yes." The proof of this is that, not only the hottest months of the year as among the other months, but again the most exceptionally hot years as among the other years,[3] and the hottest provinces, that is to say the southern ones, as among the other provinces, are distinguished by their relative fertility in murders, assassinations, blows, and woundings. Does not the coincidence of these three sorts of facts force this conviction upon us? It is quite certain that it proves that heat accounts to a certain extent for one *part* of the excess of crimes or offenses of violence shown us in months, years, and provinces having a high temperature. But only a part, and perhaps a small part. Would statisticians have established this coincidence which we at the present time establish, a few hundred or a few thousand years ago? I doubt it very much, if history does not lie. Let us bear in mind that the relative mildness of customs among northern nations is of rather recent date; that it is due to the modern movement of civilization towards the higher latitudes, there is no historical phenomenon better proved; and that, if we go back to the time of the indolent Roman civilization threatened on the North by bloodthirsty hordes, or even only as far back as the time of the crusade against the Albigenses, we shall everywhere find the colder climates relatively more fertile in bloodthirsty crimes. Violent criminality depends so little upon climate, and even upon race, that the same country, without any change taking place in its climate or the race of its

[1] "Revue scientifique" of May 28, 1888, article entitled, "La criminalité en France." In this are given two large plates and a well developed table.

[2] The enumeration of crimes committed in prison ("Criminalità carceraria") has given rise to a calendar approximately similar to this. There are, however, some differences: the greatest number of crimes against persons there occurs in *August*, and not in June. See the work of *Marro*, "I caratteri." Table on page 363.

[3] On this point *Colajanni* has raised apparently very strong objections in the "Archives de l'Anthropologie criminelle," November 15, 1886. But in the following number, Ferri has partly regained his position.

inhabitants, becomes milder, becomes enervated even in becoming civilized, or becomes bloodthirsty again upon returning to barbarism. When Greek civilization flourished in the south of Italy, in Greater Greece, when the Arab civilization was captivating the south of Spain or the Roman civilization the south of France, it was the north of Italy, the north of Spain and the north of France which was the special field of homicide.[1]

As to the movement of civilization towards the north, is it at least to be accounted for physically? Not any more than the other. The causes of it are historical and perhaps accidental; that they are social is quite certain. They are, before everything, that good fortune of scientific discoveries, of industrial, military, and political inventions, which we have been developing for three centuries in Europe, and which, by means of a thorough utilization of natural resources, which have been subdued and domesticated, have allowed regions which were previously unproductive to carry out successfully the acclimation of civilizing ideas, when the latter were withering in their cradle.

Furthermore, it is quite possible that so many inventions coming one after another to be put to account at one time, necessarily require an expenditure of bodily force which the inhabitants of the towns situated too much to the south could not supply. And this will no doubt be the case so long as the development of these novelties, as always happens in the beginning, shall continue to be rugged and difficult. The feverish agitation, the deafening racket, which appear to be an essential part of modern capital cities, lead one to suppose so. We cannot believe that Memphis or Babylon were ever habitually tuned up to this pitch. But it is permissible to believe that this is a passing crisis, and that once it has been facilitated by our actual efforts, the use of the new implements of civilization will extend even to the tropical zone. The reflourishing of civilization in the valley of the Nile and the splendid progress made in Australia justify this hope. Civilization has passed from the fine tropical regions to the temperate or cool zones for the same reason, at bottom, as wealth passes from the leisure and privileged classes to the industrious classes, a phenomenon in which no physical cause intervenes.

It therefore seems exceedingly probable to me that the action of heat plays but a small part in the predominance in the south of

[1] See the development of this idea in our "Criminalité comparée," p. 152 *et verso.*

coarse and violent crimes. I may add, in their summer predominance. In summer people live more in the open air, they travel, they come in contact with one another more; from this there arise more numerous encounters, passions more greatly excited, and more frequent opportunities for murder. This indeed is to so great an extent the principal explanation of these phenomena that it alone can account for the exceptions to the pretended rule of the influence of climate. And these exceptions are numerous. This so-called law does not apply in France,[1] as can be seen from the fine official charts of Yvernès relative to the division of bloodthirsty crimes among our Departments, excepting in Corsica and along the Mediterranean shore. Furthermore, the thing which strikes us is merely the darkness of the patches in the neighborhood of large cities, in the Departments of the Seine, Bouches-du-Rhône, Gironde, Loire-Inférieure, Nord, Seine-Inférieure, and Rhône. The more populous a town is, even though situated in the north, the more numerous are the meetings between human beings, and the more does the proportion of murders, among a given number of inhabitants, increase.

Of all the crimes against the person, the one which is manifestly the most influenced by temperature is rape or indecent assault. Among primitive peoples, there are periods of breeding-time rather clearly marked; the "Annamite breeding-time," according to Lorion, takes place in April and September. As a people become civilized, this influence disappears; at the same time the annual curve of the crime we are here dealing with is very regular. It shows an irregularity which Lacassagne says cannot be accounted for, but which seems to me to confirm the physical action revealed by itself. Stationary in February, this crime increases in March and decreases in April. It is noticeable that the annual curve of temperature generally shows a similar irregularity. Very well, the action of this external cause may be more apparent and more marked here than elsewhere. It is none the less true that it is hardly permissible to take this fact into account at all in the true explanation of this offense, so greatly

[1] I say in continental France. In colonial France this law does not apply. This is also the opinion of *Corre*. "It cannot be denied," says he, "and we will furnish the proofs in another work, that criminality against persons is slight, both as to the number of crimes and as to the nature of the assault (if we may be allowed to express the gravity of crimes by the word 'quality') among the native population of our intertropical colonies." ("Les criminels," 1889.) He has furnished this proof in his very interesting monograph on "Crime en pays créoles," (Lyons, Storck).

does it depend even more keenly upon the density of population, the intensity of urban life, and the progress of civilization. It is in the large cities, such as Lyons, or in their immediate vicinity, in the north or in the south it matters not, that it attains its greatest frequency. In the most southern regions, but regions which are sparsely populated, agricultural and firm in religious belief, it is lowered to its minimum. Besides, it has been observed [1] that it increases in proportion to the length of the days, rather than in proportion to the rise in temperature: "for it is lowered in July and August, with the diminishing of the daylight, in spite of the temperature, sometimes [and more often than not] greater than that in the month of June." But how could the lengthening of the days have any influence over this crime, if not because of the similar prolongation of social activity and the increase in the number of meetings due to its exercise?

The same considerations apply to crimes against property. What does their attaining their maximum in winter prove? That cold makes one a thief? Nothing of this kind, be it understood, has been said. It proves that want of the means of sustenance is felt especially during this season.[2] But for what reason? Because our chief nourishment consists in cereals, and because, since our passing from the pastoral to the agricultural phase of our civilization, by reason of many and accumulated inventions, we provision ourselves for winter during the summer. But, in the case of pastoral peoples, does this apply? In the case of peoples who live by hunting, the opposite is what takes place, the winter being the best season for game; it is during the winter so to speak that they gather in the harvest, and it may be assumed that among them it is preferable to steal during the summer. In their case too the best years of "harvest" are perhaps those in which famine has raged among us.

One could just as well draw up an industrial calendar as a criminal calendar, for there is no industry which does not have its busy season and its dead season; a nuptial calendar, a calendar of mortality, etc. Does it not seem that, as far as mortality is concerned at least, the action of climate, season, and race alone makes itself felt? It would be a mistake to think this, and this

[1] "Etude médico-légale sur la statistique criminelle en France," by *Chaussinand* (1881). See also "Archives," No. 5, article by *Garraud and Bernard* on "Viols et attentats à la pudeur."

[2] In the second place, the nights are then longer and the darkness is favorable to theft.

example furnishes us with an "a fortiori" argument which is worth something. No doubt, with respect to the age of from one to five years, the great infant mortality of the coast Departments of the Mediterranean — it is three times greater than that of certain other Departments — is due especially to the tropical heat of the summers in this zone, and statistics have revealed to us this very important fact, never suspected before the existence of statistics, that the highest mortality among children, as a general thing, is during August and September, the lowest in May and November. But why are fourteen Departments around Paris sadly privileged in this respect? Why are countries where industry is carried on on a large scale to be distinguished in this same way? Upon what are certain strange things dependent, the following, for example, that in certain of the Departments, for all ages the mortality among women is greater than that among men, whereas in others the converse has been shown to be the case?

The different conditions of social life can alone account for these facts. If the group of Flemish provinces in Belgium, as has been proved by Bertillon, numbers, for an equal amount of population, more dead than the group of Walloon (French speaking) provinces the cause cannot but be social also, for "these poor Flemish" have among them at the same time more insane persons, more paupers, and more illiterates. So strongly does Bertillon believe in the preponderance of social causes, even in so far as mortality is concerned, that according to him society could and ought to take some action with a view to diminishing the annual tribute paid to death by certain regions of our territory.

Still more instructive would be a comparison of the criminal calendar with the calendar of the birth rate. If you read in a statistical table that the greatest number of legitimate births takes place in February and March, and the smallest number in June, July, and December, do not be in too great haste to account for these differences by means of the aphrodisiacal action of the spring (children born in February were conceived in May) or by the refrigerating action of the autumn (children born in June and July were conceived in September and October). First of all, this explanation does not account for the lowest number corresponding to the month of December, which as far as date of conception is concerned, brings us to March, that is to say during Lent. Here the influence of habits of religion makes itself felt;

in Catholic countries people are not married during this time of the year. And de Foville [1] will tell you that in the Scandinavian countries, the maximum and the minimum are no longer the same; and this is so, he says, because in these countries "the most laborious periods, in the case of rural populations, correspond to other seasons in France." The cause of these differences is thus far more an economic than a physical one.[2]

Between the birth rate and climate one might establish a fairly constant relation, as well as between criminality and climate, and even a similar relation, the fruitfulness of marriages, just as the frequency of bloodthirsty crimes, being found to coincide in our day, because of a sort of natural compensation, with residence in hot climates. It is nevertheless recognized as being certain among the majority of the economists, from Malthus to Tallqvist,[3] that in the last analysis the social causes alone give the key to the phenomenon of population.

But how then, one will say, are we to account for the variations in the number of births corresponding to certain physical causes, and how account for the difference in the rate of progress shown by the different races? Upon this last point, let us limit ourselves to doing away with a confused state of affairs. It is not the Anglo-Saxon race which is responsible for the prolificness of England, nor the Celtic race which is responsible for the absence of prolificness of France. In Ireland the Celts are very prolific, just as the French are in Canada.[4] Every race in passing through the various phases of its civilization goes through several succes-

[1] "La France économique," 1887.

[2] This cause is, however, partly physical, and this is proved by the fact that the "maxima" and the "minima" of natural births almost corresponds to those of legitimate births.

[3] "Recherches statistiques sur la tendance à la moindre fécondité des mariages" (Helsingfors, 1886); a pamphlet filled with information of the very greatest interest and as remarkable for the firm basis of its criticism as for the extent of its researches.

[4] "Among our highly civilized populations," says *Lagneau* ("Dictionnaire encyclopédique des sciences médicales"), "race has absolutely no influence on the birth rate." The latter "depends almost entirely upon social conditions." Can we not say as much with regard to criminality? — Will anyone pretend that if the number of illegitimate children increases in France, while the lawful birth rate decreases, this is due to physical or physiological causes? It is to be noticed that the region in which the proportion of illegitimate children is the greatest, twelve out of every one hundred births (even nineteen in the Department of the Seine), is the northern region, which, as we know, is the richest and most highly civilized. And this is all the more unfortunate as this is the model region, the focal point of every spread of imitation.

sive periods of prolificness and unprolificness. It suffices if there is a conquest, a discovery of new territory, or a new article of food,[1] to awaken from its lethargy the most sterile nation and even to make its old people become prolific. If there is one influence which seems to be exclusively physiological, it is the one which is shown by statistics, either in so far as births and marriages are concerned, or in so far as crimes are concerned, with relation to the average age of married persons, of parents, and of criminals.

However, in the case of births and marriages, we know, beyond a doubt, that the degree of civilization plays a preponderating part among the determining causes of the average age[2] at which persons marry or have the greatest number of children. Reasons of an economic nature, customs, ideas, artificial needs, prevail in this respect over natural impulses. In a country such as China, where people are astonished if a man of twenty is not married and where they are in the habit of saying that a man without children is "like an apple tree without apples," the population must inevitably increase more rapidly than in France, where it is only considered proper to marry after the age of thirty at the youngest, and where those who have more than three or four children are ridiculed, unless they are pitied.

If the age of the highest number of marriages and cases of paternity is thus determined by means of sociological causes, why should not the age of the highest number of crimes also be determined in this same manner? The increasing precocity of our young assassins is a very fitting thing to confirm this opinion, which is furthermore shown by statistics, chiefly international statistics. The age of the greatest delictuosity, averaging twenty-five years, varies greatly from one country to another and from

[1] The Spanish, English, Portuguese, Italian, and German races have owed to the discovery of America or of various islands in the ocean and to the conquest of certain American or insular territory the tenfold increase of their population over-seas, and the discovery of the potato caused a rapid increase in the population of Ireland.

[2] As a general thing, the progress of civilization delays the age at which the matrimonial crisis of life takes place, but only up to a certain point. Since 1840 in England marriages have gradually become more precocious; in Sweden and Norway since 1861–1865; in France since 1850. But when civilization thus takes it upon itself to advance the age of unions, it does not for this reason cease to cause a decrease in their prolificness. This accounts for that apparent paradox in this new phase. "The decrease of prolificness keeps abreast of the precocity of marriages" (Tallqvist). This means that if ease, as the author cited points out, causes people to marry sooner, foresight on the other hand causes them to have fewer children, and *the former ordinarily accompanies the latter.*

one period to another. Civilization has a tendency to advance this age, and race seems here not to play at all an important part. The proportion of persons imprisoned who are minors, out of one hundred of all ages, is two in Prussia, ten in France, eight in Italy, twenty in Belgium, and twenty-seven in England. These last two numbers, as compared with the others, absolutely contradict, let us observe in passing, the current prejudice as to the reputed retarding temperament of northern peoples. But let us add that the proportion of offenses committed by minors is decreasing, under the influence of education, in England, whereas, in France, it continues to increase; and this is all the more unfortunate for us, because the proportional number of minors, in view of the decrease in the prolificness of marriages in France, is becoming smaller in our country.

Now, when we see a natural influence as strong as that of age itself masked and often altered by causes of a social nature, how can we doubt but that far lesser influences, for example that of the seasons or of the time of day, are themselves also recast and completely changed by surrounding society? I might seek for the proof in the fact, which has been partially established, that, in passing from surroundings which are less densely populated and less civilized to surroundings which are more densely populated and more civilized, from the country to a town, from the past to the present, the curve of suicides, births, marriages, crimes, etc., is found to be less and less sensitive to physical influences of this order, and under this head shows less strongly marked variations. The curve of travel, for example, the difference between the number of journeys by day and by night, between the number of journeys in winter and in summer, has become less since the substitution of locomotives and steamboats for stage coaches and sailing vessels.

But this is only partially true. In certain respects, the contrary might be upheld. There comes a time when a civilization having reached its zenith finds an advantage in not doing violence to the nature of things, although this might be quite possible, and in conforming to indications shown by climates, seasons, and the time of day, instead of not taking them into account at all. Although industry taken as a whole is less dependent upon rain and fine weather, and upon geographical and geological peculiarities, than agriculture, it is none the less true that neither industry nor agriculture, in becoming perfected, have a tendency each day to free themselves more and more from these external conditions.

Far from it; the more agriculture progresses, the more does it make its processes, what it creates, and its operations subordinate to the weather and the nature of the soil; the more the art of war progresses, the better does it adapt itself to accidents of soil and to meteorological and other circumstances; the more the building industry develops, the more does it take into account climate, northern or southern exposure, etc. Only, to conform in this manner to nature is to adapt nature to one's ends and to oneself, and it does not by any means follow that nature plays any part in industrial works.

In the same way, the more marriage and paternity become artificial and become clothed with the social livery, the more, beyond a certain point at least, are the natural conditions of a happy union and of an advantageous heredity taken seriously into consideration. From the middle of the present century, for example, almost everywhere in France the benefit of getting married a little earlier in life has been appreciated, and statistics show this salutary change.

Is this not the same, perhaps, in the matter of crimes? The more the offense becomes an industry, and a clever industry, the more do the clever thieves, and the fierce murderers themselves, know how to await the hour, the place, and the season which are most favorable to their plans. From this fact there arises a more frequent repetition of certain offenses in certain seasons and at certain times of the day. But this does not in the least prove that the season and time have been accomplices or fellow-perpetrators of these crimes. Furthermore, what I am now saying will be all the more true as the proportion of professional or habitual crime shall increase and that of accidental crime shall decrease. But the movement in this direction is, unfortunately, attested by the statistics of the number of recidivists, *whose regular and universal increase* is one of the most serious facts of our present times. Where is the professional vagabond who does not so arrange as to rove about, beg and steal during the season of fine weather, and to have himself arrested in autumn or in the winter?

Wars take place in the springtime with far more regularity than do murders in summer. Is this as much as to say that the influences of temperature and vegetation have decided that there shall be a fight? Paper mills are situated on the banks of streams, iron works in the vicinity of veins of iron and coal, with far more regularity than knife blows are localized in southern Italy or Spain; is it any the less true that industry is a thing essentially social and not physical in so far as its causes are concerned?

If we may be permitted to do so, we will again for a moment compare the birth rate and criminality. Neither does a family have, on the average, all the children it might have, nor does a man, even the worst recidivist, commit all the offenses he could commit. Thus the number of the children of a nation, and the number of the crimes and offenses of a nation as well, are an expression of the action of a cause or several causes of a restrictive nature. Thus the criminologists misstate their problem. The question is not to discover why such and such a nation shows such and such a number of offenses at such a date, but why it shows only this number of offenses. Perhaps the analogy which I have established will be rejected, under the pretext that there is a natural force which drives us directly to paternity, whereas there is no such force which drives us directly to crime. But this distinction is fallacious. Not one natural impulse suggests to us the desire of becoming a father; if sexual inclination results in the procreation of children, it is not this object which it has primarily in view. Similarly we have an innate desire for well being which, also indirectly, may lead us into theft, swindling, and abuse of confidence, and an innate feeling of pride which, in certain cases, may lead us to commit murder for the sake of revenge. It is quite certain that sexual inclination does not, taken by itself, impel us any less to adultery than it does to paternity; and it is even noticeable that, impelling us less and less towards paternity, it draws us more and more towards adultery. A strange sight, let me parenthetically remark, is that of a wealthy, active, enlightened, and prosperous society, which is always more sterile in children and more prolific in offenses; of a society which has not all the children, but all the artificial needs which it can support, and which buys itself every luxury, except that of a large family!

If, however, the individual listened only to himself, and only obeyed the dearest wish of his being, the desire to perpetuate himself, logic ought to advise him to follow a different line of conduct; and in proportion as incredulity wins him over, as the dream of posthumous immortality haunts him less, he ought the more greedily to seek to live again in his sons because he is no longer given any other means of surviving himself. But the contagion exercised by surrounding examples, by artificial pleasures, is so strong that it makes him forget even this fundamental wish; his foresight enlarges without ceasing, but it never ceases to become shorter; it extends to all the many caprices which he has to satisfy, but is limited by the horizon of his short life; and one might say *that a modern society has all the children which it can support, once it has supported all its artificial needs.* It is not so easy to formulate the law of criminality; but it does seem that the increase of artificial needs suggested, and the increasing concern of satisfying them, ought to be reckoned among the principal causes of both of these phenomena. The French Departments as compared with one another, and the provinces of Europe as well, as compared with one another, have revealed to Tallqvist a continuous and complete correspondence between the relative prolificness of marriages and the relative number of savings bank pass books and fire insurance policies. A similar cause, the progress of foresight — as I have defined it — seems to him, with reason, to account for these various similar effects.[1] Now countries having a low birth rate seem to be distinguished by more crimes against property and fewer crimes against persons;[2] countries having a high birth rate show the reverse. The same thing accounts for this; greed, the expression of foresight directed towards the pursuit of well being, must, as it increased, have increased the number of thefts and decreased the numbers of the population.

The question of the "physical factors" of an offense, if it be examined thoroughly, raises the general question as to what part is played by these agents within the entire compass of social science. This is a many-sided problem which is reproduced with variations in law, in philology, etc. However, we can say that the discussion has revealed the pre-eminence of the "social fac-

[1] The increasing sterility of marriages also accompanies the progress of learning. Let us add that since 1872 even the number of marriages has regularly decreased in France from 8.8 for every one thousand inhabitants to 7.4 ("Revue scientifique," March 8, 1890).

[2] In *Guerry's* large atlas (Moral Statistics) we notice especially that the English provinces with a low birth rate show a pronounced increase in the number of offenses committed upon property. In France this increase is expressed by means of the following figures. In the eighteen Departments in which the birth rate is highest, for over one hundred crimes against persons, we have 135 crimes against property; in fifty other Departments where it is less, the proportion of crimes against property becomes 175; in eighteen Departments where the birth rate is still lower the proportion is 202; and in the Department of the Seine, where the birth rate is the lowest, the proportion is 445. This is very significant.

tors." On this point Montesquieu has once and for all been overthrown. If there is any one branch of human activity which is favorable to the development of his point of view, it is assuredly not the Law, as he has attempted to show, but Language,[1] as this complex system of articulations and sounds is the most unconscious of the modes of action by means of which our energy is expended.

Again, there have been frequent attempts to explain by means of thermic, hygrometric, and climatric differences, the phonetic changes, and those laws of phonetics which are so precise, those of Grimm for example, that by reason of their very strictness they recall the laws with which the physicist is concerned. On this subject, an Italian philologist, Ascoli — for Italy seems to have a marked predilection for this sort of explanation — speaks of "philological isothermal lines."[2] But nothing could be more vague and insufficient than this appeal here made to the exact sciences. There is a tendency to overthrow even the pretension to account for the majority of the phenomena in question by means of ethnological influences, by certain conformations of the throat and the mouth which are peculiar to certain races. In any event the delusion of characterizing each human race by means of a language or a family of languages which is peculiar to this race has been completely dissipated. When the principle of imitation shall have been applied to languages, to its fullest extent and to its greatest depth, which has not yet been done, it will be seen that the laws of details laid down by philologists, phonetic laws, laws of habit and of analogy, and the many others, are to be accounted for by means of this general tendency, which is eminently social, either to imitate others, whether relatives or

[1] While on the subject I will say with regard to this that I do not know why the bad habit has been formed of construing philology as being foreign to sociology. If, expressly and consciously, philology had been made a part of sociology, it being in our opinion the foundation of the former, the danger of treating social science from a naturalistic point of view would have been avoided as well as that of confusing things which are social with things which are vital. It would clearly have been seen that the moment when a man *speaks* is that in which he *associates himself*, and thus this would have led to a recognition of the fact that the elemental and essential factor is imitation, which plays so vital a part in the formation of the life of languages first and then of religions.

[2] See an interesting work by *Bourdon*, entitled, "L'Evolution phonétique du langage," in the "Revue philosophique" of October, 1888. The author, like many philologists of that time, finds himself compelled greatly to extend, but still not sufficiently to my way of thinking, the principle of imitation as the key to the interpretation of philological phenomena.

strangers, whether consciously or unconsciously, or on the other hand, and once the impulse has been given, to imitate oneself, a thing which leads to mechanical habits of speech and to the analogous simplifications which result therefrom.

As to the causes of each phonetic or grammatical variation which takes place consciously or unconsciously, and which day by day is circulated among the entire nation when imitation deigns to take it up, are we to believe that they are chiefly physical and vital? No, if we stop to realize that, on the one hand, this incessant production of little philological inventions is due to accident and to the intensity of social life, and, on the other hand, that they have no chance of being reproduced and propagated unless the upper classes and the great cities adopt them. In passing from the south to the north or the north to the south, from a Latin mouth to a Celtic mouth, or from a Celtic mouth to a German mouth, a language becomes refracted by the regular transmutation of such and such consonants into such and such other consonants, almost like a ray of light is refracted in accordance with such and such an angle by passing through such and such a lens. But the laws of this philological refraction, however exact they may be, no more give the key to the formation of languages in its essentials than do the laws of optic refraction the formula of the formation of light. Light is due first of all to the combustion which takes place at the point of the ray's departure, at its focus, and then to the vibratory elasticity of the ethereal medium which produces its expansion into rays. This combustion is to this elasticity what inventive force in our societies, studied under no matter what aspect, is to imitative passiveness.

If such has been or ought to be the fate of the principal physiological and biological explanations even in the matter of language, all the more should we set them to one side in matters of religion, of law, of industry and art, and of crimes as well. The first mythologists — just as the first philologists and criminologists — did not fail to connect the diversity of gods, of myths, and of rites with that of climates and races, as being cause and effect. The religious man, according to this hypothesis, would only have known how to deify the familiar or peculiar atmospheric phenomena, at the most the flora and fauna of his habitat, according to the mode of deification invariably suggested by the peculiarities of his hereditary and specific instincts. This naturalistic point of view is discredited; it has been found inadequate to account for anything more than the varying accessories of a given theme, which has remained ever the same throughout its passage from race to race, from climate to climate, and has been due to social causes entirely.

It has thus, little by little, given way to theories which have continued to be sociological, either to that theory which makes of the mythologies a morbid excrescence of languages, or to that of the generalized euhemerism of Spencer, which has this much about it which cannot be denied, that every striking, rising, eruptive personage, every teacher, every inventor brought to light is glorified, and that every glorification pushed to extreme is an apotheosis.

Or again, to systems which perceive in the human god the incarnation, if not of an inventor, at least of an invention, for example of that great and fruitful primitive invention the domestication of animals, symbolized in the worship of the cow. Or else, finally and as a general thing, to an entirely historical explanation of the succession and the transformation of religions owing to accidents which have taken place in the past, such as defeats or conquests, or the struggle between or mingling of different civilizations. It might also have been noticed that the constant, universal passing from religions of castes to religions of proselytizing, or rather in each one of them, from the closed phase to the open phase, is, in the last analysis, no more than one of the forms assumed by that great social fact, which we shall deal with later on, of *imitation-custom*, of imitation still servilely attached to physiological heredity, giving way to *imitation-fashion*, to imitation free and triumphant.

Why has not Taine's theory as to the combined action of climate, race, and time, a theory of which Ferri's law of three factors is, after all, no more than an application to criminality, been able to satisfy the requirements of historians? Because the originator of this law — who, moreover, in his latest historical works, which are perhaps his masterpieces, has been careful not to make any use of it — has not reserved a sufficient part for individual and accidental genius, and especially for the social conditions under which it appears, is developed and becomes prolific. He has shown a talent worthy of admiration in his philosophy of Art, a talent sufficient to bring to light the physical influences which affect the evolution of sculpture and painting, and, assuredly, his theory might have seemed to have free play within this domain. At the same time, does what he tells us about the characteristics of the Dutch school of painting in its palmy days, tell us the reason why, the climate of Holland having remained the same, its art only flourished during the period of its political and commercial greatness? The prosperity of printing in Holland in the seventeenth century must also have some apparent physical explanation to account for it; but is not its true cause the freedom of thought of which this nation enjoyed the monopoly at this time, and which caused so many eminent minds to flock to it? [1]

Artistic expansion, in every civilization, becomes ripe, at the time when, a society having just completed its vintage of discoveries and inventions brought in from all sides, the fermentation of these civilizing elements, in order that they may agree, begins. It is the ebullition which reveals and is an auxiliary of this work within. So long as this phase of the autonomous development of societies, in no matter what latitude, lasts, the inspiration to be derived from the surrounding fauna and flora are, like all the others, — far less, assuredly, than those derived from religion, — utilized by the artist; but the source of art does not lie in this. Criminality, in its intermittent outbreaks, — without making mention of its habitual course, — also has its special time. It also breaks out in times of crises, when the civilizing elements are not in accord. Only, instead of working towards the harmonizing of these elements, it impedes it; for their fermentation it endeavors to substitute that of disturbing elements.

[1] One word more, to go back to the theory of Montesquieu, which has again been taken up during the last few years in so talented a manner by Mougeolle. If the geographical circumstances had in history the hereditary importance over the development of peoples which historians attribute to them as a general thing, the ancient Mexicans and the ancient Peruvians being inhabitants of the sea coast and possessing a great expanse of sea coast must have been essentially a maritime people as the Carthaginians, the Venetians, and the inhabitants of London were. However, they knew nothing of navigation. Note that the Mexicans should have explored in the interests of commerce (and they were traders at heart) that "American Mediterranean," as the sea of the Antilles is called. They should have taken possession of that sea. They should have done this, all the more because, having absolutely no beasts of burden, navigation seemed necessarily to offer to them the only means of transportation. Well, in spite of all this they did not navigate. Why? The answer is simple. Because they did not have the *good fortune* to think of a few of the inventions necessary for navigation.

§ 62. (IV) Physiological influences. Race and sex.

What has just been said with regard to physical influences in general makes it permissible for me to say but a few words about physiological influences in particular. Incitement to crime, whether of social or other origin, is only felt by individuals who are more or less organically predisposed to feel it; and the regularity of the figures of statistics show us that, among a given race, these predispositions from birth break out according to a numerical proportion which remains practically constant, in spite of the unceasing renewal of the population. Classified from the point of view of greater or lesser stature, the various categories which make up a population, as has been shown by Quételet, are divided into proportions symmetrically arranged about the average height and almost invariably reproduced. Classified from no matter what other point of view, they form a hierarchy which is no less invariable. *It is therefore necessary*, it would seem, that there should be, during each moment of time, a determined number of giants and a determined number of dwarfs; and also, *it is necessary* that at each moment of time there should be a certain number of generous natures and a certain number of perverse natures. These are natural compensations.

At the same time, when we look into the matter more closely, we perceive slow movements under this apparent immobility; the proportion of persons of small stature, for example, is not the same at various periods of time, as has been proved by the measurement of conscripts. Furthermore, just as a better military organization has allowed of the employment of conscripts of a stature formerly judged to be too small, it may well happen that a more perfect social organization should one day come to turn to account certain native perverse tendencies. Finally, if we go back to causes, we shall find that the proportion of dangerous natures is the effect of historical antecedents. The proportion of homicidal natures is larger in Corsica and Sicily than it is in Milan and Bordeaux, but this difference is not dependent upon race; the Corsican race, the Sicilian race (a very complex metal moreover, result of many fusions, just as Corinthian brass) would actually furnish a quite different contingent if the *clan spirit* and the *maffia* had not for a long time past fashioned these races after its own image, or if the ideas prevalent on the Continent which are hostile to this spirit had for several centuries past, and not but yesterday, penetrated to these islands.

This consideration greatly weakens the bearing of an objection formulated by Ferri against Colajanni. "It is evident," he tells us,[1] "that as between the northern provinces and those of the south, of Italy, for example, the difference in social surroundings is not so enormous as is the difference between the frequency of the most serious crimes against the person. From this it follows that the great difference between these provinces with regard to bloodthirsty crimes cannot be due to anything, for the most part, excepting climate and race." That which Ferri here calls the race, just as so many other writers do, is nothing but the result of history, the accumulated legacy of social habits which have passed into the blood. It is certain that there is no more powerful physiological influence upon criminality than that of sex. Criminality among women is actually, and not merely apparently, very much less than it is among men. Taking an equal number of their respective population, according to the official report of 1880, the men number annually five times as many accused as the women, and six times as many apprehended.

It is instructive to compare with this result that furnished by Marro, according to Théophile Roussel, upon the comparison of punishments incurred by boys and girls in their respective schools. Out of a hundred boys, nine or ten are punished for larceny; out of a hundred girls, *not one.* Out of a hundred boys, fifty-four are punished for quarrels accompanied by acts of violence; out of a hundred girls, seventeen. The thing which effectively shows us the innate moral superiority of woman is that this endowment is manifested chiefly during her minority and in rural surroundings, that is to say, before she comes in contact with the masculine contagion which perverts her during the course of her life, and especially of an urban life. In fact the result of English statistics as to the number of minors and adults of both sexes, sentenced from 1861 to 1881, is that, among minors, the criminality of the girls was about one sixth that of the boys, and that, among adults, that of the women was a half or a third that of the men. According to Mayr, the statistics of Bavaria show that the participation of women in offenses is larger among urban and more dense populations. But at the same time, do not the figures prove that the physiological influence which we are dealing with, in spite of its singular and undeniable

[1] "Archives de l'Anthropologie criminelle," January, 1887.

power, has a tendency to be itself masked and neutralized by social influences? [1]

Let us observe, with regard to this, one of the peculiarities of statistics. Computed to cover a period of ten years, the number of women killed by lightning is found to be approximately one half that of men killed in the same manner. Is this due to the more sedentary, more domesticated life led by women? In any event, this cannot be dependent upon anything other than the peculiarities of their social life, and cannot be dependent at all, I assume, on their physical life.

To sum up, the fact revealed by statistics that certain seasons or certain climates coincide with a certain recrudescence or a certain decrease of certain crimes no more proves the reality of the *physical causes* of crime than does the fact revealed by anthropology of a greater recurrence of ambidextrous, left-handed, or prognathous persons among malefactors prove the existence of a *criminal type* in the biological acceptation of that word. But this negative conclusion cannot satisfy us; [2] and the physical or physiological explanation of crime having been set aside, we have now to show along what lines the laws of crime are to be sought. We shall find them in a special application of the general laws which appear to us to govern social science.

[1] Between the criminality of men and that of women the distance is greater in Italy and less in England, greater in the country and less in cities. Messedaglia accounts for the first result by means of the more active participation of the English woman in public life. Colajanni is of the opinion that economical conditions, here as everywhere, play a predominating part. In this he might very well be mistaken. Truly from this point of view the fate of woman is not worse in Great Britain than in Italy, nor in cities than it is in the country, where the housewife has to undergo so many privations. The difference in ideas seems to me to be of greater importance; for example, we must not forget that the relative religiousness of woman as compared with man becomes less in proportion as she becomes civilized and urbanized. Perhaps this is why to a certain extent, although she gains more, at the same time she becomes demoralized at least for a time.

[2] With regard to this great insufficiency from the naturalistic point of view, of the explanation by means of race or climate, I will refer the reader to the substantial and conclusive demonstrations collected by *Colajanni* in the two volumes of his "Sociologia criminale."

2. Preponderance of Social Causes

§ 63. (I) **The tendency towards imitation, its force and its forms, its study by means of the phenomenon of crowds. How a suspicion soon becomes a conviction among a crowd. Genesis of popularity and unpopularity. The spirit of sect and the spirit of the group. The group, as well as the family, a primitive social factor; double origin of societies.**

Before anything else, we ought summarily to define and analyze the powerful, generally unconscious, always partly mysterious, action by means of which we account for all the phenomena of society, namely imitation. In order to judge of its inherent power, we must first of all observe its manifestations among idiots. In them the imitative inclination is no stronger than in ourselves,[1] but it acts without encountering the obstacle which is met with in our ideas, our moral habits, and our wishes. Now, a case is cited of an idiot[2] who "after having taken part in the slaughtering of a pig took a knife and attacked a man." Others carry out the imitative tendency in setting fire to buildings.

All the important acts of social life are carried out under the domination of example. One procreates or one does not procreate, because of imitation; the statistics of the birth rate have shown us this. One kills or one does not kill, because of imitation; would we today conceive of the idea of fighting a duel or of declaring war, if we did not know that these things had always been done in the country which we inhabit? One kills oneself or one does not kill oneself, because of imitation; it is a recognized fact that suicide is an imitative phenomenon to the very highest degree; at any rate it is impossible to refuse to give this character to those "suicides in large numbers of conquered peoples escaping by means of death the shame of defeat and the yoke of the stranger, like that of the Sidonians who were defeated by Artaxerxes Orchus, of the Tyrians defeated by Alexander, of the Sagontines defeated by Scipio, of the Achaeans defeated by Metellus, etc."[3]

After this how can we doubt but that one steals or does not steal, one assassinates or does not assassinate, because of imitation? But it is especially in the great tumultuous assemblages of our cities that this characteristic force of the social world ought

[1] As a general thing, as we know, it is not impulses which are strong in the case of the insane, even in the case of those who are called "impulsives"; but it is the brakes within which are weak.

[2] "La folie héréditaire," by *Saury*.

[3] "Le suicide dans l'armée," by *Mesnier*.

to be studied. The great scenes of our revolutions cause it to break out, just as great storms are a manifestation of the presence of the electricity in the atmosphere, while it remains unperceived though none the less a reality in the intervals between them. A *mob* is a strange phenomenon. It is a gathering of heterogeneous elements, unknown to one another;[1] but as soon as a spark of passion, having flashed out from one of these elements, electrifies this confused mass, there takes place a sort of sudden organization, a spontaneous generation. This incoherence becomes cohesion, this noise becomes a voice, and these thousands of men crowded together soon form but a single animal, a wild beast without a name, which marches to its goal with an irresistible finality. The majority of these men had assembled out of pure curiosity, but the fever of some of them soon reached the minds of all, and in all of them there arose a delirium. The very man who had come running to oppose the murder of an innocent person is one of the first to be seized with the homicidal contagion, and moreover, it does not occur to him to be astonished at this.

There is no need for me to recall certain never to be forgotten pages of Taine's dealing with the fourteenth of July and its consequences in the provinces.[2] How can these things be so? In the most simple manner imaginable. The manner in which the mob acts shows us the force under the domination of which it became organized. Let us imagine ourselves carried back to the time of the Commune; a man wearing a white blouse, crossing a square, passes close to an over-excited crowd; he looks like a suspicious person to someone. In a moment, with the rapidity of a conflagration, this suspicion spreads, and instantly, what happens? "*A suspicion is enough*, all protest is useless, every proof is a delusion; *the conviction is profound*."[3] Supposing that each one of these people had been alone in his own house, never could a mere suspicion in the mind of each one of them, without proofs to support

[1] Of course, it necessarily follows that these men assembled together should resemble one another on some essential points such as nationality, religion, social class.

[2] Read again what is said about the massacres of September ("Révolution," vol. IV, pp. 295 *et seq.*). Among the Septemberists "some having come with good intentions are seized with vertigo at the contact of the bloody whirlwind, and, by a sudden stroke of revolutionary feeling, are converted to the religion of murder. A certain Grapin, delegated by his section to save two prisoners, sits down beside Maillard, and passes sentences with him during sixty hours." — There must without doubt also have been many such men as Grapin during the night of St. Bartholomew.

[3] Maxime du Camp.

it, have been changed into a conviction. But they are together, and the suspicion of each of them, by virtue of imitative force, keener, and acting more promptly in times of emotion, is reinforced by the suspicions of all the others; the result of which ought to be that, from being very weak, a belief in the guilt of the unfortunate fellow suddenly becomes very strong, without the shadow of an argument being necessary. Reciprocal imitation, when it is exercised over *similar* beliefs, and, generally speaking, over *similar* psychological states, is a true multiplication of the intensity proper to these beliefs, to these various states, in each one of those who feel them simultaneously.

When, on the contrary, in imitating one another, several persons exchange *different* states, which is what ordinarily takes place in social life, when, for example, one communicates to the other a taste for Wagnerian music and in return the other communicates to him a love for realistic fiction; these persons no doubt establish between themselves a bond of mutual assimilation, just as when they express to each other two similar ideas or needs which take root in this manner. But in the first case, the assimilation is, for each of them, a *complication* of their internal state — this is essentially an effect of civilization — and in the second case the assimilation is, for each of them, a mere *reinforcement* of their inner life. Between these two cases there is the musical interval between unison and a chord. A mob has the simple and deep power of a large unison. This explains why it is so dangerous to associate too much with minds which reflect one's own thoughts and one's own feelings; in doing this one soon arrives at the *sect spirit*, which is entirely analogous to the *mob spirit*.

The war madness, that intermittent attack which peoples suffer, can be accounted for by means of the preceding statements. In a country in which civilization has multiplied its relations, that is to say developed imitative force, thirty or forty millions of men are exchanging their fancies and their conceptions, their passions and their desires. The inner state of each one of them in this way becomes complicated, as a consequence of the dissimilarity between classes, interests, habits, and minds which have a tendency to become fused together. From this there result the ardor of cupidity, the fever of luxury. But at the same time, upon one point, their inner state ought merely to be reinforced by their being brought into contact with one another; namely in that which touches the feeling which a hostile nation, or one reputed to be such, inspires in them. This hatred, as compared with all the other desires put together, would be extremely weak in each one of them if they were by themselves; but it is common to all; they express it to one another; the imitative reinforcement must thus be exercised over it in particular and give rise, from time to time, to sublime or extravagant outbursts of patriotism which, in the very midst of a world of reason, to the great surprise of the wise, break out with a force in proportion to the progress of civilization. Why be astonished at this? It is inevitable.[1]

Let us return to the phenomenon of mobs; it is interesting from the point of view of social embryology, because it shows us by what means a new society has been able, and often has been compelled, to spring into existence outside of the family; I do not say maintain itself, once it has come into existence, without the aid of the family. There are, we say, two distinct germs of societies, the family and the mob; and, according as it shall have had one or the other as its principal source, as it shall have increased in its course by affluents derived from one or the other of them, a nation will clothe itself with absolutely different characteristics. No doubt the two origins resemble each other in many ways. In both cases, the society is the product of a suggestion, and not of a contract. A contract is the meeting of several wills born independently of one another, and which have happened to agree; a pure hypothesis. A suggestion is the product of wills which are born agreeing with the superior will from which they proceed; such is the primitive social fact. Every mob, like every family, has a head and obeys him scrupulously.[2] But the super-

[1] The elective genesis of the most inexplicable popularity and unpopularity is another excellent example of the part played by imitation in social life. When several successive elections take place with regard to one man or one idea, the vote of one Department manifestly carries that of another, and the enthusiasm for or against is as irresistible as a rising tide. After having been favorably regarded many times, the most ordinary man appears to be a great man and everywhere encounters the sincere enthusiasm of people who did not know him, but who heard him greeted with acclamation around them, also sincerely by a crowd to whom he is just as much an unknown; or else it is just the other way, he is suspected, then spurned, and then treated like the very worst scoundrel and the indignation which he inspires in honest property holders for no apparent reason would go as far as murder, should he be so unfortunate as to show himself before them. The history of "Boulangisme" is very instructive in this respect.

[2] One can see in these remarks in "Etudes sur les mœurs religieuses et sociales de l'extrême Orient," by *Alfred Lyall* (Thorin, 1885) how, even in India, where the tie of blood seems at first sight to be the only social bond, the prestige of a celebrated individual, of an ascetic famed for his austerity, of à dreaded brigand, suffices to rally around him a clientèle of companions and to form a new caste.

stitious and constitutional respect of the son for his father in the ancient household is one thing, and the infatuation of a day aroused by a leader of riots is quite another thing. When the family spirit, whether agricultural or rural, dominates in the social life, imitation-custom reigns there exclusively, with that majestic particularism and serenity which were characteristic of the Egyptian and the Chinese world; when the mob spirit takes its place, imitation-fashion effects its levelings and its changes, its assimilations of vast extent and its transformations in short periods of time. In the country the family-society predominates, the population is only kept up or increased by means of the domestic peopling; in towns the mob-society predominates, from all sides come people detached from their home and confusedly brought together. This is partly why I thought it best to attach so much importance, in the preceding chapter, to the distinction between urban brigandage and rural brigandage. It is not immaterial to know whether the inclination to crime is the fruit of a bad family education or of a dangerous companionship. It is always either a family, or a sect, or a café full of comrades, which drives to crime the individual who is wavering; and, in this last case, the enthusiasm which carries him away recalls, to almost the very highest degree, the popular current which drives a rioter to commit murder.

§ 64. (II) The laws of imitation. Men imitate one another in proportion as they are in close contact. The superior is imitated by the inferior to a greater extent than the inferior by the superior. Propagation from the higher to the lower in every sort of fact: language, dogma, furniture, ideas, needs. The great fields of imitation; formerly aristocracies, today capitals. Similarity of the former and the latter.

After these few words as to the force and the forms of imitation, we must set forth its general laws, which must be applied to crime as well as to every other aspect of societies. But the limits of this work will only allow us a brief indication of the subject. We already know that the example of any man, almost like the attraction of a body, radiates around himself, but with an intensity which becomes weaker as the distance of the men touched by his ray increases. "Distance" should not here be understood merely in the geometrical sense, but especially in the psychological sense of the word; the increase in the relations established by correspondence or by printing, of the intellectual communications of all kinds between fellow-citizens scattered over a vast territory, has the effect of diminishing in this sense the distance between them. Thus it may happen, let us repeat, that the honest example of an entire surrounding but distant society may be neutralized in the heart of a young vagabond by the influence of a few companions. From the economic, philological, religious, and political point of view, it is the same. In the vicinity of the largest cities there are still to be found villages, having but slight relations with them, where the old needs and the old ideas are preserved, where they order their cloth from the weaver, where they like to eat brown bread, where they speak nothing but dialect, where they believe in sorcerers and witchcraft. . . . This consideration must never be lost sight of.

Now instead of taking each example by itself, let us examine the connection between several examples and let us seek to find the result of the exchange. First of all, however mean and however despised an individual may be, repeated contact with him does not fail to stamp the highest and the proudest persons with a certain vague tendency to copy him. We have the proof of this in the contagion of *accents;* the proudest master, if he lives alone in the country with his servants, eventually borrows some of their intonations and even of their phrases. It is thus that the coldest body sends heat to the hottest body. But, just as in reality the heating of the hot body by the cold body is approximately nothing if it be compared with the great heat imparted to the cold body by the hot body, similarly one can often ignore, the more often even, in our societies, the impressive action exercised by the example of slaves upon their masters, of children upon adults, of the laity upon the clergy (in the prosperous days of the theocracy), of the ignorant upon the literate, the ingenuous upon the clever, the poor upon the rich, the plebeians upon the patricians (in the prosperous period of the aristocracy), of the inhabitants of the country upon the inhabitants of cities, of the provincials upon the Parisians, in a word, of the inferior upon the superior, and only take into account the opposite action, which is the true explanation of history. There is during every period a recognized superiority, sometimes wrongly recognized as such. It is the privilege of the man who, richer in needs and ideas, has more examples to give than he has to receive. The unequal exchange of examples, such as it is governed by this law, has the effect of causing the social world to progress towards a leveling state which may be compared to that universal uniformity of temperature which the law of the radiation of the heat of bodies has a tendency to establish.

It sometimes happens, too often in fact, that the political and military power is found in the hands of the nation or the class having the fewest civilizing examples to show. In such a case as this, the class or the nation which is in subjection, believing itself to be superior to the one which rules it, limits itself to a submission but refuses to be assimilated. This is one of the frequent causes of acts of oppression and of bloody revolts. For the conqueror, before everything, either wittingly or unknown to himself, wishes to be copied, and does not believe his victory to be a real one as long as this is not done; so greatly does he feel that imitative contagion is the very best social action. Also he strives in every manner, by brutal violence or by oppression disguised in some way, to force upon the vanquished, not only his yoke, but his own type.

Philip II, for example, made use of the former against the Moors of Andalusia. They were the most industrious, the richest, the most civilized, and not the least faithful of his subjects. But they jealously guarded their national usages, their manner of dressing, of eating, of living, without allowing the Spanish customs to penetrate among them. Everything which was said against them at that time, all the hatred which they inspired in the people and the clergy of the conquering race, arose from this fact. "A victorious people," Fourneron says correctly on this subject, "will always have grievances against those who profit by the laws without becoming absorbed into their unity." [1] That is to say, against those who obey but do not imitate themselves.

The decrees which Philip II, in 1566, enacted against the Moors to the applause of all Christians, had as their real object a compulsory imitation by the Moors of the Christians in everything and for everything. "After the first of January following," says the author cited, "the Moors could possess neither weapons, nor slaves, nor costumes after their own fashion . . . they had immediately to provide themselves with doublets and breeches, to cease to hide under the 'habarah' and the 'feredjeh' the faces and shoulders of their women, who were compelled thenceforward to

[1] This author adds: "The same repugnance is observable even today against the Jews among the Christians of the Danube and against the Chinese among the Americans of the West."

wear caps and farthingales . . . forget their own language and learn Spanish within a period of six months . . . etc." Here we see demented despotism, and we know the sea of blood it caused to flow. But, during the periods and among the nations who boast the most of their democratic tolerance, do we not find a reigning sect, Puritan or Jacobin, pursuing the same object, at bottom, by taking possession of the national education and molding the children in the same form as its own, or simply, without decrees and without battles, by excluding from every branch of their employ, by excommunicating in a thousand ways, anybody who persists in having *a style* which is not its own?

It is none the less true that imitation imposed upon people in this manner scarcely ever spreads, and never sinks in very deep; in other words, it is the *social superior*, the person with most ideas of a civilizing kind, even when he is distinct from the political superior and opposed to the latter, who eventually prevails, excepting in cases of a radical extermination such as was that of the Moors in the sixteenth century.

History abounds in illustrations of this truth. Go into the home of a peasant and look at his household effects. From his fork and his glass to his shirt, from his andirons to his lamp, from his axe to his gun, there is not one piece of his furniture, of his clothing, or one of his implements, which, before having come down to his cottage, was not originally an object of luxury for the use of kings or warrior chiefs, or ecclesiastical chiefs, then of the lords, afterwards of the citizens of towns, and lastly of the neighboring landowners. Draw this peasant into conversation. You will find he has not a single idea on law, agriculture, politics, or arithmetic, a single sentiment of family or patriotism, a single wish, a single desire, which was not originally a peculiar discovery or initiative, propagated from the social heights, gradually down to his low level. His language, the French which he is beginning to speak correctly, is an echo of the neighboring town, itself an echo of Paris just as the dialect which he still speaks (let us assume that we are dealing with the south of France) had been communicated to him from the neighboring castles, themselves modeled after the Provençal courts, or as he had started to speak Latin after the time of Julius Caesar because the nobility of Gaul had been eager to copy the language of the conquerors. His very hatred of the Old Régime was whispered to him by the leaders of the Old Régime; his need of equality comes to him from the Jacobin clubs which in turn had received it from the salons of the philosophers where the innovations of Rousseau were discussed by fine ladies and clever men. His jealous love of the land comes to him from the great feudal landowners whose soul it was and whom his ancestors, for centuries, had as neighbors and as masters, — a twofold reason for imitating them.

It is especially in fostering the spread of example that a social hierarchy is useful; an aristocracy is a fountain reservoir necessary for the fall of imitation in successive cascades, successively enlarged. If industry on a large scale has become a possibility in our day, if the diffusion of needs, of tastes, of identical ideas in the hearts of immense masses of people has opened up the vast outlets which it needs, is it not to the old inequalities that we are indebted for this existing equality?

But let us beware of thinking that this movement is going to cease; in democratic times the work of the nobility is carried on, and on a larger scale, by capitals.[1] The latter in many ways resemble the former. The nobility, in their days of splendor, shine by reason of wit, luxury, generosity, courage, gallantry, and a spirit of enterprise; they purchase these brilliant gifts by furnishing a larger contingent to madness, crime, suicide, the duel, illegitimate births, to vices and maladies of every sort. Capitals are no less luxurious, no less ruinous, no less gay and full of innovation. They show the same egoism and the same insolence; they have a profound contempt for the provinces in return for the profound admiration which they themselves inspire in the former, and treat them in precisely the same manner as the gentlemen of former days used to treat the common people, who were only too happy to pay their debts and for their extravagances; they also show a lower birth rate and a higher death rate; and, owing to the cankers which gnaw them, to tuberculosis, syphilis, alcoholism,

[1] Conversely, we find the work of capitals carried on by the nobility which they have created and which survives them. Everything is relative in fact, and by capitals we must understand, whether in the midst of the forests of ancient Germany or among the primitive Latins, a borough greater in size than the neighboring villages. Here is born and is always formed a body of patricians. With his usual penetration, Niebuhr has reduced the fundamental contrast of Roman history, that between the Patricians and the Plebeians, to the distinction which serves as its source, between "Rome-city" and "Rome-country." This contest, to tell the truth, is the foundation of every history. Each day under our eyes grows the conflict in which we see it assuming its latest form; the electoral duel between the workman and the peasant. It has its source finally in the human organism where muscle, which rural life nourishes too much, separates and is united to sinews, which the urban life has developed to excess.

pauperism, and prostitution, they would inevitably perish if, like every living aristocracy, they were not renewed very quickly by the influx of new elements.[1] They maintain themselves by means of immigration as did the Roman patriarchate by means of adoption. Thus the moralist of today, in order that he may predict what the morality of tomorrow will be, should keep his eye on the examples furnished by great cities, just as the moralist of yesterday was right in being concerned with what took place in the midst of courts, salons, and castles.

§ 65. (III) Application to criminality. Vices and crimes were formerly propagated from the nobles to the people. Examples: drunkenness, poisoning, murder by command. Deliberations of the Council of Ten. Counterfeit money. Pillage and theft.

Let us see how all this applies to our subject. Strange as it may seem, there are serious reasons for maintaining that the vices and the crimes of today, which are to be found in the lowest orders of the people, descended to them from above. In every nascent or renascent society when the producing of wine becomes difficult or limited, drunkenness is a royal luxury and a privilege of the aristocracy. It is quite certain that the kings of Homer's time got drunk far more often than did their subjects, the Merovingian chiefs than their vassals, and the lords of the Middle Ages than their serfs. Even as late as the sixteenth century, in Germany "the celebrated autobiography of the knight of Schweinichen furnishes a proof that the coarsest drunkenness did not dishonor a person of rank." [2] He tells us as a matter of course that, the first three nights after his marriage, he went to bed in an absolute state of intoxication, as did all the guests composing the wedding party.

The smoking habit, at present so widespread in every sort of surroundings, perhaps already more widespread among the people

[1] Just as the nobilities of the Old Régime, democratic capitals today are still the conservators of the duel. In my study on this subject I thought I had shown that the duel had become an essentially urban phenomenon and that except for a few large cities this prejudice would rapidly have disappeared. From 1880 to 1889, out of 598 duels among civilians registered in the Ferréus Annual, 491 originated in Paris, according to my reckoning. Of the others, 107 originated in Marseilles, Nîmes, Lyons, Limoges, etc. No country duel exists, so to speak, just as though honor in the country were of too inferior a kind to be deserving of a recourse to arms against the party who offends it. The kind of urban duel which predominates is the literary duel, a rather inoffensive kind, after all.

[2] "Recherches sur divers sujets d'économie politique," by *Roscher*.

than among the socially elect, where they have begun to combat this passion, was propagated in the same manner. James I of England, Roscher tells us, put a very heavy tax upon tobacco in 1604, "because," says the law, "the lower classes, incited by the example of the upper classes, impair their health, taint the air, and corrupt the soil." [1] The irreligiousness of the masses, which today here and there contrasts with the relative religiousness of the last survivors of the old aristocracy, is just as much due to this same cause. Vagabondage, under its thousand and one existing forms, is an essentially plebeian offense; but by going back into the past, it would not be very difficult to connect our vagabonds, our street singers, with the noble pilgrims and the noble minstrels of the Middle Ages.

Poaching, another hotbed of crime, which in the past, together with smuggling, has played a part which may be compared with that played by vagabondage at the present time, is still more directly connected with the life of the lords. One ought to read, in Taine's "Ancien régime," of the importance of poachers in the eighteenth century in all the countries where there were forests. For the very reason that hunting was a feudal privilege, the wretch who indulged in it by main force, with an audacity and a passion hard to realize, was driven to it less by reason of his poverty than because of the vague delusion that he would to some extent ennoble himself. At this time there were poaching parties in imitation of the great hunting parties of the king; poachers to the number of from twenty-five to fifty often exchanged murderous shots with the gamekeepers, and in this manner served their apprenticeship as brigands.

Poisoning is now a crime of the illiterate; [2] as late as the seventeenth century it was the crime of the upper classes, as is proven by the epidemic of poisonings which flourished at the court of Louis XIV, from 1670 to 1680, following the importation of certain poisons by the Italian Exili. The Marquise de Brinvilliers is the direct ancestress of the common Locustes of our villages. At the table of every king at first, and afterwards of all the principal lords, during the Middle Ages and as late as the sixteenth century, it was always customary that no dish should be offered the master without previously having been tasted,

[1] Pipes were smoked at the court of Louis XIII. (See *Quicherat*, "Histoire du Costume," p. 478.)

[2] There are still exceptions to the rule, for example that dramatic Ain-Fezza case which has just come to an end while I am correcting the proofs of this page.

"tried," out of fear that it might be poisoned. This characteristic shows the former frequency of this crime in courts and castles, especially in Italy. Italy in the Middle Ages was the nation after which the others were modeled.

Must not murder by bravos, by "bravi," so much used in Germany and Italy in the Middle Ages, have been the transition phase which homicide passed through in descending from the highest stratum of society to the lowest? The fact remains that the power to kill, from which was derived the right to kill, has been, in every primitive society, the distinguishing indication of the upper classes. The "Grands jours d'Auvergne," however pleasant they may have been made out in the valuable account given by Flechier, are sufficient to show us what were in this respect, even until the seventeenth century, the tendencies of the nobility in backward countries.[1] The evolution of the political assassination is instructive. There was a time when kings, the heads of republics, themselves assassinated; for example Clovis. What is more, it was their near relatives whom they killed by preference; parricide, fratricide, uxoricide, cold blooded in-

[1] It was not only in Auvergne, it was in many other provinces also that those terrible extra-judicial tribunals met; and against whom were their forces always directed? Against the bandits of the nobility. In our day when an exceptional form of justice is brought into play, for example in 1810, it has only to punish brigands who have been recruited from the lowest ranks of the people. In the sixteenth century, during the religious wars, kings, queens, princes, great vassals, gentlemen, all brave men, moreover, thought they had a right, not only to kill in a duel their enemy who had been overcome, but to assassinate him, either from motives of vengeance, or for ambition's sake and sometimes through greed. (See especially "Ducs de Guise," by *Formeron.*) In those days one became famous through the number of bold assassinations one had committed, for example Baron de Vittaud, whom the gentle Marguerite de Valois herself went to see at the Augustine Convent in order to confide to him the mission of killing Du Guast, the king's favorite, who had outraged her. Philip II decorated and ennobled his bravos. The massacre of St. Bartholomew is only the best known of the bloody orgies of this time. The further back we go into the past, the more do the customs of the scum of the nobility, I do not say of its élite in normal times, everywhere resemble those of the Sicilian or Corsican bandits of our day. Let us add it is true that the extraordinary number of fatal duels or of homicides, properly so-called (for at that time it is hard to distinguish between duels and assassinations in many cases) committed during the sixteenth century and again under the Fronde by the nobility, is due to a great extent to that monopoly of the right of wearing a sword which was so fatal to them. There were gentlemen of the Old Régime, like the Corsicans of today, who were turning to murder owing to the habit of carrying weapons, so much so that by forbidding them to do so their criminality was suddenly diminished by three fourths under the Second Empire. To the habit of wearing a sword was related that of going on horseback in the streets, which, given up toward the end of the sixteenth century, had also (see Voltaire) a great homicidal influence.

fanticide, after the manner of a Tropmann, were the Merovingian specialty, as can be seen from each page of the writings of Gregory of Tours.

Later on, the princes commit assassinations which are paid for; this is especially proved by the archives of Venice. Lamansay, who has consulted them,[1] has found in them, from 1415 to 1768, more than one hundred deliberations of the Council of Ten relating to commissions of this sort. Here is a sample taken at random. "1448, September 5. The Council of Ten charge Lawrence Minio to inform the person who is unknown that he accepts the latter's offer which consists in putting to death Count Francis [Sforza], and that, after the execution, he can promise him from ten to twenty thousand ducats."[2]

Finally there comes a time, — and fortunately as a general rule far sooner than in Venice, — when men of the State would blush to make this sort of bargain; and this is the time when regicides and tyrannicides spontaneously spring up from the hot-headed populace. It is noticeable that the great recrudescences of private homicide, as far as we are able to judge with respect to a past lacking in statistics, have immediately followed the outbreak of external wars or civil wars, that is to say the great debauches of official homicide called "reasons of State." Is there not reason to believe, finally, that the cruelty of the old justices, who were so bloodthirsty, was a terrible example solemnly given by the upper classes of society, to ferocious minds, and that the excesses of public vengeance may have aroused or stimulated those of private revenge?

Arson, the crime of the lower classes today, was one of the prerogatives of the feudal lords. "Did we not hear the Margrave of Brandenburg boasting one day of having, during his lifetime, burned one hundred and seventy villages?"[3] Counterfeiting today takes refuge in a few caverns in the mountains, in a few underground places in towns; we know that for a long time it was a royal monopoly. Now governments limit themselves to sometimes putting false rumors in circulation. Finally theft, so degrading in our day, has had a brilliant past. Montaigne

[1] "Revue historique," September and October, 1882, article on "Assassinat politique à Venise."

[2] Jean-Marie Visconti had bravos of another sort; he let loose his dogs upon the citizens of Milan.

[3] "L'Allemagne à la fin du moyen âge," by *Jean Janssen* (French translation, 1887).

tells us, without being very indignant about it, that many young gentlemen of his acquaintance, to whom their fathers did not give enough money, got funds by stealing. Why should they have had any scruples on the matter when, at this same time, the king, Henry III, plundered and ransomed as he saw fit the merchants of Paris; when it was customary in the best disciplined armies to plunder captured towns and to extort enormous ransoms from prisoners of war, even of a private war, captured as a result of ambushes and betrayals? The sequestration of persons,[1] so much used quite recently among the Sicilian brigands, strangely resembles this proceeding of extortion, just as their "abigeato" recalls the military "razzias."

In one of the popular German songs of the sixteenth century, republished by Janssen, we read that the brigandage of the nobility is intolerable, that gentlemen seem to consider stealing as "an honorable action" and they go so far as to teach it "just as children are taught to read." Werner Roleswinck has supplied us with ample details as to the manner in which young gentlemen were brought up to steal in Westphalia (1487). When they went on a campaign, they sang, in the dialect of their country: "Let us steal, let us plunder without shame! The best people in the country do it!" The same customs, in less violent but more crafty form, as was fitting, were imputed to the legists; here the difference between rural theft and urban theft is felt.

In every plan of reform in Germany during the fifteenth century, the "brigandage of the nobility" is mentioned. A chronicler of the same period says that "the brigand knights make the roads very unsafe." Goetz of Berlichingen and Frank of Sickingen are, in the sixteenth century, brilliant personifications of this seigniorial criminality. In Italy the spectacle was at this time similar; the owners of castles plundered and held to ransom, throughout their fiefs, travelers, merchants, and boatmen. In France we are comparatively privileged in this respect; our nobility and especially our royalty, with some exceptions becoming more numerous during the sixteenth century, owing to the Italian contagion, were of a mildness and a probity which were remarkable among all the others. None the less is it true that our kings had

[1] In the course of a criminal trial which was brought to my notice by a distinguished archaeologist, the Vicomte de Gérard, and which was carried on in 1653–54 before the inferior court of Sarlat, I note that one of the victims was incarcerated for eight days in a dungeon in the castle of M——, on bread and water and only obtained his liberty upon the payment of a large sum of money.

hardly any scruples about indulging in arbitrary confiscation, and that our gentlemen, even during the seventeenth century, if we are to judge by a thousand deductions drawn from the literature of the times, had very broad notions on the subject of delicacy. In the "Bourgeois gentilhomme," Dorante, who represents the type of the elegant cavalier, of the fashionable lover, commits a veritable abuse of confidence to the prejudice of Jourdain; he undertakes for the latter to carry a very valuable diamond to Dorimène (a peculiar commission moreover), and he gives it to her as coming from himself, Dorante. Here we have a little trick which it did not seem improper at that time to attribute to a courtier. However, we know whether Molière was a good courtier or not. In the memoirs of Rochefort, we read of a characteristic which proves that the great lords of the time of the Fronde made sport, not merely of killing, but of stealing. One day, he tells us, when he was in happy company "it was suggested that they go and rob on the Pont-Neuf; this was a form of amusement which the Duke of Orléans had made fashionable at that time." Rochefort says, however, that he had some hesitancy about this; at the same time he looked on, perched up on the bronze horse. "The others began to waylay the passers-by and took four or five cloaks. But, someone who had been robbed having gone and complained, the archers came and our fellows took to their heels."

And yet we say that the last descendants of these pickpockets of feudal times are now the most unblemished representatives of French honor and honesty! If heredity were the principal "factor" as far as morality is concerned, could this be as it is? Furthermore, everywhere in Europe, until the sixteenth century, there existed the right to the estate of a deceased alien, a right which was in truth one of stealing, for the benefit of the lords, and affecting all those who were shipwrecked upon their coasts. This propagation from those above to those below applies to urban crime and rural crime equally well. When, in a country such as Sicily, we see country brigandage flourish by reason of a continual recruiting among the lower agricultural classes, we may be sure that at an earlier period the upper rural classes, which at the present time limit themselves to protecting this bold plundering, themselves used formerly to practice it. Similarly, when a band of obscure insurgents terrorizes a capital and holds a government in check, let us recall the fact that there was a time when statesmen were not ashamed to carry out the massacres and annoyances which they suppress in our day.[1]

Finally, there is no need for me to recall the fact that during all the periods of their prosperity, monarchic or aristocratic courts, just as capitals at the present time, were a school of adultery, of license and moral corruption for the rest of the nation. Every offense against morals has as its cause the examples which have come from above. Rape, even more than plunder and burning, was the great diversion of the old warriors, of the military and dominant class, at a time when a castle or a town was captured and at once sacked. Brantôme cheerfully relates these ferocious orgies. Of how many criminal assaults has the habit of rape and plunder in wartime, considered for centuries as a right of war, been the cause even in times of peace and in the very midst of industrious and agricultural people!

What has just been said does not imply that there was a time, even during the most barbarous period, when murder, theft, rape, and arson were a monopoly belonging exclusively to the higher ranks of the nation; but it does mean that when a man of the lower ranks was found to be a murderer, a thief, a "strupator," an incendiary, he stood out by reason of the terror which he inspired, ennobled himself to a certain extent, and broke into government circles. In barbarous times — that is to say, times of *social illogicalness*, of isolation and of chronic hostility — every active, enterprising, and adventurous man hopes to become the leader of a band, just as, in a century of peace and of great agglomerations, he hopes to become the *head of a household.* Then, provided his criminal industry prospers, he succeeds in having himself proclaimed king, as was done by that Marcone, a brigand of Calabria who, in 1560, had himself styled "king Marcone." This thing, which has often happened in Italy, may serve as a partial explana-

[1] With regard to the history of Spanish literature, *Brunetière* ("Revue des Deux Mondes," March, 1891), observes that the chivalrous romance was the forerunner of the knavish romance, which dealt with the exploits of brigands and swindlers. In literature there was but a step between such men as Amadis aux Cartouche and Amadis aux Mandrin. Are not these latter in their own way "a sort of knight errant"? Or else should we say that in proportion as a society is formed, becomes organized and regulated, it is the knights of former times who become the beggars of today? . . . Could there not be a peculiar way of interpreting the point of honor which would be to do no work with one's two hands and, not having a farthing, in wishing to live as a gentleman? In our day this point of honor would very quickly lead people to the convict prison or the gallows. In the time of Charles V history tells us that it just as easily led them to the conquest of Mexico or Peru.

tion of the origin of feudalism, not only of Christian feudalism, but of every sort of feudalism, for example Greek and Hindu feudalism.[1] "The little [Italian] governments which originated [in the fifteenth century] through some exploit of brigandage, are very numerous and of a savage character" says Gehbart. Does not this essentially criminal character of the ruling classes, in Italy during the fifteenth and sixteenth centuries, to a certain extent account for the very distressing spread of sanguinary criminality among the Italian lower classes of our day? And do not we Frenchmen to a certain extent owe our lesser propensity to homicide, to the relatively mild character of our former rulers?

§ 66. (IV) At the present time they are propagated from the great cities to the country. Women cut to pieces. The lovers' vitriol.

While crime formerly spread, like every industrial product, like every good or bad idea, from the nobility to the people, and while the nobility, in those remote times, drew to itself the audacious and criminal elements of the people, today we can see crime spreading from the great cities to the country, from the capitals to the provinces, and these capitals and great cities having an irresistible attraction for the outcasts and scoundrels of the country, or the provinces, who hasten to them to become civilized after their own manner, a new kind of ennobling.[2] For the time

[1] Moreover, let us not forget that this criminal contagion of the aristocracy has at all times been compensated for, and more often than not, advantageously, especially in the eighteenth century by their beneficial contagion. The peculiar character with which the virtues as well as the vices of a people clothe themselves, is derived by these people from their former chiefs. Although the sentiment of chivalrous honor became vulgarized in France, where it was expressed by means of too frequent duels; and although lofty pride and independence today characterize the Spaniard, energy and a love of freedom the Englishman, this is not a mere question of race. In this we may see the consequences of a time-honored influence exercised by the nobles of these different nations. Obviously it is by imitating the classes which used to be the upper ones, that every Spaniard aspires to be a hidalgo and that the most plebeian of Frenchmen will fight a duel today. In former times single combat was a privilege of the aristocracy, as was the honor of knighthood.

[2] Let us observe, while on the subject, that the substitution of capitals for aristocracies as the social summit destined to spread the various currents of imitation according to the law of their progress from above to below is itself perhaps a consequence of this law. Is not emigration from the country to the city, which has for more than a century caused the great centres to preponderate, perchance connected with the emigration, under the Old Régime, of the country nobility to the court? Under Henry IV, as is seen in the case of Olivier de Serres, the French nobility still lived upon their landed properties. After the time of Louis XIII we find a movement of concentration by the great lords to the court of the king.

being this latter fact is a fortunate one for the provinces, which are being purified by means of this emigration and passing through an era of comparative security. Never, perhaps, in rural regions has there been less fear of assassination and even of robbery with violence than at the present time. But unfortunately the attraction of the great cities for criminals is closely connected with the influence exercised by them over the remainder of the nation, with the fascinating power their example has in all matters. As a consequence it is to be feared that the benefits derived from this betterment of conditions in the provinces is but temporary. The capitals send to the provinces not only their political and literary likes and dislikes, their style of wit or folly, the cut of their clothes, the shape of their hats and their accent, but they also send their crimes and their misdemeanors.

Indecent assault upon children is an essentially urban crime, as is demonstrated by its chart; in its spread it is seen to form a dark spot around the great cities. Each variety of murder or theft invented by evil genius is born or takes root in Paris, Marseilles, Lyons, etc., before becoming widespread throughout France. The series of corpses cut to pieces began in 1876 with the Billoir case and was for a long time confined to Paris, Toulouse, and Marseilles; but it was carried on in the Departments of Nièvre, Loir-et-Cher, and Eure-et-Loir.[1] The feminine idea of

This tendency has been criticized and with good reason; but while criticizing it, its critics have unconsciously and universally imitated it. The lesser nobility which could not go to court compensated themselves for this lack of power by concentrating in the larger or smaller towns of their neighborhood, where they observed the manners and the amusements of the court; or else assembled together in some castle, richer and more hospitable than the others, an imitation in miniature of Versailles. At the same time the rich townsmen, financiers and magistrates, came together around the court in Paris, or around the provincial aristocracies in each one of the little "Faubourgs Saint-Germain" which was included in nearly every town in France. (On this subject see "La ville sous l'ancien régime," by *Babeau.*) Finally, the workmen, the very peasants, began to look upon the towns as the country gentlemen of former times looked upon the court. For the latter the court was the Eden they dreamed of, the country which most abounded in game as far as good sinecures were concerned, of pleasant and refined pleasures to be sampled; and it is because this conviction has for a long time prevailed that the town has become little by little for our farmers a terrestrial paradise, the place where all profit is made without work and where every pleasure is to be found.

[1] See "Contagion du meutre," by *Aubry*, pp. 137 *et. seq.* In England and even in France, Billoir had had precursors, but this was a fact of which he probably was unaware. The English Billoir was called Greenaer, and he himself had been preceded by Theodore Gardelle and Catherine Hayes. (See "Causes célèbres de l'Angleterre," by *Lewis*, 1884). Consult also "Dépeçage criminel," by *Ravoux*, with notes and commentaries by *A. Lacassagne.* (Lyons, Storck.)

throwing vitriol in the face of a lover is entirely Parisian; it was the widow Gras who, in 1875, had the honor of inventing this, or rather of re-inventing it. But I know of villages where this seed has borne fruit, and the peasant women themselves now try their hand at the handling of vitriol.[1] In 1881, a young actress, Clotilde J——, threw vitriol over her lover, at Nice. "When she was asked at what time she first thought of avenging herself, 'since the day,' she replied, 'when I read *in a Paris newspaper* an article dealing with the revenge of women.'"[2] Another instrument of feminine hatred is the revolver; its use in a much talked of case in Paris was very soon followed by a similar shot at Auxerre.[3] In 1825, in Paris, Henriette Cornier cruelly put to death a child of which she had the care; not long afterwards, other children's nurses yielded, for no other reason than this, to an irresistible desire to cut the throats of their employers' children.

With regard to thefts the same thing applies. There is not a single means of swindling employed at village fairs which did not first see the light of day upon a sidewalk of Paris. "There were," says Corre (in "Crime et suicide"), "following the Pranzini and Prado cases, a few attempts at imitating them on a small scale carried out upon prostitutes. But what more striking example of suggesto-imitative assault could there be than the series of mutilations of women, begun in the month of September 1888 *in London*, in the Whitechapel district! Never perhaps has the pernicious influence of *general news* been more apparent. The newspapers were filled with the exploits of Jack the Ripper, and, in less than a year, as many as eight absolutely identical crimes were committed in various crowded streets of the great city. This is not all; there followed a repetition of these same deeds outside of the capital and very soon there was even a spreading of them abroad. At Southampton attempt to mutilate a child; at Bradford horrible mutilation of another child; at Hamburg murder accompanied by disemboweling of a little girl; in the United States disemboweling of four negroes [Birmingham], disemboweling and mutilation of a colored woman [Milville]; in Honduras disemboweling . . . etc. The Gouffe case had its almost immediate counterpart in Copenhagen. . . . Infectious epidemics spread

[1] It often happens that because of their clumsiness they disfigure themselves through the spurting of the liquid over their own face.

[2] *Paul Aubry, op. cit.*

[3] The Clovis Hugues case followed by the Francey case.

with the air or the wind; epidemics of crime follow the line of the telegraph."

It may be objected, it is true, in looking at the chart of French criminality, that many rural centres, far away from the great centres, are nevertheless making progress in the matter of crime.

But let us study this chart closely, let us go into detail, and, after having seemed to depart from the preceding reflections, we shall be compelled to come back to them. We shall see that the influence exercised by the example of the great cities over criminality is not only direct, as we have just pointed out, but at the same time and more especially indirect, like that of the old nobility, through the spread and the attraction of their pleasures, their luxuries, and their vices, a forerunner of and a preparation for the contagion of their offenses. They attract the country people because the latter began by imitating them in everything. Thus the progress of this imitation may be measured by the progress of rural emigration, which is almost entirely directed towards Paris or the other great centres. An exodus within and without which is ever increasing, because the proportion of the rural population as compared with the total population is constantly decreasing, and, in less than twenty-five years, has been lowered from three-quarters to two-thirds.

Now when we say change of place we almost always mean change of class as well; and when one is out of one's sphere, socially, it is not long before one is beyond the pale of the law. In 1876, it was calculated that, out of every 100,000 Frenchmen who had stayed at home, there were eight accused of some crime; that, out of the same number of Frenchmen who had emigrated to the interior of the country, there were twenty-nine; that out of the same number of foreigners residing in France, there were forty-one. The more detached from his native soil and his family a man is, the more is he led astray. When he once more acquires a fatherland and a family, he at once becomes better. For example: "The Department of Nord[1] has two or three times as many naturalized foreigners as the Department of Doubs, and the criminality of its immigrants is one-fourth as great."

This is not all; the example of the great centres not only affects persons who are young, active, enterprising, and who hasten to them; it also affects, it deeply and invisibly stamps the individuals who have stayed at home; and, if one of the latter,

[1] See "La France criminelle," by *Henry Joly*, p. 61.

through the cultivation of vines, through industry or through speculation, becomes rich and raises himself above the others, the first use he will make of his fortune will be to copy some Parisian, in so far as will be consistent with his natural rusticity, and to awaken to this ungainly and tormenting imitation all his neighbors. They are rural townsmen who are an outcome and a counterpart of the citizen gentlemen of the Old Régime. It is as though a caricature of Paris itself had appeared in the midst of the village. This applies to all those farmers who have become rich too quickly in the Department of Hérault, through wine growing, and in Normandy through even the breeding of cattle, as well as to the commercial upstarts who have spread everywhere.

§ 67. (V) The crime chart of France, drawn by Joly. Its divisions by watersheds, fields of criminality; Hérault, Normandy, Eudes Rigaud.

But let us once more look at the chart. I do not mean the one [1] where each Department is colored according to the number of accusations and charges which have taken place within it, without any distinction being made between the accused and the persons apprehended who are natives of the Department, and those who have come from somewhere else. Joly has rendered a great service to our studies by drawing up a chart [2] the shades of which are graduated according to the proportionate number of accusations and charges directed against persons who are natives of a Department, whether they be prosecuted within it or outside of it. In this manner, to each Department is attributed all the criminality, internal and external, which can be imputed to it, and nothing more than this; its own impelling force towards good or towards evil is thus clearly expressed.

Now, it is a remarkable thing that this chart, the most correct and the most complete expression of the criminality of the Departments, also shows us the widest and the clearest distribution of it. We no longer have the scattering and the checkerboard effect of the old charts; there are great masses which begin to take on a physiognomy. It has seemed to me that the Departments of the same shade or of a similar shade were grouped, approximately,

[1] For example the first chart of *Yvernès* joined to the "Compte général" of 1888 and giving a summing up of the "Criminalité générale" from 1878 to 1887.

[2] This chart is published with "France criminelle," to face page 44. Its component parts were supplied by *Yvernès'* second chart coupled with the "Compte général" of 1887. However, the latter is only based upon rough figures, not reduced to the same unit of population.

within the limits of the same watershed; the valley of the Seine is very dark, and it is quite apparent that the focal point of this spreading darkness is a large black spot, Paris. In contrast with this the entire valley of the Loire, or pretty nearly so, is pure white. The Loire waters the Departments of Allier, Cher, Nièvre, Loiret, Loir-et-Cher, Indre-et-Loire, Maine-et-Loire, and Loire-Inférieure. With the exception of the Department of Loiret, which is tinted gray, no doubt because of the city of Orléans, all these Departments are conspicuous for their relative morality. The same thing applies to the entire valley of the Charente, including the Department of Vendée. I might say as much of the valley of the Garonne, did not the proximity of Bordeaux blacken the Department of Gironde; it is surprising that Toulouse, an old *customary law* town and one which has remained stationary, it is true, does not darken the Department of Haute-Garonne. All the Departments watered by the Saône are white, excepting the first one, a frontier Department and, as such, rather dark. There takes place along the border between the two States a sort of endosmosis and exosmosis of criminal immigration and emigration of suspects which is expressed in higher figures in the general account of justice.[1] Finally, there are none of these Departments until the valley of the Rhône is reached which, for the most part, do not show a light shade of color, at least on the left bank. Naturally we must make an exception of the Department wherein Lyons is situated, and the one including Marseilles.

Furthermore, we must not be astonished at seeing the same level of morality prevail in the valley of the same navigable watercourse and in the region which is contiguous to it. Let us remember that the rivers were for a long time the only means of communication between men, the natural vehicle of examples, and that in so far as customs, industry, and fashion as well as morals are concerned, they have in the long run brought their entire course to the same level.[2] This is said out of fear that

[1] It is not only the fact of the bad choice made by these wandering people which causes their greater criminality; but assuming the same degree of immorality, we know that a person will always feel less scruple about robbing or even killing a man who is foreign to the locality in which he lives, or even where he is temporarily staying, rather than a fellow-countryman.

[2] Another example. Look closely at chart 21 of the "Atlas de statistique financière de 1889," which gives the sales of beverages, you will see the same shading separately extending over the entire basin of the Loire, the entire basin of the Dordogne and of the Garonne.

some partisan of *physical factors* might depend too much upon this quasi-hydrographic division of French criminality. But the thing which is worthy of notice is, after all, the favorable effect upon morality of the agricultural or semi-industrial wealth of rich countries, by the old and solid wealth arising out of the land and labor.[1] Such being the rule, the great exception shown by the valley of the Seine around Paris, and more especially Normandy, stands out all the clearer, and shows, at least partly, the effect produced by the capital, just as on a lesser scale the exception of the Departments of Gironde, Rhône, and Bouches-du-Rhône shows the effect of Bordeaux, Lyons, and Marseilles.

Normandy is the region of France which is the oldest and most persistent in crime, although it is one of the most prosperous materially. Better still, its most barren regions, as has been pointed out by Joly, of the Departments of Eure and Calvados, and which lie to the east of these two Departments, are the least criminal, a fact which seems to contradict our previous remark; but which is only too clearly accounted for by reason of the lesser participation of these regions in the demoralizing influences which prevail in its more fertile regions. Here the example of the farmer who has through speculation in cattle become rich the quickest — because the *superior* who is now imitated is the *richest*, and the richest is generally, in our day, *one who has become rich* — arouses among his fellows, angered at feeling themselves his inferiors, a deplorable emulation which is expressed by means of an imitation of his comfort, his greed, his drunkenness, and his Malthusian foresight. Here we see two effects of a same cause: the progress of cupidity and an increasing concern to model oneself "per fas et nefas" after those who have enriched themselves. Let us draw a comparison between what goes on here and what takes place at the other end of France, in the Department of Hérault. Since 1860, that is to say, since the time when its easy and rapid acquiring of wealth began, this Department, which used to be classed among the whitest, has become more and more shaded, until today it is one of the very darkest.

In this Department the District which has grown most wealthy, that of Montpellier, is the one which has grown the worst; and,

[1] Even countries which are rapidly acquiring wealth would also benefit themselves, when their increasing wealth is the fruit of labor. Twenty years ago the Breton Departments were reckoned among the thirty most criminal ones; today they are numbered among the thirty least criminal ones. And during this interval Brittany has been noted for the progress made in its agriculture.

within this District, the obvious centre [1] of criminal inflammation is the port of Cette, the most prosperous town of that part of the country. "It may be said that three-quarters of the inhabitants of the Department of Hérault are individuals who suddenly became very wealthy." In this case you will say, what part can the influence of the great cities play, and especially that of Paris? A larger part than one would suppose.[2] Too rapid acquiring of wealth is a sort of higher change of class, which is no less dangerous for the individual taken out of his class than is the other sort, and which is far more dangerous for the public. Now, there are men out of their class of this sort as of the other sorts. The great city or the example of the great city draws them and dazzles them; the example of Paris especially, where persons of this sort out of their class abound more than anywhere else, because, nowhere else does speculation, which is often fraudulent, result in such large or such quickly acquired fortunes.

Furthermore, this must not make us forget the part, in fact ever a preponderating one, played by custom and tradition, by paternal and hereditary examples, in the particular aspect with which the vicious or delictual manifestations of each province, even the most *modernized* of them, are clothed. One never models oneself after the urban stranger to such an extent that one does not still more resemble one's father, who was himself previously modeled after the noble or the cleric who lived near him. We must therefore combine these two sorts of imitation of the superior in order to have an approximately complete idea of the reality. In Normandy, for example, the criminality and the immorality of the peasants of our day remind us to an astonishing degree, in many of their characteristics, of the disorders of the Norman clergy, regular and irregular, as they are brought back to us in so temperate a manner by the pastoral visits of the Archbishop Eudes Rigaud in the thirteenth century.[3] These joyous Chapters, these shrewd monasteries, through which this holy man conducts us, ought rather to have had a Rabelais for a visitor. Drunkenness and luxury, indolence and violence, greedy epicureanism and cupidinous laziness were already the cause of all

[1] See *Henry Joly, loc. cit.*

[2] Assuredly we should also take into account the part played by immigration of foreign workmen and of alcoholism, as in the case of the Department of Bouches-du-Rhône.

[3] "Registrum visitationum archiepiscopi Rothomagensis," (Rouen, 1852, *in quarto*).

their faults. They were great gamblers, rather litigious, but not very vindictive for the period, and still less hospitable and charitable. These characteristics have remained the same deep down, in spite of the change of appearances. Instead of cider and alcohol they used then to get drunk on wine. Their luxuries consisted among the monks in sometimes having shirts, often cushions and curtains of striped serge; among the nuns in wearing girdles with iron ornaments on them.

We have made some progress since those times. Both monks and nuns, at least before the appointment of the pious bishop and at the beginning of his episcopacy, had numerous bastards, just as their great-grand-nephews do. On the other hand, it is noticeable that nowhere did Eudes Rigaud find the convents filled; where there should have been twenty monks, there were twelve or fifteen at the most. It is quite clear that the priors, from an eminently egotistical reckoning of an economical order,[1] sought to limit their spiritual family as much as possible, just as the Norman fathers of present times seek to limit their carnal family, at least their legitimate one. In fact, this monastic Malthusianism has more than one analogy with existing Malthusianism and, like the latter, does not hinder an increase in the number of illegitimate children. I will pass over many other similarities of this same kind. The result of all this seems to be that, from the Middle Ages down to our own times, the Norman has remained about the same, perhaps after the image of the classes who used formerly to rule him and whose influence still persists in the effects produced by more recent models.

There are still provinces in France where this influence does not play any very striking part. The Departments of the central mountain range, especially that of Lozère, show dark shades which are in disadvantageous contrast with the general whiteness of the country of the plains. We must be careful not to confuse the offenses of these mountainous regions, an abiding place for the old morality, with those of the urban regions. Imitation of the superior still takes place in them under its old form which is aristocratic or domestic. The father who is religious, violent, vindictive, and more often than not a poacher, and in this himself an imitator of his former leaders the lords,[2] is the type after which the son is

[1] This calculation appears very clearly in certain places, especially page 92.

[2] As is observed by Joly, Lozère numbers, in spite of the small number of its inhabitants, more offenses related to hunting and fishing than any other Department.

modeled, and to a certain extent this criminality of the mountaineers, which is chastely savage, all revenge and anger, may be considered as a consequence and a vulgarization of the feudal criminality, such as the "Grands jours d'Auvergne" have shown it to be. Corsica is included within the same category. Brittany could also have been included, before the contemporaneous improvement in its morality.

But this archaic form of criminality is perceptibly on the decline, and wherever on the chart we see the shading becoming darker, we may be sure that imitation of rural ancestors has had its place taken by imitation of urban strangers or urbanized neighbors. If in dealing with the whole of a large country such as France, we could split up the rough totals of statistics into their real and vital elements, we would plainly see, as Joly so well expresses it, that beneath these figures there are in reality a thousand little hearths of unperceived contagion or of beneficial effects no less hidden, which have been lighted or extinguished here and there, in some commune or some village. The rise and fall established by the statistician are no more than the algebraic sum of these small positive and negative quantities. Then we ought to recognize the importance of the imitation of a superior. It will be seen that each one of these hearths is a social superiority of a good or bad standard, a fortune or an esteem well or badly acquired, which come to light among a population up to this time buried in the routine of their traditional vices or virtues. But it will also be perceived that, if these hearths appear to have sprung up spontaneously, this spontaneity is only apparent. The very coincidence of their similar appearance shows that they have borrowed their first flame or spark from some central fire, which is called the great city.[1]

[1] The contagious influence of Paris is very perceptible in the Department of Creuse. This Department, if only the offenses committed within it by its sedentary population are taken into account, is to be distinguished by its whiteness. If one counts the convictions pronounced outside of its limits, that is to say, in Paris, against its population of masons who are periodically emigrating and of which an ever increasing proportion goes to live in Paris, it will descend to the forty-seventh place. It has been since 1865 and especially since 1864 that these workmen have given up all idea of returning to their domicile of origin. The annual number of arrests of workmen coming from Creuse, which take place in Paris, has increased during the interval from 1860 to 1886 from 172 to 543. — With regard to the Department of Haute-Vienne, this number has increased during this same period from 78 to 268; for the Department of Seine-Inférieure, from 304 to 1057; for the Department of Vosges, from 98 to 371, etc. One will be able to judge of the extent of the moral ravages due to this cause, when one finds that only one-third, or approxi-

§ 68. (VI) Criminality of great cities. Progress of homicide. Murder because of greed alone. Rape and indecent assaults upon adults and upon children. Abortion and infanticide. Alleged law of inversion between crimes against property and crimes against persons. Both increase in the same proportion in great cities. At the same time civilization improves mankind. How can this be reconcilable?

The study of the criminality peculiar to great cities of contemporary times is thus brought especially to our attention as the least uncertain means of learning about the future criminality of States. Now, criminal statistics upon this point are not very reassuring. At the same time we must not be too greatly alarmed. As a matter of fact, the capitals are an aristocracy in process of formation, as is shown by their rapid growth. From 1836 to 1866 the population of Paris doubled, while that of France increased by one-eighth. Like every growing aristocracy, they have the fever which accompanies growth; they abandon themselves with frenzy to every excess, to every extravagance. Their infatuation is displayed with the hypocritical enthusiasm of which they are the object. But every aristocracy, once it has become established and has grown up, becomes wise, and when their superiority in rank begins to wane, their virtues are revealed; there is nothing which can equal the charm of intercourse with them when they have lost their power. After the time of Louis XIV, the nobility and the clergy of France, having come under the royal yoke, began to set an example of gentle and peaceful habits. It must certainly have been imitated like that of their politeness, and this beneficial effect, which is fitted to destroy in a great measure the moral evil which was imputable to the upper classes in the past, will perhaps explain to us why, on the eve of the Revolution, the criminality of France, excepting in times of want and famine, and outside of regions demoralized by the scourge of poaching, seems to have been very slight. "Brigands and robbers in France became more and more scarce in the eighteenth century," at this time "the safety of the high roads astonished English travelers," [1] especially Young.

It will, perhaps, some day be like this with our aristocrat-capitals, after some successful insurrection of the provinces. For capitals, like aristocracies, work unconsciously towards

mately, of the population of Paris is born in Paris. (Upon all these points see *Joly, loc. cit.*)

[1] *Babeau,* "La vie rurale dans l'ancienne France."

making themselves useless and inoffensive, by the very prolonging of their action. Depopulated, ruined, powerless, but not stripped of their former halo of glory, they will keep the supremacy in art and taste, the prestige of honor, which survives the overthrow of a nobility. Their best flowering, aesthetic and pure, will be reserved until their decline. Such was Athens vanquished under the Roman Empire; such in her turn was Rome, after the barbarian invasion. In the meantime, it must be admitted that, from the point of view of vice and crime, they offer a sad spectacle. No doubt, as Mayr points out in their favor in his "Statistica e vita sociale," they can make the excuse that, in their case, the proportion of adults from eighteen to fifty years of age, that is to say of a suitable age for crime as well as for action, is very perceptibly greater than in the country, where, on the contrary, the number of old persons and children is proportionately greater.

But this is only an extenuating circumstance, assuming that it is not an aggravating circumstance; it is really not worth while for the great cities to draw to themselves the most active and strongest part of the nation, if it be only to direct that force and that activity along the paths of evil. Over and above all this the difference pointed out is, though significant, not sufficient to justify that between the various sorts of criminality which I have been comparing. In the first place, in so far as crimes properly so called are concerned, that is cases taken before a jury, if we, like Bournet,[1] draw up a table of crimes against property and a table of crimes against the person showing on each of them, by means of three distinct curves, the annual number of accused persons from 1826 to 1882: first, in the whole of France; second, in the rural communes; third, in urban surroundings, that is to say in every agglomeration of more than two thousand souls, we find that, whereas the first curve and especially the second one have gradually been lowered during the course of this half century, the third one has been gradually getting higher *in both tables* at once. Moreover I ought to point out that the decrease in the number of crimes, even in the country, is a deception of statistics and does not in any way indicate an actual decrease of criminality in the true sense of the word. Many acts called crimes by the Code of 1810 have been classed as misdemeanors by later laws, and to this legislative changing of a crime to a misdemeanor is added the daily in-

[1] "La criminalité en France et en Italie," (1884), pp. 103 *et. seq.*

creasing habit of carrying out this same change judicially, practiced at the bars with the assent of the courts and the prisoners.[1]

Taking advantage of this observation I may add that if, still following Bournet, we study separately the criminality of the Department of the Seine, in other words of Paris, from 1826 to 1882, we are struck by a remarkable fact, not very likely, it seems to me, to confirm the hypothesis of the necessary amelioration of morals by the progress of civilization; which fact is the increase in the number of crimes of a bloodthirsty nature.[2] They have become almost three times as numerous in Paris while they have decreased by one-third in the country and increased slightly in the other cities. Without going so far back as 1826, I find that in 1857 there took place five murders and nine assassinations in Paris, that in 1887 there took place sixteen murders and thirty-six assassinations, and that during this interval we have a series of figures between these two, increasing irregularly, but nevertheless increasing, and more rapidly as one can see, than the increase in the population of Paris.[3] Now let us compare this result with that shown by violent criminality in the whole of France between 1856 and 1880. In order to eliminate a disturbing element which has often affected the accuracy of calculations of this nature, I have been careful to deduct the figures covering Corsica. Having made this deduction, I have found that the five years from 1856 to 1860 gave a total of 1299 murders and assassinations, and that the five years from 1876 to 1880 raised this number to 1533.[4]

[1] I will refer the reader for proof of this fact to my "Criminalité comparée."

[2] In his "Contribution a l'étude de la statistique de la criminalité de 1826 à 1880," (1884), *Socquet*, in spite of his inclination to plead the cause of the cities, admits on page 17, that "violent criminality has considerably decreased in the country and greatly increased in cities." He speaks of "great" criminality in the legal sense of the word, and we know what must be understood by its purely apparent decrease, we also know that its increase, where it does make its appearance, is for some reasons even greater in reality than in appearance.

[3] See various years of the "Compte général de l'Administration de la justice criminelle en France." (National Printing Office.)

[4] This applies to our neighbors, be it understood, as well as to ourselves. Illing, a high secret counsellor of the regency, has undertaken the task of proving the increase of criminality in Prussia. He has had no difficulty in doing so. Furthermore, says *Georges Dubois* on this subject in the "Bulletin de la Société des prisons" (1886, p. 874), "all the functionaries of the penitentiary administration, civil employees and ministers of religion, agree in recognizing [in Prussia as in France] that the moral evil of which criminality is the unfortunate expression is developed, *not only through the increase in the number of crimes, but also through the intensity of the perversion which these crimes reveal.*"

This is an increase of about one-fifth while violent criminality in Paris trebled, that is to say, passed from 14 to 45.

This would lead one to suppose that the actual increase is far greater than the apparent increase. I must point out one thing which, although a very simple matter, seems to have escaped the statisticians. In order to ascertain whether the number of homicides, thefts, or other misdeeds had increased or diminished from one period to another, it was deemed sufficient at one time to look up the number of judicial sentences bearing upon these offenses, without stopping to realize that, even though followed by an acquittal, cases of this sort none the less showed the carrying out of a delictual act, committed, it is true, by some person other than the person accused or the person apprehended. But did this matter, from the point of view of morality or immorality generally? In our day this has been felt, and now it is the number of accusations or apprehensions, and not of convictions, which is consulted.

However, does this suffice? Certainly not. As a matter of fact, today, just as previously, no account is taken in the calculation of any offenses excepting those which have resulted in a prosecution before the courts, either at the instigation of the public prosecutor directly, or by virtue of a mandate of transfer given by the examining magistrate or an order of transfer made by the chamber of indictment.[1] But how many complaints and examinations there are, which, although setting forth a very serious crime or misdemeanor, such as an assassination, a murder, a considerable theft, finally end in being classed as not prosecuted, in the pigeonholes of the public prosecutor's office, or at least in a decree of no ground for prosecution. All this must therefore be included in the sum total of criminality if an accurate rendering of it is required. This has never been done so far as we know.

Now, if this gap be filled in, here is what is found. In the first place, the total number of crimes and misdemeanors which have not been prosecuted as stated above has constantly increased. Its average figure per annum, for the five years from 1846 to 1850, was 114,014; for the period from 1861 to 1865, 134,554; for the period from 1876 to 1880, 194,740; and for the period from 1881 to 1885, 225,630. If we analyze these figures, we shall find that the yearly average of assassinations which got no further than the threshold of the courts was, from 1861 to 1865, 217; from

[1] [This corresponds to the Grand Jury in America and England. — Transl.]

1876 to 1880, 231; from 1881 to 1885, 253; that the yearly average of murders was for the first of these periods 223, for the second 322, and for the third 322; that for the same periods the average number of wilful blows and wounds inflicted and not prosecuted, was successively 12,000, 16,397, 18,234; that of cases of arson (wilful or supposed to be accidental) 12,683, 13,186, 16,470; that of thefts 41,369, 62,223, 71,769; that of swindlings 4044, 5998, 7633; that of abuses of confidence 3336, 6453, 17,760; that of forgeries 373, 696, 637; let us add that of public outrages of decency, 800, 1087, 1088; of outrages committed against public officers, 1843, 2669, 2217, etc.

Now let us add together, for each one of the periods covered, the average number of crimes or misdemeanors for which sentence was pronounced and for which sentence was not pronounced. Here is the number of crimes and misdemeanors for which sentence was not passed, for the successive five year periods from 1861 to 1865, 1876 to 1880, and 1881 to 1885: assassinations, 175, 197, 216; murders, 105, 143, 186; blows and wounds, 15,520, 18,446, 20,851; simple theft, 30,087, 33,381, 35,466; swindling, 3314, 2993, 3502; abuse of confidence, 2800, 3378, 3696, etc.[1] Now add together the two series of real averages. The total will be:

Assassinations . . .	392	428	469	(Let us add, in 1887, 433)
Murders.	328	465	508	*600*
Blows and wounds .	27520	32843	39082	41039
Simple theft	71456	95604	*107235*	*105344*
Swindling	7358	8991	*11135*	*11689*
Abuse of confidence	6136	9831	*15456*	*16048*

I omit the other figures which are no less significant. The ones given will be sufficient to make us appreciate the pretended decrease in the number of bloodthirsty crimes in our time, there being no doubt as to the enormous increase in the number of offenses of a crafty or sensual nature. Now, the rapidly increasing progress of crimes of violence themselves, as is shown from the figures pointed out, ought beyond a doubt to be imputed to the great cities. In fact, on the one hand, we know that, in so far

[1] The series is thus carried on during the following years, 1886, 1887, 1888: assassinations, 234, 234, 214; murders, 174, 186, 179; blows and wounds, 22,069, 21,065, 21,842; simple theft, 34,457, 35,349, 37,505; swindles, 3595, 3581, 3718; abuses of confidence, 3824, 3919, 4040, etc. It is rather a surprising thing to see certain newspapers following the "Journal officiel" of January 31, 1891, praising results of this kind. The paper "Le Matin" of February 12, 1891, emphasizes these figures in order to bring out once more the current error relative to the pretended decrease of criminality on a large scale.

as cases in which sentence is pronounced are concerned, the proportionate share contributed by these great cities is larger; on the other hand, it must seem extremely probable that, in so far as cases in which sentence is not pronounced are concerned, this same thing applies "a fortiori." The increase in the latter could not be accounted for if it were only rural populations which were being considered. It is especially in the great cities that conditions favorable to the "incognito" or the flight of malefactors are found and are more numerous.

Let us dispose of an objection which is only one of detail. It may be said that, among the homicides which are not prosecuted, a certain number have not been prosecuted because it has been shown that they were neither crimes nor misdemeanors. This is true; but on the other hand, among the deaths reputed to be accidental, the number of which has increased more than three-fold in the last fifty-eight years,[1] and among the suicides which have increased from 1759 in 1827 to 7902 in 1885, and 8202 in 1887, how many concealed homicides have there been! If we admit that during this half century the proportion of mistakes in calculation has remained the same, we ought to admit that, assuming only (and this is very little) *one* homicide wrongly classed among a *thousand* accidental deaths or suicides, the increase under this head would be very perceptible. But I calculate it to have been far greater.

Again how many true suicides there are which, true suicides though they be and in another sense, are in reality murders! How many unfortunates who kill themselves are killed as well by treacherous competitors or able swindling speculators who have ruined them, by the slanderers who have disgraced them, by all

[1] From 1781 in 1826–30 the annual average number of accidental deaths has gradually increased to 13,309, in 1881–85. Perhaps there has been a tendency too hastily to attribute to the increase in the number of machines, to the feverishness of progress, this enormous increase. I understand that the development of railroads has caused the number of accidents which are directly due to them to increase from 25 in the period 1841–45 to 366 in the period 1876–80, that the progress of urban circulation has caused the number of dead bodies found in the streets to increase from 873 in the period 1836–40 to 2619 in the period 1876–80. But why in the period 1840–80 has the number of deaths called accidental *through drowning* almost doubled, increasing from 2887 to 4130? At any rate let us admit that on the average *one* death called accidental out of one hundred is a hidden crime, and we will see how greatly this will increase the number of homicides. Let us add that, from 1830 to 1889, the number of unidentified bodies received at the Morgue slowly increased from 325 to 906 (*Macé*, Mon Musée criminel").

those honest contemporary assassins who from a distance, unseen and unpunished, strike down their victims! [1]

Furthermore, the number of murders and assassinations is of less account than the motives which may have inspired them.[2] Their motive has changed in France and consequently has greatly changed their nature. The proportion of murders and assassinations due to greed, according to the official report of 1880, has almost doubled: from 1826 to 1880, it rose from thirteen per cent to twenty-two per cent; the proportion of those which have arisen out of domestic discussions has undergone a similar increase from fourteen per cent to twenty-one per cent, whereas homicides due to revenge decreased from thirty-one to twenty-five per cent.

Now, is it not especially in the great cities, where more often than not the murderer and his victim are unacquainted with each other, that greed is what inspires murder or assassination? From this point of view, the Department of the Seine and that of Corsica are the exact opposite of each other; and there is nothing in common between the murderers and the assassins of these two French Departments excepting their name, between the vindictive and rural homicide of the one, and the greedy and urban homicide of the other. The latter sort occurs more frequently, as is inevitable. But, however striking the contrast may be, it is none the less true that the same law of imitation of the superior by the inferior accounts for these two opposed terms. In fact, it is a mistake to look upon the cult of family vengeance, bequeathed by heredity, as a primitive sentiment, innate in man; nothing is more inconsistent with the careless and forgetful character of savages than this tenacious and persevering remembering of an injury. Just as an immediate revenge is natural, so is revenge after the expiration of a long time unnatural. The intense domestic pride, which is shown by the "vendetta," could only have been a privilege of the aristocracy in the beginning. That is why the people of olden times, who created their divinity after the image of their leaders, looked upon revenge as the will of the gods. To be steadfast in seeking a collective revenge is, in societies which are still barbarian and even among three quarters of the civilized world, a manner of being ennobled. Assassinations from motives of revenge are very

[1] This is all the more probable and the number of suicide-homicides of this nature should be increased, according to statistics, in the same proportion as that of suicides due to financial losses or domestic losses increases.

[2] "Compte général de l'administration de la justice criminelle en France," 1880.

frequent in Corsica, in Sardinia, and in Spain, only because the family spirit has remained remarkably strong in those countries. But as this solidarity of ancient origin is dissolved by the individualism of modern and urban origin, the need of enjoyment is substituted for that of making oneself respected or feared, the need of money for that of vengeance. It is therefore not surprising that in capitals homicide from motives of greed should flourish.

But, among crimes against the person, it is rape or indecent assault upon children which ought especially to be charged up against great centres. With an uninterrupted regularity, a thing which distinguishes the statistics of every imitative propagation,[1] the annual number of these abominable crimes has increased in France from 136 in 1836 to 791 in 1880; it has become five times as great. Socquet (*op. cit.*) is compelled to acknowledge that this enormous increase applies principally to cities, and especially that the share contributed by cities in the matter of this crime is far greater than that contributed by rural districts. The Departments which here rank first, taking their population into consideration, are those which include the great centres, those of Seine, Nord, Seine-Inférieure, Gironde, Rhône, Bouches-du-Rhône, etc. The rural Departments rank last.[2] This is an essentially masculine and senile crime, as well as an essentially urban one; the more it increases, the more, it seems, does the age of those committing it increase; the proportion of persons accused sixty years of age and over is on the increase, and shows the effects of a pathological cause. But is it not because libertine habits, under the sway of urban excitation, have become general and firmly rooted among youths and mature men that middle aged and old men are more and more given to this monstrous aberration of the sexual instincts,[3] which is the result of a life of debauchery?

[1] In the same way this regularity is to be observed each time a new product, or a new industrial article is placed in circulation and is carried from one person to another. The relative statistics of the sale of this article, for example, of smoking tobacco, coffee, etc., increase so regularly that one can foresee what the progress will be in the future. If there are any doubts as to the imitative character of suicide, and as to the part played by imitation even in madness, it would only be necessary to observe the regular rise of the curve of suicides and cases of mental alienation.

[2] See the thesis of *Paul Bernard*, a pupil of Lacassagne, "Les attentats à la pudeur sur les petites filles," (Lyons, Storck, 1887).

[3] The last few years have shown a slight decrease in this crime, but it would be rash to base any serious hope upon a numerical oscillation which is perhaps accidental, and which perhaps is also merely apparent, this crime being one of

A thing which at first sight seems surprising is that indecent assaults upon adults have slightly decreased (from 137 to 108), whereas indecent assaults upon children less than fourteen years old have increased five-fold. What does this signify? This decrease has, at bottom, the same meaning as this increase. As a matter of fact, committed without any violence, that is to say with the consent of the object of them, upon persons more than thirteen years of age classed as adults, these same acts, which would be prosecuted as assaults if they had been accompanied by violence, are not prosecuted under the law. Now, there can be no doubt, according to the increasing number of attacks upon children, but that adults also are subjected to attacks which are more and more numerous. If this is so, the decrease in the number of prosecutions for assaults upon adults simply proves that adults offer less and less resistance, being affected by the surrounding depravity. The increase in the number of assaults upon children does not, moreover, warrant us in thinking that children offer more resistance; the contrary is proved by the indulgence of the jury with regard to this crime in particular, for the testimony of the victim is more often than not favorable to the accused. But in this case consent does not prevent a prosecution.

The rather large proportion of crimes or offenses committed by minors of both sexes is another characteristic trait of urban criminality. The precocity of young people in the matter of vices as in the matter of talent and aptitude of every kind is greater, as we know, in the great cities than in the fields. This is to be accounted for by the remarkable sensitiveness of youth to the effects of imitation. We can thus attribute to the increasing influence of the great centres the ever growing contingent contributed to the supply of crime by delinquents from sixteen to twenty-one years of age. The number of boys of this age accused or inculpated has quadrupled in less than fifty years: from 5933 in 1831, it has increased to 20,480 in 1880. The number of girls of this same age has been almost trebled; it has increased during this same period of time from 1046 to 2830. This *progress* has continued. In 1885 the number of boys amounted to 25,539, and that of girls to 3149. To be quite frank, this is appalling.[1]

those which allow the courts the greatest latitude in estimating them. If the wave of indulgence which is coming over the public should be felt, even by magistrates, it is not surprising that at the present time they should *class, as not to be prosecuted,* a number of cases which would, a few years ago, have given rise to a prosecution.

[1] England, in this respect, as in many others, is advantageously distinguished

On the whole, what is shown by all these figures is the voluptuousness, the increasing dissoluteness of our customs. The increasing number of abortions and infanticides confirms this inference. With regard to abortion, it is so difficult to discover it that any pretensions to stating it in figures are rather chimerical. However, let us observe that through unaccountable oscillations, it still perceptibly increases (8 in 1826, 20 in 1880), and that out of one million rural inhabitants there were found, from 1876 to 1880, four accused of this crime, whereas, out of one million inhabitants of cities, there were fourteen.[1]

Infanticide escapes the investigation of the law far less often than does abortion; also, since at least 1831, it progressively ascends without interruption until 1863 (average number from 1831 to 1835, 94; average number from 1856 to 1860, 214), and although, after this date, it is slightly lowered, this is owing to the law of 1863, which changes into a mere misdemeanor called suppression of children facts which previously would have been classed as infanticide. Furthermore, the decrease is slight and followed by an increase (average number from 1856 to 1860, 186; average number from 1876 to 1880, 194).[2] I am perfectly aware that, according to our statistics, for an equal number of rural inhabitants and of urban inhabitants the country plays a greater part in this crime than do the cities. But it is according to the place of the child's birth whether rural or urban that the accused are thus classified, without taking into account their residence in the country or the city before their crime. How many girl mothers are there born among the fields who would not have become criminals had they never lived in some city? Even without moving, how many country people there are who are subject in everything to the inspiration, the suggestion of cities!

Once more statistics are here no more than hieroglyphics which we have to decipher by the aid of our knowledge acquired from

from the Continent. From a statistical table given by *Colajanni* (see his "Sociologia criminale" Vol. II, pp. 77–95), it appears that, in this island country the proportion of male minors, during the period from 1861 to 1881 has decreased from 7373 to 4688, and that of female minors, from 1428 to 795. The same exceptional decrease is to be observed in Spain. We should also note that the fewer children people have, the worse is their bringing up. In England, families have remained sturdy and numerous.

[1] *Socquet, op. cit.*, see especially on this subject the "Recherches sur l'avortement criminel," by *Gaillot*, pupil of Lacassagne, (Lyons, 1884).

[2] "Compte général de l'administration dé la justice criminelle en France," 1880.

other sources. The increase of infanticide is so closely connected with that of immorality, the acknowledged field of which is urban life, that it is not permissible to attribute to this crime, whatever may have been the birthplace of its perpetrators, a rural origin.

It would be a mistake to believe, as do several prominent members of the Italian positivist school, that a law of inversion governs the mutual relations between crimes against the person and crimes against property, and that, where one sort increases the other decreases. As far as France is concerned, the charts of Yvernès, together with his official report upon criminal statistics from 1826 to 1880, show, Department by Department, a perceptible concordance, rather than any disagreement, between the geographical distribution of these two sorts of crimes. Neither do the tables of Von Liszt for the German Empire[1] show this sort of antagonism which has been imagined. Between these two sorts of criminality there is a direct and not an inverse ratio. As to Italy, Bodio has drawn up very detailed charts[2] which, if examined attentively, do not offer any support to the theory of his fellow-countrymen. I see by them, for example, that, colored white on the chart of "omicidi," the region about Siena is also colored white on the chart of "reati contra la proprietà," that the province of Rome shows more or less dark shading, but always dark, on both charts, just as do Sardinia, Sicily, etc. Corsica, it is true, seems to confirm the ingenious proposition with which we are dealing; all black on the murder chart, it is all white on the theft chart. But this is a good example to give of the illusions to which statistics lay us open.

One might think, according to these charts, that this island is the Department of France where property is most respected. There is no Department where it is less respected. One seventh of the territory of this island only consists of forests and thickets because of the obstacles placed in the way of the cultivation of the soil by inveterate habits of plunder and marauding. I can say the same thing of Paris, to which I will now return after this detour. Crimes against property appear to have diminished by one half (the annual average, from 519 in 1825 to 1827 dropped to 261 in 1876 to 1882). But let us take into account the laws of 1832 and 1862, which classed as misdemeanors so many former crimes, and the judicial changing of a crime into a misdemeanor,

[1] "Archives de l'Anthropologie criminelle," No. 2. Charts are given with

[2] "Archives de l'Anthropologie criminelle," No. 5.

which shows a very marked preference for crimes against property. Now let us look at the table of misdemeanors; we shall find that the number of simple thefts — among which many are to be found, the aggravating circumstances of which the prosecuting magistrates have not thought it best to reveal — has kept on increasing in Paris, as well as the number of swindles and abuses of confidence.[1] A few indications will suffice. From 1865 to 1885, the number of thefts increased, almost regularly, from 3205 to 5364; the number of swindles from 532 to 803; the number of abuses of confidence from 921 to 983.

On the whole, the prolonged effect of large cities upon criminality is manifested, it seems to us, in the slow substitution, not exactly of guile for violence, but of greedy, crafty, and voluptuous violence for vindictive and brutal violence. Through them, through the fever of pleasures which they stimulate, every intense civilization, unless care be taken, will inevitably run to a conflict of appetites, mortal enemies of one another. How can we be astonished that they imprint their stamp upon crime? How can we wonder even that they stimulate it? They act as a stimulus for madness, and what is more, for genius, that other pretended nervous affection, into which nature most certainly enters far more than it does into the producing of criminal "neurosis." In his "Uomo di genio,"[2] a curious book, as bulky and no less interesting than his "Uomo delinquente," Lombroso has placed a chart of Italy showing the geographical distribution of talent and of artistic genius in the peninsula. The thing which strikes me is their distribution around the old capitals, Florence, Rome, Genoa, Milan, Parma, Palermo, Venice, etc. It is exceedingly probable that this is the same in all countries. In our own it is certain that the result of the statistics of Jacoby is that the number of remarkable men furnished by each Department is directly connected with the density of their population and the proportional importance of their urban population. This is not the only good side of the urban medal; but what an obverse it has![3]

[1] See the various volumes of the "Compte général de l'administration de la justice criminelle en France."

[2] Under this title *Lombroso* published (1888) the fifth edition greatly enlarged of "Genio e follia."

[3] A fact which, were it clearly proved and based upon sufficient statistics would be one which would reassure us, is the decrease in *military criminality*. This is a new subject upon which *Corre* ("Archives de l'Anthropologie criminelle," March 15, 1891) is one of the first to have ventured. He devoted himself to showing numerically the offenses which were exclusively military and offenses of the com-

In spite of all this, our thought would be misinterpreted if it were deduced from it that in our opinion civilization, necessarily, drives man to madness and depravity.

Although vengeance may be a nobler motive than self-interest, it is a menace to the security of persons and property in quite another way. If we compare the barbarian phase with the civilized phase of a society, we ought to congratulate ourselves upon having been born during the latter. Scotland, during the time of the clan feuds, was one of the most bloodstained lands in Europe; today this country is a shining example because of the exceptional mildness of its customs.[1] Since Italy has positively and absolutely become a part of the stream of modern life, bloodthirsty crimes as well as those against property are found to be decreasing in number year by year; this is proved by the statistical tables of Bodio. Spain in becoming modernized has shown the same result. The two charts of the geography of crime, already mentioned, of Von Liszt, show a gradual darkening of the shading in Germany as one passes from west to north, that is to say from the most enlightened and wealthiest regions to the oriental and Slavonic portion where comparative ignorance and poverty prevail. In the matter of crimes against property as well as those against persons (leaving aside any consideration of motive), these latter

mon law. Setting aside the former, which are also important from our point of view, and of which moreover the proportion has itself decreased by about one-third in the last fifty years, he found that the French army showed one common crime or offense in 1839 for every 466 men, in 1849 for every 483 men, in the period 1865–66 for every 436 men, and in the period 1885–86 for every 738 men. This improvement is certainly due to the service having been made compulsory for everybody. Before this the power of substitution encumbered the regiments with substitutes recruited from the dregs of the population. In proportion as the distinction between the nation and the army came to be done away with, it was natural to expect to see the characteristics peculiar to the army, whether good or bad, lose their prominence. Military criminality, just as military suicide — if not the military duel — has thus decreased. Now although in spite of its decrease it may still be greater than that of the rest of the nation, though this is disputed by Corre, we must nevertheless be rejoiced that this new advance has already become so marked, at least in France. In fact, the prestige of the army in our democracies has become no less contagious than that of capitals, and has shared with the latter the heritage of the nobility of the Old Régime. The true aristocracy of our day are the officers of our regiments who are obeyed and imitated by everybody more and more, everybody being or having been a soldier. The distinction between the *soldier* and the *civilian* corresponds to a certain extent to that between the *inhabitant of the city* and the *inhabitant of the country*. A regiment is a very compact and very well ordered town.

[1] Out of 100,000 inhabitants, Italy numbered from ten to eleven homicides in 1880, Spain numbered from seven to eight, France from one to two, and Scotland *less than one-half*.

provinces, having but recently emerged from barbarism, show a larger number than do the western and northern provinces. Even Berlin, for a capital, presents a moderate criminality,[1] excepting in so far as outrages against morals are concerned, in which matter naturally it ranks first, just as Paris does in France.

In glancing over the comparative criminal statistics of Europe,[2] we at once perceive that the most bloodthirsty countries are the least civilized ones; southern Italy, southern Spain, Hungary, etc. This has also been the case, it would seem, in the past. During the Middle Ages, Germany was the least civilized country in Europe. It was also one of the most criminal. Male criminality, in fact, must have been truly appalling in Germany; for we have been given, with regard to female criminality in the same country and at the same time, the following admission of Conrad Celte, a publicist of the fifteenth century; after having spoken of the frightful punishments to which women were subjected (sewn up in sacks alive and buried under the earth, walled up alive, etc.) he adds: "All these penalties and all these tortures do not prevent their heaping crime upon crime; their perverse minds are more fruitful in imagining new crimes than are those of the judges in thinking of new punishments."

How then are we to reconcile the improvement in morals which everywhere is a result of civilization with the demoralization aroused by the example of great cities, the summits and the sources of civilization? The contradiction can, I believe, be reduced to an ambiguity. But before attempting to smooth away this difficulty, we ought to consider a few developments, after which

[1] "Archives de l'Anthropologie criminelle," No. 2, p. 187 and No. 5. *Bodio's* table of the international statistics of criminality. See also the substantial pamphlet of *Bosco* on "Gli Omicidii in alcuni stati d'Europa" (Rome, 1880).

[2] According to *Wyzewa*, however ("Revue des Deux Mondes," May 1, 1891, "La vie et les mœurs en Allemagne"), there has been in process of formation for the past twenty years in Berlin a new society of business men of untrustworthy financiers of officials and employees, who with the army of working-men have introduced new habits which "now spread from man to man through the rest of the Empire." The old peaceful and honest society has ebbed.

The example of the capital of Germany having become so contagious, it is well to look at the new aspect with which crime has been clothed.

"The army of crime is, in Berlin, a real army, with an organization which is entirely military. In this respect, as in the case of the Fire Department and the Postoffice and Tramways, Berlin will soon become the foremost of cities: there is not a single kind of swindling in Europe or America which is not practised by eminent specialists, allied together, as is necessary for persons acting in concert."

The police are left behind by crime; they have remained traditional and old-fashioned.

it will be smoothed away of its own accord. This problem, which has been so much discussed, of the relations which exist between the progress of civilization and the movement or the change in criminality, will have to be stated before it can be solved. We will state it in another way. Criminality always being, in its characteristic form and its realization in fact, a phenomenon of imitative propagation, the question is, whether the many other phenomena of imitative propagation, which taken all together are called civilization — academic diffusion of knowledge, domestic or ecclesiastical diffusion of beliefs and rites, diffusion of political ideas by the newspapers, diffusion of the requirements of consumption through contact with comrades, diffusion of industrial or artistic aptitudes and talents, by the life of the studio, the office, the trade, etc. — foster or impede the progress of the propagation of crime. Or rather, the aim is to discover, if that were possible, which among these various spreadings of example which are called instruction, religion, politics, commerce, industry, are the ones that foster, and which the ones that impede, the expansion of crime.

§ 69. (VII) By means of another of the laws of imitation; the law of insertion, the alternate passing from fashion to custom, an irregular rhythm. Examples drawn from the history of languages, of religions, of industries. The same law applies to feelings of morality or immorality.

The manner in which we state the question already shows that in our opinion crime is a peculiar social fact, but after all a social fact like any other.[1] It is an off-shoot of the national tree, but a branch nourished by the common sap and subject to the laws which are common to all. We have seen that, taken by itself, it grows in conformity with the rule of imitation from *above* to *below*, just as do all the other fruitful and useful branches of the same trunk. We might have added that, again like them, it becomes changed or develops through the intermittent insertion of new buds or new grafts of *imitation-fashions* which come to replenish and nourish, sometimes to drive back, a stock of *imitation-*

[1] *Aristotle*, in his "Politics," expresses himself as follows: "The raising of flocks and herds, agriculture, *brigandage*, fishing and hunting, these are the means of *natural* industry available to man for the procuring of his subsistence." If we concede to the economists that all wealth which is not acquired as the fruit of labor is the result of plunder, whether brutal or disguised in some manner, we can form an accurate idea of the enormously important part played by crime in the social functions.

customs, but they themselves have a tendency to take root, to swell the legacy of custom and tradition. Every industry feeds itself in this manner by means of an afflux of improvements, innovations today, traditions tomorrow. Every science, every art, every language, every religion, obeys this law of the passing from custom to fashion and the return from fashion to custom, but custom which has expanded. For with each step in advance taken by it the territorial domain of imitation becomes larger, the field of social assimilation and of human fraternity expands, and it is not, as we know, the least salutary effect of imitative cause from the point of view of morality.

Here a few explanations will be necessary. At the beginning, or rather at each beginning of history, what do we find? As many dialects, as many forms of worship, as many embryonic systems of law, as many industrial or artistic processes, as many standards of morality, let us add as many kinds of vices and crimes, as there are families or groups of families. And in the end, when the same whirlwind of civilization has for a long time commingled all these tribes, what do we find? A common language, a common religion, or a science in common, a common body of law, a common form of government, an industry in common, a common art, a common standard of morality, and finally, a standard of immorality and a criminality which are uniform, spread over the entire continent where the distinct elements used to exist in the beginning.[1]

How has this change taken place? If we observe its phases we shall see; for it is not enough to say that warfare and victory have in the long run resulted in this unity; they only aroused it. Conquest can account for the subjection but not for the assimilation of the vanquished; but by breaking down the barriers between the tribes which it amalgamates into towns, and later on those between the towns which it binds together into federations, and still later those between the federations which it organizes into States, and into States which become larger and larger, it opens the door, from century to century, to the prestige of the foreigner, which becomes superimposed upon the prestige of the ancestor.

Furthermore, the door never stays open very long to the

[1] On the other hand, although in the beginning it was found that everything differed according to locality, yet everything remained practically unchanged from one century to another, there were many differences but little differentiation; and in the end everything became uniform everywhere, but everything went through a rapid change: it seems as though the difference in time and the difference in space are the counterpart of each other.

invasion from outside, the infatuation for words, for gods, for laws, for trades, for maxims, for tastes, for vices, and for crimes which are external. One will always find a dialect, a religion, a body of law, a standard of morality, a form of aestheticism, a form of depravity or brigandage, after having extended its rule owing to this widening of its field, with jealousy shutting itself up behind ramparts which have become more extensive but once more insurmountable, and there becoming perpetuated through the sanction of custom alone. From this there arises that peculiar resistance offered by a local, provincial, or national dialect or worship, in the interval between salutary epidemics of fashion, to the importation of phrases or beliefs taken from its nearest neighbors. For example, in primitive Germania, before the invasion, each little people had its dialect, its vocabulary, its law, etc. The result of the invasion was to let loose upon these tribes themselves a current of *fashion* which compelled them to imitate the prestige of the vanquished. All their institutions then became partly Romanized or Christianized, as did their languages, under the influence of the universal impulse. Nevertheless it is true that their new religion, their new languages, their new civil and criminal law, etc., very soon became just as exclusively dear to them as the customs of their ancestors had been.

But I will pass over those Merovingian and Carolingian times which were so obscure, at the same time pointing out that the reign of Charlemagne is remarkable, like the period of the invasions, for a great overthrow of the inclosing walls of the law, politics, industry, and other matters, under the blows of a powerful agent of renovation. Afterwards the frontiers became once more established, and each nationality was again shut up within itself. But if by nationality is to be understood less a political division than a social reality, we shall see that, since the Merovingian age, nationalities, groups of individuals which have become sufficiently like one another, have already diminished in number and increased in extent.

The heroic period of the Crusades, before the time of Saint Louis, marks another great tornado of external imitation of every kind. This was the time when several new and broad streams of imitation, having their source in a number of inventions and discoveries of the greatest importance, for example of the rediscovery of the Roman law, of Aristotle partly exhumed, of the idea of the Gothic style of architecture or the heroic song, overflow and cover with their silt all local customs, all social philosophies or religions, all local styles of architecture and literature, drowning some and reviving others. Then follows a period of comparative rest under Saint Louis, when the kingdoms which have grown become separately organized, and when the great schools of jurisprudence, philosophy, architecture, and poetry become concentrated and limited, are transmitted and perpetuated in the same manner as a hereditary legacy, a national or regional tradition. The Renaissance, the discovery of America, and the Reformation put an end to this work of formation, and under their torrential deposit of countless novelties quickly transformed languages, beliefs, sciences, letters, arts, and commerce. Instead of a transformation there would have been an absolute overthrow, had not the seventeenth century come to bind up the sheaf of this harvest, and, as a traditional consolidation of its progress, sanction it. Then comes the eighteenth century, and, with the same enthusiasm but on a still larger scale, it takes up once more the work of the sixteenth. But already, in our own day, do we not feel that the flood of cosmopolitism raised by our French philosophers is subsiding, and that the end of our century is working to separate the nations, grown very large it is true, just as much as the age which preceded it had contributed towards uniting them?

To each branch or to each subdivision of social activity we ought separately to apply in detail the law of this irregular, but continuous, rhythm, were it not for the fact that this subject would lead us too far afield.[1] There would be many corollaries to be deduced from it; I will do no more than point out one of the most simple, but not the least worthy of notice from the point of view of the future of morality. A traveler who traverses a still savage or barbarian archipelago or continent everywhere meets with small groups of people, so greatly attached to their ancestral institutions that at first sight everything about them appears to be aboriginal. Each one of these groups is convinced that they have their own particular language exclusively their own, that they "drink in their very own glass" every religious, political, and artistic idea which they may have acquired.

However, in covering an extensive region, this traveler notices

[1] It would be a very poor interpretation of the facts to see in this rhythm an example of Spencer's rhythmic movement, that is to say, an action followed by a reaction. Let us be careful not to confuse *action* and *reaction*, the latter destroying the former, with *sowing* and *taking root*, the latter of these carrying on and forming the completion of the former.

that, in spite of the difference in race, the languages of these various peoples, today hermetically sealed, betray a common stock of roots, their religions a common stock of legends and mysteries, their arts a common stock of implements, methods, and subjects, etc. Should he desire, in the face of this remarkable similarity, to cling to the hypothesis of aboriginality from which he started, he will find great difficulty, as they did before the advent of Darwin,[1] in reconciling the resemblance between the species of a common genus, of a common family, or of a common order, with the hypothesis of their having been created independently. He will temporarily escape the difficulty by explaining all these correspondences of parts and analogies shown by the comparative anatomy of societies, by means of the presumed identity of human nature and the assumed invariableness of its necessary development in all times and at all places. But taken in detail this conception results in an absurdity, and it is contradicted by an observation of our civilized and half civilized nations, among whom we can establish similar correspondences of parts and analogies the cause of which is to us sufficiently clear.

It is with the energy befitting an ancestral custom that Catholicism, for centuries, has continued to exist in Ireland and Brittany; nevertheless we know the names of the missionaries who imported and spread it in those countries by the help of a great impulse of opinion hospitable to the foreigner, hostile to men's ancestors, similar to our revolutionary crises. Everywhere, in the whole world, the steam engine has been installed in workshops and factories of every kind which have become, in less than a century, local, hereditary, and ineradicable industries, in the very spot where the tourist sees them today. But we know that the steam engine came to us from Watt, that it spread little by little, starting with a little corner of England, and that, wherever workmen venerate it as an ancestor, it was at first received as an intruder. There has not been a single weaving machine, spinning machine, or sewing machine, which has not shared this same fate. National though it be in Germany, music was brought there from Italy; however Grecian Greek sculpture may be, Greece received the germ of it from the Orient or from Egypt; however original Etruscan art may have been, it was imported from Phoenicia.

[1] Let us observe in passing that the law of Malthus and Darwin, the tendency of each species to spread itself and also to vary indefinitely, without doubt requires a completion by means of a tendency, not contrary, but consecutive to and alternating with the former, a tendency to become fixed.

Many an expression, many a construction in our language, originally introduced from love of neologism, is only kept later on from love of archaism. There is not one literary innovation which, having become general, does not take on a classic appearance, otherwise called a traditional one.

It is useless to insist any further. We can draw the conclusion that every social matter, that is to say, all individual initiative, every special method of thought, feeling, or action, put in circulation by a man, has a tendency to be spread through fashion, among primitive peoples as well as among those who are civilized, and after having become widespread, to take root in the form of a custom, among civilized peoples as well as among primitive ones.

The thing which concerns us is to observe that it is not merely language, dogma, industrial and artistic instruments and talents, but moral or immoral feelings, moral or immoral habits as well, which have a tendency to become general and to become fixed in this manner.

How many African tribes, among whom drunkenness has already been raised to an institution, received from us, less than a hundred years ago, their first drink of spirits, and only took it with a grimace! How many millions of Europeans there are who resemble these savages in this! The bad habit of smoking, with which the whole of Europe and all the old world became innoculated from a few American colonies, has everywhere become acclimated to such an extent that the cigarette has become in Spain what the pipe of peace was among the Red-Skins, a national emblem. The bottle, which used formerly in all countries to be devoted to drunkenness, also becomes a sort of fetish, just as the gun, in Sicily and Corsica, is the object of a holy veneration [1] due to the traditional homicides of which it is the instrument, or as the flint knife of the Aztec sacrificer, used to open human victims in accordance with the rites, was an object of religious veneration. The "phallus," worn round their necks by Roman children under the Empire, symbolized the cult of that religion of pleasure which, coming from Syria, had taken possession of Rome and all romanity and had there so soon taken such firm root.

An epidemic of vice as well as one of virtue never fails soon to become *predisposed*. There is not a virtue, barbarian or civilized, hospitality or probity, bravery or industry, chastity or benevolence,

[1] "A man lends neither his gun nor his wife," says a Sicilian proverb. The gun comes before the wife.

which, today firmly rooted in the morals of a people, was not brought there yesterday or the day before. There is no atrocity, no oddity, no corruption, no superstition, — anthropophagy, religious murder of old men and the sick, tattooing, sorcery, divination by means of dreams or auguries, massacre of a political adversary or confiscation of his possessions, interrogatories by torture, the duel, the jury, the inquisition, etc., — which, wherever it is found to be established as a constitutional evil, did not begin by being an exotic germ brought by a social current of air. What an absurd thing the duel is! And with what ancestral authority it is imposed upon civilized people, upon whole continents![1] At the same time is it possible to have any doubt but that originally it was, like every form of ordeal, like the "Wergeld," the invention of an individual, very unworthy of its great success? Assuredly, the notion of a judgment from on high being obtained by means of a combat between the two parties litigant, when the only reason for going before a court is to avoid fighting, could not have come into existence spontaneously in so many places at once.

It would therefore be a mistake to suppose that every people among whom is found endemic the habit of devouring their captives, of sacrificing the old men, of selling or killing the newly born, of treating slaves with inhumanity and, in the first place of having slaves at all, or else of becoming passionately attached to the bloody games of the circus, to burning at the stake, or to bull fights, are born cruel. Or that people given to pederasty, such as the Arabs or the Greeks, are born infamous; or that people, classes, devoted by national custom to stealing domestic animals, to smuggling, to usury, to financial speculation, are born thieves. The truth is, rather, that they have become so through unfortunately allowing the microbe of some disastrous foreign example to penetrate among them.

It would be a mistake of the same kind to imagine that the

[1] It is even impressed upon the minds of the learned men who concern themselves with it. In his pamphlet "Du duel au point de vue médico-légal" (Lyons, Storck, 1890), *Teissier* is of the opinion that dueling is *necessary* in the army. Just as though the Roman armies, to whom the duel was never known, had been lacking in discipline and courage. — This writing includes, moreover, several interesting statements, for example the following: that since 1878 there have taken place in France 647 duels which were not military, and that there has been, on an average, one death in seventy-seven duels, and that the greatest number of duels take place in the spring, and the smallest number in autumn. Can anybody be found who will account for this regular maximum and minimum by means of the action of physical factors? If not, I wonder why the same explanation would not better apply to suicide and homicide.

native kindness, honesty, and modesty of the civilized population of our Europe is a sufficient protection against the invasion and the acclimation of certain forms of cruelty, of corruption, of abominations, at the very mention of which they become scandalized. The more civilized a people are and the more they are subject to the domination of fashion, the more suddenly and rapidly does the avalanche of example sweep down from the heights of the cities to the lowest rural depths. The various people of the Roman Empire, peacefully settled about their blue sea, were the mildest, the most humane, even the most enervated, that the world ever saw until the eighteenth century in France, and yet they could not do without seeing thousands of gladiators slaughtered at every great festival, because it was the custom in the city of Rome, which had received this custom from Taranto, I believe.

Thus it is that our eighteenth century wound up in the butchery of the French Revolution, each murder in Paris being at once repeated in Paris itself and reverberating soon in massacres or robberies throughout the whole of France. This was nothing more than a *fashion*, but it had a perceptible tendency to become strengthened into a tradition through the authority of its "great ancestors." The unfortunate part of it is that, whenever any crime or vice can be authorized by means of the example of one's ancestors, it appears to be excusable, even respectable and patriarchal, which obtains for it the sympathy of everybody and the indulgence of the jury. Such are knife blows ("coltellate") in Italy, assassinations through revenge in Corsica, the "sfregio" in Naples, or, in certain localities which have become too commercial, forgery of commercial documents, or elsewhere voluntary setting fire to houses by the owner himself to the injury of the insurance companies. There are cantons and districts in which this last crime is perpetrated so frequently that the companies refuse to renew fire insurance policies.

The "sfregio" is used by Neapolitan lovers just as the "vitriol" is used by French mistresses; it allows the former to force people to marry them by threatening a scar on the face, just as the latter do by means of the threat of a burn which will be still more disfiguring. Both of these disfigurations had in the beginning the character of an epidemic, then, at least the first of them, an endemic character. The razor cut on women's faces has become such a national institution around Naples that, according to

Garofalo,[1] "there are villages where not one young girl, unless she be protected by her ugliness, has a chance of escaping it if she does not make up her mind to marry the first man who proposes to her." Even the jury looked upon this old usage with such favor that it had to be compelled to do its duty. Imperial Rome looked upon the games of its Circus and its Amphitheatre as being so innocent that it was honestly and sincerely scandalized at the human victims sacrificed by the Druids, in about the same way as we take umbrage at the polygamy of the Arabs without stopping to think of the prostitution in our great cities. England carried on a campaign against the slave-trade without the slightest hesitancy about allowing thousands of children and women to be buried alive in its coal mines. In order to perceive the odious character of a custom, it must be contemplated from without and from a distance. We reproach the savages who poison their arrows, and we exhaust our brains to devise strange engines of destruction, grape-shot, torpedoes, which in the twinkling of an eye can sink the most formidable vessel of war and mow down two hundred thousand men in an hour on a single battlefield.

There is nothing to equal the progress of our political and military inhumanity, unless it be the depth of its unconsciousness; our newspaper polemics breathe nothing but deadly hatred; instigation to murder, the glorification of assassination, no longer astonish anybody in them. But it is especially in the direction of fraud that condoned crime has developed. The inroads made by immorality upon morality, by dishonesty upon honesty, are as continuous as they are imperceptible. The tendency, in drawing-rooms, seems by preference to be, as we are aware, to go to the extreme limit of respectability, and to strive to extend that limit; so much so that after a certain length of time, in a very lively society, a person can only continue to be respectable by saying the most indecent things possible. The part played by this tendency in gatherings for pleasure is the same as that played by ability in serious matters. It is carried to the extreme limit of honesty and causes this vague dividing line to recede so far that, in certain highly civilized and very busy communities, one can with perfect honesty indulge in the very greatest dishonesty, with the consent of general opinion. If it were not for the courts, do you not suppose that the tendency of wine merchants to color their goods with

[1] "La Criminologie," French translation, 1888, p. 280.

aniline, in other words to poison their customers, would very soon become an ineffaceable tradition, a customary practice in storage sheds, like "stock clauses" in the deeds of conveyancers?

§ 70. (VIII) The meeting of different currents of imitation; their struggle or their concurrence governed by the laws of social logic and expressed by means of statistics.

To sum up, vices and crimes, like honest needs and habits, like ideas and words, like all kinds of imitative repetitions, conform to that unlimited law of progression which has unlimited persistence, and which governs the social world and the living world at one and the same time. But this law, in both instances, does no more than to express a tendency sometimes seconded, sometimes checked, by meeting analogous tendencies, auxiliaries on the one hand and rivals on the other. It is possible, I believe, to formulate the fundamental reason for these examples of assistance and conflict, and we shall now see that the question whether, and in what manner criminality is fostered or opposed by teaching, by religion, by science, by industry and wealth, by art and the beautiful, can be answered by appealing to the general laws which govern the mutual relations between religion, for example, and science, or between science and industry, or between various industries or various arts among themselves. But these abstract terms do not tell us anything very definite; let us come down to familiar and explanatory details. Two distinct spreadings of example, emanating from distinct and often very distant cerebral centres, may happen in their wanderings to come together in some one man's brain. They are *two rays of imitation* which *interfere.* We can in fact denote as a ray that closely bound series of men, each in turn a model and a copy, who have, so to speak, passed from hand to hand, a common idea, a common need, a common process, from the inventor of it to the individual who is contemplating it. They are really linked together like the atoms of ether which transmit the same light vibration to one another. I will assume that we are dealing with a scientist, in whom there come together two of this sort of rays, one which, from Cuvier down to him, carries with it a belief in the independent creation of each species, the other which, from Darwin down to him, carries with it a belief in the relationship of species.[1]

[1] The contagion of beliefs and desires from man to man offers so great a resemblance to the contagion of actions, and is so far implied in the latter, that

Obviously one of these two rays must be arrested in him, for these two beliefs are contradictory; one says "yes," the other "no." If, however, by some chance, he had not just at first been conscious of this contradiction, as often occurs in the case of contradictions which are no less absolute between certain religious dogmas and certain scientific theories, which do not seem to disturb one another in the least in certain complex minds, the arrest in question would not take place. But, sooner or later, every contradiction must become apparent. On the other hand, if in the brain of an astronomer there meet the belief, descended from Newton to him, in stellar attraction, and the belief descended from Leverrier to him, in the discovery of Neptune, his first belief will be reinforced, because the second one, coming from an independent source, affirms exactly what the other affirmed, says "yes" where the other says "yes," a thing which is called a confirmation. The interference, in this case, is a stimulus, where, in the first case, it was an impact.

Let us suppose the case of a doctor who, having a love of railway travel, a special desire having come down to him in a straight line from the first travelers to have boarded a car, has at the same time an ardent desire to cure his patients, a professional desire, transmitted to him through a line of physicians going back to Hippocrates. These two desires conflict in him, they too are contradictory, but in another way, in the sense that one prevents the other from attaining its object. Each one of them, with regard to the object of the other, is an obstacle. To satisfy one would be *not to* satisfy the other; one, in so far as its realization is concerned, thus implies a denial of the other; one "wishes yes," the other "wishes no." If, on the other hand, the two desires are in accord, as, for example, in the case of a provincial candidate, the desire to become a Deputy and the desire to go to live in Paris, we can say that one confirms the other, a realization of the former implying a realization of the latter.

I apologize for spending so much time on such clear and simple cases, but they alone will enable me to clear up difficult and obscure cases.

I believe I am able to designate the former as well as the latter by the name of "imitation." Imitation-belief and imitation-desire, it is true, are involuntary, whereas imitation-action is voluntary, but they are conscious also and equally connected with personal identity. The inner consciousness of a person is often better expressed by the nature of the most inevitable convictions and passions than by those of the most well thought out actions. That is why the latter, no less than the former, leave a man absolutely responsible from our point of view.

Now let us suppose the case of a man no longer merely believing and desiring, but acting; then it is that the contradiction between his beliefs and his desires is bound to show itself. Whether he speak or act, he is compelled to choose between the conflicting ideas or passions by which he is swayed. But at this very moment does he not find himself to be embarrassed in other ways? No, the embarrassment is always the same, only under a different name. In order to express the same idea, the same belief, two words or two figures of speech are open to him; *two rays of verbal imitation* the distinct origin of which it is often possible to determine as being in two well known writers who introduced these different phrases into the language; and these two rays clash. Why? Because the question for the speaker is which is the better of two manners of speaking.

Now, to maintain that one of them is better is to *deny* that the other one can be better. Similarly, in order to realize the same desire, to manufacture the same product, to satisfy the same need of consumption, two means, two ways of proceeding, two articles are before the man about to act, the manufacturer, the consumer; these two processes, these two articles emanate from entirely distinct inventors. They are, for example, the paddle-wheel and the propeller for steam navigation, millstones of flint and millstones of steel for grinding wheat, gas or electricity for lighting, wheat or corn as a food, etc. The question here is which is the most advantageous process or article; to choose one is to say that that one is and the other is not. Besides, leaving aside the object which they fulfill for the time being, a process, an article, a tool, a certain piece of work, an action, they do not contradict one another any more than do two notions thought of "in the air," apart from any affirmative or negative proposition.

Again, for every use in which it does not compete with the propeller, the paddle-wheel can be propagated without the propagation of the propeller interfering with it; similarly, the flint millstone, except in so far as the grinding of wheat is concerned, and electricity, except in so far as lighting is concerned, can be propagated without in any way being interfered with by the propagation of the steel millstone or of gas; the employment of one word does not hinder the employment of another word outside of the acceptations of them which are synonymous. And yet again in the same way, the development of suicide cannot check the development of homicide except in so far as, as in the Orient, homicide and suicide are two different means of avenging oneself upon one's enemy. We deceive ourselves if we pretend to find in our Europe, as Ferri and Morselli do, a law of inversion in the progress of these two scourges which are so absolutely different among us. This illusion has been dissipated.[1] Finally, in the same way, if the expansion of labor in a nation forces back the expansion of stealing, it is because and in so far as labor and stealing are two different means *together open to the same individual* of acquiring money. Among the lazy and the degenerate, who do not wish to or cannot work, this choice, or this conflict, does not occur.

In so far as they are concerned, the progress of laborious activity does not in any way interfere with fraudulent activity; it is even possible that the former may be indirectly favorable to the latter if, through industrial and intellectual overdriving, it exhausts the working class or the intelligent class and increases the number of cases of degeneracy or incurable laziness among these classes. It is in this way that the spread of the railroads has not in any way resulted in injuring that of locomotion and traction by means of horses; for although on the one hand it did away with stage-coaches, on the other it has increased the occasion for short trips in omnibuses or carriages, in the case of which one has no choice between horse motive power or steam motive power.

Whatever may be the case, we can lay down this principle: every time statistics show us between two simultaneous propagations, for example between that of a religion and that of a science, between that of instruction and that of the crime of poisoning, between that of forethought and that of the birth rate, a very plainly marked inverse ratio, the one advancing as the other recedes, this indicates that one implies the denial of some of the things which the other affirms as being essential, although it may often be hard to discover where this implied and inner contradiction lies. And on the other hand, every time statistics show us between two simultaneous propagations, for example between that of fire insurance policies and that of arson, between that of vagabondage and that of thefts, between that of urban life and that of indecent assaults, a very clear parallel, we can be sure that one implies the confirmation of one of the points which the other affirms, or the pursuit of one of the objects which the other pursues. Thus society, in both cases, and there remains only one more case,

[1] See our "Criminalité comparée."

that of heterogeneous propagations which cross without producing any effect, just like so many resonant waves in the air, has paused to analyze itself; it has sought to do away with an antithesis in order to strengthen a synthesis. It has taken a step in advance along the road of that logical unity a systematic dream of which is its soul, just as the soul of the philosopher is the slow and loving elaboration of his system, fallacious perhaps, but certainly captivating!

§ 71. (IX) Application of these ideas first of all to the influence of teaching upon criminality.

I have said that society, in its incessant struggle and competition in the field of imitation, carries on a work which is the result of logic; should I not have said rather a work which is the result of finality? Let us say both at once; but it is logic which enlightens teleology, as it is geometry and algebra which enlighten mechanics, and not vice versa. To tell the truth, there is not a single act which is not the expression of some silent proposition. For a Mahometan, to wash oneself is to attest the truth of the Koran; for a Christian, to give alms is to attest the divinity of Christ and the immortality of the soul; for the husbandman, to labor is to affirm that the earth is the source of all wealth; for the artist, to model, to paint, to write verses is to maintain that the chief reason why nature exists is that she may furnish subjects for statues, landscapes, or poems for the sculptor, the painter, and the poet. Also, every merely theoretical idea, even one which, contradicting some one of these affirmations, spreads till it reaches the agent, the parent-belief of which it denies, has a tendency to exhaust the source of its action; and there is nothing more powerfully efficacious than this incessant influence to which scarcely anybody pays any attention.

Now do not vice and crime imply, like every other line of conduct, possibly to a lesser degree, a particular belief, a certain theory of life, if not of the universe, inherent in the malefactor? The latter, even when he is superstitious as in Italy, has his own special positivism and pessimism, deep rooted, and which, though they have nothing scientific about them, are none the less all too logical. He only believes in money, the pleasures of the senses, force; he not only practices but he also professes the right to murder and steal like others do the right to work, and he has not waited for the advent of Darwin to look upon this life as a war in which extermination alternates with plunder. By this I do not mean to insinuate that the vulgarization of the Darwinian theories has perhaps been a ferment for criminality, at least in their lofty and pure form. For, whether materialistic or spiritualistic, every true work of art is an act of belief in the divinity of art and in the duty of mortifying oneself and dying for art's sake.[1] Thus it is quite certain that it is not the diffusion of the scientific spirit, nor that of the artistic sentiment which is of such a nature as to encourage crime; they tend to exhaust its source, and, though it may happen that Darwinism is translated by nihilists and realism by pornographers, neither Darwin nor Zola are responsible for this circumstance.

Nor is religious sentiment the proper thing to confirm the coarse "credo" of the criminal soul; this sentiment is the most absolute denial of it and still its strongest adversary. Although Christianity especially may be itself translated by impostors, and sometimes degenerate, as a very great exception, into superstitions which even look upon crime with favor, in medals worn on the necks of brigands, in prayers offered up for the success of a uxoricide, yet it is none the less true that, even in our western Europe, murderers and thieves are generally to be distinguished by their relative irreligiousness.[2] But there is one sentiment which,

[1] In thus tracing back to the man of science the responsibility for crimes which a perusal of his writings might suggest to a scoundrel, the author of the "Disciple" has taken a point of view as false as it is commonplace, and which is entirely unworthy of his splendid talents. He has less right than anybody to blame the denial of free will, a thing which is also denied in every one of his novels, the fundamental theory of which is based upon the all-powerfulness of psychological heredity. In order to carry on the idea of his "Disciple," he ought indeed in his next work to make a study of the evil influence exercised by writers of fiction and not by the philosophers upon their readers. His own works, I fear, with their abundance of voluptuous details, from which is to be gathered the lasting impression that a life of love, even of a love which is a lie, is the only life worth living, must have led into temptation many young men and many women; and I doubt whether the authors of the determinist theories have as many cases of adulteries upon their conscience, or of other crimes due to love which may have led to a more serious and a different type of wrongdoing.

[2] The statistics of *Marro* on this subject (*op. cit.*) deal with too small numbers to have any very great weight in this question. Nevertheless it results therefrom that among male delinquents forty-five per cent regularly attend mass, and among normal men fifty-seven per cent (Italians). Among female delinquents, this same numerical difference is very much more decided, the question of religion being of more moral importance in the case of their sex than it is in the case of ours (see p. 421). Is it not to a great extent to the religiousness of women as compared with men that we must attribute the enormous difference between masculine and feminine delictuosity? The delictuosity of the latter shows us a proportion which varies between *one-tenth* and *one-third* of ours. . . . In the "Revue philosophique" (May, 1890) I contrasted on this subject the contradictory explanations given by Colajanni and Joly, and I believed, while having a predilection for the second,

in becoming generalized, should it be developed in the mind without a sufficient counterweight, agrees with one of the principles dear to delinquents. This is what we might call the mercantile sentiment, the worship of gold and immediate enjoyment to the exclusion of everything else.

Thus, although habits of industrial labor, wherever they enter into competition with habits of stealing, excel in counteracting the latter as being a contrary and inferior means of attaining the same object or of expressing the same view of life, it may happen that the progress of industrialism, indeed, by redoubling the desire of this object or the belief in this view, will give rise to an increasing number of offenses. In this same way the extension of the railways, while over-stimulating the passion for travel, has indirectly contributed towards increasing the circulation of carriages themselves, whether public or private, and towards developing coach building in the long run, although the railway car is the exterminator of the public or private carriage wherever it enters into competition with the latter; and the history of industry is full of similar examples. Although the printing press exterminates the copyist wherever it is to be found competing with him, printing, in developing a love for reading and a worship of the characters of the alphabet, has in the long run increased the number of scribes occupied in copying or in recopying in offices. Although the manufacture of textiles by means of machinery may have killed all the weaver's stalls in its vicinity and wherever the products of both enter into serious competition in the mind of the consumer, yet the progress of the former, by developing the need

which is entirely religious, rather than for the first, which is entirely economical, that I was substituting for both of them a personal and a different interpretation, as follows: The morality of woman would be due to her subjection, like that of the negroes in our colonies before their emancipation; and this is why in proportion as she works out her own emancipation, in passing from rural surroundings to urban surroundings, from a less civilized country, such as Italy, to a more civilized country, such as England, her criminality increases and becomes more nearly equal to that of man. — But upon reflection I am still less satisfied with this hypothesis than I am with Joly's, which is that although the Frenchwoman has been emancipated for the last half century, her relative criminality has decreased from twenty to fourteen per one hundred persons accused or charged with some crime; whereas it ought to have increased according to my hypothesis. But this decrease agrees very well with Joly's explanation because for the last half century the distance which with us exists between the two sexes, from the point of view of religious belief, and practice has certainly been growing greater. We find the criminality of women becoming almost equal to that of men in the Breton Departments where men are almost as religious as women, and in more highly civilized surroundings where women are almost as lacking in religion as men.

of being properly dressed and the idea of personal dignity connected with this care as to one's clothing, has caused an increase in the number of the latter in many rural districts where the product of the former has not as yet penetrated but where its spirit is already beginning to make itself felt. For the needs and the ideas stimulated by some means of production which is advancing often go ahead of it, as a result of a contagion from one person to another which is more rapid than the increase in its outlet. This very unequal progress of these two spreadings of imitation, the imitation of objects and the imitation of means of attaining those objects, the imitation of ideas and the imitation of expressions of those ideas, are worthy the notice of the economists. It would account for many things in their field;[1] in ours, it should not be lost sight of when we come to study the relations between criminality and teaching, education, wealth, labor, etc.

It is useless to repeat what has been said on all sides as to the inefficiency, an established fact today, of primary instruction, considered by itself and leaving aside religious and moral teaching. This result ought not to surprise us. To learn to read, to write, to count, to explain a few elementary ideas of geography and physics, does not in any way counteract the silent ideas implied in delictual tendencies, does not in any way combat the object which they seek, does not suffice as a means of proving to a child that there are better means than crime of attaining this object. Only, all this may supply crime with new resources, may modify its methods of proceeding, which become less violent and more crafty, and may sometimes strengthen its nature. In Spain, where the proportion of illiterates to the entire population is two thirds, only about one half of them have any part in the general criminality.[2]

[1] For example, the commercial invasion of the Mediterranean world by the Phoenicians, of the Christian world by the Venetians, and of the entire world by the English, the need of consumption of certain products having spread more rapidly during each period than the needs and the talents of production with relation to these same articles. Everywhere and always a circumspect nation has profited by the longer or shorter interval which occurs between the creation of the former needs and that of the latter among each one of the peoples who serve as an outlet for them. Then these latter, in order to consume that which they cannot or will not yet produce themselves, have only a choice between two decisions: submit to the price set by the foreign manufacturer or conquer him in a war and compel him to manufacture for nothing. This latter option, which is frequently found in history, is exemplified in private life by stealing, forgery, and murder due to greed.

[2] "La criminalidad en España," by *Imeno Agius*, "Revista de España," October, 1885, February, 1886.

Marro has shown that, among the delinquents examined by him with so much care, the proportion of individuals who had had primary instruction is as high as seventy-four per cent, whereas, among the honest people with which he compares them, this proportion was only sixty-seven per cent. But how would it be possible for the humanization of the mind by higher education not to have a moralizing influence? One does not attain such lofty, such rugged truths, without having long trodden the way of right, overcome fatigue and avoided false steps; there is no form of moral discipline superior to this exercise and this close application of the mind towards a pole which has nothing in common with the aspect of an evil mind. What need is there of statistics here? I know well that although, in France, the liberal professions, taking into account the number of the special class of population which goes to make them up, furnished a very small contingent of the tribute of crime so long as they were mingled with landowners and persons of independent means, this is no longer the case since they have been segregated from the latter. It has now been found that the proportionate amount of criminality among them is very great, being represented by the figure 28 out of 100,000 souls, whereas that of farmers is only 16 and that of landowners and persons of independent means but 6. I also know that in Prussia, and possibly in Italy, statistics have shown the same results.

But what does this prove if not that all the moral benefit of higher studies is turned into harm when they no longer serve any purpose but that of earning money, in callings where competition is more fierce and the dangers are more numerous than anywhere else? One thing at least is noticeable and that is that the one of the so-called liberal professions which a man can enter without this high degree of theoretical preparation, the profession of notary, has stood out among them all for some time past owing to the frightful progress made in its delictuosity. The dismissals of notaries, which in 1881 were still only from 18 to 25 a year, have increased by degrees to 75 in 1887.

A recent writer [1] sees in the pleasure of contemplation which is afforded by the work of art, an antidote for the pleasure of action which is experienced in the realization of some glorious undertaking incarnated in some military leader or some statesman. He thus gives expression to the political or military decadence of peoples

[1] *Emile Hennequin*, "Critique scientifique," (Didier, 1888).

among whom literary and artistic culture is in progress; and he adds that the decline in violent criminality in a given place from the moment when the taste for literature slips in, is to be accounted for in the same way. This comparison is not lacking in fairness. It is certain that the need of strong emotions, when it is satisfied among a coarse class of readers as is actually the case among certain admirers of the realistic novel, no longer needs to seek satisfaction in rape and assassination actually carried out. Also, far from being ordinarily an exciting cause of crime, as was thought by reason of the nature of its subjects, contemporary literature — I do not say that which consists in reports of the proceedings in criminal courts — is rather a derivative of criminal instincts. Unfortunately the same thing cannot be said with regard to its effects upon vice, which it stimulates beyond any doubt.

Now, vice often causes a predisposition to crime. But the progress of a crime is less rapid than that of the vice with which it is connected. Furthermore, even in so far as the latter is concerned, the effect of the most immoral literature is perhaps more apparent than real, although most assuredly real, for here as everywhere "the dream dispenses with the deed."

§ 72. (X) In the second place, to the influence exercised by work and industry.

I will not stop to demonstrate how a child is made moral by means of the education it receives at home. As to the influence of work, about which only a few words have been said by the way, this question merits a more thorough scrutiny. Poletti [1] has given us an original theory on this subject which already has been keenly discussed in France [2] and in Italy. Without again taking up this discussion which has been exhaustive, we ought to point out what is, from our point of view, the truth which results therefrom. Poletti comes to his decision from observing that the total number of crimes and misdemeanors in France trebled in half a century and from finding a similar increase in all our civilized countries. He believes himself compelled to conclude therefrom, it is true, that the progress of our industrial civilization is connected with the progress of criminality; but his admiration for

[1] "Il sentimento nella scienza del diretto penale," (Udine, 1882).

[2] "Revue philosophique," our article on criminal statistics (January, 1883). Of the Italian positivist school, especially Ferri and Garofalo gave their separate support to the criticism formulated in this article.

our industrial civilization does not suffer therefrom. Why? Because, according to him, though industry may be an incitement to commit offenses, this incitement causes the number of offenses to increase more slowly than it does itself, and this smaller increase is equivalent to an actual relative decrease. In France (it is the statistics of our country that are responsible for this ingenious way of looking at it) from 1826 to 1878, imports increased from 100 to 700, exports almost as much. Statements of successions to real and personal property have also furnished figures which increased from 100 to about 300. From the above comparisons and from many other similar ones, it may be deduced that the public wealth of France, that is to say, its productive activity, quadrupled during this same interval of time. Now, its criminality only increased from 100 to 254. Therefore, for the same number of acts of a productive kind, there was a less number of destructive acts committed in 1878 than in 1826; therefore the *net* amount of crime, if I may be allowed so to interpret the thought of Poletti, has appreciably diminished, while its *gross* amount was increasing. Here there are two errors superimposed upon each other; one which consists in considering as a regular, permanent, and inevitable effect of industrialism, an evil which is connected with it accidentally, indirectly, and temporarily. The other in deliberately closing one's eyes in order to demonstrate to oneself that this evil is a benefit. Through one of them, the author shows that he is very hard on industrialism; through the other, that he is very partial in its favor. The first of them makes him flatly contradict Spencer, according to whom,[1] in a society founded upon industry, the criminals must be "very scarce, if not inappreciable in number," and though in this Spencer may be contradicted by statistics, it is none the less true that labor, taken by itself, leaving aside the bad influences due to the consumption of its fruits in certain cases, is perhaps the most powerful moralizing agent.

The second makes him contradict reason. I will admit for the time being that civilization gives rise to crime just as the vibration of the ether gives rise to the sensation of light; but because, according to a famous rule of the psychophysicists, this sensation only increases as the logarithm of its exciting cause, does it follow that when I light nine candles instead of three, or twenty-seven instead of nine, I see any less clearly from the fact that the in-

[1] "Principe de sociologie," Vol. III, p. 814 of the same French translation.

tensity of my vision has only increased from two to three or from three to four? We cannot judge of the criminality of a nation or of a period, as we would estimate the insecurity of some means of transportation. No doubt we have a perfect right to say that, in spite of their annual, and yearly increasing, contingent of accidentally killed and wounded, the railroads are a mode of locomotion becoming less and less dangerous because the ratio of accidental deaths and maimings to the number of kilometres covered is ever decreasing. But why have we a right so to express ourselves, to calculate the unsafeness of journeys, not from the number of accidents taken by themselves, but from the ratio between this number and the number of trips? The reason is that there really is a connection, a necessary and indissoluble connection, between the increasing number of journeys and the taking place of a few accidents from time to time. Even though all the employees and all the travelers might have their minds set constantly on avoiding accidents, these would inevitably take place; whereas, if everybody always sincerely wished that there should be no crimes, there would not be any. The foresight and the carefulness of employees and of travelers supposedly remaining constant, one can say that, the greater the increase in the number of trains, the greater will be the increase in the number of accidents as well. But, public morality remaining constant, and all other circumstances remaining as they are, will there be more crimes the more work increases?

"A priori," one can say the contrary; and "a posteriori," one finds the proof of this when, by chance, one finds himself in the conditions required in order to see the influence of work taken by itself over delictuosity, independently of every other disturbing influence. One may suppose that, from 1860 to 1867, the morality of post office employees has remained the same, and that the nature of their work had not changed, but its intensity has greatly increased; the number of registered letters in particular has increased two and one half times. However the number of these letters which have disappeared annually, in other words which have been stolen, has gradually decreased from 41 to 11. This is due to the fact that force of professional duty increases in proportion to the frequency with which it is carried out and ought, as a consequence, to prevail more and more over the force of bad instincts, if we assume that the latter has not varied.

A professor would be astonished were he to be asked whether, as his class becomes more studious, it lays itself open to a greater number of punishments.

Only there is work and work; and if in a more studious class, the work is badly distributed, being excessive for some whom it enervates and injures, and insufficient for others for whom it is no more than a recreation, or if it is badly managed, directed towards unhealthy compositions and readings which stimulate the senses and vanity and carry to the verge of frenzy the desire for premature pleasure or emulation with a view to obtaining prizes, in such a case, it may well happen that the progress made in the work is accompanied by a progress in lack of discipline, in academic vices, and faults of various kinds.

An analogous phenomenon occurs in our cities where the madness for luxury outstrips the increase in salaries, and where offenses of an indecent nature have increased six or seven times in number while the public wealth only increased to three or four times what it had been before. The socialists are therefore right when they partly impute to the unjust division or the unfortunate direction of productive activity, the moral evil which grows with it, and which, moreover, does not diminish when the former declines. For since the time at which Poletti's information with regard to the prosperity of France ceased to apply, this unequal division has no longer increased, it has rapidly become less, as we know only too well, but crime has continued its ascending progress with a more marked vehemence. So after all nothing remains of the law laid down by this distinguished writer, and it is contradicted by all statistics.

Delictuosity, as Garofalo has pointed out, is so out of proportion to commercial activity, that England, where crimes and misdemeanors are decreasing, is the nation most remarkable for the extraordinary increase in its commerce, and Italy and Spain, where criminality is greater than it is in the chief countries of Europe, come far behind the former country as far as the development of business is concerned. Let us add that in France the most laborious class in the nation beyond any doubt, is the peasant class, and it is one of the least criminal classes as well for an equal number of the population, in spite of the unfavorable conditions under which this class has to exist. Let us conclude that work is in itself the enemy of crime, that if it fosters crime, it is owing to an indirect action, and one which is in no way necessary, and that its relations with crime are analogous to the mutual relations between two sorts of work which are antagonistic to each other. Once again, *criminology* is nothing more than a case of sociology such as we understand it to be. It is the general law of political economy dealing with the production of merchandise that ought to be applied to the production of offenses if one wishes to account for the vicissitudes of this special kind of industry.[1]

This is all the more true since crime, in becoming localized among certain categories of persons without class, or degenerates, becomes more and more a career. In this respect, we are confronted with an apparent difficulty. On the one hand, malefactors associate together less and less in carrying out their operations, as is proved by statistics when we come to compare, from 1826 to our own time, the number of accusations and the number of accused. These two figures, of which the latter always necessarily exceeds the former, have been approaching each other a little, from which we might infer that, carried out in a more isolated manner, crime appears to be more of an accident, and less a habit or a profession. But, on the other hand, the regular, uninterrupted, and inevitable progress of recidivism in every European country, expressly attests the contrary. In passing, we may remark that, under the old system, on the other hand, the number of the fellow-perpetrators of any crime was very large, whereas recidivism properly so called seems to have played but a small part in the criminality of those times. During every famine, during every time of dearth, the bands which were organized, consisting in from forty to fifty men sometimes, pillaged and ravaged everything; but these bands would then disperse.

After all is said and done, this inverse ratio between the numerical importance of these bands and recidivism has nothing strange about it. The first fact is to be accounted for by means of the unceasing progress made by the police, and not in any way by means of a progress in morals; and the second fact is really alarming. More accidental while it was at the same time more general, the crime of olden times had the characteristics of an

[1] Jacoby is not willing to concede the possibility of striking the level of the morality of a people from the figure which represents their criminality. I would answer in fact that this level must be far lower than statistics would indicate in a country where it shows us deplorable results. In countries where there are persons suffering from goitre, — Jacoby himself has said this, — even persons who have not goitre as a general thing have larger necks, so much so that shirtmakers in these localities are in the habit of making all collars larger. Thus it is that, in a depraved nation, moralists have a wider sleeve.

epidemic; modern crime, more circumscribed and more deeply rooted, progressing slowly and continually, has the appearance of a constitutional evil.

Where is the progress of the repetition of offenses more marked than elsewhere? In great cities, because, having reached a certain point in density and size, these forests of men enable malefactors to find once more, under the form of cafés and unlicensed dwellings, their caves of former times. "In forty cities which have over 30,000 inhabitants," says an official report, "there is to be found one recidivist for every three hundred and seven inhabitants, whereas in cities having a smaller population only one recidivist is to be found for every seven hundred and twelve inhabitants." But it is especially in cities having a population of more than 100,000 that the proportion of recidivists, with relation to the number of either the population, or of persons sentenced, rises to a level which is significant. In these cities the number of offenses is legion, but, conversely to ordinary armies whose maxim is to disperse in order to live and to concentrate in order to act, this hidden army disperses in order to act under the vigilant supervision of the police and gathers itself together in order that it may live on its plunder. It is none the less a very flourishing corporation at this present time, and we can readily understand why this is so. "Upon what does the fact of some particular trade being prosperous generally depend?" I asked in a former work. "First of all upon the fact that it pays better, then upon the fact that it costs less, finally, and especially, upon the fact that the ability to exercise it and the necessity for exercising it have become less rare or more frequent. Now all these circumstances have combined in our time to foster that particular industry which consists in plundering all the others." [1]

"While the quantity of things which can be stolen or obtained by swindling, and of pleasures which can be obtained by theft,

[1] To despoil them, that is to say to develop them *without reciprocity*, in this alone criminality differs from other trades. It is, we may say, an industry whose progress is helped by the progress of all others, by virtue of the *law of outlet* of J.-B. Say, the result of which is that every production of a new article stimulates the production of others, even sometimes, as we have said, the production of previously existing articles which the new article is destined to replace. In this respect there is an absolute analogy between the trade of crime and every other trade. But the trade of crime has this peculiarity that it serves no other trade, excepting the contraband professions which exist because of it. It is true that this last exception is of very wide extent: does not the lower order of newspaper exist through chronicling the reports of the criminal courts, and were crime to cease, would not their printing off be lowered prodigiously?

rape, swindling, abuse of confidence, forgery, and assassination, has increased during the last half century out of all proportion, the prisons have been better ventilated, improved all the time as to food, quarters, and comfort, judges and juries have shown greater clemency day by day. Thus the profits have increased and the risk has become less, to such an extent that, in our civilized countries, the profession of pickpocket, of vagabond, of forger, of fraudulent bankrupt, of assassin even, is one of the least dangerous and the most profitable that a lazy man can adopt. At the same time the social revolution has increased the number of persons out of their class, of those who are restless, a hotbed for crime, and of vagabonds whose number has quadrupled since 1826."[1] And as charitable instincts have not made much headway in our bustling society, the condemned who are still honest after having committed their first crime, "discharged prisoners wavering between the example offered by the majority of society, honest but inhospitable, and that of the little criminal fatherland which is quite ready to naturalize them, end by necessarily taking this direction as girl mothers naturally turn to prostitution." I wonder to what figure the criminality of the centuries which have passed would have been raised if so many causes at once had seconded the boldness of criminals, who must have been exceedingly brave to have dared run the risk of incurring the penalties of those times. There were a few adulterous women even at the time when they were stoned and public opinion condemned them; is it surprising that at the present time there are many?

Of crime as of every industry, one can say that the most apparent obstacles or means of assistance placed in its way are not always the most real ones. This means that, according to what has been said above, the closest and the most effective *contradictions* and *confirmations*, those which are most fitting to overthrow or to support a theory which is to be inferred from a plan, are not always the most obvious ones. Seldom is the best means of developing an industry to pay it a bounty; seldom is the best means of ruining an industry to place a tax upon it. Also, I must agree with Ferri in recognizing that the most certain means of overcoming crime is not to punish it by much more severe penalties, and I will add that the prospect given delinquents, of prisons more pleasant to live in, is not the thing which best

[1] "Revue philosophique," article on criminal statistics, January, 1883.

accounts for the increase in the number of offenses. Protective or prohibitive tariffs are none the less a powerful weapon in the hands of governments, the only one indeed which they can use with facility and speed in the interest of those industries which are dear to them and to the injury of those industries which they look upon with suspicion. The example of the German Empire and the United States is there to prove the efficaciousness of this sport of kings. The police laws, the laws of procedure and of penal justice are analogous to prohibitive tariffs; used in the right way by strong powers, they produce an effect which is apparent, sometimes more superficial than deep-seated, but often a decided one. And as, after all, this sword of justice is the only direct instrument at the immediate disposal of public authority in its struggle with the enemy within, its importance requires that we give it a chapter to itself. So here we but mention it in order not to forget it.

If it were possible to create genius by decree, the most infallible means of doing away with any given sort of crime, as well as of causing any given industry to flourish, would certainly be the bringing to light of certain great discoveries, powerful fields of a new spreading of example and having no apparent connection with either crime or labor. Unfortunately nothing is more the result of chance than these vital ideas, and nothing is more impossible to foresee than their consequences, for the contradiction or the confirmation which they bring to bear upon established habits, upon prevailing ideas, are indirect and implied, complex and confused, until the time when, in being realized, they are revealed. When Papin discovered the motive power in steam, who could have guessed that the industrial greatness of England was embodied in this discovery in the form of a germ, a discovery which was a "sine qua non" condition of the discovery made by Watt? In the same way, in discovering America could Christopher Columbus have dreamed that the consequence of his marvelous voyage would be a perceptible decrease in the criminality of England? Yet according to the historian Pike, this is a matter of which there can be no doubt. He attributes to the discovery of the New World, as a result of the purifying current of emigration to which it gave rise, the very marked improvement in morals, and the decline of brutality in England towards the close of the seventeenth and eighteenth centuries. The American Eldorado, in fact, has exercised over every adventurer in quest of a "vita nuova" a fascination which may be compared to that of the Holy Land during the Middle Ages. The enthusiasm for transatlantic colonization has been the crusade of modern times, and, like the crusades of the past it has made the continent more healthy.

§ 73. (XI) **In the third place, to the influence of poverty or wealth.**

The influence of wealth and poverty upon crime is a question which is at one and the same time distinct from and dependent upon the question which deals with the influence of labor.[1] It is the favorite battle ground of the two rival factions of the positivist school, the socialist faction and the orthodox faction. According to Turati and Colajanni, the real cause of the crimes committed by the poor, would be their poverty, just as, according to Ferri the true cause of many of the crimes committed in summer, would be the temperature. Although Ferri is not able to support his hypothesis, does he at least succeed in overthrowing that of his adversaries? In "Socialismo e criminalità" he tries hard to do so, and Garofalo, after him, in his "Criminologie" does the same. In a rather striking table,[2] the former of these writers shows us that in France, from 1844 to 1858, year by year, the *increase* or the *decrease* in the price of grain, of meat and wine, has corresponded to the *increase* or *decrease* in violent or lascivious criminality. The years during which people drink the most are those during which they kill the most. Thus well being would seem to be a source of offenses against persons; while on the other hand it would seem to act as a contributing cause of the decrease in offenses against property.

Garofalo is not even willing to grant this last concession. "It is true," he tells us, "that theft, which is the coarsest manner of violating the rules of property, is spread on a far larger scale among the very lowest classes of society; but it is counterbalanced by forgery, by fraudulent bankruptcy and by the extortion of the upper classes; and these misdeeds are nothing more than just so many varieties of a common *natural offense*." In support of this assertion he invokes Italian statistics of 1880 in which he finds, although not without debatable instances, that 14,524 offenses can be imputed to laborers and 2011 to property holders, which gives us

[1] I will take the liberty of referring the reader on this point to my article "Misère et criminalité" published in the "Revue philosophique" in May, 1890.

[2] "Socialismo e criminalità," p. 77.

a proportion of eighty-eight to twelve, whereas the proportion of laborers to property holders among the population of Italy is as ninety is to ten. Therefore the rich have contributed more than their proportionate share of the total criminality of Italy.

I shall take the liberty of attaching quite another import to a passage from the official report upon the criminal statistics of France from 1887 on, in which it is stated that, out of every hundred thousand inhabitants of each one of the following classes taken by itself, there are found annually twenty accused belonging to the servant class, that is to say,[1] to one of the poorest of them, and twelve accused belonging to the liberal professions, including that of property holders and of persons of independent means. As to the poorest class of all, that of vagabonds and vagrants, it furnishes one hundred and thirty-nine accused. It is true we also find twenty-one accused who deal in commerce, twenty-six who live by industry, which is a very high figure in view of the rather large profits realized in these professions between the two dates given, and only fourteen accused living by agriculture, which is a very low figure taking into account the relative poverty of farmers.

But is it not possible to reconcile these results which appear to disagree? Let us not forget that the desire to acquire wealth being the ordinary motive of an offense, and the one which is ever preponderating, as well as the only motive of industrial labor, the possession of wealth ought to drive from crime even the most dishonest man, as it ought to drive the most laborious man from industrial labor — for it is a contradiction to desire what one already has — at least if the gratification of this desire has not been over-excitement, as often happens, but only to a certain extent and not in every instance. Now, in bustling centres, where, owing to a mutual feverishness, a constant acquiring of wealth rather than wealth itself is the object pursued, fortune is like those fiery liquors which excite thirst even more than they

[1] Let us observe on this subject the rapid increase of the number of domestic servants. In Paris their number has increased from 112,031 in 1871 to 178,532 in 1881. This is all the more unfortunate as, according to Parent-Duchâtelet in particular, this class "furnishes a large contingent to prostitution" as well as to criminality. — Is it not surprising that at a time when the need of equality, the overthrow of all superiority is making so much headway, relative servitude is thus rushed into? Is there less pride than envy at the basis of the need of leveling with which we are dealing, and will this allow these facts to be reconciled with the increasing laziness and greed which cause the easy profits of domestic service to be sought?

satisfy it. To this no doubt, as well as to the agitation which exists in these centres, is due the fact that their delictuosity is equal to that of servants.

Similarly, in a licentious society, in large cities, in agglomerations of working men, indecent assaults are more numerous in proportion as the pleasures of the senses are more easy of access. But one might lay it down as a principle that, wherever wealth is an obstacle to business, it is also an obstacle in the way of crime, in about the same manner as political power ceases to be dangerous as soon as it ceases to be meddlesome and ambitious. This is the case among property holders in the country, whether great or small, among persons of independent means and even among the greater part of the liberal professions, wherever they are, as in France, not very absorbing or feverish. Satisfied with his relative well being, a man remains in them carrying on his intellectual labors in a half-hearted sort of way, labors which are artistic rather than mechanical, honorary rather than mercenary, and abstains from criminal means of obtaining an increase in his income which he to a certain extent desires. The French peasant, as a general rule, participates in this moderation of desires, and, grown rich through his sobriety, his stoicism, his economy, and through his patch of ground the ownership of which he finally acquires, he is happier than the millionaire, the feverish financier, or the politician, who is compelled because of his very millions to use them as the material for his unsafe speculations, his swindles and extortion on a large scale. The most prosperous farmers are, moreover, the most honest ones, as a general thing.

Let us not talk of wealth and poverty, in fact not even of well being and misfortune. Let us speak rather of happiness and sorrow, and let us be careful not to deny this truth as old as the world itself, that the excuse offered by the evildoer is often that he is unfortunate. Though sons of the present century, let us acknowledge, whatever it may cost our *filial* pride,—for nothing is more respected than this very parentage, — let us acknowledge that, under its brilliant exterior, our society is not a happy one, and, though we had no further assurance of its great evils than its numerous offenses, without even contemplating its increasing number of suicides and cases of madness, without heeding the cries of envy, suffering, and hatred which predominate in the uproar of our cities, yet we could not call in question its sorrows.

What is the cause of this suffering? It is the disturbance

within, the illogical and unstable condition of our society, the internal contradictions which give rise within it to the very success of its unprecedented discoveries and inventions, piled one upon another, food for contradictory theories, sources of frenzied, egotistical, and antagonistic needs. In this obscure gestation the need of a great "Credo," a great common goal makes itself felt; this is the Creation before the "Fiat Lux." Science increases the number of ideas, it elaborates a high conception of the Universe, with regard to which it will in the end, I hope, bring us to a state of agreement. But where is this high conception of life, of human life, which it stands ready to make the prevalent one? Industry increases the number of products, but where is the collective work which it engenders? The pre-established harmony of interests was a dream of Bastiat, the shadow of a dream of Leibnitz. The citizens of a State furnish one another with scientific or other kinds of information, but do it for the benefit of their rival interests; the more they thus mutually render assistance to one another, the more do they feed their essential contradictions, which may have been as deep rooted in former times, but which could never have been as conscious, as painful, and as a consequence, as dangerous. In what do they all work together? On what subject do they all collaborate?

If we seek to find the desire which is common to them all, with respect to which they do not quarrel with one another, we shall discover but one: to make war on one's neighbor. Our century has so far devised nothing better than this ancient and fierce solution of the problem of rival interests which consists in obtaining order by means of disorder, agreement among individuals by means of the conflict of nations. Assume the peace of the world to have been assured by the final triumph of one State, as under the Roman Empire, and then tell me how, there being no external war, we would be able to escape civil war. From time to time, when, through a sudden expansion of suffrage, the enlarged body of voters, like lakes which have suddenly become seas and are astonished at their own flood, are agitated by great collective movements, it is thought that they are about to give birth to the Messiah. But they are no more than a swaying to and fro in one spot, the backward and forward motion of a vast swing. At certain periods, in the Egypt of the Pharaohs, during the Christian Middle Ages, the warlike outlet for men's passions was not the only one; there was mingled with it, and militating against it, their unanimous convergence towards an imaginary pole which in reality united them, towards a point situated outside of and above the real world, towards the life to come, a sort of *virtual focus* of desires. They did not merely work together to kill the enemy, but that they might live again in the happiness of which they dreamed. Today in so far as "salvation," as a unanimous and saving dream, a star of refuge is concerned, we can no longer depend upon art, philosophy, the higher culture of the mind and the imagination, the aesthetic life, yet in reality, we have here an unlimited America left to mankind and one which will offer them an undivided field, which can be indefinitely extended without ever coming in contact with its limits, without lawsuits or battles, long after all the plains of the Far West and the Plata shall have been tilled and peopled with hostile farmers. The worship of art, plastic and superficial to be sure, was the ruling passion and the safeguard of the Roman Empire, if we are to judge by the luxuriant extravagance of statues, frescoes, and monuments, and of artistic utensils which make its smallest provincial towns stand out in sharp contrast to ours. But our times could not be content with this feast of the senses; they demand an art of a more serious nature, more intense pleasures of the mind; as yet this exists but in outline, and many a "lustrum" will roll by before a majority of mankind will take refuge in this future terrestrial paradise, supposing this should ever happen.

§ 74. (XII) And fourthly, to the influence of civilization in general.

The question whether or not civilization, — a collective name for instruction, education, religion, science, art, industry, wealth, political order, etc., — causes the amount of criminality to diminish is ambiguous. This word has two meanings; or rather all civilization passes through two stages. A first stage during which inventions and renovating initiative flow together haphazard; we have arrived at this stage in Europe at the present time. A second stage when the afflux becoming exhausted, its elements begin to act in concert and have some system. Now a civilization may be very rich without being coherent; this is so in the case of ours. Or else very coherent without being very rich; this was the case in the ancient town or the community of the Middle Ages. But is it by means of its wealth or its cohesion that it repels crime? By means of its cohesion beyond any doubt. This cohesion in religion, in science, in every form of work and power in every different sort of initiative, mutually strengthening one another, either actually or apparently, is in reality an absolute coalition against crime; and even though these fruitful branches of the social order, to continue my metaphor, but feebly combat the off-shoot, their concord suffices to draw away from it all the sap.

As long as republican Rome kept her civilization, the rather simple elements of which had with ease been welded into a compact mass, Roman morality held its own. But from the end of the Punic wars, when the Asiatic worship of Cybele was brought to Rome with Greek art, disorder, confusion of minds and of wills began to make their appearance. The inevitable signs of corruption begin to appear; the accusation of embezzlement brought against Scipio Asiaticus, who could not defend himself and was only acquitted by being pardoned, the revelation of those bloody orgies, of the bacchanalia which were the occasion for so many capital executions, the epidemic of arson against which the Senate had to take severe measures. If the morals of this great city of olden times never improved, is it not because the continuous arrival of exotic religions, of heterogeneous civilizations, did not leave her any time to put a little order into this chaos? Stoicism such as it was when it flourished under the Empire of the second century of the Christian era, made an attempt to do this, and its attempt is analogous to that of Protestantism in times which were no less incoherent. This attempt consisted in acquiring new vigor from the sources, and in reconciling the austere virtues which early citizenship alone upheld, with the new cosmopolitanism, an undertaking as impossible as that of importing the virtues of the early Church into the midst of the modern world, or the reconciling of the Mosaic dogmas with the encyclopaedic knowledge of today. The invasion of Christianity into the Empire met with an incomparably greater success [1] in fusing into a whole a portion of its altered and recast elements, at least in the Byzantine Empire which had itself, in spite of its puerile senility, an original and coherent civilization of its own to which its duration bore witness. Now, as compared with Rome, Byzantium was moral in spite of the fact of its bad reputation.

It is not the progress of civilization, it is the suffering of these

[1] In the same way the invasion of French rationalism in the eighteenth century was fruitful *for the future* in quite a different way from the Protestant Reformation.

critical times which is given expression in the derangement of minds and the perversity of actions. With the increase in mental alienation which is observable in our day, and which is undeniable,[1] one may compare the recrudescence of trials for sorcery which marks the end of the sixteenth century. The civilization of that time was, like ours, a brilliant one. Sorcerers and sorceresses were neurasthenics consulted by clients who were a little mad themselves. The universal practice of having recourse to divination, pacts with the devil, nocturnal revels, all these reveal the despair of a society which no longer knows "of which saint to become a votary." Our own society is plunging itself into suicide and madness, our fathers knocked at the door of hell.

Must we curse these critical times? No, for they are the necessary passage to a state which is sometimes better. And we must not, moreover, be alarmed or pained beyond measure at seeing an increase in our ranks of those exceptional beings whom the alienists call "degenerates," minds lacking in equilibrium, consciousness without energy. A thing which ought to reassure us is the very pronounced connection, still obscure but certain, which discerning observers have discovered between this decadence and the loftiest exaltation.[2] That is why to these men the flame of genius is a suspicious thing, and, when they see it shining somewhere, like the flame of fire-damp, they expect to see some explosion of madness in the descendants.

[1] If the enormous increase in the number of cases of madness treated in asylums or in private houses — an increase which, from 1836 to 1869, according to Jacoby's statistics, has amounted to 245 per cent — was due to a large extent to the progress in mental medical science and to the increasing solicitude of families or of the government for the treatment of the insane, we would find the increase in the number of insane cared for in asylums corresponding approximately to that of sick persons of all kinds treated in the hospitals. For surely no one will pretend that the progress of the succor given by hospitals has more especially been applied in the case of insane asylums, and that cities, the State, or individuals have shown themselves more generous in the creation or the endowment of the latter than in the endowment or creation of hospitals or ordinary hospices. Now, according to *Jacoby's* table ("Sélection," p. 414), the number of insane cared for in asylums has increased *three or four times as rapidly* as that of patients in hospital institutions. Thus it is proved that the progress of madness is not apparent but real.

[2] Such is the truth hidden beneath the mistake made by Poletti. The same causes which, during the first stages of civilization, cause industrial and scientific inventions to succeed one another rapidly, which is a source of prosperity, cause cases of madness and even a falling into crime to increase. But let us be careful not to confuse with this *succession of inventions* the *development of labor* which springs from them through contagious imitation and which is destined to continue after their mine shall have become exhausted. China no longer furnishes any inventions, but continues to labor more than ever.

But let us ask ourselves whether this word "degeneration," used to designate a filiation of anomalies some of which consist in the keenest outburst of intellect, is a happy and a just expression. Have we any social degeneration here? Yet social progress is owing to an agglomeration of this sort of degeneration. Is there even any vital degeneration? I do not admit that there is, and I do not know whether one would not be justified in seeing in these anomalies, in these anatomical and physiological peculiarities which have, as they say, the "marks of degeneration," just so many attempts to escape from the prison of race, in conformity with that potent wish of variation which is the basis of life and the only reason why these monotonous repetitions exist. This wish is repressed by the regular type of the species or race, a limited tissue of characters uniformly repeated wherein individuality, should it wish to be perpetuated without trouble, must allow itself to be imprisoned as it were in an iron cage. But were this wish ever stifled, the progress of life itself would cease as well as that of our societies. Every variation in an individual is a new race projected, a new species in embryo.[1]

From this point of view, could one not interpret the anomalies, the peculiarities pointed out by anthropologists among the insane, criminals, and men of genius, by applying to them the general rules laid down by Darwin with regard to the "Variations in Animals and Plants," perhaps the most weighty of his books? For example, would not civilization, especially during its fever of increase, act on the human type like domestication acts on the types of animals and vegetables? Domestication is a kind of animal or vegetal civilization, just as civilization is a kind of human domestication.

Now, on the one hand, in becoming domesticated, a race loses a great deal of the fertility which it had in a natural state, but, on the other hand, "animals and plants," the great naturalist tells us, "have varied infinitely more than all the forms which in the natural state are considered as distinct species." Every domesticated species has immediately given signs of a "variableness which is fluctuating, indefinite," a sort of fruitful madness of the type which is soon to produce the most marvelous and

[1] Examine some individual variation, it will be found to consist in the more or less marked atrophy or hypertrophy of some organ. Assume that this excess or this defect is pushed to extreme, and by virtue of the law of organic correlation you will find that a general reform of the organism will follow. Every peculiarity possessed by an individual is unconsciously due to this fact.

most fixed adaptations. Similarly, a race in becoming civilized becomes disturbed but is emancipated, and rushes in every direction outside of itself and sometimes surpasses itself. It is possible, after all, that nature did not make the human brain with a view to civilization, and that to this fact is due the progress of madness during the progress of civilization. But, by this means, the brain adapts itself little by little to its better employment. Nor has nature made the human eye with a view to reading, writing, a close scrutiny at a distance of twenty centimètres, and from this fact results the frequency of near-sightedness which spreads in proportion as knowledge is diffused; but this is not a sufficient reason for us to burn our books; and it is worth noticing that far-sightedness is adapting itself to this new form of work.

§ 75. (XIII) Analogies offered by the historical transformation of offenses with that of industries, of languages, of religions, of law, etc. At first *internal* changes in each sort of crime, which has nominally remained the same, general meaning of this transformation. Importance of this consideration in criticizing impartially the judges of the past. Irreversibility of the transformation pointed out above.

In everything I have said so far, I have limited myself to showing that, whether in the manner of its spreading and taking root, whether because of the nature of its conflict or agreement with other kinds of social activity or existence, with the other currents of example, criminality conforms to the general laws which govern societies. But so far we have made a study only of various groups of *coexisting* imitation, especially of the work-group as existing beside the crime-group. It remains for us to complete this table by briefly pointing out that inventions, *successive* imitations the chain of which forms the history of crime, have been substituted for or added to one another in conformity with the rules of social logic bearing upon the substitution and the accumulation of inventions, and of successive imitations [1] in general. In other words, what we are now concerned with is to sift out the analogies which are to be found in the historical changes which have taken place in crime, and the changes which have taken place in industry, I might even add in law, in language, in religion, etc. But as these matters are only of secondary

[1] I can equally well say *invention* or *imitation* here, for I only mean to speak of inventions which have succeeded, *been imitated* in a certain larger or smaller way, and during a longer or shorter period of time; the others do not count from the social point of view.

interest to us from the point of view of penal law, I will not dwell upon them.

I will limit myself first of all to pointing out that, considered as to its inmost, its elementary details, every social transformation always consists in the *logical duel or the logical coupling together* of two inventions, one of which, the new one, either contradicts the other or else confirms it, is an obstacle in the path of the other either in better attaining the same object, or in creating an object contrary to the object of the other, or else comes to the assistance of the other, either by adding to it some method of perfection which does not alter the nature of the other, or in strengthening and generalizing the need, the object to which it responds. Here we have the simple and general rule, absolutely without exception, which governs social transformism; and it is obvious that crime is subject to this rule.

At each step in the history of murder, for example, we find the bronze axe entering into competition with the flint axe, the iron axe with the bronze axe, the matchlock with the cross-bow, the revolver with the pistol, just as at each step in the history of locomotion we find the wheel with spokes being substituted for the solid wheel, the wagon with springs for the one without springs, the locomotive for the stage-coach.[1] Or else we find murder by reason of filial piety opposed successively in some island by each one of the new religious ideas; Christian, Buddhist, Mahometan, which no longer allow one to consider the homicide of his aged parents as the first duty of a good son; just as we find pious pilgrimages to the tomb of some saint successively combated by each one of the new doctrines or the new fashions which decrease the faith in the virtue of pilgrimages and the need of carrying them out.[2]

We also know that it is as a result of small increases always consisting in a new process grafted on to a group of previously

[1] Or as at each moment during the existence of a language we see the person who speaks this language make rapid choice between two expressions, one old and one modern, and the philological change which results in the long run from an infinite number of similar choices. Probably it is thus that the *article* has come to be substituted for the *declension*, "caballus" for "equus," etc., in the formation of the Romance languages. Does not political life also consist at each moment upon each question, in a conflict between *two* opinions one of which says "yes" and the other of which says "no"? Has anybody ever seen a three-sided fight? There have never been more than two rival elements face to face at the base of every change.

[2] Or just as we see a word fall into disuse because the idea of which it is an expression has been replaced by some other idea which has invaded men's minds.

existing processes that burglary or the making of counterfeit banknotes are ever being perfected, like photography or the electric telegraph. Or else that the development of cattle stealing in a given section of the country, of the stealing of bills to bearer in another, depends upon the aid rendered these crimes by each importation of new breeds of cattle or each putting in circulation of new negotiable instruments which pass from hand to hand, by contributing to increase a greed for this form of wealth; just as metallurgy receives a new impetus with each new use discovered for iron, from whence results a greater demand for this metal. Owing to the alternate or combined play of these various logical operations, criminality, in all countries, changes in nature and aspect from one age to another. One might think, looking at the matter from a distance, that the same kinds of offenses have always been in existence. But the same thing can be said with respect to the various kinds of industry. From all time there have existed an industry for the production of food, another for the production of clothing, others for shelter, for weapons, for ornaments, for art. Does this make it any the less true that the processes for obtaining food, equipment, amusement, etc., have varied greatly from the time of the Troglodytes of Eyzies up to our own times, and the processes for poisoning, arson, swindling, of homicide even, no less? Especially is it any the less true that an industry, while having apparently remained unchanged, while having kept the same processes, has become greatly altered, if it no longer answers the same needs, but has adapted itself to new functions, if, for example, a certain method of building, which was formerly intended to be used for the housing of the statues of Greek gods and to fulfill the needs of public worship, now serves to shelter litigants or to flatter the vanity of some individual, or if carpets formerly made for Arabs to recline upon under tents in silence are now manufactured for the feet of ladies who chatter in a drawing-room?

The same thing applies to crime. There are thefts and thefts, knife blows and knife blows, arson and arson. Setting fire to another's house for the sake of revenge has nothing in common but its name with setting fire to one's own house out of greed. I have already pointed out how much suicide, as well, differs from itself, according as it is an act of religious fanaticism as in India, a means of having one's enemy accused of crime as in China, a heroic means of rehabilitation as in China again, or an act of despair as in Europe. When societies first come into existence, hatred and hunger, or at the most physical love, are the inspiration for every crime; later on passions which already begin to be less elemental, religious fanaticism, family vengeance, conjugal jealousy, the sentiment of man's or woman's honor, finally the desire of luxury, of comfort, of dissipated pleasures, of the voluptuousness of cities, become the predominating motives.

What difference does it make that, in two different periods, a thing which is not strictly accurate moreover, people have killed and stolen after the same fashion? The soul of the offense has changed. French statistics of the year 1880, in telling us how, in less than a half century, the proportion between the various motives of crime, whether vengeance, jealousy, honor, or cupidity, has been completely altered, show us the strength of the internal causes which impel this change. Conversely, it may often happen that the same need is satisfied in industry by the most dissimilar products, and, in crime, by acts which are apparently not similar at all. In such a case as this there has taken place a true criminal metempsychosis. The Polynesian warrior who buys heads which have been severed from bodies to make of them a lying trophy and thus gain the esteem for himself which is the result of his apparent exploits, does not differ very greatly from the European who buys a decoration for a money consideration and at the price of some suspicious bargain.

We must not forget that internal revolution affecting certain crimes under the illusive permanence of their surface, if we wish to judge justly of the past. For example, have we any right to pity the people of those times when society had no interest in the punishment of homicide and plundering and left to the family of the outraged person the care of avenging the death or the physical injury which had been inflicted upon it? Instead of without proof attributing to those times the absurdity of not having felt the most keen interest in them, we should do better to see in this peculiarity of their criminal procedure a proof that the habitual criminality of those times differed greatly from that of ours.

Everywhere and always, among the newest peoples, whenever a particularly audacious murder or robbery even is committed under the inspiration of a motive of such a nature that everybody must fear that this act will be repeated should it go unpunished, everybody will instinctively join hands in order to secure the punishment of the guilty person. We know what lynch law is in America. In every society in process of formation there is spontaneously established some similar custom, which takes the place of our public prosecutor's office. I conclude from this, as among certain peoples and at certain periods, among the Alemanni, for example, murder and theft were punished only by the family of the victim, that these offenses were generally acts of vengeance provoked by an enmity existing between families, as is the case in Corsica. It is the same with respect to the homicides committed in Cochin China by the Annamites, in Algeria by the Arabs; rage, jealousy, resentment are the abundant sources of these crimes, as we are told by Lorion and Kocher. The proof of this lies in the fact pointed out by both these learned men, which is that the Annamites, and the Arabs as well, kill one another but do not kill Europeans.

On the other hand, in our day and in our Europe, if crime is less frequent, it is to be dreaded in quite another way; we are aware, beyond the shadow of a doubt, that the murderer who has feloniously broken into the house of an old lady to kill and rob her would just as soon enter anybody's house if he were set free. Each one is therefore interested in his punishment; and if our society as a whole takes upon itself his prosecution, there is nothing for us to boast about in this. In the last analysis this but proves that cupidity has become the usual motive of assassination. Besides, when a brigand who was a menace to all made his appearance in olden times, the feeling of common danger always set up against him, just as against some monster which had to be exterminated, a revengeful hero, a Hercules. The public vengeance is incarnated in his person by means of myths or legends.

Again, the rule of prosecution which was exclusively a family matter was not without significant exceptions. Among the Alemanni, for example, there were certain crimes prosecuted and punished with death by the entire nation. But what were these crimes? Desertion, cowardice, and notoriously bad morals.[1] Obviously this was because these crimes were the only ones the example of which seemed to be a contagion of such a nature as to become general and not local. Had homicide at that time been inspired by cupidity, would they have omitted to add it to this

[1] *Thonissen*, in his fine work on the "Loi salique," says that this list furnished by Tacitus is perhaps incomplete; but he himself when he attempts afterwards to enumerate crimes not included within pecuniary compensation by the Salic Law, and which are punished by the extreme penalty, finally finds five. "Treason, desertion, cowardice, regicide, and infamous morals."

list where today it could not fail to rank first? We learn from an edict of Childebert, in the year 596, that, in his time, there were in Gaul brigands and robbers, assassinating and plundering on the high roads. Now these latter, by the terms of this edict, are barred from pecuniary composition; the judge must have them bound and executed. No doubt all this expression of the royal will did was to regulate a previously existing practice. But the necessity, not recognized until that time, of modifying by means of a legislative enactment the old Germanic law, confirms what was said above as to recrudescence and also as to the transformation in criminality during the Merovingian period.[1]

This character, becoming less and less proud, vindictive and passionate, and more and more voluptuous, studied and greedy, with which crime has been clothed in passing from barbarism, I do not say from savagery, to civilization, is due to the general causes which, in the whole order of things, have caused to predominate in civilized man as compared with barbarian man, design over passion, a wish for well being over pride. Pride especially, pride of blood, family pride rather than individual pride, is like a very precipitous psychological mountain which the wear of every social contact has resulted in denuding, of slowly lowering for the benefit of that alluvium of artificial needs and voluptuous refinements which has never ceased to grow at its foot.

Every form of art and every form of industry has felt this great mental movement. Painting, sculpture, music, architecture, poetry, have all begun by having as their sole object the glorifying of a king, a hero, or a god, and as their only motive the glory of the artist, and have ended by answering above everything to the need of comfort or refined pleasure which has spread among the public, as well as to the need of pecuniary success and not merely honorary success, which is gaining in ascendancy even over the hearts of artists themselves. Every industry, — with the exception, be it understood, of those which satisfy the coarsest needs, and which I will compare with the stealing of food or acts of

[1] In reading the "Origines indo-européenes," by *Pictet*, in the midst of all the conjectures which are there accumulated, one is struck at seeing how much the relative analogies under the name of *murder* and of *theft, but especially of murder*, in all the Aryan languages, are concise, correct, and incontestable. This fact certainly supports the opinion which looks upon homicide, and homicide not for greed, as the customary crime of barbarian times. *Fraud*, on the other hand, or abuse of confidence only gives rise in the work in question to philological similarities which are few and doubtful.

anthropophagy necessitated by famine, — every industry begins in the same way by working for the greatness of the great and for the most part for the honor of the artisan, and ends in the same way by catering to the tastes of everybody for a compensation which is entirely mercenary. To the extent that the luxury of barbarian times aimed at magnificence and ostentation does the luxury of later times aim at elegance and grace,[1] at gentleness and simplicity. Again, just as the danger of murder in olden times was only to be dreaded within a narrow circle about the murderer, similarly the usefulness of old industries was only appreciated, and with good reason, by a limited number of persons, by the few families for whom the workman especially intended his work. Nowadays the entire public feels an interest in the prosperity of our new industries as in the repression of our new forms of offense.

Let us note that these changes cannot take place inversely. This is a remark which we shall have occasion to make again elsewhere. We could no more conceive, unless there should be an overthrow of our civilization and its place were taken by a new society, of a return of our greedy, lascivious, and subtle criminality to the passionate, proud, and brutal criminality of our ancestors, than we could conceive of a return of our contemporary dramas to the tragedies of Rotrou, or of Racine even, and to the mysteries of the Middle Ages, or of our paintings showing scenes from everyday life to the frescoes of monastic chapels, or of our railway laborers to the "frères pontifes" of the Middle Ages, who built bridges and roads for charity, or to the masons of the Gothic cathedrals, or even of our analytical languages, so convenient for the use of everybody, to the synthetic languages of former times, complicated, sonorous, and pompous, and well suited to an aristocracy of leisured and speech-making citizens. This *irreversibility* is the characteristic of every natural transformation, not only organic, but physical as well. There is not a creature which has retrograded along the road of life, there is not a river which has flowed back to its source. Why? More often than not we do not know; but it seems that, in so far as the social world is concerned, the bearing of the laws of imitation readily accounts for the impossibility of this retrogression. The necessity of their application assumes this.

[1] See *Roscher* (*op. cit.*) and *Baudrillart*, "Histoire du luxe."

§ 76. (XIV) In the second place, change in the accusation, crimes which have become torts, and have then been legalized, or vice versa. Comparison with the variation in values. General meaning and irreversibility of these slow revolutions. Garofalo's theory of the "natural offense."

In passing from one civilization to another, or in going over the successive phases of a single civilization, we find certain acts descending from the rank of great crimes to that of lesser offenses and becoming finally lawful if not praiseworthy, — for example from the Middle Ages down to the present, religious free-thought, blasphemy, vagabondage, poaching, smuggling, adultery, sodomy, — or on the other hand, from being lawful, from being praiseworthy sometimes, as they used to be, becoming slightly offensive and finally criminal,—for example, from ancient times down to the Middle Ages, abortion, infanticide, pederasty, fornication.

This double movement of transformation which consists, not like the previous one, in the changing of the motives for the same act which is always looked upon as an offense, but in the different qualifications of a common act which sometimes allowed and sometimes punished, takes place under the action of the unconscious logic which governs every transformation of a society, and which has a tendency to place beliefs in harmony with needs, and both beliefs and needs in harmony with actions. It is owing to this fact that, when a new belief, such as the Christian faith, or when a new need, such as that of political emancipation, arises out of all proportion, this general uneasiness which denotes the rupture with the old system of desires and ideas is the rule which governs conduct. From this there result currents of opinion or passion which, like marine currents, tend towards the re-establishment of the equilibrium which has been disturbed.

The transformation with which we are here dealing may be compared with that which takes place, being governed by the same causes, in the value of natural or manufactured objects. When Christianity became spread throughout the Roman Empire, the temples, the statues of gods, the lascivious paintings, the amphitheatres, the thermal baths themselves, which had previously been of very great value, and a sufficient justification for the most lavish extravagance, rapidly depreciated to such an extent that they became an encumbrance which had sometimes to be demolished at great expense. Thus, later on, a heresy of a thousand persons was sufficient to reduce to nothing the value of the images of the saints which filled the Eastern Empire, and bring into play the hammer of the iconoclasts. We know that, at the Bourse and the "Hôtel des ventes," it is not a so-called law of supply and demand, but the explanation itself of this pretended law, an opinion which may be false or true, a capricious judgment circulated among the general public, which causes the current price of the stock of some company, the pictures of some master, or the furniture of a particular period to rise and fall. A certain book which used to be sold for its own weight in gold can no longer find a purchaser. The library of Alexandria was infinitely precious to the inhabitants of that city; to Omar it was a nuisance.

No doubt, though needs and actions conform to ideas, ideas in their turn are modeled in the long run after needs and actions,[1] but only in the long run. It is not true that the nature of the acts which are judged to be useful or injurious, virtuous or criminal, and the scale of their gradations, are determined by nature and the relative intensity of the needs which are a concomitant part of each age. They are rather related to an ideal of honor or a counter-ideal of dishonor, both conceived of *in reference to* and not in imitation of general needs, which are not present but past ones. The honor and the dishonor of a certain time correspond with the needs of the time which has immediately gone before; these are sentiments which survive their cause and become strengthened even after the latter has disappeared. Chivalrous honor was never more keenly felt than under Louis XIII, when chivalry had already lost its reason for existing. Was there ever a time when so many duels were fought, although social interest had never been more opposed to this epidemic?

The unfolding of religious beliefs, as well as of scientific truths, is to a great extent independent of the parallel development of needs, in spite of the fact that the former feels the effects of the latter, and the subordination of the latter to the former, consequently of human conduct to human thought, seems to me to be the dominant factor in history. For example let us try to ascertain what has been, during each phase of a society, the act reputed to be the greatest crime; we shall find that it is the act which is

[1] Among the Athenians, according to Lysias, insulting a magistrate, even when he was in the exercise of his duty, was only punishable when it took place within the precincts of the Court where this magistrate was sitting. According to Thonissen, this is to be accounted for by the habits of slander and free speaking which were common among the Athenians.

most repugnant to the prevalent dogma. We shall also find that the possession deemed to be the most precious is the one which satisfies the need which is most in conformity with this dogma.

During the theocratic phase, to touch an object which is tabu, an *impure* animal or man, to worship any god other than the god of the tribe or the town, to allow the sacred fire to go out, to blaspheme, to infringe the custom dealing with the burial of relatives (who become gods after their death), not to sacrifice upon their graves the human or animal victims called for by the rites: these are the greatest crimes. For the disciple of Zoroaster, the greatest crime is to bury the dead; their bodies should be exposed to the dogs and birds of prey. For the Greeks, the greatest crime is not to bury the dead. During these same periods, a divine talisman (Minerva's veil at Athens, the shields which came down from heaven at Rome, the black stone of Mecca), a relic of the god, of a saint, an object of worship: such are the possessions most highly valued. The greatest *treasure* of the Middle Ages was what we still call, through a survival in language, the "Treasure of the Churches." Thus one of the most lucrative forms of swindling of those times was the industry of the sellers of false relics and indulgences, as at present it is the industry of the sellers of shares of stock. Even profane furniture had to be modeled after the furniture of the churches in order to have any value, and luxurious chairs looked like choir stalls.

Moral sentiment depended so much upon religious belief, during the period with which we are dealing, that not only in Egypt and in India, but almost everywhere, at a time when a regard for human life outside of that of members of the tribe was unknown, a respect for animal life was pushed to the extreme of attaching to the killing or wounding of certain animals a character which was criminal in the highest degree; long before there were humanitarians there were "animalitarians," to make use of the expression of Letourneau. This was because superstitious ideas were suggested by the odious, queer, and enigmatical appearance of wild beasts or reptiles which were the object of general veneration. However, the spread of religious belief has had better effects than these. When, in a tribe where a scruple would be felt about killing the members of that tribe but none about killing strangers, there was introduced a religion of proselytizing, it was no longer only one's fellow-countryman, but it was one's *co-religionist* whom one spared, and the killing of whom was judged to be a crime. "How could a believer," Mahomet was wont to say, "ever kill another believer?" He does not merely say "another Arab." If infanticide is unknown in Cochin China to the extent that it is not provided for in the Annamite Code, it is because the girl mother is not in the least discredited in that country, but on the other hand is able to get married much more readily, into those families where they are anxious to have children in order that they may perpetuate the worship of their ancestors.[1] Here we have a superstition which has checked an injury and a crime.

During the monarchic phase of societies, the greatest crime is high treason, rebellion against the authority of the king; the greatest possession is the royal favor, a smile and some present from the monarch. Everything, both in clothing and in valuable furniture, is modeled after the royal palaces.

However, let us observe that this phase is added to the previous one rather than substituted for it. Also theocratic sentiment still prevails in this phase. In fact we can judge of the nature of the crimes looked upon as being the most serious at different times by considering those crimes most often punished by the death penalty. Now we find from the archives of the royal court of Stockholm, according to d'Olivecrona, that during the seventeenth century, "the court pitilessly imposed the death penalty for sorcery, for sacrilegious and blasphemous speeches against God, for perjury, and for the sin of sodomy," but that, "a composition could be paid for homicide upon condition of a fine which accrued for the benefit of the king."

We find the same contrast in England during the sixteenth, seventeenth, and eighteenth centuries, as well as in France. In England, where they were so lavish of the death penalty, "few persons were executed for murder." During the feudal phase the greatest crime is "félonie," that is to say treason against one's lord; the finest possession a knight's spurs; everything not having a seignioral stamp about it is of no value. Until the sixteenth century, there existed feudal crimes, which have since disappeared, among others hunting and fishing, which are now mere misdemeanors or rather special infringements. In our democratic century of individualism, the greatest of crimes is homicide, whatever may be the status of the victim; the possessions most sought after are the electoral offices, gratification of the senses and comfort;

[1] See *Lorion* on this subject (*op. cit.*).

everything takes on an appearance of realism, of individualism, of popularization. Even art bends in the direction of this form and measures the value of its works according to their popularity. In Boutillier's time (fifteenth century), the uniting together of laborers with a view to increasing their wages was a capital crime;[1] at the present time it has become the exercising of a right, almost a duty. It is to be observed that at Athens, laziness in the case of a poor man was a misdemeanor; in the case of the rich a wasting of the family estate in luxury and debauchery. This last law may seem to be opposed to the democratic spirit of the Athenians; but the democracy of ancient times understood the cult of the family in a different manner than ours, and thought it a duty, no less than did the aristocracy, to watch over the preservation of the home.

I will point out, without insisting very much upon it, the manifestly irreversible character, to a large extent, of the changes which have taken place in criminality from the point of view which we have just been studying, that is to say, in correlation to revolutions in ideas the retrogression of which could not even be conceived of. This is so in certain cases at least, for example when the spirit of democracy (whether under a monarchic form or not) comes after the feudal spirit, and especially when a better religion comes after a form of worship which is inferior, a more advanced science or industry after a more rudimentary science or industry. It is quite certain that a nation having been seriously converted to Christianity would never give it up for a coarse form of worship, such as that of the Polynesians, and consequently would not think of regarding as criminal something which it looked upon as being lawful formerly, that is to say, for example, the fact of touching an object which is tabu. It is just as certain that a nation having attained our present degree of enlightenment would never go back to punishing with any kind of a penalty the act of casting a spell over a field or of assassinating some one in effigy to the accompaniment of mystic words, and that a society raised to the level of our contemporary luxury, the slow deposit of so many discoveries and industrial inventions which have come within the reach of all, would never think of putting a woman in prison for wearing a silk dress. Here, and in every example of this sort, and they can be cited by thousands, it is manifest that the impossibility of returning to the accusations of the past is dependent

[1] *Du Boys*, "Histoire du Droit criminel chez les peuples modernes," Vol. I.

upon the impossibility of replacing our beliefs, our knowledge and our habits, our ideas and our forces, in the last analysis our discoveries and our inventions, with those of former times.

But there are also a large number of changes which have taken place in the accusation which have as their cause, without being dependent upon any new discoveries or inventions, the mere imitative expansion of those which were already known. In this new sense, the irreversible character of the transformations with which we are dealing is still more manifest, for the waves of imitation are ever advancing and know no ebb. In proportion as neighboring or distant peoples progress along the way of reflecting one another more and more, we know that the moral sphere of each one of them expands and tends to embrace all the others, and this mere enlargement of the sphere of duty causes the appearance or disappearance of numerous forms of crime. When the inhabitants of a seacoast have entered into relations with the foreigners who navigate their seas, they no longer consider lawful, murder, the enslaving of persons who are shipwrecked, or even the capture of vessels which are driven ashore upon their coasts. They decree laws and penalties for the repression of these inhuman acts, and thenceforward there never will be any thought of striking this article from their statute books. Let us not forget that the greatest moral benefit of civilization has been less the perfecting in us of natural feelings of justice and kindness than the indefinite extension of the limits of their application beyond the confines of the family, the tribe, the town, and the fatherland.

There has been nothing of more essential importance in the history of humanity than this gradual opening up of new horizons in the conception of what crime is, this idea having originally been confined within the circle of the hearth, and it is clear that thus it can never again go back to its infancy of olden times. The first step which had to be taken was by far the most difficult, and it would be impossible sufficiently to bless the ingenuous inventors — for in this the presence of new ideas was a necessity — who thought of the most ingenious devices for overcoming the difficulty. By means of the symbolical forms of adoption, by means of certain ceremonies such as the mingling of drops of blood to seal an alliance, they made it possible for the family to expand artificially, when already, be it understood, a certain degree of social similitude had come to be established between this family and the outside elements which were to be incorporated into it. A proceeding which is especially peculiar is the following, which Marco Polo saw practiced by the Tartars. The families wishing to become united celebrated a marriage between two of their dead just as though they had been alive, and, from that time on, a tie of relationship, or relationship by marriage, was thought to bind them closely together. These polite and salutary fictions are certainly worth as much as those of our codes, traps within which the spirit of the jurist lies hidden.

Let us add that, owing to these expedients and to many others, the imitative progress of civilization does not result merely in an increase in the number of offenses under the guise of acts which were previously not considered as being of a delictual character. It also produces the opposite result, the doing away with offenses formerly regarded as such, because ignorance is the chief source of the prejudices which cause non-injurious acts to be looked upon as criminal, and because it is impossible that in reflecting one another more and more people should not enlighten one another more and more every day. Thus, either by virtue of the laws of imitation, which we know, or by virtue of the laws of invention (which compel the most simple inventions, for example, to precede the more complicated ones, or the crudest ones to precede the most perfect ones), the metamorphoses of crimination form a series which, taken as a whole, it would be impossible to reverse.

Now let us ask ourselves whether, in the midst of all these transformations, there is no fixed point. We have said a few words as to the theory of the "natural offense" outlined by Garofalo; by this he understands the outrage perpetrated, in all times and in all countries, against a certain average feeling of pity and justice the limits of which it is very difficult for him even approximately to determine. In spite of the unrestricted limits which may be given it, this notion, as we have already pointed out, fundamentally implies an undeniable truth. But it ought to be better defined, and our point of view will supply us with the means of so doing. Not every similarity existing between living beings is of vital origin, that is to say, the result of repetition by means of heredity. There are many of them, called functional analogies by anatomists, and, moreover, treated by them very loftily and with the most absolute scorn, which occur between animals and plants belonging to types not related to one another, or at least which make their appearance by virtue of causes quite other than the tie of blood. Such is the vague resemblance between the wing of the insect and that of the bird; such is the fact that animals of all branches, in being developed according to their special order of progress, acquire a head and senses, a stomach and members, etc.

All this is of some importance, but there is not an anatomist who will do these coincidences the honor of placing them in the same rank as those similarities, often very obscure and hard to perceive, yet due to heredity, which they call correspondence of parts. In the same way, all the similarities which exist between social beings are not of social origin, and have not imitation as their cause; there are some, and a great number of them, whose spontaneous appearance is due, as among several heterogeneous societies, to the suggestion of the same organic needs, to the grasping of the same external conditions for the purpose of utilizing them.[1] Even though not related, two languages have this much in common, that they distinguish between nouns and verbs, that they decline and conjugate. Even though not connected with the same mythological source, two religions may possess solar or lunar myths and deify bravery in men or fecundity in women. Even independently of all common tradition, two governments may be republican or monarchic.

One can, if one will, call *natural religion,* that common basis which several religions are found to have, and as well, although this does not always amount to the same thing, the things which remain approximately invariable in each of them in spite of the greatest changes which may occur in them. Will one perchance say that these are the faith in a divine principle and a future life? This has been said, but not without laying open those who have made the statement to having it contradicted by many facts. One can also, though not without a certain extravagance, call *natural language* the ensemble of ways of speaking, of the inventions of philology, by means of which all idioms are related to one another without being aware of it, and always will be related to one another.

Finally, I do not see anything incongruous in denoting as *natural offenses,* those acts which the organic impulses of human

[1] In this case let us observe it is repetition by generations (heredity), combined with repetition of undulation (a form of repetition which is peculiar to all physical agencies) which accounts for the similarity which cannot be accounted for by imitation. Of the three forms of repetition which I distinguish one at least is always at the basis of every similarity.

nature, in so far as it is identical everywhere and always, have caused to be perpetrated everywhere and the opposition of which to the fundamental conditions of social life has in all times and at all places caused them to be disapproved and stigmatized. I will add that the name of *natural rights* given those powers of action without which social life would be an impossibility, is neither more nor less justified, and that it also has its reason for existing, understood in the way of which we have just been speaking. And I even believe that one could just as well define the idea of a *natural penalty;* retaliation, above everything, is deserving of this name. A remarkable thing is that the Egyptians, the Red-Skins, and the African negroes all separately conceived of the idea of cutting off the noses of adulterous women, an idea naturally suggested, I suppose, by the desire to make hideous those whom their beauty had caused to transgress. The Aztec vestals, just as the Roman vestals, were buried alive when they violated their oath of chastity. On the other hand, not only is retaliation spread over the entire earth, and often, as we can see, under similar forms, sometimes also, as we have seen, under symbolical forms, symbols of a symbol, but it is kept up with remarkable energy throughout all the metamorphoses of the penal law. Now again, does not the resistance which the people are bringing to bear upon the complete abolition of the death penalty depend upon the fact that it is only applied in the case of assassins? Thus, as you can see, I do not repel the parent idea of the natural offense, but I define it in explaining it, and it will not be found amiss that, without in this respect sharing the contempt professed for functional analogies by anatomists, I do not dwell upon it immoderately.

However, this explanation must itself be explained and developed. There are three different ways in which we may interpret, in every social order, those non-imitative similarities to which the idea of *what is natural* is unconsciously applied. Sometimes these spontaneous resemblances are looked upon as being especially connected with the beginning of the independent social evolutions between which they occur. In this sense, natural language, natural religion, natural law, natural government, natural industry, and natural art, could only have existed in all their purity during primitive times, and would ever be changing, like the background of a picture becoming more and more covered with various kinds of figures. Sometimes, on the other hand, we are told of those things which are termed natural as being rather things which are ideal and rational, like ultimate causes understood in the way Aristotle understood them. It is when their development is ended and not at its inception that these various languages must be intended to bring out their conformity with a common natural grammar, the various systems of civil and penal law, their conformity with a common natural law, etc.

Finally, instead of noticing the non-imitative similarity of certain determined states, whether they be initial or terminal, the similarity of their succession may rather be maintained, and as our evolutionists are doing, an attempt may be made to condense into one formula of development common to the most diverse societies, the settled series of their transformations. I admit that, of these three interpretations, which are moreover all more or less acceptable in a varying degree, I have a preference for the second. I believe it to be more consistent with the facts, less fundamentally mystic in spite of appearing to be otherwise, and alone susceptible of being reconciled with the aspirations of reason, which are in reality positive themselves, and the data furnished by experience. If in the theory of Garofalo on the natural offense we must see a first step towards that positive idealism, I welcome it by that title, and I hasten to welcome it, not as a summing up of the conceptions of crime of the past, — for this summing up would be singularly inaccurate, — but as the plan of future conceptions of crime, destined, let us hope, to become simplified and rectified in this sense or in a more intellectual sense, but still in one which approaches this thought.

§ 77. (XV) In the third place, changes in criminal procedure. Same order as that of the succession of tools. Irreversible order.

Just as the motive and the nature of crime have greatly altered from age to age, so have the ways in which these crimes have been committed; and this latter transformation, merely because it is more superficial than the others, is none the less deserving of some attention. Here again, crime has conformed to the general course of social evolution. Let us first of all observe that agricultural industry is distinguished from industry properly so called by its characteristic attachment to traditional usage. Rural criminality is to be distinguished from urban criminality by this same characteristic. In the second place, progress in industry has consisted in obtaining the greatest possible useful effect with the least possible expenditure of human energy, that is to say, in replacing man by instruments which become more and more responsive and less and less costly, in other words, by living energies or substances first of all, then by inorganic ones, and often enough, if one goes into detail, by animal energies or substances at first, then vegetable ones, then physical, and finally chemical ones.[1]

Without being invariable, this order is sufficiently frequent to be worthy of notice. Stones for grinding grain at first operated by slaves, then by horses, were afterwards operated by wind and water power. Locomotion was at first effected by transportation on the backs of slaves, in palanquins, or on horseback, on donkeys, camels, and elephants, or in wagons hauled by horses, later on by means of steam, the result of the combustion of fossil plants (coal).[2] In the future perhaps it will be by compressed air or electricity. The offerings or sacrifices to the gods were first human, then animal, and finally vegetable before becoming entirely metallic. The important thing was always to obtain the same advantage at the lowest possible price. The horns of domestic animals in early times served various purposes, such as window panes, drinking vessels, etc., a great number of the purposes now served by glass. Formerly light was obtained by burning tallow or fat (Nero thought of this in having Christians burned for the illumination of his festivals) before it was obtained by means of torches, with olive oil or other oleaginous seeds, and finally with mineral oils or gas. Bourdeau, in his "Forces de l'industrie," has pointed out striking examples of this order. In the beginning letters were sealed with an animal product, bees-wax; then with Spanish wax, a vegetable product, or with sealing wafers or

[1] The distinction of an age, such as it is understood by archaeologists, is nothing but the incomplete expression of this law, if one stops to think that the age of unhewn *stone* or hewn stone and then of *bronze* and *iron* (these latter being substances which are chemically obtained), were preceded by an age of *wood*, in which the only weapon and tool was the stick, and in still more primitive times by an age when man was reduced to his own semi-animal strength alone, or to that of his fellow-beings whom he had subjugated. — But instead of construing this succession of periods as a general division of history or of prehistoric times, it is more accurate and more interesting to see in it before everything a series of phases just passed through by each industry separately and at periods which differ very widely.

[2] There are exceptions. For example, navigation was first of all effected by means of the arms of rowers, then by means of sails, and finally by steam. Here the third term, of vegetable origin, ought, it would seem, to change places with the second. But in reality this case comes within the general rule of the maximum effect being obtained by the minimum effort.

paste. From the use of animal ivory there has been a change to the use of vegetable ivory, etc.

Crime has progressed in the same manner. For animal poisons, ordinarily used by savages who dip their arrows in the venom of snakes, have been substituted in current usage, vegetable poisons, which were in vogue during the Middle Ages, and today mineral poisons, phosphorous and arsenic. The first assassins must have knocked down and strangled their victims with their bare hands, later on set ferocious dogs upon them, or brought them down with arrows, operated by means of the elasticity of wood, and still later made use of the explosion of gunpowder and dynamite. The progress of hunting, connected with that of warfare, here throws light on that of murder, the murderer like the warrior having begun by being a hunter of men. Now, the first Nimrods pursued their quarry themselves, then they had it pursued and caught by a dog, or by birds of prey, and then by an arrow from their bow and a bullet from their gun. The coursing dog must necessarily have preceded the pointer; the latter only became a possibility after weapons throwing a missile had become perfected, he being but an accessory of this type of weapon. At a time before the beginnings of history, we have reason to believe that man in battles, and homicidal attacks as well, employed as an auxiliary, before any of the weapons throwing a missile had become sufficiently perfected, the strength of wild animals which had been tamed, such as the dog who was half jackal, the tiger even and the lion, which animals had been domesticated at the Assyrian court.[1] It is hard to conceive what purpose could have been served by the dog, a wild animal which had scarcely been tamed, at this dawn of humanity, unless it were to fight for its master. The *offensive* dog must have come before the *defensive* dog. And this is not all; homicide by order, by bravos, which corresponds to industry carried on by slaves, must have been in existence even before homicide carried out by dogs, tigers or lions.

In the case of theft, a maximum of effect with a minimum of effort has been attained less through an alteration in methods, although these have greatly changed, than through an alteration in the nature of the objects stolen. At first, flocks were stolen, as is still the case in Sicily; then crops, which were already less troublesome and just as lucrative; finally, money, banknotes, and

[1] Several Roman emperors, as we know, had themselves drawn in their triumphal chariots by domesticated lions.

bills to bearer, which, though small in bulk, were the equivalent of many head of cattle. But if in swindling, as commonly understood, we see nothing more than a species of theft, we yet perceive that the historical succession of the methods of stealing corresponds to that of the stolen objects.[1] Between the stealing of a flock, even between the stealing of the sheep of Polyphemus by Ulysses, the most crafty hero of ancient times, and the stealing of several millions by an untrustworthy financier of today, who makes the public his dupes by means of the lies in his newspapers, there is the same distance as there is between the death of Caesar from Brutus' dagger and the explosion of a nihilist bomb under the train of the Czar.

One word more as to homicide. According to the statistics of Bournet,[2] I find that in Italy, out of 2983 crimes of a bloodthirsty nature committed in 1888, by far the greater proportion are murders committed by means of knives, stilettos, daggers, clubs, agricultural implements, and other sharp or cutting instruments which require a more or less marked amount of human energy. The total number of crimes of this sort is 1815, whereas murders committed by means of firearms number but 824. In Corsica and in Sicily, the converse is true. In Corsica, especially during the period from 1836 to 1846, we reckon 371 homicides by means of a gun or pistol and 69 by means of a knife or stiletto. Thus homicide in Italy, and in Spain as well, or even in France,[3] seems, as far as the means employed are concerned, to be behind homicide in Corsica and Sicily. Are the nations most advanced in industry the most backward in the matter of crime? However this may be, it does not prevent the weapons of warfare from progressing at the same pace as do the implements of industry, and by virtue of the same scientific progress, as we know only too well in Europe.

Among many warlike people, whom the contagion of surrounding industrialism does not reach, the progress in the matter of armament does not fail to make itself felt. How many islanders

[1] Swindling is more and more developed rather than ordinary theft, for the same reason that indirect taxes are every day becoming more important than direct taxes. This is because indirect taxation is the most perfect form of taxation in the sense pointed out. — This change seems to be irreversible.

[2] "Criminalité en France et en Italie."

[3] During the period 1856–73 we find in France 457 murders carried out by means of knives, stilettos and swords, and only 273 committed by means of guns and revolvers; from 1836 to 1880, the part played by the pistol increases and that played by the stiletto decreases.

we see who, having remained savages in all other respects, are already making use of guns! It is also noticeable that the more primitive weapon, just because it is the oldest, is considered the noblest. In Italy the knife is a more noble instrument than the gun.[1]

In the matter of armament as in the matter of implements the progress is obviously irreversible. It is useless to prove it.

§ 78. (XVI) A summing up of the chapter. Characteristics which differentiate crime from the other social phenomena. Crime and war. Historical passing from the unilateral to the reciprocal.

To sum up this entire chapter, we have every right, it seems to me, to conclude that criminality without any doubt, like every other branch of social activity, implies physiological and even physical conditions, but that, like industry especially, it is to be accounted for better than in any other way, by the general laws of imitation, in its local color as in its special force at each period of time, in its geographical distribution as in its historical transformations, in the varying proportion of its various motives or the unstable hierarchy of its varying degrees as in the succession of its changing methods. We have mentioned the importance in our opinion attaching to this demonstration, from the point of view of penal responsibility, from which it results that the offense is an act emanating not merely from the living being, but from the personal individual, such as society alone can make him and cause him to increase in number in its image; from the person more identical with himself, up to a certain point at least, as he is more similar to others; the more willing and conscious as he is more readily impressed by example, just as the better it breathes, the stronger the lung is. It has been said that our body is a small quantity of condensed air, living in the air. Can it not be said that our soul is a small quantity of society incarnate, living in society? Born from society, it lives by means of society; and if the analogies which I have perhaps at some length enumerated are correct, there is no reason why its criminal responsibility should be misunderstood any more than its civil responsibility, which latter is undisputed and assuredly incapable of being disputed.

Moreover, let us clearly understand each other on this important point. I will not deny that, to a greater or lesser extent, the

[1] Among the Annamites and the Chinese, decapitation with the sword is considered a national art, which it would be a shameful thing to allow to degenerate.

physical or physiological provocations to commit an offense have acted as the determining cause of the will; but their action, being only partial, does not prevent the delinquent from being responsible. On the contrary, they compete with one another, on their part, to demonstrate that he is responsible. No doubt, if they acted by themselves upon the individual, he would not be socially responsible, because this would reveal in him a being absolutely alien to the society of other men; but he might continue to be responsible individually. By this I mean that the condition of social similarity, required by our theory of responsibility, would not really be fulfilled, but that the condition of individual identity, which is above all requisite, might be realized, in spite of the inevitable necessity of external influences.

Without doubt one can see, to a certain extent, in the criminal calendar, and in general, in all statistical tables where a connection is shown between exciting causes of a physical or vital nature and a recurrence of certain crimes, a *sociological* confirmation of the physio-psychological hypothesis as to the similarity of the will to reflex action. The will, according to this theory, only differs from reflex action in the number of the psychic elements, of the memories interposed between the initial exciting cause and the final reaction, which is called voluntary when one has lost consciousness of the complex tie which exists between these two terms. Thus statistics would give us back this lost consciousness, or rather, it would enable us to acquire this consciousness which we have never had by causing us to put our finger on our secret springs.

Now, this much having been admitted and to a certain extent proved, it is quite certain that responsibility based upon free will falls to the ground. But based upon identity, upon individual *character*, it survives, on condition that social similarity be not lacking. For the exciting cause which has been received has only acted because it has been found to be in accord with the demands of the character; this conformity is one of the necessary intermediaries between the first and the last term of the series. Besides, the true nature of reflex action, even the most simple and of the lowest form, would be misinterpreted if there were seen in it merely a phenomenon of causality without any finality. This elementary reflex, the reflex of organization, to use Richet's term, is the employment of the exciting cause with a view to realizing the ends of the species, of the physical organism. When will is present, "acquired reflex," the reaction is the employment of the exciting cause with a view to the attainment of the individual ends of the person. Let us not forget this mystery of the person; especially let us guard against denying it. To affirm the existence of the unknown, is not this often the only means of turning our lack of knowledge to account? However this may be, should the reflex be greater, the voluntary act would still be ours. But besides this it belongs to society, and, as such, makes us accountable to society, when the exciting causes which have brought it about are partly or mostly social ones.

I would not wish to leave the subject without giving warning that the analogies herein developed as existing between crime and the other social phenomena, especially industry, must not make us forget the differences which exist between them. Crime is a social phenomenon like any other, but a phenomenon which is at the same time anti-social, just as a cancer participates in the life of an organism, but working to bring about its death. And, in fact, if Mitschlerlich was able to say that "life is a corruption," a bitter saying justified to a certain extent by the new school of chemists, according to whom the "chemical diminution of putrefaction and those of the intra-organic combustions offer the greatest analogy," we have a right to say also, as a consequence, that corruption is a part of life, but of the life which kills. Crime is an industry, but a negative one, which accounts for its extreme age; as soon as the first product was manufactured by a laborious tribe, there must have been formed a band of plunderers.[1] A brother and a contemporary of the industry which it fosters, crime does not originally seem to have been any more a disgrace than industry itself. They have developed along the same lines, by both passing from the unilateral form to the bilateral form.

In the beginning, industry was the result of services which were not paid for, given for nothing to the chief by his subjects, to the master by his slaves; by becoming mutual, it has become commerce, an exchange of services. Crime, in becoming mutual, has become warfare, an exchange of injuries. Just as barter and sale is the bilateral form of the gift, so is the duel the bilateral form of homicide,[2] and war the bilateral form not only of homicide, but

[1] Scarcely does the mind of a child commence to affirm when it begins to deny. These negative propositions take their laws from logic, like affirmative propositions; but they are not susceptible of the same development, if we remember the theory of the syllogism. Nevertheless, denial is a leaven which is useful for the mind.

[2] Just as suicide is the premeditated form of it. The new criminologists

of plunder, theft, and arson; it is the highest and the most absolute possible expression of crime which has become a mutual affair. The unfortunate part of it is that, although this complex form of crime has made its appearance, simple crime, crime properly so called, has not disappeared. But the same thing is true with regard to simple industry, a partisan of slavery, which does not give way without resistance to free and salaried industry, and in certain countries succeeds in prolonging itself indefinitely alongside of the latter. It is none the less true that free industry is the born enemy of slavery, and that militarism is the born enemy of brigandage. Spencer, as we saw above, was right when he saw in military development the source of penal repression.

This is so for the very reason that war is a result of crime, the soldier a result of the brigand, as the workman is a result of the slave. This derivation is not a doubtful one. The further back we go into the past, the more does the boundary between the army and the plundering band become effaced. In the sixteenth century even, in the civilized States of Europe, there was no hesitation in looking upon brigandage as entitling a man to military advancement. The Spanish army, the best disciplined of all those of that time "found included in its ranks," Forneron tells us, "assassins or brigands who had given themselves up. Sometimes the brigands who were carrying on their trade in the Catalonian mountains allowed themselves, at a time when their trade seemed to be most dangerous, to be formed into companies under the command of one of their leaders, who received a captain's commission, and to be incorporated as a unit into some previously existing regiment. Some useful crime would obtain for a man the rank of an officer."

Until the seventeenth century, even in France, the royal garrisons of towns "were looked upon as a veritable scourge [1] and, whereas now towns ask for the privilege of having a barracks,

have taken pleasure in going beyond the limits of their subject in order to occupy themselves with suicide, a suburb of which they seek to make a city ward. I see no reason why they could not just as well concern themselves with the duel, another phenomenon which is no less dangerous. It is too bad that the elements are practically lacking in so far as statistics of the duel in the army are concerned. Certainly the frequency of dueling should be no less remarkable in the army, as compared with the civilian population, than the frequency of suicide. If the dominion of example is not doubtful, in so far as suicide is concerned, suicide being an epidemic which has often in a few days decimated fanatic or terrorized populations, it is still more manifest in so far as the duel is concerned.

[1] *Babeau*, "La ville sous l'ancien régime," Vol. II.

they used formerly to endeavor to avert this danger; this privilege was appreciated only by those upon whom it was not conferred. The bands of Germans, Italians and Swiss who were in the pay of France conducted themselves during the religious wars and the Fronde as though in a conquered country. The French companies did not behave any better. They all held their prisoners for ransom and plundered defenseless villages." Everywhere armies, even the regular ones, have begun by inspiring as great a dread in their fellow-countrymen as in the enemy.[1]

With regard to this matter, Thucydides is particularly instructive. What he tells us about the remote times in Greece can be generalized. When among the islands of an archipelago, there was one, a nest of pirates like the others, which began to dominate the group by means of the very powerfulness of its piracy, its domination was made complete by ridding the seas of its former colleagues. This is what was done by Minos, according to the Greek historian. "He deported the malefactors who occupied the islands and into most of them he sent colonies." Thus we see that deportation is not an invention of modern times. "Assuredly," adds Thucydides, "those of the Greeks and barbarians who dwelt upon the mainland near the sea, or who occupied the islands, had no sooner become able to visit one another by means of their vessels than they gave themselves up to piracy.... The most powerful men of the nation were placed at their head. They surprised unwalled towns and gave them over to plunder. And there was nothing shameful in this trade, it even resulted in some glory for those who practiced it. The Greeks also carried out a similar brigandage on land, and this old usage still exists in a great part of Greece, among the Locrians-Ozoles, among the Etolians, among the Acarnanes and upon all that part of the continent. It is owing to this brigandage that the custom of always being armed has remained firmly established among the inhabitants." [2]

[1] "The Chinese recruits," says *Maurice Jametel*, "are in many cases brigands who hasten to take advantage of the opportunities offered them of continuing their exploits under the banner of the Son of Heaven."

[2] Is this criminal origin of warfare by any chance to be included among the number of causes which account for a fact revealed by statistics, that is, in every country, the very striking increase in the number of military criminals, as compared with the number of civil criminals? At any rate, there are many other causes which concur in accounting for this fact. The army is composed of elements which are exclusively masculine, young, celibate, which form a population brought to the very highest degree of density, all of them conditions which cause a pre-

It is really a surprising thing to find developing side by side during the progress of history, with an increasing breadth and power, on the one hand this exchange of property, this competition between different kinds of produce, which is commerce, and on the other hand, this exchange of injuries, this impact of destructive agencies, which is warfare!

The enormous difference between the simple and the complex, the unilateral and the bilateral, established in this manner between crime and warfare ought not, moreover, to astonish us; this method is a customary one in social logic. Between slavery and the condition of wage earners, between gift and sale, between the command and the contract, between the subjection of woman to man as a result of primitive marriage and their mutual fettering as a result of modern marriage, between homage, which is politeness not reciprocated, and politeness, which is mutual homage, etc., there is no lesser abyss than between murder and combat. It is certain that crime, at the present time at least, serves no useful purpose, and is injurious to everything, whereas war has a very serious reason for existing, one which is inherent in the very heart of society; and in spite of Spencer's error on this subject, the military development of a people is far more often in direct ratio than in inverse ratio to their industrial development. Can it be deduced from this that, before the first wars, murder and theft were in some way of use? Yes, if it be true that the simple is the means of the complex. Was it not necessary to pass through slavery before arriving at the mutual help accorded one another by workers, through the prostrations of subjects of olden times before their king or their lord, before arriving at our bow-

disposition to crime. Also, soldiers are responsible for the addition of a number of special crimes and misdemeanors to the crimes and misdemeanors of the common law. Whatever the case may be, we can state that out of 10,000 men, the French nation supplies an annual average of forty offenses and the French army an average of one hundred and seven offenses. The Italian army furnishes one hundred and eighty-nine. From 1878 to 1883, the increase in criminality in the army in Italy was very rapid. It advanced from 3491 crimes or misdemeanors to 5451, whereas civil criminality remained approximately stationary. (*Setti*, "L'Esercito e la sua criminilità," Milan, 1886). I will recall the fact that suicide in the army is much more widespread than in the rest of the nation. This is the same with regard to dueling ("Du suicide dans l'armée," by *Mesnier*, Paris, 1881). In 1862 suicide in the French army was *four times* greater for an equal number of the population, than in the country as a whole; but as it has been decreasing in the army while increasing among the nation to such an extent that it *trebled* in fifty years, this evil finally in 1878 was only *one-half again* as great as it was in the whole of France. Furthermore, the proportion of suicides in the army increases in proportion as we ascend the scale of social status.

ing in the street? Was it not necessary to go through the system of command and obedience, of the domestic, political, and religious autocracy, before attaining the system of contract, mutual command, and mutual obedience? Without aggressions, without spontaneous rapine, in the early stages of history, would there ever have been later on conquests and great States, an essential condition of every high, peaceful, and honest civilization? The truth of the matter is that crime has become an evil without anything to compensate for it since it has advantageously been replaced by militarism and warfare. An army is a gigantic means of carrying out, by massacre and pillage on a vast scale, the collective designs of hatred, vengeance, or envy, which one nation stirs up against another. Condemned under their individual form, these odious passions, cruelty and greed, seem to be praiseworthy under their collective form. Why? First of all, because they quell many little internal conflicts though they bring about an external one; also, because they lead to a warlike solution of this very difficulty, and to the increase in territory as a result of the peace which is bound to follow. The effect of militarism is to exhaust the criminal passions scattered through every nation, to purify them in concentrating them, and to justify them by making them serve to destroy one another, under the superior form which they thus assume. After all is said and done, war enlarges the sphere of peace, as crime formerly used to enlarge the sphere of honesty. This is the irony of history.

But, in truth, if this is so, I cannot resist indulging in one reflection. In a time like the present, when militarism has so greatly overflowed, is it not doubly distressing to have also to state the proofs of the overflow of crime? It seems as though, if our criminality began to decrease, as it should do, this would not be too great a detriment to our armaments and our military contingents which are every day increasing.

CHAPTER VII

THE JUDGMENT

§ 79. The place occupied by criminal procedure and penal justice in social science. Production and exchange of services, production and exchange of injuries.

§ 80. Historical evolution of criminal procedure, which corresponds to that of religious thought or irreligious thought. Proof by ordeals and the duel at law. Proof by torture. Proof by the jury. Proof by expert testimony. Propagation of each of these methods by procedure through imitation-fashion, and then consolidation through imitation-custom.

§ 81. Criticism of the jury system. The future of expert testimony. Necessity for a special school of criminal magistrates.

§ 82. Impossibility of requiring absolute conviction on the part of the criminal judge; possibility of approximately estimating the degree of his belief and usefulness of this estimate though it is an imperfect one. *The point of conviction,* its variations and their causes.

§§ 83–86. Criticism of some reforms proposed in the matter of definition of crimes. (I) Premeditation in case of homicide. History. Holtzendorff's theory. The book of Alimena. A consideration of motives. (II) Attempt. Why a likening of attempt with a crime which has been carried out is repugnant to common sense. (III) Complicity.

§ 79. The place occupied by criminal procedure and penal justice in social science. Production and exchange of services, production and exchange of injuries.

"One must be a revolutionist in physiology, but a conservative in medicine," an eminent contemporary physiologist was wont to say.[1] One could just as well say, be a revolutionist in social science but a conservative in politics and in criminal justice; and this wise counsel would contain a large portion of the truth. However, it would be impossible as well as unwise to raise any question of politics, and in the same way any question of penal law, in the practical innovations which a revolution in ideas has for some time past been giving rise to and making ready. Every new form of pathology implies a new form of therapeutics. Positivist *criminology* has as its necessary consummation a positivist penalty. Here the new Italian school holds a good hand against its adversaries. Already, from the utilitarian point of view, it has completely overthrown the theory of responsibility as based

[1] *Charles Richet,* "Revue scientifique."

upon free will; but it has been less fortunate in its efforts to found a better theory.

On the other hand, starting from the point at which we have now arrived, not only has this school dealt legislative, judicial, and penitentiary institutions, constructed according to the classic principles, and especially the institution of the jury and our prisons as they exist at present, the hardest blows which they have ever received, but it has also firmly established the foundation and planted the first landmarks of reforms which it will be useful to attempt. According to our method, which is theoretical and critical at the same time, we are going to weigh these ideas less by examining them separately and one by one, than in elucidating them by means of others and giving them the place in a general system which seems to belong to them. But first of all we shall have to define the nature of the bond which connects procedure and penal justice with social science as an object, and the connection which exists between the energy expended in judicial examinations, in the hearings held in criminal courts or correctional tribunals, and the other forms of public activity.

Social life is nothing more than an interlacing and a tissue of the following two kinds of facts: the production or the exchange of services and the production or the exchange of injuries. Man is born with a sense of recognizing favors and wishing to be avenged for wrongs. He is constrained to return gift for gift, blow for blow just as a child does; and the progress of civilization has consisted, not in changing the nature, but in regulating, generalizing, and facilitating the manifestation of these two tendencies. Just as social life has substituted for the system of the voluntary gift, which is irregular and arbitrary, a giving in return for some other gift, the system of barter, and then that of purchase or sale according to a uniform course, which is made an essential condition of any great commercial progress; so it has substituted for the system of vengeance which is capricious, changeable, and intermittent, the system of retaliation and later on punishments which are less coarse and regulated by custom or the law.

Now at each moment, and during whatever phase of this twofold development, societies everywhere show us, in the fields as in the cities, in a camp as in the "agoras," a varied picture of thrusts and parries in words or in actions, following immediately and without any previous proceeding, compliments being returned for compliments, injuries for injuries, smiles or offensive looks for similar facial expressions, and services or injuries by other useful or injurious actions. This spontaneous exchange, which is rapid or at least not impeded, of good or bad actions, is the normal and customary thing. For every bargain which brings you before the civil or consular courts, how many bargains are there which are settled without difficulty, how many payments are made in cash without any delay! For one insult for which the person insulted thinks he ought to demand redress in the correctional courts, how many outrages there are which are wiped out then and there, either by some stinging reply or in some other manner!

Thus, as we see, the importance of criminal proceedings would be misunderstood if they were to be separated from the more extended group of which they form a part, just as one would erroneously estimate the part played by civil actions if one did not reinstate them, under the head of a peculiar and difficult species of a kind infinitely greater in scope, in the economical life of the country. The penalties imposed by courts and tribunals form a part of those innumerable punishments which have followed immediately, or without any legal discussion, the misdeeds to which they correspond, a verbal punishment for some insolence, the discharging of a faithless servant, the expelling of a dishonest gambler, dismissal of functionaries who have incurred suspicion, reprisals by parties, and finally, war among nations. Thus it is that the profits and the advantages sought by the two parties in a civil altercation, and obtained by one of them as a result of the judgment rendered, come to form a part of those innumerable remunerations, such as the price of merchandise sold, wages, fees, farm rents, appointments, and benefices of all kinds which are collected without any difficulty. A civil action is a solution of difficulties accidentally incurred, either in an exchange of services, or reciprocal advantages, or in the acquiring by one of the parties of a piece of property which the other party prevents his obtaining, or which compensates him for an involuntary injury occasioned by the other.[1]

[1] Here we have three varieties of procedure. Every demand for the payment of a sum or the carrying out of an obligation, every amendment in an action for distribution, etc., is included within the first. The complainant says: "I have rendered you a service, render me a service in your turn according to our agreement or according to the law." The second kind includes actions of abandonment, of surrender of immovables, questions of party walls, etc. The complainant says: "You prevent me from having the enjoyment of my property, of getting out of my property the service which I expect, leave my property to me." The third can be reduced to a demand for damages.

In these three cases, even in the last one, although it serves as a transition to criminal trials, the point in issue, for the plaintiff, is always to prosecute, not for an injury received by somebody else, but for his own property. The personal element is, to such an extent, the vital object of actions of this kind, as of economic life in general, that the courts will refuse to take cognizance of them without any further examination when this motive is not apparent. Conversely, a criminal action is the settlement of difficulties which have arisen, either in the exchange of injuries between the parties litigant (society, on the one hand, which through its representative claims that it is injured, and on the other hand the accused whom society in its turn wishes to injure, with the object of obtaining expiation, intimidation, or correction, it matters not), or in the taking place of some injury which one of the parties wishes, without provocation, to inflict upon the other (this is what takes place in cases of unjust and malicious prosecution). Here the object directly contemplated by the demand is the detriment to the defendant, to the guilty one, with a view sometimes to his later betterment; as to the advantage to the plaintiff, that is only the indirect and mediate, I will not say the secondary object of the action.

In this way is to be accounted for, by means of the analogy briefly pointed out herein, between the two species of exchange, the confusion existing in early times between the two forms of procedure, penal and civil, which both being begun by a private action, were formerly carried out according to the same forms and before the same judges. But in spite of the similarity, their gradual separation is also to be accounted for by the divergency in their object, and their dissimilarity, which becomes very great, is to be accounted for by other considerations. There are in fact, between injuries and service, from this point of view, obvious differences.

First, it is always the most serious injuries, such as murder, wounding, theft, arson, etc., which give rise to criminal prosecution, because these are the ones for which it is most difficult, and most often forbidden, moreover, to take vengeance without a judgment having been pronounced. But it is not always, or even ordinarily, the greatest services which give rise to civil actions; great commercial houses carry on business with one another on an enormous scale without there being any need for the law to intervene. That is why, although the proportion of bilateral injuries, compared with that of mutual service, has ever been decreasing during the course of civilization and still continues to diminish in our own time, the importance of criminal law compared with that of civil law seems sometimes to increase. It would be a mistake to deduce from this increasing importance that civilization has retrograded.

In the second place, in the majority of legal proceedings arising out of the occurrence of voluntary injuries, society is greatly interested in bringing them and prosecuting them itself. But it is not interested, or it is not interested to the same extent, in bringing civil actions which arise out of the rendering of services. However, one might at first sight wonder at this difference. It is only right that every product should be paid for, that every service should be recompensed, because it is an important thing to encourage the reproduction of this product or of this service, or, in other words, not to discourage it; it is only right that every misdeed should be punished, because it is an important matter to prevent or to hinder the repetition of this injurious act. This is the utilitarian explanation of reward and also of probity, of vengeance and of penal justice as well.

Now, without for the time being investigating whether or not this point of view excludes a more sentimental justification, whether the punishment "ne peccetur" is or is not reconcilable with the punishment "quia peccatumest," or a reward in view of some future benefit is reconcilable with a reward because of some past benefit, we may well ask ourselves why society believes itself to have less interest in fostering the production of services than in preventing that of injuries; and why, as a consequence, it does not take upon itself the burden of setting in motion the rights of each one of us, of bringing actions against our recalcitrant debtors, just as it takes upon itself the duty of avenging the more serious injuries of which we have been the victims. The truth of the matter is that a people would suffer still more from a suspension of their industries, from a paralyzing of their credit than they would from an increase in the number of crimes. And when this people sees its credit, its industrial development threatened by some crisis, by strikes, by an epidemic of bankruptcies and failures, it will not fail to take the proper measures to arrest this scourge. For example it will intervene, sometimes on one side and sometimes on the other, in the wars which take place between the organizations of employees and organizations of employers for the settlement of the wage scale.

But the most ineffective means of accomplishing this would be an exercise by the State itself of private functions; the best thing in a case of this kind is to allow individuals to settle their own difficulties. It is in their power thenceforth by being more prudent in their investments and their sales for credit, to prevent the loss and lack of remuneration of which they complain, and their neighbors as well can derive a useful profit from this lesson. But is it in the power of a victim of an offense or of his fellow-citizens without the assistance of the public powers to prevent the malefactor, emboldened by remaining unpunished, from soon committing fresh crimes? The exercise of public power in criminal matters and not elsewhere is thus very well justified, although the reason for this difference does not at first sight clearly appear.

Finally, from the point of view of procedure — and this for the time being is what we shall deal with — another difference obtrudes itself. Except in the very rare cases of an anonymous benefit the person rendering a service is always known, and it is scarcely necessary to carry out any very minute and prolonged investigation to discover a benefactor. But the perpetrator of an injury more often than not is careful to conceal himself, and he is not discovered without some effort being made. The true counterpart of an ordinary criminal action would seem to be a civil action in which the plaintiff would have to prove to the defendant, in spite of the absolute or partial denial of the latter, that he, the defendant, had obtained some great advantage for the plaintiff and so compel him to accept payment.

This hypothetical case may have been realized, but we must recognize the fact that it is not a very frequent one. As a general thing it is on the question of law and not on the question of fact that the disagreement of the parties in a civil action is based; and when parties are "at issue upon the facts," the contested point is not ordinarily to know whether one of them has committed an act of encroachment, for example, or has used an unlawful right of way, but it is to discover whether this act has really been committed. In the criminal action, it is not the question of law, it is the question of fact which ordinarily is the issue between the public prosecutor and counsel for the defense, and the fact to be cleared up is not the actual occurrence of the crime or the offense, of the homicide or the theft which incriminate the man, but it is the commission of this act by the accused. The problem of legal proof is thus important in quite a different way in criminal trials than it is in civil trials, and of quite a different nature.

§ 80. Historical evolution of criminal procedure, this corresponds to that of religious thought or irreligious thought. Proof by ordeals and the duel at law. Proof by torture. Proof by the jury. Proof by expert testimony. Propagation of each of these methods by procedure through imitation-fashion, and then consolidation by imitation-custom.

To seek out the perpetrator of a crime and prove his guilt, this problem which for us is of rather secondary theoretical interest after all, must have been the most interesting form of gymnastics of inductive logic at its inception. Above every scientific problem there was nothing that could more keenly arouse curiosity and stimulate investigation than the solution of this problem. It was still, as it had been in the previous period of savagery, a man hunt, but under a better and more enlightened form. Later on the interest in this search decreased, but it has never ceased to be very keen. Thus it is not surprising that man has in all times, and especially in the very oldest times, called to his assistance in the clearing up of this mystery every actual or imaginary, positive or mystic resource which was offered him. No doubt witnesses have always been heard, suspected persons have been interrogated, the condition of the locality has been ascertained, and indications of all kinds have been collected; the confession of the accused has always been regarded as a striking proof of his guilt. But besides this, each period has had its especially preferred kind of proof, its characteristic method; and we must take care not to think that the confession has always been the "king of proofs." Do you suppose that the decision of an oracle bringing an accusation in the heroic times of Greece, or that the carelessly carried out proof of the boiling water or the red hot iron, in the roughest days of the Middle Ages, had not just as much probative force as the confession itself? Each age perceptibly reflects in the criminal procedure which characterizes it the fundamental belief which animates it, that is to say, its most universal and undisputed belief; so that the series of legislative and judicial changes upon this point corresponds to the changes in human thought itself.

Mystic in the beginning, suffering from hallucinations, drunk with illusions and pride, human thought peoples the entire universe with gods, but with gods who are solely occupied and preoccupied with the affairs of mankind. This thought is incarnate in a nature of which every living being or apparently inanimate being has eyes with which to see man, a mysterious language in which to commune together about man, and even to communicate with him sometimes and to reveal the answer to the problems which torment him, because of his crimes or the secret of his future. Thus the same spirit which permitted divinations by augurs or sorcerers to become widespread and to be strengthened during long centuries must have fostered the diffusion and the taking root of the examination of criminals by means of ordeals.

Admitting that the good or bad actions, past, present, or future, of each one of us are the chief concern of the surrounding divinity and constitute its entire relative omniscience, it is just as natural to consult this divinity in a symbolical manner as to the guilt or innocence of the accused as it is on the question of the victory or defeat of a general on the eve of battle. Then man consulted the red hot iron, the boiling water, the cards or the dice, the blind fate of weapons, dreams which are all just so many divine revelations, as we today consult our medico-legal experts, or, I should say, as we shall consult them tomorrow, when science having become fixed and dogmatized shall perhaps have become an idol in her turn and shall give us oracles unanimously invested with an infallible authority. Ordeals are to a certain extent the divine-legal expert testimony of the past.[1] They correspond to the mythological phase of the human mind,[2] just as our actually

[1] However, we ought here to make a distinction which has already been pointed out above and which has always been too much neglected. It is only for the discovery of crimes committed by one tribe upon another, by one family upon another, and by one class upon another, that the necessity of ordeals or the oath imposed upon the accused has been felt. Here we have the reason. During the times of the "vendetta," it was impossible (this impossibility still exists in Corsica, Sicily, among the Ossetes, etc.) to find witnesses who were not doubtful, that is to say who were not relatives, as a result of the fact that disinterested spectators and strangers to the quarrel could feel absolutely no indignation against the perpetrator of the crime committed outside the family or the "gens." From this dearth of testimony there results the necessity of having recourse to ordeals or the oath (which is itself a sort of ordeal). But with respect to "intra-familial" crimes, this necessity is not felt, for in these cases honest witnesses can be found as easily as in our own time.

[2] Let us add that they form a part of the legal formalism customary among primitive peoples, and which is to be accounted for in the creation of rights but not in the discovery of facts. The very early peoples have a formalistic law for the same reason that they have a language consisting of gestures. Their formalism when it is a matter of setting up an agreement is an excellent means of proof, as their gestures are an excellent means of expressions. On the other hand, it impedes their search for offenses just as their gestures are an obstacle to the exactness of their reasoning. Besides this, their formalism has been greatly

existing expert testimony has begun to correspond to its scientific phase, which is just beginning to come into existence.

But, between these two superstitions, one of which was puerile and chimerical and the other of which will be, I hope, serious and to a great extent the truth, consequently the more profound, there have been others which have subjugated mankind and set their stamp upon his penal institutions. When, for example, still being religious, but having recovered from the delirium of divination, the people of Europe of the twelfth and thirteenth centuries ceased to have faith in the duel at law and other chimerical proofs, a relative positivism, which is also felt in the scholastic philosophy of dry reason, closely following Aristotle, at that time demanded the employment of a more rational mode of examination, that is the inquisitorial system. At the same time, this period of dry and hard rationalism had its own particular superstition, the superstition of force, and it is by force that this system claimed that it discovered the truth, by the force of the syllogism of the theological schools, being the force of torture in matters of criminal law.[1]

This period lasted, owing to an extraordinary prolongation of the universal blindness, until the eighteenth century. The confession of the accused having taken on a very great importance which it never possessed to this extent, either before or after this period, the most approved method of getting at this very best form of proof was torture. Then the softening of customs and the revival of men's minds repelled this savage absurdity; but another superstition, the optimistic faith in the infallibility of individual reason, of common sense, of natural instinct, created in Europe, after the example of England, the jury, an assumed revelation of the truth by a non-enlightened and unreasoning

exaggerated, as has been demonstrated by *Dareste* in his splendid work on the History of Law.

[1] This sort of coarse and cruel positivism or rationalism which assumes the predominating use of torture, perhaps accounts for the fact that it never played anything but a secondary part in theocratic Egypt, and the fact that in primitive Greece and Judea it nowhere appears. Neither in Homer, nor in Hesiod, is it dealt with, any more than in the Bible. The Greeks from the time of Rhadamanthus, according to Plato, imposed the oath upon the accused; the latter, like all his fellow-countrymen, was convinced that the gods never left perjury unpunished, and so absolute was this belief which was suggested by unanimous example, at least before the first murmurings of philosophy, that this taking of the oath might seem to be a surer means even than torture of dragging a confession from a guilty man. Scepticism had for a long time invaded the Roman Empire when an abuse of torture prevailed there against even free men themselves.

conscience. Proof by jury ought to have been conceived of during the century in which the verdict of common sense, regarded as the touchstone of truth, served as a foundation not only for the Scottish philosophy, but for every philosophy, and in France suggested the dogma of the sovereignty of the people. Here is the position which we now occupy, while waiting till the expert, who, for the time being, is a corrective and antidote for the jury, shall have become its successor and shall continue to increase in strength.

If this picture is correct, there will be no absolute necessity of going any further in order to justify the attacks directed by Ferri, Garofalo, and all the new Italian or even French school, against the institution of the jury. A just and profound feeling of the needs of the present time is the inspiration of these critics, just as it is the inspiration of efforts attempted by these same innovators with a view to extending, to regulating, to perfecting, to consecrating the judicial functions of expert testimony. It is only to be regretted that they have not seen fit simultaneously to approach and include the entire question of judicial proof which is such an arduous one, and have forgotten on this point, as on many others, the teachings of Bentham.[1] But we shall go back to this. Let us continue.

In England we have first ordeals and then the jury, on the Continent first ordeals, then torture, then the jury, and soon we shall have expert testimony. Such have been, or will be, the successive talismans devised for the discovery of the truth in the demonstration of justice. Do not be shocked because I thus place the jury upon the same basis as torture or the duel at law; you will soon be convinced that it has taken their place and that it should be considered their equivalent, infinitely preferable to them I admit, in spite of all the reproaches it has incurred. What I have meant to say is this, that everywhere and always when some great crime takes place, there arises, with regard to the question of who the guilty man is, or whether the accused is guilty or not, a general need of enlightenment, which prejudices people towards a more or less marked credulity. This credulity seeks and finds its object, which is furnished it by the idolatry prevailing at that time; it will grasp at something or some person who is reputed to be infallible; then it will shift to something

[1] We know the "Traité des preuves judiciaires" by *Bentham,* in two volumes edited by Dumont (1830).

else; but during these changes from age to age it remains, deep down, always the same. Formerly it consisted in the probative force of the judgment of God, later on that of torture, even yesterday that of the verdict of any twelve men brought together in a lay council, when the adage "Vox Populi vox Dei" met with scarcely any denial.

It would not be very difficult for me to show now that the irregular transformation of criminal procedure is a phenomenon of imitation like any other, governed by the same laws and especially subject to the same rhythm of alternating fashion and custom. In the late Middle Ages, before the thirteenth century, we find the greater portion of barbarian Europe — with the exception of Spain and Italy, unless it be temporarily and incompletely — under the sway of procedure by accusation and the practice of the duel at law, among other ordeals. Furthermore, each province, if not each fief, had its own particular customs, its special forms of ordeal, not to mention the benefit of clergy, which made a large portion of the population only amenable to the Church courts, ecclesiastical tribunals soon destined to serve as a model for the lay courts,[1] after having themselves been fashioned after the Roman law, from which they borrowed the written interrogatory.

In spite of all this, a certain uniformity of legislation had already become established at this remote period, which would imply, during this time of local particularism, a rather strong impetus of exterior imitation in the matter of the criminal law. There must have taken place then the same thing which we know took place later, in the thirteenth, sixteenth, and eighteenth centuries, when the various peoples, still disregarding the other examples offered by their neighbors, were hastening to copy their institutions in the matter of penal justice, probably because it is these institutions which are the most striking when seen from afar. There is nothing which stands out more at a distance than a gallows in a landscape.[2] Let him who can explain how, without

[1] Among the Greeks, as in the Middle Ages, the criminal justice of the lay courts followed the criminal justice of the ecclesiastical courts and so was modeled upon it. I therefore do not understand how it is that Thonissen is surprised at finding, among the contemporaries of Homer, a criminal procedure against murder and theft, still in a rudimentary state, whereas crimes of a religious nature were subject to a "vast system of repression, where every requirement was provided for, where every detail was regulated, from the legal policy which defined offenses to the inevitable intervention of the judge who made certain of their punishment."

[2] In monarchic France, a unification of the law by the gradual substitution of

the contagion of being carried away by example, men, even barbarians, even when a prey to the most acute delirium of mysticism, which, moreover, is in itself inexplicable, otherwise than by means of an imitation contagion, could have had all together the idea of having the accuser and the accused fight a duel in order to judge, according to the result of the fight, whether or not the accusation was well founded. Obviously, such an absurd idea as this cannot have spread without a universal predisposition for the supernatural; but just as obviously, without its propagation, at some certain date across the frontiers, this territorial expansion could never be accounted for. However, thus established as a fashion, the duel at law and the other judgments of God were kept up by custom and with an energy of resistance which was peculiar, until a new practice succeeded in coming to light.

This new means of examination, which is perhaps a little less cruel, but far more absurd than the preceding one, is, as we know, torture. I say that it was scarcely more cruel; for proof by the red hot iron, by the boiling oil, and even by the duel, was quite equal in point of the suffering inflicted to torture by means of the wooden horse, the boot, or the water; and proof by dreams or the duel was even more perilous.[1] And I add that it was far less absurd; for it was based I believe upon a psychological intuition of a certain depth. The most untruthful man, in fact, has a natural impulse to tell what he knows, and, if he does not tell it or tells the contrary, it is only in bringing into play his self-control which assumes an expenditure of brain force — our contemporary psychologists would say of force of restraint — being made in this manner.

Now, in inflicting on this man physical torment, the greater part or the whole of his energy is compelled to devote itself to resisting the pain, and thenceforth his secret should escape him, unless there is some obstacle to prevent its doing so. Therefore, when it is known that a man is cognizant of the truth with relation to what is being asked him, the torture which is inflicted on him can and ought to be efficacious.[2] Where the absurdity begins

ordinances for Customs, by the gradual infringing of the royal judges upon the domain of the seigniorial judges, took place in criminal law first of all; every province already administered justice for criminals in the same way, as they still perserved in civil law their distinctive originality.

[1] The emperor Claudius was induced to condemn to death several persons by merely having witnesses brought before him, who stated that they had dreamed that these persons wished to assassinate him!

[2] Armies on a campaign have often successfully inflicted torture upon spies and fugitives whom they have arrested. Highwaymen are, or used to be, in the

to enter into the matter is when this terrible means is applied to people who cannot possibly know anything. However this may be, moreover, history tells us that, like magic, like sorcery, like anthropophagy, like human sacrifice, and like everything which is absurd or cruel, but which corresponds to some great absurdity or cruelty which is already a prevailing one, procedure by means of the torture spread universally and with truly great rapidity. Torture and the secret investigation are the most prominent characteristics of inquisitorial procedure, which, introduced in the thirteenth century by the jurists of the royal jurisdictions, whose influence increased unceasingly, in the end, in the sixteenth century invaded the whole of Europe with the exception — apparent or partial — of England alone.

How was this transformation carried out? Here there cannot be the slightest doubt we are progressing in the full light of history. The field of this contagion was a corner of Italy whence, towards the middle of the twelfth century, the discovery, the exhuming of the Roman law which had been half buried, by the criminologists of the school of Bologna, caused a disturbance in all the feudal tribunals and upset their small customary systems of jurisprudence. Furthermore, it was in the superior courts of justice that this innovation had its inception, then it became more common in the inferior courts.[1] In Spain as early as the end of the twelfth century the activity of the criminologists of Bologna was being felt. Scarcely had they been opened when the schools of Italy became filled with Spanish students. "There soon," says Esmein, "they forgot, they set aside the natural laws, 'fueros' and national customs, in order to follow the Italian maxims." The laws of Alphonso the Wise did no more than sanction these changes. In Germany, it was not long before the influence of Italy became

habit of proceeding in the same manner. "A majority of these gentlemen," says Voltaire, while ironically attributing to them the invention of torture, "are still in the habit of squeezing the thumbs, burning the feet, and questioning by means of other torments, those who refuse to tell them where they have their money." Here we have the reason for the "question" (torture). It is obvious that everyone knows where he has his money.

Esmein, in his learned history of criminal procedure, cites examples of numerous brigands who, on being subjected to torture, divulged thousands of crimes which were unknown. The psychological observation mentioned above applies to them. There is still another more palpable explanation of torture. It is that keen and present pain to be escaped, whether it be at the price of the convict prison or the scaffold in the near future, makes a man forget the future suffering which is to come after it.

[1] *Du Boys*, "Histoire du Droit criminel chez les peuple modernes," Vol. I.

paramount.[1] "Procedure, resulting from the Roman law and the Canon law as it had become fixed by the Italian doctors, makes rapid progress [in the fifteenth and sixteenth centuries]."

Torture, Esmein again tells us, was used "after the example of the Italians"; the German doctors gained all their knowledge from the Italian doctors of whom they were but imperfect copies. This epidemic of the Middle Ages must have been a very irresistible one to have reached even England, so conservative in its ancient usages. The English, it is true, boast of never having recognized torture, and have made us believe it; but under Edward I, at the time when it was becoming widespread upon the Continent, they began to practise that reinforced torture, with death added to it, which they called "la peine forte et dure"[2] and which prevailed for several centuries in this country of all the liberties. In France, where the civilization of Italy under every form rapidly made its way, especially at the time of the expedition of Charles VIII, there can be no doubt that direct inspiration from the Italians dictated the royal ordinances of 1498, of 1539, of 1560, of 1566, and of 1577, which paved the way for the great ordinance of 1670.

Thus everywhere, the prestige of ancestral institutions, of methods designed by men's ancestors, having declined, there was substituted for it, from the thirteenth to the sixteenth centuries, the prestige of the Italian institutions, of inventions which were the fashion.[3] Now it is a remarkable fact that however odious torture may have been and in spite of its foreign origin it promptly took root as a national custom, to such a point that the French ordinances referred to above, which prescribed or sanctioned the use of torture, were several times approved of by the States General and by the assemblies of the notables. The three orders always met

[1] See on this subject, and they are well justified sometimes, the lamentations of *Jean Janssen* ("L'Allemagne à la fin du moyen âge").

[2] See *Du Boys* on this subject. When an accused would not confess, he was put back in prison, stretched out on his back with an enormous weight on his chest, left almost without anything to eat or drink, and if he persisted in denying his crime, *until he died*, he was considered innocent. This was a great advantage for his memory. The English might have borrowed other things than torture from us, just as we ourselves could have borrowed other things than the jury from them.

[3] The acknowledged motive for the employment of torture was everywhere that "on the one hand ordeals and compurgations were no longer believed in and that on the other hand, it was not desirable to pronounce sentence upon mere indications, however strong they may have been." The confession had to be obtained at any price, or else proof that it was impossible to obtain a confession.

on this ground, as an exception to be sure, in a unanimous concert of eulogies! Even in 1614, "we find in the 'Cahiers' wishes expressed which tend to increase the harshness of procedure."

At the end of the eighteenth century again, torture had many illustrious defenders. Just as bull fights in Spain have ended by becoming the chief occupation and the principal business of certain persons, or the games of the Circus in Rome, one has no difficulty in finding in Europe, during the sixteenth and seventeenth centuries, dilettanti in the art of torture, such as Perrin, Dandin de Racine, or Hessels de Gand, one of the commissioners of the Duke of Albe during the revolt in the Netherlands. "He was industrious," says Forneron ("Histoire de Philippe II"), "but his predominating passion was the sight of torture. He loved to see the accused suspended by his hands, raised by the pulley, disjointed, spitting blood, beginning to make admissions, retracting them, completing them on each fresh turn of the pulley." This cruelty had thus become very much acclimated everywhere, just as had formerly the duel at law, and even more widely in this sense, that it prevailed with greater uniformity over a large number of persons amenable to the courts. But for the same reason that men became disgusted with the duel at law towards the twelfth century, they became disgusted with torture after the last century. Then a new epidemic raged, the English fashion of the jury.

The jury does not in any way come from the German forests; it came into existence in 1215, as has been demonstrated by Du Boys and other authors,[1] owing to the embarrassment experienced by the itinerant justices of England in doing without the ordeals which the Lateran Council had just prohibited. Whereas upon the Continent the idea of torture suggested itself as being the proper thing, the English, with infinitely more sagacity no doubt, devised the expedient of assembling twelve of the neighbors of the accused[2] when he did not admit his guilt, and regarding "their *conviction* relative to the existence and the perpetrator of the crime" as being the equivalent of the judgment of God. This was all the more natural, as for a long time past the embryo of the

[1] See especially his "Histoire du Droit criminel de la France," Vol. II, p. 555, *et seq.*

[2] As to this rather obscure origin of the English jury, one can still consult *Mittermayer* ("Traité de la procédure criminelle," French translation, especially p. 419). His explanation differs slightly from *Du Boys'*, but in the last analysis it can be reconciled with it. See also the "History of the English People," by *Green*.

jury, under the name of "proof by the country," existed in the English system of bringing an accusation; and this form of proof was placed in the same category as that of "proof by battle." The accused had the right of choosing between these two.

In this manner the fact that the ordeals and the jury were the equivalent of each other is attested. We must recollect that at this period men were prone to believe that the Holy Ghost was present at every reunion of Christians carried out with any solemnity; a jury might seem to be a species of council inspired from on high. Even the jury was destined to furnish the illusion of certainty. A presumption of oracular infallibility was attached by religious belief, as later on by philosophical and humanitarian belief, to decisions, *the grounds of which were not stated.* Furthermore, from its origin as we see, the verdict has only been, as it is still in our day, a supreme act of opinion, a "constat" of fact, and not a judgment properly speaking; and if it is gradually assuming the appearance of a decree, and if the jury is in reality being substituted for the criminal court, it is owing to a real usurpation of the function of the latter.

The English juries were to so great an extent looked upon as mere witnesses, in early times, that until the time of Edward III in the fourteenth century, absolutely no testimony could be brought before them, and even in our own time, in England, when the accused confesses, the jury is incompetent because then the proof is complete. It is because the jury is a species of inspired witness that it has never been asked to state the grounds of its verdict and that this idea is even repelled just as much as the idea of a decree without any grounds would be repelled. In fact, has a witness any need to state the grounds of, or to *prove* his allegations, which are just the very proof which is being sought for?

At the beginning of the French Revolution, France found herself in an embarrassing position similar to that of the "justitiarii itinerantes" of 1215; torture having been done away with, it became necessary to find a substitute for it. It is certain that at this time the example of England which had in various ways become the aim of the French philosophers, who were the fascinating and shining innovators of the last century, was the determining motive for the importation of the jury into France first of all, and then by contagion into the majority of the European nations, and beyond the seas into South America. This fashion, in fact, has spread much farther than did that of torture; it covers half the globe.[1]

It was knowingly, furthermore, that the English jury was imported into France. "The 'Cahiers' of 1789," says Esmein, "had demanded judgment by a jury in criminal matters; they recommended that a study should be made of English institutions. It is, indeed, England which will be imitated. Men will even progress so far along this way that they will sacrifice, in order that the imitation may be complete, some of the best creations of French genius,"[2] for example, the institution of the public prosecutor. The framers of the proposal for the Constituent Assembly "sacrificed traditional institutions for the principles of English procedure"; which did not however prevent, in France and everywhere, the jury from becoming in its turn the most sacred of the customs which it is impossible to interfere with under penalty of the greater excommunication. This custom, which took root so rapidly, has a firm popular support in routine, and in the most ineradicable of routines, that which takes good faith for progress. Even in science itself it numbers eloquent defenders as stubborn, and as sincere in spite of their learning, as was Muyart de Vouglans, at the end of the eighteenth century when he passionately defended the cause of torture.

But here again a new wind is blowing; for some years past there have been arising on all sides objections, timid at first, then formal accusations, serious reasons, crushing statistics, against the fantastic and senseless power, which continues to exist, owing to the blind veneration of everybody. Its unfitness is being shown, its contradictions and its blunders are being laughed at; it is being treated just as men began to treat the Sibyl, with its rebus which was no more incomprehensible than certain verdicts in the later times of paganism. There is no rascal who fears it any longer, and no honest man who respects it. Its absolute discrediting, if not its end, is in sight. Now we must estimate the bearing of the reproaches which have been directed against it.

[1] A strange thing indeed is this enthusiasm suggested in the most refined and artificial century, and the one most enamored of rationalism and of the fictitious in everything, that is our eighteenth century in France, for the criminal procedure of England, that is to say for what is most archaic and unpolished in the matter of procedure!

[2] Let us note that Esmein is a very strong partisan of the jury.

§ 81. Criticism of the jury system. The future of expert testimony. Necessity for a special school of criminal magistrates.

The ignorance, fear, ingenuousness, versatility, inconsistency, and partiality in turn servile or carping, of juries have been superabundantly proved. A thousand characteristic traits have been cited, but let us pass over these anecdotes, however instructive they may be.[1]

Any man, whatever his profession, and provided his morality is not too far below the average, is eligible to serve on a jury; if by any chance he should be suspected of having any legal ability he is at once challenged. His worth lies in his incompetence. After this, how can we be astonished at his insufficiency? This curious sort of magistrate is chosen by lot.[2] This was no doubt a very wise guarantee during the superstitious times when a providential character was attached to the man chosen by fate[3]; but a thing which is still more hazardous than the choice of the individuals who make up the jury is the character of their decision. Their decision depends, first of all, upon the greater or lesser amount of eloquence indulged in by counsel, and what eloquence it is! The criminal court rooms seem to be a school of all the common grounds of old-fashioned forms of rhetoric. Furthermore, their decision depends upon influences which are less admissible and even more dangerous. In Sicily, according to Garofalo, the jury is the slave of the maffia; in Naples of the camorra[4]; in the Romagna of political passion against the existing government;

[1] *Lacassagne* ("Revue scientifique," December 29, 1883) gives us the following personal recollection. After a verdict of acquittal in a case of infanticide where there had been a great deal of discussion about the foetus there is found on the desk of the jurymen the following note made by one of them: "The *fetusse* is the child." The chief interest in the case for him was to add this idea to his knowledge. I have been given by the foreman of a jury the following piece of information: that in a very serious case, out of seven "oui," one of the jurymen having written "voui," it was thought necessary to vote over again. Then there were only six "oui," the man who had written "voui" having written "non" because he knew how to write "non" but not how to write "oui" . . . etc., etc.

[2] In the opinion of Turgot, this was a sufficient reason for rejecting the establishment of the jury.

[3] Why twelve jurymen, rather than ten or twenty? The predilection for this number, in a century saturated with the decimal system, would be incomprehensible, were we not aware of the mystic virtues which used to be attributed to certain numbers and especially to this number twelve.

[4] The jury in Italy seems to be worse than elsewhere. It can be bought. In France we would not see, the evening after an acquittal, the jurors taking part in a celebration given by the accused. This fact is pointed out by Garofalo as having actually occurred at Polenza in 1879.

in Spain, not long since, of the "mano nera." Let us add, in Corsica, of the clan spirit and the bandit spirit; in France, of the spirit of opposition, or the party spirit, of the press and of the spectators. In Russia, as elsewhere, the jury is careful not to condemn persons of high rank. Even in England it quails before a verbal or written threat.[1]

However, the English jury is the best in the whole world; it is relatively severe, it is full of deference for the presiding judge, and it sometimes consults jury manuals which have been compiled for its use; with us people do not waste their time writing books of this kind. In spite of all this the English jury scandalizes the English public by its unreasonable acquittals. Even Lord Kingsdown said in the House of Lords in 1859, "that it would be better to abolish the institution of the jury than to maintain it such as it is."[2] Taine, in his "Notes sur l'Angleterre," has collected similar complaints. Now they go even further; in 1884 James Stephen, one of the eminent lawyers across the Channel, wrote a book condemning the jury, which met with great success. This institution being thus treated in its own birthplace, we cannot be surprised when we hear that in Corsica, sometimes, when the victim of an assassination does not seem to have been sufficiently avenged by the verdict, his relatives, "when the sitting of the criminal court is over, complete the work of the jury with their rifles,"[3] and that in New York, in 1884, the repeated indulgence of the jury brought about a sanguinary street riot in which fifty persons were killed.[4] We also know that on March 15, 1891, at New Orleans, eleven out of nineteen accused persons were massacred by the exasperated populace because the jury, by whom they were to be tried, was suspected of having been intimidated. The habit, I was going to say the institution of "lynching," that American monstrosity, is an offspring of the jury, for which it serves as a barbarous antidote; "similia similibus." It might be thought that this atrocious and summary form of procedure was due to the anarchistic state of the first Colonists, and that as a consequence it would gradually disappear as civilization pro-

[1] See the characteristics mentioned in a little pamphlet, "Institution du jury," by *Emile Bouvier* (Lyons, 1887), p. 33. In certain states of North America, according to Du Boys, it has been thought necessary, when the accused was a Free Mason, to authorize the accuser to object to a jury of Free Masons.

[2] *Loiseleur*, "Les crimes et les peines."

[3] *Arthur Desjardins*, "La loi de Lynch" ("Revue des Deux Mondes," May 15, 1891).

[4] "En Corse," by *Paul Bourde*.

gressed. But American statistics have proved that this is not the case at all. They show us "in 1884, 103 legal executions as against 219 lynchings; in 1885, 108 against 181; in 1886, 83 against 133; in 1887, 79 against 123; in 1888, 87 against 144; in 1889, 98 against 175." [1] The proportion of lynchings thus is ever on the increase.

I might remark parenthetically, that these examples show to what an extent the jury lacks even the doubtful merit of reflecting public opinion. Under the absorbing effects of the advocate, the twelve jurymen are weaned away from popular feeling, just as a little sea water placed in a vessel is no longer affected by the movement of the tides. Nor does the jury to any greater extent possess the political qualities attributed to it, for I know not what reason. In times of disturbance, and even under normal conditions, in cases where a question of politics is involved, the jury is either servile or rebellious, and as much to be feared in the latter case as it is in the former. Sometimes it is a "tribunal of terror," as Mittermayer says, for example, in France under the Revolution and the Restoration, and in England during the sixteenth and seventeenth centuries. Sometimes an instrument in the hands of a faction and an encouragement to all the excesses of journalism, it has demonstrated that there can be no true independence and impartiality without a certain degree of intelligence. It was the Athenian jury, the tribunal of the Heliasts, which condemned Socrates and Phocion to death; it was an English jury which sent Thomas More to the scaffold. "In France the great argument against the death penalty is the unjust condemnation of Lesurques, another victim of the jury." It may well be believed that, if we had had the jury in the France of former times, prosecutions for sorcery and heresy which were so great a subject of reproach, and justly so, against the magistracy, would have been far more numerous and more severely judged. If enlightened magistrates, numbering men of superior mind among them, could not escape this aberration, to what limit might not an ignorant jury have gone? In the English Colonies in North America these prosecutions were especially terrible against heretics and sorcerers, according to Mittermayer; it is to be noticed that the jury in these colonies conformed in every way with the jury of the metropolis.[2]

[1] *Enrico Ferri*, "Nuovi orizzonti."

[2] "In some of the Alpine valleys, subject to the ecclesiastical jurisdiction, as for example that of Abbondanza in Chablais and of Chamounix at the foot of Mont-Blanc, criminal justice was carried out by the people, through the intermediation

We find that the jury can be severe where it ought to acquit; we also find that in religion as in politics, it leaves much to be desired. Mittermayer recognizes the fact that, "at a time when the public powers are corrupt and the judge is a coward or has been intimidated, the jury would not be of any great assistance in defending personal liberty." But if this is so, then what good is it?[1] For, on the other hand, it must have been recognized by experience that, as applied to common law crimes, when they break out with great intensity, it is despairingly powerless, as Sicily and Corsica know only too well. When the First Consul resolved to put an end to the rural brigandage which was rife in many parts of France, he was compelled to have the brigands tried by special courts.

Moreover, every time there is a desire to insure the carrying out of the law, the jury system must be checked. From this arises the growing employment of summary convictions, which is equivalent to a partial and gradual suppression of the jury. As to urban brigandage, it openly scorns the jury; is not the overflow of crime in our large cities partly due to this cause? If there is some subject on which the jury is competent, it must indeed be with regard to matters affecting the honor of individuals. "Especially in questions of honor, where conscience speaks louder and more plainly than the law, no jurisdiction could be equal to that of the jury," says Beaussire in his "Fondements du Droit." Yes, in theory, but let us see how it works out in practice. "It is, however, impossible," he adds, "to conceal from oneself how powerless this jurisdiction has shown itself to be in our country, *especially in questions of this sort*, to protect the material and moral interests of which it is the arbiter." For this, it is true, there would be a remedy according to the late lamented professor;

of the heads of families who were called 'hommes de coutumes,' because they were the guardians of the old customs of the country." We must not think that these "hommes de coutumes," sitting as a jury, were more lenient than ordinary magistrates. We find them in 1462 condemning to torture by fire a great number of men and women prosecuted for heresy and "a poor woman called Perroneta de Ochiis, accused of carnal relations with the devil, was before being burned, seated naked during the twentieth part of an hour [three minutes] on red hot iron." ("Cibrario," Vol. I, p. 140.)

[1] In 1890 the party in power in France, in spite of their traditional infatuation for the jury, found themselves compelled to make a great legislative effort in order to take away from it jurisdiction over newspaper offenses. Its arguments are unanswerable. Very well, but if it has just been decided that the jury is incompetent in these cases which have always been considered its particular specialty, "a fortiori" haste should be made to proclaim its incompetence in every other respect.

and that would be the establishment of a special jury; but what would this special jury be, excepting a tribunal of experts, that is to say, the very jurisdiction which is destined, as we are about to see, partly to take the place of the jury? And if the necessity of a special class of men makes itself felt here, why not elsewhere as well?

The thing with which the jury is most unanimously reproached is its weakness. Its proverbial indulgence is not only scandalous because of the frequency with which it occurs, and often shameful because of the cases in which it is applied, but it is even more injurious by reason of its object. This indulgence is exercised in dealing with the species of crime which it is most important to repress in places where it is in vogue. According to Jacoby, the American jury is as indulgent for every sort of fraud as the Italian jury is in cases of stabbing, or the Corsican jury in cases of shooting. It is in the southern provinces of Italy, where crimes of a bloodthirsty nature have mounted to an appalling figure, that the Italian jury shows them the most favor; it is in the regions of Italy and France where theft predominates that the Italian and French juries show the least degree of severity towards thieves.[1] I mean relative severity; theft is in fact the only offense that juries, which are generally composed of property holders, feel the need of punishing.

Furthermore, they are very careful to contradict themselves afterwards, by absolving in emulation of one another forgeries, abuses of confidence, and fraudulent bankruptcies, all forms of theft upon a large scale. In Brittany, they are very severe in cases of infanticide; apparently because there this crime is very rarely met with and has more reason for its existence than elsewhere, owing to a fear of disgrace. In regions where this crime is commonly met with, and where girl mothers have less to fear the flaying of public opinion, which is as charitable in their case as is the jury, the latter will acquit them as a matter of course. It was important that the jury should act with severity in the first case of "lover's vitriol" in order to forestall a repetition of this crime; its desire to please has made an epidemic of this evil. More than this. In 1887, a jury of the Department of the Loire acquitted, in

[1] "Certain members of the Tribunal of Marseilles tell me that, not only is fraud honored, but that one sees defrauders who have confessed acquitted by the jury." (*Joly*, "La France criminelle," 1890.) Ah! If the magistracy should dare to indulge in a single enormity of this kind, what an outcry there would be against it! But the jury can take any liberty.

spite of the evidence, a girl who had assassinated her mother in order to rob her.

In vain are the laws as to selecting the jury increased in number; nothing has come of it. To the power of taking into consideration extenuating circumstances which has been given the jury, can soon be joined that of taking into consideration very extenuating circumstances; nothing will come of it. The whole institution of the jury is defective in its foundations. If we stop to think of all the homicides, and all the infanticides, and all the cases of theft, and all the cases of arson, the cases of forgery, and the cases of abuse of confidence, and all the cases of rape, which, had it not been for the jury, would not have existed, one can be pardoned for going so far as to say, that it has done more harm to society even than torture.

Why then, one will ask, does it offer such firm resistance to the attacks made upon it? Is it because it is indissolubly bound up in parliamentary institutions? I cannot see where this tie comes in.[1] Is it because, in spite of everything, it has been an advance in our civilization? It has been such an advance, but it is no longer one. There is nothing more progressive than the jury, yet nothing more stationary, so long as the magistracy, inspired by provincial emulation, which is to be accounted for by the imitation of one another by its members, carried off their feet in a current of an accumulation of useful examples, does not cease to fulfil its functions, at least in certain respects, — I am not speaking of cases of misdemeanor, — with an increasing zeal, intelligence, and accuracy, attested by statistics.

It is true that the proportionate number of acquittals by juries has gradually decreased, from thirty-seven per cent in 1831 to seventeen per cent in 1880; but this result is due, as the official report of 1880 informs us, to "the scrupulous attention which the magistrates bring to bear more and more in the examinations of cases before granting an order to have them tried before a court of competent jurisdiction," and also to the use of summary convictions which only permits of the more serious and more fully proven crimes coming before the jury. Therefore let us not mention progress or liberty in speaking of the jury; its power lies elsewhere. This power consists in the difficulty in the way of replacing the jury.

Here we have the true reason for the existence of the jury,

[1] The same thing was said about the national guard, as long as it lasted.

without reckoning the force of habit. In fact, what shall we put in its place for the time being, unless it be our present magistracy? Now, in spite of the praise which has just been accorded it, this magistracy is not really prepared to take its place.[1] Among the innovators, Garofalo is the one who has felt this the most, perhaps because he himself is a magistrate. If he rejects the idea of confining to the judicial body the responsibility of judging great criminals, it is not, be it understood, because he adheres to the commonplace paradox on the danger of knowledge which might bias a man's mind and on the danger of professional experience which might steel a man's heart; just as though before everything it were not necessary for a man to be a surgeon in order to perform a surgical operation!

The thing with which he reproaches his colleagues is precisely that they have not the experience and the knowledge which his school deems necessary, and not without reason, for the correct administration of criminal justice. They are jurists, and this is what they should be, because with the exception of a few examining magistrates, their duties practically consist in absorbing themselves exclusively in civil cases and they have not time to give other cases any more than a small part of their attention. At the law school they only learn criminal law as an accessory of the civil law; they only study it *from the civil point of view,* from the syllogistic point of view, without any regard for the psychological or physiological realities, without bothering themselves about, or questioning the relation between crime and natural science any

[1] In spite of everything the greater enlightenment and indulgence could not fail to be felt as a blessing, if henceforth the magistracy were substituted for the jury. Not only would the advantage of a fixed jurisprudence be found in it, that is to say of a justice equal for all, and would the scandal of successive and diametrically opposed verdicts in absolutely similar cases be avoided, but, besides this in many cases, it is safe to say that the guilt or even the innocence of the accused would be very much more surely ascertained. For example, in 1841, in the La Roncière case, an error of law, which today has become an obvious one, owing to the progress made in cerebral pathology, was committed to the injury of the accused, who, on the faith of a hysterical woman subject to hallucinations, was condemned to ten years hard labor. The details can be found on this subject in the last book of *Liégeois,* "De la suggestion" (Douai, 1889). At present, even before a jury, this monstrous sentence would probably never have been pronounced. But even in 1841, it could not have failed to have been repugnant to a criminal court composed of enlightened councillors. In fact, the president of the assize court said at that time: "That he would rather have had his throat cut than sign the verdict of guilty." In this respect he had a premonition of the final order handed down in this case, unfortunately too late, by Brouardel, Legrand du Saulle, Liégeois, and other good justices.

more than about social science, about degeneracy and madness any more than about progress and civilization. Also the manner in which they deal with correctional cases, with an indulgence sometimes almost as lamentable as that of the jury, with an abuse of the lighter penalties which officially is reckoned among the causes of the progress of recidivism, might cause a serious hesitation in requiring them to determine criminal cases. "The existing judges," said Garofalo, "are perhaps, among all the government officials, those least fitted to carry on this work. Accustomed from the very nature of their studies not to take any account of man, they only occupy themselves with formulae. For the [civil] law is absolutely indifferent to everything regarding the physical and moral qualities of individuals; the goodness or the wickedness of a creditor cannot have the slightest influence upon the validity of his claim. This strictly legal character is very far removed from penal science, which has as its object the struggle with a social malady, that of crime. The member of a court which is called upon to pass judgment in a penal matter preserves all his habits; it is not the individual who attracts his attention, it is the legal definition of the facts which concerns him."

There will be no limit to his subtleties, for example, those based upon our Article 405, and he will decide that a mere untruth is never sufficient to constitute the "fraudulent trick" required by this article in a case of swindling. The smallest piece of paper put in evidence by a swindler in support of his allegations will thus render him liable to be condemned, whereas the best laid plot of verbal trickery will mean that he will be encouraged by being acquitted. In spite of my very profound respect for the Court of Cassation, I take the liberty of believing that there are ways of lying which might fool the sharpest man, and that in cases of this sort every one of them should be separately examined. I also take the liberty of believing that, when uttered by an accused, whose deplorable tendencies have already been proved by the written evidence in his case, by his antecedents, by his answers and his general attitude during the hearing, the least subtle falsehood is exceptionally serious and, in certain cases, demonstrates the necessity for a repression. This is not the only case in which a civil judge trying a criminal case could be led into error by force of his habits. Sometimes they will lead him to the surprising judgments which lead into error the public itself, inclined to interpret them too severely. The public has no knowledge of the pleasure "sui generis" which the lawyer has in arguing from the point of view of his habitual syllogistic logic in order that he may thwart the conclusions of moral sense and prove to the ignorant that, where they see an offense, a swindle, a theft, or an abuse of confidence, there was merely "civil fraud."

"Finally, the judge readily forgets that the penalty which he is inflicting, ought, before everything, to serve some useful purpose; that this useful purpose is attained in various ways, according to the individual dealt with, and that consequently it is an examination of individuals which should determine the nature and extent of the penalty." Why has the judge condemned some man to six months imprisonment rather than to a week or a year? Because he remembers having, a week or a month ago, in a similar case, or one which *appeared* to be similar, pronounced a similar sentence. We need seek no further reason. When he thus falls back upon his "jurisprudence," it is in order to disguise his absolute despotism and to conceal it from himself. To tell the truth, he is out of his element in a criminal court.[1]

Now see this same man sitting in a civil court; here he once more finds his guiding star. There is no question of procedure too fine and too Byzantine to captivate him, and in the solution of which he will not take delight in discovering a "delicate" side. If, by chance, the question is a new one, which at the present time means that it is trifling and insignificant to a high degree, his interest becomes a passion, and between the lawyer and himself the matter then becomes a feverish competition of research and

[1] It is not certain that the existing magistracy, were it to be substituted for the jury, would be more severe than the latter in all its decisions taken together. It certainly would be more fair towards the world in the measure of its relative severity or indulgence. An advantage which is not to be despised in a time which claims to be impregnated with such a thirst for equality. Mr. de Holtzendorff observes that in Holland, during the years which preceded the complete abolition of the death penalty, the magistrates, passing judgment alone and without the assistance of juries, showed themselves still more indulgent, and more prone to pronounce acquittals in order to avoid inflicting capital punishment which was repugnant to them, than did the juries of neighboring countries. The great difference at present existing between the jury and the magistracy from this point of view would seem to be, I believe, the following. The jury, being more ignorant, is before everything the echo of an opinion already formed, already existing in popular prejudice; the magistracy, being more enlightened, would be more a reflection of opinion which was in process of formation. One can rest assured that if, in the eighteenth century, in France, crimes had been submitted to a verdict of a jury and not to the order of the councillors in the Parliaments, who were generally tainted with the fashionable sentimentality or by "philosophism," capital executions and horrible torture would have been far more lavish.

subtleties, of searches among the court orders and the authorities in order to arrive at the solution of so rare a case as this, and to enrich the collection of legal literature with this variety which has not yet been classified.

Let us not be amused at this great seriousness, let us not even too much regret the expenditure of time and of intellectual force buried in this labor. The settling of a uniform and complete jurisprudence is only attained at such a price as this, and it is not too high a price to pay for so precious a possession for the insuring of public security. But the very next day in the criminal court, the scene is quite different. Ugly faces, I admit, but expressive ones, physiognomies which are just so many social or pathological conundrums to be solved, pass before the inattentive looks of the court and the bar. Neither the lawyer nor the judge notice the serious problems offered by these unfortunates nor see any use in thoroughly investigating their past, and sometimes consulting some efficient medico-legal expert with regard to them, or else some former prison keeper, nor even of instituting an investigation. This would require too much time and too much expense.

Now, if it were a question of some hedge or road of no special value about which the two parties litigant were disputing, an adjournment to the locality would be ordered, a colored diagram of the place would be drawn up by a draughtsman, nothing would be too expensive. But here it is only a question of throwing some light on the darkest obscurities of the mind, and this same judge, who believing himself to be unable to make a sketch of a field, or incapable of verifying the fact of two examples of handwriting resembling each other, yesterday called in the doubtful assistance of a land expert or school teacher, today believes that he can get along perfectly well without the assistance of an alienist. Yet, a century which claims to be a wise one owes it to itself, it seems to me, to use some judgment in passing upon the crimes which are so numerous in it. Certainly, if the magistracy of the Old Régime, in this resembling that of the new, had not justified a better opinion of itself in civil, than in criminal cases, it is very probable that we would long since have been enjoying the benefits of a civil jury, to the joy of business men.

The intelligence and capacity of the personnel of the judiciary have nothing to do with the case. A magistrate of the average intellectual ability, should he be deprived of dealing with law-suits and given the special work of dealing with crimes, will as a general thing very soon become a very fair examining magistrate. But it is the alternate mingling of the two occupations which is to be deplored. Where has that encyclopaedic judge who must take an interest in alternately disentangling the quibbles of parties litigant and reading the eyes of malefactors and excelling in both been found, or at any rate, is there any hope of discovering him in all the courts? One may be quite sure that if he has one of these abilities he will be lacking in the other; and that, should he possess the vigor and the subtle logic required for the handling of civil cases, he will be lacking in the psychological depth and keenness required for the study of delinquents. Now or never is the time to apply that famous principle of the division of labor which political economy, though exaggeratedly it is true, vaunts in its own field.

Therefore let us clearly distinguish between the two forms of magistracy, one criminal and the other civil. Let us specialize and localize each of them in its own particular task.[1] For example, let us no longer require that the public prosecutor should take part in civil hearings, where ordinarily he simply wastes his time, except when he makes some motion and causes his colleagues to waste theirs,[2] and where historical reasons — shall I dare to add, a certain unconscious need of symmetry which he satisfies by standing before the clerk of the court — alone account for his presence.

Finally, let us not have correctional chambers, but special correctional courts just as we have special commissaries of police who are not at one and the same time justices of the peace or arbitrators. But first of all, would it not be a good thing to begin by having these future judges, who no less than our police officers should be men of competence through long experience, undergo a special apprenticeship? Even in the school of law perhaps it would be a good thing to compel young men who felt that they

[1] The expedition of civil cases would profit just as much as that of criminal cases. A magistrate begins by filling his calling for a short time at the bar, then he sits as president, as councillor and exercises functions for which he has not been prepared in the least. The ignorance of law which is even held up as a reproach in the case of the magistracy is due to this fact. It is very urgent that an end should be put to this abuse, in spite of a few brilliant exceptions to the rule.

[2] The civil conclusions of law of the public prosecutor are a useful experience for him; very well, but however brilliant they may be, they tire the judge to no purpose, he having already made up his mind after having heard the pleas of both sides and the answers of counsel. In certain cases, the law requires these conclusions, but practice shows us here, as well, their absolute uselessness. More often than not the magistrate who is prosecuting "relies upon the wisdom of the tribunal."

had a "criminological" calling regularly to visit malefactors in prison and to make a psychological if not physical, and before everything, biographical and domestic study of some of these persons, a kind of moral vivisection. They should be compelled to be members of the protection societies which are still so deficient, and perhaps because of their youth they would be better received by the prisoners than is generally the case with those serious persons or persons invested with an official character among whom this commission chooses its members.

A wish of this kind was expressed at the Congress of Rome. Can the idea be realized? No, practical men will say. Practical men are those who think that everything is impracticable, just as men of good taste are those among whom the fastidious are always to be found. However, it is quite possible that in this they are right; but from this proposition or from others of a similar kind we can at least gather this much, that in the last analysis it is a very important matter to have an apprenticeship for criminologists. On all sides we see being founded during the last few years, at Rome (in the old convent of Regina Coeli), in Switzerland, in Sweden, in Denmark, and in Germany, normal schools intended for the education of prison employees; and yet nobody can understand the urgency, and they would not even deign to discuss the idea, of including in our higher education a special section for magistrates who are the men who have to obtain the inmates for these same prisons and supervise these same employees.

Once this deficiency has been overcome, and these reforms have gone into effect, the time will have come, we believe, to deprive the jury of the functions which it fulfils so badly, and to confer them upon justices who are elected for life, and made ready for the part to be played by them by means of a sufficient term of probation. In these functions, we must draw a distinction on the one hand between the power which the jury has always possessed, of constituting "proof in fact" by itself, and on the other hand the power which it acquired later on or usurped of being "judges of the facts," even judges of the law, and indirectly of the penalty.[1] All this latter part of these attributes should be

[1] Since the jury, as a consequence of this usurpation which has been sanctioned, hands down regular judgments it ought as a consequence to be held bound to give the reasons for its verdict. So long as its verdicts passed as the expression of an oracle, having of themselves probative force, it was permissible, strictly speaking, to accept these decisions without any "whereas" or "grounds." But a judgment, or an order, must state its reasons; this is an essential part of it; it is

conferred once more upon the magistrates. As to the first part, forgotten and unperceived today and formerly the only or the principal part, on whom is it to be conferred; who shall be in this sense the successor of the jury? I have already named the scientific expert.

Medico-legal expert testimony goes far back into the past. As early as the thirteenth century it begins to appear, either before the ecclesiastical tribunals or before the royal judges. An edict of Philip the Handsome [1] later sanctioned its use; the "Caroline," that is the penal code of Charles V, required that doctors and surgeons should make an examination and draw up a report in criminal cases, and a writ of Pope Pius V (1565–1572) "solemnly proclaimed the competence of men who practised the art in the estimation of facts of a medical nature in ecclesiastical matters."[2] In prosecutions for witchcraft, especially in that of Joan of Arc, the medical expert is brought in to decide whether the cause of the madness is not perhaps a natural one, and sometimes he saves the victim from the stake.[3] In the seventeenth century, there appeared the great work of Zacchias, entitled "Questiones medico-legales," where penal responsibility is studied in its most difficult aspect, such as the influence of epilepsy, or somnambulism, etc.

But this beginning, which was already remarkable because of its precocity, was far from forecasting the importance which legal medicine was to attain in modern times. At the beginning of our century, legal medicine was still accessible to any physician; at the present time it has become a true special branch of science, a very high and difficult form of specialization. Chairs in this science

the most elementary and sure guarantee of the wisdom and justice of the sentences pronounced by the judiciary. Now, if there is any desire to see the institution of the jury crumble before long under universal ridicule, let juries be compelled to set forth, or at least to point out in writing, the reasons for their opinion. I do not ask for anything more; and yet I only ask the minimum of the requirements to which the man amenable to justice has a right, and which have never been refused him in a civilized country, except by those who invented the jury.

[1] In 1391, Count Amadeus of Savoy, having died under circumstances which justified the belief that he had been poisoned by some quack, two physicians were called in to give their opinion upon this question, and their opinion was in favor of the accused. (See *Cibrario,* "L'Economie politique au Moyen âge," Vol. I, p. 296 of the French translation.)

[2] *Linas,* "Dictionnaire encyclopédique des sciences médicales." Articles on the insane and legal medicine.

[3] In the 123rd book of the "Histoire de de Thou" (1599) one finds throughout the narrative accounts of a person possessed by the devil, together with a medical examination and medical dissertations on this subject. The doctors were already in conflict with the theologians at that time.

are becoming more and more numerous, its laboratories are more and more sought after, and the masters who teach it are becoming more and more renowned. The constant increase in the powers conferred upon experts, especially upon medico-legal experts, is not only one of the wishes of the new school of criminologists, but it is also one of the tendencies of judicial practice. It is also a strange thing, as Henri Coutagne has rightly pointed out ("Lyon médical," June 24, 1888), that, in order to safeguard private and purely pecuniary interests, our Civil Code provides not only for cases of obvious madness which may result in depriving a man of his civil rights, but even for cases of semi-madness which is sufficient to have a judicial council provided for him, whereas our Penal Code, which has as its object the protection of our most serious and most general interests, only condescends to take into consideration cases of obvious madness. And it is at least peculiar that the law, in civil matters, has made the establishment of any cerebral disorder subject to one of the most complicated forms of procedure, whereas in criminal matters, it has omitted to make any regulations as to proofs of this kind.

Already, in several countries, and particularly in Germany, there exists a "tribunal of super-arbitrators." This institution has the approval — a sign of the times — of a distinguished examining magistrate, Guillot, according to whom it will fulfil the requirement of ending the spectacle of "magistrates and lawyers, one as incompetent as the other, discussing before juries [still more incompetent authorities assuredly], the most delicate problems of medicine and toxicology." A jurist only finds one objection to this [1] and it will be as well to state it. "The establishment," says he, "of a separate commission of learned men such as the tribunal of super-arbitrators would be a direct attack upon the principle of the sovereign power of the jury." This is perfectly true, but it will indeed be necessary to pass through this stage, unless we are always to remain backward in a line of scientific progress which cannot be disputed and in which other rival nations have gone ahead of us. In one way or another, science will finally prevail over ignorance, even predominating ignorance. Such is the new power, increasing every day, before which the jury is bound to disappear.[2]

[1] "Gazette des Tribunaux," April 29, 1887.

[2] Then it is to be feared that expert testimony will in its turn become the object of a superstitious belief. For nothing here below is infallible, not even science. In a poisoning case in which I was examining magistrate, the first experts discovered

Thus I fully approve on this point of the criticism formulated by the positivist school, and I partly approve of its suggestions. But only partly. Though the "right" of this school, represented by Garofalo, does not go beyond an acceptable reform in its hopes, the "left," under the impulse of Lombroso, seems disposed to go much farther. His adversaries credited him with strange pretensions. All tribunals having been done away with as well as the jury, we would see taking their place commissions of alienists, judges from whom no appeal would lie, who "after having seen the accused, heard his statements, felt his head, and minutely examined his organs,"[1] would send him for the rest of his life to a "manicomio criminale" should he be so unfortunate as to present certain physical characteristics. It must be admitted that, although this is a slander, it is not an entirely inexcusable one; imprudent statements have been the cause of it.

Far removed from pitfalls of this kind, Ferri, however, hopes that the entire discussion, before criminal courts, will some day be reduced, after the incriminating fact has once been proved, to a determination as to what category of delinquents a condemned man should be placed in, and consequently to defining the kind of penalty or rather the treatment which he ought to undergo. But

in the organs of the victim a very perceptible quantity of alum and from this came to the conclusion that the poisoning resulted from a lack of power to digest this substance. Nothing could have been less acceptable "a priori" than such a hypothesis as this. The experts on the other side proved that these learned men, although very worthy in every other respect, had found alum in the organs which had been examined by them "because they had put some alum there without knowing it." Alum is a combination of aluminum and sulphuric acid which had eaten into the china of the vessels in which they were operating.

In a recent case, tried at Tours, an innocent man, since recognized to be such in a very striking manner, was condemned to a month's imprisonment upon the report of three experts who had *unanimously* sworn to the identity of his writing with that upon the incriminating document. Still more frequent, if we are to believe *Paul Bernard* ("Archives," No. 26), must be the mistakes in diagnosis relative to what he calls "false sudden deaths." This passage is worthy of note, because it supports the hypothesis which I set forth in a previous chapter as to the rather large number of homicides which were called accidental deaths. "An old man," says he, "is found dead upon a public road; the physician called in examines the body and, there being no traces of violence, comes to the conclusion that this is a case of sudden death due to apoplexy or to the rupture of an aneurism. In a certain number of cases where this diagnosis does not satisfy the law, it has happened that when the autopsy has been performed the expert has found severe lesions which had absolutely no connection with the alleged cause of death. . . . What mistakes must have been committed and perhaps what a large number of criminal deaths have thus escaped the investigation of justice!" Observe that, since 1835, the number of sudden deaths has greatly increased.

[1] "Il professore Lombroso" by *Guilio Nazari* (Oderzo, 1887).

first of all, it will be necessary to reach some kind of agreement as to the classification of malefactors, and we know that agreement in this respect does not prevail among the innovators. We know, also, that their inclination leads them to curtail the part played by moral causes. As far as we are concerned, expert testimony, even when organized in the form of a body, ought never to be anything more than a superior means of obtaining information placed at the disposal of the law, a sort of *legal proof* of a new kind; and though the expert should be a physician or a naturalist of a certain type, the judge should before everything be an enlightened moralist, psychologist, and sociologist at one and the same time. Our premises logically lead us to this conclusion.

§ 82. Impossibility of requiring absolute conviction on the part of the criminal judge; possibility of approximately estimating the degree of his belief, and usefulness of this estimate though it is an imperfect one. The point of conviction, its variations and their causes.

I cannot leave this subject without pointing out the striking contrast which exists between the greater importance which is attached to the question of proof in legal practice, and the very secondary part which it plays in the theories of the criminologists, even of those whom their positivism ought to accustom to look more closely into facts. A crime has been committed. More often than not its perpetrator is unknown or merely suspected; and what is then the first precaution which ought to be taken? It is to gather together all the information on the subject, a long and arduous task in which there is displayed an art which it would be very difficult to formulate scientifically. But now I will assume that this work has been accomplished. Some man has been accused of the crime and brought before some court. Then there are two problems to be solved: 1st. Up to what point has it been proved that the accused has committed the act which has been imputed to him? A question which, in the inmost conscience of each juryman or judge, signifies: "Up to what point am I convinced that the accused has committed this offense?" 2d. Admitting that he is the perpetrator of this offense, to what extent does this prove that he is dangerous and ought to be punished?

Now, of these two problems the former is already so difficult to solve, and as a general thing is so imperfectly solved, that it absorbs the attention of the magistrate and the lawyer and the result is that the other question is rather neglected. On the other hand, in the writings of the theorists, it is always assumed without the slightest doubt that the first of these questions has been solved, and it seems that they concern themselves only with the second. That is why scholastic discussions, whatever may come of them, will never have the practical, vital influence which it is feared or hoped they will have. The principal effort of the lawyers and the examining magistrates of the courts themselves will always be to carry on a work of inductive or deductive logic in order to succeed in coming to some conclusion, and they will only be occupied briefly or secondarily, assuming the accused to be guilty, in measuring the amount of his guilt, or, if you prefer, of his "temibilità." If the new school were to bring into the law new elements of knowledge, if it could seriously suggest that its anthropological description of the malefactor would be a serious presumption against the accused, it would beyond dispute be entitled to the honor of being a reformative agency. As a matter of fact, all legal progress has been accomplished in the direction of more easy, or prompt, or complete proof, and all the modern inventions and improvements have served this end; telegraph, post, railroad, photography, just as have the ingenious devices more especially adapted to this object, the "casier judiciaire," the Bertillon method, the apparatus of Marsh and Mitcherlisch, etc., all of which are just so many powerful instruments of investigation and, so to speak, physical, or mechanical examining magistrates. In fact, a treatise on proof, even though written by a Bentham, is not sufficient to bring about improvement in the discovering of a delinquent. Here as everywhere progress has only been a result of large or small inventions.

However, it would not be idle to speculate on this subject and it is unfortunate that nobody has thought of doing so. This forgetfulness is caused by an infatuation for the absolute which has caused philosophers to make so many blunders. In their claim of attaining, like the geometricians, necessary truths or, like the theologians, articles of faith, metaphysicians have learned to scorn, under the contemptuous appellation of probabilities, moral proofs and empiricism, all the degrees of belief less than that superlative intensity of conviction which they have called certitude. Everything or nothing; anything which is not absolutely demonstrated has no value in their eyes. As long as it remained imbued with this prejudice, philosophy failed to recognize its principal reason for existing, which is that it should rely on sciences in order to round them out and to build over their gaps the arches of its hypotheses, and as a consequence, to effect the enlargement of their formulae at the expense of the weakening of their proof. It is probability, and not certitude, which is the proper department and field of operation of philosophers.

But, on the other hand, it is not hard to account for the fact that during such times as Plato's and the seventeenth century when mathematics were practically the only sciences which flourished, and during the Middle Ages when theology was the supreme science, philosophy in this double commerce should have contracted the habit of considering as unworthy the notice of the learned men and consequently of the philosophers, everything which was not absolutely certain, everything which did not have the emphasis of a dogma or a theorem. Similarly, having been formed under the sway of this scholastic disdain, the criminal law of the Middle Ages, and especially that of the time of Louis XIV, on principle, had to require, on the part of a judge who pronounced a sentence, a conviction which was absolute, ideal, and unlimited, and which, moreover, was required by the expiatory and sacred character of the punishment. Also, for fear he should delude himself on this point, he was forbidden to say that he was convinced except in those cases in which he was lawfully reputed to be so. From this there arose the theory of "legal proofs," the last existing trace of which in our penal laws is the prohibition of the criminal judge taking into consideration certain testimony of relations, relatives by marriage, or servants.

But, we know what pitfalls we are liable to stumble into if we fix our gaze too high. Nowhere are people satisfied with mere frivolous arguments and nowhere are they contented to take so little trouble in the matter of proof as in the philosophical schools most infected with truth "a priori" and beyond dispute. Never were sentences so lightly pronounced and upon the slightest indications as in the heyday of legal proofs when the judge pretended that he only took into consideration absolute certainty which was not susceptible of any greater or lesser degree. However, the feeling of this fact in men's experience, that conviction has its degrees, and that belief is a quantity, dominated the judge and even the legislator without their knowing it.

For example, when the accused, who had been subjected to the torture while existing proofs were held in reserve, had undergone this torture without making any confession but the depositions of witnesses afterwards established his guilt, he was sentenced just as though he had made a confession, with this difference, however, that he could not be sentenced to a capital punishment. Why this lessening of the penalty, if it were not because the certainty attained from mere evidence was judged to be less absolute than certainty obtained by means of the confession? In our own time the full penalty is still always spared the perpetrator of the most monstrous parricide if it be not very conclusively proved that this crime can be imputed to him. As a general rule, it seems, impliedly to everybody, that the severity of a sentence ought to be proportional, not only to the enormity of the crime or the danger of its being repeated as the theorists would have us believe, but furthermore to the convincing force of its proof.

It is now time to take into account those calculations, those inmost "analyses" to which, unconsciously, one's personal beliefs are subjected. Are they valid? Are they reasonable?[1] For the last two centuries, that is to say, since the tremendous development of sciences which are to a certain extent conjectural, either natural sciences or social sciences, — geology, paleontology, archaeology, and astronomy studied by means of spectrum analysis, comparative philology, mythology, etc., — has surpassed the slower advance of the mathematical sciences, or has at least occupied a more important position alongside of them, philosophy has admitted that its object is to navigate the undulating surface of what is probable without ever coming to land at what is certain, and it has learned to be satisfied with this. The criminologist doctrines ought to profit by this example and take into account the doubts, the presumptions, and the weak convictions of judge or jury, just as philosophers place a value upon increase or decrease in the general belief of the learned world with regard to a disputed theory, such as the simian descent of man or the bacteriological origin of certain illnesses.

Bentham, in a passage from his work on proof which has not been sufficiently noticed, has incidentally put forth the idea that each judge ought, in giving his opinion in favor of conviction, to express by means of figures the degree of his belief, and that there

[1] As to the possibility of measuring the extent of belief, and of desire as well, see two articles published by me in the "Revue philosophique" in August and September 1880.

should be an acquittal if the total of all the figures added together is not equal to a *minimum* number fixed by the law. It has been objected that this system would give a very obstinate judge an abusive advantage, and this objection has appeared to be overwhelming. So little is this really the case that our university examinations, for example those for the baccalaureate, which so seldom give occasion for objections, are a realization of Bentham's idea. Here everything which is possible has been done exactly to proportion the opinion of the examiner, that is the degree of his belief in the capability or the knowledge of the candidate; and this position has been arrived at in a way which is satisfactory to all the parties interested. Is this belief easier to measure than the belief of a judge or a jury in a man's guilt? I do not mean to say that all that is necessary is to transport from the sphere of the university to the sphere of the judiciary the proposition with which we are here dealing. But I do believe that there is no excuse for rejecting "a priori" every attempt at a similar system of reckoning in the courts.

If this attempt were to be made, then it would be easier to perceive the existence of an opportunity of adopting a projected reform pointed out by the Italian innovators and which would consist in fact in generalizing a Scottish custom. In Scotland,[1] the jury may pronounce a verdict of acquittal in one of two ways; either by saying "not guilty," or by saying "not proven." Nothing could be more reasonable than this distinction, especially if belief is a quantity. Surely it is just as practical to distinguish, if there is an acquittal, between an affirmation of innocence and a refusal to affirm guilt for lack of sufficient belief in it, as, when there is a conviction, to distinguish between a pure and simple conviction and a conviction with extenuating circumstances. Often, in taking into account extenuating circumstances, the judge or the jury really mean that they are not sufficiently convinced to pronounce a conviction pure and simple.

If we admit that a very high degree of probability, which is more or less close to certainty, makes an accused person *condemnable*, it still will remain to determine, in so far as possible, this *point of condemnability* and to point out the relation of its variations to those of certain influences. In fact this point varies; there is a great distance between the vague suspicion which causes a man's head to be cut off in times of revolution or war and the

[1] See *Mittermaier's* work on the jury.

profusion of accumulated charges which the law believes necessary in ordinary times before condemning to a week's imprisonment, with the consent of the public, some powerful personage and one of previous good character. The judge's conviction, it is true, may have been just as intense in the former as in the latter case, but it is obvious that it is a creature of his passion, of his desire of being convinced, just as in the second case it has long been prevented from coming into existence, owing to his desire not to be convinced.

Let us assume the judge to be indifferent, disinterested, and impartial. Ought he not, especially if he has been brought up in the utilitarian school, to deem sufficient, in certain cases where the need of repression is keenly felt in the interest of the public safety, such an amount of conviction as, in other cases, ought not to suffice in his eyes? To put it in more general terms, is not this minimum of conviction which is exigible in inverse ratio to the social need of repression? There would seem to be no doubt as to the affirmative if this problem were not in reality interpreted as follows: Ought the judge to require less strong proofs according as the act is more serious? Or ought he, on the other hand, to require them to be that much stronger?

According to the humor of juries this difficulty is solved sometimes in one way and sometimes in another. When some horrible crime, such as an assassination in a railway carriage, appalls the public, it seems that the cause of this common terror must at any price be discovered, and that the individual who happens to be most greatly compromised, or on whom suspicion most strongly rests, sometimes without any good reason, ought to be the scapegoat. The jury remains subject to this unconscious impression just so long as the speech of the public prosecutor continues to retrace for them the details of the crime and revives in them the horror which it evokes. But, with the very first words of the counsel for the defense, their indignation changes to pity, they no longer give the crime a thought, they think of the penalty which will follow their verdict, they see the dreadful cleaver falling on the head of this weeping man surrounded by his children. Then it seems to them that the force of the proof ought to be in proportion to the severity of the punishment, that is to say, to that of the crime. Torn by these two conflicting sentiments, they end by acquitting or by pursuing a third course which consists in conviction with extenuating circumstances, however aggravating, however horrible may be all the circumstances of the crime in their own opinion.

However, what solution would we have adopted? It would be with the object of putting an end to all this embarrassment of conscience that it would be a good thing to allow the jury the power of answering not only "yes" or "no," but furthermore by "non liquet." Furthermore, we believe that on principle the requirements of proof ought to increase in proportion to the gravity of the crime; for, if society is more interested in having crime punished in proportion as this crime is more serious, it is especially interested in being sure that this punishment shall be a menace only to the criminal, and it ought to avoid the risk of a mistake in proportion as the punishment is a more terrible one. Let us add that society is not a reasoning being, that it is composed of persons who have not only a feeling of interest, but the care of their honor and who would blush at committing an injustice through fear or through motives of egoism, and who even though feeling anxiety, because of some danger, are often pleased to incur it out of a spirit of generosity. These persons desire that their representative, the administrator of justice, should resemble them and that he should not disgrace them while protecting them.

§ 83. Criticism of some reforms proposed in the matter of definition of crimes.

We do not believe that it is advisable to expatiate any more upon matters concerning the judgment. But, after having made a study of the legislative reforms proposed with regard to it by the new school, we will have to discuss its ideas of reformation in so far as incrimination is concerned, although it may well seem contrary to logical, or rather chronological, sequence to deal with this subject after the preceding one. Without taking into account this objection, let us examine the criticisms of the innovators relative to the aggravating circumstances offered by premeditation as well as their theories on attempt and complicity.

On this first point they happen to agree with the jury, who generally take into account the excusable or shameful, passionate or greedy, motive for homicide,[1] and not the secondary question

[1] It is not only the jury, but it is the magistracy as well, which, to as great an extent as it can, fills up at this point the tremendous gap existing in the law. The public prosecutor, in classifying under the name "homicides due to negligence" or "blows and wounds having occasioned death unintentionally," many true murders, has certainly drawn the reason for his decision from a consideration

of whether it has been premeditated. This unconscious jurisprudence of the jury has been put into a system outside of the school of which we are speaking, by Holtzendorff originally, and later by Mancini (1868) before being adopted by Garofalo. In a rather recent book [1] a writer of eclectic temperament, but a strong sympathizer with the positivist reformers, has summed up and systematized the work of his predecessors, and added to it a statement of the legislation of the entire world upon the subject with which we are now occupied.

§ 84. (I) Premeditation in case of homicide. History. Holtzendorff's theory. The book of Alimena. A consideration of motives.

From antiquity, we find two different points of view appearing, which, from age to age, from people to people, are reproduced and can serve to demonstrate to us the power of example in the domain of legislation. Although still badly stated, the distinction between simple homicide and premeditated homicide was recognized by the Romans, perhaps even by the Greeks. They have handed it down to us and we have passed it on to the criminal codes inspired by ours. But among the barbarians a very different and characteristic distinction is found. Homicide for revenge committed openly and fearlessly is excused; only secret and cowardly homicide is punishable and is considered assassination according to the Ripuarian law. The same predominant importance attached to the consideration of motives is to be observed in the following provisions. In Russia, a code of the eleventh century punishes with greater severity homicide committed without drawing one's sword from the scabbard; in Sweden the ancient laws invoked the most horrible penalties for the murder of a man who had been unable to defend himself. Everywhere during the ages of barbarism, it is cowardice which is punished in the case of murder. At the time of the crusades, feudal Europe distinguished among the cowardly forms of homicide a form which was even more cowardly than the others, homicide to order, and kept for that its very greatest punishments.

of determining motives. *Enrico Ferri,* in his "Omicidio-suicidio," rightly points out the very small number of prosecutions against lovers who, having resolved to kill themselves together, have partly carried out their resolution and one of whom has survived the other. As a general rule no one will be willing to consider the survivor as a murderer, and though it be averred that he has killed someone, as he killed this person with their consent and out of despair, he is not even prosecuted.

[1] "La premeditazione in rapporto alla psicologia, al diritto, etc." by *Bernardino Alimena* (Turin, fratelli Bocca, 1887).

Now the Roman point of view was formulated with accuracy in the "Caroline" (1532) and, with a constancy more worthy of notice as it is less justified, it is repeated in every legislation of our time, excepting in the English law or those systems derived from it. How does it happen that the very simple and very reasonable idea of proportioning the gravity of murder less in accordance with the degree of foresight and reflection encountered than with the nature of the passions and tastes which have driven the murderer to reflect and to look ahead has not offered itself to a single modern legislator? How does it happen that premeditated murder has seemed to everyone as synonymous with murder committed in cold blood, — just as though the strongest passion was not precisely the most calculated and the most fitting one to foster long drawn out plans, — and that murder which is not premeditated has seemed to everyone as necessarily committed during an attack of excusable madness, just as though the thief who is taken by surprise and who reluctantly and without having wanted to, beforehand, kills, was moved by hatred, jealousy or fanaticism?

The absolute sway exercised by imitation has alone been able to close men's eyes to these obvious truths. Let us especially notice the code drawn up in 1870 for the State of Panama (Colombia). Here another species of imitation, that of the enervating indulgence which is rife upon the continent of Europe, has been added to the preceding one. Simple homicide is punished with from four to six years imprisonment, premeditated homicide with from six to eight years, or from eight to ten years, and never more. As we see, it is high time for the wind to change its direction.

Is this as much as to say that the provisions of English legislation which, being the last echo of the barbarian laws referred to above, stand by themselves, as we have said, and are distinguished from the others to the advantage of the former? No; the aggravating circumstances which constitute "murder," the English equivalent of assassination, lead to peculiar results. Whether voluntary or not, it does not matter, a murder is called a "murder" if it has been committed as a result of gratifying a bad motive or pursuing some unlawful object. For example, according to an eminent English lawyer consulted by Alimena, there is a "murder" when a man, who has gone upon his neighbor's land to steal one of his hens, fires a shot intended for this fowl, but shoots the owner; the "malicious" character of the motive which inspired the perpetrator of this accidental murder is sufficient to place him among assassins. However peculiar this conception may be, it has, with variations, penetrated every body of law which England has inspired, in Canada, in the greater part of the United States, in Malta, in India,[1] etc. More than this, that other peculiarity of English legislation which is that homicide is presumed "murder until the contrary be proven,"[2] has permeated almost every American code. Such is the power of imitative impulse. Can one be astonished that it dominates criminals, when it sways legislators themselves to such a point as this?

Now, without taking either of these two points of view, Holtzendorff is before everything concerned with determining motives. He classifies them into three categories. 1st. Motives of an economical order (cupidity). 2d. Motives of a sexual order (love, jealousy, libertinage). 3d. Motives of a hateful and vindictive kind (political or religious fanaticism, private or family vengeance). This classification leaves much to be desired. Ambition is not included in it, and fanaticism, whether political or religious, should furthermore not be confused with revenge and hatred from which it is often separated[3] and from which it is always distinguished by that intensity of depraved conviction, of perverse sincerity, which is peculiar to it. Whatever the case may be, according to this author, it is only when premeditation concurs with motives of the first category that it reveals a deeper perversity, but not when it is combined with motives of the last two kinds.

Furthermore, according to German statistics, homicides through greed are three times more frequently premeditated than simple homicide, whereas homicides through hatred and revenge are twice as often simple as they are premeditated;

[1] Other peculiarities of the Anglo-Indian Code: the man who has supplied the fire to light the funeral pyre upon which a Hindu widow wishes to die is not guilty of murder if she is more than eighteen years old; if she is less than eighteen it is a case of murder.

[2] During very early times when a belief in a posthumous and terrible punishment for perjury existed, it often seemed natural to put the burden of proof upon the accused, who *ought* to prove his innocence because he always *could* by taking an oath with "oath-helpers."

[3] There are Russian sects which advocate not only "suicide in a body," out of piety, but even infanticide after the manner of Abraham. (See an article by *Anatole Leroy-Beaulieu* in the "Revue des Deux Mondes" of May 1, 1888.) "In 1870 a moujik bound his son of seven upon a bench and opened his abdomen, then assumed an attitude of prayer before the sacred images. 'Dost thou pardon me?' he asked the dying child. 'I pardon thee and God also,' replied the victim offered as a sacrifice." Here fanaticism has attained the height of a paroxysm and is perfectly free from all hatred.

homicides due to sexual passion hold the middle course, but they incline to the side of premeditation. A curious thing is that some statistics of Quételet's give the same results for France, except that murderers inspired by greed furnish premeditation with a contingent six times and not merely three times as great. I will ask to be allowed only to accept these figures under the privilege of inventory. I deem it certain that almost all homicides are desired for a longer or shorter time before they are carried out; but according to their nature, it is more or less easy to prove this. For homicides due to cupidity it is generally very easy, for homicides due to hatred and revenge it is very difficult, — and, according to their nature also, the public prosecutor is more or less disposed to raise against them, if there is any doubt, this aggravating circumstance, — homicides with love or with revenge as their motive inspire a great deal more indulgence in the accuser himself than do murders with greed as their motive. To this is due, to a great extent at least, the statistical statement above.

Nor must we think, that, because from 1825 to our own time, in France the numerical proportion of murders with relation to that of assassinations has been decreasing, murderers have progressed in foresight and in criminal calculation. No, the practice of changing a crime into a misdemeanor, whether in its legal form since 1832, or in its judicial form, expresses the thing far better; an increasing number of murders have passed into the column of blows and wounds which have occasioned death unintentionally.

Finally, although a statistical table of Quételet's (contradicted it is true by a German statistical table invoked by Holtzendorff) says that after the age of thirty or thirty-five murderers commit more premeditated homicides than simple homicides, must we hasten to conclude from this that criminals, as they advance in age, substitute guile for force? Here again the preceding consideration, seems to me to be applicable. However, let us admit that all these numbers are correct; let us especially admit the first numerical results given above, relating to murderers through greed, through sexual passion and vengeance. It will follow that the vilest kind of murder is ordinarily the one committed upon most reflection. But, is it because it has been the subject of reflection, and only because of this, that it is vile? Let us clearly distinguish between two problems which seem to me to have been confusedly raised by legislators and authors. The degree of relative responsibility of various agents who commit a similar act is one thing, and the degree of relative gravity of various acts committed by equally responsible agents is another. An agent is all the more responsible, as we know, in proportion as he is more completely given up, assimilated, to his acts; in this respect it is useful to know whether he has formed his plan in advance.

Furthermore we must note that certain kinds of madness, for example, hypochondria, melancholia, where the patient turns over and over his fixed idea, are very far from excluding premeditation. The epileptic during his period of semi-insanity premeditates a great deal. But a misdeed is the more serious in proportion as it shows in the author of it a more dangerous nature, that is to say, one which menaces a greater number of interests or interests deemed to be the most precious ones according to locality and time. A fault has a symptomatic value especially. Now is to *premeditate* within oneself a symptom of a dangerous nature? This depends not only upon the thing which is premeditated, but upon the passion which drives one to premeditation. Greedy premeditation of murder is a danger for everybody; vindictive premeditation of murder is a danger for a limited number of people, and if the vengeance in question is roused by unjust wrongs, a danger which it is in the power of each one to avoid by never wronging anybody unjustly. Thus the legislative mistake has consisted in taking into account premeditation by itself, leaving aside motives without which premeditation is only a fictitious aggravation. Its artificial character clearly appears in certain cases which have nothing exceptional about them.

For example, it often happens that an outraged husband premeditates killing his wife's lover should he meet him in his own house, or that a man is resolved to kill his enemy the first time the latter shall take the liberty of saying the slightest thing to offend him. Here the premeditation is conditional; if the condition is fulfilled through some act of the victim's, will one say that there has been murder or assassination? To tell the truth, there has been neither one nor the other in the strictly legal sense. Thus we should be far more concerned with motives and far less concerned with premeditation.

If this circumstance had, taken by itself, the importance which is given it in matters of homicide, it ought, for the same reason, to play a similar part in the matter of theft and arson. But this is not the case at all; legally, premeditated theft is not contrasted with simple theft, nor premeditated arson with simple arson, although assuredly there do exist cases of arson and of theft which have been planned far ahead, as there are cases where they have been carried out on the impulse of the moment. However, perhaps there was some occasion in the matter of theft, rather than in the matter of homicide, to take into consideration the question of premeditation. If, in fact, as Alimena very reasonably contends, premeditation is of importance especially when it is coupled with cold-bloodedness, it is rarely so in the case of murderers and it is almost always in the case of thieves that it ought to be important to take it into account. Therefore, instead of seeking to ascertain the principal aggravating circumstances of the fraudulent taking in the means which the malefactor has employed, for example, breaking in or scaling, it would have been possible, whatever the means employed, to inflict a greater penalty for theft for which greater preparation had been made.

From this point of view I will style simple theft the act of a peasant who, happening to pass along a road and seeing a ladder near the window of a house which at the time is empty, climbs the ladder, takes a sack of grain and flees; and I will style qualified theft a case of pickpocketing committed by one of the men who work at fairs and markets, who, without any breaking in or scaling whatsoever, but with a skill quite professional and only with difficulty acquired, with a simplicity of ways and means which is quite a work of art, pilfers your wallet or your pocketbook from your pocket. Unfortunately this would be to take just the opposite point of view from the legal terms.

Furthermore, a consideration of motives seems to me just as vital in the matter of theft as in the matter of homicide; to the former as to the latter the threefold classification of Holtzendorff, as corrected and completed, is applicable. It is not always greed which makes the thief steal; it is often lust or a heated spell of passion; sometimes, also, it is hatred, vengeance, or envy. This last case is rarely met with in normal times; but not as rarely as one might suppose. Certainly Duval, the so-called anarchist, who used to plunder a private residence, found in this, besides the pleasure of enriching himself, the pleasure of impoverishing a "bourgeois." But, on the other hand, during times of disturbance, during external or civil wars, theft from animosity and reprisals become most frequent. When the soldiers and even the officers of an army of invasion, in defiance of the most elementary international law, plunder the residents of a country, the pleasure they have in stripping them of their goods is at one and the same time a greedy and a cruel one. This is so true that sometimes what they cannot carry away they smash, in order thus to avenge the humiliation which they themselves or their fathers have been subjected to. Obviously, however severe the judgment of history should be upon these cases of plundering, it cannot go so far as exactly to compare them with the cases of embezzlement inspired by greed alone.

§ 85. (II) Attempt. Why a likening of attempt to a crime which has been carried out is repugnant to common sense.

Although the new school may have happened to agree with the jury, "grosso modo," in its way of looking at premeditation, they absolutely disagree with regard to the question of attempt. According to this school, an attempt to commit a crime "ought to be considered the same as the crime itself when the danger arising from the act of the delinquent is as great," [1] a thing which occurs when his plan was well put together, but was not carried out simply because of unforeseen obstacles, "independent of the will," as stated by the French law, which is here approved of by our reformers.[2] But, as we know, a jury will never refuse its partial or absolute indulgence to the perpetrator of an assassination or a theft which has failed. Nobody has been harmed, therefore why inflict any punishment? It is curious to find that on this point the positivist school only takes into consideration what takes place within the man, that is, the resolution formed by the agent, and rejects as being contaminated with coarse materialism that excessive concern for the physical action with which it reproaches certain of the leaders of the spiritualistic school, in Germany and Italy, particularly at Carrara.

[1] *Garofalo*, "Criminologie."

[2] Does not the influence of Roman law upon ours make itself felt here? "The law 'Cornelia de Sicariis' punishes attempt at homicide in the same manner as it does the crime which has been carried out. This was the same in the case of parricide approved by the law 'Pompeia de pariicidias.' Under the empire, in the matter of crimes of high treason, they even went much further than this and jurisprudence punished even acts of preparation." The same was true with regard to crimes of violence punished by the law "Julia de vi," and for the crimes of intrigue and forgery. But, "in so far as private offenses were concerned, which were four in number, the 'furtum' or theft, the injury 'injuria,' the 'damnum' or damage provided for by the law 'Aquilia' and rapine 'rapina,' their nature excluded on principle all incrimination in the case of a simple attempt at theft." In fact in the Roman law "there was absolutely no general system as to the attempt." (*Humbert*, see "Conatus," "Dictionnaire des Antiquités.")

At the same time there is really nothing contradictory in this. If the penal law has as its basis social interest, it ought indeed to strike at, not the accomplished crime, which is only of interest to the victim and his family, but it ought to strike at the psychological source of other possible future crimes. It is because they have embraced the cause of society more consciously and more resolutely than anybody else that the innovators in the matter of the penal law have found themselves led to their theory of attempt. This theory will be better and better received, we believe, as the memory of the old private action shall be more completely blotted out and the fundamental reason for the public action shall be better understood. This theory has not yet been universally accepted, and to prove this it will suffice for me to recall the embarrassment of the majority of criminologists in facing a problem similar to ours; that is the problem of homicide through mistake. I have resolved to assassinate Paul, I seek him and find Peter, whom I kill, believing him to be Paul. Now am I guilty of assassination or of voluntary homicide? This question has been the subject of an infinite number of subtleties, and systems have multiplied ever since the time of the Digest. However, it is clear that, as far as society is concerned, Peter's life is worth as much as Paul's life. An assassin who has killed the former without wishing to is therefore just as guilty as though he had voluntarily killed the latter, as he thought he was doing. Consequently, the solution of the question from the social point of view is quite simple, and, if difficulties have seemed to arise, it can only be because people have unconsciously taken the point of view of the time when the penal action was brought, not by the nation, but by the family; for most assuredly, Peter's family cannot show that the killing of the latter was a voluntary one. Therefore this act could at that time have given rise to an action for damages only.

Now, that which applies to the offense committed through mistake also applies to the offense which through accident is not accomplished, that is to say, it applies to the attempt. An assassin has done everything required for the killing of Peter, but, owing to a providential chance, he has not been able to succeed. This is very lucky for Peter, and under the Merovingians, Peter would not have been able, without being laughed at, to maintain that the "Wergeld" was due him as it would have been due to his family if his assassination had really been carried out; but if this is lucky for Peter, is it an equally fortunate thing for society? No, society is still menaced by the proven wickedness of the malefactor, and this menace is just as great as though this wickedness had attained its object; it will even become greater if, in order to make the criminal participate in some way in the unforeseen chance of his victim, he is rewarded for his success by being given a semi-exemption. Consequently there is every occasion, it seems to us, to welcome the new ideas on this point, as on so many others.

It is no less true that this absolute likening of criminal attempt to accomplished crime is repugnant to popular sentiment; and outside of the reason that I have just given, I think I can perceive another, but not a better one. That which popular sentiment requires in a penalty is not only that it shall be effective in the future, in preventing a later repetition of the act which has been punished, but it is also to wipe out an injustice done in the past by establishing a compensation for the unlawful pleasure which the crime has afforded its perpetrator. Again, being unconsciously inspired by this spirit, judges are prone, everything else being equal, to impose a heavier sentence upon the thief in proportion as the sum stolen is a greater one, in spite of the fact that the temptation was one which was proportionately stronger and, from the point of view of free will, must have lessened the man's guilt. If, the crime having miscarried, the criminal has not enjoyed the thing he wanted, the penalty is lacking in the second part of its usefulness in the eyes of the masses. And no doubt this is the true hidden reason for the repugnance which they feel in seeing the perpetrator of an attempt punished as severely as the perpetrator of an act that has been accomplished.[1] Moreover, we must not confuse this desire for a suffering by way of compensation with the feeling which has suggested retaliation. One is exactly the opposite of the other, one requires that the guilty man shall suffer what he has caused another to suffer; the other that he shall suffer in proportion to the pleasure he has had. But, from a rational point of view, one is no better justified than the other, and the conscience, as it becomes more enlightened, ought to resist this persistent need of symmetry which makes it seek in the actual suffering a *counterpart* of its past pleasure after having formerly made it seek in the suffering of the guilty man an

[1] Also when we see, for example, the Roman law punishing the attempt to seduce a married woman (see *Humbert, loc. cit.*) in the same manner as a seduction which has been carried out, there is scarcely anybody who will not cry out against it.

opposite, so to speak, of the suffering of his victim. The justification of the punishment is a definite thing, as we shall soon see.

§ 86. (III) Complicity.

On the question of complicity, we have only a word or two to say. Here again the guiding principle of the new school, which is that, in passing judgment, it is necessary to take into account not the abstract thing called the offense, but the living being called the delinquent, shows us its excellence; and the opposite principle leads one to an absurdity. The accomplice, says the law, ought to be punished in the same way as the principal perpetrator. Just as the penal likening of the attempt to the completed offense is understood, because there is the same amount of perversity in both cases, is the penal likening of the accomplice to the principal perpetrator little understood, because these two different individuals differ, perhaps profoundly, by reason of their physical and moral nature, their characteristics and their passions, and the unequal and dissimilar danger which their exemption would cause. Without taking these considerations into account, French jurisprudence decides "in abstracto" that the accomplice is affected by the same aggravating circumstances which apply to the perpetrator in person (a servant of the man robbed for example), so that, had he himself been the principal in the crime, he would have been punished less severely than he actually is, because of his complicity. After this one can well be astonished that it does not make the accomplice profit by the extenuating circumstances inherent in the person of the principal (a minor of sixteen for example). In reality, the magistrates have no guiding thread in this obscure labyrinth;[1] and it seems to us that the new school is not mistaken in proffering them its torch, even though this torch is still rather smoky. The new school, as we know, is far from having arrived at a fixed idea of a classification of malefactors.

I will add a last consideration. The co-operation of several persons in the commission of a theft or murder is an aggravating circumstance. Obviously, the legislature, in enacting this very wise provision, did not take the point of view of the theory which makes free will the basis of responsibility. It took the point of view of social interest, which demanded energetic measures for presenting the recurrence of an especially alarming act, the

[1] A few examples of the digressions of the Court of Cassation itself in these matters may be found in the "Délits et les peines," by *Acollas*, pp. 68–69.

associating together of the malefactors. But if the degree of guilt were to be measured by the degree of liberty, this association ought to be looked upon as an extenuating circumstance, either for all the associates at the same time if they mutually suggested the plan in which they worked together with one another, or for those among them who were carried away, if a majority of them were carried away, by a leader.

From our point of view, on the contrary, this criminal bond ought generally to bring about an increase in the punishment of all of them. For the fact of having chosen the depraved influences of his companions in preference to the influences of a hundred other honest comrades shows ordinarily that, in the case of each one of the fellow perpetrators or accomplices of a crime, there exists a depravity which is innate or acquired, or at any rate inherent in his person itself. This is not the case when an honest individual is violently carried away by the example of everybody, when for example a soldier participates in the revolt of his entire regiment, or massacres, rapes, burns in a village, as a result of seeing others around him massacre, rape, and burn.

CHAPTER VIII

THE PENALTY

§ 87. Efficaciousness of penalties. Proofs and examples.
§§ 88–90. Historical Summary. — (I) Changes in the penalty which universally lead to changes in the method of proof. Four phases. Gradual moderation of penalties. (II) Price and penalties; a constant antithesis. The scale of offenses and the scale of penalties. A new phase in political economy as well as in the penal law.
§§ 91–94. Rational Basis. — (I) Penal law based upon utility or opinion? (II) The penal law and the relief-board ought to be derived from principles not contradictory to each other. (III) The various penitential systems. The "manicomio criminale." The necessity of segregation of prisoners based on their social origin. (IV) Transportation, the cell, the Irish system. Comparison and conclusion.

§ 87. Efficaciousness of penalties. Proofs and examples.

Here we stand, at the end of our researches, facing the practical problem which must be solved by applying the principles already discussed. The object is to discover what are the best existing penalties, or, if no good ones exist, what are the necessary penitential reforms. But, before deciding whether or not it is best to attempt a solution of this question, we ought to decide another, that is to say, we should seek to discover the value of the theory of Enrico Ferri [1] and of a large portion of his school as to the almost absolute inefficaciousness of any penalties. If this idea has been proved to be correct, why should we then waste our time studying the penal system? It may seem singular, as we have already pointed out, that the innovators, keenly seeking to

[1] I am speaking of Ferri the professor. But when Ferri the deputy speaks in the Assembly, as a legislator as practical as eloquent, he is careful not to underestimate the importance of the penalty. This is sufficiently proved by his speech, of May 28, 1888, where, for example, we read the following passage: "England, with a population almost equal to ours, with twenty-eight million inhabitants, has forty thousand prisoners, of whom fourteen thousand are in penitentiaries and industrial schools (whereas Italy with thirty million inhabitants has seventy thousand prisoners, of whom five thousand are minors who are in the penitentiaries); *and this for the reason that England is the most severe country in Europe in dealing with adult malefactors. . . .*" Ferri adds ". . . and the one showing the most clemency for young malefactors, and showing the greatest care in the case of abandoned children." You will notice how much this last remark bears out our theory upon the preponderance of the social causes of crime.

define and to obtain a prevalence for their reform ideas within the prisons as well as within the Faculties of Law, began by proclaiming in a measure the uselessness of the very object towards which they are striving. But it is none the less true that logic compels them, once they have laid down the principle of the predominance of the physical and anthropological factors of the offense, to deduce from this that the prospect of a penalty, which is but a small portion of the social factors, the entire group of which is itself an unimportant portion of the three groups of factors united, exercises over the delinquent an effect which is of the very slightest.

Conversely, for the same reason, the preponderating importance which we have accorded to social causes logically prohibits us from accepting this conclusion. Thus this point is worthy of our notice. The mistake against which I am arguing is inherent, I repeat, in the very foundation of the doctrine of Ferri and especially of Lombroso, and lies in their too naturalistic manner of interpreting criminal determinism. The inefficaciousness of penal laws in their opinion plays the same part as the inefficaciousness of civil laws in the theories of the classical economists. According to the latter the civil laws are almost powerless in hindering the course of the economic laws which have absolutely governed the production and the redivision even of wealth. This is an illusion which is in process of dissolution.

The proofs advanced by Ferri and his pupils in favor of their opinion are of two sorts, reasons and facts. Lack of foresight is one of the psychological characteristics of the malefactor and especially of the born malefactor; therefore he very seldom has in his mind, when acting, any thought of the penal risk about to be incurred, or else this thought is present, but in the form of an image so feeble that this paper dike cannot for a moment stem the torrent of passion. Here we have their argument "a priori." On the other hand, statistics have sometimes shown that, when repression becomes more severe, criminality has increased rather than decreased, and that, repression having become less severe, criminality has remained stationary or has decreased instead of increasing. Here we have their argument of fact. Neither one nor the other of them will bear examination.

In the first place, however lacking in foresight criminals may be, they are no more so than are school boys. However, will anybody deny the efficaciousness of punishments in schools? I know that they seem useless in the case of the best pupils, and without any permanent effect, if they are not repeated, in the case of a few undisciplined boys; but three-fourths or four-fifths of a class will feel the effect of this brake. Do away with punishment, you will see. Even the scholars who are never punished would be idle if they were sure that they could not be punished. Now it is noticeable that the faults of school boys are themselves a result of Ferri's three factors; the children who commit them always yield either to their lazy or insubordinate temperament, or to the influence of certain seasons, — in the spring, if I have not been misinformed, peccadillos in schools increase, — or to the effect of bad examples around them. It is none the less true that these three causes combined can easily be overcome by an intelligent application of a few punishments. Are criminals any more lacking in foresight than lovers? I do not believe this is so either.

Now what do statistics show us on this subject? According to Mayr,[1] though France shows but seven or eight illegitimate births out of one hundred, whereas many other countries reputed to be more moral, for example Bavaria, have shown twenty-two and still show twelve or more,[2] this difference is due in a great measure to the article of our Civil Code, which prohibits any investigation as to paternity. Indeed, all the provinces of Germany where this provision is in effect stand out, according to him, by reason of their small proportion of illegitimate children, and, everywhere that an investigation of paternity is made, the proportionate number is greater. Thus, even in the supreme intoxication of passion, lovers do not entirely lose their heads. Though a woman in love with a man may be led, irresistibly, it is said, to throw herself into his arms — certainly more irresistibly than an assassin is driven to kill his victim — yet it suffices for this woman to know that in case her lover shall abandon her later on, she will have no right to make him share in the possible consequences of their love, for an anticipation of this double possibility, one part of which must seem so improbable to her and the other so distant, to restrain her a great many times when she is on the precipice of her desire.

"A fortiori" one must believe that the thought of the scaffold or of imprisonment has a very considerable weight in the mental

[1] "La Statistica e la vita sociale."

[2] Paris only furnishes a contingent of twenty-six per cent, which is very little for a capital; in Vienna this proportion rises to fifty per cent.

balance of a malefactor who hesitates in the carrying out of his criminal designs. In reality, the articles of the Penal Code are of very great concern to delinquents, just as the articles of the Civil Code are of very great concern to litigious people. To give one example among a thousand. Spanish counterfeiters and their accomplices, who are very numerous, know very well, according to Gil Maestre, that Article 301 of their Penal Code punishes with a mere fine the carrying of counterfeit money when it does not amount to more than 125 "pesetas"; also they are very careful never to carry with them more than a sum equal to or less than this amount.[1] It has often been said and repeated that the majority of assassins who were guillotined had witnessed executions, and this fact has been cited as an unexceptionable proof of their lack of foresight or of their fearlessness. But in their remarkable desire to witness scenes of the carrying out of the death penalty cannot one see, before everything, the indication of a fixed idea, of a constant fear or anxiety which they compel themselves to overcome? The unfortunate thing is that only too often they succeed in doing this.

We know, according to statistics, that the number of cases of poisoning decreased very rapidly towards the middle of this century, from the time when discoveries in chemistry and toxicology made it possible more surely to discover the causes and the perpetrator of this type of crime. The fear of being prosecuted and sentenced has thus prevented many persons from committing this crime. The amount of the penalty with which this crime is punished has not increased, but the probability of receiving this penalty has increased, which amounts to the same thing. It is therefore certain that poisoners, at least, are people who are possessed of foresight. Moreover, an advance in civilization is always accompanied by an advance in foresight; consequently were it to be admitted that penalties are not very efficacious at the present time, there would be every reason to rely upon their increasing efficaciousness in the future. But, even in the most remote past, can anyone seriously believe that the former equivalent of the penal law, which was the family vendetta, was not possessed of a certain virtue in the way of repression, and that criminality would not have overflowed all the known bounds if

[1] Alongi, who has such a far-reaching knowledge of Sicilian malefactors, tells us that, in spite of the terror inspired by the chiefs of these bands, their strongest feeling is a fear of the rural police.

primitive humanity, instead of raising vengeance into a duty, had made a universal practice of pardoning injuries? Everywhere the first legislators repressed the disorders of their times by severe penalties whose salutary effect is unanimously attested by chronicles and legends.

The powerlessness of the penal law in general is a paradox which evidently belongs to the "nuova scuola," [1] just as the powerlessness of the press was a fitting paradox for Emile de Girardin. But the powerlessness of an exaggerated penal law is a common ground which is recognized everywhere, and which is not any the more true on this account. For example, after having recalled the fact that, on the very eve of the French Revolution, printing, colportage, and the sale of works opposed to religion or the royal authority (Declaration of 1758) were punished by death or the galleys for life, Loiseleur [2] adds: "A lesson full of teachings! The century during which these severe measures were promulgated was the very one in which the pamphlet had a commanding voice and governed men's opinions, was the century of every temerity of the pen, and of every aggression of men's thought. So true is it that too severe a penalty acts directly contrary to its object and drives men to do the very things which it is intended to prevent." Just as though it were really a prospect of the galleys or the scaffold which had driven the encyclopaedists to write what they did! Loiseleur forgets that, a few pages before these lines occur, he has just told us of the tortures of the Spanish Inquisition, a severe repression, if there ever was one, and one which attained its object only too well in rooting out of the most liberal and proudest soil every germ of independence of mind. If the penalties decreed against the freedom of the press were scarcely increased in the second half of the last century, it was because they were no longer applied; and they were no longer applied because they were condemned by opinion, and opinion condemned them because in France there had started a free-thinking propaganda which had its field where? In two neighboring countries where there was no penal law to punish the liberal writer, in England and in Holland. Let us assume that England and Holland, from the sixteenth century on, had been governed by a criminal legislation as severe

[1] This school has had predecessors in this matter also; in the Memorials of the States General of 1789 (see *Arthur Desjardins'* book on this subject) we find the nobility of Soule affirming the inefficaciousness of all penalties excepting the death penalty. This is precisely the opinion of Lombroso.

[2] "Les crimes et les peines" (1863).

as that of France in the matter of intellectual dissent, and we shall find that Voltaire could never have been born among us or would have perished miserably in the depths of some galley.

Ferri has too easy a triumph through the aid of a few examples in which it is seen that penalties of an extravagant atrocity were far from obtaining an effect proportioned to their degree of horror, because no dishonor was connected with the accomplishment of the deeds punished by them. Such have been the penalties so often decreed against duellists, poachers, and smugglers. Again, we know through Voltaire that though Louis XIII failed in his efforts to suppress the duel, Louis XIV entirely succeeded in doing so. After 1663, "his fortunate severity," says he, "little by little corrected our nation and even the neighboring nations who conformed to our wise customs after having taken our bad ones. There are in Europe today but one hundredth the number of duels that there were in the time of Louis XIII." But the scaffold, the convict prison and the prison are nothing; the great, the eternal, the invisible penalty is the dishonor followed by social excommunication. Can anyone deny the power of that penalty? One might just as well deny the power of the interdicts put forth by Innocent III or the political power of opinion, that anonymous and universal government. From this it follows, we may say in passing, that if the criminalists who are too preoccupied with the anthropological factors, in this resembling the too indulgent moralists, their adversaries, diminish by their explanation of crime the disgraceful character which is attached to it, though thenceforth they even demand against it the most severe penalties, they will nevertheless have lowered the strongest barrier which is opposed to its progress.[1]

Is this as much as to say that being flayed by opinion can suffice? It would be a great mistake to think so. In the first place, there are crimes, even very serious ones, that opinion in certain countries or certain localities does not flay, precisely because owing to a long period of previous impunity they have become very widespread; assassinations in Corsica, voluntary arson in many communes, even forgery among merchants involved in debt. What would happen if, in the matter of murder, theft,

[1] Ferri observes, in support of his theory that gambling debts, although they have no legal sanction, are a species of debt more frequently paid than any other. But it is just because the law does not protect them that the all-powerful tribunal of public opinion has taken them under its special protection, by making people consider it a very dishonorable thing not to pay these debts.

forgery, and swindling, as in the matter of cheating at play, the only penalty should be blame and expulsion from a more or less restricted circle of persons? In the beginning, opinion would be just as severe as it is now; but little by little, the number of delinquents having increased, it would relax, would show itself more indulgent to the most contagious forms of offense, and it might indeed happen, were the majority to favor dishonest people, that a certain consideration would come to be attached to the forms of dishonesty in vogue.

The same thing applies to the usefulness of penalties as applies to so many other forms of usefulness; there is usefulness which is seen and usefulness which is not seen. I will grant Ferri that penalties have not the immediate virtue which is commonly attributed to them. In the immediate future, they perhaps often only serve to reassure honest people, an advantage not to be despised. But indirectly and in the long run, their power is still greater than the people themselves can have any idea of.

Where the efficaciousness, even immediate and direct, of repression becomes obvious, is everywhere that, as in France in 1775,[1] in Sicily since 1877, in Greece for the last twenty years, in Italy under Sixtus V (1585–1590),[2] a few energetic measures overcame to a great extent the most deep-rooted criminal habits. I would like to ask Ferri, who is practically a Florentine, if he thinks that the severe measures decreed by the terrible ordinances of justice in 1294 against the magnates of Florence were ineffective? They attained their object very well, as every similar severe measure did in the other Italian republics. Their strength lay in fear says Perrens. "Any of them who wished to give up the rule by fear was lost. Venice remained prosperous for such a long time only because she recognized in terror the source of her power and that she took great care not to give it up." In Athens severe

[1] In 1775 there occurred in France a recrudescence of brigandage, even in the neighborhood of Paris. By a Declaration of May 5, brigands were brought under the jurisdiction of the Provosts who applied the death penalty in their case. Brigandage ceased.

[2] It is true that after his reign, from 1590 to 1595, Roman brigandage broke out again, in spite of a redoubling of measures of repression. In five years five thousand capital executions took place at Rome according to the statement of the Venetian ambassador. But this must certainly be due to the fact that this period of time included four interregnums, the periods which are always favorable to the rebellion of ungovernable natures. The bandits and the papal armies often fought with equal forces on each side. The executions in question were on the whole merely a carnage of war which would be bound to stir up criminal reprisals and not to discourage crime.

penalties were inflicted on the official who did not render a sufficient account of his administration; and Greek history shows us the preventive effect of this threat. Nor is there any doubt that the death penalty being made a part of a proposed decree contrary to pre-existing laws has prevented many bold innovations. It is enough to convince one of this to notice how, in fact, social and religious institutions were persistently maintained among the Athenians in spite of the notorious instability of these people, in spite of their need of innovation, which was kept up by their seafaring and commercial life, and by their continual relations with so many nations who were so unlike them.

Now contrast with the Athenians the French people, who, though not so active in the long run, and very much less prone to innovation and more prone to a spirit of conservatism, owing to the nature of their sedentary life, which was not suitable to adventure, though it might be for colonization, have undergone in less than a century the very greatest social upheavals. Did the severities of the Inquisition perchance serve no purpose? According to the archives of the Spanish Inquisition, more than three hundred thousand persons were condemned to death or the galleys in the course of three centuries, but principally during the fifteenth and sixteenth centuries by this terrible tribunal. Leaving to one side the horror of this spectacle, I deduce from this that this country must at that time, during its heroic period, when its genius covered the entire world, have given proof of a remarkable independence of mind equal to this prodigious activity in order to have furnished such a number of rebels against religious orthodoxy. It is perhaps because in that country men's thoughts were exceptionally liable to become enfranchised that the Inquisition flourished there with so much lustre. Neither in France nor in Italy did the necessity for such a suppression of men's consciences appear to be felt. Well, we know what became of intellectual beliefs and fruitfulness after this rather prolonged reign. The fires of the Inquisition attained their object.

It is possible to judge of the efficaciousness of penalties by comparing it with the results of lack of punishment. There have been armies having no disciplinary punishments, no dungeons or execution platoons; in every instance they soon became a horde. If, in a large city, the police becomes disorganized or relaxes its vigilance momentarily, one very soon finds that the streets are no longer safe. When, in 1819, Cardinal Consalvi decreed that every murderer should be set free on condition that after having committed his first crime, he would not go to swell the ranks of the brigands in the mountains, the result was that [1] knife blows and stabbings with the stiletto "showered from one end of the Church lands to the other." The predecessor of Sixtus V, Gregory XIII, had shown a similar weakness; this weakness had been followed by a similar result.

In every country, when a somewhat prolonged state of anarchy, for example in France during the Hundred Years War, the Religious Wars, and the French Revolution, has emboldened criminals, crime multiplies. The "Livre de Vie" of Bergerac,[2] a manuscript which is to be found among the archives of that town, contains, for the edification of posterity, an official account of the murders, cattle stealing, and exactions of every kind which took place in the surrounding country, a country today one of the most peaceful, from 1378 to 1382, at a time when the rivalry between the English and French factions who were fighting for the country left a free rein to evil passions. The list makes one shudder. In the sixteenth century, murderers, owing to the factional troubles, always had a hope of remaining unpunished; to this is due in part, one may well believe, the long drawn out epidemic of assassinations which were the desolation of these dreadful times.[3] Taine has sufficiently brought before our eyes that river of crimes which the French Revolution let loose; let us only mention it in order not to forget it. Animated with quite a different spirit, Perrens shows us the same spectacle in his "Histoire de Florence"; and, just to mention one characteristic, in 1301, after the victory of the "Blacks," the acts of brigandage committed in the town and in all its territory are beyond number. "During four days, the bands were spread over this country, devastating, pillaging, burning splendid houses and the properties of the wealthy. Just as in the town, there were killed and wounded." At the time of the tumult of the "Ciompi," in 1378, the same bloody scenes were enacted. No doubt here we must make a liberal allowance for the part played by the force of example; but, had it not been absolutely certain that no punishment would follow, would the force of example have arisen, or even the first impulse?

Without going so far back as this, let us recall that which took

[1] "Le brigandage en Italie," by *Dubarry*.

[2] "Bulletin de la Société archéologique du Périgord," 1887.

[3] See "Sentiments moraux au XIVe siècle," by *Arthur Desjardins, passim.*

place at the foundation of every American town, those towns marvelously and suddenly built up through the caprice of an adventurer or the discovery of some miner. San Francisco came into existence in 1848 from one of these chance happenings with incalculable results; towards this El Dorado flowed the emigrants of the entire world, the mingled scum of every civilization. Then there was no police force; also, in spite of the tremendous ease with which wealth might be acquired by digging for nuggets or working in the mines, and the manifest uselessness of having recourse to murder and theft in order to make one's fortune, the trade of crime prospered to such an extent that we see "the spectacle of an organization of malefactors operating in broad daylight, having their president and their vice-president chosen by election, their headquarters in a place called by them 'Tammany Hall,' parading the streets of the town with a band, and banners. . . . and starting out on a certain Sunday with the pillage and the destruction of an entire section inhabited by the Chilians."[1] This condition of affairs lasted until the time when the men who desired order joined together in the exercise of a vigorous repression. Later on new bands were formed, it is true, and in 1856 the power was in their hands, but once again a coalition of the better element and a few capital executions were sufficient to purge the young city. It is in this practical school that we ought to study the penal law.

The same thing applies, it seems to me, to the effect of penalties upon criminality as applies to the effect of prices on consumption. The consumption of the article does not decrease in proportion to the rise in its purchase price. Sometimes it drops far more rapidly than the price rises; this is the case with articles which satisfy feeble and fictitious needs; sometimes it drops very much more slowly; this is the case with articles which are absolutely necessary, and which satisfy strong and natural needs. Similarly, that which I am quite willing to call luxurious criminality, in other words all sorts of offenses taken together — thefts, abuses of confidence, forgery, arson, indecent assault, even murder — which are inspired by a desire, to a great extent artificial, of libertinage or well-being and not by hunger, vengeance, or love, ought, it seems to me, to be very sensitive to the brake of repression, and very rapidly to decrease when the severity of this brake increases. But criminality which is to a certain extent necessary, that is that portion of murders, thefts, etc., brought about by poverty or by

[1] "L'Océan Pacifique," by *de Varigny* (1888).

all-powerful passions, must obviously resist the increase in penalties very much better. There must inevitably come a time when the price of certain objects will in vain become an extravagant one, the number of their few consumers is not sensibly diminished, the latter being monomaniacs whom no expense can prevent from gratifying their disordered fancy. Such are the criminal insane or semi-insane, the monomaniacs of crime, whom no punishment can deter. But these latter are an exception; the more civilization advances, the more will the proportion of crimes of the first category, as well as that of merchandise which is a luxury, increase. The importance of penalties like that of prices is thus ever on the increase.[1]

§ 88. Historical Summary.

I think that what I have said above proves that penalties, even though imperfectly applied as they are, render a service to society. But, in order that they shall render it a still greater service, in what direction ought they to be reformed? This problem is being studied now more than ever; it has been the inspiration for many fine works buried under the mountains of fastidious books which we will not attempt to remove here. It seems to me that, without any very elaborate preparation, we should be in a position to solve this problem. But before admitting the absolute justice of much of the criticism of our reformers against the existing systems of penal law and before outlining their projected reforms, let us begin by putting them in their true place according to our customary method of glancing retrospectively over the transformations which have taken place in the penalty.

[1] One can attempt to demonstrate the inefficaciousness of precautions for the prevention of accidents, for example, railroad accidents, by advancing the same reasons advanced for proving the inefficaciousness of penalties. Is it not, however, certain that it would be possible, upon condition of greatly increasing measures of precaution, to diminish by one-fourth, one-third, one-half, perhaps three-fourths the number of persons killed as a consequence of collisions between carriages in the streets and trains upon the rails? This much is certain; but it is also certain that the decrease in the number of accidents would not keep pace with the increase in the number of precautions taken; *it would move more slowly*, more and more slowly, and there would come a time when the *minimum* of accidents would in reality have been attained, for, in order to decrease this number to however slight an extent, it would be necessary to impose upon people loss of time, thought and money, greater in *social value* than the few lives spared by this means.

§ 89. (I) Changes in the penalty which universally lead to changes in the method of proof. Four phases. Gradual moderation of penalties.

These changes are very closely bound up in the changes which have taken place in proof, or, if you prefer, in criminal procedure, which has been dealt with above. In fact there exists a bond, during each phase of legal evolution, between the nature of the proof which "gives their tone" to the others and the character with which the penalty has a tendency to clothe itself. I have distinguished four species of proofs which have been, or which are beginning to be, in vogue: ordeals, torture, the jury, scientific expert testimony. Now to the first of these corresponds a penalty which is *expiatory:* so much so that the offering of a victim to the gods sometimes dispensed with a capital execution. To the second, that is to torture, corresponds a penalty which is essentially one of intimidation and which is *exemplary:* the wheel, quartering, burning at the stake, tortures which were more horrible than ever. To the third, that is to proof by means of the popular conscience, by the jury, corresponds a penalty which is mild and pretendedly *correctional.* Finally, what is the penalty which is going to correspond to the fourth, to proof by dogmatized science, that is, to expert testimony? Is it not a penalty, before everything *sanitary,* either because it strives to eliminate from the social organism elements which cannot be assimilated, foreign bodies, or because it strives to heal the mental and moral disorder of patients who are called malefactors? This is what we shall soon see. These four phases may be divided into two groups which scarcely resemble each other at all, but which nevertheless have common characteristics.

The first is like the third, in this way, that a mystic belief, a belief in divine revelation or belief in the infallibility of the human conscience, the worship of the supernatural or the religion of humanity, serves as their inspiration. In the same way the second and the fourth, in spite of their very great dissimilarity in so many other respects, have both a rather pronounced air of utilitarian and rationalistic reaction against previously existing mysticism. For the Romanists of the thirteenth to the sixteenth centuries, dazzled by the still recent discovery of the Roman law and the Roman world, the best penalty was the one which conformed most to the principles of that "written reasoning" which they deciphered avidly; for our learned men, for our contemporary naturalists, intoxicated with so many natural truths revealed one after another, the best form of penalty could not be founded upon anything except the natural sciences.

I do not pretend, moreover, that the series of these four phases, although assuredly irreversible, is invariable; one of the links in the chain may be lacking or can be replaced. It may also happen that it will be extended beyond the last link. Finally, we know that the one first pointed out was preceded by still more ancient aspects. In Homer, in Hesiod, the question of pecuniary composition is dealt with, but no trace is yet found, says Thonissen,[1] "of that religious purification which, at a more recent period, was thought indispensable before allowing the individual who was so unfortunate as to have spilled human blood, access to the Agora and the temples." In fact in the "Iliad," "the perpetrator of homicides mingles with citizens and foreigners without placing any taint upon them." Thus the mystic conception of expiation must in Greece, as elsewhere, have followed the utilitarian conception,[2] which was pre-eminently positivist, of buying back and of pecuniary reparation. Here religious mysticism has seemed to be and has in fact been an advance over barbarian utilitarianism, just as the latter had itself been an advance over that sort of domestic mysticism which imposed a vengeance which could not be bought off as the most sacred of duties.

We ought also to observe that, in passing from the old polytheism to Christianity, the idea of expiation became very greatly changed and that this change has itself a manifestly irreversible character. Expiation, an appeasement of the wrath of offended deities, always took place among the Greeks and Romans of the most remote times as soon as the penalty in conformity with the rites had been inflicted upon the guilty man or upon some of his family. But the Christian God is only appeased, the transgression in His eyes is only atoned for, when the penalty is accepted by

[1] However, there is some doubt as to the justification of the inference drawn from this silence.

[2] Pecuniary composition must have been an invention of cold, calculating, practical men who met with difficulty in making their positivist manner of utilizing crime prevail over the innate feeling of indignation and of vindictive justice. We have already mentioned that exclamation of a Danish warrior who, in a popular song cries out: "Who would formerly have dared to take money as the price of his father's assassination?" This *new* custom was revolting to them. In the Book of Numbers Moses forbids anyone "to receive any ransom for the murderer in order that he should escape the death which he has merited." Among the Semitic races, Thonissen tells us, the relatives who gave up vengeance for a sum of money were stained with indelible infamy.

the guilty man as a just punishment to which he voluntarily resigns himself. The "voluntary penalty," the "penance," is a conception the originality of which no longer strikes us, but one which was sufficient to stamp the Christian world with its own particular impress.[1] It is necessary for the guilty man to wish to be punished in order that he shall be cleansed of his transgression, just as it was necessary for him to wish to commit his transgression in order to have been stained by it. This punishment of self by self is in fact the only one which is a sure indication of a regeneration of one's being. In wishing for his punishment, the sinner takes it upon himself, and consequently throws off his sin which he took to himself when he wished it. It would be a contradiction for a man to continue to hold as his own his sin when he had taken to himself the penalty which is essentially a negation of the wish for the sin.

The entirely sociological and materialistic expiation of primitive times was in accord with the family collectivism and barbarian coarseness of those times, just as the entirely psychological and spiritualistic expiation of the Christian era is in accord with the lofty individualism with which its coming has been marked. Punishment ceased thenceforth to have a value of its own; its only value is as a symbol of a mental condition. It is quite possible, without having been punished, for a man to have undergone a *conversion* in his heart; but who is there who, having undergone no penalty, can prove to others and to the guilty man himself that this conversion has actually taken place? The penalty has thus become simply an external and social manifestation of remorse, remorse reinforced at the same time as it is attested by the visible and traditional form intelligible to all, with which it clothes itself. Unfortunately, the penalty understood in this manner only prevails in ages of belief; it is exceedingly rare in our present time prisons and there is no hope that it will ever flourish in them again.

An advance which is perhaps not essentially irreversible, but which, owing to its continuity from half way through the Middle Ages at least, is deserving of notice, is the gradual moderation of

[1] This does not mean, moreover, that the germ of the penance did not exist before the time of Christianity. It is exceedingly probable that at all times and in all countries, crimes committed by a man against a member of his own family, of his own limited social group, aroused in him remorse and a need of punishing himself, of carrying out a sort of "auto-vendetta" against himself. But in our western world the original part of the Christian conception consisted in making this apply outside of the family and making it universal.

penalties.[1] It seems as though severity were in inverse ratio to the degree of civilization. This is no doubt why, as long as the clergy were more enlightened than the lay world, the ecclesiastical courts were distinguished for their relative and unanimously recognized indulgence,[2] although the logic of dogma ought, it would seem, to have driven them to accentuate even more than the lay courts the expiatory and cruel side of punishment. However this may be, in this the penal law resembles therapeutics. Before the time of Ambroise Paré, the limbs of the wounded were plunged in boiling oil. For the violent remedies of former times, bleeding, trephining, setons, frightful amputations, have by degrees been substituted a milder treatment and surgical operations not only more rarely carried out but less painfully. And at the same time cures came to be better and better effected. Would that we could say as much of the curative properties of milder punishments!

However, the change pointed out corresponded to a very general need because it has been extended not only to academic, but to mystic penalties as well,[3] in spite of their relative mildness. Even as late as the fourteenth century, the confessors did not give as a penance "paters" and "aves" to be recited. They ordered people to fast for entire months and for entire years, to flagellate themselves, etc. The *mitigation* at that time brought to bear on their severity will give some idea of their customary harshness. For example, in time it was allowed "to exchange one year of penance for three thousand lashes with the recitation of a psalm with every hundred." [4] Theodore, Archbishop of Canterbury, in the ninth century, had already drawn up a sort of tariff of these exchanges. These exchanges in the end, in fact, became regular sales, as can be seen from the rates of the Roman

[1] With regard to the *moderation* (and also the *gradual replacing*) of penalties, see my article on "Carnevale" ("Archives de l'Anthropologie criminelle," July 15, 1890, p. 450).

[2] For example, when Jacques Cœur, so unworthily rewarded for his patriotic services, was prosecuted in the lay courts of Charles VII, he solicited, but in vain, the favor of being judged by the ecclesiastical tribunals in his character (which was more or less doubtful) of a cleric. See on this subject "Jacques Cœur," by *Pierre Clément*. (Didier.)

[3] On the other hand it is a curious thing to see certain deliberative assemblies which have just voted reforms in the examination of criminals or in the penal code, in conformity with the increasing clemency, place at the disposal of their president more severe parliamentary penalties. Though one may share in the feeling of the uselessness of penalties in general, yet one will not cease to believe in the power of those which one feels to be necessary.

[4] *Jusserand*, "La vie nomade," according to Hardy. "Registrum palitinum dunelmense."

penitentiary. Thus the result brought about was the system of "indulgences," a system of pecuniary composition with Heaven, a mystic "Wergeld," the late apparition of which tends to confirm the idea that the ancient "Wergeld" itself had nothing primitive about it.

Furthermore, we must be careful not to mistake a mitigation of the penalty for its decadence and its disappearance. This is a mistake which Carnevale seems to me to have fallen into in the chapter of his "Critica penale" entitled "Décadence de la peine." [1] The idea there developed by him is that, during the progress of civilization, the legal, political, and moral, if not the religious auxiliaries of and substitutes for, the penalty are ever becoming more pronounced, but that the penalty properly so called is ever becoming less pronounced, and there will gradually come a time, far distant, when it is bound to disappear entirely.

However, deep down, the spirit of the penalty, the true penalty, is general reprobation, for the same reason that true government is public opinion. And it would be possible to write upon the so-called "decadence of government" a chapter based upon just as good reasoning, and reasoned out in the same manner, as those pages devoted by this learned Italian to the decadence of the penalty, because we do not find the government by opinion being developed. In fact, in the same proportion as the physical side of the penalty decreases, its spiritual side stands out, and is strengthened just as everywhere among political powers on the decline, whether under the monarchic or other form, the social power of opinion is ever growing. I will admit that compassion for misfortune may progress to such a point as to absorb all indignation against the unfortunate. But there is nothing more humiliating than this sort of compassion for the one who is its object, and who with characteristic vanity would rather incur hatred than this disguised contempt, preferring a hundred times to inspire fear rather than pity. The more this pity increases, owing to its redoubled intensity in the mind of everybody, and owing to the number of those persons feeling it at one and the same time, persons who are members of a particular section of the public which the advance in means of communication and in news as disseminated by the press is ever enlarging, the more will this

[1] "Criticate penale," by *Emmanuele Carnevale* (Lipari, 1889). The paragraph which follows is an extract of the report which we gave on this bulky pamphlet in the "Archives de l'Anthropologie criminelle," No. 28.

increasing feeling of pity, as lacking in contempt as possible, be dishonoring, heavy, and intolerable for the vain delinquent who becomes more and more vain because he becomes more and more urbanized. The larger this group of the public becomes, no matter what happens, the more pronounced and distressing becomes the disrepute of the man who is the subject of public blame, even though he be the subject of public pity.

§ 90. (II) Price and penalties; a constant antithesis. The scale of offenses and the scale of penalties. A new phase in political economy as well as in the penal law.

It will never be possible to form an adequate idea of the penalty without comparing it with its opposite, the price. We saw above, by means of the tariff of indulgences and pecuniary composition, the power of the tendency which drives men to reduce everything to figures, to reduce everything to measurements, even evils and suffering, and to convert penalties into prices or, to put it better, to look upon penalties as prices *reversed*. We have already pointed out the latter antithesis in comparing the effect of price on consumption, and on the production of offenses as well.

But in many other respects this parallel is continued. To put this in more general terms, we may state that every society, unconsciously, in establishing its system of punishments, has yielded up to a certain point to the need of modeling this system upon its system of recompenses.[1] This instinctive and irregular symmetry must be taken into account in order to give their practical value to the ideas of the Italians on indeterminate penalties and their banter at the expense of those criminologists who have

[1] An exchange of injuries seems to have been as natural, in the beginning, as an exchange of services, and no doubt it preceded the latter. "We see among the various savage tribes," says *Spencer* ("Sociology," III, p. 659), "that on principle external warfare had as its object the carrying out of an equalization of damages of the same nature. Among the Chinooks, when one side has a greater number of killed than the other, it must be indemnified by the other or else the war will continue." This is a true exchange of blood. "Among the Arabs when the two parties wish to make peace they count up their dead and the one who has the greater number receives the price of blood prescribed by custom." To an act of politeness, the shadow of a service, it is customary to reply by another act of politeness that is, in the same coin. Similarly, when an injury has in the course of time changed in character and has only preserved the appearance of its former reality, it is replied to by a *mock* revenge. Among the Australians, for example, the abduction of a woman of the tribe by a neighboring tribe has ceased to be looked upon by the woman's tribe as a true offense; but as it is a pretended offense, honor requires that reparation should be obtained by a *symbolical retaliation*. (See as to this, *Letourneau*, "Evolution du mariage," p. 112.)

gone to so much trouble "a priori" to proportion the amount of fines, or the number of months of imprisonment, to the supposed gravity of the offense. It must be admitted that nothing can compare with the strangeness of this hierarchic scale of offenses traced by the law in order to balance a hierarchy of penalties no less strange and no less chimerical,[1] the greatest of which are often the least effective. It may well be asked whether, in this respect, any advance has been made by our contemporary codes over the Salic Law. The rate of pecuniary composition was determined in each case by the Salic Law according to unvarying and easily understood principles, as has been shown by Thonissen; the rate is always trebled, for example when the case is one of an injury to one of the king's companions or to a woman who is pregnant.

But though we may seek to discover why, in certain cases, our Penal Code has fixed such and such a maximum of imprisonment and fine, rather than any other, yet we will not perceive any other fundamental reason than the arbitrary will of the legislator, which is to be interpreted and rounded out by the arbitrary will of the judge. The law does not seem to have had any concern, says Holtzendorff, "excepting for a certain symmetry of figures, or rather for an aesthetic arithmetic of penal law, combined with precautions intended to avoid the point at which common sense would be impressed with the injustice of the penalty." The consequence of this is that each penalty, capricious and variable, and not being justified in the eyes of the public, is discredited and is considered by malefactors merely as an unfortunate accident, a professional risk which must be incurred. But, would the best remedy for this state of things be, by chance, to do away at one fell swoop with all proportionality between the penalty and the gravity of the offense? Yes, upon condition of substituting for it a proportionality obvious to everybody and which can be realized by the malefactor himself, between the penalty and the perversity of the delinquent.

Unfortunately, this new species of proportionality would be still more difficult to establish and justify than the preceding one. Nevertheless, an attempt in this direction must necessarily follow.

[1] The need of this *equation between the offense and the penalty* is so absolute in minds dominated by the ideas of the classic school that we find this formula and this concern once more in a book filled in other respects with new and often excellent views, "Devoir de punir," by *Eugène Mouton*, a former magistrate. This prejudice, perhaps the only survivor from the wreck of the judicial illusions of the author, prevents his admitting of an increase of the penalty because of recidivism.

The penal legislator of the Old Régime, of 1678 for example, pursued an ideal of justice, severe in its dealings, by virtue of which he compelled the judge to pronounce sentence when certain proofs, called legal ones, were furnished him and to acquit in the opposite case, no matter what his inmost conviction might be. And when he did pronounce sentence, to pronounce a certain fixed penalty, which was invariably determined beforehand. His chief concern was to leave the least possible margin to the caprice of the judge. Thus there was apparently obtained — and an appearance which satisfies public opinion is no small matter in these cases — a perfect equality of treatment of accused persons,[1] and for those who were sentenced, an exact correspondence between the degree of their offense and the degree of their punishment. But, the falseness of this appearance having been disclosed to the public, this system had to be changed; contemporary legislators place almost no limit [2] over the power of the judge in so far as proof is concerned, and only restrict this power in so far as the penalty is concerned between very wide limits, which are ever being widened by the optional admission of extenuating circumstances.

Now what has been the result of this? The law having left to the courts the care of finding the compass which they lacked, the latter, as much at sea as the law, have only been able to secure forgiveness for their unguided power through an unlimited indulgence, and thus their very weakness is born of their absolute power. The irrational and uncertain character of the penalty has thus become obvious, whereas formerly it was hidden. So much the better, but upon one condition, which is that the necessity of making a greater effort to escape this regrettable condition and prepare for a new state of things should finally be felt, a state of things where the penalty will be justified by reason in the opinion of everybody, and not only apparently justified as formerly, but really justified.

The lines along which this change is to be made have already been pointed out to us by our previous antithesis between the recompense and the punishment, the price and the penalty. In

[1] I mean for accused persons who are in the same social category. Furthermore penalties were not equal, as we know, in the cases of the noble and the commoner.

[2] The only remaining vestige of legal proofs is the prohibition placed upon the judge of hearing certain witnesses or of giving any weight to their testimony, because of their relationship or household ties with the accused. Bentham, for reasons which are very strong but far too severe, criticises this legislative provision.

the first place, during every period, during our century as during past centuries, a particular kind of penalty seems necessary to the legislator, and we must notice the fact that the nature of this predominating sort of penalty is always related to the nature of the most valued kinds of possessions. During the ages of religion, when no wealth can be compared with divine favor, excommunication is the very severest penalty. Draco, the terrible Draco, thought he was very severe when he decreed that the murderer should be driven from the temple and should not be allowed to touch either the lustral water or the sacred vessels.[1]

In other times, and in other surroundings, the disgracing penalties — branding, the pillory, degradation, etc. — are the most to be feared, because consideration is the most cherished wealth in minds whose pride is their strongest resource. The indications of infamy are, moreover, reckoned in the *opposite way* to indications of honor. Among the Visigoths, it being a matter of honor for a free man to wear long hair, scalping, that is to say, removal of the skin of the top of the head, was a punishment employed which was deemed to be a capital one.[2] With purely individual honor, such as it is understood to be today, can be contrasted only individual dishonor; but to the family honor of former times corresponded the dishonor of an entire family through the fault of an individual,[3] and this solidarity did not astonish anybody. As a general thing people have become less irasçible, which is not an evil, but less sensitive, which is regrettable, on the question of honor, that is in the domestic meaning of the word; and this is proved by noticing how much today "the legal protection of honor" leaves to be desired.[4] Also in the nineteenth century the disgracing penalties no longer play a leading part; this part now belongs to penalties which deprive a man of his liberty. To tell the truth, however, it is less a deprivation of liberty than a deprivation of physical love which makes the malefactor dread imprisonment.

Now in proportion as the need of independence and voluptuous

[1] A terrible punishment among the Cambodians, says Lorion, is a refusal of burial. This is the same among the Chinese, who cannot conceive of any higher recompense for their services than that of the prospect of a fine mausoleum and will send each other at the first of the year a coffin as a New Year's gift.

[2] This was combined with flagellation. In the "Schwabenspiegel" we still see *the tonsure and the whip* inflicted together upon the robber.

[3] See on this subject *Joly*, "Les lettres de cachet" (Paris, 1864).

[4] See on this subject a study by *Beaussire*, "Revue des Deux Mondes," December, 1887.

freedom has developed, imprisonment, which during the Middle Ages was not a penalty properly speaking and was only employed as a means of preventive detention, has under various names which are practically synonymous invaded almost the entire field of the penal law. Let us add to this the fine. But a thing which ought to surprise us is that this pecuniary penalty has advanced so little during this century in which money plays so great a part. If this penalty has developed so little,[1] it is no doubt because of the habitual insolvency of malefactors. At the same time is there not some means, in spite of this, of doing away with this anomaly? It will be enough if I set forth a suggestion very skilfully advanced by Garofalo.[2]

The delinquent condemned to a term of imprisonment should remain incarcerated until, through his labor, he shall have saved a certain sum of money, deemed sufficient to indemnify his victim. In such a case as this the imprisonment would be no more than an accessory and a condition requisite for this payment, which payment would be thus converted into the principal penalty. Thus would be avoided the scandalous reckoning of those filibusters who say to themselves when rifling the safe of the bank which employs them: "After all, this million is well worth the five or six years imprisonment of which it makes me run the risk."

These compulsory damages of which I am speaking would have another advantage over the fine, that is the advantage of being an act of justice. Very often a thief is not entirely insolvent; but in this case, the little he has is employed in paying the fine to which he has been sentenced to the State and the man robbed is more to be pitied than if the sentence had never been pronounced. "It is immoral," says Fioretti[3] on this subject, "that the government should gain an advantage from and be enriched as a conse-

[1] For a long time past, publicists have demanded an extension of pecuniary penalties (see on this subject *Prins*, "Criminalité et répression," and *Michaux*, "Question des peines").

[2] See his pamphlet entitled, "Riparazione alla vittima del delitto" (Fratelli Bocca, 1887). Moreover this idea is not as new as one might think. As early as 1783, Catherine II applied it in Russia. The length of the term of imprisonment instituted by her was not fixed in advance. "The condemned," says *Boullaire*, a former magistrate ("Bulletin de la Société des prisons"), "had to repair the damage caused and pay the expenses of his keep by the result of his labor." At the Congress of Stockholm just as at the Congress of Rome, the question of indeterminate penalties was made the subject of serious study. See the report of *Van Hamel*, the distinguished professor of law at the University of Amsterdam. (Published in the "Bulletin de la Société des prisons," 1888.)

[3] See the Transactions of the Congress of Rome.

quence of the very offenses which it is held bound to prevent," as though to console itself, but at the expense of the victims, for not having prevented them. Fioretti is of the opinion that all fines ought to be concentrated into a general fund which would serve to indemnify poor persons who had been robbed. Féré [1] goes further than this; he expressly proposes the foundation of an association of insurance against injury from theft. A realization of these suggestions would, I fear, have the disadvantage of increasing the number of robberies, just as insurance policies against fire have increased the number of cases of arson. This same reproach cannot be applied to Garofalo's proposition; and although de Aramburu [2] has a very poor estimate of the profit to be derived from the labor of prisoners, I know of prisons in France, if not in Spain, where labor is carried on with a certain amount of activity which would surely be doubled if the term of the imprisonment were dependent upon it. Let us at least retain this much of this suggestion, that is that during our age of recompense, which is essentially of a pecuniary nature, pecuniary penalties are deserving of a privileged position, far greater than the one which they actually have at the present time.

Let us carry our parallel still further. If we pass from the nature of penalties to their amount, we see that, like prices, they pass through three different phases. During the first period the price, whatever it may be, is proportional, not to the extent of the benefit considered by itself, but to the greatness of the man under obligation who pays it off. And in the same way the penalty is proportional, not to the seriousness of the offense, but to the dignity of the person outraged who is revenged for it. From this arose the conception of Hell, an eternal penalty proportional to the infinite greatness of God; and of Heaven, an eternal recompense due, not to our slight merit, but to the infinite goodness of God. From this also there arose, when royal power had become established in the feudal world, the atrocity of the punishments demanded by the august character of the king, who claims to have been injured by the delinquent. This is equivalent to saying that reward played a very important part in payments and revenge in punishments.

The kings of the Old Régime gave evidence of their nobility either by their excessive gifts, which had no connection with the services rendered them, or by the penalties inflicted by them,

[1] See "Dégénérescence et criminalité." [2] "Nueva ciencia penal."

which were no less intemperate. A gentleman of the court of Francis I, having taken the liberty of playing a prank upon a lady, the king sent for him in order to have him hanged within the hour. The gifts of princes and lords were of the same kind. They were none the less the price of bravery and merit, but a price which was not fixed, in which the character of the present and the gratitude was of more importance than that of the reward. The remuneration which the great lord owed his faithful vassals consisted above everything in the hospitality which he offered them,[1] a splendid hospitality if he were rich and powerful like the Duke of Burgundy, a frugal and stingy one if he were but a poor country gentleman. This did not matter. Whatever the value of the vassal's services, he had to be contented with this welcome, which varied according to the fortune of his liege lord, and the obligation of each to the other was discharged after this unequal exchange of the evidences of devotion and indications of affection had taken place.

In the same way the cruelty of the punishments which a lord had at his disposal, and especially of those which he employed, was measured by the degree of his position, and the distinction between the three forms of justice, the high, the middle, and the low, originally can have had no other cause than this. But little by little, as the Middle Ages came to an end, that which the lords appreciated in the services of a vassal, a servant, or a merchant came more and more to be their usefulness, and less and less the fidelity or servility which were joined thereto. Then there began a remuneration of everybody's services otherwise than in banquets, receptions, and entertainments; they began to be paid for. At the same time legal punishments had a tendency to become more precise, to become more uniform, as prices did. It is none the less true that, until the downfall of the Old Régime,[2] the prices of objects which were identical showed the greatest diversity in

[1] This was their recompense, just as that of the saints was to sit at table with God, the permanent guest of the banquet of divine Joy. The forms of celestial remuneration were invented in fact, according to the pattern of terrestrial remuneration, just as the punishments of Hell are a reflection of the horrible penalties which were a dishonor to the period in which they were conceived. The effect has become the cause in its turn, and, owing to an inevitable reaction, the cruelty of the punishments of Hell must have contributed to increasing that of the legal penalties. These latter seem to us insanely cruel, but they must have seemed mild to those who compared them with the steaming boilers and the red hot tongs of demons carrying on their work throughout eternity to punish these same crimes.

[2] See "Prix en 1780," by *Léon Biollay* (Guillaumin, 1886).

different provinces, and that similarly the penalties within the jurisdiction of different parliaments, and often even of different "presidials," had remained very unequal. On the other hand, in each locality, prices, like penalties, did not vary. Today, on the contrary, prices as well as penalties vary more chronologically but are more uniform geographically.

The thing which characterizes this second period, in spite of everything, is the tendency to contemplate more indifferently, with neither gratitude nor indignation, which does not mean with neither esteem nor blame, admiration nor scorn, both the services and the offenses, leaving to one side the servant and the delinquent, and geometrically to seek the conditions of the *equivalence* between the services and the prices on the one hand, the offenses and the penalties on the other. This is the golden age of political economy as founded by Adam Smith; it is the golden age of the criminal law as fashioned by Beccaria as well. While the classic economist formulates the so-called unchangeable laws which determine at each moment what a product is *worth*, its *fair price*, the classic criminologist is racking his brains to define what an *offense is worth*, its just penalty, just in all times and in all places.[1] Economic progress seems to consist for the one in a gradual decrease of penalties. There are no doubt many divergencies in their different points of view, but what they both maintain is that the work should be appraised, leaving aside all question of the workman. From this we get the axiom, "To each one according to his works." The penal law, on the whole then, is treated as though it were exactly the converse of the condition of people receiving salaries.

This is the point we have reached, and that is why a criminologist may seem out of place in proposing to disturb this fine superficial order of things, or what is still left of it, in order to inaugurate a third phase. But has not this phase already begun in economics, owing to the socialistic and realistic pressure of these latter times? Behind the book the author is being sought more and more, behind

[1] *Mittermaier*, in spite of his historic learning, is imbued with this idea. In his treatise on the death penalty I find this curious note: "A capable French magistrate, Mouguier, justly points out, in his treatise on the criminal courts, that the penalty which surpasses by even one atom the seriousness of the crime is unjust." No more than the author whom he cites does Mittermaier seem to doubt of the possibility of estimating *almost to an atom*, the amount of penalty which is equivalent to a given amount of offense. In his opinion, as in the opinion of all his school, the double scale of offenses and penalties expresses something which is as much an eternal truth as Euclid's axiom on parallel lines.

the picture the painter, behind the score the musician. Behind the labor, which was the essence of the old economists, one seeks the laborer; it is to their needs or their passions, to their power or their capacity, rather than to their work, that their recompense ought to correspond in whatever form it may be, — appointments, fees, reputation, literary success, decoration, etc., — in order to attain the true object of the recompense, which in the last analysis is less to reward a past service than to encourage a repetition of it in the future. In the play or the novel of a budding author, it is less the new masterpiece, more often imperfect, which is welcomed than a new talent perceived through its imperfections; he is exalted, he is surfeited that he may hasten to surpass himself.

The highest promises of ability in political orators and statesmen are applauded with the same amount of exaggeration. Glory is no longer the reward of genius, it is rather the feverish stimulation of genius, its intensive culture by the public. "To each one according to his needs," or rather "to each one according to his talents"; sometimes one, sometimes the other of these two mottoes prevails, but the former of them is on the decline or is only realized apparently and as to detail, in order to facilitate transactions, though the increasing need of expedition in business is responsible for the habit in ordinary life of estimating impersonally small services, without taking into account the amount of labor expended by those who do them. Though in the stores the necessity of a uniform price for everybody, in spite of the unfairness which this equality conceals, is felt more and more, yet ask yourself why this uniform and impersonal price has risen so rapidly in the case of a certain article, in the case of a certain piece of furniture made in Paris, for example, and you will see that this price has been necessitated by the demands of the workmen based upon their taste and their ability, upon their needs and their ballots. Had the price been any lower they would have refused to work. Thus, though each workman as an individual is paid for his work, the workmen collectively are paid rather for their needs or their talents. The same thing applies to that *equal penalty for all*, which seems to demand a speedy form of repression in the overworked courts, where there exists, so to speak, a penal tariff, three months' imprisonment for one kind of misdemeanor, and six months' imprisonment for another. In reality, the punishment is less impersonal than it appears to be, and the courts are compelled, though they scarcely ever succeed in doing it, to regulate the price of each category of the condemned. "To each one according to his perversity," such is or should be the penal motto.

Furthermore, besides this petty form of offense, are to be found the real crimes, exceptional misdeeds, which are not tabulated, similar to those "exceptional services," or services called such, which will bring a man an exceptional reward. Here, each delinquent is examined separately, with insufficient enlightenment, we know, as the examiners are juries, but at least with the requisite intention. A man saves your life, a railroad employee prevents the derailment of a train, these are types of labor which are not paid for in days' wages. Every time the good will of the agent is evident and the utility of his action predominates, there arises the occasion for these exceptional prices, just as the uniting of a manifest wickedness and a serious injury will be the occasion for greater penalties. It is not even necessary that the injury should be very serious and that the usefulness should play a predominating part. The personality of the agent is always of such a preponderating importance in our eyes that, even without having received any special benefit or suffered any great damage, we feel ourselves bound to mete out surpassing rewards or punishments when, through the repetition of small pieces of work, which are well and imperturbably carried out or of petty offenses which invariably recur, a nature eminently good or perverse comes under our observation.

Thus a good employee who is regular in his habits has a right to a raise, an exceptional salary in place of his customary salary; a good servant, when his wages have been paid up to date, is often surprised at not being mentioned in his master's will, a good workman who has given proof by his ability, however without any especially prolonged action, may aspire to become his employer's partner. Similarly, a good delinquent, a man who has committed a series of petty thefts, of small swindles, of trivial indecent assaults, and has shown his inborn perversity, though he may perhaps have not yet assassinated anybody nor committed highway robbery, in one word a recidivist, ought to have a particular kind of treatment at the hands of the criminal courts. He is then punished, not for his past offenses, let us observe, but simply because of the future offenses which he would commit if he were not punished.

Thus it is that in giving a raise to an honest employee, a man thinks rather of the services he will render, owing to this favor, and which he would not render were it not conferred. Thus we see that, when closely scrutinized, the point of view of our new criminologists does not disturb the desired symmetry between economic evolution and penal evolution. However, is this as much as to say that a past offense, were it certain not to be repeated, should remain unpunished? And would this not be the same thing as saying that a past service, were it certain never to be repeated again, would be deserving of no recompense? No, as our evolutionists are well aware, there are rudimentary and useless organs, relics of the past, which organic progress is powerless to do away with.

But of these two questions which I have just asked, the first is less offensive than the second. We would consent to leave unpunished a misdeed, the impunity of which would cause no danger, rather than to leave some benefit unrecompensed. Why? Perhaps because the evolution of the penalty is in this sense already further advanced than is that of the price. It has taken a decisive step which the evolution of the price has not yet and perhaps never will take. Although a fixing of the price is due, to a great extent, sometimes to custom and sometimes to fashion, it comes within the domain of private matters. On the other hand the penalty is fixed by the courts, organs of the social power. Thus the penalty is the symmetrical opposite of what the price would be, if, in conformity with the most exaggerated communistic desires, every sale, every individual transaction having been suppressed, the entire community were to take upon itself the responsibility of paying for the services rendered by its members to one another, and were to prohibit them from paying one another, as at present they are forbidden to carry out justice on one another.

If, however, a thing surely little to be desired, this great and radical economic change should take place, the idea of price would be greatly altered, almost as the idea of the penalty was altered from the time when it ceased to be a private revenge and became first of all a public vengeance, an image of the former, and then something still more refined, or still more subtilized. It is probable that, according to the hypothesis where society takes upon itself the remuneration of every service rendered its members, as it now assumes the burden of punishing the injuries which they have suffered, we would soon find theorists criticising the proportionality of the compensations to the services as being an obsolete and mystic conception. They would have no difficulty in proving that the State should be concerned, not with services rendered, extinguished and vanished, but services to be rendered, the only ones in relation to which it can act. That the man who performs a service, or *makes an attempt to serve* should, in consequence thereof, be paid by reason of the future work of which he has shown himself to be capable. That the object of the remuneration is not to realize a sort of retaliation backwards, but to stimulate production, either in encouraging the one remunerated, or in giving the other citizens the enticement offered by his example; that therefore the service must not be looked at by itself, no attention being paid to the laborer, but there should be established categories of producers rather than categories of products, on the one hand producers through habit and temperament, to be picked out with care and given stimulating honors and pay for life, on the other hand producers through opportunity, to be compensated less liberally.

As we see, this third phase of the social system of remuneration and punishment, which we have just outlined, is exactly the opposite of the first, and the second seems to have served only as a transition from one to the other. During the first phase, which was entirely one of passion, it was the person of the man who bound himself and not that of the benefactor which was of importance, or rather it was the person of the victim and not that of the malefactor. Besides, it seemed as though there were no concern in the ardor of his gratitude or resentment, except with the service or the injury which was past, and not at all with the service or the injury which was to come in the future. In the third phase, which was entirely one of reckoning, only the person of the producer and his future production were thought of, or the person of the malefactor and his future crimes. But, deep down, the contrast pointed out is more apparent than real. Under the most sincere recognition, under the most passionate revenge there is an unconscious utilitarianism,[1] an ulterior purpose deaf to the

[1] I do not mean to say by this that these feelings have arisen *principally* owing to the domination of the idea of usefulness. This would be a great mistake; here are two proofs of this among a thousand. Everybody, under the Old Régime, was truly convinced that with the exception of the king there was absolutely no man more useful and more indispensable than the executioner. Everybody in ancient Egypt was convinced that the most useful man was the embalmer, by whom bodies were preserved in view of the future resurrection. And yet the horror inspired by both these men who were deemed to be necessary was such that they were compelled to fly as quickly as possible after having fulfilled their task, in order to escape being torn to pieces.

future, which has existed through all time, and of which every society must have been conscious in the long run.

Can we say, by analogy with the idea mentioned above by Carnevale, that the social transformation towards which we seem to be progressing leads us to a gradual *decline in the price?* Assuredly, even in the most perfect phalanstery, there always will be purchases and sales, in spite of the many ideals which have been formulated in this respect; there always will be at least remuneration for services in the form of a *written acknowledgment* and especially let us hope, under the form of praise and consideration for the skillful and industrious producer. Here we have the spiritual side of the price; it has already become almost the only one at the disposal of artists and authors, let us hope that it will progress in its development every day.

I must also call attention to the application of the preceding antithesis to a solution which has already been pointed out several times in this work, but which it will not be out of place to repeat. The further back we go into the past, the more pronounced do we find this great economic fact, the importance of which the economists are beginning to realize. There are two prices for the same article, one for the people of the tribe, later on the members of the same nation, the other for the foreigners with whom intermittent commercial relations are held on certain market days and in certain chosen places. This latter price is the only one controlled by the mere conflict of interests in conformity with the wishes of the classic economists. The first price regulated by custom takes into account the solidarity which binds the members of a common social group and sets a limit to the abuses of their mutual exploitation. Although apparently it has been gradually effaced, this distinction still exists, it is still very pronounced in certain watering places, and, if we compare the international commerce of the great modern States with their internal commerce, we will perceive that it has lost none of its former clearness.

Now, just as there always have been and there still are two prices, is it not true that there are two penalties, one for the outside enemy, the other for the adversary within, just as there are two standards of morals, an external one for war, for diplomacy and politics, for all our relations with those whom we consider foreigners because of the difference in nationality or simply in caste or class, the other internal for our relations with our social fellow-countrymen? The unfortunate thing is, that all too often, during the past, penal justice treated the malefactor, even when a native of the country, as though he were an enemy and also that the evolution of the penal law seems to have had revenge alone as its basis.

But it is none the less true, when the chief of the barbarian tribe, or even the savage tribe, is really a dispenser of justice, that when he represses an assault committed by one of his people against another member of the great family over which he governs, his chief concern is quite different from that which sways him when he seeks to revenge an injury caused by a member of a foreign tribe. In the latter case, social defense is his only concern, and he takes vengeance on the guilty man or on his brother, it matters not. But, in the other case, it is not a matter merely of defending society against the guilty man who is moreover here considered as an individual and is distinguished from his relatives, but it is necessary, if possible, to *reconcile* him to society. If this is impossible, then the case is the same as the preceding, and then the penalty, but only then, can be entirely one of utility. While pursuing its course in our day, let us notice, penal evolution has a tendency to carry us back to the true cradle of the penalty, to that individual penal law which was a moralizing, and before everything a spiritualizing one, that is to say, consisting in censure and disgrace which was characteristic of the domestic justice of the earliest times, but extending it to all delinquents.

I would regret having lingered so long over these preliminaries, did not a statement which is of some importance arise out of them. Assuredly our reformers have wasted less time than we did a short while ago with historical matters and, without any concern for precedents, they have treated *objectively*, as realists and naturalists, the problem of the penalty. Very well; it so happens that their solution, in so far as it is acceptable, is the logical consequence of the previous solutions disdained by them, that it was called forth by the solutions, that it takes its proper place at the proper time just as they did, and that here we have its greatest merit and the cause of its success. When men believe that they are only responding to their little individual reasoning it is really mighty social logic which is leading them. The individual exerts himself, his surroundings are his guide.

§ 91. Rational Basis. (I) Penal law based upon utility or opinion?

Let us, however, endeavor to look our subject in the face with the naked eye, so to speak, without the aid of the eyeglasses of history. The penalty ought to be adapted to its object. Very well; but what is its object? A decrease in the number of offenses, we are told, because such is the interest of all. Yet however simple and clear at first sight may be the idea of basing the penal law upon general utility, it presents, as we have already seen, difficulties and obscurities upon reflection. Why, in fact, should the lawfulness of the penalty depend upon utility rather than upon the general wishes of the public? I can say the same thing of the lawfulness of governments which have both these kinds of support, either one after the other, or simultaneously. What is the most lawful power, the one which governs through opinion, or the one which, even better than and in spite of opinion, seeks to gratify public interest? It would be the latter, could it be maintained for any length of time without making opinion conform to itself. But, on the whole, the national will, spontaneous or by suggestion, is the only permanent basis of governments; does not this same thing apply to civil or penal systems of law? The pretension, even the intention, which is very sincere moreover, and sometimes very well founded, of being useful to the people, despite the will of the people, is what is called absolutism in politics; in penal law this is called utilitarianism.

Now one is just as stable and lasting as the other. In fact, if this be made the object of the penalty, a decrease in the number of offenses implies a conformity of the penalty to opinion rather than to the interests of the majority. For is it not opinion, as given expression by the legislator, which has stamped certain actions rather than certain other actions with a delictual character and reckoned their degree of relative delictuosity? Garofalo might, as an objection to this, advance his theory of the natural offense; but the natural offense is only sanctioned by the various systems of law in so far as they see fit to do so.

Whenever the legislator has attempted, whether in the making certain acts criminal, or in the penal sanction of certain prohibitions, to run counter to public opinion, it seldom happens that he has not been defeated by it, or if he triumphs over it, that he has not lived to regret it. Sometimes he makes some particular action into an offense, because this action is the result of a national vice which he thinks ought to be repressed. Sumptuary legislation, as Roscher remarks, was chiefly directed in Rome against gluttony. In France, under the Old Régime, against luxury in personal adornment, so characteristic of the French;

in Germany, against the passion of drunkenness and bacchanalian contests where bets were made as to who could drink the most. Thus a certain kind of lavishness was given a delictual character wherever, because of surrounding example, it was the one most liable to be condoned. Animated with the same utilitarian spirit, the old legislation on the subject of the duel treated this subject with very great severity, because the trend of customs to be overcome was so firmly rooted. Adam Smith thought it unjust that the more the customs duties were raised, the more severe became the penalty against smugglers; for in this way, he said, the government punishes them more severely after having led them more into temptation. He might have added that, the greater the temptation, the more indulgent is the public toward those who have yielded to it. On the other hand Bentham was of the opinion that the severity of penalties against smuggling ought to be in proportion to the increase in duties, in order that the fear of punishment should always serve as a counterweight to the desire for profit.

Now, which one of them was right, the lawyer who spoke as a utilitarian, or the economist who spoke as a moralist, imbued with the idea of justice such as it is conceived to be by public opinion? For one the raising of customs duties is an extenuating circumstance, for the other an aggravating circumstance. Here there is an absolute contradiction between the penalty based upon utility and the penalty based upon public opinion. Now, for a long time it is true, it seems to have been the feeling of utility which prevailed in the majority of legal systems, for the most frightful punishments were decreed against smugglers. But nine times out of ten these enactments remained a dead letter. Sentences which are not a dishonor to anyone have, in fact, as their common destiny invariably to become exaggerated; *not being a dishonor, the penalty should be all the more a corporal punishment because it is of so little effect by itself.* This excess soon becomes such a crying one that it can no longer be tolerated. Does this mean that in countries such as Corsica and Sicily, where murder and assassination are condoned by the public, I advise the legislator and the judge to imitate the cowardly indulgence of the jury? No; in such a case as this, it is general opinion, the opinion of Europe, upon which justice should depend in combating local and insular opinion and in the end making it conform to the former.

Based on public opinion, the penalty seems to me to be justified in quite a different manner to that in which it is justified when based upon utility. To the interest of the majority will ever be opposed the interest of the rebellious minority. The interest of the professional thief will always be stealing, in spite of the contrary interest of the honest portion of the population. Though needs and desires may be spread by imitation, they will not allow themselves to be denied, and their very unanimity will only increase their hostility. It is by coming in contact with very honest people that many a swindler has cultivated a passion for enriching himself, which drives him to dishonesty. Now, by what right can the desires of some be sacrificed to the desires of others, if there is no need to be concerned with anything but human desires, if usefulness is the only good? And by what right can a man who has been sentenced be looked upon in any way except as one who has been overcome? But in being spread by contagion, ideas conform to and confirm one another to such an extent that the opinion of the honest majority in the end wins over even this minority and compels it, in its inmost heart, to admit itself guilty, notwithstanding its boasting.

However, it is this opinion which must be judged from a theoretical point of view, should the only result be to suggest a reform within it, if this be necessary. Then I ask why we want it to be free from all indignation and hatred against the malefactor and guided by the coolest calculation? I question whether the vulgarization of the positivist and utilitarian opinion on this matter would be the best means of attaining the useful and positive object which is attributed to the penalty. To see in the criminal only a dangerous being and not a guilty man, an invalid or a sick man and not a *sinner*, and in the punishment only a process of elimination or repair and not a stigma, is the same thing as wishing that criminologists, and following them the entire public, should bring to bear upon crime and the penalty an intellectual judgment, free from every emotion and all blame.

But the very school which proposes all these reforms is the one which excels in bringing to light this truth, that intelligence by itself is inert, and that sentiment alone is the motive power of people and of societies. When we shall cease to hate and stigmatize the criminal, crime will multiply. Besides, I repeat, for what reason should we deem it necessary, were it possible to do so, to remove from hatred and indignation their most natural object, crime, at the risk of causing them to overflow upon other objects, and of dangerously deflecting towards other ends, in our political or religious controversies, for example, those eternal sentiments of the heart? I am willing to admit that crime, being subject to the universal determinism, is as natural a fact as any other. But the anger which possesses us at the sight of a criminal action and the desire of revenge with which we are at once filled against its perpetrator are entirely natural phenomena as well. Why should they be deemed irrational? Why should they be blamed when it is thought that crime itself is not to be blamed? If it be claimed that these sentiments imply a mistake, the mistake of believing in the freedom of the criminal agent, then our theory of responsibility proves the contrary. Does a man suppress a sensation, an optical or acoustic illusion by proving that it is deceptive? The best taught color-blind man sees green and red as one color, although he knows that these colors are different. Similarly the most determinist of husbands heaps his scorn and rage upon his unfaithful wife, although he may know that she could not help deceiving him.

However, let us draw a distinction. If the irresistible cause of this infidelity appears to him to lie in the very nature of his wife, in her temperament and character combined, no argument will be able to have any effect upon his indignation and his thirst for revenge. If, on the other hand, it can be proved to him that the misconduct of his wife is the result of an attack of temporary madness, his contempt might be changed to pity or to sorrow. Similarly again, if one could prove to the victims of certain crimes and to the onlooking crowd that the perpetrators of these crimes are poor unfortunates, attacked with masked epilepsy, with imperfect nutrition of the brain, it might be that in time the public conscience would cease to demand a dishonoring of these luckless creatures. But, in admitting that the feelings of reprobation and of the necessity of purification, with which we are here dealing, can be weakened and converted into charitable compassion, is it a good thing once again thus to cut down the strongest dike which stands in the path of the progress of social evil? From a utilitarian point of view we must answer no. Why, on the other hand, should we answer yes, were it not for the fact that there is an aestheticism, a hidden idealism at the base of utilitarianism?

The conception of a penal law free from all vengeance and all hatred is a very old one in the history of spiritualism. As early as the third century, Gregory of Nazianzus affirms that, "God does not take vengeance by punishing the wicked, He calls them to Him and wakens them from the sleep of death." To Gregory of Nyssa, also, the thought of an eternal hell is intolerable. He dreams of a final and immense amnesty. "At the end of time," according to him, "every penalty will be expiated, every soul will be justified. The devil himself will be included within the work of universal salvation." [1] This same generous inspiration has been continued down to our day, as we have seen, to Fouillée and Guyau. The utilitarians have breathed it in with the surrounding air; and it is as being contrary to this ideal, it is as stained with moral ugliness, that they hate hatred, even when it is useful. They, more than they think, resemble the Egyptians who abhorred the embalmer, the French who execrated the executioner, while at the same time appreciating the fact that both the embalmer and the executioner were the persons most indispensable to the State.

From this I draw the conclusion, not that the utilitarian doctrine ought to get rid as quickly as possible of the aesthetic and moral elements which have found their way into it, — for the conception of the useful cannot stand alone and is dependent upon the conception of the beautiful, the physically beautiful and the morally beautiful, — but that it is illogical apparently to proscribe moral ideas when in reality and unknowingly the inspiration is drawn from them and that it is impossible not to be inspired by them. It is a strange thing that while the positivist innovators in the matter of penal law are unwilling, they say, to hear any mention of right, duty, guilt, merit, and unworthiness, even when these words are filled with a new meaning; and when these old organs are employed in the fulfilment of new functions according to the processes of life, the innovators, who are no less positivists in political economy, the socialists of the body, give as the essential characteristic of their innovations the introduction of moral ideas in the order of economic phenomena. The latter have over the former the advantage of having a consciousness of their tendencies.

[1] *Adolphe Franck*, "Essais de critique philosophique," 1885. I will allow this citation from Franck to stand, although according to the "Monde" of December 29, 1890, — in a very kindly article however, — it contains "an error very easily verified." I am sorry for this. I uphold his statement here because it expresses a feeling which has been shared by more than one mystic of the Middle Ages, especially by the disciples of *Joachim de Flore* in his "Evangile éternel." See *Guerardt* on this subject in his "Italie mystique."

§ 92. (II) The penal law and the relief-board ought to be derived from principles not contradictory to each other.

Let us not forget that the question of crime and the question of labor are closely united. Let us not forget, either, that the problem of the penal law is closely bound up in the problem of public charity. Pauperism and criminality, which are united to each other through mendicancy and vagabondage, are two evils of a different nature, but are equally injurious to society. Society would therefore be contradicting itself were it to solve one of these two great problems by means of principles contrary to those which serve it for the solution of the other, in showing itself, for example, pitiless and concerned with its own interest alone in the treatment of criminals, when it lavishes upon the lazy, and not merely upon the disabled, the treasures of its charity. To what extent ought society to cure the sick, artificially to nourish the malingerers and parasites? Is it to the same absolute extent to which it is interested in their cure or their preservation? If this were so, society should not concern itself with them. But society believes, it feels that it has duties towards them. Why has it not duties towards malefactors as well? [1] Thus it is not enough to say that the object of society, in punishing them, ought to be a decreasing of the number of offenses; were this the sole object, it would allow of hateful penalties.

Society should have still other ends in view. The amelioration of the guilty man, if it be possible, or if this is impossible, and the immediate elimination of the guilty man is not judged to be necessary, his more or less costly feeding and support until the end of his days. That society has a right to protect itself, like each one of us, is admitted, but more than any of us it is sufficiently wealthy to be able to pay for the luxury of kindness. What is this impassive and heartless collectivity, as bare of pity as of indignation, which is advised to strike down like a butcher that which bothers it, or unconcernedly to cast it out beyond the seas, and which at the same time is forbidden to stigmatize the very thing which it is told to crush or to expel? Which of us does not recognize himself in it? It was the principles of the old political

[1] Conversely one can just as well ask, as society does not believe that it ought to suppress the sentiment of pity which the unfortunate inspire in it, although this costs dear, why ought society to believe that it has to suppress the feeling of indignation, which according to this hypothesis is useless but less costly surely, which criminals arouse in it?

economy, based upon the free play of competing egoisms, which led Darwin to his theory of vital competition, and it is as pupils of Darwin that the new criminologists speak, but the new economists have revealed the narrowness of these doctrines and brought about the necessity for motives other than egoism, for production even, and for the redivision of wealth, and have sought foundations for justice other than the triumph of the strongest.

In fact, the generous efforts which have been made up to this time to bring about penitential reform give the lie to the utilitarian principles of the latest reformers. What are so many penitential colonies, so many prisons having cells, so many protection societies, so many costly plans and projects, tried one by one in almost every civilized State with a view to solving the penal question, if not, as Prins very well puts it, "the organization of a sort of socialism by the State for the benefit of delinquents," and not merely for the benefit of society? The elimination of the delinquent, when he is recognized to be incurable, is important; the reparation of the offense, when it is possible, is also important.

But a thing which is still more important to the mass of honest people, and which in the last analysis accounts for the concern felt by it, in the evil-doing minority, is the need which this body of the honest people feels of spreading among this minority the example of its own honesty, even though this propaganda should cost it dear and bring it in almost nothing. This kind of instinctive devotion to one's specific type is so essential to every living or animated being that no one is conscious of the degree of self-denial implied in this expansion of one's self. This zeal for converting is, after all, nothing more than a variety of the instinct of propagation, but this instinct is a sort of natural apostleship which causes every creature, whether organism or nation, universally to spread its faith in itself. To have children, to found colonies; a bad calculation, were it calculation, for individuals and for the State. But these are duties rather. Similarly, to improve the guilty, to civilize bandits, is difficult and costly, and could not be called a good investment of the time and money expended. But this is an obligatory extravagance.

Therefore, let us feel no regret at this generosity, and at any cost let us continue our attempts with a view of fulfilling our ungrateful task. But before everything let us thoroughly imbue our minds with this truth, a bit commonplace I admit, yet which is little known, that the best conceived penitential mechanism, the most ingeniously arranged one, is yet inefficacious if it is not carried out by a faithful personnel. If the English punishment of transportation met at the beginning of this century with a marvelous success, it was to a great extent owing to the intelligent philanthropy of the first governors, Philip, Hunter, and Macquarie. Everywhere that the separate cell system, mitigated by frequent visits to the cell and rounded out by a vigilant guard when the cells are left, has been practised with love and charity it has produced excellent results in Europe as in America, for example, in Belgium; in the North, it is true, far more than in the South, if it be compared with imprisonment in one room and not with the Irish system, which is certainly superior to it. Everywhere else it has failed; it has only prevented the prisoners from mutually perverting one another at the cost of debilitating them separately, it has only substituted consumption for corruption.[1]

Since 1853 the system of penal servitude, which might better have been called[2] a system of continual and gradual liberation, has been extolled with great reason. It has succeeded exceedingly well in Ireland, where a personnel of picked men has been entrusted with its application,[3] and not quite so well in England, where this condition, it seems, was not fulfilled to the same extent. It will be the same with every other method. Let no one say that devotion to duty is an exception; hard to meet with in our day. Our society is better down below than it is on its surface; it has, like jewel cases, as Joubert would say, "its velvet on the inside." Maxime du Camp has furnished superabundant proof of this in his later writings, which everybody has read. Had Madame Boucicaut made her will at the time of the Roman Empire, she would certainly not have thought of founding or endowing charitable societies, of relieving the invalids, or of enriching the poor. She would have bequeathed a few million sesterces to Lutetia for the construction of an amphitheatre, a

[1] Even in Belgium its results are not certain. See *Beltrani-Scalia*, "Réforme pénitentiaire," pp. 189 and 204.

[2] Of course we must not confuse *penal servitude* with which we are here dealing, with the sort of penal servitude in use under the Merovingian kings and about which we can read interesting details in the "Alleu" of *Fustel de Coulanges* (1889), pp. 280 *et. seq.* At that time slavery was a penalty often inflicted, for example upon those, and they were numerous, who could not pay the "Wergeld."

[3] And in Saxony as well, where Holtzendorff applied this system. In Ireland its efficaciousness is splendid; from seven hundred and ten in 1854 the number of convicts has little by little decreased to two hundred and forty-one in 1875 (*Beltrani-Scalia*).

few more million for the construction of a theatre, and the rest of her fortune for the annual purchase of wild beasts, gladiators, and actors intended for the amusement of the Lutetians. The worthiness of our time — let us add, to be just, the worthiness of the Christian centuries which have preceded it — may be estimated by means of this hypothesis and this antithesis.

It ought to be possible to bring together in a prison the worst human brutes and the finest types of men, such men as Cartouche and Vincent de Paul. Let search be made for the latter; in the end they will be found, just as in the end the former are found. Then it will be possible to attempt the necessary reforms, which all tend on the whole to widen the arbitrary powers given directors, inspectors, and the employees of penitential establishments.

§ 93. (III) The various penitential systems. The "manicomio criminale." The necessity of segregation of prisoners based on their social origin.

There is no need for me to go into detail as to the numerous systems adopted or suggested. But the principles set forth all through this book will admit of our estimating from a general point of view their relative value, by pointing out the conditions which they ought to fulfil. In the first place, those criminals should be segregated who, according to the opinion of a medical commission, have acted under the compulsion of a more or less strongly marked madness. The creation of a "manicomio criminale," of a "criminal sanitarium," is a necessity in so far as these men are concerned.[1] Between the ordinary madhouse and the prison properly so called, this intermediate asylum would offer society the protection which the first of these types of establishment could not secure it to the same degree, and which the second one could only give at the expense of justice. As to the suggestion sometimes made of replacing all prisons by this "manicomio" we will not discuss that. The realization of such an idea would have the double disadvantage of inflicting upon unfortunate madmen an unjustifiable injury in treating them like malefactors and of doing too great an honor to malefactors by confusing them with madmen. Were it to be averred that criminality, from the physiological point of view, is a variety of madness or degeneracy, it would be none the less certain that, from the social point of view, there would be a wide gap between an unfortunate lunatic who, having committed a homicide, is inconsolable

[1] See the pamphlet of *Semal* on "Prisons-asiles" (Brussels, 1889).

during his lucid intervals at having killed one of his fellow beings, and a professional assassin incapable of repentance.

Having made this first selection, we must now make another, no less delicate and no less important. There will be a great danger, in fact, in mingling together pell-mell delinquents for whom crime is their principal and only profession and those who, gaining their living by some honest trade, have accidentally committed some fault or have even repeated some crime a second time through weakness. Rather than continue to mingle them together, it would be better to do away with the only segregation that has been established up to this time, that of the sexes. Assuredly, the coarse pastorales of the penitentiary to which this promiscuity would give rise would be preferable to the lessons in crime, to the mutual depravation and to the corruption against nature which are fostered by our existing prisons, where the prisoners are all together. Therefore, it is important to keep at least a separate part of the prison for chronic delictuosity. If the separate cell system were applied to all, this division by categories would lose, it is true, much of its interest; under this system each prisoner has a prison of his own. But is not the usefulness of the cell keenly felt in the case of professional delinquents, or those at least whose incurableness has been demonstrated after a certain time by proof?

No, patients who are corrupt to their very bones have no need to fear the "decay of imprisonment." It may be said, it is true, that a prison where the prisoners are all together provides professional malefactors with the opportunity of getting to know one another better and of forming or strengthening their "professional syndicate." Here we have a great danger, but one less serious than it seems, for they never lack for meeting places, even when they are at large. As to delinquents through accident, it is clear that they ought to be protected from all contact, from all communication, if not with one another, at least with incorrigibles. It is to these latter that the cell is of use, it is they as well who ask for it as a favor, and, if it is not granted them, the least that can be done is to set apart for them a separate place from that where prisoners of the former category are shut up.

But in establishing these distinctions it will not be sufficient to take into account, as has been said and as everybody is correct in saying, the professional or accidental character of the prisoner's delictuosity. It would also be necessary, according to the statements set forth in the previous chapters of this work, to have some concern for his social origin, that is to say, before everything else, a concern as to whether his origin is rural or urban. At the present time sufficient attention is not given this matter; into a prison yard, in the midst of thieves and swindlers of the great cities who are viciously refined and who speak the language of the gutter with the purest accent, a poor peasant, speaking a dialect, guilty of some brutal rape, of arson, or of a shot fired in revenge, is thrust,[1] and then people are astonished at seeing him come out in a few years a far more dangerous man than when he went in! But this is inevitable. The prestige of the inhabitant of the city over the inhabitant of the country is exercised even in prison, or, to put it better, in prison more than elsewhere. For nowhere else are persons in such close contact with one another. Our reformatories for children and youths are seminaries of criminals, as is well known;[2] and the causes of this are many, but among these causes must be reckoned as one of the first a forgetting of the truth which I have just recalled.

In fact, professional criminality, in very civilized countries, has become almost exclusively urban, and the country no longer harbors any but delinquents through opportunity, if we except a few marauders. Also the disadvantage which I have pointed out is only experienced as an exception in prisons where recidivists throng. But in so far as Sicily, Corsica, and many other provinces are concerned, this is not the case; also even in the most *urbanized* regions the part played by the rural element among the beginners in crime or misdemeanors is considerable. Therefore, everywhere, it is worth while to create special establishments for prisoners who have come from the country,

[1] However, the importance attached to this statement had been for a long time pointed out by *Léon Faucher* and *Ferrus*. The latter in his book on "Prisonniers" (1850) admits that Léon Faucher, in taking this point of view, that is to say in looking upon convicts in towns and convicts in the country as "two distinct races," and in giving "this great difference in character as the fundamental basis of his classification," is, among all the eminent minds which have been concerned with this subject, "the one which has come nearest to fulfilling the conditions of a true penitential reform." It is true that Ferrus extols above all others his own classification, a very vague and defective one, entirely psychological, but he believes that each of these views completes the other. The truth underlying his thought is the usefulness and the necessity mentioned by him, long before the Italian authors, of *individualizing* the penalty as far as possible.

[2] See the "Mondes des prisons," by Abbé *Georges Moreau*, former almoner of the Grande-Roquette. See also "Bulletin de l'Union internationale de Droit pénal," February, 1891, and elsewhere.

and to organize for their employment the agricultural labor which is suitable for them. These ought to be "penitentiary farm schools," according to the expression of Michaux. Mettray and other agricultural colonies are already a partial realization of this idea.

Unfortunately, in the majority of our prisons, whether those having cells or the contrary, the lusty arms of our country men are given I know not what ridiculous employment of the industrial idler. Perhaps it would be better to force them to remain idle. In fact, an endeavor is made to teach them some urban trade, as though it were a duty to foster by means of the prisons an emigration from the fields to the great centres,[1] which emigration is precisely one of the principal irrigation canals whence the tree of crime draws its sap. Just for a moment recall the hasty sketch of crime given above. Formerly vagabondage, a fruitful current of crime, was recruited in the fields; the "Routiers," the "Jacques" of the Middle Ages, were not citizens but villagers. All the nomads and the adventurers who, under false cowls, retailing false relics, infested the roads at that time, were serfs who had tired of the plow. All the adventurers of that period, at some time or another, went to swell the band wandering over the roads or the band which remained in one place, in the neighboring caves or woods. Today all these sharpers of many forms and many shades, all these gypsies, these frequenters of gambling houses, these jugglers at fairs, these prostitutes disguised as harquebusiers or as café singers, even these basket-makers and traveling tinkers, these innumerable varieties of suspicious travelers and beggars who plow our roads, are the scum of the cities, though they may have been born in the country. For, when one of our farmers or one of our farmgirls has a desire to leave their own class, they begin by going to the neighboring large town as formerly they used to have themselves enrolled in the nearest troop of brigands, and after having passed through a sufficient stage of alchoholism, of idleness, and of prostitution, they set out to roam the country. Rural emigration to the cities is thus one of the tributaries of contemporary criminality, and the public powers should tend to impede it and not to assist it.

[1] On this subject *Prins*, in "Criminalité et répression," indulges in reflections which are perfectly just, which we are glad to endorse as we are the majority of the practical conclusions to which he has come, owing to his long experience. *Michaux*, in his "Question des peines," p. 233, also expresses the wish for prisons "in the country, for the convicts of agricultural origin," and his authority is of the very greatest weight.

Now, having become accustomed for several months consecutively, in his cell, to making poor wooden shoes or cloth slippers, a young peasant on being set free would blush to go back to labor; and, having become a bad cobbler from being a good laborer, he is lost to his native soil, which would perhaps have put him on his feet again. But here again we have but a secondary aspect of the question; the great evil is the mingling together in our prisons of prisoners socially *heterogeneous*, of whom the less evilly inclined cannot but get worse from contact with those who are more evilly inclined. I give this latter name to the inhabitants of cities for "corruptio optimi pessima."

If we are thoroughly convinced of the preponderance of social causes in the hatching out of offenses, we will thus take the social origin of delinquents as the principal, I do not say the only, basis of their classification. As there do not yet exist, and will not for a long time in France, in spite of the Law of 1875, a sufficient number of cells to accommodate all the prisoners, and as, moreover, if there were enough cells, the disadvantage of the separate cell system universally applied and not mitigated, that is, applied day and night, would very soon be perceived, it is advisable to inquire what prisoners ought to, or can with least danger, be left together at least during a few hours of work or recreation.

My answer is that it will be those who, having before their offense lived the same kind of approximately honest life, have ready-made subjects of conversation, other than their misdeeds. What is the use, according to the system employed at Auburn, of condemning to a Pythagorean silence an incendiary, a murderer, and a burglar, sitting side by side and all three of whom are peasants? [1] You may be sure that, if they did talk to one another, it would be to converse about the aspect of the coming harvest, whereas alongside of them a group of workingmen would no doubt discuss politics.[2] Surely there would be nothing very corruptive in such conversations as these. But when you force one of these country people to live with one of these townsmen, what do you expect they will converse about, unless it be the judges who have

[1] I say peasants or country landowners; this makes no difference. I do not mean to say that they should in prison pay any attention to differences in class, but, a thing which is far more important, to the difference in professional surroundings.

[2] *Prins*, in "Criminalité et répression," seems to take this point of view. He sees no danger (p. 165) in having two farmers who have become criminals by accident working side by side. Besides, Prins, like ourselves, believes that rural recidivists and urban recidivists should be segregated, and I am glad to see that Michaux also advises this same segregation.

sentenced them, and the facts which brought about their sentence? Crime is their only topic in common, this is the only subject which each suggests to the mind of the other. This memory would be salutary if it were accompanied with humiliation, which is what the Bavarian Code of 1813 aims at, according to which Code the prisoner ought to undergo every year, on the anniversary of his crime, an additional punishment of a week's confinement "alone and in darkness." But when fellow prisoners in their conversation celebrate the memory of their misdeeds, it will be on the other hand to glorify them.

§ 94. (IV) Transportation, the cell, the Irish system. Comparison and conclusion.

Two great penitentiary inventions have come to light, or rather have been developed in the last century, and are still competing as to which one shall be used in the various States: *penal colonies*, of which transportation is only an important variety, and the *cell*. We are under the necessity and we are at present in a position to choose between the two or to give each one its due. Under the form of transportation the former, of English origin, at first aspired to be the only and universal panacea for crime, after the great success which it met with in Australia. Later on the cell, imported from America, stirred up an infatuation which was no less absolute and was set up in competition with the colony. Between regeneration brought about by a change of air and labor carried on in common, either beyond the seas or even in some distant part of the national territory, and regeneration brought about by isolation and meditation, there seems to be nothing in common.

But more recently, and as often happens in the case of two industrial, philosophical, or artistic inventions, one of which, the new, is claimed to supplant the other, the old, the struggle between colonies and the cell has been seen to result in a treaty of peace and their rivalry to end in an agreement. Each one of them has had its share, the cell, petty delinquents, transportation, great criminals, or else they have been successively applied, like other penalties, to similar categories of malefactors who, having first undergone the punishment of solitary confinement, are released that they may then be transported in certain cases beyond the seas. However, the third idea, that of conditional liberation, has gradually been added to the two mentioned above, or at least to that of the cell; from this we get the composite system known under the name of the "progressive system." As a general thing there is a tendency to recommend the cell at the outset of every penalty, just as bed and diet are prescribed at the beginning of every medical treatment in cases of rather serious illness, but this is only for a time which is not absolutely determined upon in advance, and the maximum of which, one or two years at the most, ought alone to be fixed by the judge.[1] Whatever severity there may be in this compulsory seclusion — for the saying which springs from imitation, "cella continuata dulcessit," was not thought of by a prisoner — would confer upon this system an exemplary and intimidating character which, according to our principles, should never be lost sight of in penal matters; and on the other hand the brevity of this punishment, thus undergone as a mere prelude, would protect it from the reproaches that it might have incurred had it been prolonged without mitigation during a number of years.

Furthermore, the cell, however tight shut it may be, results only in absolute isolation for those prisoners who like it. The others, perched all day at the bars of their window or with ear glued against their partition, have a thousand ways of talking to one another; they communicate just enough for it to *go to their heads*, to change their boredom into exasperation, and not enough to gratify the innate need of sociability.[2] The compulsory cell at night for everybody, the optional cell in the daytime for the majority, this, therefore, it seems to me, is the medium to be adopted. Besides, without a certain freedom of communication between prisoners, how shall we learn to know them from their conversation and their relations and to distinguish those who can be reformed from the incorrigibles?

It is peculiar that the first idea of the two penitentiary systems in question was suggested by the monastic orders. What is the clearing of a desert island or coast by deported convicts if not the

[1] Everybody also agrees that the cell is best in the case of preventive detention. This is the opinion of Beltrani-Scalia in spite of the reasonable antipathy which he feels against the separate cell system as applied to long terms of imprisonment. His book on "Riforma penitentiaria in Italia," although it already is dated a few years back (1879), has not lost anything in importance. He authoritatively pronounces himself in favor of the Irish system.

[2] You can find some curious information as to the means of communication employed between prisoners in adjoining cells, in the "Notes d'un témoin," memoirs of a former political prisoner, *Emile Gautier*, published in the "Archives de l'Anthropologie criminelle," September 15, 1888.

equivalent of what often took place in Europe in the Middle Ages, that is, the transportation of a multitude of monks who were diggers and laborers into an unhealthy country which was soon made healthy and fertile, and where they laid the first foundations of towns which are flourishing today? We can, without too greatly humiliating the voluntary penitents of those times, compare with their work of civilization the Australian colonies of our unwilling penitents. In the same way, what is a prison which has cells, if not a criminal cloister? [1] The first prison with cells established at Rome in 1703 by Pope Clement IX was conceived after the fashion of a convent. From Rome this germ passed into America, where it was developed by the Quakers of Pennsylvania.

Now, not only is the prisoner's cell thus copied from the monk's cell, but the struggle which has taken place between the cell system and transportation recalls, to a certain extent, the competition existing in all times between the contemplative orders and the active orders, the Anchorites and the Cenobites.[2] The controversy, it is true, seems today to have been settled in favor of the former, and the transportation system seems to have lost ground instead of gaining it. To tell the truth, proceedings of this kind are interminable because the question has been badly formulated. If our ideas as to the importance of imitation are correct, a serious and true moral reformation of the majority of convicts can only be expected as a result of their prolonged contact with honest people. To isolate them from one another is to prevent them from corrupting one another,[3] and we are quite ready to recognize that, when it has been said of a prison that it does not deprave the prisoners, even this is to give it great praise, which is deserved by only a very small number of them; but one can

[1] We must notice, as Beltrani-Scalia does, that the penitentiary system of the church in the Middle Ages was, not the separate cell system properly so-called, in spite of the current belief on this point, but a progressive system of conditional liberation.

[2] *Labor* seems to me to imply a living together in a penitential establishment; just as *solitude* seems to imply *idleness*. This does not mean that the prisoner cannot to a certain extent be employed in his cell, but true labor, useful employment of energy, especially under the agricultural form is only possible as a general rule, in the open air and in work yards. "Let us remember," writes a true partisan of the separate cell system, "that the exercise of every profession is possible in a cell." Every profession excepting that of agriculture.

[3] A prison warden states that "to keep three fallen women imprisoned together is, in spite of the supervision which can be exercised, to increase their shamelessness as its cube." Here we have in a humorous form the mathematical application of the laws of imitation.

hope for still better things. If the penitential system ought to be before everything a medical treatment of the "maladies of the will," it cannot attain this object by enervating the patients. Diet alone is not sufficient to restore a constitution, a good system of treatment is necessary also; the cell only makes a man better if it is liberally open to a stream of kindly disposed visitors, and visitors who are welcome to the prisoner.

Unfortunately, this last requirement is more difficult of fulfilment. So long as the poor are not members of the protection societies, they will not be very efficacious, as Madame Arenal justly remarks. The hope which had been based upon the visiting of prisoners by magistrates, lawyers, and other persons of an official or semi-official character which was more or less apparent, and, at any rate, of a different social class, has not been fulfilled, according to Maxime du Camp.[1] At the present time the protection societies do not any more, unless on rare occasions, seek the convict in his prison; they wait until he comes of his own accord to them in a special asylum after he has been set free. Again, we ought to observe that "spontaneous departures from the asylum are far more frequent in summer than in winter." This means that the inclemency of the weather may alone determine released convicts to overcome the repugnance which this charitable hospitality inspires in them.

If this is the case, it is thus not while in the cell that the convict can really gradually begin to improve morally; it is only after he has left his cell. But then the difficulty of having any effect upon him is very great and everyone vaguely feels that this is the knotty point of the penal problem. In fact, malefactors are game of a particular species, very hard to capture, which no one knows what to do with after it has been captured, and which it is as dangerous to set free as it is embarrassing to keep. One might just as well make a sick man who has been in bed several months get up and send him for a walk out of doors as to make the liberated convict pass suddenly from a hermetically sealed cell to absolute liberty, or rather to make the convict turn to recidivism. Under these conditions relapses are inevitable. People have tried in every way to manage the transition here mentioned, that is, to take every precaution with regard to this moral convalescence.

If we are to believe the ardent supporters of deportation, the

[1] See his article on "Patronage des libérés," "Revue des Deux Mondes," April 15, 1887.

best thing to do is to send beyond the seas the chrysalis from the cell, transformed into a migratory butterfly. Owing to the miraculous virtue of the voyage, labor and liberty in a new land, honest people would very soon arise from this chaos of dishonesty by coming in contact and conflict with one another, and in these hearts, already prepared by the purification of isolation, social regeneration would take place. The success achieved, let us observe, has only come up to these enthusiastic promises to the extent which was to be expected according to our point of view. English transportation succeeded very well in Australia and even in America, where Maryland did not have so much cause to complain, in spite of its keen protest on this subject, of the convicts which the mother country sent there each year.

But we must not forget that these people transported were English; they were not in the least the miscreants that our transported convicts were; far from that, they were petty delinquents for the most part. The English law ordered transportation for every sentence of more than three years imprisonment. In view of the severity, until the reign of Queen Victoria, of that legal system which punished with hanging the stealing of a sheep, we may well believe that a very slight offense was sufficient to bring down upon its perpetrator the slight penalty of three years imprisonment. Nor should we forget that the prosperity of Australia dates from the day when the stream of free immigration of colonization by honest men finally became greater than penal colonization which was abhorred by the former and expelled by it. The experiments tried at Norfolk and in Van Diemen's Land with the convict element alone have clearly demonstrated [1] the impossibility of creating order out of disorder. Also we must not be surprised that our colony of Numea, where the convict element predominates, is far from being equal in prosperity to Botany Bay. If, however, out of all the contradictory information received from Numea we begin to perceive the possibility, I will not say probability, indeed, of a certain success in the future, it is because the population of independent colonists sometimes welcomes the convicts sent there. It is also because a large number of these released convicts have opened stores, inspired confidence, made money, and encouraged the newcomers to follow in their footsteps.[2] The

[1] See on this subject Michaux.

[2] See "Chronique de Nouméa," "Archives de l'Anthropologie criminelle," No. 2. But according to the speech of Labiche in the Senate (February 5, 1855), out of twenty-two hundred persons transported to Guiana, François, Deputy from

latter, but lately a band of strangers in the society of their native land, feel themselves to be integral members, in spite of their past and upon condition of their fairly good conduct in the future, of a new and different society, swayed by a new kind of opinion.

Now here we see, as everywhere, the contrast of the indulgence of a society for the faults which do not affect it, and its severity with regard to those in the results of which it has an interest. "Though men readily forget in our penitential colonies," says an eye witness, "last year's crime, which resulted in a change of hemisphere for the convict, by way of compensation they demand a severe rule in the case of new faults. Each one of them feels himself attacked or threatened when suddenly the news of an assassination committed in the country spreads," and public opinion is not satisfied unless the death penalty is inflicted upon the guilty man. The Kanakas, on these occasions, join the convicts in the search for the malefactors, and it is a strange spectacle, this, "of cannibals competing in the work of justice with men who pretend to be civilized."

In spite of all it has been possible to say in its favor, transportation has serious defects. A paradise hoped for by the worst criminals, a hell feared by the best ones, it is not in the least exemplary nor intimidating. It cannot compare, for the sequestration of dangerous and incorrigible malefactors, with a good house of detention upon the mainland; and one can, one should in fact, inquire whether, when it does act as a regenerative influence, it does not do so at a far higher price than it would cost to form a well thought out organization of conditional liberty upon the national territory, a thing everywhere at the present time being attempted and made a study of. Applied under the name of "banishment" in the case of incorrigible petty delinquents, it has another disadvantage. In colonies, practically the only work is agricultural labor.

Now, this type of labor is perhaps available to the majority of great criminals transported, among whom the rural element

this Colony, reckoned only three who had been set free who became the first of a stock of honest men, and Chessi, the Governor, counted ten. It was replied officially (Session of February 11, 1885) that in Guiana out of sixty-five hundred persons transported during only four years, there were one hundred and thirty who became good men. This figure seems to be beyond dispute. In spite of everything, this is not very encouraging. The recent book of *Léon Moncelon*, Delegate from New Caledonia to the Superior Colonial Council, under the title of "Le bagne et la colonisation pénale," paints a most pessimistic picture of our New Caledonian House of Correction.

predominates, but it disconcerts and discourages recidivists who have been banished, and urban malefactors in general. I read in the "Bulletin de la Société général des prisons" that in November, 1887, out of three hundred recidivists banished to the Isle of Pines with the intention of making colonists of them, there was not one man who was a farmer by profession or birth. Now, a man is born a peasant just as he is born a poet, he does not become one.

Furthermore, transportation or banishment can never be anything more than a provisional expedient. The egoism which makes us cast off our criminal detritus upon our neighbors is of ancient date. Formerly, the penalty of banishment outside of the limits of its jurisdiction was pronounced by each parliament so that the various provinces used to exchange their bandits; the abuse of this exchange came finally to be realized. A refined variety of the old banishment and consequently of modern transportation was "unclassing," a penalty under which the man sentenced was driven out of his class and introduced into a new class. This is what the nobility did with regard to its members when it degraded them and deported them, so to speak, into the Third Estate, a thing of which the latter complained[1] with justifiable pride in the Memorials of 1789, rather like Australia has protested, finally, against the sending out of convicts. Conversely, in Florence, we have found the people, in order to humiliate the magnates, inscribing in the register of the nobility the names of murderers and thieves. Thus to a greater extent than we are aware, we are carrying on the old system when we believe ourselves to be carrying out an innovation.

More modest in appearance, the idea of conditional liberty combined with that of protection societies is new and fruitful in quite a different way from transportation. Under the Crofton system, an Irish variant of penal servitude, conditional liberation is preceded by a period of gradual emancipation, the various stages of which the prisoner goes through more or less rapidly according to his conduct, as shown by notes kept on that subject. Thus it seems prudent to interpose between the cell and liberty, even conditional liberty, a period of "limited freedom" so to speak. However this may be, imprisonment looked upon as an initiation to liberty, such is the new idea, paradoxical in appearance, which is gradually making its way in the world,

[1] See the "Cahiers des Etats Généraux et la législation criminelle," by *Arthur Desjardins.*

but especially under the form of conditional liberation. The conception of this conditional liberation originated in France, where it was applied, in the case of prisoners under age, in Paris under the Government of July.[1] The excellent results which it brought about [2] suggested to England, soon imitated by Italy, Germany, the majority of the Swiss Cantons, the Netherlands, and Austria, its no less happy application to adults; and our country, which had already, moreover, instituted a sort of special conditional liberation in the cases of persons deported, finally decided in 1885 [3] to take part in the movement which had originated from its own impulse. The only new thing about it consists in commuting a portion of the sentence, a quarter, a third, or a half, never more, of the prisoner who has seemed to deserve this favor of the law, owing to his good conduct while in prison. The door of his dungeon is open to him before the expiration of his sentence, but with this threat, that, if he does not behave himself when he gets out, if he gives any new cause for complaint, he will be once more imprisoned, without being given a trial, for a length of time equal to the term of imprisonment which he had been let off. His fate is therefore in his own hands; thenceforth he has a means of obtaining freedom to look forward to other than escape or pardon; but, to a great extent also, it depends upon the police and the management of prisons.

In the opinion of du Boys, this is the disadvantage of this system; it "to a certain extent deprives justice, for which is substituted the abitrary will of the administration, from the moment when the guilty man has been sentenced." No one will deny this disadvantage; it is as incontestable as it is inevitable: as soon as the condemned man is submitted to a series of examinations in prison which determine the amount of his sentence which shall be carried out according to the decision of a commission, the men who go to make up this commission are given a latitude in estimating the facts which they may very well abuse. Once more this proves that too much exaction cannot be shown in the

[1] [This refers to the government of Louis Philippe inaugurated August 7, 1830. —Transl.]

[2] Before this innovation, the proportion of relapses among the class of convicts with which we are here dealing, during the year in which they were set free, was seventy per cent; afterwards it fell to *seven per cent.*

[3] We ought to point out the session of the Senate of March 22, 1884, where the question with which we are here dealing was thoroughly gone into in the fine speeches of Herbette and Bérenger, so thoroughly competent in matters of this sort.

choice of men called upon to become the examiners and the liberators of prisoners. For Garofalo and his school, however, the danger resulting from this extra-judicial power ought to have nothing alarming about it. Thus we come to a practical realization up to a certain point, in our contemporary systems of law, of the idea of indeterminate sentences suggested by this author, but formerly put into effect by the Inquisition, which, in pronouncing a sentence, always reserved to itself the power of increasing or lessening the penalty according to the subsequent conduct of the condemned.

England was at first aroused at the idea of seeing let loose in her very midst, like so many prematurely unmuzzled dogs, the convicts which she was accustomed to send afar into her colonies. Liberated convicts have sometimes seemed to justify this feeling by reason of their new crimes, and the boldness of their meetings, where they did not fail to hold discussions. But finally the fact had to be recognized that, owing to the measure which had been adopted, criminality in England had diminished.[1] There is no possible doubt that the protection offered honest society by the sword of Damocles always hanging over the head of the man conditionally set free is preferable to the elusive security which was formerly obtained by the supervision of the police. But this is not enough; something more is expected from the new method, that is, the moral improvement of the man released.

Now, as we know, we can only hope for this if this man is brought into contact with honest examples. This purpose is fulfilled, or should be fulfilled, by protection societies, which through their authorized recommendations have the recluse of yesterday, today a free man, who has no means of support, admitted to some farm, factory, or work-shop, or into a family where his past will be known but never recalled. One can get some idea of the service which this family protection is intended to render by those already rendered in certain countries, in Scotland, Belgium, and Germany, by family protection of the insane. Féré [2] thus names a system of treatment which consists in isolating the insane from one another without sequestrating them, and in separating them from their own family, where, more often than not, they breathe the unhealthy air of semi-insanity, and without confining them in asylums. Thus they are separately confided

[1] Session of the Senate of March 22, 1884, reported by Bérenger.
[2] See "Revue scientifique" of November 5, 1887.

to the care of families who are strangers to them, where each one, under a periodic supervision of a physician, forms a part of the household, upon the payment of a remuneration which is always very much less than the board in sanitariums. In Gheel, a little Belgian town of five thousand inhabitants, this method has been employed since the seventh century and is connected with a pilgrimage to the sanctuary of St. Dymphne, the patron saint of madmen. It has succeeded so well that, on the first of January, 1883, sixteen hundred and sixty-three patients were undergoing the treatment which has just been described. More recently, in April, 1884, in the province of Liège, at Lierneux, this example was followed; it has met with complete success.

Féré believes that he is justified in basing great hopes for the future on this and other similar attempts. I do not know whether or not they are slightly exaggerated; in any event, when we here find a prolonged contact with sanity sometimes sufficing to cure madness, how can we have any doubt as to the salutary influence that a prolonged contact with honesty, owing to the protection of liberated prisoners, is destined to produce upon the criminal?

However, there is one important thing to be observed. The results which are justly to be expected from conditional liberation, even rounded out by an extension of the protection system, would never be attained if the tribunals and the courts had not constantly suggested, in pronouncing a sentence, a provision for its probable mitigation by an anticipated liberation, and if, consequently, they did not form the habit of inflicting penalties which were nominally far more severe. Already, and with reason, complaints have been made as to the abuse of short sentences, one of the causes of the progress of recidivism; what would happen if they became shorter and shorter still through indirect means? The gradual lessening of punishment is one thing, a sort of historical law; their progressive curtailment is another.

In his speech of May 28, 1888, in the Italian Chamber, Ferri cites the following remark of the English commission appointed in 1878 to make a study of the results attained by the various systems of penal law: "Delinquents fear more the length of the sentence than what it will be [that is to say than its severity]." Thus a tendency to prolong the term of imprisonment, even in continuing to make it less severe, supposing that this has not already been done to excess, would at one and the same time conform to the progress made by pity and the increasing need of repression. Or rather, there is occasion, it seems to us, purely and simply to suppress or shorten still further the short terms of imprisonment (of less than three months), sometimes replacing them by a simple "judicial warning" in the case of a man's first criminal offense and sometimes by cutting them down till they consist almost entirely in the dishonor of having passed twenty-four hours in jail, except that then the long terms of imprisonment kept for cases of relapse should be considerably increased in length. Were it more rarely applied and with greater severity, we would find the dishonoring character of imprisonment accentuated more and more, this character which is now being partly lost because imprisonment has become so common and yet which is nevertheless the principal cause of its efficaciousness as a preventive measure. The time when the means of punishment at a society's disposal are less and less of a dishonor is also a time when the honors which it has to offer are esteemed less and less of an honor. These are both bad symptoms.[1]

We must also try to form an accurate idea of the progress which has led to the gradual and almost absolute suppression of forms of punishment which are called corporal,[2] a very unfortunate expression moreover, every punishment, as Beaussire and Eugène Mouton remark, resulting in a direct or indirect attack upon life and physical health. Whatever happens, a penalty will and should always involve suffering. At this point we must forestall

[1] Since these lines were written the Bérenger law of March 27, 1891, has to a great extent fulfilled the wishes which are expressed in them. We know that according to this law persons sentenced for the first time are given the advantage of a provision which allows the judge to suspend the carrying out of their penalty for five years; if during this period they are not sentenced again, their penalty is never carried out. But this lessening of the penalty in so far as they are concerned is compensated for by an increase in the penalty in the case of recidivists. For a long time past the positivist school of penal law has demanded a reform in this direction and it may congratulate itself on having brought it about. (See with reference to the law here dealt with a commentary in the "Journal des Parquets," 1891, No. 5.)

[2] Because of its peculiarity I call attention to the following proposition. *Schopenhauer* expresses the wish that *all miscreants should be castrated* and all insane women placed in a convent. In a note he cites an extract from the "Mélanges" by *Lichtenberg*, where it is said: "In England, it was suggested that thieves be castrated. This idea is not a bad one, the penalty is a very harsh one, it makes people contemptible but not incapable of finding employment, and if theft is a hereditary failing, it will no longer be transmitted. Furthermore, their courage is lessened and as in many cases it is sexual instinct which leads to larceny, here we do away with one more opportunity for it." ("Le monde comme volonté," Vol. III, p. 388 of the Burdeau translation). From the *utilitarian* point of view I can find no answer to such arguments.

a superficial illusion. No less than the lightening of penalties does their simplification seem to be a result of civilization. Compare the elaborate collection, the horrible museum of old instruments of torture and suffering and torments without number, which fill the annals of the penal law, with the simplicity and the uniformity of our means of repression which are always becoming more simple and more uniform; death pure and simple without aggravation, the fine, imprisonment, and hard labor.

But in reality the most important of these penalties to be considered, that is, imprisonment, inflicts upon the condemned — and unfortunately upon the man held as a preventive measure — a varying degree of suffering. From the psychological point of view it is always increasing, for this suffering consists in preventing him from satisfying the more and more complicated needs which a civilized, and especially a city life, develops among malefactors as it does among their fellow-citizens. The prisoner who is from the country suffers far less in this sense, in the same prison, for he is deprived of fewer things. This term "imprisonment" is an abstract title given to the most varied and dissimilar forms of deprivation. The deprivations for the peasant of going to dig, to labor, and to drink at the inn; for the workman of going to the shop, talking politics in the café, visiting his mistress, going on strike, etc.; for the man of luxury of the upper class travel by rail, smoking excellent cigars, making love to and winning the hearts of pretty women, etc.

This suffering which results in deprivation is constantly increasing, and although the positive suffering, physical if you will, may indeed decrease, the former will be sufficient to make a term in houses of detention more insupportable than ever. In the same way, though the death penalty, owing to the suppression of every form of preliminary suffering and the perfection in the future of the method of carrying it out, be reduced to a mere deprivation of life, yet it will not cease to be more and more terrifying if the pleasure of life by chance goes on increasing, through the complication of forms of enjoyment and the increasing abundance of the good things of life. It is perhaps because civilization each day adds some new variety to the flora of pleasure, that it can better and better afford to condemn the guilty to penalties which are in some way negative. During barbarian times when there are very few pleasures to be indulged in, it cannot possibly be sufficient to punish by the mere suppression of some of these pleasures, whence arises the necessity in those times of resorting to corporal punishment.

CHAPTER IX

THE DEATH PENALTY

§ 95. The problem of the death penalty. Fictitious enthusiasm raised by the idea of its abolition. Reaction against this.

§ 96. Theoretical and religious importance of the question. Effect of Christianity and influence of Darwinism. One of two things must be adopted: either abolish the death penalty in order to substitute something else for it, or else make it milder in order to extend it.

§ 97. Is it desirable to extend it? Weakness of the ordinary argument against the death penalty; irreparability, possibility of legal mistakes, pretended inefficaciousness. Statistics on this subject: their improper interpretation.

§ 98. Arguments to the contrary. Escape of the condemned who have been pardoned. Another consideration. Inconsistency of the general public: while opposed to the legal death penalty they are favorable to the extra-judicial death penalty. Another contradiction: the progress of militarism, the increasing extermination of inferior races, and the gradual dispensing with the scaffold. Utilitarianism ought to take into account the suffering of unsatisfied public indignation.

§ 99. But utilitarianism would logically carry us much too far. Society should not be more egotistical, taken as a whole, than should the individual. Protestation of the feelings: increasing horror aroused by the death penalty, or by the existing methods of carrying it out. The doing away with war and the abolition of the scaffold. Robespierre and Napoleon. The death penalty is abolished in the very cases where the utilitarian doctrine most demanded its being retained: in political matters.

§ 100. Utility of an experiment to be tried for definitely solving the question. As a third method radically change the manner of carrying out the death penalty. The "Phaedo" and the guillotine.

§ 95. The problem of the death penalty. Fictitious enthusiasm raised by the idea of its abolition. Reaction against this.

The most impure wine has its dregs, which are even more impure than it is and of which it must be cleared. The prison which has the worst inmates has a few persons in it so inhuman and so obviously incorrigible that it is important to segregate them. What is to be done with this riffraff of society? These persons who have never known pity will be unable to feel remorse; it is puerile to think of fining them. The only object of a penalty, in so far as they are concerned, ought to be that of putting an absolute end to the series of their crimes and, if possible, of intimidating their imitators who still remain unpunished. But how is this object to be attained? Kill them! says Nature to Society. Kill them! says the past of humanity to the present through the hundred voices of history. Nature, on a vast scale by its slaughter of the feeble and the conquered, by its extravagance, by its famines, by the claw and the fang of its ravenous beasts who serve it as executioners, applies the death penalty. Whoever either cannot adapt himself, or does not adapt himself, sufficiently well, or does not adapt himself quickly enough to the conditions of his existence, is at once sacrificed by nature.

Human beings of all times have followed this example; man's first tools were weapons; homicide was his first art. The death penalty is a thing so absolutely lawful in the eyes of primitive peoples that, when they ask themselves this difficult question: "Whence comes death?" (I mean natural death, the only one which astonishes them, for violent death seems perfectly natural to them) one of the solutions most generally suggested in their minds consists in believing that man, who originally was immortal, has become mortal as the result of an infraction of some one of the thousand foolish directions with which the rituals of savages are filled.[1] Each people, each section of a people, each church, each coterie, seems to have known but one way of doing away with its adversaries or its dissenters: extermination. To this is due the carnage of battlefields and the carnage of the scaffold. Because of a difference of one "iota" between two catechisms, because of a hair's breadth between two political beliefs, it has spilled and it will continue to spill floods of blood upon the ground. It seems, to tell the truth, that after this the question of whether we shall or shall not continue to decapitate a few hardened malefactors in order to get rid of them is not worthy of discussion. However, this is not at all the case. It is not merely because of its difficulty of solution that this problem which has been so discussed is always worthy of attention, it is especially because of the gravity of the principles upon which its solution depends.

I am well aware that this problem has been the subject, at a

[1] At a time when people are convinced, as all primitive people are, — what I mean by this is, since the dawn of history, without attempting to form any opinion as to prehistoric times, — that every illness, even a mere cold, is a divine punishment for some sin, it is natural to deduce from the fact that everybody must die, even the most perfect, even those most free from faults during the entire course of their life, the conception that everyone is punished for sins committed previous to this present life, sins committed either by the individual himself (metempsychosis) or by his ancestors (reversibility of demerit). To this no doubt is due, at least in part, the explanation of *original sin*.

period which is still quite recent, of an enthusiasm out of proportion to its intrinsic importance. There can be no better example of human silliness than the frankly fictitious passion lavished upon this subject. The idea of the abolition of capital punishment has assumed a political aspect which has contributed no little to its intermittent diffusion. At each great awakening of a political party it comes back into favor, so that it is at the very moment when men are ready to kill one another for a slight difference of opinion or interest that they most loudly proclaim the inviolability of human life, even when there are the most serious reasons for taking it.

In 1848 the current of abolition was so powerful that it prevailed in the legal system of three German States, the Duchies of Oldenberg, Anhalt, and Nassau, and in Switzerland in the Canton of Fribourg, and not long after in that of Neuchâtel. No one knows why, about 1860, when the war in Italy was but the forerunner of the German conquest, on the eve of the terrible battles whose menace was hanging over Europe, a new impetus of enthusiasm for the destruction of the scaffold was everywhere seen, as though there could be nothing more urgent for the honor of civilization than to wipe out this blood-stain. The Italians, or at least it would seem so, in their state and national crisis and with their usual wealth of homicides, must at that time have been occupied with quite different matters; yet they are remarkable for their zeal in the cause of abolition. The champion of this dogma was Ellero (the preceptor of Enrico Ferri), who in 1861 founded a review for the express purpose of spreading his beliefs, which were vigorously contested, moreover, by the Hegelian Vera. After them come the Germans, and in theory it is curious to find them so jealous of human blood, even that of a criminal, and so rabid in their unwillingness that justice should continue to wield the sword. The standard-bearer of abolition in Germany is Mittermaier, a convert, for in the beginning he had been a partisan of the death penalty. In 1865, just one year before the battle of Sadowa, his work on this subject was translated into French and created quite a sensation among our lawyers. Surely it is more comprehensible that Belgium, with its peaceful customs, should have taken part in this movement and that in 1865 a society should have been formed in that country with the exclusive object of stirring up public opinion in this direction. There is no country, even to Sweden, which has not felt the counter effects of this fever, the germ of which, moreover, had been inoculated in that country long ago by the charitableness of its mild legislation. At the Diet of 1862 abolition was voted for by the peasant class and was defeated, but by a small majority,[1] by the clergy and the nobility. Nothing can show better than this divergency of votes, be it said in passing, the truly democratic nature of this nation, among whom innovations spring from the people.

On the whole, before 1870, or rather before the Darwinian doctrine met with its great success, the suppression of the executioner was, under the sway of general enthusiasm, the universal wish of enlightened minds, and especially the fixed idea of persons who, at the same time, would erect an altar to Robespierre, Marat, and Saint-Just. Even at the present time, among the most pronounced abolitionists of our parliamentary assemblies, we shall find many duellists who, because of some trivial injury, boast of the desire and believe they have a right to kill their adversary in the lists, while at the same time refusing to allow society a right to execute assassins.

Fashions change like the winds; the fashion which we are here discussing is obviously on the decline and a current in the opposite direction is beginning to overcome it. The theory of natural selection has seemed, with reason, to justify the death penalty; again, although the votaries of the Darwinian and Spencerian school of penal law are divided upon this point, as has been proved by the discussions which took place at the Congress of Rome, yet the majority are in favor of retaining capital punishment. The chief concern, even outside of this school, is no longer to abolish but to modify the greatest of punishments, by the discovery of some wise means which will cause death without suffering. The general preference seems to be in favor of a powerful electric shock. We may expect some day to see societies or reviews founded with the object of bringing about this transformation in the death penalty and its development, just as but a short time since they were founded in order to bring about its abolition.

This new species of propaganda will very likely meet, like the former, with resistance difficult to overcome. Death stamps every custom and every fashion which has had it as its object

[1] In 1867 the question was once more discussed and it was possible from this to obtain some idea of the versatility of the various assemblies, even the northern ones. In 1867 one of the two chambers voted, by a very large majority, for abolition, and the following year the same chamber, composed of the same members, voted against it, the other chamber voted against it both times.

with a sacred character which is the cause of the impelling force of the former and the invincible tenacity of the latter. Each country clings to its traditional instrument of execution as it does to its funeral rites. That is why the process, perhaps the most generally used for the execution of persons condemned to death, is the most simple and primitive of all, hanging.[1] They hang people in England, the United States, Austria, and Russia. Then comes strangulation. They strangle people in the Orient, Spain, and Italy. Then comes, or perhaps is equally favored, decapitation, whether by means of the axe or by means of the guillotine. The axe, which is more brutal than the guillotine, but made more respectable by reason of its antiquity, is used in Germany, Denmark, Norway, Sweden, Finland, and Switzerland. It has not been possible to have the guillotine adopted outside of France, excepting in Greece, Belgium, Bavaria, and Hamburg. Of all French innovations none has met with less success in spite of its indisputable superiority over the method of decapitation by the axe, if not over hanging and strangulation. I have already pointed out that in China and in Cochin China, decapitation with a sword is a national art. It would be difficult to substitute for this diversity a single kind of execution. It may well be asked whether the virtue of intimidation which belongs to the death penalty is not to a great extent due more to the method of carrying it out as prescribed by custom, just as the prestige of the rural policeman is due to his hat.[2]

§ 96. Theoretical and religious importance of the question. Effect of Christianity and influence of Darwinism. One of two things must be adopted: either abolish the death penalty in order to substitute something else for it or else make it milder in order to extend it.

It is therefore certain that at various times the importance of the question with which we are here concerned has been overestimated in various ways owing to public enthusiasm. It is none the less true that this enthusiasm is itself due to the influence of some great religious or philosophical doctrine prevailing in men's minds and in process of penetrating to their very hearts.

[1] See on this subject an interesting article by *Henri Coutagne*, in the "Archives de l'Anthropologie criminelle," No. 3. See also the international investigation opened by the "Société générale des prisons," a few years ago. Its "Bulletin" gives the result of this investigation in its February and December numbers in 1886.

[2] Military executions are always carried out by the firing of a volley; in Servia even persons civilly condemned are shot.

We have just seen the immediate effect exercised by Darwinism upon the solution of this problem. Consequently it is a problem worthy of being at all times considered because it is connected with the gravest doubts, due to the curiosity of the human conscience. Cournot [1] is right in pointing out that the active propaganda during our century for the abolition of slavery, and for the abolition of the death penalty as well, is inspired by "a sort of religion of humanity," of which the founder of positivism, Auguste Comte, gave the formula and claimed to be the high priest. Neither is Charles Lucas [2] wrong in maintaining that, with regard to the question of the death penalty, the struggle taking place is between the Christian and the pagan civilizations. In fact, the religion of humanity, humanitarianism, or to put it more concisely, socialism in the highest meaning of that word, is the quintessence of Christianity, its oldest incarnation and its most pure expression. There is at the bottom of this worship of society made divine, a natural social conception of the universe. Love, kindness, a need of sympathy similar to that which persons associated together feel for one another, and which makes them imitate one another without ceasing, is given as the underlying principle of this world; justice, reciprocity of service among persons associated together is given as its object.[3]

To this point of view there is opposed a conception which I will very willingly call the naturalistic one, the idea of nature being attributed, according to the ordinary acceptation, to the external and hostile relations of living beings not associated together rather than to their inner relations of organic solidarity. The old polytheism was especially naturalistic in this sense. At the beginning of things it placed chaos and the struggle of the elements; at the end of things the conquest of the former and the suppression of the latter. Then upon this type it built up the relations of small societies among themselves, of associates with one another, and could not, as a consequence, raise itself to the conception of a universal society. Whereas the contrary doctrine, in accounting for the outside universe by means of the social union, has a tendency to strengthen the latter and to make its

[1] "Considérations sur la marche des idées," Vol. II; p. 269.

[2] Report of the Academy of Moral Sciences on the "Peine de mort," by *d'Olivecrona*. (1868).

[3] The pardon must have antedated justice, because the unilateral, as we have already seen above, must always go before the bilateral. The pardon, affection, are the gratuitous *giving* of sympathy and service; justice is the *exchange* of them.

domain universal. Therefore, from this point of view, we may consider the propagation of the Darwinian theory in the last few years as a direct return to the pagan spirit, as Lucas would say.

Now, must not every religion and every philosophy which, under a mythological or scientific form, makes the heart of the whole matter the innate disorder, the initial conflict, and only sees a victory after a struggle in every form of harmony, inevitably result in a justification of the conqueror and the executioner? It is a fact that the progress of Darwinism has encouraged an appalling revival of the military spirit and has checked the abolitionist movement which was recently so powerful. It is none the less certain that pagan antiquity, even at its zenith, was pitiless to its convicts as to its vanquished foes. Let us stop to think of the nineteen thousand persons condemned to death whom Claude caused to be brought on one single occasion from the various provinces of the empire to ornament one of his celebrations! Not only does this figure astonish us by the annual number of executions which it assumes, but furthermore, this idea, which was then a customary one, of making the punishment of the condemned serve the purpose of public entertainment is the expression of a cruel, a candid manner of extending and pushing to its limit penal utilitarianism, which, by contrast, makes our most utilitarian criminologists of the present time look like sentimentalists.[1]

Against these legalized horrors the stoic morals and Christian beliefs inaugurated a reaction which, without always being effective, did not fail to leave its impression upon morals and laws. Tertullian forbade the faithful to accept duties in pursuance of which it would be necessary to pronounce the death sentence. St. Ambrose, who was less exacting, ordered the judges to abstain from Holy Communion for several days after having pronounced a death sentence. In spite of its severity, the Theodosian Code already, on certain points, enacted a few modifications of the old Roman penal system. The Canon law everywhere introduced a moderation of penalties. No doubt these scruples and these modifications did not prevent the burning and massacre of heretics, Albigenses, or Huguenots, and the belief in hell strengthened the official position of the executioner. But in spite of all, this breeze of clemency wafted over Europe with Christ, as it had spread in

[1] In very remote times we find that the utilitarian commutation of penalties was far better understood by Shabak, who, says Maspero, replaced the death penalty by that of labor on the public works. But in Mexico as in Rome, the massacre of prisoners was the occasion for a joyous celebration.

India with Buddha, has never entirely ceased to be felt. In the Middle Ages it seems to have changed into a wind in the opposite direction, but on the whole, for a barbarian and warlike time, was not this period less severe than had been the imperial period, considering it was one of peace and civilization? There can be no doubt of this when we stop to consider that the revival of Roman law was then distinguished by a still more acute attack of legal cruelty and madness.

Finally, in the eighteenth century, the true, the pure Christian inspiration is reanimated and impregnates the materialism of Diderot as well as the spiritualism of Jean-Jacques. To tell the truth, I do not believe that this inspiration is prepared to halt before the hypothesis of natural selection. But the question is to know whether it has not now accomplished enough and whether it is best to go any further in this direction. At the same time, this point is a more serious one than it appears to be at first sight; for, from the historical point of view, to cease to advance in one direction is almost the same thing as would be a movement in the opposite direction. Owing to the same reasons which must have determined the legislator not to crown the past work of Christianity or spiritualism by overthrowing the last scaffolds which still remain standing, it will not be long, perhaps, before we logically retrograde little by little, appearing to be making a scientific innovation along the bloody path of the vast legal slaughters dear to ancient paganism and more modern neo-paganism. If anyone can prove the necessity of continuing to guillotine ten or fifteen criminals in France, England, or elsewhere, it will not be difficult soon to prove the urgency of striking down a hundred or a thousand through the agency of electricity or chemistry. Legislative progress is the most terrible and the most inexorable of machines. Individual logic has its fears and hesitates sometimes before a precipice; social logic, never.

Looked upon from this point of view, which has nothing chimerical about it, the question is replete with practical conclusions for the future and theoretical difficulties for the present. This point of view is no longer the subject of oratorical dissertation, it is the very crux of the social question in its most perplexing part. Our system of repression is obviously in a state of transition, nothing could be more unstable than its present equilibrium. The third course, upon the threshold of which we have momentarily hesitated and which consists in keeping the executioner, but on condition of not using his services, or to keep him just sufficiently busy for him to be able to preserve the appearance of having some reason for existing, cannot be prolonged beyond certain limits. Also, the abolitionists have really too free a rein when they do their best to prove the uselessness of this sinecure. Their criticisms are directed against capital punishment as applied today. But they do not seem even to suspect the possibility of a more extensive application of it; which would render useless or demonstrate the erroneousness of a great proportion of their argument.

However, one of two things must occur: either the instrument of the supreme punishment shall be swept away, or there shall be erected such a number of them that the annual number of executions shall be equal to the number of persons excommunicated from the social world, of anti-social beings condemned to eventual *elimination.* There is no middle course. Out of at least a hundred true monsters who appear each year before the courts of our country, there are seven or eight, eight or ten, who, either because they have been dealt with by a less indulgent jury, or because their petition for a pardon was presented at an unfavorable time, or after a number of other pardons had been granted one after another, or else because their case had more publicity because of the fact that it was tried at a time when the public mind had no special occupation, are victims of the inevitable sacrifice. Are they any more perverted and rotten than the others? Not always; at any rate the difference between the former and the latter in this respect is so slight that it is not a sufficient reason for the very great inequality with which they are treated. It would be better to leave to fate, according to the old Roman usage, the task of carrying out this decimation of the criminal legion; at least one would have the courage thus to admit frankly and publicly that these few executions are a homage rendered to the principle of intimidation pure and simple, without being complicated by any idea of justice. But, if we must recognize that we kill simply to cause fear, then we must kill a sufficient number of people to cause a great deal of fear, in accordance with the needs of repression.

Can this be possible? Is not the irregular progress which has led us by degrees to the extreme moderating of all penalties in general and to the extreme lightening of the death penalty in particular, one of those irreversible changes of which history has shown so many examples? Perhaps; for it is due to that gradual and continual assimilation which, making us sympathize more and more with our fellow beings, who are ever becoming more worthy the name, stays our hand, held ready to strike them, more and more every day. This is, therefore, a direct and inevitable result of those laws of imitation which absolutely govern societies; it is also their result, but indirectly, in so far as it proceeds from those religious or philosophical doctrines which I have called socialistic doctrines.

These doctrines, in fact, only come into existence in accordance with history when civilizing assimilation has unified some vast region of the globe. The whole of India had already become one, even though not united at the time when it was possible for Buddhism to come forth. The world known to the ancients had already become almost entirely Romanized before it was possible for Christianity to spread over it. Europe had already become almost entirely modernized before it was possible for the French rationalism of the eighteenth century or for Kantism to flourish. Briefly, it is only when spontaneous imitation from man to man has extended afar its tissue of spiritual similarities, that is to say social similarities, and developed the need of sympathy while satisfying that need, that the advent of a spiritualistic and proselytizing, humanitarian and cosmopolitan religion or philosophy, founded on love and the universal brotherhood in God or without God, in a God conceived in the image of man or in some other ideal of humanity, becomes possible.

At this point the objection may be offered at first sight that this is a fallacy, that it is war or conquest, according to the Darwinian method of perfection, which brought about this Roman peace, this vast and homogeneous Romanism, without which neither the Christian bud of Judaism nor the stoical offshoot of polytheism could have blossomed. It is war and it is conquest which have brought about our modern European unity, without which the liberal deism of such a man as Voltaire, the moral idealism of such a man as Kant, or even the scientific humanitarianism of such a man as Auguste Comte would have died at their birth. So that these great majestic formulae of a pre-established order, divine or inevitable of the universe, would be confronted with a denial of themselves in the very conditions under which they made their appearance or achieved their success.

But this point of view is superficial. In reality would war and conquest ever have accomplished anything other than to divide up and pulverize humanity to infinity, instead of collecting it into sheaves, if before, during, and after battles and victories, the instinct of sympathy which causes men, even when fighting, to reflect one another in everything, had not been continually acting? It is this "madreporic" work, so to speak, which, through all the volcanic eruptions of battles, forms the vast strata of societies. Whoever imitates other men, in other words, whoever speaks, prays, thinks, labors, or amuses himself, is carrying out an elementary act of sympathy, is imperceptibly binding himself to his models, and is making ready a future alliance between his descendants and theirs. Such is the first germ and the initial element of *altruism*, which, later on spreading under higher manifestations, little by little improves the human race. The labors of war are only useful to the extent to which they serve this fruitful instinct by overcoming obstacles in its path. Without this instinct nothing social can exist, not even war.

May I be forgiven for this apparent digression? If we will stop to think it over thoroughly, perhaps we shall find that my reply given above goes straight to the heart of social Darwinism and ricocheting, it also strikes natural Darwinism. For if the struggle for existence plays but a secondary part, and furthermore, I believe, but a temporary part, in the development of peoples, why should we hasten to attribute to it a preponderating and incessant action in the development of organisms? In reasoning thus by analogy, or rather by induction, from the known to the unknown, one is tempted to predict a short life, I will not say for transformism, but for the mechanical and insufficient form which Darwin has for the time being given it. If this be so, it is unfortunate to think that the glory of this great man, so well deserved in so many respects, may suffer therefrom. But to make up for this, this fire of materialism and division which the influence of his ideas has contributed to stir up will suffer still more, and also we may well believe that the spilling of human blood, even when legal, even when judged to be useful, will inspire an increasing horror.

§ 97. Is it desirable to extend it? Weakness of the ordinary argument against the death penalty; irreparability, possibility of legal mistakes, pretended inefficaciousness. Statistics on this subject; their improper interpretation.

However, let us admit that this conjecture is an illusion and that the irregular course by means of which we have progressed to the almost entire destruction of the scaffold can be retraced. Then, I ask, is it desirable that we should retrace it? Let us examine the question, setting aside any decision which may have been arrived at, and in the first place, let us hear the opponents of the death penalty. In truth, the greater part of their arguments are so weak that it would be impossible to account for their success, did not their very weakness show the religious origin, as has been said above, of their inspiration. There has never been a time when apologetics have shone by reason of their dialectics. The death penalty has been seriously reproached for causing an irreparable injury in case of error; just as though its irreparability were not a "sine qua non" condition of the absolute security which it is expected to insure and were not, moreover, a characteristic common to every other penalty, or nearly so.

The death penalty has also been reproached because of the innocence of those against whom it has sometimes been invoked; as though such a thing as absolute certainty could possibly exist in this world. The legal errors which send an innocent man to the scaffold are surely less frequent, says Vera, with good reason, than the surgical errors, as a result of which a useless and irreparable amputation of a limb takes place, which is sometimes fatal, and always painful. Among judicial errors we rarely find any which have led their victims to the scaffold; nearly all of them have merely resulted in sentences to hard labor. In order to find a single one in Italy which resulted in death, Musio, president of the Senate Commission in 1875 for the new project of the Penal Code, was compelled to go back as far as 1840. Legal errors of which no mention is made, those which consist in acquitting guilty men, are infinitely more numerous, we may be sure, than those with which the press and the criminal courts resound. An objection which seemed a formidable one, but only when one is imbued with the idea that the penalty ought before everything to be proportional to the offense, is that the death penalty, since the doing away with its barbarian refinements, does not permit of any varying degree. However great may be the difference in the crimes for which it is invoked, it remains the same. Thus it cannot fulfil the required mathematical equation. Just as though this object were a very important one when we cast out pell-mell beyond the seas great assassins and petty thieves, criminals and recidivists, the former being called transported convicts, the others being known as exiles, but in other respects, both being subjected to the same treatment! After all, the thing which we have a right to expect from a remedy is that it shall be proportional to the illness; or is it not rather, that it shall be the proper remedy for the curing of the patient, who in this instance is the social body?

The answer to this has been an attempt to prove the inefficaciousness of capital punishment. This clever paradox has made an impression, in spite of several curious contradictions. It is maintained that the most terrible of criminal penalties is possessed of every virtue, and yet — the remark is Seti's[1] — the preventive power of social and religious penalties, which are assuredly less intimidating, is recognized. When the death penalty is lavishly used, its enemies never fail to say that the various peoples are becoming accustomed to it and are no longer affected by it. When it is rarely applied, as in our day, they say that the probability of incurring it sinks to insignificance in the minds of malefactors. However, we must choose between these two contradictory criticisms. It might be answered that the very rarity of this punishment adds to its efficaciousness. It might be added that a murderer today has about as much chance of being guillotined as a soldier has of being shot. Now, however slight this risk of death may be, it is never a matter of absolute indifference, even to the bravest and most seasoned trooper.

According to Holtzendorff, the death penalty has no effect upon the hardened malefactor, because the successful carrying out of the first murders committed by him with impunity, gives him more courage, than the fear, greatly diminished, of the guillotine or the gallows, takes away from him. This is ingenious, but if it were true it would be no less certain, and the author recognizes this fact, moreover, that upon the novice in crime the prospect of the gibbet does have a salutary effect. In spite of such an admission, this eminent criminologist goes so far as to maintain elsewhere that, if persons who had been executed could come back to life, even the recollection of their frightful sufferings would probably not prevent them from starting in to commit crimes all over again. He cites the case of an assassin who was hanged, but not properly hanged, — for they do a great deal of hanging, but do it very badly in England, — who, saved by a miracle, was again sentenced later on to hard labor for other crimes. I will take the liberty of looking upon this fact as being curious rather than as having any probative force.

[1] "L'Esercito e la sua criminalità," by *Auguste Seti*, (Milan, 1886).

One of Holtzendorff's most weighty arguments against the death penalty is the following. One result of the death penalty is to call attention to the crimes which it punishes, to dramatize the carrying out of the criminal procedure, of which it may be the final issue, and consequently of *advertising* them in the press; from this there springs up an unhealthy enthusiasm in the public which stimulates *the spirit of imitation* among candidates in the field of crime. Thus the death penalty excels in increasing, by virtue of example, the very homicides which it punishes.

Is this really true? Would the accounts of legal proceedings be read any the less if the rivals of Troppmann, Lemaire, Pranzini, and d'Eyraud could only be condemned to hard labor for life? Is not the true source of the ardent interest which criminal cases inspire before everything the especially horrible and exceptional character of the crime committed? However, we must admit that the cases of Troppmann, Lemaire, Pranzini, and Prado would have interested us less if we had not known that the life of a man was at stake. The argument in question has thus some real value; the accused who has the blade of the guillotine hanging over his head becomes for that very reason an interesting personality, and to a certain extent a romantic one. But does this mean that the fear of coming to a like end does not lessen the tendency to follow in his footsteps? And besides, would it not be easy, if people really wanted to, to remedy the disadvantage pointed out by prohibiting the publication in the periodical press of the proceedings of the criminal courts?

Naturally here statistics have been called in and their figures have seemed conclusive. Tuscany has had the privilege of furnishing the writers mentioned above with one of their favorite arguments. Since 1787, with the exception of a short period, the death penalty has always been abolished in that country, either in law or in fact. Now, says d'Olivecrona, according to du Boys-Aymé, "official opinions, as well as the testimony of persons worthy of belief, agree in proclaiming that the cessation of capital executions has not been followed by an increase in the number of crimes, and that public safety is considered as infinitely greater in Tuscany than in the rest of Italy." In America, it is true, in the State of Rhode Island, Mittermaier admits, there took place a considerable increase in the number of assassinations after the suppression of capital punishment; but he pretends that this was not so in the State of Michigan. In this he is contradicted by an

American correspondent of the "Société générale des prisons," who, in 1886 (see his "Bulletin"), published the results of an investigation carried on throughout the world with regard to the death penalty and its results. This correspondent "is compelled to state that the number of sentences pronounced as a result of crime is on the increase," but, being an abolitionist, "he does not attribute this increase to the abolition of the death penalty." One invokes or rejects the testimony of figures according as they may or may not agree with one's opinion.

Mittermaier adds that the two German Duchies and the Swiss Cantons where, in his time, the death penalty had not yet been re-established, did not have to admit after its suppression that there was any recrudescence of homicides. But the Cantons where it was re-established — and there were actually at least eight of them — were compelled to admit this owing to the evidence of deplorable results. In Finland, according to d'Olivecrona, the same experiment undertaken in 1826 does not seem to have succeeded any better. Now if this be so, then I ask why the death penalty was once more re-enacted. In countries where the death penalty has been maintained, it is applied less and less as we know; has criminality on a large scale increased proportionally? In Sweden, where it has been possible to collect statistical statements on this subject, for the last century and a half they have gradually passed from one execution out of forty-eight thousand inhabitants in 1749, to only one execution out of three hundred thousand inhabitants in 1818, whereas the proportion of serious crimes has decreased. Out of a population of fourteen millions of inhabitants in 1834, England, Holtzendorff tells us, reckoned nine hundred and twenty-two death sentences, three thousand sentences to deportation and hard labor, and ten thousand seven hundred and twenty-one prison sentences.[1] Thirty years later, the population having increased to nearly twenty-three millions,

[1] Until the year 1780 in England, legislation reckoned two hundred and forty kinds of crimes punishable with the death penalty which was either compulsory or optional for the judge, including the various crimes of stealing, "although," says Holtzendorff, "observation would have shown that cut-purses preferably selected an execution as a time for stealing." According to the investigation of the General Society of prisons, which we have already mentioned, the death penalty is on an average actually carried out five times for every one hundred death sentences in Germany, fifty in England, eight in Austria, and seventy or seventy-five in Spain, etc. In France today this figure amounts to but twenty-two out of one hundred. During the entire course of the Second Empire the proportion did not decrease; it remained steady at the figure of fifty or fifty-five per hundred.

the number of sentences to hard labor was only fifteen hundred and fourteen and that of prison sentences nine thousand three hundred and eighteen. Thus, repression under its most cruel and dreaded forms there became very much milder, and security increased in proportion. One would be inclined to believe that, if the death penalty serves any purpose, it is to multiply crimes and not to prevent them. The abolitionists have not retreated before this paradox. They point out that the execution of Gamahut was immediately followed by the crime of Marchandon, and it is quite true that these two cases resemble each other very much.

For us as for Seti, this surprising similarity only proves one thing, which is the force of the tendency towards imitation, because the necessity of imitating crime overcame, in the case of Marchandon and other criminals placed in the same situation as he was, the fear of incurring punishment. I also am well aware that on the very day of the execution of the bandit Rocchini, an old man fell under the hand of the assassin in the commune of Zigliara. But he was a Corsican, we must remember, and this homicide seems to me like a defiance of the law by a brigand, of a "vendetta" carried out upon the executioners; unless it was, as the public is convinced, an act inspired by a sort of ferocious justice, as a remedy for the insufficiency of a previous sentence pronounced by an Assize Court. If this be so, all that it is possible to conclude from the coincidence pointed out is that, had there been a death sentence, an assassination would have been avoided. The abolitionists still point out such and such a small country where the death penalty having been re-established there were a few more crimes committed the following year. They show a contrast offered by the statistics of Belgium, where, while from 1832 to 1835 criminality increased in the Province of Brussels, the scene of many executions, it decreased by almost one half in the Province of Liège, which province did not see the erection of the scaffold once between those two dates.

But in order to reduce to their proper value these numerical results, let us recall the fact, as Holtzendorff very cleverly points out somewhere, that "the figures of statistics resemble the writing of the Semitic languages," where the reader has to fill in as best he can the lack of vowels. The vowel which is here lacking, I believe, is the following fact. The general rule is, that when a nation, whether great or small, decides to do away with the death penalty, it is because for some time past, criminality of a violent nature has been decreasing more or less rapidly owing to various causes. After the abolition of the death penalty, these causes have not ceased to act, but they forget to tell us whether from that time on the movement in the direction of a decrease in criminality with which we are dealing did not also lose some of its impetus.

Conversely, when a country after having done away with the scaffold re-establishes it, it is because the already perceptible increase of serious crimes under the sway of impulse and influence of some kind has seemed to make it necessary. It is not surprising that, in spite of this restoration, the impulse and influence in question have preserved a sufficient amount of energy sometimes to keep on causing an increase in the number of assassinations and murders; but has this increase been more or less rapid than it was previously? On this point we are not enlightened. After all, fear of the gallows, the sword, or the guillotine, is only one of the motives fit to paralyze the effect of passions which drive a person to crime. Statistics which give us pell-mell the action of these complex causes have not been able, so far at least, to throw any decided light upon the problem with which we are dealing. The groups of figures to which the abolitionists have recourse in order to demonstrate the uselessness of capital punishment remind me of the manner in which Colajanni thought he was able to prove the harmlessness of alcoholism. We know beyond any doubt that alcoholism has a demoralizing effect and that the death penalty has a terrifying effect, although statistics give us no very clear information on this point.

However, the language of figures is not without some eloquence here and there; we have already seen the lesson taught by them in Rhode Island, Michigan, and elsewhere. Furthermore, Bravary, a former Belgian Attorney-General, maintains that in his country an epidemic of arson and assassination came into existence as a consequence of a prolonged suspension of the death penalty, when it was suddenly stopped after a few executions had been carried out in 1843. How many military revolts have been smothered, how many political conspiracies crushed, by a few severe measures of a similar kind! Garofalo believes himself authorized, with the figures at his disposal, to prove that everywhere the scaffold had been overthrown, in Austria for example, the evidence of the deplorable results brought about by its overthrow had compelled the government to restore it. But why have we any need to ask of statistics what the rules of criminal associations could tell us far better if this were necessary? When malefactors associate together they ordinarily subject themselves to a Draconian code, the only penalty in which is death. Now there are scarcely any laws better obeyed than theirs, although there have been few as harsh.

§ 98. Arguments to the contrary. Escape of the condemned who have been pardoned. Another consideration. Inconsistency of the general public: while opposed to the legal death penalty they are favorable to the extra-judicial death penalty. Another contradiction: the progress of militarism, the increasing extermination of inferior races, and the gradual dispensing with the scaffold. Utilitarianism ought to take into account the suffering of unsatisfied public indignation.

The most ardent partisans of abolition have been compelled to make concessions which are rather important. In the first place, they cannot deny the fact of the very frequent escape of malefactors sentenced to death and whose penalty has been commuted into hard labor for life. They also recognize the fact that these men who thus escape have often committed fresh murders, beginning with that of their keeper. But they hope to remedy this by means of an effective penitentiary reform, the necessity of which, in fact, is felt more in proportion as the death penalty is less frequently made use of. Also they agree that it will always be a good thing to show no pity in the execution of captured pirates, mutinous sailors, and in time of war not only insubordinate soldiers, but also, adds Holtzendorff, spies and traitors, even when they are civilians, arrested by an *army of invasion* seeking to defend itself against the "fanaticism" (meaning the patriotism) of a hostile population. The fellow-countrymen of this eminent author, a few years after these lines were written, made extensive use of the prophetic authorization which they contain!

Finally, Holtzendorff observes that homicide due to greed being more coldly calculated than homicide due to revenge, the intimidating effect of capital punishment ought to prevent the former far more effectively than it does the latter. But homicide due to greed, as we know, is increasing among our civilized societies. The result is that the deterrent effect here spoken of ought each day to be more efficacious.

A reason in favor of the scaffold having great weight seems to me to be the following. When social transformations are such, as happens during periods of really progressive civilizations, that the advantages connected with the trade of murder are on the decrease, then the usefulness of the death penalty ought to increase. In fact, I concede to Holtzendorff that, in view of the ease with which this penalty can be escaped, and the delay in the criminal trials of which it is the final outcome, the prospect of a punishment which is so improbable or at least so remote is not able to stay the hand of an assassin who is strongly inclined to commit murder, owing to the attraction of a profit far greater than honest labor, with an equal expenditure of effort, could obtain for him.

But, when the profit which attracts him becomes very much less, and when the honest trades become far more lucrative, when, furthermore, his natural savagery has become milder or been weakened as a result of the prosperity around him, and his lack of foresight has decreased with his ignorance, the scales of the motives which urge him towards good and towards evil begin to oscillate, the heavier tray is but a little heavier and, more often than was the case formerly, a very slight weight added to the other tray may suffice to overbalance it. Consequently, there may and there ought to come a time during the course of social progress when the threat of the death penalty, even rarely pronounced, will oppose an almost insurmountable dike to the current of criminality.

Does this mean that we must retain the death penalty, at least as it is now carried out? I have already pointed out a few of the difficulties which its retention offers; the first is, I repeat, to strengthen the remains which are left without making the additions demanded by distributive justice and which would gradually cause it to assume its former dimensions. It seems that stated in this way, and thus understood, in the form of a radical dilemma, of a choice between everything or nothing, capital punishment is in quite another way worthy of examination and proper to justify the hesitations of men's thoughts, especially of positivist thought. All the more so as it will furnish us with a remarkably concise comparison between the principle of social utility and other principles and will clearly show us its insufficiency.

In the first place, I will say that as history can never bear to stand still, a prolongation of the existing "statu quo" is an impossibility, and that we must either go on to the very end of the path of clemency followed for the last century, or make a decided retrogression along the bloody road of the past. I make this statement because the death penalty, applied as it is now, is no longer anything but a losing number in a lottery for the one man who undergoes it out of the thousand who deserve it almost as much as he does. Furthermore, I maintain that the idea of restoring to the death penalty a portion of its former domain, to make of it the great annual mowing down of all the scoundrels in a country, has "a priori" nothing absurd about it, though it may be revolting; at any rate has nothing in it contrary to the positivist and utilitarian principles, the application of which is extolled, nor even to the socialistic principles, the realization of which is every day extended. The death penalty has decreased by degrees, in the same proportion as the feeling of responsibility and of guilt have become weaker. This is one of the causes, and perhaps not the least of them, of the moderation, or to put it better, the softening of the penalty. Therefore if we succeed in re-establishing the notion of responsibility, of guilt, upon a new foundation, it is probable that there will follow a strengthening of penalties and a more pronounced return in the direction of capital punishment.

Furthermore, recognized as being unfit for social life, the great incorrigible criminal should be excluded from society, as everyone will admit, but social life more and more absorbs organic life to such a point, that, outside of the former, existence becomes more and more an impossibility. Therefore exclusion from society is today more than ever an impossibility, except by means of the scaffold. Also I will point out an extraordinary contrast; on the one hand, the increasing repugnance of the public, as represented by the jury, — leaving out the slight reaction during the last few years, — in applying the death penalty; on the other hand, an increasing tendency of the public, of which the jury is also the echo, of condoning, of praising the action of a man who has been dishonored or a woman who has been betrayed, who takes vengeance with a revolver. Thus the death penalty legally pronounced and carried out is ever becoming more repugnant; but the death penalty pronounced extra-judicially by an individual is ever becoming less repugnant. This contradiction must be done away with.[1] One of two things must happen: either the public will continue to applaud the man or the woman who, under

[1] Though Voltaire was a declared adversary of the death penalty, getting into a controversy with J. J. Rousseau was sufficient provocation for him to write, in speaking of the latter, that it is necessary "*capitally* to punish a vile sower of sedition;" rather a strong statement coming from him, as Faguet very justly remarks.

interesting circumstances, make themselves executioners, and then it ought to approve of the legal executioner fulfilling his duties; or else it will be in favor of the doing away with this terrible officer, and in this case it ought to show severity towards ordinary citizens who usurp his functions.

Finally, individual rights are being sacrificed more and more to collective interests or those called such. Perhaps you may say, it is true, that, if rights of property are being respected less and less by the socialism of the State, the protective guarantees of the lives of the people against the encroachments of power, against the desires of the social Moloch, are better assured. The State, like the individual, in becoming more civilized, would thus feel a greater hesitancy about killing and less hesitancy about stealing. But, the extension of military service to include all citizens by means of compulsory enrolment with a view to the battles which are ever more murderous, proves the falsity of this distinction. I am struck with a contrast of quite a different nature. Whereas the death penalty was freely used in former times, and at the same time on a battle-field, the number of dead was insignificant; now the number of capital executions is very low, but the slaughter of war has increased lamentably. Here we have a strange compensation, a crying anomaly. And what a death is that of our modern soldiers, disemboweled by the explosion of a shell, struck by a bullet in the jaw! The pincers, the wheel, quartering, all the tortures of former times have their equivalents today on a fetid plain where groan and writhe thousands of wounded amid corpses. And no one is scandalized when the perpetrators of these horrors consecrate them, when the victorious generals in their hymns to war glorify these massacres, thanking God and proclaiming their usefulness, even their necessity, as the remedy for the evil of human over-production. A Europe which could listen to these savage theories without protest has forfeited all right to pretend to faint like a sensitive woman when anybody suggests killing without pain a few hundred, I do not say honest people, but evil-doing brutes with the semblance of human beings.

Whether it be due to degeneracy,[1] or atavism, to nature or to

[1] It is true that, if the criminal were a degenerate in the proper sense of the word, the death penalty might be deemed useless up to a certain point, as being but another means of bringing about that sterility to which a family which has begun to decay and degenerate must inevitably come. But it has not at all been proved that degeneracy is the true explanation, still less the only explanation, of delictuosity.

education, the criminal is an inferior being. The fate of inferior races, as it is regulated in theory by the Darwinian thinkers, in practice by the European colonizers, is the fate which is due them, unless logic is a meaningless word. When, in every quarter of the globe, there rises and is extended, is regulated and hastened the inundation by the white race of the varieties of men whom we judge our inferiors, even those who in their time have been the most noble ones; when the inhabitants of Oceania melt before us like snow in the sun; when out of several million native Americans there will soon remain but a few thousand; when in Africa we hunt down the negro and even the Arab like a wild animal; it seems to me in truth that the general feeling of pity at the thought of executing an always relatively small number of malefactors is really lacking in opportuneness. Yet the man who thinks that he is giving expression to "advanced" ideas by carrying to the extreme the purification of the inhabitants of this planet by means of the direct or indirect, but gigantic and systematic destruction of races other than ours, would be afraid that he would be considered a reactionary if he showed himself favorable to the progress of the scaffold.

But such obvious inconsistencies are not long lived. Before everything let us be logical. If Christian charity is to be reproached, as some have dared, with having contributed towards the physical bastardizing of the human race by artificially prolonging, by means of hospitals and charities, the life of sickly organisms which were destitute and parasitical, and by allowing them to reproduce themselves, they and their infirmities, conversely and consequently we ought to praise the cruelty of the old criminal justice which, by a prolonged elimination of perverse natures, contributed largely towards the moral purification of the people. Lombroso has been bold enough to go to this length.

If one wishes to be a positivist and utilitarian in real earnest, it is necessary, no doubt, to take into account the horror which the scaffold inspires in the condemned, the mental tortures of the unfortunate who is dragged bare-necked like a woman at a ball to the legal butchery. This horror, these tortures are an evil to be avoided unless they serve to prevent a greater evil. But as a consequence we must especially take into account this greater evil, the danger which otherwise many honest and useful lives will incur, and also the indignation, the moral suffering which the honest crowd and the family of the victim feel when a guilty man does not receive the punishment, which, as they think, his crime merits according to the ideas which they have formed and which they value very highly.

It may be said that this feeling of indignation is unreasonable, contrary to science, and the emotion felt by this multitude or this family would suddenly cease if the truth underlying the determinist principles were demonstrated to them. I do not believe this at all; but admitting this, can positivism and utilitarianism, I cannot say it too often, allow themselves, without detracting from their own dogmas, to consider a painful feeling as not existing when it is founded on a mistake? If we take this direction, moreover, why not go a step further? Perhaps it would not be very difficult to prove that the final horror and agony of the man condemned to death are themselves contrary to reason and science. What! He complains! Why, he is being spared the refinements of that final punishment which we must all incur, that "exquisite death," as the old executioners used to say, which will be inflicted upon us by the agony of death preceded by some terrible illness. He is going to die, after all, the easiest death, that is to say, the quickest one.

As to death itself, has it been rationally and scientifically proved that it is an evil? Not at all, if we are to believe the ally of utilitarianism, that is, our fashionable pessimism. Either it is only a comedy, and I will not so insult it, or it is the justification not only for suicide, but for hanging, decapitation, shooting, drowning, and the executions of all times. Furthermore, one cannot refuse to concede to this discouraging philosophy a certain amount of truth. Nature and society, everything lies to us, everything deceives us. Our life is one long unconscious illusion, reproduced each morning, renewed each season. There is not one of our thoughts which is not an error imposed upon us by the deception of our senses or our fellow-beings or our mind or our knowledge. There is not one of our feelings, not one of our passions, especially if it be deep rooted and absolutely incurable, such as love, which is not a fraudulent deviation of our energies by a chimerical hope, a sort of eternal swindle by which we are always caught.

Therefore, if this be so, why be afraid of death? Why should our fears be any less false than our hopes? The fear which death inspires in us is too strong not to have something fantastic and of the impostor about it. In the last analysis it is no more invincible than the belief in the objective reality of space and time, the categorical forms of thought. After having broken or counteracted these prisms, after having broken even the spell of desire, O! philosophers, shall we remain the dupes of fear?

§ 99. But utilitarianism would logically carry us much too far. Society should not be more egotistical, taken as a whole, than should the individual. Protestation of the feelings: increasing horror aroused by the death penalty, or by the existing methods of carrying it out. The doing away with war and the abolition of the scaffold. Robespierre and Napoleon. The death penalty is abolished in the very cases where the utilitarian doctrine most demanded its being retained: in political matters.

All this may be true, syllogistically perhaps there is no answer to it, but one's heart resists and protests, the heart has its own reasons, which reason, it has been said, knows nothing of, or to put it better, which sooner or later reason is compelled to recognize. When the heart feels itself repelled by a principle it is because it foresees the consequences of such a principle. Let us see how far the principle of utility will carry us in this instance. In the first place, it seems now to be generally agreed that capital punishment should be admitted only in murder cases; but why should it be applied only to murderers? Death, assuming it to be an evil, is not the only evil, nor the greatest of evils. From the utilitarian point of view does not the happiness of the living matter as much or even more than their number? To keep their number from decreasing by preventing homicide is all very well; but to keep their well being from decreasing by preventing theft, (which is always an unproductive consumption and often a destruction) is just as good, and perhaps better. It is by reason of a kind of unanimous and truly strange homage to the ancient law of retaliation, that after having given up the death penalty as a weapon against theft, forgery, arson, and rape, legislators deem it to be indispensable as a weapon against homicide. In this last intrenchment, where it is still defended by an unconscious motive of symmetry, it seems to everybody to be almost impregnable. Let us assume that the wishes of a large portion of the new school had been realized in the matter of penal law; then there would not be, so to speak, more than two penalties, death for the murderer, and the fine or compulsory pecuniary reparation (in prison) for the thief. This would be a complete return to the old system of retaliation in all its extent and all its simplicity, freed from its peculiar accessories.[1]

But in this case what are our pretended novelties? Atavism? If retaliation, as there can be no doubt, is a conception which has served its purpose, let us not merely scorn it verbally, let us forget it in our laws and consequently either let us drive the scaffold from its last foothold, or let us cease to restrict the menace of it to murder and assassination. There is always and everywhere something dearer in the last analysis than life. Sometimes it is religious faith or feudal fidelity, and then it will not seem strange that heretics should be burned and traitors or cowards hanged as assassins are. Sometimes it is honor, and then it is thought natural to wipe out the slightest insult in blood, to stone adulterers, whereas a brigand is spared. Sometimes again it is money, and then theft ought to be repressed as severely as homicide. Observe, also, the enormous expense with which the support of prisoners encumbers the budget. It is quite certain that it would be a useful measure for a society composed of honest people to save these expenses or to decrease them by sacrificing a large portion of those anti-social beings who impose these expenses upon it.

Unfortunately logic requires that we go still further. It demands that the lazy and the parasites who are supported by the community should be sacrificed; the same thing applies to invalids, and to sickly and deformed children. This is not all. If the sacrifice of a life is lawful when it prevents the total sum of social assets possessed by the survivors from decreasing, why should this not be the case when it must serve to increase its wealth? From this point of view it would not be difficult to justify vivisection practised on man, such as had been inaugurated, it would seem, by the Emperor Frederick II, assuredly the most "advanced" mind of his time. The vivisection of animals may suffice the experimental physiologist when he seeks to find the secret of

[1] Let us add that, for the repression of offenses which consist in slander by the public press, a type of offense peculiar to modern times and which is every day increasing, so far only one punishment seems to have been accepted by everybody, though it may not be an efficacious one, that is, the compulsory publication of the judgment which stigmatizes the slanderer. Thus, to slander in some legal way, to rob the robber in some way (by dispossessing him or taking from him by force the fruit of his labor), to make the murderer die; here we have our system of repression. No doubt it is a far cry from this system to the time when blasphemers had their tongues pierced and incendiaries were burned, but not so far as one might be led to suppose. This system of ours is retaliation reduced to the very greatest possible degree of reasonableness, but it still remains retaliation.

functions or anomalies common to all living beings. But for a study of the higher functions of the brain and the treatment of mental maladies,[1] experiments upon man himself would seem indispensable, and the sacrifice of a few hundred insane, by bringing about the localization and the absolutely certain connection of various forms of madness with their causes, would in the future save the lives of thousands of patients today destined to die.

I am carrying to an extreme, and as though wantonly, you may say,[2] the theory which I am endeavoring to overthrow. But if social utility is everything, and if the rights of the individual are nothing, or, to be more precise, if society is nothing more than a collection of interests and appetites, an *algebraic sum* of benefits and injuries, and not a bundle of reciprocal sympathies and assurances which are called duties and rights when they are looked at objectively, are not my deductions, though carried to extreme, perfectly correct? Moreover, are you quite sure that if the odious manner of experimenting which I have thought of really existed, and it were a question of its abolition, this abolition would not meet with energetic resistance inspired by the interests of "human collectivity"? Let us remember the difficulty experienced in uprooting from our customs, in the most sentimental of centuries, torture, that legal vivisection of the accused and the witnesses.

However, this last example is to some extent a consolation because it proves on the whole that society is not an entirely egotistical being, but that, like the individuals of which it is composed, it has its moral or aesthetic repugnances and knows how to enforce them when occasion requires, for its own interest, whether mistaken or not. This is exactly the point I wanted to arrive at. Let us speak frankly. The defenders of the death penalty reason

[1] Let us add phthisis and syphilis.

[2] I might push this theory still further, and not without having some historical proof to bear me out. Were not those zealous magistrates who, under Louis XIV, sent people in batches to the convict prison when the royal galleys needed rowers, utilitarians to the highest degree? And was it not by virtue of this same feeling of the *needs* of their time, of the needs of the people this time and not merely of the monarch, that the Roman tribunals increased the number of death sentences in the arena when the sovereign people complained that they had not a sufficient number of gladiators whose death they could witness? "The number of pretended criminals who were present in the arenas during that period," says Friedlænder, "was so great as to cast great doubt upon the justice of the orders which sentenced them. Thus the king of the Jews, Agrippa, had brought into the arena of Berytus on one single occasion fourteen hundred unfortunates who were all accused of having deserved death." All this, without mentioning the prisoners of war who were sent to the "Imperial schools of gladiators."

with great force, both in fact and in law, and I have demonstrated the weakness of the arguments opposed to them. As for me (if philosophers can be allowed to say "I" sometimes, as poets are always allowed to do), the answer I would give them, the best reason which I can find in the last analysis is the following.

The death penalty, at least such as it is or has been practised up to the present time, is repugnant to me; it has a repugnance for me which I cannot overcome. I have for a long time tried to overcome this feeling of horror, but I have not been able to do so. If all those who refuse to admit the arguments of the partisans of the scaffold will be sincere with themselves, they will likewise recognize that their chief objection is their disgust in contemplating legal murder face to face, but especially under the existing form which is most in use: decapitation. We read the figures of Bournet, the syllogisms of Garofalo, and we are ready to agree with these abstract statements. But when the concrete reality stands before us or rises in our imagination, the erected scaffold, the last morning preparations, the unfortunate man who is strapped to a plank, the falling triangular blade, the bleeding trunk, and the cannibal frivolity of the populace which has run to feast itself on this scene of authorized slaughter,[1] there are no statistics or lines of reasoning which will hold against the loathing which we feel. This repulsion, this heartsickness, is not a peculiarity of certain natures; a great number, an ever increasing number of our contemporaries feel this way. Of the very ones who in their utterances approve of the death penalty in theory, there are more than half who, upon witnessing an execution, would spare a condemned man if they possibly could. It may be, however, that the numerical majority has not yet been won over to the side of nervous or sensitive people, but in proportion as civilization refines our thoughts and purifies our hearts, the time is coming when, assuredly, their feelings will become law. In the meanwhile their position is the same as that of those minorities which always have taken the initiative in great reforms in all sorts of matters, particularly in the matters of penal law. Trials for sorcery, the penalty of flogging, prosecutions against heretics, as Holtzendorff remarks, were done away with under the domina-

[1] We learn from the Journal of Barbier that when the executioner "had completely beheaded at one blow" an unfortunate condemned, it was customary to applaud. During the execution of Lally "the people clapped their hands," says Mme. du Deffand. All this happened during the most sensitive and humane of centuries.

tion of feelings which, in the beginning, the mob was far from sharing. It is all very well to conform to a popular feeling, and especially it is very clever, but to alter that feeling is better.

We were saying a little while ago that we ought to take into account in positivist calculations the suffering due to the indignation felt by the honest crowd who deem insufficient the penalty inflicted upon the malefactor; and we must recognize the fact that this suffering is still often felt in our own time when an assassin is condemned to any sentence other than death. But, for the same reason, we will now add that the pain of the pity and horror felt in the hearts of most men who have reached a certain degree, and not even a very high degree, of intellectual and moral culture, at the sight or even the picture of the scaffold, as moreover it is raised by a painting of a battle-field, is also worthy of consideration. And, when these men hold the power in their hands, is it not their right and their duty to cause their way of feeling to prevail over that of the crowd, of energetically resisting the cries of honest rage which demand the death of a guilty man [1] as well as the attacks of blind patriotism which drive a nation into war with a neighboring country? A modern statesman should do everything which can be done with common decency to avoid warfare from afar. Should he not do everything to prepare himself, prudently if possible, to abolish the death penalty? He ought certainly to improve his penitentiary system, especially in so far as the measures to be taken as a protection against the escape of great criminals are concerned, this being a "sine qua non" condition of its abolition, as is recognized by Mittermaier, Charles Lucas, and Holtzendorff.

The question whether in fact the death penalty can be entirely done away with and the question as to whether war between

[1] There are countries, for example certain parts of Sweden (see *d'Olivecrona*, "Peine de mort," p. 174), where they are convinced that persons can be cured of every malady and every infirmity, principally that of epilepsy, by drinking the blood of executed criminals. To this is due in recent times, in 1865, those mobs of the sick and infirm, thirsting for blood, around the foot of the scaffold. Will it be said that a civilized statesman ought to take into account popular feeling on this point? "During the Middle Ages," says Rambaud, "the best bone setter seems to have been the executioner; as he understood so well how to break limbs, therefore he ought to understand how to mend them." Here we have the usefulness of the executioner observed from a point of view which is now rather neglected. Should the legislator of former times have taken into account the popular belief on this point and have kept up the punishment of the wheel in order not to deprive the people of the surgical skill, more or less real, that this horrible exercise gave or was thought to give him?

civilized nations can entirely disappear, are almost of the same order and ought to be solved by means of analogous considerations. So true is this that the interruption and then the retrogression of the abolitionist current have coincided in our century with the objectionable return to militarism in 1870. Is perpetual peace any more than a chimera? So seductive a chimera at any rate that its beauty can cause forgiveness for the madness of falling in love with it; and if this madness should become general, could not this dream become a reality? Against war, a coalition is being formed slowly and little by little. It is not a coalition of interests, as is often wrongly said, for the interest of an agricultural or industrial nation, it matters not which, as is being more and more felt, is to dominate its neighbors by force of arms in order later to flood them with its products, and to coerce them that it may grow rich. But, it is a conspiracy of sympathetic feelings which the habit of living in a society is developing in us, and which will indeed end, let us hope, in stifling the conspiracy of egoisms. Certainly I do not place in the same rank the two or three hundred thousand men mowed down by one of our contemporary wars and the ten or fifteen malefactors executed during one of our legal years. But there is between this last legal slaughter and the frightful military butchery with which I am comparing it, the following analogy, which is that the right of lawful defense, exercised collectively, can alone justify both of them.

Now, I state that when this right of lawful defense is exercised by individuals, it is more repugnant to them to spill blood, being given an equal danger, in proportion as they are more cultivated. A man, in becoming civilized, recedes more and more before murder, even when necessary and lawful. It costs him more and more dearly to kill in defense of his own life; he will wait, before resorting to this extreme measure, for a danger which is more and more pressing. In return, each day he takes greater precautions to see that he does not come face to face with this cruel dilemma. His prudence will increase with his mildness. Again, perhaps he will decide quickly enough to kill his enemy in the night, without recognizing him, without seeing him, by firing into his body all the cartridges of his revolver; but if a sudden light shows him the face of the man he is going to attack, he will hesitate at the risk of being shot himself. A full view of his victim will be a sufficient cause for sparing him.

You may say that this is unreasonable. Very well; but this

is an essential matter to him. Such is the individual who becomes civilized; and because the individual always models society after his own image such ought to be society in the course of its progress. The institutions, whether legal or otherwise, of our country are to the State what our members are to our mind. The State is an enlarged reproduction of our *average mind.* We want this reproduction to be exact and not distorted. In fact, more often than not it is sufficiently accurate. To mention but one proof among a thousand, it has been noticed how a gallant people, the Italians and Spaniards for instance, have always avoided the application of the death penalty in the case of women, in spite of the impossibility of justifying this difference in any rational manner. Inspired by this feeling, the Penal Code of the Argentine Republic provides that no woman can ever be condemned to death. It is to be noticed that in the judgments which we form of statesmen, a reflection of the distinctions which I have just pointed out makes itself felt to the great surprise of certain philosophers. Spencer is astonished that Napoleon, after having caused the death of almost two million men on battle-fields, should be considered as less a criminal than Robespierre, the perpetrator of twenty or thirty thousand homicides only. He might well have been astonished at a still more strongly marked contrast from his utilitarian point of view, which is, that the murder of the Duc d'Enghien is more of a blot in itself on the memory of the great captain than all the carnage of Eylau and Leipsic.

Everybody feels in fact the immense difference which exists between knowingly and voluntarily and out of hatred doing to death a certain person, whom one knows and who knows you, and to come to a decision, inspired by ambition, which will have the effect of causing the probability or the possibility of a violent death to hang over a great number of persons, but with no certainty with regard to any one of them, or, even if it were certain that an indeterminate number of people not known in advance would perish as a consequence of the decision which had been arrived at. In the first case, the natural or acquired instinct of sociability is violated in its inmost parts. In the second case it is not. No doubt the statesman who, in declaring an unnecessary war, innocently sends to certain death an uncertain but considerable number of citizens, is more injurious to the country than he would be in abusing, on one occasion only, his power to kill his enemies. But, although less injurious, he would be infinitely more odious to his people and even to history; so far is the human conscience from being utilitarian!

Similarly, though it can be demonstrated to us by statistics that the abuse by a certain president of a republic or a certain monarch of the power of pardoning persons condemned to death has resulted in a recrudescence of murders and assassinations, yet we never can be persuaded that this murderous indulgence is a crime. At the same time it would surely become criminal, if the connection established by statistics between the increase in the number of pardons and that in the number of homicides remained constant and showed that between the two there was a connection as of cause and effect, so much so that, in sparing the life of a guilty man, the head of the State was knowingly signing the death warrant of one or several innocent persons. Obviously in this case his strict duty would be never to pardon anyone; the individual most opposed to the spilling of blood, should he find himself threatened with a mortal blow, would not hesitate to fire his revolver at his assailant. But there are more doubtful and more difficult cases. Between absolute certainty and mere possibility there lies the unlimited scale of degrees of probability. The danger incurred by honest society if a malefactor or a rebel is not executed may be more or less probable. Up to what point ought it to be probable to make it the duty of the representatives of the nation to proceed with all severity? This depends, it seems to me, upon the more or less peaceful or more or less disturbed condition in which the country happens to be, and this also depends upon the varying gravity of the danger in question. In troublous times, as in time of war, a lesser probability would suffice to justify in all eyes the severe measures which would be disapproved of during normal times.

Assuming two unequal perils to be equally probable, the more serious one might alone look sufficiently probable to justify the extreme punishment, and assuming that they were not equally probable, it might be, if the more serious one is the less probable, and the more probable is the less serious, that this sort of balance between the gravity and the probability of each of them places them in the same rank in the scale of the motives proper to determine upon the cruelty of measures of repression. Septimus Severus, after the defeat of his rival Albinus, caused twenty-nine senators, convicted of having espoused the latter's cause, to be put to death. Was the fear of new revolts, which he made up his mind to prevent, sufficiently well founded to operate as a defense in his favor against the reproach of being inhuman which he brought down upon himself on this occasion? Yes, for, though these future rebellions were not at all imminent, yet they could not have failed to be very sanguinary as the preceding one had been. "If," says Duruy, "we had a little less compassion for the instigators of civil wars who are struck down by the conqueror, and a little more for those who perish in these disturbances while carrying out their duty as soldiers, we would place alongside of the twenty-nine senators executed at Rome for having played the terrible game of revolutions, the thirty or forty thousand corpses of the Roman legionaries which covered the plains of Lyons."

But this is the very thing our contemporary society has done in abolishing the death penalty in political matters, that is to say, in all cases of rebellion where the probability and the gravity of the danger in allowing the guilty to go unpunished both increase to the very highest possible degree. It is true that society has kept the death penalty intact, with all its old horror, in military matters, although, after all, politics is no more than the armament and the war of factions. It is extraordinary, we must admit, to have to discuss whether or not it is allowable to guillotine a parricide at a time when it is considered perfectly natural to have a marauding soldier shot during the course of a campaign. But aside from this very great exception, is it not remarkable that capital punishment has been reserved solely for common law crimes, so to speak; that is to say, in cases where the danger of clemency is at one and the same time of the slightest and the most doubtful, or the least pressing?

The converse could be far more readily understood from the point of view of military doctrine, and it would be perfectly right to bring up this anomaly if the law, while showing more indulgence for the perpetrators of the greatest evils, had not taken into account the relative nobility of their passions, the sincerity of their mistakes, and the dark beauty of their souls.[1] Here social utility has been

[1] However, let us not forget that the political offense, and the same may be said of the political crime, is often the expression or the issue of ordinary delictuosity. In this respect it is a good thing to take into account the evidence of a man who was formerly convicted for an offense of this kind, *Emile Gautier*. "*Out of fifty political prisoners*, taken unfortunately from the midst of the average if not the very best of the working class of a large city like Lyons, there will be found at least a *good half dozen* who in prison feel very much at home, in their element, and have a preference for convicts held for common law crimes, whom they immediately begin to imitate, by virtue of I know not what equivocal predestination.

sacrificed to social aestheticism. There is also another reason which lies deeper. As a general thing the force of a person's convictions is in inverse ratio to the number of his ideas. Therefore when the latter increase in number, the progress of civilization ought inevitably to weaken the former and as a consequence fanaticism, when it breaks out in our civilized society under the form of a more and more exceptional phenomenon, conflicts less and less with an equal and contrary fanaticism which absolutely demands the death of the enemy.

The same thing applies to those struggles between a fanatical conspirator and a sceptical government, as applies to our duels, which are rarely duels to the death. This means that, in spite of the gigantic sacrifice of our wars, a scourge proportional to our scientific powers, which are very great, and not in the least to our hatred of one another, which is weak when compared with that of the past, the tragic period of our European history is approaching its end and is bringing us to a more merciful phase. History in fact is a kind of tragedy which is in process of finally clothing itself with the aspect of a comedy, which in truth is a very serious and a very long one. By this I mean that the dialectic proceeding, which is generally made use of by social logic at the inception of a civilization, is the violent *elimination* by fire and steel of elements which are contrary to it, like those old dramas in which the only possible outcome was the dagger blow. Murders are lavishly committed during the fifth act, because, as Hegel has pointed out, each hero lives for his idea, is identical with his idea, cannot survive his idea without its being a contradiction should the idea succumb, and cannot believe that he has overcome the idea of his enemy so long as he has not killed him. That keen intensity of faith and of desire which incarnates an idea in a man and makes every conflict of ideas a mortal one is called heroism or fanaticism, according to the circumstances of the case.

At a later period, the proceeding of the *accumulation* of competing elements tends to replace the former proceeding, a thing which rather reminds us of the final reconciliation and the mutual embrace of persons, or the spontaneous conversion of a few, as the issue of a comic imbroglio. That is why the necessity of the death penalty under all its forms, war, single combat, and capital

in language, bearing, habits, turn of mind and even lack of morality, savageness, treachery, slyness, greed, thievish humor and unnatural desires." ("Archives de l'Anthropologie criminelle," December, 1888.) The author is talking about what he has seen with his own eyes.

execution, but principally in the matter of politics, is felt all the more and on a more extensive scale the further back we go into the past, and on the other hand, becomes weaker and each day less, in proportion as we advance into the future. Every time the passions and the convictions, which are brought into play in our modern struggles, by some chance are raised to their tragic level of former times, in time of war, strikes, or revolutionary crises, the death penalty regains some of the ground it has lost. But each time the work of civilization is once again taken up, it loses ground.

In the ancient times they began by killing the vanquished after the battle; then they reduced him to slavery or held him for ransom. Similarly, the old penal law punished with death the majority of its guilty persons who at the present time we condemn to imprisonment or fine. It made a special point of decapitating the political enemy on land; at the present time we deport him or exile him. For the death penalty actually undergone, at first they substituted execution by means of an effigy, just as at first human sacrifices made to the gods were replaced by pretended sacrifices under the form of offerings of animals or vegetables. We call it moderation of customs; it must also be called weakening of beliefs. It seems to me that having become sceptical, and what is worse, pessimistic,[1] a society ought to allow the best moral flower of scepticism and often of pessimism, that is pity, freely to bud and bloom within it. Neither the rebel nor the criminal deserve it I know; also it is not by virtue of I know not what metaphysical right to exist that society ought more and more to spare their lives; but it is owing to generosity or clemency. It is a good thing for society to be aware of its lofty motive; society must not be told that it has acted advantageously when it yields to a good impulse.

If then, society runs a risk, it must do so knowingly and willingly, as a man of feeling does in a similar case. An impassive

[1] The highly civilized man becomes a pessimist, owing to a reason similar to that which makes him a sceptic. In fact man, whether civilized or barbarian, never has at his disposal a budget of belief and desire which is approximately equal; divided between an ever-increasing number of ideas, his budget of beliefs is pulverized into fleeting *opinions*, without the support of any strong convictions, which makes him a sceptic, and, similarly, the increasing number of the needs among which his budget of desires is distributed gradually makes him have no great interest which can strongly affect him; that is to say annoy him, a thing which predisposes him to pessimism. An Epicurean pessimism, moreover, an enlightened scepticism which are not without a strong charm.

society which without hatred or emotion strikes down any obstacle, which knows neither vengeance nor pardon; such is once again the ideal of the utilitarians. This ideal is impossible of realization. Also, whatever they may do, society, though taught in their school, will always revenge itself and will often pardon, but its vengeance will be lacking in courage and its pardon in kindness. There will be cowardice in its intermittent reprisals, and there will be still more cowardice in its amnesties. The fear of suffering, the respect for suffering, the admiration for suffering, all are cowardly, and our century, just as those which have gone before it, has known all these things. It remains for it not to recognize, but to develop, a sentiment which has surely less danger and more of nobility in it; that is, compassion for suffering.

§ 100. Utility of an experiment to be tried for definitely solving the question. As a third method, radically change the manner of carrying out the death penalty. The "Phaedo" and the guillotine.

Finally, what we want to know is whether, after having given up sacrificing the most formidable of its enemies, political delinquents, our society can without too great risk show itself as magnanimous towards common malefactors. We want to know whether, in ceasing to strike down about ten criminals a year, it would expose an equal or a greater number of honest lives to the risk of being the victims of assassination. In case it should be proved, if not conclusively, at least with a certain degree of probability, that this excess of crime is the almost inevitable consequence of this excess of indulgence, there can be no doubt that the executioner ought to continue his work. But has this been proved? Or, to put it better, has it been proved that owing to a better police organization, at least owing to its exclusion from politics which result in its disorganization, and owing to the improvement in the penitentiary system, the death penalty could not be replaced advantageously? That is the question.

It is very far from having been answered. The abolition of the death penalty has been tried, but in little States, and the inconsistent results, though generally favorable to its retention, which this experiment has produced, perhaps make it desirable that a wider, and at the same time more methodical, attempt should be made. An author who is a great positivist, Donnat, in a curious book, suggests that the legislative assemblies should vote only that their new laws be applied for a limited number of years, after the expiration of which it could be ascertained whether it would be best to retain them as permanent measures. D'Olivecrona had expressed this excellent idea before him in regard to the question with which we are here dealing. He suggested that during ten years, for example, the death penalty should be suspended among all the great nations of Europe; that during that interval, the police, the rural police, and prisons should be the special object of the government's solicitude, and if, in any of these States, or in the majority of them, the number of serious crimes increased more rapidly than it had increased formerly, or was lowered more slowly than it had been formerly, it would be necessary without any hesitation to re-establish the scaffold as a permanent thing; but assuming the contrary to be true, it would be necessary to abolish it permanently. For the time being, doubt, strictly speaking, is permissible, and our society, moreover, has problems to solve which are still more important than this one.

But, while waiting for the decisive experiment with which we have been dealing, a third course seems to me to be inevitable; that is to moderate the death penalty without abolishing it. In this way we would continue to progress along the way of a moderation of punishments, without depriving ourselves of the service which can still be rendered by a punishment of the past, become, it is true, a rudimentary function in the present. How many similar functions there are which preserve an actual physiological importance!

After all, in the matter of severe penalties we have scarcely any choice except between these two really efficacious methods of repression: to cause death without suffering or suffering without death.[1] In other words, we ought to retain the death penalty while moderating it, or if we abolish it, replace it by a hard and painful life inflicted upon great criminals and by a frankly admitted return, not a hidden and shameful one, to corporal punishment. I could have understood the abolition of the scaffold when the penalty of whipping was still practised daily in our penitential establishments, where, moreover, its necessity was felt as a punish-

[1] William the Conqueror had a horror of the death penalty, so much so that he abolished it; but this did not prevent him from being very cruel, so that he had the eyes of rebels torn out. During this period to cause death seemed a slight thing, to cause suffering was the only important thing. Nowadays there is a tendency towards the prevalence of the opposite feeling; corporal punishment is being done away with, but we still cling to the death penalty.

ment[1] in order to compel labor. But, since it has been done away with and compulsory labor consists in doing nothing unless it be to have oneself supported at the expense of the State, a new argument and a very strong one has been created in favor of the death penalty. Would we, by chance, think it was any less preposterous to re-establish the old convict prisons, if not the bastinado and the lash, or even solitary confinement for life than invisibly and unconsciously to shock the condemned by means of an electric current? We know that this question is being made the subject of study in America and that several commissions have pronounced themselves in favor of this innovation, the experiment having even already been successfully carried out.[2]

Such perhaps, after all, will be the final result attained by the abolitionist crusade. But is this nothing? It seems to me that the day this progress, though slight in appearance, shall be realized, the greatest objection against the death penalty, which is the repugnance it inspires, will disappear. There will no longer be any corpse hanging from the gibbet, severed neck, bleeding trunk, or head with gaping arteries, no more savage and almost sacrilegious mutilation of the human form. Will it be said that death by electricity savors rather of the laboratory of physics? But, if a simpler process is sought, would death by means of certain poisons which have a sudden and absolute soporific effect before

[1] In dealing with two books ("La Guyane . . . et l'Expansion coloniale de la France"), in which two writers of the highest authority, *Léveillé* and *de Lanessan*, have shown the difficulties and the inefficaciousness of our penitentiary system in the colonies, *Rivière*, in the "Bulletin de la Société générale des prisons" (April, 1887) makes the following very just remarks: "I regret that, in works as deep as these . . . , the two learned authors so quickly pass over the very serious question of means of correction. Neither one nor the other of them suggests any practical penalty with compulsory labor. De Lanessan limits himself to recommending severity on the part of the keepers . . . Léveillé indeed mentions the enforcing of discipline; but he forgets to point out how it should be done. . . . *To replace the rope and the rod, which created and maintained in our convict prisons until 1780 a relative activity; to replace the whip* which makes of penal servitude the instrument so greatly admired by Léveillé, *is not an easy thing.* This, in my opinion, is the only weak spot in these two strong studies which could in this respect have obtained very precious information from our 'disciplinary companies' in Algeria and in the Alps at fort Baraux." Rivière adds that the question here touched upon by him in such a bold way is "the keystone of the entire penitentiary system."

[2] On July 7, 1891, there took place at New York the execution by electricity of four men condemned to death. This process fulfilled in every way the predictions of its originators. Death was instantaneous, without the slightest apparent suffering, without any disfiguration or horrible contortions, before a small number of witnesses. This result has silenced the adversaries of this innovation who had exaggerated the partial failure of a first attempt made in 1890.

becoming fatal, and replacing by sleep the final agony, inspire in a few legally appointed witnesses of this supreme issue, the publication of which, be it understood, should be prohibited, an impression which can be compared with that which the scene at the guillotine gives rise to?

What reader of the "Phaedo" is there who has experienced the slightest feeling of horror at the detailed account, the realistic portrayal of the death of Socrates? While we take part, as though we were present, at this execution of the most innocent of condemned, yet not for a moment do we have to avert our eyes. Athens even in her cruelty had her decency and her aesthetic distaste for hideous spectacles. Supposing Socrates had been guillotined on the Agora, in the midst of a populace stirred up against him by the wicked jokes in "The Clouds," instead of having drunk the hemlock, reposing on a bed in the midst of his most faithful disciples, our admiration would no longer overcome our pity when we read the "Phaedo," assuming that this book had still been a possibility. We would have been disgusted. And it would have been necessary to draw a veil over the last moments of the great philosopher, as over those of such men as Lavoisier and Bailly. Even in this there are still some lessons for us to learn from the Athenian school.

However, if objections are found to poison as well as to electricity, at least let us shoot our condemned as they do in Servia. For surely the firing squad itself is less horrible to observe than the odious invention of Guillotin, which is preferable, I admit, to decapitation with the sword or axe, and even to strangulation if not to hanging, but which is perhaps even more repugnant in its clever atrocity. Though Loye in his book on this depressing subject[1] may heap experiment upon experiment to prove to us that this is the easiest of deaths, that in spite of certain contractions, purely reflex, observable in decapitation, or of certain legends about La Pommerais, about the head of Charlotte Corday blushing with shame at the slap of the executioner, that in spite of all these things, persons who are decapitated have no time to suffer and certainly become unconscious before they have been able to feel the cold steel of the knife; though he may add that "the severing of the head from the trunk gives a public proof of death," an advantage which electrocution would not possess; yet the only

[1] "La mort par la décapitation," by *Loye*, with a preface by *Brouardel* (Lecrosnier and Babé, 1888).

reply which I will make to these final conclusions in his book is the insurmountable disgust experienced in reading it in spite of the really great value of the researches which it contains. Never has a work on poisoning or even on hanging, or the picture of the most murderous battle, been as revolting to the imagination and the heart as has this procession of severed heads. This is because physical suffering here is not the only thing to be taken into consideration. It is because there is a degree to which the desecration, even though painless, of the human body is unbearable, invincibly repelled by the nervous system of the public as well as by that of the sufferer; and assuredly the guillotine goes beyond this degree. Nothing savors more of barbarism than this bloody proceeding and, though it were proved that it is painless, yet this method of decapitation would nevertheless continue to be the most violent and the most brutal form of operation, a sort of frightful human vivisection.

This may be a sentimental feeling if you will, an aesthetic one to put it better, perhaps a religious one, but it is a feeling of the very greatest importance. The general movement for the abolition of capital punishment, up to a time not far removed from our own, is especially due, I believe, to the method of carrying it out. If the existing reaction in its favor is halting, held back by I know not what inner protest of the heart, it is still to the same cause that this effect must be attributed. Death by decapitation is unnatural, and everything which is unnatural must finally be rejected, in spite of the strongest utilitarian arguments. Let a less repulsive punishment than the guillotine be adopted, let the condemned, at least to a certain extent, have the choice of the manner in which he shall die [1] and we shall see whether the still pronounced antipathy against the greatest punishment will not change into a quite different feeling, and a great predilection for the most logical, most concise, and even, under these conditions, the most humane solution of the penal problem in so far as social monsters are concerned, until the time comes when, this species of wild beast having finally been tamed, it will be possible to think of obliterating capital punishment from our codes.

I have only one word to add as to the publicity of executions. In spite of everything which can be said in its favor, it has very

[1] "Antoninus Pius and the divine brothers [Verus and Marcus Aurelius]," says *Denis* in his "Histoire des idées morales," "had allowed the condemned man to choose the manner of death he wished; a practice which was not recognized after their time."

justly been done away with in Germany, England, Austria, the United States, Sweden, Switzerland, and Russia. In Denmark executions take place, not in the cities but in the open country, which renders impossible the sickening scenes occasioned among us by the "manifestations" organized by the vicious or criminal element in Paris at the foot of the scaffold. Finally, executions are public only among European peoples in France, Spain, Greece, Italy, and Norway, that is to say, with the exception of Norway, in southern States which are especially fond of outdoor spectacles. Must we believe that this species of mournful pomp is essentially a part of their character, like the ceremonies of their worship and the sonorousness of their eloquence? No, Spain feels no regret for its "auto-da-fé," nor Rome for the games in its Circus. Nowhere is the need of substituting an obscure death penalty, carried out before a few selected persons, for the brilliant, processional, and scandalous death penalty, felt more than among the people who are most fond of celebrity and of sunshine, even of a disgraceful celebrity and of a murderous sunshine. Nowhere will the death penalty thus transformed become less intimidating or less exemplary.

INDEX

N

R

Demand Any Rare Book at:

www.facsimilepublisher.com

if not available, give information,
our team will search and update you.

Promote Knowledge:

If you have any rare book
which is not available at
www.facsimilepublisher.com,
offer it to other readers so that others can also be
benefitted with your cooperation.
The book will be printed with your courtesy.

Print & Publish:

If you wish to get your book printed or published,
we have the service for you.

Customization on Demand:

We offer customization of books
as per the demand of the customer.

Published by

Facsimile Publisher
Ashok Vihar, Delhi-110052 (India)
Website: www.facsimilepublisher.com

Distributed by

Gyan Books Pvt. Ltd.
5, Ansari Road, Daryaganj, New Delhi-110002 (India)
E-mail: books@gyanbooks.com, Website: www.gyanbooks.com

2 222000 013295